"A new, original, necessary history, in many ways the crowning of a life's work. A professional war correspondent who has personally witnessed armed conflict in Vietnam, the Falkland Islands and other danger zones, Hastings has a sober, unromantic and realistic view of battle that puts him into a different category from the armchair generals whose gung-ho, schoolboy attitude to war fills the pages of a great majority of military histories. He writes with grace, fluency and authority. . . . *Inferno* is superb."
—*The New York Times Book Review*

"If there is a contemporary British historian who is the chronicler of World War II, it would be Max Hastings . . . [*Inferno*] is a true distillation of everything this historian has learned from a lifetime of scholarship—and more important, of real thought—on what he calls 'the greatest and most terrible event in human history.'"   —*San Francisco Chronicle*

"Compellingly different. . . . A panoramic social history that not only recounts the military action with admirable thoroughness, crispness and energy but also tells the story of the people who suffered in the war, combatants and civilians alike."   —*The Wall Street Journal*

"A relatively brief review can only begin to indicate the depth, breadth, complexity and pervasive humanity of this extraordinary book. The literature of World War II is, as Hastings notes at the beginning of his bibliography, so vast as almost to defy enumeration or comprehension, but *Inferno* immediately moves to the head of the list."   —*The Washington Post*

"*Inferno* is a magnificent achievement, a one-volume history that should find favor among readers thoroughly immersed in World War II and those approaching the subject for the first time. As the years thin the ranks of those who fought in the war, Hastings's balanced and elegantly written prose should help ensure that the bloodshed, bravery and brutality of that tragic conflict aren't forgotten."   —Associated Press

"This book is packed with fascinating and surprising statistics and facts. . . . Hastings has an extraordinary ability to throw a bucket into the ocean of wartime papers, diaries, letters and documents of every kind, and bring up something fascinating and worthwhile every time."   —*Financial Times*

"Oddly enough, good single-volume histories of the war are relatively rare. By and large, its sheer scope intimidates writers: while there are hundreds of books about individual episode, from the Battle of Britain to D-Day, surprisingly few historians have tried to pull all the threads together. But Hastings, as the author of several splendid volumes on various aspects of the conflict, is the ideal candidate to conquer this historiographical Everest. His book is at once a 'global portrait,' emphasizing events in Asia as well as in Europe, and a 'human story,' saturated in the details of ordinary people's experience. . . . Hastings has a terrific grasp of the grand sweep and military strategy of the war, showing how a combination of Russian blood, American industry and German incompetence made the allied victory inevitable. But what makes this book so compelling are the human stories. . . . This is the book he was born to write."   —*The Sunday Times* (London)

"Though the Second World War has been the subject of immense historical research, Max Hastings here demonstrates how much there is still to know. . . . Hastings draws on eye-witness accounts and anecdotes from soldiers of all armies to show graphically what the war was like for the ordinary people who fought it, and, overwhelmingly, how terrible it was for the combatants. While many of the frontline commanders of each of the belligerent powers come in for some harsh treatment for their ineptitude or bungling, the valour, heroism and, above all, the extraordinary stoicism of their troops amid scarcely imaginable pain, suffering and losses are repeatedly highlighted."
—*The Evening Standard* (London)

"[A] huge, majestic book. . . . The Second World War took place in the skies, the oceans and the lands of five different continents. It encompassed fighting in Arctic blizzards, as well as in jungles and deserts. Any military history must encompass all of this and more. And at the same time it must reconcile the grand strategy of generals and politicians with the more violent experiences of ordinary soldiers . . . Hastings shapes all these stories, almost miraculously, into a coherent narrative. Overlaid upon this tapestry is an analysis of how the war brought out the best and the worst in people, how it could be won only through the use of astonishing brutality and how it changed society forever."   —*The Sunday Telegraph* (London)

Max Hastings

INFERNO

Max Hastings is the author of more than twenty books. He has served as a foreign correspondent and as the editor of Britain's *Evening Standard* and *Daily Telegraph*. He has received numerous British Press Awards, including Journalist of the Year in 1982 and Editor of the Year in 1988. He lives outside London.

www.maxhastings.com

INFERNO

THE WORLD AT WAR, 1939–1945

Max Hastings

VINTAGE BOOKS
A DIVISION OF RANDOM HOUSE, INC.
NEW YORK

FIRST VINTAGE BOOKS EDITION, OCTOBER 2012

The Library of Congress has cataloged the Knopf edition as follows:
Hastings, Max.
Inferno : the world at war, 1939–1945 / by Max Hastings.
p. cm.
Originally published: London : HarperPress, 2010.
Includes bibliographical references and index.
1. World War, 1939–1945. I. Title.
D743.H364 2011
940.54—dc22 2011013890

Vintage ISBN: 978-0-307-47553-4

Book design by Robert C. Olsson

Printed in the United States of America

10 9 8 7 6 5 4

To Michael Sissons,

for thirty years a princely agent,

counsellor and friend

Contents

Illustrations

INSERT TWO

Japanese troops on Bataan, c. 1942. (*U.S. National Archives & Records Administration, Washington D.C.*)

Indian refugees escaping from Burma, January 1942. (*George Rodger/ Time & Life Pictures/Getty Images*)

American prisoners in the Philippines, May 1942. (*U.S. National Archives & Records Administration, Washington, D.C.: 127-N-114541*)

Crew abandoning USS *Lexington*, Battle of the Coral Sea, May 1942. (*AP Photo/Press Association*)

Japanese soldiers killed on Guadalcanal, August 1942. (*AP Photo/Press Association*)

Australian troops carrying a wounded comrade to a dressing station on Papua New Guinea, December 1943. (*AP Photo/Press Association*)

HMS *Vansittart* on convoy escort duty in the Arctic, February 1943. (*AP Photo/Press Association*)

Survivors of a U-boat sunk in the North Atlantic, April 1943. (*Photo by Jack January/USCG Historian's Office*)

WRENS wheeling a torpedo alongside a submarine at Portsmouth, September 1943. (*Imperial War Museum A 19471*)

Chinese foot soldiers, August 1945. (*Jack Wilkes/Time & Life Pictures/ Getty Images*)

German grenadier during the retreat from the Soviet Union, 1943–44. (*Keystone/Getty Images*)

The Soviet Union, 1943. (© *The Russian State Documentary Film and Photo Archive at Krasnogorsk [RGAKFD]/N. Asnina*)

Women riveters in an American dockyard, 1942. (*CORBIS*)

Twelve-year-old mill operator at the Perm Engine-Building Works, Soviet Union, 1943. (*ITAR-TASS*)

The Red Army advances. (© *The Russian State Documentary Film and Photo Archive at Krasnogorsk [RGAKFD]/Minkevich collection*)

Drawing by Zainul Abedin from his *Bengal Famine* series, 1943. (*Courtesy of Zainul Abedin*)

Maps

Introduction

This is a book chiefly about human experience. Men and women from scores of nations struggled to find words to describe what happened to them in the Second World War, which transcended anything they had ever known. Many resorted to a cliché: "All hell broke loose." Because the phrase is commonplace in eyewitness descriptions of battles, air raids, massacres and ship sinkings, later generations are tempted to shrug at its banality. Yet in an important sense the words capture the essence of what the struggle meant to hundreds of millions of people, plucked from peaceful, ordered existences to face ordeals that in many cases lasted for years, and for at least 60 million were terminated by death. An average of 27,000 people perished each day between September 1939 and August 1945 as a consequence of the global conflict. Some survivors found that the manner in which they had conducted themselves during the struggle defined their standing in their societies for the rest of their lives, for good or ill. Successful warriors retained a lustre which enabled some to prosper in government or commerce. Conversely, at the bar of a London club thirty years after VE-Day, a Guards veteran murmured about a prominent Conservative statesman: "Not a bad fellow, Smith. Such a pity he ran away in the war." A Dutch girl, growing up in the 1950s, found that her parents categorised each of their neighbours in accordance with how they had behaved during the German occupation of Holland.

British and American infantrymen were appalled by their experiences in the 1944–45 northwest Europe campaign, which lasted eleven months. But Russians and Germans fought each other continuously for almost four years in far worse conditions, and with vastly heavier casualties.* Some nations which played only a marginal military role lost many more people than the Western Allies: China's ordeal at Japanese hands between 1937 and 1945 cost at least 15 million lives; Yugoslavia, where civil war was over-

---

* Throughout this book, the word "casualties" is used in its technical military sense, meaning men killed, missing, wounded or taken prisoner. In most ground actions in most theatres, approximately three men were wounded for each one killed.

laid on Axis occupation, lost more than a million dead. Many people witnessed spectacles comparable with Renaissance painters' conception of the inferno to which the damned were consigned: human beings torn to fragments of flesh and bone; cities blasted into rubble; ordered communities sundered into human particles. Almost everything which civilised peoples take for granted in time of peace was swept aside, above all the expectation of being protected from violence.

It is impossible to detail within a single volume the vastness of the war, the largest event in human history. I have already described aspects of it in eight books, most significantly *Bomber Command, Overlord, Armageddon, Retribution* and *Winston's War.* While any work such as this should be self-contained, I have striven to avoid repetition of either anecdotage or analysis of large issues. For instance, having devoted an entire chapter of *Nemesis* to the 1945 dropping of the atomic bombs on Hiroshima and Nagasaki, it seems fruitless to revisit my own arguments. This book sustains a chronological framework, and seeks to establish and reflect upon the "big picture," the context of events: the reader should gain a broad sense of what happened to the world between 1939 and 1945. But its principal purpose is to illuminate the conflict's significance for a host of ordinary people of many societies, both active and passive participants—though the distinction is often blurred. Was, for example, a Hamburg woman who ardently supported Hitler, but perished in the July 1943 firestorm generated by Allied bombing, an accomplice to Nazi war guilt or the innocent victim of an atrocity?

In my pursuit of the human story, wherever possible without losing coherence my narrative omits unit identifications and details of battlefield manoeuvres. Maps are deliberately impressionistic rather than detailed; photos depict ordinary people, not warlords. I have tried to create a global portrait: the strategic narrative emphasises aspects of the conflict which I have not examined elsewhere, and about which there seems more to be said—for instance, India's experience—at the expense of others which have been exhaustively explored, such as Pearl Harbor and the battle for Normandy.

The Jewish genocide became the most coherent fulfilment of Nazi ideology. I wrote in *Armageddon* about the ordeal of concentration-camp prisoners, and have here instead addressed the evolution of the Holocaust from a Nazi perspective. So widespread is a modern Western perception that the war was fought about Jews that it should be emphasised this was not the case. Though Hitler and his followers chose to blame the Jews for the troubles of Europe and the grievances of the Third Reich, Germany's struggle with the Allies was about power and hemispheric dominance. The plight of the Jewish people under Nazi occupation loomed relatively small in the wartime perceptions of Churchill and Roosevelt, and less surprisingly in that of Stalin. About one-seventh of all fatal victims of Nazism, and almost one-tenth of all wartime dead, ultimately proved to have been Jews. But at the time their persecution was viewed by the Allies merely as one fragment of the collateral damage caused by Hitler, as indeed Russians still see the Holocaust today. The limited attention paid to the Jewish predicament by the wartime Allies was a source of frustration and anger to informed coreligionists at the time, and has prompted powerful indignation since. But it is important to recognise that between 1939 and 1945 the Allied nations saw the struggle overwhelmingly in terms of the threat posed by the Axis to their own interests, though Churchill defined these in generous and noble terms.

One of the most important truths about the war, as indeed about all human affairs, is that people can interpret what happens to them only in the context of their own circumstances. The fact that, objectively and statistically, the sufferings of some individuals were less terrible than those of others elsewhere in the world was meaningless to those concerned. It would have seemed monstrous to a British or American soldier facing a mortar barrage, with his comrades dying around him, to be told that Russian casualties were many times greater. It would have been insulting to invite a hungry Frenchman, or even an English housewife weary of the monotony of rations, to consider that in besieged Leningrad starving people were eating one another, while in West Bengal they were selling their daughters. Few people who endured the Luftwaffe's 1940–41 blitz on London would have been comforted by knowledge that the German and Japanese peoples would later face losses from Allied bombing many times greater, together with unparalleled devastation. It is the duty and privilege of historians to deploy relativism in a fashion that cannot be expected of contemporary participants. Almost everyone who participated in the war suffered in some degree: the varied scale and disparate nature of their experiences are themes of this book. But the fact that the plight of other people was worse than one's own did little to promote personal stoicism.

Some aspects of wartime experience were almost universal: fear and grief; the conscription of young men and women obliged to endure new existences utterly remote from those of their choice, often under arms and at worst as slaves. A boom in prostitution was a tragic global phenomenon which deserves a book of its own. The conflict provoked many mass migrations. Some of these were orderly: half the population of Britain changed residence in the course of the war, and many Americans took new jobs in unfamiliar places. Elsewhere, however, millions were wrenched from their communities in dreadful circumstances, and faced ordeals which often killed them. "These are strange times," wrote an anonymous Berlin woman on 22 April 1945 in one of the great diaries of the war, "history experienced first hand, the stuff of tales yet untold and songs unsung. But seen close-up, history is much more troublesome—nothing but burdens and fears. Tomorrow I'll go and look for nettles and get some coal."

The nature of battlefield experience varied from nation to nation, service to service. Within armies, riflemen experienced far higher levels of risk and hardship than millions of support troops. The U.S. armed forces suffered an overall death rate of just five per thousand men enlisted; the vast majority of those who served faced perils no greater than those of ordinary civilian life. While 17,000 American combat casualties lost limbs, during the war years 100,000 workers at home became amputees as a result of industrial accidents. Men who found themselves on battlefields when their nations were in retreat suffered more heavily than others who served in times of victories; Allied warriors who saw action only in 1944–45 had a far better statistical prospect of survival than, say, airmen or submariners who began operational service earlier, when their cause was faring badly.

My story emphasises bottom-up views and experiences, the voices of little people rather than big ones; I have written extensively elsewhere about the warlords of 1939–45. Contemporary diaries and letters record what people did or what was done to them, but often tell us little about what they thought; the latter is more interesting, but more elusive. The obvious explanation is that most warriors are young and immature: they experience extremes of excitement, terror or hardship, but only a small minority have the emotional energy for reflection, because they are absorbed in their immediate physical surroundings, needs and desires.

It was fundamental that only a tiny number of national leaders and commanders knew much about anything beyond their immediate line of sight. Civilians existed in a fog of propaganda and uncertainty, scarcely less dense in Britain and the United States than in Germany or Russia. Frontline combatants assessed the success or failure of their side chiefly through counting casualties and noticing whether they were moving forwards or backwards. These were, however, sometimes inadequate indicators: Pfc. Eric Diller's battalion was cut off from the main American army for seventeen days during the Leyte campaign in the Philippines, but he realised the seriousness of his unit's predicament only when this was explained to him by his company commander after the war.

Even those with privileged access to secrets were confined to their own fragments of knowledge in a vast jigsaw puzzle. For instance, Roy Jenkins, who later became a British statesman, decrypted German signals at Bletchley Park. He and his colleagues knew the importance and urgency of the work they were doing, but, contrary to the impression given in sensational films about Bletchley, they were told nothing about the significance or impact of their contributions. Such constraints were greater, unsurprisingly, on the other side of the hill: in January 1942 Hitler became convinced that too many people in Berlin knew too much. He decreed that even officials of the Abwehr should receive only such information as was necessary for their own work. They were forbidden to listen to enemy broadcasts, a considerable handicap for an intelligence service.

I am fascinated by the complex interplay of loyalties and sympathies around the world. In Britain and America, confidence that our parents and grandparents were fighting "the good war" is so deeply ingrained that we often forget that people in many countries adopted more equivocal attitudes: colonial subjects, and above all India's 400 million, saw little merit in the defeat of the Axis if they continued to endure British suzerainty. Many Frenchmen fought vigorously against the Allies. In Yugoslavia, rival factions were far more strongly committed to waging civil war against one another than to advancing the interests of either the Allies or the Axis. Large numbers of Stalin's subjects embraced the opportunity offered by German occupation to take up arms against a hated Moscow regime. None of this implies doubt that the Allied cause deserved to triumph, but it should emphasise the fact that Churchill and Roosevelt did not have all the best tunes.

It may be useful to explain how this book was written. I began by rereading Gerhard Weinberg's *A World at Arms* and *Total War* by Peter Calvocoressi, Guy Wint and John Pritchard, probably the two best single-volume histories of the war. I then composed a skeleton narrative, setting the most important events in sequence, and laid upon it the flesh of anecdotage and my own reflections. When I had completed a draft, I revisited some other outstanding recent accounts of the conflict: Richard Overy's *Why the Allies Won*, Allan Millett and Williamson Murray's *A War to Be Won* and Michael Burleigh's *Moral Combat*. I then reviewed my own comments and conclusions in the light of theirs.

Wherever possible, I have favoured relatively obscure anecdotage at the expense of justly celebrated personal recollections—omitting, for instance, the likes of Richard Hillary's *The Last Enemy* and George Macdonald Fraser's *Quartered Safe Out Here*. Dr. Lyuba Vinogradovna, who has researched my Russian material for the past decade, for this work once again identified and translated personal narratives, diaries and letters.

Serena Sissons has translated thousands of words from Italian memoirs and diaries, because Mussolini's people seem to me inadequately represented in most Anglo-Saxon narratives. I have explored unpublished Polish accounts in the Imperial War Museum archive and London's Sikorski Institute. I am once again indebted to Dr. Tami Biddle of the U.S. Army War College at Carlisle, Pennsylvania, for insights and documents derived from her own researches, which she has generously shared with me. Various friends, notable among them Professor Sir Michael Howard, Dr. Williamson Murray and Don Berry, have been kind enough to read my draft manuscript and make invaluable corrections, suggestions and comments. The foremost among modern British naval historians, Professor Nicholas Rodger of All Souls College, Oxford, read the chapter on the British experience at sea, much to the advantage of my final text. That outstanding American chronicler of the Pacific War, Richard Frank, has corrected some of my most egregious mistakes about the Eastern war. None of these, of course, bears any responsibility for my judgements and errors.

Any writer's highest aspiration, more than sixty-five years after the war's ending, is to offer a personal view rather than a comprehensive account of this greatest and most terrible of all human experiences, which never fails to inspire humility in its modern students, prompted by gratitude that we have been spared anything comparable. In 1920, when Colonel Charles à Court Repington, military correspondent of the *Daily Telegraph*, published a best-selling account of the recent conflict, it was considered sinister and tasteless that he chose as his title *The First World War*, for it presumed another. To call this book *The Last World War* would be to tempt providence, but it is at least certain that never again will millions of armed men clash on European battlefields such as those of 1939–45. The conflicts of the future will be quite different, and it may not be rashly optimistic to suggest that they will be less terrible.

Max Hastings
Chilton Foliat, Berkshire, and Kamogi, Kenya
April 2011

INFERNO

CHAPTER ONE

POLAND BETRAYED

WHILE ADOLF HITLER was determined to wage war, it was no more inevitable that his 1939 invasion of Poland precipitated global conflict than that the assassination of the Archduke Franz Ferdinand of Austria did so in 1914. Britain and France lacked both the will and the means to take effective action towards fulfilment of security guarantees they had given earlier to the Poles. Their declarations of war on Germany were gestures which even some staunch anti-Nazis thought foolish, because of their futility. For every eventual belligerent save the Poles themselves, the struggle began slowly: only in its third year did global death and destruction attain the vastness sustained thereafter until 1945. Even Hitler's Reich was at first ill-equipped to generate the intensity of violence demanded by a death grapple between the most powerful nations on earth.

During the summer of 1939 *Gone with the Wind*, Margaret Mitchell's novel of the old American South, enjoyed a surge of popularity in Poland. "Somehow, I considered it prophetic," wrote one of its Polish readers, Rula Langer. Few of her compatriots doubted that a conflict with Germany was imminent, because Hitler had made plain his commitment to conquest. Poland's fiercely nationalistic people responded to the Nazi threat with the same spirit as the doomed young men of the Confederacy in 1861. "Like most of us, I believed in happy endings," a young fighter pilot recalled. "We wanted to fight, it excited us, and we wanted it to happen fast. We didn't believe that something bad could really happen." When Jan Karski, an artillery lieutenant, received his mobilisation order on 24 August, his sister warned him against burdening himself with too many clothes. "You aren't going to Siberia," she said. "We'll have you on our hands again within a month."

The Poles paraded their propensity for fantasy. There was an exuberance in the café and bar chatter of Warsaw, a city whose baroque beauties and twenty-five theatres caused citizens to proclaim it "the Paris of eastern Europe." A *New York Times* reporter wrote from the Polish capital: "To hear people talk, one might think that Poland, not Germany, was the great industrial colossus." Mussolini's foreign minister, his son-in-law Count

Galeazzo Ciano, warned the Polish ambassador in Rome that if his country resisted Hitler's territorial demands, it would find itself fighting alone, and "would quickly be turned into a heap of ruins." The ambassador did not dissent, but asserted vaguely that "some eventual success . . . might give Poland greater strength." In Britain, Lord Beaverbrook's newspapers denounced as provocative Warsaw's defiance in the face of Hitler's threats.

The Polish nation of 30 million, including almost 1 million ethnic Germans, 5 million Ukrainians and 3 million Jews, had held borders established by the Treaty of Versailles for only twenty years. Between 1919 and 1921, Poland fought the Bolsheviks to assert its independence from longstanding Russian hegemony. By 1939 the country was ruled by a military junta, though the historian Norman Davies has argued, "If there was hardship and injustice in Poland, there was no mass starvation or mass killing as in Russia, no resort to the bestial methods of Fascism or Stalinism." The ugliest manifestation of Polish nationalism was anti-Semitism, exemplified by quotas for Jewish university entry.

In the eyes of both Berlin and Moscow, the Polish state owed its existence only to Allied force majeure in 1919, and had no legitimacy. In a secret protocol of the Nazi-Soviet Pact signed on 23 August 1939, Hitler and Stalin agreed on Poland's partition and dissolution. Though the Poles viewed Russia as their historic enemy, they were oblivious of immediate Soviet designs on them, and were bent instead upon frustrating those of Germany. They knew the ill-equipped Polish army could not defeat the Wehrmacht; all their hopes were pinned upon an Anglo-French offensive in the west, which would divide Germany's forces. "In view of Poland's hopeless military situation," wrote its London ambassador, Count Edward Raczyński, "my main anxiety has been to ensure that we should not become involved in war with Germany without receiving immediate help from our allies."

In March 1939, the British and French governments gave guarantees, formalised in subsequent treaties, that in the event of German aggression against Poland, they would fight. If the worst happened, France promised the military leadership in Warsaw that its army would attack Hitler's Siegfried Line within thirteen days of mobilisation. Britain pledged an immediate bomber offensive against Germany. Both powers' assurances reflected cynicism, for neither had the smallest intention of fulfilling them: the guarantees were designed to deter Hitler, rather than to provide credible military assistance to Poland. They were gestures without substance, yet the Poles chose to believe them.

If Stalin was not Hitler's cobelligerent, Moscow's deal with Berlin made him the cobeneficiary of Nazi aggression. From 23 August onwards, the world saw Germany and the Soviet Union acting in concert, twin faces of totalitarianism. Because of the manner in which the global struggle ended in 1945, with Russia in the Allied camp, some historians have accepted the postwar Soviet Union's classification of itself as a neutral power until 1941. This is mistaken. Though Stalin feared Hitler and expected eventually to have to fight him, in 1939 he made a historic decision to acquiesce in German aggression, in return for Nazi support for Moscow's own programme of territorial aggrandisement. Whatever excuses the Soviet leader later offered, and although his armies never fought in partnership with the Wehrmacht, the Nazi-Soviet Pact established a collaboration which persisted until Hitler revealed his true purposes in Operation Barbarossa.

The Moscow nonaggression agreement, together with the subsequent 28 September Treaty of Friendship, Cooperation and Demarcation, committed the world's two principal tyrants to endorse each other's ambitions and forswear mutual hostilities in favour of aggrandisement elsewhere. Stalin indulged Hitler's expansionist policies in the west, and gave Germany important material aid—oil, corn and mineral products. The Nazis, however insincerely, conceded a free hand in the east to the Soviets, whose objectives included eastern Finland and the Baltic states in addition to a large share of Poland's carcass.

Hitler intended the Second World War to start on 26 August, only three days after the Nazi-Soviet Pact was signed. On the twenty-fifth, however, while ordering mobilisation to continue, he postponed the invasion of Poland: he was shocked to discover both that Mussolini was unwilling immediately to fight beside him, and that diplomatic communications suggested Britain and France were serious about honouring their guarantees to Warsaw. Three million men, 400,000 horses, 200,000 vehicles, and 5,000 trains advanced towards the Polish frontier while a last flurry of futile exchanges took place between Berlin, London and Paris. At last, on 30 August, Hitler gave the attack order. At 8:00 the following evening, the curtain rose on the first, appropriately sordid, act of the conflict. Sturmbannführer Alfred Naujocks of the German Sicherheitsdienst (security service) led a party dressed in Polish uniforms, and including a dozen convicted criminals dismissively code-named *"Konserwen"*—"tin cans"—in a mock assault on the German radio station at Gleiwitz in Upper Silesia. Shots were fired; Polish patriotic slogans were broadcast across the airwaves; then the "attackers" withdrew. SS machine gunners killed the "tin cans," whose bloodstained corpses were arranged for display to foreign correspondents as evidence of Polish aggression.

At 2:00 a.m. on 1 September, the Wehrmacht's 1st Mounted Regiment was among scores roused in its bivouacs by a bugle call—some German units as well as many Polish ones rode horses to battle. The squadrons saddled, mounted, and began to move towards their start line alongside clattering columns of armour, trucks and guns. The order was given: "Muzzle caps off! Load! Safety catches on!" At 4:40 a.m., the big guns of the old German battleship *Schleswig-Holstein*, anchored in Danzig harbour for a "goodwill visit," opened fire on the Polish fort at Westerplatte. An hour later, German soldiers tore down crossing poles on the western frontier, opening the way for leading elements of the invasion force to pour forward into Poland. One of its commanders, Gen. Heinz Guderian, soon found himself passing his family's ancestral estate at Chelmno, where he had been born when it formed part of pre-Versailles Germany. Among his soldiers, a twenty-three-year-old lieutenant, Wilhelm Pruller, expressed the euphoria that suffused the army: "It's a wonderful feeling now, to be a German . . . We've crossed the border. *Deutschland, Deutschland uber alles!* The German Wehrmacht is marching! If we look back, or in front of us, or left or right, everywhere the motorised Wehrmacht!"

The Western Allies, heartened by knowledge that Poland boasted the fourth largest army in Europe, anticipated a struggle lasting some months. The defenders deployed 1.3 million men against 1.5 million Germans, with thirty-seven divisions on each side. But the Wehrmacht was far better equipped, having 3,600 armoured vehicles against 750 Polish, 1,929 modern planes against 900 obsolete ones. The Polish army had been progressively deploying since March, but had held back from full mobilisation in response to Anglo-French pleas to avoid provoking Hitler. Thus, on 1 September, the defenders were surprised. A Polish diplomat wrote of his people's attitude: "They were united in the will to resist, but without any clear idea about the kind of resistance to be offered, apart from a lot of loose talk about volunteering as 'human torpedoes.' "

Ephrahim Blaichman, a sixteen-year-old Jew living in Kamionka, was among thousands of local inhabitants summoned into the town square to be addressed by the mayor: "We sang a Polish hymn declaring that Poland was not yet lost, and another promising that no German would spit in our faces." Piotr Tarczynkski, a twenty-six-year-old factory clerk, had been ill for some weeks before he was mobilised. But when he informed the commanding officer of his artillery battery that he was ailing, the colonel responded with a brisk patriotic speech, "and told me he was sure that once I found myself in the saddle I would feel much better." Equipment was so short that the regiment could not issue Tarczynkski with a personal weapon; he did, however, receive a regulation charger, a big horse named Wojak—"Warrior."

An air force instructor, Witold Urbanowitz, was conducting a mock dogfight with a pupil in the sky over Dęblin when he was bewildered to see holes appearing in his plane's wings. Landing hastily, he was met by a fellow officer who ran across the field to meet him, exclaiming, "You're alive, Witold? You're not hit?" Urbanowitz demanded, "What the hell's going on?" His comrade said, "You should go to church and light a candle. You were just attacked by a Messerschmitt!" The nakedness of Poland's defences was everywhere apparent. Fighter pilot Franciszek Kornicki was scrambled twice on 1 and 2 September. On the first occasion he pursued a German plane which easily outpaced him. On the second, when his guns jammed he tried to clear them, roll and renew his attack. As the plane banked steeply, the harness buckles holding him in his open cockpit came undone; he fell into the sky, and found himself making an embarrassed parachute descent.

At 5:00 p.m. near the village of Krojanty, Polish Uhlan cavalrymen received an order to counterattack, to cover the retreat of neighbouring infantry. As they formed line and drew sabres, the adjutant, Captain Godlewski, suggested that they should advance on foot. "Young man," the regimental commander, Colonel Mastalerz, responded testily, "I'm quite aware what it is like to carry out an impossible order." Bent low over the necks of their horses, 250 men charged across an open field. German infantrymen fled from their path, but beyond them stood armoured cars, whose machine guns ravaged the Uhlans. Scores of horses crashed to the earth, while others raced away riderless. Within minutes half the attackers were dead, including Colonel Mastalerz. The survivors fell back in confusion, flotsam of an earlier age.

France's high command had urged the Poles to concentrate their forces behind the three big rivers in the centre of their country, but the Warsaw government deemed it essential instead to defend its entire 900-mile frontier with Germany, not least because most Polish industry lay in the west; some divisions thus became responsible for fronts of eighteen miles, when their strengths—around 15,000 men—scarcely sufficed for three or four. The three-pronged German assault, from north, south and west, drove deep into the country in the face of ineffectual resistance, leaving pockets of defenders isolated. Luftwaffe aircraft gave close support to the panzers, and also launched devastating air raids on Warsaw, Łódź, Dęblin and Sandomierz.

Polish troops and civilians were strafed and bombed with ruthless impartiality, though some victims took time to recognise the gravity of the threat. After the first wave of attacks, Virgilia, the American-born wife of Polish nobleman Prince Paul Sapieha, told her household reassuringly, "You see: these bombs aren't so bad. Their bark is worse than

The Polish Campaign

Baltic Sea

LITHUANIA

Kaunas

Vilnius

Königsberg

Danzig

East
Prussia

Minsk

RUSSIA

Bydgoszcz • Torun

Bialystok

Poznan

Modlin

Pinsk

Pripet

Kutno

Warsaw

Brest-Litovsk

Pripet Marshes

Lodz

Gora Kalvaria

Radom

Vlodava
Lublin

Kovel

P O L A N D

Chelm

Luck

Rovno

GERMANY

Vistula

Zhitomir •

Cracow

San

Vistula

Lvov

Przemysl

Dniester

German attacks 15/27 Sept.

Polish Bzura Pocket

Russian attacks 17/27 Sept.

0   50   100 miles

HUNGARY

ROMANIA

0   50   100   150 kms

their bite." When two bombs fell in the park of the Smorczewski family's stately home at Tarnogóra on the night of 1 September, the young sons of the house, Ralph and Mark, were hastily dragged from their beds by their mother and rushed outside to hide in a wood with other young refugees. "After recovering from the initial shock," Ralph wrote later, "we looked at each other and fell into a fit of unrestrained giggles. What a strange sight we were: a motley collection of youths, some in pyjamas, others with coats thrown over their underwear, standing aimlessly under the trees, playing with gas masks. We decided to go home."

Soon, however, there was no more giggling: the people of Poland were obliged to recognise the devastating power of the Luftwaffe. "I was awakened by the wail of sirens and sound of explosions," wrote the diplomat Adam Kruczkiewicz in Warsaw. "Outside I saw German planes flying at incredibly low level and throwing bombs at their ease. There was some desultory machine-gun fire from the tops of a few buildings, but no Polish fliers . . . The city was stunned by the almost complete lack of air defence. They felt bitterly disappointed." The town of Łuck belied its name: early one morning a dozen German bombs fell on it, killing scores of people, most of them children walking to school. Impotent victims called the cloudless skies of those September days "the curse of Poland." The pilot B. J. Solak wrote: "The stench of burning and a brown veil of smoke filled all the air around our town." After hiding his unarmed plane beneath some trees, Solak was driving home when he met a peasant on the road, "leading a horse whose hip was a blanket of congealed blood. Its head was touching the dust with its nostrils, each step causing it to shudder with pain." The young airman asked the peasant where he was taking the stricken animal, victim of a Stuka dive-bomber. "To the veterinary clinic in town." "But that's four miles more!" A shrug: "I have only one horse."

A thousand larger tragedies unfolded. As Lt. Piotr Tarczynski's artillery battery clattered forward towards the battlefield, Stukas fell on it; every man sprang from his saddle and threw himself to the earth. A few bombs dropped, some men and horses fell. Then the planes were gone, the battery remounted and resumed its march. "We saw two women, one middle-aged and one only a girl, carrying a short ladder. On it was stretched a wounded man, still alive and clutching his abdomen. As they passed us, I could see his intestines trailing on the ground." Władysław Anders had fought with the Russians in World War I, under the exotically named Tsarist general the Khan of Nakhitchevan. Now, commanding a Polish cavalry brigade, Anders saw a teacher leading a group of her pupils to the shelter of woods. "Suddenly, there was the roar of an aeroplane. The pilot circled, descending to a height of fifty metres. As he dropped his bombs and fired his machine-guns, the children scattered like sparrows. The aeroplane disappeared as quickly as it had come, but on the field some crumpled and lifeless bundles of bright clothing remained. The nature of the new war was already clear."

Thirteen-year-old George Slazak was on a train with a party of children travelling home to Łódź from summer camp. Suddenly there were explosions, screams, and the train lurched to a stop. The group leader shouted at the boys to get out fast and run for a nearby forest. Shocked and terrified, they lay prostrate for half an hour until the bombing stopped. On emerging, a few hundred yards up the track they saw a blazing troop train which had been the Germans' target. Some boys burst into tears at the sight of bleeding men; their first attempt to reboard their own train was frustrated by the return of the Luftwaffe, machine-gunning. At last, they resumed their journey in coaches riddled with bullet holes. George reached home to find his mother sobbing by the family radio set: it had reported Germans approaching.

Franciszek Kornicki, a pilot, went to visit a wounded comrade in a Łódź hospital: "It was a terrible place, full of wounded and dying men lying everywhere on beds and on the floor, in rooms and corridors, some moaning in agony, others lying silent with their eyes closed or wide open, waiting and hoping." Gen. Adrian Carlton de Wiart, head of the British military mission in Poland, wrote bitterly: "I saw the very face of war change—its glory shorn, no longer the soldier setting forth into battle, but the women and children being buried under it."

ON SUNDAY, 3 September, Britain and France declared war on Germany, in fulfilment of their guarantees to Poland. Stalin's alliance with Hitler caused many European communists, compliant with Moscow, to distance themselves from their nations' stand against the Nazis. Trades union-ists' denunciations of what they branded an "imperialist war" influenced attitudes in many French and British factories, shipyards and coal mines. Street graffiti appeared: "Stop the War: The Worker Pays," "No to Capi-talist War." Independent Labour MP Aneurin Bevan, a standard-bearer of the left, hedged his bets by calling for a struggle on two fronts: against Hitler and also against British capitalism.

The secret protocols of the Nazi-Soviet Pact, delineating the parties' territorial ambitions, were unknown in Western capitals until German archives were captured in 1945. But in September 1939, many citizens of the democracies perceived Russia and Germany alike as their foes. The novelist Evelyn Waugh's fictional alter ego, Guy Crouchback, adopted a view shared by many European conservatives: Stalin's deal with Hitler, "news that shook the politicians and young poets of a dozen capital cit-ies, brought deep peace to one English heart . . . The enemy at last was plain in view, huge and hateful, all disguise cast off. It was the Modern Age in arms." A few politicians aspired to separate Russia and Germany, to seek the support of Stalin to defeat the greater evil of Hitler. Until June 1941, however, such a prospect seemed remote: the two dictatorships were viewed as common enemies of the democracies.

Hitler did not anticipate the British and French declarations of war. Their acquiescence in his 1938 seizure of Czechoslovakia, together with the impossibility of direct Anglo-French military succour for Poland, argued a lack of both will and means to challenge him. The Führer him-self quickly recovered from his initial shock, but some of his acolytes were troubled. Herman Göring, commander-in-chief (C-in-C) of the Luft-waffe, his nerve badly shaken, raged down the telephone to Germany's foreign minister, Joachin von Ribbentrop: "Now you've got your fucking war! You alone are to blame!" Hitler had striven to forge a German war-rior society committed to martial glory, with notable success among the young. But older people displayed far less enthusiasm in 1939 than they had done in 1914, recalling the horrors of the previous conflict, and their own defeat. "This war has a ghostly unreality," wrote Count Helmuth von Moltke, an Abwehr intelligence officer but an implacable opponent of Hitler. "The people don't support it . . . [They] are apathetic. It's like a *danse macabre* performed on the stage by persons unknown."

The American CBS correspondent William Shirer reported from Hit-ler's capital on 3 September: "There is no excitement here . . . no hurrahs, no wild cheering, no throwing of flowers . . . It is a far grimmer German people that we see here tonight than we saw last night or the day before." As Alexander Stahlberg passed through Stettin with his army unit en route to the Polish border, he echoed Shirer's view: "None of the brave mood of August 1914, no cheers, no flowers." The Austrian writer Stefan Zweig readily explained this: "They did not feel the same because the world in 1939 was not as childishly naïve and gullible as in 1914 . . . This almost religious faith in the honesty or at least the ability of your own govern-ment had disappeared throughout the whole of Europe."

But many Germans echoed the sentiments of Fritz Muehlebach, a Nazi Party official: "I regarded England's and France's interference . . . as nothing but a formality . . . As soon as they realised the utter hopelessness of Polish resistance and the vast superiority of German arms they would begin to see that we had always been in the right and it was quite senseless to meddle . . . It was only as a result of something that wasn't their busi-ness that the war had ever started. If Poland had been alone she would certainly have given in quietly."

The Allied nations hoped that the mere gesture of declaring war would "call Hitler's bluff," precipitating his overthrow by his own people and a peace settlement without a catastrophic clash of arms in western Europe. Selfishness dominated the response of Britain and France to the unfold-ing Polish tragedy. France's C-in-C, Gen. Maurice Gamelin, had told his British counterpart back in July: "We have every interest in the conflict beginning in the East and only generalising little by little. That way we shall enjoy the time we need to mobilise the totality of the Franco-British forces." Tory MP Cuthbert Headlam wrote petulantly in his diary on 2 September that the Poles "have only themselves to blame for what is coming to them now."

In Britain on 3 September, the air-raid alarm which sounded within minutes of Prime Minister Neville Chamberlain's broadcast announcement of war aroused mixed emotions. "Mother was very flustered," wrote the nineteen-year-old London student J. R. Frier. "Several women in the neighbourhood fainted, and many ran into the road immediately. Some remarks—'Don't go into the shelter till you hear the guns fire'—'The balloons aren't even up yet'—'The swine, he must have sent his planes over before the time limit was up.' " After the all-clear, "within minutes everyone was at their doors, talking quickly to each other in nervous voices. More talk about Hitler and revolutions in Germany . . . Most peculiar thing experienced today was desire for something to happen—to see aeroplanes coming over, and defences in action. I don't really want to see bombs dropping and people killed, but somehow, as we *are* at war, I want it to buck up and start. At this rate, it will carry on for God knows how long." Impatience about the likely duration of the struggle proved an abiding popular sentiment.

In remote African colonies, some young men fled into the bush on hearing that a war had started: they feared that their British rulers would repeat First World War practice by conscripting them for compulsory labour service—as indeed later happened. A Kenyan named Josiah Mariuki recorded "an ominous rumour that Hitler was coming to kill us all, and many people went fearfully down to the rivers and dug holes in the bank to hide from the troops." The leaders of Britain's armed forces recognised their unpreparedness for battle, but some young professional soldiers were sufficiently naïve merely to welcome the prospect of action and promotion. "The effect was one of exhilaration and excitement," wrote John Lewis of the Cameronians. "Hitler was a ludicrous figure, and Pathé newsreels of goose-stepping German soldiers were a cause of hilarious merriment . . . They were pretty good at dive-bombing defenceless Spanish villages, but that was about all. Most of their tanks were dummies made of cardboard. We had beaten a much more powerful Germany twenty years before. We were the greatest empire in the world."

Few people were as clear-thinking as Lt. David Fraser of the Grenadier Guards, who observed harshly: "The mental approach of the British to hostilities was distinguished by their prime faults—slackness of mind and wishful thinking . . . The people of democracies need to believe that good is opposed to evil—hence the spirit of crusade. All this, with its attempted arousal of vigorous moral and ideological passions, tends to work against that cool concept of war as [an] extension of policy defined by Clausewitz, an exercise with finite, attainable objectives."

Many British airmen anticipated their own likely fate. Pilot Officer

Donald Davis wrote: "It was a marvellous autumn day as I drove up past the Wittenham Clumps and Chiltern Hills I knew so well, and I remember thinking that I should be dead in three weeks. I stopped to view the scene and ponder for a few minutes. [I decided that] were I to be faced by the same decisions I should still have decided to fly and join the RAF if I could." To Davis's generation around the world, the privilege of being granted access to the sky fulfilled a supreme romantic vision, for which many young men were content to make payment by risking their lives.

At Westminster, with monumental condescension a government minister told the Polish ambassador, "How lucky you are! Who would have thought, six months ago, that you would have Britain on your side as an ally?" In Poland, news of the British and French declarations of war prompted a surge of hope, boosted by the new allies' extravagant rhetoric. Varsovians embraced in the street, danced, cried, hooted car horns. A crowd gathered outside the British embassy on Aleje Ujadowskie, cheering, singing, stumbling through a version of "God Save the King." The ambassador, Sir Howard Kennard, shouted from the balcony: "Long live Poland! We shall fight side by side against aggression and injustice!"

These tumultuous scenes were repeated at the French embassy, where a crowd sang "La Marseillaise." In Warsaw that night, a government bulletin announced triumphantly: "Polish cavalry units have thrust through the armoured German lines and are now in East Prussia." Across Europe, some enemies of Nazism embraced brief delusions. Mihail Sebastian was a thirty-one-year-old Romanian writer, and a Jew. On 4 September, after hearing news of the British and French declarations of war, he was naïvely astonished that they did not immediately attack in the west. "Are they still waiting for something? Is it possible (as some say) that Hitler will immediately fall and be replaced by a military government, which will then settle for peace? Could there be radical changes in Italy? What will Russia do? What's happening to the Axis, about which there is suddenly silence in both Rome and Berlin? A thousand questions that leave you gasping for breath." Amid his own mental turmoil, Sebastian sought relief first in reading Dostoyevsky, then Thomas De Quincey in English.

On 7 September, ten French divisions moved cautiously into the German Saarland. After advancing five miles, they halted: this represented the sum of France's armed demonstration in support of Poland. Gamelin was satisfied that the Poles could hold off Hitler's Wehrmacht until the French rearmament programme was further advanced. Slowly, the Polish people began to understand that they were alone in their agony. Stefan Starzyński, a former soldier in Piłsudski's Legions, had been Warsaw's inspirational mayor since 1934, famous for making his city a riot of summer flowers. Now, Starzyński broadcast daily to his people, denouncing Nazi barbarism with passionate emotion. He recruited rescue squads, summoned thousands of volunteers to dig trenches, comforted victims of German bombs who were soon numbered in the thousands. Many Varsovians fled east, the rich bartering cars for which they had no fuel to procure carts and bicycles. A sixteen-year-old Jew, Ephrahim Blaichman, watched long columns of refugees of his own race trudging wretchedly along the road from Warsaw. In his innocence, he did not grasp the special peril they faced: despite Poland's notorious anti-Semitism, "I had never experienced anything more severe than name-calling."

Exhaustion among men and horses soon posed the main threat to the headlong German advance. Cavalryman Lance-Corporal Hornes found his mount Herzog repeatedly stumbling: "I called out to the section commander—'Herzog's had as much as he can take!' I had scarcely got the words out when the poor beast fell to his knees. We'd gone 70km on the first day, then 60 on the second. And on top of that, we'd had the trek over the mountains with the advance patrol galloping . . . That meant we'd gone nearly 200km in three days without any proper rest! Night had long fallen, and we were still riding."

The horrors of blitzkrieg mounted: while Warsaw Radio played Chopin's Military Polonaise, German bombing of the capital was now accompanied by the fire of a thousand guns, delivering 30,000 shells a day, which pounded its magnificent buildings into rubble. "The lovely Polish autumn [is] coming," the fighter pilot Wiroslaw Feric wrote in his diary, recoiling from the irony. "Damn and blast its loveliness." A pall of grey smoke and dust settled over the capital; the royal castle, opera house, national theatre, cathedral and scores of public buildings, together with thousands of homes, were reduced to ruins. Unburied bodies and makeshift graves lay everywhere on the boulevards and in the parks; food supplies, water and electricity were cut off; with almost every window shattered, glass fragments carpeted pavements. By 7 September the city and its 120,000 defenders were surrounded, as the Polish army reeled back eastwards. Its chief of staff, Marshal Edward Rydz-Śmigły, had fled Warsaw with the rest of the government on the second day of war; the army's supply system and communications collapsed. Cracow fell almost without resistance on 6 September; Gdynia followed on the thirteenth, though its naval base held out for a further week.

A counterattack on 10 September by eight Polish divisions, across the Bzura River west of Warsaw, briefly disrupted the German offensive and took 1,500 prisoners. Kurt Meyer of the SS Leibstandarte Regiment acknowledged with mingled admiration and condescension: "The Poles attack with enormous tenacity, proving over and over again that they really know how to die." Contrary to legend, on only two occasions did Polish horsemen engage German tanks. One such episode took place on the night of 11 September, when a squadron hurled itself at full gallop at the village of Kałuszyn, strongly held by the Germans. Out of eighty-five horsemen who attacked, only thirty-three afterwards rallied. The invaders used their own cavalry to provide reconnaissance and mobility, rather than for assaults: Lance-Corporal Hornes's unit advanced in column, while two men rode ahead: "They would hurry at a gallop from one hill to the next, then wave the troop on. As another precaution, lone horsemen were sent out alongside us on the ridges of the hills. Suddenly, we saw new unfamiliar contours emerging from the thick dust-cloud: small, agile horses with bobbing heads, ridden by Polish Uhlans in their khaki uniforms, long lances held with one end in the stirrup leather and the other slung from the shoulder. Their shining tips bobbed up and down in time with the horses' hooves. At the same moment, our machine-guns opened fire."

The Wehrmacht was vastly better armed and armoured than its enemies. Poland was a poor country, with only a few thousand military and civilian trucks; its national budget was smaller than that of the city of Berlin. Given the poor quality and small number of Polish planes compared with those of the Luftwaffe, it is remarkable that the campaign cost Germany 560 aircraft. Lt. Piotr Tarczsynski's artillery battery came under intense shellfire a mile from the river Warta. Tarczsynski, a forward observer, found his telephones dead; linesmen sent to investigate never returned. Without having summoned a single salvo, he was surrounded by German infantrymen who took him prisoner. Like many men in his predicament, he sought to ingratiate himself with his captors: "I can only compare my situation with that of someone finding himself unexpectedly faced by influential strangers upon whom he is completely dependent. I know I ought to have been ashamed of myself." As he was marched away to captivity, he passed several dead Polish soldiers; instinctively, he raised his hand to salute each one.

Amid popular rage against the invaders of their homeland, there were scenes of mob violence which conferred no honour upon Poland's cause. Mass arrests of ethnic Germans—supposed or potential fifth columnists—took place throughout early September. At Bydgoszcz on "Bloody Sunday," 3 September, a thousand German civilians were massacred after allegations that they had fired on Polish troops. Some modern German historians claim that up to 13,000 ethnic Germans were killed during the campaign, most of them innocents; the true figure is almost certainly much lower, but such deaths provided a pretext for appalling and systemic Nazi atrocities towards Poles, and especially Polish Jews, which began within days of the invasion. Hitler told his generals at Obersalzberg: "Genghis Khan had millions of women and men killed by his own will and with a light heart. History sees him only as a great state-builder . . . I have sent my Death's Head units to the east with the order to kill without mercy men, women and children of the Polish race or language. Only in such a way shall we win the *Lebensraum* that we need."

When the Wehrmacht entered Łódź, thirteen-year-old George Slazak was bewildered by seeing some women throw flowers at the soldiers, and offer them sweets and cigarettes. Small children shouted *"Heil Hitler!"* Slazak wrote wonderingly: "Boys I was at school with waved swastika flags." Though these welcoming civilians were Polish citizens, they were of German ancestry and now flaunted their heritage. Josef Goebbels launched a strident propaganda campaign to convince his own people of the justice of their cause. On 2 September the Nazi newspaper *Völkischer Beobachter* announced the invasion in a double-deck headline in red ink: "The Führer Proclaims the Fight for Germany's Rights and Security." On 6 September *Lokal-Anzeiger*'s headlines asserted: "Terrible Bestiality of the Poles—German Fliers Shot—Red Cross Columns Mowed Down—Nurses Murdered." A few days later, *Deutsche Allgemeine Zeitung* carried the startling heading "Poles Bombard Warsaw." The story below stated: "Polish artillery of every calibre opened fire from the eastern part of Warsaw against our troops in the western part of the city." The German news agency denounced Polish resistance as "senseless and insane."

Most young Germans, graduates of the Nazi educational system, unhesitatingly accepted the version of events offered by their leaders. "The advance of the armies has become an irresistible march to victory," wrote a twenty-year-old Luftwaffe flight trainee. "Scenes of deep emotion occur within the liberations of the terrorised German residents of the Polish Corridor. Dreadful atrocities, crimes against all the laws of humanity, are brought to light by our armies. Near Bromberg and Thorn they discover mass graves containing the bodies of thousands of Germans who have been massacred by the Polish Communists."

On 17 September, the date on which Poles expected the French to begin their promised offensive on the Western Front, the Soviet Union instead launched its own vicious thrust, designed to secure Stalin's share of Hitler's booty. Stefan Kurylak was a thirteen-year-old Ukrainian Pole, living in a quiet village near the Russian border. Retreating Polish troops began to trickle down its dusty main street on foot and on horseback, some crying out urgently, "Run—run for your lives, good people! Hide anywhere you can, for they are showing no mercy. Hurry. The Russians are coming!" Soon afterwards, the teenager watched a Soviet tank column clatter through the village: a child who lingered in its path, frightened and confused, was casually shot down. Kurylak took refuge in his family's potato pit.

Vyacheslav Molotov, Stalin's foreign minister, told the Polish ambassador in Moscow that, since the Polish republic no longer existed, the Red Army was intervening to "protect Russian citizens in western Belorussia and western Ukraine." Although Hitler had agreed to Stalin's annexation of eastern Poland, the Germans were taken by surprise when the Soviet intervention came. So, too, were the Poles. Once the Red Army struck in their rear, wrote Marshal Rydz-Śmigły bitterly, resistance could become only "an armed demonstration against a new partition of Poland." The Wehrmacht high command, anxious to avoid accidental clashes with the Russians, declared a boundary on the San, Vistula and Narew Rivers; wherever its forces had advanced beyond that line, they now withdrew.

Hitler hoped that Stalin's intervention would provoke the Allies to declare war on the Russians, and in London there was indeed a brief flurry of debate about whether Britain's commitment to Poland demanded engagement of a new enemy. In the War Cabinet, only Churchill and War Minister Leslie Hore-Belisha urged preparations for such an eventuality. Britain's Moscow ambassador, Sir William Seeds, cabled: "I do not see what advantage war with the Soviet Union would be to us although it would please me personally to declare it on Molotov." Much to the relief of Prime Minister Neville Chamberlain, the Foreign Office advised that the government's guarantee to Poland covered only German aggression. Bitter British rhetoric was unleashed against Stalin, but no further consideration was given to fighting him; the French likewise confined themselves to expressions of disgust. Within days, at a cost of only 4,000 casualties, the Russians overran 77,000 square miles of territory including the cities of Lwów and Wilno. Stalin gained suzerainty over 5 million Poles, 4.5 million ethnic Ukrainians, 1 million Belorussians and 1 million Jews.

In Warsaw, starving people still clung to hopes of aid from the west. An air-raid warden confided to an acquaintance: "You know the British. They are slow in making up their minds, but now they are definitely coming." Millions of Poles were at first bewildered, then increasingly outraged, by the passivity of these supposed friends. A cavalry officer wrote: "What was happening in the west, we wondered, and when would the French and British start their offensive? We could not understand why our allies were so slow in coming to our assistance." On 20 September, Poland's London ambassador broadcast to his people at home: "Fellow countrymen! Know that your sacrifice is not in vain, and that its meaning and eloquence are felt to the utmost here . . . Already the hosts of our allies are assembling . . . The day will come when the victorious standards . . . shall return from foreign lands to Poland." Yet even as he spoke, Count Raczyński was conscious, as he wrote later, that his words were "little more than a poetic fiction. Where were the Allied hosts?"

In Paris, Polish ambassador Juliusz Łukasiewicz exchanged bitter words with the French foreign minister, Georges Bonnet. "It isn't right! You know it isn't right!" he said. "A treaty is a treaty and must be respected! Do you realise that every hour you delay the attack on Germany means . . . death to thousands of Polish men, women and children?" Bonnet shrugged: "Do you then want the women and children of Paris to be massacred?" The American correspondent Janet Flanner wrote from Paris: "It would seem, indeed, as if efforts are still being made to hold the war up, prevent its starting in earnest—efforts made, perhaps self-consciously, by government leaders reluctant to go down in history as having ordered the first inflaming shots, or efforts made as a general reflection of the various populations' courageous but confused states of mind. Certainly this must be the first war that millions of people on both sides continued to think could be avoided even after it had officially been declared."

The French were wholly unwilling to launch a major offensive against the Siegfried Line, as Winston Churchill urged, far less to invite German retaliation by bombing Germany. The British government similarly declined to order the RAF to attack German land targets. Tory MP Leo Amery wrote contemptuously of Prime Minister Neville Chamberlain: "Loathing war passionately, he was determined to wage as little of it as possible." *The Times* editorialised in a fashion which seemed to Polish readers to mock their plight: "In the agony of their martyred land, the Poles will perhaps in some degree be consoled by the knowledge that they have the sympathy, and indeed the reverence, not only of their allies in western Europe but of all civilised people throughout the globe."

It is sometimes argued that in mid-September 1939, with the bulk of the German army committed in Poland, the Allies had an ideal opportunity to launch an offensive on the Western Front. But France was even less prepared psychologically than militarily for such an initiative; and Britain's small expeditionary force, still in transit to the Continent, could contribute little. The Germans could probably have repelled any assault without much disrupting their operations in the east, and the inertia of the French and British governments reflected the will of their peoples. A Glasgow secretary named Pam Ashford wrote in her diary on 7 September: "Practically everyone thinks the war will be over in three months . . . Many hold that when Poland is smashed up there won't be much point in continuing."

The Poles should have anticipated the passivity of their allies, but its cynicism was breathtaking. A present-day historian, Andrzej Suchcitz, has written: "The Polish government and military authorities had been double-crossed and betrayed by their western allies. There was no intention of giving Poland any effective military support." As Warsaw faced its doom, Stefan Starzyński declared in a broadcast: "Destiny has committed to us the duty of defending Poland's honour." A Polish poet later celebrated the mayor's defiance in characteristically emotional terms:

> And he, when the city was just a raw, red mass
> Said: "I do not surrender." Let the houses burn!
> Let my proud achievements be bombed into dust.
> So what, if a graveyard grows from my dreams?
> For you, who may come here, some day recall
> That some things are dearer than the finest city wall.

By the end of the campaign's third week, Polish resistance was broken. The capital remained unoccupied only because the Germans wished to destroy it before claiming the ruins; hour after hour and day after day, merciless bombardment continued. A nurse, Jadwiga Sosnkowska, described scenes at her hospital outside Warsaw on 25 September:

The procession of wounded from the city was an unending march of death. The lights went out, and all of us, doctors and nurses, had to move about with candles in our hands. As both the operating theatres and the dressing stations were destroyed the work was done in the lecture rooms on ordinary deal tables, and owing to the lack of water the instruments could not be sterilised, but had to be cleansed with alcohol . . . As human wreckage was laid on the table the surgeon vainly attempted to save the lives that were slipping through his hands . . . Tragedy followed tragedy. At one time the victim was a girl of sixteen. She had a glorious mop of golden hair, her face was delicate as a flower, and her lovely sapphire-blue eyes were full of tears. Both her legs, up to the knees, were a mass of bleeding pulp, in which it was impossible to distinguish bone from flesh; both had to be amputated above the knee. Before the surgeon began I bent over this innocent

child to kiss her pallid brow, to lay my helpless hand on her golden
head. She died quietly in the course of the morning, like a flower
plucked by a merciless hand.

Professional soldiers can seldom afford to indulge emotionalism about
the horrors of war, but posterity must recoil from the complacency of
Germany's generals about both the character of their national leader and
the murderous adventure in which they had become his accomplices. Gen.
Erich von Manstein is widely regarded as the finest German general of the
war; afterwards, he took pride in pretensions to have done his part as an
officer and gentleman. However, his writings during the Polish campaign,
as well as later, reveal the insensitivity characteristic of his caste. He was
delighted by the invasion: "It's a grand decision of the Führer in view
of the attitude of the Western Powers up till now. His offer to solve the
Polish question was so obliging that England and France—if they really
wanted peace—should have pushed Poland into accepting." Soon after
the campaign began, Manstein visited a formation which he himself had
recently commanded: "It was touching to see the staff so pleased when I
suddenly appeared . . . Cranz [his successor] told me it was a pleasure to
command such a well-trained division in war."

In a letter to his wife, Manstein described his personal routine during
the campaign, in which he served as Gen. Gerd von Rundstedt's chief of
staff at Army Group South: "I get up at 6:30, plunge into the water [for a
swim], into the office by 7:00. Morning reports, coffee, then work or trips
with R[undstedt]. Midday, field kitchens here. Then half an hour break. In
the evening after supper, which we eat together with the general staff officers as at lunch, the evening reports come in. And so it goes on to 11:30."
The contrast is stark, between the serenity of army headquarters and the
vast human tragedy its operations had precipitated. Manstein signed an
order for the German forces encircling Warsaw to fire upon any refugees
who attempted to leave: it was deemed easier to force a swift outcome of
the campaign, and to avoid a battle in the streets, if the inhabitants were
unable to escape the capital's bombardment. Yet he was a man of such personal fastidiousness that he sometimes quit rooms in which von Rundstedt
was speaking, because he recoiled from his chief's obscene language. On
25 September, he basked in a congratulatory visit from Hitler, writing to
his wife: "It was nice to see how the soldiers rejoiced everywhere as the
Führer drove past." In 1939, the officer corps of the Wehrmacht already
displayed the moral bankruptcy that would characterise its conduct until
1945.

A Polish cavalry officer, Klemens Rudnicki, described the plight of his

regiment and its beloved mounts in Warsaw on 27 September, the last
night before the city fell: "Red, glittering flames illuminated our horses,
standing quiet and motionless along the walls of the Łazienki Park, resembling saddled skeletons. A few were dead; some were bleeding, exposing
huge, gaping wounds. Kowalski's horse Cenzor was still alive, but lay with
his bowels ripped out. Not long ago he had won the Army's Challenge
Cup at Tarnopol. He had been our pride. A shot in the ear ended his
sufferings. Next day, probably, somebody needing to assuage his hunger
would cut a joint from his loins."

Warsaw capitulated on 28 September. Little Captain Krysk of Rudnicki's 3rd Squadron declared emotionally that he rejected the order:
"Tomorrow morning we shall charge the Germans to preserve the regimental tradition that the 9th Lancers never surrender." Rudnicki dissuaded him; together, the regiment's officers secreted their colours in the
church of St. Anthony on Senatorska Street, the only building still intact
amid acres of rubble. Rudnicki reflected ruefully that the Polish army
should have deployed in depth for a protracted defensive action, instead
of manning a weak forward line that was certain to be broken. This, however, would have been "at variance with our natural aspiration—and with
our military traditions and hopes of becoming a great Power."

On 29 September the Modlin army, north of Warsaw, surrendered to
the Germans, who took 30,000 prisoners. Organised resistance petered
out, the Hel Peninsula falling on 1 October; the last recorded engagement
took place at Kock, north of Lublin, on the fifth. Hundreds of thousands
of men fell into German hands, while many more struggled to flee. The
young flier B. J. Solak was moved to encounter an air force colonel sitting
beneath a tree, tears pouring down his face. Felicks Lachman was one of
many Poles whose thoughts reverted to their recent reading of *Gone with
the Wind*. Fleeing his home, he mused: "Desolate as was the Tara estate,
Scarlett O'Hara was going through fire and water to the place where she
knew she belonged. We had left, once and forever, men and things that
formed the social, intellectual and emotional environment of our life.
We were moving in a vacuum, aimlessly." After an air raid on the city of
Krzemieniec, Adam Kruczkiewitz saw in the street a hysterical old Jew,
"standing over the corpse of his wife . . . uttering a string of curses and
blasphemies, shouting 'There is no God! Hitler and the bombs are the
only gods! There is no grace and pity in the world!' "

A few Polish cavalry units made good their escape into Hungary, where
they surrendered their arms. At the barracks of the 3rd Hungarian Hussar
Regiment, exhausted fugitives were moved to find themselves greeted by
the unit's officers, led by the elderly Colonel von Pongratsch, drawn up

in full ceremonial uniform. A few days later, when the Poles left to face internment, the bewhiskered veteran embraced each one before bidding them farewell. Such old-world courtesies were welcome, because they had been banished from the pitiless universe of which most Poles now found themselves inhabitants.

Gen. Władysław Anders led his exhausted and depleted unit eastwards to escape the Germans. The men sang as they urged on their emaciated horses amid a throng of refugees and military stragglers. Then they met the Red Army, and Anders sent a liaison officer to the local Soviet headquarters to beg safe passage to the Hungarian border. The Pole was stripped of all he had and threatened with execution. Russian guns began to shell the Polish positions. Anders ordered his men to split into small groups and find their own way into Hungary. He himself, badly wounded, was captured along with many others. A Russian officer told him complacently: "We are now good friends of the Germans. Together we will fight international capitalism. Poland was the tool of England, and she had to perish for that."

Regina Lempicka was one of hundreds of thousands of Poles arbitrarily arrested by the Russians during the months that followed, then shipped to Kazakhstan. Her grandmother and baby niece died of starvation during their exile, while her soldier brother was shot. The family experience in Russian hands, she wrote later, became "a ghastly dream." As one group of Polish soldiers was marched over a border bridge by Red Army guards, a prisoner said bleakly: "We enter Russia. We shall never return." Tadeusz Zukowski wrote: "From this instant the whole world seemed to change: different sky, soil and people. A weird feeling, as if something cracked inside you had burst open, as if life left you and you suddenly dropped into a dark cave, a pitch-dark underground passage." A woman said contemptuously to a Polish prisoner on his way to the gulag, "You Polish, fascist lords! Here in Russia you will learn how to work. Here you will be strong enough to work but too weak to oppress the poor!"

Around 1.5 million Poles, mostly civilians evicted from their homes in the forfeited east of their country during the months that followed, began an ordeal of captivity and starvation in Soviet hands, which cost the lives of some 350,000. Many such families were without menfolk, because these had been summarily dispatched. On 5 March 1940, the Soviet Union's security chief, Lavrenty Beria, sent a four-page memorandum to Stalin, proposing the elimination of Polish senior officers and others defined as leaders of their society. Those held in Soviet camps, urged Beria, should be subjected to "the use of the highest means of punishment—death by shooting." Stalin and other members of the Politburo formally approved the recommendation to decapitate Poland. During the weeks that followed, at least 25,000 Poles were murdered by NKVD executioners at various Soviet prisons, each receiving a single bullet in the back of the head. The bodies were then buried in mass graves in the forests around Katyn, west of Smolensk, at Minsk, and at other sites, the largest of which was discovered by the gleeful Nazis in 1943.

Later allegations that the post-1945 Allied war crimes trials represented "victors' justice" were powerfully reinforced by the fact that no Russian was ever indicted for Katyn. In October 1939 a Pole under interrogation by NKVD officers demanded bitterly: "How is it possible for the USSR, a progressive and democratic state, to be on friendly terms with a reactionary Nazi Germany?" His inquisitor replied coldly: "You are wrong. Our policy is at present to be neutral during the struggle between England and Germany. Let them bleed—our power will increase. When they are utterly exhausted, we shall come out as the strong and fresh party, decisive during the last stage of the war." This seems a just representation of Stalin's aspirations.

Hitler, visiting Warsaw on 5 October, gestured to the ruins and addressed accompanying foreign correspondents: "Gentlemen, you have seen for yourselves what criminal folly it was to try to defend this city . . . I only wish that certain statesmen in other countries who seem to want to turn all of Europe into a second Warsaw could have the opportunity to see, as you have, the real meaning of war." Warsaw's mayor Starzyński was removed to Dachau, where he was murdered four years later. The Polish army had lost 70,000 men killed and 140,000 wounded, together with uncounted thousands of civilian dead. The German army's casualties amounted to 16,000 killed and 30,000 wounded. Some 700,000 Polish soldiers became Hitler's prisoners. An unelected Polish exile government was established in London.

Britain's Chief of the Imperial General Staff (CIGS), Gen. Sir Edmund Ironside, met Adrian Carlton de Wiart on that officer's return from Warsaw and snapped dismissively, "Well, your Poles haven't done much." This assertion reflected the frustration of British and French hopes that the Polish army would inflict sufficient injury upon the Wehrmacht to alleviate the Western Allies'. Carlton de Wiart replied, "Let us see what others will do, sir." A remarkable number of Poles made the decision to accept exile, separation from everything they knew and loved, in order to continue the fight against Hitler. Some 150,000 made their way westwards, often after memorable odysseys. This was by far the largest voluntary exodus from any of the nations eventually overrun by Germany, and reflected the Poles' passion to sustain their struggle. Exiles fleeing west were astonished by the warm reception they received in fascist Italy, where a host of people called to them, *"Bravo Polonia!"*

Before quitting his home airfield, the fighter instructor Witold Urbanowitz gave a radio and his silk shirts to the woman cleaner of his quarters and his formal evening dress to the porter, then set off by bus with his cadets, down the road to Romania; almost a year later, at the controls of a Hurricane, he became one of the RAF's foremost aces. Some 30,000 Poles, one-third of them air force pilots and ground crew, reached Britain in 1940, and more came later. One man clutched a wooden propeller, a symbol to which he had clung doggedly through a journey of 3,000 miles. Many others joined the British Army in the Middle East, after their belated release from Stalinist captivity. These men would make a far more notable contribution to the Allied war effort than had Britain to their own.

Poland became the only nation occupied by Hitler in which there was no collaboration between the conquerors and the conquered. The Nazis henceforth classified Poles as slaves, and received in return implacable hatred. As Princess Paul Sapieha crossed the frontier to precarious safety amid a throng of refugees, her small daughter asked, "Will there be bombs in Romania?" The princess answered, "No more bombs now. There's no war here. We're going where it will be sunny and where children can play wherever they please." The child persisted: "But when are we going home to Papa?" Her mother could not answer. Soon, there would be scarcely a corner of Europe that offered safe haven to either children or adults.

Hitler had committed himself to conquer Poland, but as so often, he had no clear plan for what should follow. Only when it became plain that Stalin welcomed the country's extinction did Germany's ruler decide to annex western Poland. Before the war, Nazis liked to dismiss Poland as a *"Saisonstaat"*—a temporary state. Now, it would cease to be any state at all: Hitler became master of lands containing 15 million Poles, 2 million Jews, 1 million ethnic Germans and 2 million other minorities. Among his foremost characteristics was a reflexive hatred of all those who opposed his will. This soon manifested itself against the Poles—and especially, of course, against their Jews. One day in Łódź soon after the occupation began, Szmulek Goldberg was returning from work when he "encountered chaos in the streets. People were running wildly in every direction. Somebody stopped and grabbed my sleeve. 'Hide! Hide!' he shrieked. 'The Germans are capturing Jews at gunpoint and taking them away on trucks.'" He watched trucks drive past, loaded with captives, a first earnest of Hitler's designs upon his race. Within weeks of Poland's conquest, the first few thousand of its Jewish citizens had been murdered.

In Britain, a mother named Tilly Rice who had been evacuated with her children from London to a fishing port in north Cornwall wrote on 7 October after the end of the Polish campaign: "In the household in which I live the whole thing has been received in bewildered silence . . . War is still going on, but as something distant with just occasional repercussions on the general lives of the community . . . My own reactions to the whole situation are growing more and more indifferent every day." Britain and France had declared war on Germany to save Poland. Poland was now gone, and Polish representatives were expelled from the Allied Supreme War Council, where they were deemed redundant. Many British and French politicians and citizens demanded to know to what end the war was being sustained. How could it be effectively waged? The U.S. ambassador in London, Joseph Kennedy, shrugged and said to his Polish counterpart: "Where on earth can the Allies fight the Germans and beat them?" Though Kennedy was a shameless anglophobe, appeaser and defeatist, his question was valid, and the Allied governments had no good answer to it. After the fall of Poland, the world waited in bewilderment to discover what might follow. Since France and Britain lacked the stomach to seize the initiative, the further course of the war waited upon the pleasure of Adolf Hitler.

CHAPTER TWO

NO PEACE, LITTLE WAR

IN NOVEMBER 1939, the Norwegian Nobel Committee announced that, with much of Europe at war, it had decided to award no Peace Prize that year. Yet in the eyes of many British and French people, the collapse of Poland condemned to futility the struggle to which their governments had committed them. The French army, with a small British contingent in its traditional place on the left flank, confronted German forces on France's eastern frontier. But the Allies had no appetite for offensive operations, certainly not until they were better armed. The Polish campaign had demonstrated the effectiveness of the Wehrmacht and Luftwaffe, though not yet their full power. Gen. Lord Gort, commanding the British Expeditionary Force, was appalled by the condition of some Territorial units which arrived in October to join his own five poorly equipped divisions. He said he had not believed it possible to see such a sight in the British Army: "The men had no knives and forks and mugs."

Allied deployments were critically hampered by Belgian neutrality. It was assumed that if Hitler attacked in the west, he would reprise Germany's 1914 strategy, advancing through Belgium, but King Leopold declined to offer Germany a pretext for invasion by admitting Anglo-French troops meanwhile. In consequence, the armies on the Allied left wing spent much of the icy winter of 1939 building defences on the French border which they intended to abandon, in favour of an advance into Belgium the moment the Germans attacked. The British, having only belatedly introduced conscription, possessed no large reserves of trained manpower for mobilisation, to match those of almost every continental nation. Britain's antimilitarist tradition was a source of pride to its people, but in consequence the nation declared war on the strongest power in Europe while capable of contributing only limited ground and air reinforcements to the French armies deployed against Germany. Any land initiative was dependent on the will of the Paris government. France had begun to rearm before Britain, but still awaited delivery of large orders of tanks and aircraft. The Allies were too weak either to precipitate a showdown with the Wehrmacht or to mount an effective air assault on Germany, even if they had the will for one. During the winter of 1939 the RAF staged only desultory daylight bomber attacks on German warships at sea, with heavy losses and no useful results.

Common sense should have told the Allied governments that Hitler was unlikely to delay a clash of arms in the west until they were adequately equipped to challenge him. Instead, perversely, they persuaded themselves that time was on their side. They sought to exploit their naval strength to enforce a blockade of the Reich. Gamelin spoke of launching a big land offensive in 1941 or 1942. The two governments clung to hopes that the German army and people would meanwhile "come to their senses" and acknowledge that they could not sustain a protracted struggle. In Poland, so the Allies' Panglossian thinking went, Hitler's reckless territorial aggrandisement had achieved its last triumph: the Nazis would be overthrown by sensible Germans, then an accommodation could be sought with a successor regime.

The Allies formalised their joint decision making through a Supreme War Council, of the kind that was established only in the final year of the previous European conflict. It was agreed that the British and French would share the cost of the war effort sixty-forty, proportions reflecting the relative size of their economies. France's politics and policies were profoundly influenced by fear of the left, prospective tools of Stalin. In October 1939, thirty-five communist parliamentary deputies were detained in the interests of national security. The following March, twenty-seven of these were tried and most convicted, receiving prison sentences of up to five years. In addition, some 3,400 communist activists were arrested, and more than 3,000 foreign communist refugees interned.

Among the Allies' mistakes in forging their strategy, insofar as they had one, was to focus upon strengthening their armed forces while conceding little attention to morale; ministers ignored the corrosive influence of inactivity on public sentiment. In the minds of many French and British people, the war effort seemed purposeless: their nations were committed to fight, yet were not fighting. The French were acutely sensitive to the economic strain imposed by sustaining 2.7 million men under arms. They urged on the British the virtues of action almost anywhere save on the Western Front. Mindful of France's 1.3 million World War I dead, they recoiled from provoking another bloodbath on their own territory. But their proposals for marginal operations—for instance a Balkan front in Salonika, to preempt German aggression there—found no favour in London. The British feared such a step would merely provoke the Italians to make common cause with Germany. Ministers would not even speak publicly of creating an "anti-fascist front," for fear of upsetting Benito Mussolini.

Unable to define credible military objectives, many British and French politicians craved a patched-up peace with Hitler, granted only that he should accept some face-saving moderation of his territorial ambitions; their peoples recognised this, coining the phrases "Phoney War" and "Bore War." The social-research organisation Mass Observation reported "a strong feeling in the country that the wretched war is not worth going on with . . . We can suspect that Hitler has won News-Round 1 in this war. He's been able to give his own people a tremendous success story—Poland."

It is hard to overstate the impact of months of passivity upon the spirit of France's forces. In November 1939 British corps commander Alan Brooke described his sensations on witnessing a parade of the French Ninth Army: "Seldom have I seen anything more slovenly . . . men unshaven, horses ungroomed, complete lack of pride in themselves or their units. What shook me most, however, was the look in the men's faces, disgruntled and insubordinate looks . . . I could not help wondering whether the French are still a firm enough nation to again take their part in seeing this war through." Exiled Poles, of whom some thousands were now attached to the French forces, noted with dismay the equivocal attitudes displayed by their allies: the pilot Franciszek Kornicki wrote that "both the French communists and fascists worked against us, and Lyons was full of the former. One day somebody made a friendly gesture, but another day someone else would swear at you."

A French soldier, the writer Jean-Paul Sartre, wrote in his diary on 26 November: "All the men . . . were raring to go at the outset, but now they are dying of boredom." Another soldier, Georges Sadoul, wrote on 13 December: "The days pass, interminable and empty, without the slightest occupation . . . The officers, mainly reservists, think no differently from the men . . . One feels they are weary of the war, they say and repeat that they would like to go home." On 20 February 1940, Sartre observed: "The war machine is running in neutral . . . Only yesterday a sergeant was telling me, with a gleam of insane hope in his eyes: 'What I think is, it'll all be arranged, England will climb down.'"

The British were equally baffled. Jack Classon, a young shopworker in Everton, Lancashire, wrote to a friend in the army: "The war doesn't seem to make much headway, does it? We read one thing in the paper in the morning, the denial the following day, & it's killing business. You can blame my gloom on the black curtains that drape the shop & the blued windows that stare at you when you go upstairs . . . The Curzon cinema has had for the last week or so Henry Croudson the organist as guest . . . some people are enjoying that more than the picture, his most popular number at the moment being 'We'll Hang Out The Washing On The Siegfried Line.' The audience raises the roof when he plays that."

One and a half million British women and children, evacuated from the cities amid the threat of German bombing, suffered agonies of homesickness in an unfamiliar rural environment. One of them, Derek Lambert, a nine-year-old from London's Muswell Hill, later recalled: "We went to strange beds and lay with fists clenched. Our toes found tepid hot water bottles and our fingers silk bags of old lavender inside the pillows. An owl hooted, wings brushed the window. I remembered the London sounds of distant trains and motor cycles, the breaking limbs of the mountain ash, next door's dog, the droning radio, the fifth stair groaning and the ten-thirty throat-clearing; I remembered the familiar wallpaper where you could paddle a canoe through green rapids or drive a train along sweeping cuttings . . . We sobbed in awful desolation."

Most evacuees were drawn from the underclass, and shocked rustic hosts by their rags and anarchic habits: urban children, victims of the thirties Depression, were unaccustomed to meals at fixed hours, some even to knives and forks. They were used to subsisting on "pieces"—bread and margarine, fish and chips—eaten on the move, together with tinned food and sweets. They recoiled from soup, puddings and all vegetables save potatoes. Many paraded their alienation by resorting to petty delinquency. The habits of their mothers dismayed staid rural communities: "The village people objected to the evacuees chiefly because of the dirtiness of their habits and clothes," recorded Muriel Green, a garage assistant in Snettisham, Norfolk. "Also because of their reputed drinking and bad language. It's exceptional to hear women swear in this village or for them to enter a public house. The villagers used to watch them come out of the pubs with horror. The holiday camp proprietor said: 'You should see them mop down the drink.'" By Christmas, with Britain still unbombed, most of the evacuees had returned to their city homes, to the mutual relief of themselves and their rural hosts.

If there was little substance to Britain's war effort, there were many symbols: sandbagged public buildings, barrage balloons floating above London, a rigorous blackout in the hours of darkness. Before peace came, accidents in the blackout killed more people than did the Luftwaffe: in the last four months of 1939 there were 4,133 deaths on the roads, 2,657 of these pedestrians, a figure almost double that for the same period in 1938. Many more people died as a consequence of nonhighway mishaps: some

18 percent of those interviewed by Princeton pollsters in December 1940 said they had injured themselves groping in the dark; three-quarters of respondents thought air-raid precautions should be eased. Defence regulations were so stringently enforced that two soldiers leaving the dock at the Old Bailey after being condemned to death for murder were rebuked for failing to pick up their gas masks. Two and a half million people were enrolled in civil defence.

Huge tracts of downland and urban public spaces were planted with corn and vegetables. A Wiltshire farmer, Arthur Street, ploughed up his grassland as the government ordered, and sent away his beloved hunter to be trained for harness work. Many riding horses took badly to this humble duty, but Street's Jorrocks "trotted home like a gentleman," in the farmer's words, "and since that day he has hauled the milk, pulled the broadcast during wheat sowing, and done ploughing and all sorts of jobs with no mishap . . . What he thinks about it I don't know. He has no notion of what it is that trundles and rattles behind him, and the position of his ears shows that he is somewhat worried about it. But as we have never let him down before, he reckons that we are not doing it now, and so does his war work like the gentleman he is." Farmers who had struggled to escape bankruptcy in the 1930s suddenly entered a new era of prosperity.

Seven hundred fascists were interned, though most of the aristocrats who had flirted with Hitler were spared. "It certainly is breath-taking how all these lords get away with their pre-war affiliations to the Nazi regime," complained the British communist Elizabeth Belsey in a letter to her soldier husband. If the British had emulated French policy towards communists, thousands of trades unionists and a substantial part of the intellectual class would also have been incarcerated, but these too were left at liberty. There was still much silliness in the air: the Royal Victoria Hotel at St. Leonards-on-Sea, advertising its attractions in *The Times*, asserted that "the ballroom and adjacent toilets have been made gas- and splinter-proof." Published advertisements for domestic staff made few concessions to conscription: "Wanted: second housemaid of three; wages £42 per annum; two ladies in family; nine servants kept." The archbishop of Canterbury declared that Christians were allowed to pray for victory, but the archbishop of York disagreed. While the war was a righteous one, he said, it was not a holy one: "We must avoid praying each other down." Some clergymen urged their congregations to ask the Almighty's help for charity: "Save me from bitterness and hatred towards the enemy." There was anger among British Christians, however, when in November the pope sent a message of congratulation to Hitler on escaping an assassination attempt.

Hundreds of thousands of young men who had donned uniforms

trained in England with inadequate equipment and uncertain expectations, though they assumed some of their number would die. Lt. Arthur Kellas of the Border Regiment took for granted his own survival, but speculated about the fates of his fellow officers: "I used to wonder which of them were for the killing. Would it be Ogilvy, such a nice little man, so worried about his mother in Dundee? Or Donald, so handsome, confident and pleased with himself? Or Hunt, newly married, prosperous in the City of London? Germain? Dunbar? Perkins, whom we ragged without pity? Or Bell, of whom we were jealous when he was posted off to glory with the first battalion in the line in France, first of us to be promoted to the First Fifteen, leaving behind such a pretty sister in Whitehaven? It had happened to our fathers after all. Presumably our War would be much the same as theirs."

They were so young. As the eighteen-year-old Territorial soldier Doug Arthur paraded with his unit outside a church in Liverpool shortly before embarking for overseas service, he was embarrassed to be picked out by one of an emotional crowd of watching housewives: "Look at 'im, girls," she said pityingly. " 'E should be at 'ome wit' 'is Mam. Never mind, son, yourse'll be alrigh'. God Bless yer la'. He'll look after yourtse, yer know, like. That bastard 'itler 'as gorra lot to answer for. I'd like to get me bleedin' 'ands on 'im for five bleedin' minutes, the swine."

President Franklin Roosevelt wrote to his London ambassador, Joseph Kennedy, on 30 October 1939: "While the [First] World War did not bring forth strong leadership in Great Britain, this war may do so, because I am inclined to think the British public has more humility than before and is slowly but surely getting rid of the 'muddle through' attitude of the past." FDR's optimism would ultimately prove justified, but only after many more months of "muddle through."

The next phase of the struggle increased the world's bewilderment and confusion of loyalties, for it was undertaken not by Hitler, but by Stalin. Like all Europe's tyrants, Russia's leader assessed the evolving conflict in terms of the opportunities it offered him for aggrandisement. In the autumn of 1939, having secured eastern Poland, he sought further to enhance the Soviet Union's strategic position by advancing into Finland. The country, a vast, sparsely inhabited wilderness of lakes and forests, was one among many whose frontier, indeed very existence, was of short duration, and thus vulnerable to challenge. Part of Sweden until the Napoleonic Wars, thereafter it was ruled by Russia until 1918, when Finnish anti-Bolsheviks triumphed in a civil war.

In October 1939, Stalin determined to strengthen the security of Leningrad, only thirty miles inside Soviet territory, by pushing back the nearby Finnish frontier across the Karelian Isthmus and occupying Finnish-held islands in the Baltic; he also coveted nickel mines on Finland's north coast. A Finnish delegation, summoned to receive Moscow's demands, prompted international amazement by rejecting them. The notion that a nation of 3.6 million people might resist the Red Army seemed fantastic, but the Finns, though poorly armed, were nationalistic to the point of folly. Arvo Tuominen, a prominent Finnish communist, declined Stalin's invitation to form a shadow puppet government, and went into hiding. Tuominen said: "It would be wrong, it would be criminal, it was not a picture of the free rule of the people."

At 9:20 a.m. on 30 November, Russian aircraft launched the first of many bomber attacks on Helsinki, causing little damage save to the Soviet legation and the nerves of the British ambassador, who asked to be relieved of his post. Russian forces advanced across the frontier in several places, and Finns joked: "They are so many and our country is so small, where shall we find room to bury them all?" The nation's defence was entrusted to seventy-two-year-old Marshal Carl Gustaf Mannerheim, hero of many conflicts, most recently Finland's civil war. As a Tsarist officer posted to Lhasha, Mannerheim had once taught the Dalai Lama pistol shooting; he spoke seven languages, Finnish least fluently. His hauteur was comparable to that of Charles de Gaulle; his ruthlessness had been manifested in the 1919–20 purges of the defeated Finnish communists.

During the 1930s Mannerheim had constructed a fortified line across the Karelian Isthmus, to which his name was given. He suffered no delusions about his country's strategic weakness, and had urged conciliation with Stalin. But when his countrymen opted to fight, he set about managing the defence with cool professionalism. Before the Russians attacked, the Finns adopted a scorched-earth policy, evacuating from the forward areas 100,000 civilians, some of whom adopted an impressively stoical attitude to their sacrifice: border guards who warned an old woman to quit her home were amazed, on returning to burn it, to find that she had swept and cleaned the interior before leaving. On the table lay matches, kindling wood and a note: "When one gives a gift to Finland, one desires that it should be like new." But it was a distressing business to destroy housing and installations around the Petsamo nickel-mining centre, which had been constructed with infinite labour and difficulty inside the Arctic Circle. The frontier zone was heavily booby-trapped: mines triggered by pull ropes were laid, to smash the ice in front of invaders attacking across frozen lakes.

Stalin committed twelve divisions to assaults in a dozen sectors. Most of his soldiers were told that Finland had attacked the Soviet Union, but some were disbelieving and bewildered. Capt. Ismael Akhmedov heard a Ukrainian peasant say, "Comrade Commander. Tell me, why do we fight this war? Did not Comrade Voroshilov declare at the Party Congress that we don't want an inch of other people's land and we will not surrender an inch of ours? Now we are going to fight? For what?" An officer sought to explain the perils of acquiescing in a frontier so close to Leningrad, but Moscow's strategic ambitions roused scant enthusiasm among those ordered to fulfil them, most of whom were hastily mobilised local reservists.

Stalin was untroubled. Confident that his attacking force of 120,000 men, 600 tanks and 1,000 guns could overwhelm the Mannerheim Line, he ignored his generals' warnings about the restricted approaches to Finland. Tanks and vehicles were obliged to advance on narrow axes between lakes, forests and swamps. Though the Finns had little artillery and few antitank weapons, so inept were the Soviet assaults that the defenders wrecked havoc on their columns with rifle and machine-gun fire. The snowy wastelands of eastern Finland were soon deeply stained with blood; some defenders succumbed to nervous exhaustion after mowing down advancing Russians at close range hour after hour. Soviet armour suffered 60 percent losses, chiefly because tanks advanced without infantry support. Most fell victim to primitive weapons, notably bottles filled with petrol and capped with a flaming wick, which caused them to explode into liquid fire when smashed against a vehicle. Though these had been used earlier in the Spanish Civil War, it was in Finland that the soubriquet "Molotov breadbasket," then "Molotov cocktail," first entered the military lexicon.

Mannerheim observed dryly that the attackers came on "with a fatalism incomprehensible to a European." A hysterical Soviet battalion commander told his officers: "Comrades, our attack was unsuccessful; the division commander has just given me the order personally—in seven minutes, we attack again." The Soviet columns lumbered forward once more—and were slaughtered. Some Finnish units adopted large-scale guerrilla tactics, striking at Soviet units from the forests, then withdrawing. They sought to break up the attackers' formations, then destroy them piecemeal, calling such encounters *"motti"*—"firewood" battles—chopping up the enemy. Among the heroes of the campaign was Lt. Col. Aaro Pajari, who collapsed with a heart condition in the midst of one action, but somehow kept going. Like most of his fighting countrymen, Pajari was an amateur soldier, but he achieved a notable little victory against much superior forces at Tolvajärvi. During weeks of fighting at Kollaa, the Finns deployed two French 3.5-inch guns cast in 1871, which fired black-powder charges. In the northern sector, the defence was supported by a 1918-vintage armoured train, bustling to and fro between threatened points.

The Red Army was grotesquely ill-equipped for winter war: its 44th Division, for instance, issued men a manual on ski tactics, but no skis; in the first weeks, Russian tanks were not even painted white. The Finns, by contrast, dispatched ski patrols to cut roads behind the front and attack supply columns, often at night. One Finnish jaeger regiment was led by Col. Hjalmar Siilasvuo. A peacetime lawyer, short, blond and tough, he galvanised the protracted defence of Suomussalmi village, and eventually found himself commanding a division. The Russians were impressed by the proficiency of Finnish snipers, whom they called "cuckoos." The chief of staff of Gen. Vasily Chuikov's Ninth Army produced an analysis of Soviet failures which concluded that the offensive had been too road-bound: "Our units, saturated by technology (especially artillery and transport vehicles), are incapable of manoeuvre and combat in this theatre." Soldiers, he said, are "frightened by the forest and cannot ski."

The Finns deplored everything about the manner in which their enemies made war. One desperate Russian general sought to clear a minefield by driving a herd of horses through it, and the animal-loving defenders were appalled by the resultant carnage. A man gazing on heaped Russian corpses in the northern sector said: "The wolves will eat well this year." Carl Mydans, a photographer for America's *Life* magazine, described the scene on one frozen battlefield: "The fighting was almost over as we walked up the snow-banked path that led from the road to the river . . . The Russian dead spotted the ice crust. They lay lonely and twisted in their heavy trench coats and formless felt boots, their faces yellowed, eyelashes white with a fringe of frost. Across the ice, the forest was strewn with weapons and pictures and letters, with sausage and bread and shoes. Here were the bodies of dead tanks with blown treads, dead carts, dead horses and dead men, blocking the road and defiling the snow under the tall black pines."

Around the world, the Soviet assault inspired bewilderment, increased by the fact that the swastika was a Finnish good-luck symbol. Popular sentiment ran strongly in favour of the victims: in fascist Italy, there were pro-Finnish demonstrations. The British and French saw Stalin's action as further evidence of the Russo-German vulture collaboration manifested in Poland, though in reality Berlin was no party to it. There was a surge of Allied enthusiasm for dispatching military aid to Finland. Gen. Maxime Weygand wrote to Gamelin urging this course, which in French eyes had

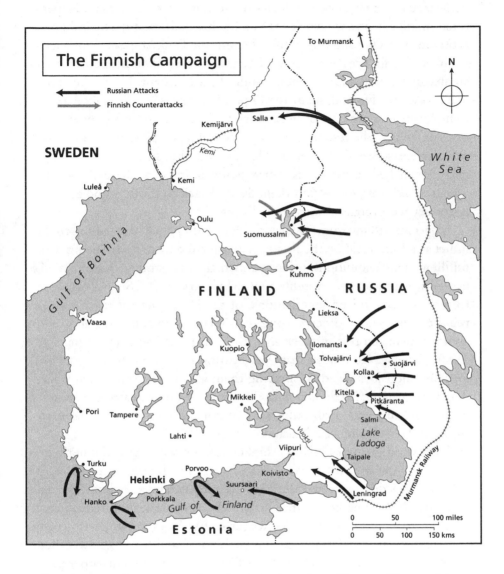

The Finnish Campaign

⬅ Russian Attacks
→ Finnish Counterattacks

the supreme virtue of moving the war away from France: "I regard it as essential to break the back of the Soviet Union in Finland . . . and elsewhere." But, while there was intense discussion of possible Anglo-French expeditions to Finland during the months that followed, the practical difficulties seemed overwhelming. If Winston Churchill had then been the British prime minister, it is likely that he would have launched operations against the Russians. But the Chamberlain government, in which, as First Lord of the Admiralty, Churchill represented a minority voice for activism, had no stomach for a gratuitous declaration of war on the Soviet Union when the German menace was still unaddressed.

Marshal Mannerheim conducted his campaign to a meticulous personal routine: he was woken at 7:00 a.m. in his quarters at the Seurahuone Hotel in Mikkeli, some forty miles behind the front, appeared immaculately dressed for breakfast an hour later, then drove to his headquarters in an abandoned schoolhouse a few hundred yards distant. In the tiny, intimate society of Finland, he insisted upon having casualty lists read aloud to him, name by name. During the first weeks of war, knowing the limitations of his army, he resolutely resisted subordinates' pleas to advance and exploit their successes, but on 23 December a Finnish counterattack was indeed launched across the Karelian Isthmus. Infantry charged forward crying *"Hakkaa päälle!"*—"Cut them down!"; lacking artillery and air support, they were repulsed with heavy losses.

The Finnish government never deluded itself that the nation could inflict absolute defeat on the Russians: it aspired only to make the price of fulfilling Stalin's ambitions unacceptably high. This strategy was doomed, however, against an enemy indifferent to human sacrifice. Stalin's response to the setbacks, indeed humiliations, of the December offensive was to replace failed senior officers—one divisional commander was shot and another spent the rest of the war in the gulag—and to commit massive reinforcements. Ice roads capable of bearing tanks were built by laying logs on trampled snow, then spraying them with water which then froze. The Finns had started the war with three weeks' supply of artillery ammunition, and fuel and small-arms ammunition for sixty days; by January, these stocks were almost exhausted.

The world greeted Finland's initial successes with awe: Mannerheim became a popular hero in western Europe, and French prime minister Édouard Daladier promised the Finns reinforcements of a hundred aircraft and 50,000 men before the end of February, but never lifted a finger to make good on his pledge. The writer Arthur Koestler, in Paris, wrote contemptuously that French excitement about Finnish victories recalled "a voyeur who gets his thrills and satisfaction out of watching other people's virile exploits, which he is unable to imitate." In Britain the left, represented by its weekly organ *Tribune*, at first offered reflexive support to Moscow's cause, then abruptly switched allegiance to back the Finns.

Churchill regarded Soviet action as direct kin to Nazi aggression. Britain's First Lord of the Admiralty exulted in Stalin's failure, declaring in a broadcast on 20 January: "Finland, superb—nay sublime—in the jaws of peril, Finland shows what free men can do. The service rendered by Finland to mankind is magnificent. They have exposed, for all the world to see, the military incapacity of the Red Army and of the Red Air Force. Many illusions about Soviet Russia have been dispelled in these few fierce weeks of fighting in the Arctic Circle. Everyone can see how communism rots the soul of a Nation; how it makes it abject and hungry in peace, and proves it base and abominable in war."

The Finns were heartened by such rhetoric. British tory MP Harold Macmillan, who visited Finland, reported a female Helsinki ticket collector saying to him: "The women of Finland will fight on, because they believe that you are coming to help them." Eight thousand Swedes and 800 Norwegians and Danes, together with a few American and British civilians, volunteered to take up arms; some reached the war zone, but none served to any effect. Britain had few enough weapons for its own armed forces, and had nothing significant to spare for a nation which might be struggling gallantly, but was not fighting the power against which it was itself making war. Thirty Gloster Gladiator biplane fighters were dispatched, of which eighteen were lost in action within ten days; the Finns were obliged to pay cash for the aircraft, a foretaste of neutral American policy towards Britain.

There was no doubt of the strength of British popular sentiment in Finland's favour, but next to nothing was done to translate this into action, save to prepare an expedition to Narvik, neutral Norway's northern ice-free port. The Allies were attracted by the notion of exploiting the pretext of aiding the Finns to land in Norway and sever Germany's winter link to Sweden's iron-ore mines. The cynicism that had characterised Allied policy during the Polish campaign thus reasserted itself. In the early months of 1940 London and Paris urged the Finns to keep fighting, because if they quit there would be no excuse for intervention in Norway. A wild French proposal to land an expeditionary force at Petsamo on the north coast was vetoed by the British, who still declined to clash headlong with the Russians.

IN MID-JANUARY, a new wave of assaults on Finland began. In one position 4,000 Russians attacked 32 Finns; they lost 400 men, but only 4 defenders survived. On 1 February, the invaders launched a massive bombardment of the Mannerheim Line, followed by infantry and armoured drives in overwhelming strength. The Finnish artillery, such as it was, had almost exhausted its ammunition, but for two weeks the defenders held their positions. An officer, Wolf Halsti, wrote on 15 February: "In the early afternoon, there appeared in front of our tent a reserve ensign, really nothing more than a child, asking if we could spare some food for himself and his men . . . he was in charge of a platoon of 'men' scarcely old enough to shave. They were cold and scared and hungry and on their way to join the troops at the roadblock in front of Lähde." Next day Halsti added: "Same reserve ensign back again, blood on his clothes, asking for more food . . . he lost both guns and half his men when the Russians broke through." Finnish suffering was matched by that of their foes, especially those trapped for weeks in encircled positions. A Russian soldier wrote on 2 February: "It's particularly cold this morning, nearly minus 35C. I was unable to sleep due to the cold. Our artillery has been firing through the night. After I woke I went for a shit, but at that moment the Finns opened fire, one bullet hitting the ground between my legs. I hadn't had a shit since January 25th."

The one-sided struggle could not continue indefinitely. The Finnish government made a last vain plea for Swedish help. The British and French offered token contingents of troops, which embarked on transports but had not yet sailed when on 12 March a Finnish delegation signed an armistice in Moscow. Minutes before this took effect, the Soviets launched a last vengeful bombardment of their vanquished victim's positions. A Finnish officer wrote to his family: "One thing is clear: we have not fled. We were prepared to fight to the last man. We carry our heads high because we have fought with all our might for three and a half months."

Carl Mydans found himself on a train to Sweden with three Finnish officers, one of whom opened a conversation with the American: "At least you will tell them that we fought bravely." Mydans muttered that he would. Then the officer's temper snapped: "Your country was going to help . . . You promised, and we believed you." He seized Mydans and shook him, screaming: "A half-dozen goddamned Brewster fighters with no spare parts! And the British sent us guns from the last war that wouldn't even work!" The Finn lapsed into sobs.

The peace which Stalin imposed bemused the world by its moderation. He enforced his prewar territorial demands, amounting to 10 percent of Finland's territory, but refrained from occupying the entire country, as he probably could have done. He appears to have been uneasy about provoking international anger at a moment when much larger issues were at stake. His confidence had also been shaken by the losses of the Red Army—at least 127,000, perhaps as many as a quarter of a million, dead, against Finland's 48,243 killed and 420,000 homeless. Soviet prisoners released by the Finns, many of them student draftees, were dispatched by Stalin to the gulag to contemplate their treachery in having accepted captivity.

The Finnish campaign was irrelevant to the confrontation between Germany and the Allies, but it importantly influenced the strategy of both. They alike concluded that the Soviet Union was a paper tiger; that Stalin's armies were weak, his commanders bunglers. After the armistice, Finland, having failed to gain useful help from Britain and France, turned to Germany for assistance in rearming its forces, which Hitler was happy to provide. The Russians learned critical lessons from the Finnish war, and set about equipping the Red Army with winter clothing, snow camouflage and lubricants for subzero temperatures, all of which would play a vital role in future campaigns. The world, however, saw only that Russian prestige had been debased by one of Europe's smallest nations.

EVEN AS FINLAND was struggling for survival, through the winter of 1939–40 the Allied armies shivered in snowbound trenches and bunkers on the frontier of Germany. Churchill, the First Lord, strove to extract every ounce of excitement and propaganda from the Royal Navy's skirmishes at sea with German U-boats and surface raiders. There was a sensational episode on 13 December, when three British cruisers met the far more powerfully armed German pocket battleship *Graf Spee* off the coast of Uruguay. In the ensuing battle the British squadron was badly mauled, but *Graf Spee* suffered damage which caused her to take refuge in Montevideo. She was scuttled on 17 December rather than risk another battle, and her captain committed suicide, an outcome promoted as a handy Allied victory. The British strove to make friends across the Atlantic, or at least to moderate their war making to avoid antagonising U.S. opinion. When Churchill heard that Americans were angered by the Royal Navy's contraband searches of their ships, on 29 January 1940 he gave orders that no further U.S. vessels should be bear-led into the British war zone, although this concession was kept secret to avoid upsetting other neutral nations whose vessels remained subject to inspection.

Meanwhile the Allied leaders and commanders wrangled: French thinking remained dominated by determination to reject a direct military challenge to Hitler; they declined even to shell the heavily industrialised Saarland, within easy range. The Daladier government, favouring an initiative as far as possible from France, was attracted by the notion of tightening the blockade of Germany through interdiction of its Swedish iron-ore supplies. To achieve this, it would be necessary to violate Norwegian neutrality, either by mining the inshore navigation route to force German ships out into the open sea, or by establishing troops and aircraft ashore, or both. Britain's prime minister and foreign secretary, Neville Chamberlain and Lord Halifax, were unwilling to adopt such a course, despite the urgings of Churchill. Many days were devoted to planning and preparing a Norwegian expedition, but action was repeatedly postponed.

Gen. Sir Edmund Ironside, head of the British Army, wrote: "The French . . . put forward the most extravagant ideas. They are absolutely unscrupulous in everything." Gamelin said afterwards: "Public opinion did not know what it wanted done, but it wanted something else, and above all it wanted action." A French naval officer and later historian, Jacques Mordal, wrote contemptuously: "The idea was to do something, even something stupid." A British scheme for mining the Rhine became a new focus of friction: Paris feared that it would provoke German retaliation.

Almost nothing about these debates was known to the Allied peoples, who saw only their armies inert in the frontier snow, digging trenches and contemplating the Germans opposite. A sense of vacuity afflicted alike young and old, national leaders and humble citizens: "Everyone is getting married and engaged, or else having babies," wrote the twenty-three-year-old Liverpool typist Doris Melling on 7 April. "Makes me feel rather stale and out of things." She was unimpressed, however, by columnist Lord Castlerosse's flippant assertion in that day's *Sunday Express* that any girl who had not found a husband by the end of the war was not really trying. "Most of my friends have made such messes of their married life—no proper homes, keeping in their jobs, and such."

Maggie Joy Blunt, a thirty-year-old architectural writer of strong left-wing convictions, lived in Slough, west of London. She observed on 16 December 1939 that what seemed to her most remarkable about the war thus far was how little it changed most people's lives:

> We have had to suffer certain inconveniences—the blackout, petrol rations, altered bus and train services, a lack of theatrical entertainment, rising cost of food, scarcity of certain commodities such as electric light batteries, sugar, butter. A number of adults are doing jobs that they have never done before and never expected to do. But there has been no essential change in our way of living, in our systems of employment or education, in our ideas or ambitions . . . It is as though we were trying to play one more set of tennis before an approaching storm descends . . . A local MP . . . remarked that he was not in favour of this "half-asleep" war. Scattering pamphlets [on Germany] is no more use than scattering confetti. I am sorry to have to say it, but we shall have to make the Germans suffer before we can make peace possible.

She and her compatriots may not have known it, but in the winter of 1939 the Nazis were troubled by many problems of their own. Germany had entered the war on the verge of bankruptcy, in consequence of Hitler's armaments expenditure. There was so little money for civilian purposes that the railway system was crumbling, and desperately short of rolling stock: two bad train smashes killed 230 people, provoking fierce public anger. Far from the Nazis having made the trains run on time, industry suffered from disrupted coal deliveries, and the Gestapo reported widespread grumbling about the faltering passenger service. The Allied blockade had caused the collapse of Germany's export markets and a serious shortage of raw materials. Hitler wished to launch a great offensive in the west on 12 November, and was furious when the Wehrmacht insisted on postponement until spring. The generals considered the weather wholly unfavourable to a major offensive, and recognised the deficiencies of their army's performance in Poland: it was short of vehicles and weapons of all kinds. As the army expanded, the 24.5 million industrial workforce of May 1939 fell by 4 million. Industrial policy was characterised by wild vacillation and arbitrary production cuts, made necessary by steel shortages.

A decision was made that would influence German armaments production for years ahead: to focus immediate effort on manufacturing ammunition and Ju-88 light bombers. The Luftwaffe convinced itself that the Ju-88 was a war-winning weapon, and the plane indeed did notable service. Later, however, lack of effective heavier aircraft became a severe handicap. The German navy remained weak—in the gloomy words of Adm. Erich Raeder, the C-in-C of the German navy, "not at all adequately armed for the great struggle . . . it can only demonstrate that it knows how to go down with dignity." Germany's paper military strength in the winter of 1939 was only marginally greater than that of the Allies. Given all these difficulties, it is remarkable that Hitler retained his psychological dominance of the conflict. His great advantage was that the Allies had made a principled commitment to confront and defeat Nazism, while lacking any appetite for the bloody initiatives and human sacrifice required to achieve this. Thus, Hitler was left to make his own weather.

In the last weeks before Germany attacked in the west, relations between the two allies became sulphurous: each blamed the other for failure to wage war effectively. French public opinion turned decisively against Prime Minister Daladier, who sought a parliamentary vote of confidence on 20 March: only 1 deputy voted against him, 239 in his support—but 300 abstained. Daladier resigned, though remaining in the government as defence minister, to be succeeded by Paul Reynaud. France's new leader was a sixty-two-year-old conservative, notable for high intelligence and physical insignificance—he stood less than five feet, three inches high. Eager to take the initiative, he now proposed a landing in Norway and bombing of Soviet oilfields at Baku. Gamelin said sourly: "After Daladier who couldn't make a decision at all, here we are with Reynaud who makes one every five minutes." France's prime minister initially supported Churchill's cherished scheme to mine the Rhine, only to be repudiated by his own ministers, still fearing retaliation. The British said that if France would not support the mining operation, they in turn would decline to join a landing at Narvik.

In the first days of April, as snow vanished from the Continent, the armies emerged as if from hibernation, looking about to discern what the new campaigning season might bring. At last, Churchill persuaded his government colleagues to support the mining of Norwegian waters. Four destroyers put to sea to execute this operation, while a small land force embarked at British ports, ready to sail to Norway if the Germans responded to the Royal Navy's initiative. London was oblivious of the fact that a German fleet was already at sea. For months, the Führer had been fearful of British intervention in Norway, because of its implications for his iron-ore supplies. His agitation acquired urgency on 14 February 1940, when Royal Navy destroyers pursued the *Graf Spee*'s supply ship *Altmark* into a Norwegian fjord to free 299 captive British merchant seamen. Determined to preempt a British initiative to seize a foothold in Norway, on 2 April he gave the final order for the invasion fleet to sail.

British ships and planes observed Germany's intense flurry of naval activity, but naval commanders were so preoccupied with their own impending mining operation that they failed to realise that these movements presaged German action rather than reaction. The Admiralty decided that Admiral Raeder's warships intended a breakout into the Atlantic to attack British sea-lanes; this caused them to deploy much of the Home Fleet many hours' steaming from Norway. Before dawn on 8 April, the Royal Navy indeed laid a minefield in Norwegian coastal waters. A few hours later, however, the Germans commenced air and naval landings to occupy the entire country. The Phoney War was over.

CHAPTER THREE

BLITZKRIEGS IN THE WEST

1. Norway

THE SMALLER NATIONS of Europe strove to escape involvement in the war. Most resisted association with Germany, which required acceptance of Hitler's hegemony, but even those that favoured the objectives of the democracies were wary of joining them in belligerence. Historic experience argued that they would thus expose themselves to the horrors of war for small advantage: the fate of Poland and Finland highlighted the Allies' inability to protect the dictators' chosen victims. Holland and the Scandinavian countries had contrived to remain neutral in World War I. Why should they not do so again? In the winter of 1939–40, all took pains to avoid provoking Hitler. The Norwegians were more apprehensive about British designs on their coastline than German ones. At 1:30 a.m. on 9 April, an aide awoke King Haakon of Norway to report: "Majesty, we are at war!" The monarch promptly demanded: "Against whom?"

Despite repeated warnings that a German invasion was imminent, the country's tiny army had not been mobilised. The capital was quickly blacked out, but old Gen. Kristian Laake, Norway's commander-in-chief, responded feebly to news that German warships were approaching up Oslo Fjord: he ordered reservists to be mustered by mail—which would assemble them under arms only on 11 April. His staff officers remonstrated, but Laake was in flight from reality: "A little exercise should do these units no harm!" he declared indulgently. German warships entered ports and began to disembark troops. The Norwegians, French and British had alike deluded themselves that Hitler would never dare to invade Norway in the face of the Royal Navy. Yet poor intelligence and misjudged deployments caused the Admiralty to forfeit its best opportunities to wreak havoc, as the Germans landed on 9 April. Thereafter, although the invaders suffered severe attrition at sea, so too did the Royal Navy at the hands of the Luftwaffe and Kriegsmarine. Norway's nearest coastline lay 400 miles from Britain, beyond range of land-based air cover. The vulnerability of ships to bomber attack was soon brutally exposed.

The most dramatic development that first morning of the campaign took place in Oslo Fjord shortly after 4:00, as the new cruiser *Blücher*, carrying thousands of German troops, approached Oscarsborg. The ancient fortress's two nineteenth-century cannons, named Moses and Aaron, were laboriously loaded. The local commander, Colonel Birger Eriksen, knowing the gunners' limitations, held his fire until the last moment. The cruiser was only 500 yards offshore when the antique weapons belched flame. One shell hit the cruiser's antiaircraft control centre, while the other smashed into an aviation fuel store, causing a pillar of flame to leap skywards. After suffering two further hits from shore-launched torpedoes, within minutes *Blücher* was engulfed in fire and listing heavily, her ammunition exploding. The ship sank with the loss of a thousand German lives.

Confusion and black comedy then overtook Norway's capital. The designated assault commander, Gen. Erich Engelbrecht, was a passenger on the stricken *Blücher*. He was rescued from the fjord by Norwegians who took him prisoner, leaving the invaders temporarily leaderless. General Laake fled the city in the wake of his staff, first taking a tramcar, then attempting unsuccessfully to hitchhike, at last catching a train. The Norwegian government offered its resignation, which was rejected by the king. The national parliament, the Storting, entered emergency session, with fierce arguments about the merits of surrender. Ministers suggested demolishing key bridges to impede the invaders, but several deputies dissented, as "this would mean destroying valuable architectural works." The British ambassador delivered a message from London promising aid, but was vague about when this might materialise. German paratroopers secured Oslo airport, and most of Norway's southwestern ports were soon in enemy hands. The first elements of six divisions disembarked and deployed, while the government fled northwards.

Among stunned spectators of the invaders' arrival was a nineteen-year-old Austrian Jewish refugee named Ruth Maier. On 10 April, in the Oslo suburb of Lillestrøm, she described in her diary a scene that was becoming a tragic commonplace of Europe: "I think of the Germans more as a natural disaster than as a people . . . We watch as people stream out of basements and crowd together in the streets with perambulators, woollen blankets and babies. They sit on lorries, horse carts, taxis and private cars. It's like a film I saw: Finnish, Polish, Albanian, Chinese refugees . . . It is so simple and so sad: people are 'evacuated' with woollen blankets, silver cutlery and babies in their arms. They are fleeing from bombs."

The Norwegians displayed implacable hostility to their invaders. Even when compelled to acknowledge subjection, they were unimpressed by explanations. Ruth Maier heard three German soldiers tell a cluster of Oslo residents that 60,000 German civilians had been murdered by the

Poles before the Wehrmacht intervened to save their ethnic brethren. Ruth laughed:

> [The man] turns to me and says: "Are you laughing, Fräulein?" "Yes." "And our Führer!," he goes all misty-eyed. "Obviously he's a human being like the rest of us, but he's the best, the best we have in Europe." The [soldier] with the sky-blue eyes—also misty now—nods: "The best . . . the best . . . !" More people come over to listen. The Norwegian says: "Are we really to believe that you've come over here to protect us? . . . That's what it says here!" He points to [a] newspaper . . . "Protect you? No, we're not doing that." But the blond interrupts him. "Yes, of course that's what we're doing." The brown-haired one thinks for a moment and then says, "Yes, actually, if we're honest about it . . . we're protecting you from the English." The Norwegian: "And you believe that?"

The faith of most Germans in the virtue as well as the expediency of their mission was fortified by its swift success. The invaders closed their grip on southern Norway, having secured communications with the homeland by occupying the intervening Danish Peninsula almost without resistance. The Norwegian Storting met again in the little town of Elverum, forty miles north of Oslo, where its deliberations were sharpened by news that the Germans had nominated a traitor to lead a puppet regime in Oslo. "We now have a Kuusinen government," declared the prime minister contemptuously: he alluded to Finnish communist Otto Kuusinen, who collaborated with Stalin's invasion of Finland. But Norway's counterpart, Vidkun Quisling, would become much more notorious, his name passing into the English language.

Four busloads of German paratroopers on their way to Elverum came under fire from a roadblock manned by members of a local rifle club; the Norwegians drove the attackers back in disarray, mortally wounding the German air attaché, Capt. Eberhard Spiller, who had been tasked to arrest the nation's leadership. The royal family and ministers decamped to the little village of Nybergsund. King Haakon VII was a tall, gaunt, sixty-seven-year-old Dane, elected monarch when the Norwegians gained independence from Sweden in 1905. In 1940, he displayed dignity and courage. At a government council held amid the deep snow of Nybergsund on the evening of 10 April, he told ministers in a high, quavering voice: "I am profoundly moved at the idea of having to assume personal responsibility for the woes that will befall our country and our people if German demands are rejected . . . The government is free to decide, but

I shall make my own position clear: I cannot accept . . . This would conflict with everything I have considered to be my duty as a king." Rather than bow to Berlin's insistence that he should endorse Quisling, he would abdicate. The old king lapsed into silence for several long moments, then burst into tears. At last, he continued: "The government must now take its decision. It is not bound by my position . . . Yet I felt it was my duty to make it known."

The Norwegians committed themselves to fight, to buy time for Allied assistance to come. Next day, 11 April, Haakon and his son Prince Olav were communing with their ministers when the Germans bombed and strafed Nybergsund in an attempt to decapitate the national leadership. The politicians threw themselves into a pigsty while the king and his aides took cover in a nearby wood. No one was killed, and though the Norwegians were shaken by the Heinkels' repeated machine-gunning, their resolve remained unbroken. Haakon was shocked to see civilians exposed to German fire. "I could not bear to watch . . . children crouching in the snow as bullets mowed down the trees and branches rained down on them," he said. He declared that never again would he seek refuge in a place where his presence imperilled innocents.

Monarch and politicians briefly discussed seeking sanctuary in Sweden, a notion favoured by the prime minister. Haakon would have none of this, and Norway's leaders moved to Lillehammer to continue the struggle. Poor, broken old General Laake was replaced as commander-in-chief by the courageous and energetic Gen. Otto Ruge, to whom a British officer paid the supreme compliment of asserting that he resembled a master of foxhounds. Norway's belated mobilisation was chaotic, since its southern depots and armouries were in German hands, but most of the 40,000 men who responded were passionate patriots. Frank Foley, the British Secret Service's man in Oslo, cabled tersely: "You cannot conceive pitiable condition material this army, but men fine types." In the weeks that followed, some Norwegians played heroic parts in their nation's defence. The country had few large towns; much of its population was scattered in communities beside deep-sea fjords, connected by narrow roads passing through defiles between mountain ranges. German, British and French commanders, alike surprised to find themselves fighting in Norway, were alike reduced to assembling intelligence about the battlefield by buying Baedeker travel guides from their local bookshops in Berlin, London and Paris.

The makeshift Anglo-French landing forces sent to Norway in the weeks following the German invasion defied parody. Almost every effective unit of the British Army was deployed in France; only twelve half-

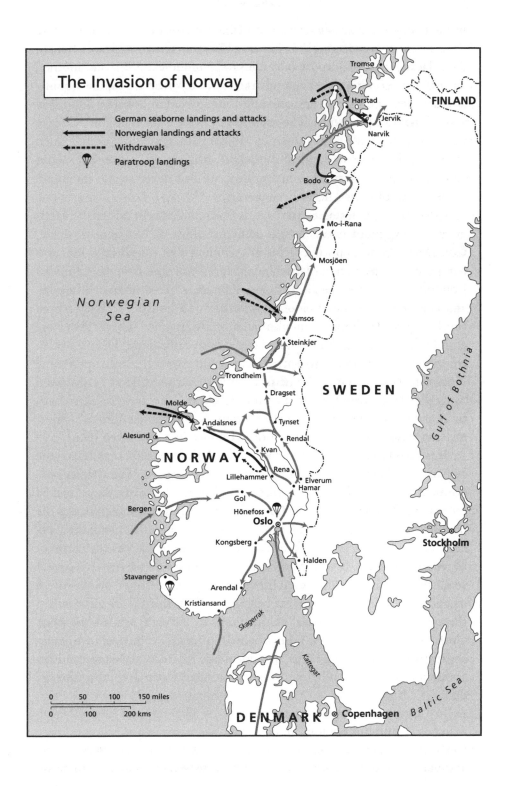

The Invasion of Norway

⟶ German seaborne landings and attacks

⟶ Norwegian landings and attacks

⟵---- Withdrawals

☒ Paratroop landings

Tromsø

Harstad

FINLAND

Jervik

Narvik

Bodo

Norwegian Sea

Mo-i-Rana

Mosjöen

Namsos

Steinkjer

Trondheim

Dragset

SWEDEN

Molde

Åndalsnes

Tynset

Alesund

Rendal

Kvan

NORWAY

Rena

Lillehammer

Elverum

Hamar

Gol

Gulf of Bothnia

Bergen

Hönefoss

Oslo

Kongsberg

Stockholm

Halden

Stavanger

Arendal

Kristiansand

Skagerrak

Kattegat

0   50   100   150 miles

0   100   200 kms

DENMARK   ○ Copenhagen

Baltic Sea

trained Territorial battalions were available to cross the North Sea. These were dispatched piecemeal, to pursue objectives changed almost hourly. They lacked maps, transport and radios to communicate with one another, far less with London. They disembarked with few heavy weapons or anti-aircraft guns, their stores and ammunition jumbled in hopeless confusion aboard the transport ships. The soldiers felt wholly disorientated. George Parsons landed with his company at Mojoen: "Imagine how we felt when we saw a towering ice-capped mountain in front of us standing about 2,000 feet high. We south London boys, we had never seen a mountain before, most of us had never been to sea."

Ashore, even where they were outnumbered, German troops displayed greater energy and better tactics than the Allies. A Norwegian officer, Col. David Thue, reported to his government that one British unit was composed of "very young lads who appeared to come from the slums of London. They have taken a very close interest in the women of Romsdal, and engaged in wholesale looting of stores and houses . . . They would run like hares at the first sound of an aircraft engine." The British Foreign Office reported in the later stages of the campaign: "Drunk British troops . . . on one occasion quarrelled with and eventually fired upon some Norwegian fishermen . . . Some of the British Army officers . . . behaved 'with the arrogance of Prussians' and the naval Officers were . . . so cautious and suspicious that they treated every Norwegian as a Fifth Columnist and refused to believe vital information when it was given them."

It is hard to exaggerate the chaos of the Allies' decision making, or the cynicism of their treatment of the hapless Norwegians. The British government made extravagant promises of aid, while knowing that it lacked means to fulfil them. The War Cabinet's chief interest was Narvik and the possibility of seizing and holding a perimeter around it to block the German winter iron-ore route from Sweden. Narvik Fjord was the scene of fierce naval clashes, in which both sides suffered severe destroyer losses. A small British landing force established itself on an offshore island, where its general resolutely rejected the urgings of Adm. Lord Cork and Orrery, the peppery, monocled naval commander, to advance against the port. Cork sought to inspirit the soldier by marching ashore himself; a notably short man, he was obliged to abandon both his reconnaissance and his assault ambitions when he immediately plunged waist-deep into a snowdrift.

In London, strategic debate increasingly degenerated into shouting matches. Churchill shouted loudest, but his extravagant schemes were frustrated by lack of means to fulfil them. Ministers argued with one another, with the French, and with their service chiefs. Coordination between commanders was nonexistent. In the space of a fortnight, six successive operational plans were drafted and discarded. The British were reluctantly persuaded that some show of assisting the Norwegians in defending the centre of their country was indispensable politically, if futile militarily. Landings at Namsos and Åndalsnes were executed in confusion and prompted relentless German bombing, which destroyed supply dumps as fast as they were created and reduced the wooden towns to ashes. At Namsos, French troops looted British stores; there were vehicle crashes caused by conflicting national opinions about right- and left-hand road priority. On 17 April Maj. Gen. Frederick Hotblack had just been briefed in London to lead an assault on Trondheim when he suffered a stroke and collapsed unconscious.

The British 148th Brigade, whose commander defied instructions from London and marched his men to offer direct support to the Norwegian army, was mercilessly mauled by the Germans before its 300 survivors retreated by bus. A staff officer dispatched from Norway to the War Office to seek instructions returned to tell Maj. Gen. Adrian Carlton de Wiart, leading another force: "You can do what you like, for they don't know what they want done." British troops fought one engagement in which they acquitted themselves honourably, at Kvan on 24–25 April, before being obliged to fall back.

Thereafter in London, ministers and service chiefs favoured evacuation of Namsos and Åndalsnes. Neville Chamberlain, self-centred as ever, was fearful of bearing blame for failure. The press, encouraged by the government, had infused the British people with high hopes for the campaign; the BBC had talked absurdly about the Allies "throwing a ring of steel around Oslo." Now, the prime minister mused to colleagues that it might be prudent to tell the House of Commons that the British had never intended to conduct long-term operations in central Norway. The French, arriving in London on 27 April for a meeting of the Allied Supreme War Council, were stunned by the proposal to quit, and demurred fiercely. Reynaud returned to Paris claiming success in galvanising Chamberlain and his colleagues: "We have shown them what to do and given them the will to do it." This was fanciful: two hours later, the British evacuation order was given. Pamela Street, a Wiltshire farmer's daughter, wrote sadly in her diary: "The war goes on like a great big weight which gets a bit heavier every day."

The Norwegian campaign spawned mistrust and indeed animosity between the British and French governments which proved irreparable, even after the fall of Chamberlain. To a colleague on 27 April, Reynaud deplored the inertia of British ministers, "old men who do not know how to take a risk." Daladier told the French cabinet on 4 May: "We should ask the British what they want to do: they pushed for this war, and they wriggle out as soon as it is a matter of taking measures which could directly affect them." Shamefully, British local commanders were instructed not to tell the Norwegians they were leaving. Gen. Bernard Paget ignored this order, provoking an emotional scene with the Norwegian C-in-C, Otto Ruge, who said: "So Norway is to share the fate of Czechoslovakia and Poland. But why? Why? Your troops haven't been defeated!" After this brief explosion, however, Ruge's natural dignity and calm reasserted themselves. Some historians have criticised his defence of central Norway, but it is hard to imagine any deployment of his small forces that would have altered the outcome. When King Haakon and his government opted for exile in Britain, the army C-in-C refused to leave his men and insisted upon sharing their captivity.

At Namsos, Maj. Gen. Carlton de Wiart obeyed the evacuation order without informing the neighbouring Norwegian commander, who suddenly found his flank in the air. After conducting a difficult retreat to the port, Ruge's officer found only a heap of British stores, some wrecked vehicles and a jaunty farewell note from Carlton de Wiart. Gen. Claude Auchinleck, who assumed the Allied command at Narvik, later wrote to Ironside, the CIGS, in London: "The worst of it all is the need for lying to all and sundry in order to preserve secrecy. Situation vis a vis the Norwegians is particularly difficult, and one feels a most despicable creature in pretending that we are going on fighting when we are going to quit at once." In the far north, the British and French concentrated some 26,000 men to confront the 4,000 Germans who now held Narvik. Amazingly, even after the campaign in France began, the Allies sustained operations until the end of May, seizing the port on the twenty-seventh after days of dogged and skilful German resistance.

The confusion of loyalties and nationalities that would become a notable feature of the war was illustrated by the presence among Narvik's attackers of some Spanish republicans, enlisted in the French Foreign Legion after being evicted from their own country. "Those officers who had misgivings about welcoming [them] into the Legion (they dubbed them all communists) were gratified by their fighting prowess," wrote Capt. Pierre Lapie. "[One of] the young Spaniards who attacked a German machine-gun post behind Elvegard . . . was mown down by fire at only a few yards' distance. Another sprang forward and smashed the head of the gunner with his rifle butt." The regimental war diary described the legionnaires' ascent of the steep hill before Narvik, where they met a fierce counterattack: "Captaine de Guittaut was killed and Lieutenant Garoux severely wounded. Led by

Lieutenant Vadot, the company managed to halt the counterattack and the Germans fell back, abandoning their dead and wounded . . . Sergeant Szabo being the first man to set foot in the town."

It was all for nothing: immediately after capturing the town and burying their dead, the Allies began to reembark, recognising that their position was strategically untenable. The Norwegians were left to contemplate hundreds of wrecked homes and dead civilians. Their monarch and government sailed for Britain on 7 June aboard a Royal Navy cruiser. Some Norwegians undertook epic journeys to escape from German occupation and join the Allied struggle, several being assisted by the Soviet ambassador in Stockholm, the remarkable intellectual Aleksandra Kollontai, to travel eastwards around the world and eventually reach Britain.

The evacuation of central Norway, under heavy air attack, shocked and dismayed the British public at home. A student, Christopher Tomlin, wrote on 3 May: "I am stunned, very disillusioned and afraid of our retreat . . . Mr. Chamberlain . . . made me believe we would drive the Germans out of Scandinavia. Now the wind is out of my sails; I feel subdued and expect to hear more bad news . . . Haven't we, can't we find, more men of Churchill's breed?" In truth, the First Lord bore substantial responsibility for the rash and muddled deployments in Norway. Britain's armed forces lacked resources to intervene effectively; their bungled gestures mocked the tragedy of the Norwegian people. But Churchill's rhetoric and bellicosity, in contrast to the prime minister's manifest feebleness of purpose, prompted a surge of public enthusiasm for a change of government, which infected the chamber of the House of Commons. On 10 May, the prime minister resigned. Next day King George VI invited Churchill to form a government.

THE GERMANS SUFFERED the heaviest casualties in the Norwegian campaign— 5,296 compared with the British 4,500, most of the latter incurred when the carrier *Glorious* and its escorts were sunk by the battle cruiser *Scharnhorst* on 8 June. The French and a Polish exile contingent lost 530 dead, the Norwegians about 1,800. The Luftwaffe lost 242 planes, the RAF 112. Three British cruisers, seven destroyers, an aircraft carrier and four submarines were sunk, against three German cruisers, ten destroyers, and six submarines. Four further German cruisers and six destroyers were badly damaged.

The conquest of Norway provided Hitler with naval and air bases which became important when he later invaded Russia, after which he exploited them to impede the shipment of Allied supplies to Murmansk.

He was content to leave Sweden unmolested and neutral: his strategic dominance ensured that the Swedes maintained shipments of iron ore to Germany, and dared not risk offering comfort to the Allies. Yet Hitler paid a price for Norway. Obsessed with holding the country against a prospective British assault, until almost the war's end he deployed 350,000 men there, a major drain on his manpower resources. And German naval losses in the Norwegian campaign proved a critical factor in making a subsequent invasion of Britain unrealistic.

The British were chiefly responsible for conducting Allied operations in Norway, and must thus bear overwhelming blame for their failure. Lack of resources explained much, but the performance of the Royal Navy's senior officers was unimpressive—the shocking incompetence of *Glorious*'s captain was chiefly responsible for the carrier's loss; the weakness of British warships' antiaircraft defences was painfully exposed. The 10 and 13 April attacks on German destroyers at Narvik, and later evacuations of Anglo-French ground forces, were the only naval operations to be creditably handled. British conduct towards Norway was characterised by bad faith, or at least a lack of frankness which amounted to the same thing. It is remarkable that the Norwegians proved so quickly forgiving, becoming staunch allies both in exile and in their occupied homeland. No action within British powers could have averted the German conquest, once the Royal Navy missed its best chance on 9 April. But the moral ignobility and military incompetence of the campaign reflected poorly upon Britain's politicians and commanders. If the scale of operations was small compared with those that would soon follow, it reflected failures of will, leadership, equipment, tactics and training which would be repeated on a much wider stage.

The campaign's most important consequence was that it precipitated the fall of Chamberlain. Had there been no Norway, it is overwhelmingly likely that he would have retained office as prime minister through the campaign in France that followed. The consequences of such an outcome for Britain, and for the world, could have been catastrophic, because his government might well have chosen a negotiated peace with Hitler. But only posterity can thus discern a consolation for the Norwegian débâcle which was denied to all the contemporary participants save the victorious Germans.

2. The Fall of France

ON THE EVENING OF 9 May 1940, French troops on the Western Front heard "a vast murmuring" in the German lines; word was passed back that the enemy was moving. Commanders chose to believe that this, like earlier such alarms, was false. Though the German assault upon Holland, Belgium and France began at 4:35 a.m. on 10 May, it was 6:30 before the Allied C-in-C, Gen. Maurice Gamelin, was awakened in his bed, five hours after the first warning from the outposts. Following the long-anticipated pleas for assistance that now arrived from governments in Brussels and The Hague, neutrals in the path of the German storm, Gamelin ordered an advance to the river Dyle in Belgium, fulfilling his longstanding contingency plan. The British Expeditionary Force's nine divisions and the best of France's forces—twenty-nine divisions of First, Seventh and Ninth armies—began rolling northeastwards. The Luftwaffe made no serious attempt to interfere, for this was exactly where Hitler wanted the Allies to go. Their departure removed a critical threat to the flank of the main German armies, which were thrusting forward further south.

The defences of Holland and Belgium were smashed open. In the first hours of 10 May, glider-landed Luftwaffe paratroops secured the vital Eben Emael fort, covering the Albert Canal—built by a German construction company which obligingly provided its blueprints to Hitler's planners—and two bridges across the Maas at Maastricht. Even as Churchill took office as Britain's prime minister, German spearheads were rolling up the Dutch army. Meanwhile, southwestwards, some 134,000 men and 1,600 vehicles, of which 1,222 were tanks, began threading their way through the Ardennes forest to deliver the decisive blow of the campaign against the weak centre of the French line. Germans joked afterwards that they created "the greatest traffic jam in history" in the woods of Luxembourg and southern Belgium, forcing thousands of tanks, trucks and guns along narrow roads the Allies had deemed unsuitable for moving an army. The advancing columns were vulnerable to air attack, had the French recognised their presence and importance. But they did not. From beginning to end of the struggle, Gamelin and his army commanders directed operations in a miasma of uncertainty, seldom either knowing where the Germans had reached, or guessing whither they were going.

Disproportionate historical attention has focused upon the operations of the small British contingent, and its escape from Dunkirk. The overriding German objective was to defeat the French army, by far the most formidable obstacle to the Wehrmacht. The British role was marginal; especially in the first days, the BEF commanded the attention of only modest German air and ground forces. It is untrue that France's defence rested chiefly on the frontier fortifications of the Maginot Line: the chief purpose of its bunkers and guns was to liberate men for active operations farther north. Scarred by memories of the 1914–18 devastation and slaughter in their own country, the French were bent upon waging war somewhere other than on their own soil. Gamelin planned a decisive battle in Belgium, heedless of the fact that the Germans had other ideas. The French C-in-C's gravest mistake in the early spring of 1940 had been to move the French Seventh Army to the left of the Allied line in anticipation of the Belgian incursion.

French vanguards crossed into Holland to find that the Dutch army had already retreated too far northeastward to create a common front, while the Belgian army was falling back in disarray. Gamelin's formations fought hard in the significant battles that followed in Belgium: although short of antiaircraft and antitank guns, they had some good tanks, notably the SOMUA S35. In a long slogging match at Hannut between 12 and 14 May, 165 panzers were knocked out, for the loss of 105 French tanks. The French front on the Dyle remained unbroken. But its defenders were soon obliged to fall back, because they found their right flank turned. The Germans, gaining possession of the Hannut battlefield, were able to recover and repair most of their damaged armour.

For the first two days of the campaign, the French high command was oblivious of its peril: a witness described Gamelin's demeanour as positively jaunty, "striding up and down the corridor in his fort, with a pleased and martial air." Another observer spoke of the C-in-C as "in excellent form with a big smile." Now sixty-seven years old, as Marshal Joseph Joffre's chief of staff in 1914 he had been widely perceived as the architect of France's triumph in the Battle of the Marne. A self-consciously cultured figure, he enjoyed discussing art and philosophy; also intensely political, he was much more popular than his future successor, the splenetic Maxime Weygand. Gamelin's crippling weakness was an instinct for compromise: he strove to avoid making hard choices. Anticipating *"une guerre de longue durée,"* a protracted confrontation on the frontier of France, he and his subordinates were confounded in May 1940 by events unfolding at a speed beyond their imaginations.

The Germans had committed seventeen divisions to demonstrate against the Maginot Line in the south, twenty-nine to seize Holland and northern Belgium, and forty-five, including seven panzer, to attack in the centre, then swing northwest towards the Channel coast after crossing the Meuse, cutting off the French and British in Belgium. Only half of the German attacking troops were fully trained, and more than a quarter were reservists aged over forty. The principal burden of defeating the French army rested upon 140,000 men of the panzer and mechanised divisions making the vital thrust across the Meuse. The first German troops reached the river at 2:00 p.m. on 12 May, having seen scarcely a French soldier since they broke clear of the Ardennes; they had thus far conducted a march rather than an attack. The Meuse line was defended by reservists of Charles Huntziger's Second Army. On the morning of 13 May, these French troops suffered a devastating bombardment by more than a thousand Luftwaffe aircraft, attacking in waves. This, the first such attack of their war, did little material damage but impacted severely on morale. A soldier wrote: "The noise of their engines is already enormous and then there is this extraordinary shrieking which shreds your nerves . . . And then suddenly there is a rain of bombs . . . And it goes on and on! Not a French or British plane to be seen. Where the hell are they? My neighbour, a young bloke, is crying."

A French staff officer at Sedan wrote: "The gunners stopped firing and went to ground, the infantry cowered in their trenches, dazed by the crash of bombs and the shriek of the dive-bombers; they had not developed the instinctive reaction of running to their anti-aircraft guns and firing back. Their only concern was to keep their heads well down. Five hours of this nightmare was enough to shatter their nerves." Soldiers, like most human beings in all circumstances, react badly to the unexpected. Through the long winter of 1939–40, there had been no attempt to condition the French army to endure such an ordeal as it now experienced.

Most of the command telephone system was destroyed in the air attacks. Early that evening of 13 May, there was a "tank panic" three miles south of Sedan. The local commanding general left his headquarters to investigate wild shouting outside, and found a scene of chaos: "A wave of terrified fugitives, gunners and infantry, in cars, on foot, many without arms but dragging kitbags, were hurtling down the road screaming 'The tanks are at Bulson.' Some were firing their rifles like lunatics. General Lafontaine and his officers rushed in front of them, trying to reason with them and herd them together, and had lorries put across the road . . . Officers were mixed in with the men . . . There was mass hysteria." Some 20,000 men decamped in the Bulson panic—six hours before German forces crossed the Meuse. In all probability, their flight was prompted by frightened men mistaking French tanks for enemy ones.

The first German river-crossing parties suffered heavily at the hands of French machine gunners, but handfuls of determined men reached the western shore in dinghies, then waded through swamps to attack French positions. A sergeant named Walther Rubarth led a group of eleven assault engineers to storm a succession of bunkers with satchel charges and grenades. Six of the Germans were killed, but the survivors opened a breach. Panzergrenadiers ran across an old weir linking an island to the two banks of the Meuse to establish a foothold on the western side. By 5:30 p.m.,

German engineers were building bridges, while rafts ferried equipment across. Some French soldiers were already retreating, indeed fleeing. At 11:00 p.m., tanks began clattering across the first completed pontoons: the German sappers' achievement was as impressive as that of the assault troops.

The French response was painfully sluggish, absurdly complacent. It was suggested to General Huntzinger that the German assault was unfolding like that on Poland. He shrugged theatrically: "Poland is Poland . . . Here we are in France." Told of the Meuse crossings, he said: "That will mean all the more prisoners." Earlier that day, Gamelin's headquarters declared: "[It] is still not possible to determine the zone in which the enemy will make his main attack." But that night Gen. Joseph Georges, commanding the northeastern front, telephoned Gamelin to say that there had been a rather serious upset—"*un pépin*"—at Sedan. At 3:00 a.m. on 14 May, a French officer described the scene at Georges's headquarters: "The room was barely half-lit. Major Navereau was repeating in a low voice the information coming in. General Roton, the chief of staff, was stretched out in an armchair. The atmosphere was that of a family in which there has been a death. Georges got up quickly . . . He was terribly pale. 'Our front has been broken at Sedan! There has been a collapse.' He flung himself into a chair and burst into tears." An officer described Gen. Georges Blanchard, commander of First Army, "sitting in tragic immobility, saying nothing, doing nothing, but just gazing at the map spread on the table between us."

The decisive moment of the campaign came later that morning. The German crossing of the Meuse need not have been calamitous, had it been reversed by a swift counterattack. But French troops assembled lethargically, then advanced hesitantly and piecemeal. Attacks by 152 bombers and 250 fighters of the RAF and the French air force failed to damage the German bridges, while costing heavy losses—31 of 71 British bombers failed to return. Flight Lt. Bill Simpson's single-engined Battle caught fire when it crashed, and he was dragged half naked from the flaming wreckage by his crew. Sitting shocked on the grass nearby, he stared at his hands "with unbelieving terror . . . The skin hung from them like long icicles. The fingers were curled and pointed, like the claws of a great wild bird—distorted, pointed at the ends like talons, ghostly thin. What would I do now? What use would be these paralysed talons to me for the rest of my life?"

By nightfall on 14 May three French formations around Sedan had collapsed, their men fleeing the battlefield. One of these was the 71st

Division. A notorious episode passed into legend, of one of its colonels who sought to check fleeing men and was swept aside by soldiers crying: "We want to go home and get back to work! There is nothing to do! We are lost! We are betrayed!" Some modern historians question the reality of this incident. Pierre Lesort, another officer of the same formation, retained a different and more heroic memory of the day: "I saw very well, about 800–1000 metres on my left, an artillery battery . . . which never stopped firing at the diving Stukas which ceaselessly attacked it; I can still see the little round clouds which its guns created in the sky around the swirling planes which continuously dispersed and returned . . . As for the reactions of the machine-gunners in my company, we never stopped shooting desperately at the planes." Yet Lesort acknowledged the progressive erosion of morale: "It must be said that this control of the sky by the Germans for these two days made the men discontented and impatient. At the start it was just a sort of grumbling: 'Christ, there are only German planes, what the hell are ours doing?' But on the following days . . . one felt the growth of a kind of helpless resentment."

Through the succeeding days, French armour launched desultory attacks on the Meuse bridgehead from the south. Gamelin and his officers made another disastrous and probably irrecoverable mistake: they failed to grasp the fact that von Rundstedt's spearheads did not intend to continue their advance west into the heart of France, but instead were racing north, for the sea, to cut off the British and French armies in Belgium. The Germans' "expanding torrent" was now advancing across a front sixty miles wide. The French Ninth Army, charged with defending the region, had almost ceased to exist. The advancing panzer columns were acutely sensitive to the risk of an Allied counterattack on their flanks, but the French high command lacked the will or the grip to initiate such action, as well as means to carry it out. It is mistaken to suppose that the French army offered no significant resistance to the German offensive in 1940: some of Gamelin's units made energetic and successful local attacks, and paid a heavy price in casualties. But nowhere did the French deliver assaults of sufficient weight to halt the racing thrusts of von Rundstedt's armour.

Pierre Lesort described "an immediate impression of total disorder and shameful despair. Belongings pushed on bikes, helmets and guns out of sight, and the appearance of dazed vagrants . . . By the side of the road a man was standing alone, immobile. Wearing a black cap and short cassock: a military chaplain . . . I saw that he was crying." Another soldier, Gustave Folcher, wrote of encounters with men of broken units from the north: "They told us terrible things, unbelievable things . . . Some had come from as far as the Albert Canal . . . They asked for something to eat and drink; poor lads! They streamed on endlessly; it was a piteous sight. Ah, if those enthusiasts who go and watch the magnificent military parades in Paris or elsewhere could have seen on that morning this other army, the real one . . . perhaps they would understand the suffering of the soldier."

A SENSE OF UNREALITY at first pervaded French public consciousness as the familiar world began to disintegrate. The Russian-born Jewish writer Irène Némirovsky described in her autobiographical novel of 1940–41, *Suite française*, the disbelieving response in Paris to news of stunning German advances: "Even though the reports were terrible, no one believed them. No more so than if victory had been announced." But as the truth began to be understood, panic swept the nation. Among the most terrible aspects of those days was the massed flight of civilians, which impacted as disastrously on military communications as upon soldiers' morale. The people of eastern France had suffered German occupation in 1914; they were determined to escape another such experience. Much of the population of Rheims fled, only one-tenth of Lille's 200,000 inhabitants stayed in their homes, and just 800 of Chartres's 23,000 people remained after the cathedral city was heavily bombed. Many places became ghost towns.

Throughout eastern and central France, army units found themselves struggling to deploy for action amid huge columns of desperate humanity. Gustave Folcher wrote:

> The people are half-mad, they don't even reply to what we ask them. There is only one word in their mouths: evacuation, evacuation . . . What is most pitiful is to see entire families on the road, with their livestock they force to follow them, but that they finally have to leave in some cattle-pen. We see wagons drawn by two, three or four beautiful mares, some with a young foal which follows at the risk of being crushed every few metres. The wagon is driven by a woman, often in tears, but most of the time it's a kid of eight, ten or perhaps twelve years old who leads the horses. On the wagon, on which furniture, trunks, linen, the most precious things, or rather the most indispensable things, have been hastily packed up, the grandparents have also taken their place, holding in their place a very young child, even a newborn baby . . . The children look at us one by one as we overtake them, holding in their hands the little dog, the little cat or the cage of canaries they didn't want to be separated from.

Eight million French people abandoned their homes in the month following the onset of the German assault, the greatest mass migration in western European history. Those families who stayed in Paris found themselves repeatedly driven into shelters by alarms: "They had to dress their children by torchlight," wrote one of those who experienced them.

Mothers lifted small, warm, heavy bodies into their arms: "Come on, don't be afraid, don't cry." An air raid. All the lights were out, but beneath the clear, golden June sky, every house, every street was visible. As for the Seine, the river seemed to absorb even the faintest glimmers of light and reflect them back a hundred times brighter, like some multi-faceted mirror. Badly blacked-out windows, glistening rooftops, the metal hinges of doors all shone in the water. There were a few red lights that stayed on longer than the others, no one knew why, and the Seine drew them in, capturing them and bouncing them playfully on its waves.

In the week that followed the German crossing of the Meuse, the invading armies maintained an almost ceaseless advance, while the Allies conducted in slow motion every activity save retreat. The British held the French overwhelmingly responsible for their predicament, but some of Gort's officers adopted a more enlightened view, understanding that their own BEF had little to be proud of. "After a few days' fighting," wrote an Irish Fusiliers officer, John Horsfall, "part of our army was no longer capable of coordinated measures, either offensive or defensive . . . We could not lay these . . . to the charge of our politicians, [they were] failings that were strictly our own . . . Within our army the fault lay in the mind, and really one must wonder what the Staff College was about in those pre-war years."

The disparity between the battlefield performance of the German and Western Allied armies would prove one of the great enigmas not merely of the 1940 campaign, but of the entire conflict. Thomas Mann once described Nazism as "mechanised mysticism." Michael Howard has written: "Armed as they were with all the military technology and bureaucratic rationality of the Enlightenment, but fuelled by the warrior-values of a largely invented past, it is not surprising that the Germans held the world at bay through two terrible wars." Though these remarks reflect important truths, they seem an incomplete answer to the question: why was the Wehrmacht so good? Its senior officers had fought in World War I, but for more than a decade thereafter the German army was almost moribund. It gained no interwar combat experience. Meanwhile, many British rankers as well as officers participated in low-intensity operations on the North-West Frontier of India, or in Irish or colonial skirmishes.

The inescapable conclusion is that the British Army's role as an imperial gendarmerie impeded its education and adaptation for large-scale war. Brushfire conflicts emphasised the handling of small forces, the regiment as the focus of operations. They demanded limited effort, sacrifice and tactical thinking. Some officers were, in Michael Howard's words, "highly professional within a tiny environment." But throughout the conflict Churchill's generals suffered from the lack of any coherent system of instruction for higher command, such as the British Army belatedly acquired only thirty years later. The Wehrmacht, re-created in the 1930s from a mere cadre, embraced new ideas and prepared and conditioned itself solely for continental war. Its officers displayed greater energy, professionalism and imagination than most of their British counterparts; its men proved highly motivated. An institutional discipline pervaded the German army's battlefield conduct at every level, and persisted throughout the war. Its commitment to counterattack, even in adverse circumstances, amounted to genius. The concept of conducting war *à l'outrance*, pursuing to the last gasp the destruction of the enemy, seemed to come naturally to Germans, as it did not to their British or French opponents. On the battlefield, Allied soldiers, reflecting the societies from which they were drawn, prided themselves on behaving like reasonable men. The Wehrmacht showed what unreasonable men could do.

IN THE MAY 1940 BEF, John Horsfall deplored a lack of good maps and the failure to cover the retreat by local counterattacks and inflict substantial damage on the German spearheads; to deploy artillery effectively; or adequately to brief those at the sharp end: "Our soldiers just need to know in simple terms what they have to contend with." Horsfall and his comrades became bewildered and disgusted by their long trek back from Belgium and through northeastern France, during which they watched a substantial part of their army, and most of its commanders, fall apart. "It was a rotten march," he wrote, "and the [Fusiliers] were progressively broken up by lost and sometimes disordered fragments of other units surging in on us from the side roads . . . There was over-much to brood upon . . . One could not fail to be aware of the loss of grip somewhere in our army. Our men knew it soon enough, and it became the task of the officers to stifle the subject—or laugh at it . . . Something pretty bad was happening. But it was no more the fault of our regiments than the shambles of the Crimea had been . . . I saw no reason . . . why that critical retreat was not effectively controlled."

Meanwhile, French commanders appeared to inhabit a fantasy world. Gamelin's staff officers marvelled to see him at lunch in his headquarters on 19 May, joking and making light conversation while his subordinates despaired. At 9:00 that night, about the time the first panzers reached the Channel at the mouth of the Somme, on Reynaud's orders Gamelin was replaced as France's military leader by seventy-three-year-old Gen. Maxime Weygand. The new supreme commander realised that the Allies' only chance was to launch counterattacks from the south and north against the German flanks in the vicinity of Arras, to break the encirclement of Belgium and northeast France. Sir Edmund Ironside, the British CIGS visiting from London, reached the same conclusion. Meeting two French generals, Gaston Billotte and Georges Blanchard, at Lens, Ironside was disgusted by their inertia. Both men were "in a state of complete depression. No plan, no thought of a plan. Ready to be slaughtered. Defeated at the head without casualties." Ironside urged an immediate attack south towards Amiens, with which Billotte promised to cooperate. Ironside then telephoned Weygand. They agreed that two French and two British divisions would attack next morning, the twenty-first.

Yet Gort never believed the French would move, and he was right. When the two weak British formations advanced next day they did so alone, and without air support. The Germans were initially thrown into disarray as Gort's columns struck west of Arras. There was fierce fighting, and the British advanced ten miles, taking 400 prisoners, before the attack ran out of steam. Erwin Rommel, commanding a panzer division, took personal command of the defence and rallied his surprised and confused units. Matilda tanks inflicted significant German losses, killing Rommel's aide-de-camp (ADC) at his side. But by then the British had shot their bolt; the attack was courageously and effectively delivered, but lacked sufficient weight to be decisive.

On the morning of that same day, 21 May, even as the British were moving towards Arras, Weygand set off from Vincennes for the northern front, in hopes of organising a more ambitious counterstroke. After waiting two hours at Le Bourget for a plane, the C-in-C's trip descended into farce. Arriving at Béthune, he found the airfield deserted save for a single scruffy soldier guarding petrol stocks. This man eventually drove the general to a post office where he was able to telephone the army group commander, Billotte, who had spent the morning searching for Weygand around Calais. The C-in-C, after pausing for an omelette at a country inn, used a plane to reach the port, then crawled by car along roads jammed with refugees to meet Belgium's King Leopold at the Ypres town hall. He urged the monarch to hasten his army's retreat westward, but Leopold was reluctant to abandon Belgian soil. Billotte said that only the British, thus far scarcely engaged, were fit to attack. To Weygand's anger—for he wrongly saw a snub—Lord Gort did not join the meeting.

When the BEF's commander belatedly reached Ypres, without much conviction he agreed to join a new counterattack, but said that all his reserves were committed. He never believed any combined Anglo-French thrust would take place. Weygand later claimed that the British were bent on betraying their ally: this reflected a profound French conviction, dating back to World War I, that the British always fought with one eye on their escape route to the Channel ports. The British, in their turn, despaired of French defeatism; Weygand was thus far right, that Gort believed his allies hopelessly inert, and was now set upon salvaging the BEF from the wreck of the campaign. Later on that bleak night of 21 May, Billotte was fatally injured in a car crash, and two days elapsed before a successor was appointed as Northern Army commander. Meanwhile, the breakdown of Allied command communications became comprehensive. After a meeting with the French army group commander the previous day, the British CIGS, Sir Edmund Ironside, wrote: "I lost my temper and shook Billotte by the button of his tunic. The man is completely beaten." Gort told King Leopold on the evening of the twenty-first: "It's a bad job." At 7:00 p.m., Weygand left Dunkirk by torpedo boat in the midst of an air raid, eventually regaining his headquarters at 10:00 a.m. next morning. Throughout every hour of his futile wanderings across northern France, German tanks, guns and men continued to stream north and west through the great hole in the Allied line.

The supreme commander now succumbed to fantasy: reporting to Reynaud on the morning of 22 May, he seemed in an almost jaunty mood. "So many mistakes have been made," he said, "that they give me confidence. I believe that in future we shall make less." He assured France's prime minister that both the BEF and Blanchard's army were in fine fighting trim. He outlined his planned counterattack, and concluded equivocally: "It will either give us victory or it will save our honour." At a meeting in Paris on 22 May with Churchill and Reynaud, Weygand exuded optimism, claiming that a new army of almost twenty divisions would conduct the French counterattack from the south to restore the link with the BEF. Both the army and the attack, however, were figments of his imagination.

On the night of the twenty-third, Gort withdrew his forces from the salient they held at Arras. This caused the French to assert that the British

The Last Phase of the 1940 French Campaign

German controlled
Weygand Line
Front Line
Maginot Line

were repeating their selfish and pusillanimous behaviour of 1914. Gort's decision represented only a recognition of reality, but Reynaud failed to tell Weygand that the British were preparing to evacuate the BEF. Gort told Adm. Jean-Marie Abrial, commanding the Dunkirk perimeter, that three British divisions would help to screen the French withdrawal. After Gort's departure for England, however, his successor in command, Maj.

Gen. Harold Alexander, declined to make good on this commitment. Abrial said: "Your decision dishonours Britain." Defeat prompted a welter of such inter-Allied recriminations: Weygand, told of the Belgian surrender on 28 May, expostulated furiously: "That king! What a pig! What an abominable pig!"

The British, meanwhile, had begun to evacuate the BEF from the port and beaches of Dunkirk. "It was evident to one and all that a monumental military disaster was in progress," the Irish Fusiliers officer John Horsfall wrote with weary resignation. "Therefore we could take refuge in history, knowing that this was not only to be expected but actually the commonplace experience of our army when tossed recklessly by our politicians into European war." Sergeant L. D. Pexton was one of more than 40,000 British soldiers taken prisoner, after a rearguard action near Cambrai in which his unit was overrun: "I remember the order 'Cease Fire' and that the time was 12 o'clock," he wrote afterwards. "Stood up and put my hands up. My God how few of us stood up. I expected my last moments had come and lit a fag."

THE DUNKIRK EVACUATION was announced to the British public on 29 May, when civilian volunteers from the Small Boat Pool joined warships rescuing men from the beaches and harbour. The Royal Navy's achievement during the week that followed became the stuff of legend. Vice Adm. Bertram Ramsay, operating from an underground headquarters at Dover, directed the movements of almost 900 ships and small craft with extraordinary calm and skill. The removal of troops from the beaches in civilian launches and pleasure boats forged the romantic image of Dunkirk, but by far the larger proportion—some two-thirds—were taken off by destroyers and other large vessels, loading at the harbour mole. The navy was fortunate that, throughout Operation Dynamo, the Channel remained almost preternaturally calm.

Arthur Gwynn-Browne, a soldier, poured out in lyrical terms his gratitude for finding himself returning home from the alien hell of Dunkirk: "It was so wonderful. I was on a ship and any ship yes any ship is England. Any ship yes any ship I was on a ship and on my way to England. It was wonderful. I kept quite still and the sea breezes I swallowed them, no smoke and burning and fire and thick grey oil smoke hazes, but sea breezes. I swallowed them they were so clean and fresh and I was alive it was so wonderful." Many men arrived in England fearful of their reception, as flotsam from one of the greatest defeats their country had ever suffered. A company quartermaster, Walter Gilding, wrote: "When we went ashore I thought everybody was going to shoot us, especially as being regular soldiers, we'd run away . . . But instead of that there were people cheering and clapping us as if we were heroes. Giving us mugs of tea and sandwiches. We looked a sorry sight, I think."

John Horsfall had the same experience:

At Ramsgate we met for the first time the unbelievable feat of improvisation achieved by the armed services and civil authorities acting in concert. Here was Britannia to greet us with the wand of a fairy and her mantle of magic; here, too, was a brief flash of history. Dimly conscious of it, we were deeply touched and knew immediately the national mood of defiance which brought down Napoleon and would destroy Hitler too. The warmth of the reception in this ancient seaport was inspired . . . An endless series of trains were awaiting and charming ladies with tea and other comforts. But fatigue and reaction were hard on the emotions, and we may have been less than responsive.

The legend of Dunkirk was besmirched by some uglinesses, as is the case with all great historical events: a significant number of British seamen invited to participate in the evacuation refused to do so, including the Rye fishing fleet and some lifeboat crews; others, after once experiencing the chaos of the beaches and Luftwaffe bombing, on reaching England declined to set forth again. While most fighting units preserved their cohesion, there were disciplinary collapses among rear-echelon personnel, which made it necessary for some officers to draw and indeed use their revolvers. For the first three days, the British were content to take off their own men, while the French held a perimeter southwards and were refused access to shipping. On at least one occasion when poilus attempted to board vessels, they were fired on by disorderly British troops. Only when Churchill intervened personally did ships begin to take off Frenchmen, 53,000 of them after the last British personnel had been embarked. Most subsequently insisted upon repatriation—and thereafter found themselves forced labourers in Germany—rather than remain as exiles in Britain.

A British soldier based at Dover barracks, David McCormick, saw little romance in his own contribution to the evacuation, described in a letter home on 29 May: "We . . . are woken & taken down to the docks at 1:45 a.m., where we undergo physical strain & mental torture until 8:30 carrying corpses about & loose hands & brains are all in the day's work. I feel very upset & sometimes feel like crying when I am down there. It is all so pointless & I hate the callousness with which it is treated by the majority of our people who chiefly go down to see what they can pinch in the way of cigarettes & money."

The navy suffered severely at Dunkirk, losing six destroyers with a further twenty-five damaged. Its worst day came on 1 June, when three destroyers and a passenger ship were sunk by air attack and four others crippled. Thereafter, the Admiralty felt obliged to withdraw its large warships from the evacuation. The RAF was often cursed by soldiers and sailors for its supposed absence from the skies; every man at Dunkirk learned to dread the repeated Stuka attacks. Yet Fighter Command made a major contribution to holding the Luftwaffe at bay, at the cost of losing 177 aircraft during the nine days of the evacuation. As the Germans sought to impede Dynamo, their pilots declared themselves more hard-pressed by fighters than at any time since 10 May. The Luftwaffe's effort against the departing British fell far short of Göring's hopes and promises, and this was as much due to the RAF as to its own bungling. After 1 June the Luftwaffe redeployed most of its aircraft to harry the French, making the final phase of the evacuation much less costly than the first.

The towering reality was that the BEF got away. Some 338,000 men were brought back to England, 229,000 of them British, the remainder French and Belgian. The withdrawal and evacuation were widely held to be Gort's personal triumph; but while the C-in-C indeed gave appropriate orders, success would have been unattainable had not Hitler held back his tanks. It remains unlikely, though just plausible, that this was a political decision, prompted by a belief that restraint would render the British more susceptible to peace negotiations. More credibly, Hitler accepted Göring's assurance that the Luftwaffe could finish off the BEF, which no longer threatened German strategic purposes; and the panzers needed rapid refit before being urgently redeployed against Weygand's forces. The French First Army conducted a brave stand at Lille, which contributed importantly to holding the Germans off the Dunkirk perimeter; it was understandable that British soldiers showed bitterness towards their allies, but Churchill's army had performed little better than Reynaud's in the continental campaign.

Dunkirk was indeed a deliverance, from which the prime minister extracted a perverse propaganda triumph. Nella Last, of Lancashire, wrote on 5 June: "I forgot I was a middle-aged housewife who sometimes got up tired and who had backache. The story made me feel part of something that was undying and never old—like a flame to light or warm, but strong enough to burn and destroy rubbish . . . Somehow I felt everything to be worthwhile, and I felt glad I was of the same race as the rescuers and res-

cued." The British Army salvaged a professional cadre around which new
formations might be built, but all its arms and equipment had been lost.
The BEF left behind in France 64,000 vehicles, 76,000 tons of ammunition, 2,500 guns and more than 400,000 tons of stores. Britain's land
forces were effectively disarmed: many soldiers would wait years before
receiving weapons and equipment that rendered them once more fit for a
battlefield.

IT IS SOMETIMES supposed that, when the BEF quit the Continent, the campaign ended, which is a travesty. In each day's fighting between 10 May
and 3 June, the Germans had suffered an average of 2,500 casualties. During the ensuing fortnight, their daily loss rate doubled to 5,000. A soldier
of the French 28th Division wrote defiantly on 28 May: "It seems that the
Germans have taken Arras and Lille. If this is true, the Nation must redis-
cover its old spirit of 1914 and 1789." Some units remained committed
to fight, some Frenchmen shrugged off the despair of their commanders.
One of Brig. Charles de Gaulle's men wrote: "In fifteen days we have carried out four attacks and we have always been successful, so we are going
to pull together and we will get that pig Hitler." A soldier wrote on 2 June:
"We are really tired, but we have to be here, they shall not pass and we
shall get them . . . I shall be proud to have participated in the Victory of
which I have no doubts." Even some foreign governments were not yet
convinced of France's final defeat. On 2 June Mussolini's foreign minister,
Galeazzo Ciano, flaunted the Italian regime's boundless cynicism when he
told the French ambassador in Rome: "Have some victories and you will
have us with you."

In the last phase of the campaign, forty French infantry divisions and
the remains of three armoured formations faced fifty German infantry
and ten panzer divisions. Thirty-five of Weygand's generals were sacked
and replaced. The French army fought better in June 1940 than it had
done in May, but it was too late to redeem the initial disasters. Constantin
Joffe of the Foreign Legion expressed surprise at the manner in which the
Jews of his regiment distinguished themselves:

> Many of them were small tailors or peddlers from Belleville, the work-
> man's quarter of Paris, or from the ghetto of the Rue du Temple. No
> one would have anything to do with them at [the training camp of]
> Barcares . . . They spoke only Yiddish. They looked as if they were
> afraid of a machine-gun, they seemed to be in perpetual fear. Yet under
> fire, if volunteers were needed to fetch back munitions under a heavy

shelling or if lines of barbed wire entanglements had to be up at night fairly in front of the enemy guns, these little men were the first to offer their service. They did it quietly without swagger, perhaps without enthusiasm; but they did it. It was always they who, up to the very last moment, brought back our arms from an abandoned post.

Wehrmacht commanders expressed admiration for the manner in which some French units fought in early June to defend their new line on the Somme. A German diarist wrote: "In these ruined villages the French resisted to the last man. Some 'hedgehogs' carried on when our infantry was twenty miles behind them." But on 6 June the front was decisively breached, and by the ninth von Rundstedt's tanks were driving into Rouen. Next day, they broke the Aisne line as the French government left Paris; the diplomat Jean Chauvel set fire to the chimney of his office in the Quai d'Orsay as he burned a mass of papers in its fireplace, one of many such symbolic bonfires of his nation's hopes. There were fears that, with the administration gone, socialist workers from the suburbs would march into the capital and proclaim a new Commune. Instead, when so many inhabitants had fled, there was only a macabre tranquillity: on 12 June in a smart Paris street, a Swiss journalist was bemused to meet a herd of abandoned cattle, lowing plaintively. The fall of the capital two days later caused the Austrian writer Stefan Zweig, a Jew now in remote exile, to write: "Few of my own misfortunes have dismayed me and filled me with despair as much as the humiliation of Paris, a city that was blessed like no other with the ability to make anyone who came there happy."

The great flight of civilians west and south continued by day and night. "Silently, with no lights on, cars kept coming, one after the other," wrote Irène Némirovsky, "full to bursting with baggage and furniture, prams and birdcages, packing cases and baskets of clothes, each with a mattress tied firmly to the roof. They looked like mountains of fragile scaffolding and they seemed to move without the aid of a motor, propelled by their own weight." Némirovsky described three hapless civilian victims of air attack: "Their bodies had been torn to shreds, but by chance their three faces were untouched. Such gloomy, ordinary faces, with a dim, fixed, stunned expression as if they were trying in vain to understand what was happening to them; they weren't made, my God, to die in a battle, they weren't made for death."

RAF fighter pilot Paul Richey saw a Luftwaffe bomb fall upon four farmworkers as they tilled a field: "We found them among the craters. The old man lay face down, his body twisted grotesquely, one leg shattered and a savage gash across the back of his neck, oozing steadily into the earth. His son lay close by . . . Against the hedge I found what must have been the remains of the third boy—recognizable only by a few tattered rags, a broken boot and some splinters of bone. The five stricken horses lay bleeding beside the smashed harrow, we shot them later. The air was foul with the reek of high explosive."

In those days when Europeans were still losing their innocence, British pilots were stunned by the spectacle of Messerschmitts machine-gunning refugees. Richey met a fellow airman in the mess: "A disillusioned Johnny almost reluctantly said, 'They *are* shits after all.' From this moment our concept of a chivalrous foe was dead." Pvt. Ernie Farrow of the British Army's 2nd Norfolks likewise recoiled from the carnage wrought by Göring's knights of the air: "All along the road were people who had been killed with no arms, no heads, there was cattle lying about dead, there was little tiny children, there was old people. Not one or two, but hundreds of them lying about . . . We couldn't stop to clear the road . . . so we had to drive our lorries over the top of them, which was heart-breaking—really heart-breaking."

At Reynaud's new refuge of government, the Château de Chissay, on the Loire, his mistress Hélène de Portes was seen directing visitors' cars, clad in a red dressing gown over pyjamas. Her impassioned influence was exercised to persuade the prime minister to agree to an armistice. Reynaud wrote sadly later, after Portes's death in a car crash, that she "was led astray by her desire to be in with the young . . . and to distance herself from Jews and old politicians. But she thought she was helping me." Portes's mood reflected that of much of her nation. At Sully-sur-Loire, a woman, red with anger and excitement, shouted at a French officer standing in front of a church: "What are you waiting for, you soldiers, to stop this war? Do you want them to massacre us all with our children? . . . Why are you still fighting? That Reynaud! If I could get hold of him, the scoundrel!"

At the headquarters of the Wehrmacht, euphoria prevailed. Gen. Edouard Wagner wrote on 15 June: "It should really be recorded for the history of our times and of the world how [Wehrmacht chief of staff Franz] Halder sits at the million-scale map and measures off the distances with a metre-rule and already deploys across the Loire. I doubt whether [Gen. Hans von] Seeckt's synthesis of 'cool judgement and warm enthusiasm' has ever found such brilliant reality as in the General Staff in this campaign . . . However, in spite of everything the Führer has earned the glory, for without his determination things would never have reached such an outcome."

On the evening of 12 June, Weygand proposed seeking an armistice. Reynaud suggested that he and his ministers might retain office in exile, but Marshal Philippe Pétain dismissed the notion. On the sixteenth, Reynaud accepted that most of his ministers favoured capitulation, and resigned in favour of Pétain. The marshal broadcast to the French people next morning: "It is with a heavy heart I say to you today that it is necessary to stop fighting." Thereafter, few French soldiers saw much purpose in sacrificing their lives on the battlefield.

Yet there were a few gallant, futile stands. An infantry battalion near Châteauneuf stubbornly held its positions. Another episode became enshrined in the legend of France: as columns of refugees and deserters from the army fled across the Loire, the commandant of the French cavalry school at Saumur, a hoary old warhorse, Col. Daniel Michon, was ordered to deploy his 780 cadets and instructors to defend the area's bridges. He assembled them all in Saumur's great amphitheatre and announced: "Gentlemen, for the school it is a mission of sacrifice. France is depending on you." One pupil, Jean-Louis Dunand, who had abandoned architectural studies in Paris to become a cadet, wrote exultantly to his parents: "I am so impatient to be in the fight, as are all my comrades here. Times a hundred times more painful await me, but I am prepared to meet them with a smile."

The local mayor had already lost his own soldier son on the battlefield. Knowing that Pétain intended surrender, he pleaded with Michon not to make ancient Saumur a battlefield. The colonel contemptuously dismissed him: "I have an order to defend the town. The honour of the school is at stake." He sent away his eight hundred horses, and deployed the cadets in "brigades," each led by an instructor, on a twelve-mile front at likely Loire crossing places; they were reinforced by a few hundred Algerian infantry trainees and army stragglers, supported by a handful of tanks. Just before midnight on 18 June, when leading elements of the German cavalry division led by Gen. Kurt Feldt approached Saumur, they were greeted by a barrage of fire. A German officer advanced beside a French prisoner carrying a white flag, in an attempt to parley. But this provoked shots and explosions which killed both men. Thereafter, as German artillery began to bombard Saumur, fierce little battles erupted along the length of the line.

Some of the defenders acted with a heroism no less memorable because it was self-consciously theatrical. A cadet, Jean Labuze, questioned the order to hold until the last, saying despairingly, "One is ready to die, but not to die for nothing." His officer responded, shortly before himself being killed: "No one dies for nothing. We shall all die for France." Another officer, at Milly-le-Meugon, roused the parish priest from his bed at midnight in order that his pupils might be shriven before facing death; some 200 took communion in the darkened village church before fighting resumed. The Loire bridges around Saumur were blown by the defenders, and throughout 19 and 20 June, repeated German attempts to cross in small boats were beaten off.

But the invaders instead crossed the river up- and downstream, outflanking Saumur; the last positions held by men of the cavalry school, around a farmhouse at Aunis, three miles southwest of the town, were overwhelmed. Scores of cadets and instructors were wounded or killed, including the former architectural student Jean-Louis Dunand. Another of the dead at Aunis was a young soldier named Jehan Allain, before the war a rising organist and composer: Allain had already won a Croix de Guerre in Flanders, experienced evacuation from Dunkirk and returned from England to fight again, before meeting his death. Sheets of an unfinished musical composition were found in the saddlebag of his motorcycle.

Even as the battles around Saumur were being fought, disgruntled soldiers and civilians looked on, mocking and upbraiding the defenders for their folly, and for causing needless slaughter. But following France's surrender, as unhappy old Colonel Michon abandoned his positions and led a column westwards in the hope of continuing the struggle elsewhere, patriots embraced the story of his little stand. At Saumur at least, they said, some soldiers had behaved with honour; monuments were erected to such men as Lt. Jacques Desplats, who died with his beloved Airedale terrier Nelson defending the island of Gennes under Michon's command. Militarily, the actions of 19–20 June meant nothing. Morally, to the people of France they eventually came to mean much.

Most of the army meanwhile awaited captivity. Lt. George Friedmann, a philosopher in civilian life, wrote: "Today among many French people, I do not detect any sense of pain at the misfortunes of their country . . . I have observed only a sort of complacent relief (sometimes even exalted relief), a kind of base atavistic satisfaction at the knowledge that 'For us, it's over,' without caring about anything else." The French political right applauded the accession of the Pétain regime to power, one of its adherents writing to a friend: "At last we have victory." As the marshal himself travelled the country in the months following the armistice, he was greeted by huge, hysterically applauding crowds. They believed that nothing the Nazis might do could be as terrible as the cost of continuing a futile struggle. The fact that Churchill persuaded the British people to an alternative judgement, to defiance of perceived reality, prompted enduring French envy, resentment and bitterness.

THE CONQUEST of France and the Low Countries cost Germany almost 43,000 killed, 117,000 wounded; France lost around 50,000 dead, Britain 11,000; the Germans took 1.5 million prisoners. The British were granted one further miraculous deliverance, a second Dunkirk. After the BEF's escape, Churchill made the fine moral but reckless military decision to send more troops to France, to stiffen the resolve of its government. In June, two ill-equipped divisions were shipped to join the residual British forces on the Continent. After the armistice, because the Germans were overwhelmingly preoccupied elsewhere, it proved possible to evacuate almost 200,000 men from the northwestern French ports to England, with the loss of only a few thousand. Churchill was fortunate thus to be spared the consequences of a folly.

Britain's ambassador to France, Sir Ronald Campbell, wrote in valediction after the collapse: "I should . . . describe France as a man who, stunned by an unexpected blow, was unable to rise to his feet before his opponent delivered the 'coup de grace.'" In the decades that followed French defeat, there was intense debate about alleged national decadence, which had caused such an outcome. That summer of 1940, the bishop of Toulouse thundered: "Have we suffered enough? Have we prayed enough? Have we repented for sixty years of national apostasy, sixty years during which the French spirit has suffered all the perversions of modern ideas . . . during which French morality has declined, during which anarchy has strangely developed."

Modern staff-college war games of the 1940 campaign sometimes conclude with German defeat. This causes a few historians to argue that Hitler's triumph on the battlefield, far from being inevitable, might have been averted. It is hard to accept such a view. In the years that followed the 1940 débâcle, the German army repeatedly demonstrated its institutional superiority over the Western Allies, who prevailed on battlefields only when they had a substantial superiority of men, tanks and air support. The Wehrmacht displayed a dynamic energy entirely absent from the 1940 Allied armies. Contrary to popular myth, the Germans did not conquer France in accordance with a detailed plan for blitzkrieg—lightning war. Rather, commanders—and especially Guderian—showed inspired opportunism, with results that exceeded their wildest expectations. If the French had moved faster and the Germans more slowly, the outcome of the campaign could have been different, but such an assertion is meaningless.

In 1940 the Germans were not obliged to divert large forces to an eastern front, as they were in 1914 when France was allied with Russia. Despite the indisputable superiority of the invader's air arm, Allied defeat was the consequence less of material than of inferior morale; with rare and isolated exceptions, at every level Allied responses to German initiatives lacked conviction. Winston Churchill was almost alone among Anglo-French directors of the war, as well as among soldiers on the battlefield, in being willing to demand a struggle to the last man. French politicians and generals, by contrast, adopted a rationalist view: they identified limits to the damage acceptable to the population and fabric of their country to avoid bowing to a foreign invader, as often before in history France had been compelled to bow. Relatively few French soldiers felt willing to sacrifice themselves for the cause, because they had faith neither in their national leaders nor in their commanders; the country had endured forty-two chronically weak governments between 1920 and 1940. Gamelin wrote as early as 18 May: "The French soldier, yesterday's citizen, did not believe in the war . . . Disposed to criticise ceaselessly anyone holding the slightest amount of authority . . . he did not receive the kind of moral and patriotic education which would have prepared him for the drama in which the nation's destiny will be played out."

Irène Némirovsky wrote reflectively in 1941, looking back on the collapse: "For years, everything done in France within a certain social class has had only one motive: fear . . . Who will harm them the least (not in the future, not in the abstract, but right now and in the form of kicks in the arse or slaps in the face)? The Germans? The English? The Russians? The Germans won, but the beating has been forgotten and the Germans can protect them. That's why they're 'for the Germans.' " Very few Frenchmen in 1940 and afterwards followed the example set by tens of thousands of Poles—fighting on in exile, even after their country had been defeated. Only in 1943–44, when it became plain that the Allies would win the war and German occupation had proved intolerably oppressive, did French people in large numbers offer significant assistance to the Anglo-Americans. In the years of Britain's lonely defiance, French forces offered determined resistance to Churchill's armies and fleets wherever in the world they encountered them. Few even among those who did not fight against the British chose instead to fight with them: the French aircraft carrier *Béarn*, for instance, laden with precious American fighter planes, took refuge in the French Caribbean colony of Martinique from June 1940 until November 1942.

Among the shocked spectators of the collapse of France was Stalin. Molotov sent Hitler a dutiful telegram offering congratulations on his capture of Paris, but in Moscow the Nazi triumph provoked horror. All Soviet strategic calculations had been founded upon an expectation that a protracted bloodbath would take place on the Continent, which would drastically weaken Germany as well as the Western powers. A Russian diplomat in London later remarked indiscreetly that, while most of the world weighed Allied and German casualties against each other, Stalin added the two together to compile an assessment of his own balance of advantage. Nikita Khrushchev described the fury of Russia's warlord at Pétain's surrender: "Stalin was in a great agitation, very nervous. I had seldom seen him in such a state. As a rule he seldom sat in his chair during meetings, usually he kept walking. On this occasion he was literally running around the room, swearing terribly. He cursed the French, cursed the English, [demanding]: 'How come they allowed Hitler to thrash them?'"

Stalin probably expected eventually to fight Germany, but anticipated at least two or three years' grace before a showdown. The Soviet Union had embarked on a massive rearmament programme that was still far from fulfilment. Stalin believed that Hitler gained too many material advantages from their relationship to breach the Nazi-Soviet Pact, at least until Britain was occupied. The German navy enjoyed access to northern Russian ports. Vast quantities of corn, commodities and oil flowed from the Soviet Union to the Reich. Even after the French surrender Stalin remained anxious to avoid provocation of his dangerous neighbour, and constructed no major fortifications on his western frontier. Instead, he exploited the chaos of the moment to increase his own territorial gains. While the eyes of the world were fixed on France, he annexed the Baltic states, where in the year that followed the NKVD conducted savage purges and mass deportations. From Romania, he took Bessarabia, which had been Russian property between 1812 and 1919, and the Bukovina. At least 100,000 Romanians, and perhaps as many as half a million, were deported to Central Asia, to replace Russian industrial workers conscripted into the army. Amid events in the west, few people outside the world's foreign ministries noticed the human catastrophe created by Stalin in the east; to that extent, Hitler's lunge across western Europe served Soviet interests. But Russia's warlord recognised the outcome as a calamity almost as alarming for his own nation as for the vanquished Western powers.

Italy entered the war alongside Hitler on 10 June, in a shamelessly undignified scramble for a share of the spoils. Benito Mussolini feared Hitler and disliked Germans, as did many of his fellow countrymen, but he was unable to resist the temptation to secure cheap gains in Europe and the Allied African empires. Mussolini's conduct inspired the derision of most of his contemporaries, friends and foes alike: he coupled himself to Hitler because he sought for his country a splendour he knew Italians could not achieve alone; he wanted the rewards of war, in return for a token expenditure of blood. To his intimates in May and June 1940, he repeatedly expressed hopes that a thousand or two Italians might be killed before a peace settlement with the Allies was signed, to pay for the booty he wanted.

On the eve of commencing hostilities with France, Mussolini asserted privately his intention to declare war, but not to wage it. Unsurprisingly, this minimalist approach precipitated a fiasco: on 17 June, when the French had already asked for an armistice, he abruptly ordered an attack on the Franco-Italian border in the Alps. The Italian army, wrong-footed by the sudden transition from manning fixed positions to launching an offensive, was briskly repulsed. The Duce's delusions and confusion of purpose persisted thereafter: he expressed hopes that the British would not make peace until Italy had been able to make some show of contributing to their defeat, and that the Germans would suffer a million casualties before Britain was overrun. He wished to see Hitler victorious, but not all-powerful. All his dreams would perish in a fashion that would have rendered Mussolini an object of pity and ridicule, had not his delusions cost so many lives.

On 20 June, Franz Halder wrote complacently: "I just cannot comprehend what more the political leadership could want of us, and which of its wishes have remained unfulfilled." Hitler's army adjutant, Col. Georg Engel, recorded: "The C-in-C [Gen. Walter von Brauchitsch] had his hour of the triumph with the Führer when he announced the end of operations and preparations for an armistice. He briefed the F[ührer] on the urgent need either to make peace with Britain or to prepare and carry out an invasion as soon as possible. The Führer is sceptical and considers Britain so weak that, after bombing, major land operations will be unnecessary. The army will move in and take up occupation duties. The F[ührer] comments that 'One way or another . . . [the British] will have to accept the situation.'"

Among the more unlikely spectators of the German victory parade in Paris on 22 June was a bewildered nineteen-year-old English girl, Rosemary Say, who found herself trapped in the French capital:

The war machine rolled down the Champs Elysées: gleaming horses, tanks, machinery, guns and thousands upon thousands of soldiers. The procession was immaculate, shining and seemingly endless . . . like a gigantic green snake that wound itself around the heart of the broken city, which waited pathetically to be swallowed up. There was a huge crowd of onlookers, most of them silent but some cheering. My [neutral American] companions were like small boys: calling out the names of different regiments, exclaiming at the modern tanks and whistling at the wonderful horses. I was quiet, fully conscious that I was caught up in a moment of history. Even so, I felt no grand emotions . . . But as the hours passed and the seemingly endless spectacle continued, I began to feel a little ashamed at having accepted the invitation. I thought of my family and friends back in London, and of the fears for the future they must have.

Before the Germans attacked in the west, the Allies had wanted a long war, believing this would serve their best interests by enabling them to mobilise both American support and their own industrial resources against Hitler. The fall of Norway, Denmark, France, Belgium and Holland seemed to show that instead, the Nazis had achieved a swift and conclusive triumph. Few people anywhere in the world saw that Germany's armistice with France, signed in the historic railway carriage at Compiègne on 22 June, marked not an end, but a beginning. The scale of Hitler's ambitions, and the stubbornness of Churchill's defiance, had yet to reveal themselves.

CHAPTER FOUR

BRITAIN ALONE

AN RAF FIGHTER PILOT, Paul Richey, wounded in France, was flown home by mail plane in the first days of June: "I looked down on the calm and peaceful English countryside, the smoke rising not from bombed villages, but lazily from cottage chimneys, and saw a game of cricket in progress on a village pitch. With my mind still filled with the blast and flame that had shattered France, I was seized with utter disgust at the smug content-edness England enjoyed behind her sea barrier. I thought a few bombs might wake up those cricketers, and that they wouldn't be long in coming either." Richey echoed the resentment many men and women feel, on coming fresh from the horrors of war to encounter those spared from them. He was right that the people of southern England would not long enjoy their cricket undisturbed. But, when summoned from their pitches, almost without comprehension until their national leader enthroned their experience in majestic prose, they inflicted upon Hitler's Germany one of the decisive repulses of history.

Churchill's speech to the House of Commons on 18 June 1940 has been so often quoted that it sometimes receives only the nod due to glorious rhetoric. But its closing words repay attention, because they defined for the rest of the war the democracies' vision of their purpose:

> What General Weygand called the battle of France is over. I expect that the battle of Britain is about to begin. Upon this battle depends the survival of Christian civilisation. Upon it depends our own British life, and the long continuity of our institutions and our empire. The whole might and fury of the enemy must very soon be turned on us. Hitler knows that he will have to break us in this island or lose the war. If we can stand up to him, all Europe may be free and the life of the world move forward into broad, sunlit uplands. But if we fail, then the whole world, including the United States, will sink into the abyss of a new Dark Age, made more sinister, and perhaps more protracted, by the lights of perverted science. Let us, therefore, brace ourselves to our duties and so bear ourselves that, if the British Empire and Com-

monwealth last for a thousand years, men will still say, "This was their finest hour."

It is striking to contrast the prime minister's appeal to "brace ourselves to our duties" with the strident demands of Germany's warlord, in similar circumstances in 1944–45, for "fanatical resistance." Grace, dignity, wit, humanity and resolution characterised the leadership of Britain's prime minister; only the last of these could be attributed to Hitler. In the summer of 1940, Churchill faced an enormous challenge: to convince his own people and the world that continued resistance was credible. Sergeant L. D. Pexton, thirty-four years old, was a prisoner in Germany when he wrote on 19 July: "Heard today that Hitler had broadcast some peace terms and that Churchill had told him what to do with them . . . Hope they do patch up some sort of terms as everyone here wants it, and to get home." Pexton's view was obviously influenced by experiencing defeat in France, and thereafter finding himself at the mercy of the victorious Nazis. But in Britain, too, there were those—especially among the commercial classes and the ruling caste, best informed about the nation's weakness—who continued to fear the worst. It was Churchill's epic personal achievement to rally them in support of the simple purpose of repelling invasion.

The latter months of 1940 were decisive in determining the course of the war. The Nazis, stunned by the scale of their triumphs, allowed themselves to suffer a loss of momentum. By launching an air assault on Britain, Hitler adopted the worst possible strategic compromise: as master of the Continent, he believed a modest further display of force would suffice to precipitate its surrender. Yet if, instead, he had left Churchill's people to stew on their island, the prime minister would have faced great difficulties in sustaining national morale and a charade of strategic purpose. A small German contingent dispatched to support the Italian attack on Egypt that autumn would probably have sufficed to expel Britain from the Middle East; Malta could easily have been taken. Such humiliations would have dealt heavy blows to the credibility of Churchill's policy of fighting on.

As it was, however, the Luftwaffe's clumsy offensive posed the one challenge which Britain was well-placed to repel. The British Army and people were not obliged to confront the Wehrmacht on their beaches and in their fields—a clash that would probably have ended ignominiously for the defenders. The prime minister merely required their acquiescence, while the country was defended by a few hundred RAF pilots and—more importantly though less conspicuously—by the formidable might of the Royal Navy's ships at sea. The prime minister's exalting leadership secured public support for his defiance of the logic of Hitlerian triumph, even when cities began to burn and civilians to die.

The prospect of an imminent invasion was less plausible than Britain's chiefs of staff supposed and Churchill publicly asserted, because the Germans lacked amphibious shipping and escorts to convoy an army across the Channel in the face of an immensely powerful British fleet and an undefeated RAF. Hitler's heart was never in it. But intelligence about his means and intentions was fragmentary: decryption of enemy cipher traffic at Bletchley Park* lacked anything like the comprehensive coverage achieved later in the war. Much German activity, or absence of it, on the Continent was shrouded from London's knowledge. British service chiefs, traumatised by the disaster in France, attributed almost mystical powers to the Wehrmacht.

Privately, Churchill was always sceptical about the invasion threat, but he emphasised it in his rhetoric and strategy making throughout 1940–41, as a means of promoting purposeful activity among both his people and the armed forces. He judged, surely rightly, that inertia and an understanding of their own impotence would be fatal to the spirit necessary to sustain morale, and to his hopes of inducing the United States to enter the conflict. There must be no return to phoney war: since defence against prospective invasion was the utmost the home army could encompass, he projected this as its principal task for many months after it became plain that the danger had passed.

Following the fall of France, the prime minister's ruthlessness was first displayed against his recent allies. One morning in July 1940, armed Royal Navy parties boarded French warships in British harbours to demand their surrender. At Devonport, officers of the submarine *Surcouf* resisted, starting a gun battle in the control room during which one French and three British sailors were killed. Three-quarters of French servicemen in Britain, including most of those rescued from Dunkirk, insisted on repatriation, a choice in which the British indulged them. French alienation increased after a British ultimatum to their battle squadron at Mers-el-Kébir was rejected on 3 July. Churchill was determined that Pétain's fleet should not support a German invasion of Britain. Adm. Marcel-Bruno Gensoul refused either to renew the war alongside the Royal Navy or to accept neutrality under British guard. Adm. James Somerville thereupon sank or shelled into wreckage three of Gensoul's ships, killing 1,300 sailors. Churchill feared that the assault might cause the Pétain regime

* For an explanation, see pp. 357–58.

actively to ally itself with the Nazis, though this did not dissuade him from giving the fire order. Vichy did not become a formal belligerent, and a few remote African colonies "rallied" to Brig. Gen. Charles de Gaulle's "Free France" in London. But French forces vigorously resisted every British encroachment on their territories until the end of 1942.

It seems mistaken to suppose that the policies of Pétain, and the widespread support they commanded, represented mere fallout from French defeat. The Vichy government welcomed the opportunity to impose what Michael Burleigh has called "a regressive moral, political and social agenda in which authority and duty would trump liberty and rights." Pathological hatred and fear of the left—and of Jews—caused almost all of aristocratic, commercial and bourgeois France to back Pétain until German oppression became intolerable and Allied victory plainly inevitable.

The Luftwaffe air assault on Britain which began in July 1940 offered Churchill's people their best opportunity to engage the Germans on favourable terms. The only class of ground or aerial weapons system in which the British had near parity with their enemies in quality and quantity was the single-seat interceptor fighter. The RAF's Hurricanes and Spitfires were handicapped by clumsy tactical doctrine and .303-calibre machine-gun armament with inadequate destructive power, but squadrons were controlled by the most sophisticated radar, ground-observer and voice-radio network in the world, created by an inspired group of civil servants, scientists and airmen. If the equipment and performance of Britain's army remained unsatisfactory throughout the war, Churchill's nation far surpassed Germany in the application of science and technology: mobilisation of the best civilian brains, and their integration into the war effort at the highest levels, was an outstanding British success story. The RAF had developed a remarkable system of defence, while their opponents had no credible system of attack.

The Luftwaffe's commanders suffered from a confusion of objectives which persisted throughout the summer. Gen. Albert Kesselring opposed the assault on Britain, preferring instead to seize Gibraltar and gain dominance of the Mediterranean; Hitler initially vetoed bombing of British cities, while Göring rejected attacks on southern ports, which would be needed for the Wehrmacht's landings. The Luftwaffe sought to gain dominance of the airspace over southeast England by destroying Fighter Command, and embarked on an incoherent campaign to achieve this by sending bombers to attack airfields and installations, escorted by fighters which were expected to shoot down RAF planes as easily as they had done in France. Intelligence, a chronic weakness of the Third Reich, was woeful: the Germans had no understanding of Fighter Command's detection and control network. They themselves had developed radar—*Dezimator-Telegraphie*, as they called it, or *DeTe* for short—before the British, and their sets were technically more advanced. But they failed to link them to an effective ground-based air-direction system, and never imagined that Fighter Command might have done so. Throughout the war, institutionalised hubris dogged the Nazi leadership, which was repeatedly wrongfooted by Allied technological initiatives; if Germans had not built a given weapon or device, they were reluctant to credit their enemies with the wit to do so.

Col. Joseph "Beppo" Schmid, head of Luftwaffe intelligence, was a charlatan who told his chiefs what they wished to hear. Göring had neither a strategic reserve of aircraft nor manufacturing resources with which to create one. The Germans conducted the Battle of Britain with stunning incompetence, founded upon arrogance and ignorance. If the RAF made its share of mistakes, Air Chief Marshal Sir Hugh Dowding and his most important subordinate, Air Vice-Marshal Keith Park, the New Zealander commanding 11 Group, displayed a steadiness of judgement amounting to brilliance, entirely absent across the Channel. The Germans began their campaign with two assets: a modest superiority of aircraft numbers and a corps of experienced combat veterans. They failed to concentrate these, however, against the vital targets—radar receivers, fighter stations and supporting installations.

The Battle of Britain opened with July skirmishes over the Channel, as the Germans attacked coastal convoys and the RAF responded. Hitting a precision target from the air was difficult. A dive-bomber pilot attacking a 750-foot ship from astern, for instance, had only a 1.5-second margin of error in pressing his bomb release, which from abeam fell to a quarter of a second; it was a tribute to the skills of German Stuka pilots that they inflicted severe losses on British convoys. But the Ju-87s flew even more slowly than the RAF's Battle bombers, which had been destroyed wholesale in France, and it was now the turn of the British to exploit enemy vulnerability: Stukas suffered slaughter wherever Fighter Command encountered them, and eventually had to be withdrawn from the battle.

A Spitfire pilot, Geoff Wellum, described the racing sensations of air combat:

All at once, crossfire, heavy and pretty close at that. Bloody front gunner. My target, concentrate, the target. Looking at him through the sight, getting larger much too quickly, concentrate, hold him steady, that's it, hold it . . . be still my heart, be still. Sight on, still on, steady . . . fire NOW! I press the gun button and all hell is let loose;

my guns make a noise like tearing calico . . . I get the fleet impression of hits and explosions of the glass nose of my Dornier and of Brian's Spitfire breaking away, its oil-streaked belly visible for a fraction of a second. Keep firing, Geoff, hold it. For Christ's sake break off or you'll hit him; too close, this. I stop firing, stick hard over. I even hear his engines as he flashes by inches overhead. Bloody hell, this is dangerous!

In mêlées in the sky, it was often remarkable how few aircraft either side destroyed. Over a Channel convoy on 25 July, for instance, scores of British and German planes exchanged fire, but only two Spitfires were shot down, and one Messerschmitt Bf-109. RAF pilots had received scarcely any training in air fighting, an art the Germans mastered over Spain and Poland, and the defenders were now obliged to learn by experience. Early in the battle, it became apparent that the overwhelming majority of "kills" were achieved by a handful of each side's best men: the top 3.5 percent of Fighter Command's pilots made 30 percent of all claims for aircraft shot down, and the Luftwaffe's aces accounted for an even higher proportion of kills. Exceptional eyesight, marksmanship and nerve to get close were the decisive factors.

The RAF strongly discouraged the cult of the "ace," and of personal scores, but the Luftwaffe energetically promoted them. Such stars as Adolf Galland, Helmut Wick and Werner Molders were said by resentful comrades to suffer from *"halswah"*—the "sore throat" on which they were eager to hang the coveted ribbon of a Knight's Cross—as all three did when their score of kills mounted. Galland, a supremely effective air fighter but also a selfish and brutal one, had no patience with weaklings in his command. One day on the radio net a frightened German voice wailed, "Spitfire on my tail!" and then again a few moments later, "Spitfire still behind me! What should I do?" Galland snarled, *"Aussteigen, sie bettnasser!"*—"Bail out, you bed-wetter!"

Air combat, unlike any other form of warfare, engaged exclusively very young men, who alone had the reflexes for duels at closing speeds of up to 600 miles per hour; by thirty, they were past it. Commanders, confined to headquarters, issued orders. But outcomes hinged upon the prowess of pilots in or just out of their teens. Almost everything they said and did in the air and on the ground reflected their extreme youth; on 17 August Lt. Hans-Otto Lessing, a Bf-109 pilot, wrote exultantly to his parents, describing his unit's hundredth alleged "victory" like a schoolboy reporting the success of his football team: "We are in the Geschwader of Major Molders, the most successful . . . During the last few days the British have been getting weaker, though individuals continue to fight well . . . The Hurricanes are tired old 'puffers' . . . I am having the time of my life. I would not swap places with a king. Peacetime is going to be very boring after this!" One of the despised "puffers" killed him the following afternoon.

The RAF's Paddy Barthrop said afterwards: "It was just beer, women and Spitfires, a bunch of little John Waynes running about the place. When you were nineteen, you couldn't give a monkey's." British pilots partied relentlessly at night, youth overcoming exhaustion. Pete Brothers said, "We used to booze dreadfully." One day when his squadron was stood down in bad weather, the airmen adjourned to the bar, only to find themselves scrambled when the sky cleared. "I shall never forget taking off and thinking, 'That button . . . turn it that way . . . switch on gunsights . . .' We were all absolutely tanked. Mind you, when we saw black crosses, you were instantly sober."

They cherished their aircraft as magic carpets into the sky. Bob Stanford-Tuck said: "Some men fall in love with yachts or some women, strangely enough, or motor cars, but I think every Spitfire pilot fell in love with it as soon as he sat in that nice tight cosy office with everything to hand." Similarly, Bob Doe on his first sight of his new plane: "Our hearts leapt! We walked round it, sat in it, and stroked it. It was so beautiful I think we all fell a bit in love with it." Fighter Command's British pilots fought alongside contingents of New Zealanders, Canadians, Czechs, South Africans and a handful of Americans. The 146 Poles who participated in the Battle of Britain formed the largest foreign element, 5 percent of overall RAF pilot strength. Their combat reputation was superb, rooted in experience and reckless courage. "When you seen [*sic*] the swastika or black cross on the aircraft," said one of them, Boleslaw Drobinski, "your heart beat much quicker, and you decided that you must get him or you get shot yourself. It's a feeling of absolute . . . vengeance." This was not bombast. When Poles later attacked Germany, they chalked messages on their bombs—"This is for Warsaw," "This is for Lwów"—and meant it.

Popular adulation was heaped on the aerial defenders of Britain, expressed everywhere airmen met civilians—as they often did, at evening after fighting in the sky above towns and villages. The applause of ordinary people meant much to the pilots amid their exhaustion and losses. "There was tremendous kindness," said one young man afterwards. "It was a lovely feeling. I've never felt that Britain was like that again." Soldiers muttered jealously about the RAF's "Brylcreem boys"; the Wehrmacht had a similar phrase of its own for the Luftwaffe—*"Schlipssoldaten,"* "neck-tie soldiers." For the rest of the war, fliers of all nations retained a glamour denied those who fought on the ground.

Fighter Command was acutely sensitive to the loss of its experienced pilots: ten Hurricane aces—men who had shot down five or more enemy planes—were lost between 8 and 19 August, then a further twelve between 20 August and 6 September. Novice replacements were killed at more than five times this rate; casualties were especially high in squadrons that continued to use the rigid formations RAF official doctrine prescribed for "Fighting Area Attacks." Units fared better whose commanding officers promoted flexibility and initiative. Pilots who flew steady courses died; those who stayed alive dodged and weaved constantly, to render them-selves elusive targets. Three-quarters of downed British fighters fell to Bf-109s, rather than to bomber gunners or twin-engined Bf-110s. Sur-prise was all: four out of five victims never saw their attackers; many were hit from behind, while themselves attacking a plane ahead.

"People who stayed in a burning cockpit for ten seconds were over-come by the flames and heat," said Sgt. Jack Perkin. "Nine seconds and you ended up in Queen Victoria Hospital in East Grinstead in Dr. Archie McIndoe's burns surgery for the rest of the war. If you got out in eight seconds you never flew again, but you went back about twelve times for plastic surgery." Hurricane pilot Billy Drake described the experience of being shot down: "It was rather like having a motor-car accident. You can't remember what the hell happened." Both sides suffered heavily from non-combat mishaps, born of momentary carelessness or recklessness by tired and often inexperienced young men: between 10 July and 31 October, 463 Hurricanes suffered such damage, sometimes total and fatal. As many as one-third of both Dowding's and Göring's overall losses were accidental.

Few pilots who bailed out offshore were recovered: a man in a dinghy looked pathetically small to rescue-launch crews scouring the Channel and North Sea. Ulrich Steinhilper gazed below as he flew back over the Channel from a September mission: "Our track across those wild waters became dotted with parachutes, pilots floating in their lifejackets, and greasy oil slicks on the cold water showing where another Me109 had ended its last dive. All along the coast near Boulogne we had seen 109s down in the fields and on the grass, some still standing on their noses." Nineteen German airmen drowned that day, while just two were picked up by floatplanes.

The chivalrous spirit with which the British, at least, began the battle faded fast. David Crook returned from a sortie in which his roommate had been killed, and found it strange to see the man's possessions just where he had left them, towel hanging on the window. "I could not get out of my head the thought of Peter, with whom we had been talking and laughing that day. Now he was lying in the cockpit of his wrecked Spitfire at the bottom of the English Channel." That afternoon, the dead pilot's wife telephoned to arrange his leave, only to hear the flight commander break news of his death. Crook wrote: "It all seemed so awful. I was seeing at very close quarters all the distress that casualties cause." After Pete Brothers's squadron was engaged a few times and he had lost friends, he abandoned his earlier notions that they were playing a game between sporting rivals. "I then said, 'Right, these are a bunch of bastards. I don't like them any more. I am going to be beastly.'" Very early in the struggle, pilot Denis Wissler wrote in his diary: "Oh God I do wish this war would end." But few of the young men who fought for either side in the Battle of Britain stayed alive through the five-year struggle that followed it. To fly was wonderful fun, but a profound and premature seriousness overtook most aerial warriors in the face of the stress and horror that were their lot almost every day they were exposed to operations.

Through August the Luftwaffe progressively increased the intensity of its assaults, attacking Fighter Command airfields—though only briefly radar stations. Air Chief Marshal Sir Hugh Dowding, C-in-C of Fighter Command, began the battle with an average of 600 aircraft available for action, while the Germans deployed a daily average of around 750 serviceable bombers, 250 dive-bombers, and over 600 single-engined and 150 twin-engined fighters, organised in three air fleets. Southeast England was the main battleground, but Dowding was also obliged to defend the northeast and southwest from long-range attacks.

The first concerted bombings of airfields and installations took place on 12 August, when the Ventnor radar station on the Isle of Wight was put out of action. The Luftwaffe intended "Eagle Day" on 13 August to be decisive, but in thick weather this degenerated into a series of poorly coordinated attacks. The Germans mounted their heaviest effort two days later, on the fifteenth, dispatching 2,000 sorties over England, losing 75 aircraft for 34 British, 2 of those on the ground. Raiders flying from Scandinavian airfields—too remote for single-engined fighters—suffered especially heavy losses, and the day became known to German airmen as "Black Thursday." The two sides' combined casualties were even higher three days later, on 18 August, when the Luftwaffe lost 69 planes against Fighter Command's 34 in the air and a further 29 on the ground.

Both air forces wildly overestimated the damage they inflicted on each other. But the Germans' intelligence failure was more serious, because it sustained their delusion that they were winning. Fighter Command's stations were targeted by forty Luftwaffe raids during August and early September, yet only two—Manston and Lympne on the Kent coast— were put out of action for more than a few hours, and the radar receivers were largely spared from attention. By late August the Luftwaffe believed Fighter Command's first-line strength had been halved, to 300 aircraft. In reality, however, Dowding still deployed around twice that number: attrition was working to the advantage of the British. Between 8 and 23 August, the RAF lost 204 aircraft, but during that month 476 new fighters were built, and many more repaired. The Luftwaffe lost 397, of which 181 were fighters, while only 313 Bf-109s and Bf-110s were produced by German factories. Fighter Command lost 104 pilots killed in the middle fortnight of August, against 623 Luftwaffe airmen dead or captured.

The RAF's Bomber Command has received less than due credit for its part in the campaign: between July and September it lost twice as many men as Fighter Command, during attacks on concentrations of invasion barges in the Channel ports and while conducting harassing missions against German airfields. The latter inflicted little damage, but increased the strain on Luftwaffe men desperate for rest. "The British are slowly getting on our nerves at night," wrote the pilot Ulrich Steinhilper. "Because of their persistent activity our AA guns are in virtually continuous use and so we can hardly close our eyes."

Göring now changed tactics, launching a series of relatively small bomber attacks with massive fighter escorts. These were explicitly designed to force the RAF to fight, especially in defence of airfields, and for the German planes to destroy it in the air. Dowding's losses were indeed high, but Luftwaffe commanders were dismayed to find that each day, Fighter Command's squadrons still rose to meet their attacks. Increasing tensions developed between 11 Group, whose fighters defended the southeast, and 12 Group beyond, whose planes were supposed meanwhile to protect 11's airfields from German bombers. In late August and early September, several stations were badly damaged. Why were 12 Group's fighters absent when this happened? The answer was that some of their squadron commanders, Douglas Bader notable among them, favoured massing aircraft into "big wings"—powerful formations—before engaging the enemy. This took precious time, but in arguments on the ground the "big wing" exponents shouted loudest. They were eventually given their heads, and made grossly inflated claims for their achievements. The outcome was that the reputation of Keith Park, commanding 11 Group, suffered severely from RAF infighting that in September became endemic, while 12 Group's Trafford Leigh-Mallory—more impressive as an intriguer than as an operational commander—gained influence. Posterity is confident that Park was an outstanding airman, who shared with Dowding the laurels for winning the Battle of Britain.

Many of the RAF's young fliers, knowing the rate of attrition Fighter Command was suffering, accounted themselves dead men, though this did not diminish their commitment. Hurricane pilot George Barclay's 249 Squadron was posted to one of the most embattled stations, North Weald, in Essex, on 1 September. A comrade said bleakly as they packed for the move, "I suppose some of us here will never return to Boscombe." Barclay himself took a slightly more optimistic view, writing in his diary: "I think everyone is quite sure he will survive for at least seven days!"

At the end of August, the Germans made their worst strategic mistake of the campaign: they shifted their objectives from airfields first to London, then to other major cities. Hitler's air commanders believed this would force Dowding to commit his last reserves, but Britain's leaders, from Churchill downwards, were vastly relieved. They knew the capital could absorb enormous punishment, while Fighter Command's installations were vulnerable. The men in the air saw only relentless combat, relentless losses. George Barclay wrote to his sister on 3 September in the breathless, adolescent style characteristic of his tribe: "We have been up four times today and twice had terrific battles with hundreds of Messerschmitts. It is all perfectly amazing, quite unlike anything else . . . One forgets entirely what attitude one's aeroplane is in, in an effort to keep the sights on the enemy. And all this milling around of hundreds of aeroplanes, mostly with black crosses on, goes on at say 20,000ft with the Thames estuary and surrounding country as far as Clacton displayed like a map below."

Sandy Johnstone "nearly jumped clean out of my cockpit" on getting his first glimpse of the massed Luftwaffe assault of 7 September. "Ahead and above a veritable armada of German aircraft . . . Staffel after staffel as far as the eye could see . . . I have never seen so many aircraft in the air all at one time. It was awe-inspiring." At the outset, German airmen derived comfort from flying amid a vast formation. "Wherever one looks are our aircraft, all around, a marvellous sight," wrote Peter Stahl, flying a Junkers Ju-88 on one of the September raids. But he and his comrades quickly learned that security of mass was illusory, as formations were rent asunder by diving, banking, shooting Hurricanes and Spitfires. By late afternoon of the seventh, a thousand planes were locked in battle over Kent and Essex. The Germans lost forty-one aircraft on 7 September, while Fighter Command lost twenty-three. As in all the campaign's big clashes, the British had the best of the day.

Ulrich Steinhilper, flying a Bf-109, was one of many pilots who, between spasms of intense fear and excitement, was struck by the beauty of the spectacle they created: over London one September day, he gloried in "the pure azure-blue of the sky, with the sun dimmed by the sinister smoke penetrating to extreme height; this interwoven and cross-hatched by the con trails of fighters locked in their life-and-death struggles. In among this, the burning balloons and the few parachutes in splendid and incongruous isolation." The Luftwaffe's 15 September onslaught was unaccompanied by the usual feints and diversions, so that Fighter Command was in no doubt about the focus of the threat, and could throw everything into meeting it. Squadrons were scrambled to meet the raiders in pairs, intercepting as far forward as Canterbury, while the Duxford "big wing" engaged over east London. That afternoon, the Luftwaffe's second attack also met strong defending fighter forces; in all, 60 German aircraft were shot down—though the RAF claimed 185. Between 7 and 15 September, the Luftwaffe lost 175 planes, far more than German factories built.

The assault remained incoherent: the attackers had begun by seeking to destroy the RAF's defensive capability, then, before achieving this, switched to attacking morale and industrial targets. Their relatively light bombers carried loads which hurt the British, but lacked sufficient weight to strike fatal blows against a complex, modern industrial society. The RAF did not destroy the Luftwaffe, which was beyond its powers. But its pilots denied the Germans dominance of the Channel and southern England, while imposing unacceptable losses. Fighter Command's continued existence as a fighting force sufficed to frustrate Göring's purposes. Throughout the battle, British factories produced single-engined fighters faster than those of Germany, a vital industrial achievement. Fighter Command lost a total of 544 men—about one in five of all British pilots who flew in the battle—while 801 Bomber Command airmen were killed and a further 200 taken prisoner; but the Luftwaffe lost a disastrous 2,698 highly skilled airmen.

Churchill's personal contribution was to convince his people, over the heads of some of their ruling caste, that their struggle was noble, necessary—and now also successful. The Battle of Britain exalted their spirit in a fashion that enabled them to transcend the logic of their continuing strategic weakness. "Our airmen have had a gruelling time, but each day that passes the more magnificently they seem to carry on the fight," wrote an elderly backbench Tory MP, Cuthbert Headlam, on 20 September. "It is odd to see how much we owe to so small a number of young men—here are millions of us doing nothing while the battle is being decided over our heads by a chosen band of warriors drawn from here, there and everywhere . . . They must be a superb body of men . . . one would like to know the difference in material strength of our RAF and the Luftwaffe: some day presumably we shall know—and then, more than ever, I expect, we shall salute the gallant men who are now doing such untold service for their country."

Britain's people endured the nation's ordeal with some fortitude. Those who lived outside conurbations were spared from Luftwaffe attack, but fear of invasion was almost universal. If Churchill was committed to fight to the last, he was also brutally realistic about the implications of possible failure and defeat. Brig. Charles Hudson attended a senior officers' conference in York in July which was addressed by Anthony Eden as secretary for war. Eden told his audience that he had been instructed by the prime minister to take soundings about the army's morale. He proposed to ask each general in turn whether, as Hudson recorded, "the troops under our command could be counted on to continue the fight in all circumstances . . . There was almost an audible gasp all round the table." Eden intensified the astonishment when he said that "a moment might come when the Government would have to make, at short notice, a terrible decision. That point when . . . it would be definitely unwise to throw in, in a futile attempt to save a hopeless situation, badly armed men against an enemy firmly lodged in England." He asked how troops might respond to an order to embark at a northern port for Canada, abandoning their families.

Hudson wrote: "In dead silence one after another was asked the question." The almost unanimous response was that most regular officers, NCOs and unmarried men would accept such an order. However, among conscripts and married men, "the very great majority . . . would insist either on fighting it out in England . . . or on [staying behind to take] their chance with their families whatever the consequences might be." In other words, senior officers of the British Army believed that, in the face of imminent defeat, many of their men would make the same choice as had French soldiers—to give in, rather than accept the uncertainties and miseries of continuing the struggle in exile. Hudson concluded: "We left the conference room in a very chastened mood." Neither he nor most of his colleagues had contemplated the prospect that fighting on to the end might mean doing so from a foreign country, with Britain vanquished. Churchill accepted such a contingency; but in this, as in much else, Britain's prime minister was willing to contemplate extremities of sacrifice from which many of his fellow countrymen flinched.

Hitler might have attempted an invasion of Britain if the Luftwaffe had secured control of the airspace over the Channel and southern England.

As it was, however, instinctively wary of the sea and of an unnecessary strategic gamble, he took few practical steps to advance German preparations, beyond massing barges in the Channel ports. Churchill exploited the threat more effectively than did the prospective invaders, mobilising every citizen to the common purpose of resisting the enemy if they landed. Signposts and place-names were removed from crossroads and stations, beaches wired, overage and underage men recruited to local Home Guard units and provided with simple weapons. Churchill deliberately and even cynically sustained the spectre of invasion until 1942, fearing that if the British people were allowed to suppose the national crisis had passed, their natural lassitude would reassert itself.

Uncertainty about German intentions persisted through that summer and into autumn. Among the population at large, fear was mingled with a muddled and excited anticipation, all the keener because the prospect of fighting Germans in the fields and villages of England seemed so unreal. One aristocratic housewife injected some of her hoarded stockpile of Canadian maple syrup with rat poison, destined for German occupiers. To the dismay of her family, however, after some weeks she forgot which tins had been treated, and was obliged to deny the delicacy to her disappointed children. The Wiltshire farmer Arthur Street caught something of the pantomime element in people's behaviour, in an account of his own workers' and neighbours' conduct on 7 September, when a warning was transmitted to the Home Guard that German landings were imminent:

> The Sedgebury Wallop platoon was on the job that night, and marched seventeen bewildered civilians to the local police station because they had forgotten their identity cards. But at 0700 the farmer in Walter Pocock woke up, and he suggested to his shepherd that he might abandon soldiering for shepherding for half an hour. "You'll be wanting to see your sheep, but take your rifle and ammo," he advised. "The fold's only ten minutes walk away, and I'll send for you the moment anything happens." "I'low me sheep'll be all right eet awhile," reported Shep. "The day's fold were pitched eesterday, an' although young Arthur be but fifteen, I've a-trained 'im proper. Any road, I bain't gwaine till the 'All Clear' be sounded." At about 11 o'clock, when the word came through that the real or imaginary threat of invasion had passed, grumbling was rife. "Bain't 'em reely comin', sir?" asked Tom Spicer wistfully. " 'Fraid not, Spicer," replied Walter. "Jist wot I thought," growled Fred Bunce the blacksmith. "There bain't no dependence to be put in they Germans."

Those Wiltshire rustics enjoyed a luxury denied to the peoples of continental Europe. They could mock their enemies, because they were spared from the ghastly reality of meeting them: on 17 September Hitler gave the order indefinitely to postpone Operation Sealion, the Wehrmacht's plan to invade Britain. The British people and the pilots of Fighter Command saw only a slow, gradual shift during October from massed daylight air attacks to night raids. Between 10 July and 31 October, the Germans lost 1,294 aircraft, the British 788. Hitler had abandoned hopes of occupying Britain in 1940, and also of destroying Fighter Command. He committed his air force instead to a protracted assault on Britain's cities which was intended to break the will of the population. The Luftwaffe chose as primary targets aircraft factories, together with London's docks and infrastructure. Due to the limitations of German navigation and bomb aiming, however, in the eyes of the British people the attacks became merely an indiscriminate assault on the civilian population, a campaign of terror.

The "blitz," which the defenders dated from 7 September, was far harder for Fighter Command to repel than daylight attacks, because the RAF had few night fighters and only primitive air interception radar. Churchill incited the feeble antiaircraft-gun defences to fire at will to hearten the population, as indeed they did—but with little impact on the raiders. Between September and mid-November, an average of 200 Luftwaffe aircraft attacked every night save one. In that period, over 13,000 tons of explosive and incendiary bombs were dropped on London, Bristol, Birmingham, Portsmouth and other major cities, at a cost to the Luftwaffe of just seventy-five aircraft, most of them victims of accidents.

The blitz imposed on city dwellers mingled fascination, terror, horror and eventually acceptance of a new normality. A London woman wrote of one raid: "The bombs came down in a cluster, close together . . . Bomb explosions have a mesmeric attraction dating possibly from firework displays of one's childhood, and I watched the first two explode. Unless it lifts an entire building in the air, the burst of an ordinary high-explosive bomb is not in itself a grand spectacle, as a major fire can be; its upward streaks of yellow or red look as crude and banal as a small boy's painting of them." Muriel Green, a Norfolk village dweller, wrote with notable sensitivity for a girl of nineteen about her thoughts as she heard German aircraft passing overhead, on their path to some British city, the night after the devastating 14 November attack on Coventry: "I wonder what the pilots feel. After all somebody loves them even if they are Nazis, and they are risking their lives and fighting for their country the same as our men that go bombing. Poor Coventry people. How bitter and hopeless they must feel today. How long can it go on? How many years must all live in fear of the unknown horrors that so many of us have not yet experienced?"

The bomber assault, which continued until Hitler began to withdraw aircraft for the invasion of Russia in May 1941, inflicted heavy damage on British city centres and ate deep into the spirits of millions of people who endured many nights huddled in shelters with their families and fears. It cost the attackers, flying from airfields in northern France, only 1.5 percent aircraft losses per sortie. This was a much lower casualty rate than the RAF later suffered bombing Germany, because the British had farther to go. Some 43,000 British civilians were killed and a further 139,000 injured. But throughout the winter of 1940–41 the Luftwaffe lacked a credible strategic plan, together with the aiming accuracy and bomb loads necessary to inflict decisive damage on British industry. The young scientific intelligence officer R. V. Jones played a critical role, by identifying the Germans' radio navigational beams and showing the way to jam them. Production was disrupted by alerts, and some important plants were damaged; tens of thousands of homes were destroyed, along with ancient buildings, churches and other landmarks. But, to a remarkable degree, the population of Britain learned to get on with its business amid air bombardment. "Human casualties were quieter than I had expected," wrote Barbara Nixon, an actress turned Finsbury air-raid warden.

> Only twice did I hear really terrifying screaming, apart from hysteria; one night a [railway] signalman had his legs blown off and while he was still conscious his box burst into flames; it was utterly impossible for anyone to reach him and it seemed an age before his ghastly, paralysing screams subsided. Usually, however, casualties, even those who were badly hurt or trapped, were too stunned to make much noise. Animals, on the other hand, made a dreadful clamour. One of the most unnerving nights of the first three months was when a cattle market was hit, and the beasts bellowed and shrieked for three hours; a locomotive had been overturned at the same time and its steam whistle released. The high-pitched monotonous tone, coupled with the distant roaring of the bullocks, was maddening.

In an age when much local transport was still horse-drawn, some city stables borrowed from country custom and acquired a goat, which horses would follow in an emergency. One night when the premises of a big City of London firm of carters were set ablaze by bombs, 200 of its horses were led to safety. Yet while Britain's "blitz spirit" was real enough, so too were the misery and squalor that bombardment imposed. Bernard Kops, a small boy who later became a playwright and novelist, wrote: "Some people . . . recall a poetic dream about the Blitz. They talk about those days as if they were a time of a true communal spirit. Not to me. It was the beginning of an era of utter terror, of fear and horror. I stopped being a child and came face to face with the new reality of the world . . . Here we were back on the trot, wandering again, involved in a new exodus—the Jews of the East End, who had left their homes, and gone into the exile of the underground."

A strand of traditional British silliness helped the afflicted: a London vicar asked a fellow occupant of his basement shelter whether she prayed when she heard a bomb falling. "Yes," she answered, "I pray, Oh God! Don't let it fall here." The vicar said, "But it's a bit rough on other people, if your prayer is granted and the thing drops, not on you, but on them." The woman replied, "I can't help that. They must say their prayers and push it off further." Air-raid shelters in old buildings swarmed with lice and bugs. In the big subterranean shelters of the inner cities, there was ugliness generated by drunken men and women, bitter quarrels and fights, filth inescapable where there were no lavatories.

Most people agreed that the struggle bore hardest upon the elderly and the very young, alike uncomprehending. Barbara Nixon again: "Neither had any idea what it was all about; they had never heard of Poland . . . and Fascism was, at most, a matter of that wicked beast Hitler who was trying to blow us up, or murder us all in our beds." Ernie Pyle, the great American correspondent, wrote from London in January 1941: "It was the old people who seemed so tragic. Think of yourself at seventy or eighty, full of pain and of the dim memories of a lifetime that has probably all been bleak. And then think of yourself now, travelling at dusk every night to a subway station, wrapping your ragged overcoat about your old shoulders and sitting on a wooden bench with your back against a curved street wall. Sitting there all night, in nodding and fitful sleep. Think of that as your destiny—every night, every night from now on."

A seventy-one-year-old Londoner, Herbert Brush, described how a woman friend had been to her doctor, "as evidently her nerves have gone wrong with the strain of driving a car under war conditions. On her way to Cambridge she came under machine-gun fire from the air and had to hide in a hedge. Then at Norwich there were several bombs dropped in the vicinity during the night. The doctor says she has shell-shock and has made her up a strong tonic and recommended complete rest for a fortnight." In a narrow sense, this woman's response to relatively slight peril was unimpressive; but human beings measure risk and privation within the compass of their personal knowledge. It was meaningless to assert to an English suburban housewife that Poles, Jews, French refugees and, later, soldiers on the Eastern Front suffered much worse things than she had. She knew only that what was happening to her was dreadful in comparison with all her previous experience of life. Only a few exulted in it, like thirty-year-old gardener, pacifist and conscientious objector George Springett. In the first weeks of war, he had regularly dosed himself with Sanatogen nerve tonic, but now he no longer felt the need for it: "I've had really first-class health since the blitz started!"

Among the heroes of the campaign were the men who learned by trial and error to deal with unexploded bombs, of which there were soon a plethora in Britain's cities. One of the more remarkable was Jack Howard, the Earl of Suffolk. Early in the war, this maverick boffin, thirty-four in 1940, secured himself a roving commission in the Scientific Directorate of the Ministry of Supply. In that role, one of his more notable feats was to evacuate from Bordeaux, after the French surrender, £3 million in industrial diamonds retrieved from Amsterdam, a group of France's most brilliant scientists, and the country's entire stock of Norwegian heavy water, indispensable to making an atomic bomb. In the autumn of 1940, this self-consciously eccentric figure chose to appoint himself to Bomb Disposal.

Suffolk formed his own squad, which included his pretty secretary Beryl Morden, and outfitted a van from his own resources. Thereafter, dressed in a Stetson hat and flying boots or occasionally a pilot's helmet, and invariably affecting a nine-inch cigarette holder, he addressed himself to defusing bombs, and especially to exploring German delayed-action devices, which were fitted with increasingly sophisticated antitampering devices. His courage and imagination were undisputed, but some UXB men deplored his casual indiscipline. On 12 May 1941, at London's "bomb graveyard" in Erith Marshes, the earl was addressing a ticking Type 17 delay fuse when the bomb exploded, taking with it "Wild Jack" Howard and thirteen other personnel rashly clustered around, including the beautiful Beryl Morden. His death was lamented, but it was widely held that his insouciance had caused the gratuitous loss of his companions. UXB work penalised amateurs.

A different sort of embarrassment was caused by another UXB man, Bob Davies, a prewar drifter from Cornwall. He had acquired some technical experience during travels around the world, which he parleyed into an emergency commission in the Royal Engineers. Early one morning in September 1940, Davies commanded a squad sent to address a one-ton bomb which had buried itself deep in the road in front of St. Paul's Cathedral during a raid in the night. The engineers quickly found themselves in difficulties when overcome by gas from a fractured main, which caused them to be briefly hospitalised. Resuming work, they dug all night, until a spark ignited gas from another main, burning three men.

The press got hold of the story—and the threat to the cathedral. The *Daily Mail* used the opportunity to applaud the courage of the UXB squads: "These most gallant—and most matter of fact—men of the RE are many a time running a race with death." Deeper and deeper Davies's men dug, until almost eighty hours after it fell, they reached the bomb, twenty-eight feet into the London clay. A heavy cable was attached, with which a lorry sought to extract the huge menace. This snapped. Only when two lorries took the strain on a second cable did the bomb slowly rise to the surface. It was lashed to a cradle and driven through the streets of London to Hackney Marshes, where it was detonated. The explosion blew a crater a hundred feet wide.

A flood of publicity followed about Davies and his team, who became famous. A headline asserted: "A Story That Must Win a Man a VC." Davies and the sapper who found the bomb and saved St. Paul's were indeed awarded the newly created George Cross, for civil acts of heroism. Only in May 1942 did an unhappy sequel take place: Davies was court-martialled on almost thirty charges involving large-scale and systematic theft throughout his time in charge of his UXB squad; he had also exploited his role to extract cash payments from some of those whose premises he saved from bombs, compounded by later passing dud cheques. More embarrassments followed: it emerged that the St. Paul's bomb did not, as claimed by the media, contain a delay fuse, so it was much less dangerous than had been alleged; and Davies did not himself drive it out to Hackney. The officer served two years' imprisonment, being released in 1944. The perils of UXB work were indisputable, and the Cornishman undoubtedly did some brave and useful work. But a lesson of his story was that scoundrels as well as heroes played their parts in the blitz, and some people were a tangle of both.

HITLER'S AIR ASSAULT on Britain ranks second only to the invasion of Russia among his great blunders of the war. After June 1940 many of Churchill's people, especially in high places, recognised their country's inability to challenge Nazi mastery of the Continent. If they had merely been left to contemplate British impotence, political agitation for a negotiation with Germany might well have been renewed, and gained support from the old appeasers still holding high government office. The unfulfilled threat of air attack, on an annihilatory scale widely anticipated and feared in 1939, could have influenced British policy more strongly than the reality of an inconclusive one.

The prime principle of employing force in pursuit of national objectives is to ensure that it is effective. The Germans failed to achieve this against Britain in 1940–41, a first earnest of one of the great truths of the conflict: while the Wehrmacht often fought its battles brilliantly, the Nazis made war with startling ineptitude. The Luftwaffe, instead of terrorising Churchill's people into bowing to Hitler's will, merely roused them to acquiesce in defiance.

Posterity sees the period between July 1940 and the spring of 1941 overwhelmingly in terms of Britain's air battle against the Luftwaffe, yet that engaged only a small proportion of Germany's military resources. For the remainder of Hitler's warriors, and almost the entire army, this became a curious time of idleness comparable with the earlier Phoney War. To be sure, there were conquered nations to be secured, fruits of victory to enjoy—above all those from France. In Berlin, "The first effects of the war were not the traditional ones of decay and scarcity," wrote the American correspondent Howard Smith, "but a sudden leap upwards in visible prosperity. Berlin charwomen and housemaids, whose legs had never been caressed by silk, began wearing stockings from the Boulevard Haussmann as an everyday thing—'from my Hans at the front.' Little street-corner taverns began displaying rows of Armagnac, Martell and Courvoisier."

German war industry, still performing relatively sluggishly, needed time to produce tanks, planes and ammunition to replace those expended in the continental campaigns. The army spent the winter conducting a vast expansion programme—between May 1940 and June 1941 it grew from 5.7 million to 7.3 million men, from 143 divisions to 180. Beyond brandy and stockings, there was important industrial booty to be garnered from the conquered territories, especially railway wagons. Nazi occupation precipitated a drastic decline in economic activity which persisted across most of Europe until the liberation, though French armaments factories made a useful contribution to the German war effort.

Hitler spent much less time than the British supposed contemplating the Luftwaffe's operations against them. He never visited its airfields on the Channel coast. Instead, for most of the autumn and winter he was wrestling with his fundamental strategic dilemma: whether to consolidate Germany's western victories and invade Britain in 1941, or instead to follow his strongest inclinations and turn east. On 31 July 1940, long before the Luftwaffe attack on Britain reached its climax, at the Berghof he told his generals of his determination to attack Russia the following May. Thereafter, however, he indulged more months of vacillation. The German navy pressed for major operations to expel Britain from the Mediterranean, by seizing Gibraltar through Spain and the Suez Canal through Libya. In advocating this course, naval C-in-C Adm. Erich Raeder was supported by Gen. Walter Warlimont, head of the Wehrmacht's strategic planning section. Following an important commanders' conference in the Reich Chancellery on 4 November, Hitler's army adjutant, Gerhard Engel, wrote that the Führer seemed "visibly depressed . . . at the moment he does not know what to do next."

The western option had still not been finally and formally rejected in November when Molotov, Stalin's foreign minister, visited Berlin. The Russian displayed an appetite for further Soviet expansionism which roused German ire, expressing Moscow's interest in the future of Romania, Bulgaria, Poland and even Greece. He enquired whether Sweden's continuing neutrality suited the common purposes of Germany and the Soviet Union, and was sharply told that it did. His remarks emphasised that if Hitler still had unfulfilled territorial ambitions, so too did Stalin. By the time Molotov boarded a plane home, Hitler was confirmed in his earlier conviction: Germany should attack Russia the following year.

From his own perspective, he had no choice. The German economy was much less strong than its enemies supposed—only slightly larger than that of Britain, which enjoyed a higher per capita income. It could not indefinitely be sustained on a war footing, and was stretched to the limits to feed the population and arm the Wehrmacht. Hitler was determined to secure his strategic position in Europe before the United States entered the war, which he anticipated in 1942. The only option unavailable to him was that of making peace, since Churchill refused to negotiate. Hitler persuaded himself that British obstinacy was fortified by a belief that Churchill might forge an alliance with Stalin, which could make victory over Germany seem plausible. Thus, the Soviet Union's defeat would make Britain's capitulation inevitable. If Germany was destined to engage in a death struggle with Russia, it would be foolish to delay this while Stalin rearmed. On 18 December, Hitler issued a formal directive for an invasion, to be launched at the end of May 1941.

Hitler saw three reasons for striking: first, he wished to do so, in fulfilment of his ambition to eradicate bolshevism and create a German empire in the east; second, it seemed prudent to eliminate the Soviet threat before again turning west for a final settlement with Britain and the United States; third, he identified economic arguments. Ironically, Russia's vast deliveries of raw materials and commodities following the Nazi-Soviet Pact—which in 1940 included most of Germany's animal-feed imports, 74 percent of its phosphorus, 67 percent of its asbestos, 65 percent of its chrome ore, 55 percent of its manganese, 40 percent of its nickel and 34 percent of its oil—convinced Hitler that such a level of dependence was intolerable. That summer, a poor German harvest made necessary the import of huge quantities of Ukrainian wheat. He became impatient to appropriate the Soviet Union's cornbelt, and thirsty for the oil of the Caucasus. Only late in the war did the Allies grasp the severity of their enemy's fuel problems: petrol was so short that novice Wehrmacht drivers could be given only meagre tuition, resulting in a heavy military-vehicle accident rate. Even in 1942, the worst year of the Battle of the Atlantic, Britain imported 10.2 million tons of oil; meanwhile, German imports and synthetic production never exceeded 8.9 million tons. Thus it was that Hitler made seizure of the Caucasian oil wells a key objective of Operation Barbarossa, heedless of the handicap this imposed on operations to destroy the Red Army, by dividing Germany's forces. He envisaged the invasion of Russia as both an ideological crusade and a campaign of economic conquest. Significantly, he confided nothing of his Russian intentions to the Italians, whose discretion he mistrusted. Throughout the winter of 1940–41, Mussolini continued to nurse happy hopes of a victorious peace following his own conquest of Egypt. It was a striking characteristic of Axis behaviour until 1945 that while there was some limited consultation between Germany, Italy and Japan, there was no attempt to join in creating a coherent common strategy for defeating the Allies.

In the last weeks of 1940, therefore, while the British people supposed themselves the focus of the Nazis' malignity and headlines around the world described the drama of the blitz, Hitler's thoughts were far away. His generals began to prepare their armies for a struggle in the east. As early as November, an Estonian double agent told the British SIS representative in Helsinki what he had learned from an Abwehr officer: "German command preparing June campaign against USSR." The SIS man commented dismissively on the implausibility of such an indiscretion, saying, "Possibly statement made for propaganda purposes." Even had this report been believed in London, the British could have done nothing to shake Stalin's complacency and promote Soviet preparations to meet the threat.

For a year following France's surrender scarcely a single German soldier fired a shot in anger. There was a protracted lull in ground operations, a loss of impetus unapparent at the time but critical to the course of the war. Hitler took no meaningful steps towards converting the largest military conquests in history into a durable hegemony. The German navy was too weak either to support an invasion of Britain or to sever its Atlantic lifeline; the Luftwaffe's campaign against Britain had failed. It seems flippant to suggest that Hitler determined to invade Russia because he could not think what else to do, but there is something in this, as Ian Kershaw has observed. Many more Nazi battlefield successes lay ahead, but some generals privy to their Führer's intentions already understood the Third Reich's fundamental difficulty: anything less than hemispheric domination threatened disaster; yet Germany's military and economic capability to achieve this remained questionable.

Hitler's continental triumphs caused the democracies to overrate Germany's strength, while persuading his own nation rapturously to rejoice in their victories. The German people had entered the war full of misgivings, which by the winter of 1940 were largely dispelled. The Luftwaffe's failure against Britain troubled few: a young pilot, Heinz Knoke, described the thrill of finding himself among the vast audience in the Berlin Sportpalast addressed by Hitler on 18 December. "I do not suppose the world has ever known a more brilliant orator than this man. His magnetic personality is irresistible. One can sense the emanations of tremendous willpower and driving energy. We are 3,000 young idealists. We listen to the spellbinding words and accept them with all our hearts. We have never before experienced such a deep sense of patriotic devotion towards our German fatherland . . . I shall never forget the expressions of rapture which I saw on the faces around me today."

Yet such triumphalism was wildly premature. Germany's 1940 victories created an enormous empire, but while this could be pillaged to considerable effect, it was administered with dire economic incompetence. Germany, contrary to widespread perceptions, was not an advanced industrial state by comparison with the United States, which it lagged by perhaps thirty years; it still had a large peasant agricultural sector such as Britain had shed. Its prestige, and the fear it inspired in the hearts of its enemies, derived from the combat efficiency of the Wehrmacht and the Luftwaffe, the latter being much weaker than the Allies knew. Time would show that these forces were inadequate to fulfil Hitler's ambitions. If Britain at the end of 1940 remained beleaguered, Germany's might rested on foundations much less solid than the world supposed.

WINSTON CHURCHILL in the winter of 1940 persuaded his people that they had achieved something heroic and important when most were bemused to learn that they had done anything at all. "The Prime Minister has been saying nice things about us fighter boys in the House of Commons," wrote Spitfire pilot Sandy Johnstone on 18 November. "He says we have just won a famous victory although, to be honest, I don't think any of us has been aware that there has been that sort of battle going on!" Churchill imbued with grandeur Fighter Command's triumph and the nation's display of resilience under German air bombardment. He did not, however, say how Britain might advance from defying the Luftwaffe to overcoming the Nazi empire, because he did not know.

Edward R. Murrow, the great American broadcaster, told his CBS radio audience on 15 September that there was no great outpouring of public sentiment following news that bombs had fallen on Buckingham Palace; Londoners shrugged that the king and queen were merely experiencing the common plight of millions: "This war has no relation with the last one, so far as symbols and civilians are concerned. You must understand that a world is dying, that old values, the old prejudices, and the old bases of power and prestige are going." Murrow recognised what some of Britain's ruling caste still did not; they deluded themselves that the struggle was being waged to sustain their familiar old society. The privileged elite among whom Evelyn Waugh lived saw the war, the novelist wrote, as "a malevolent suspension of normality: the massing and movement of millions of men, some of whom were sometimes endangered, most of whom were idle and lonely, the devastation, hunger and waste, crumbling buildings, foundering ships, the torture and murder of prisoners . . . [which] had been prolonged beyond reason." Few of Waugh's friends understood that the "suspension of normality" would become permanent in its impact upon their own way of life.

Churchill's single-minded commitment to victory served his country wonderfully well in 1940–41, but thereafter it would reveal important limitations. He sought the preservation of British imperial greatness, the existing order, and this purpose would not suffice for most of his fellow countrymen. They yearned for social change, improvements in their domestic condition of a kind which seemed to the prime minister almost frivolous amid a struggle for global mastery. The Lancashire housewife Nella Last groped movingly towards an expression of her compatriots' hopes when she wrote that summer of 1940: "Sometimes I get caught up in a kind of puzzled wonder at things and think of all the work and effort and unlimited money that is used today to 'destroy' and not so long ago there was no money or work and it seems so *wrong* somehow . . . [that] money and effort could always be found to pull down and destroy rather than build up." Mrs. Last was middle-aged, but her children's generation was determined that once the war was won, money would be found to create a more egalitarian society.

Churchill never defined credible war aims beyond the defeat of the Axis; when the tide of battle turned, this would become a serious weakness of his leadership and a threat to his domestic popularity. But in 1940–41 his foremost challenge was to convince his people that the war could be won. This became more difficult, rather than less, once the Luftwaffe was vanquished: thoughtful people recognised that the nation remained impotent to challenge German dominance of the Continent.

George Barclay, a Hurricane pilot, described an intense discussion between young fliers and senior officers in his airfield mess on Sunday, 29 September 1940, and recorded their conclusions: "The British people are still fast asleep. They haven't begun to realise the power of our enemies and that they have to give their 'all' . . . That we need dictatorial methods to fight dictators . . . That we shall eventually win the war, but it will be a hell of a job and more so unless we pull ourselves together." The message, an eminently sensible one, was that the British must try harder. Many more frustrations, sorrows and defeats lay ahead, and George Barclay himself would lie dead in a desert funeral pyre, before Hitler provoked into armed resistance a sufficiency of enemies to encompass his undoing.

CHAPTER FIVE

THE MEDITERRANEAN

1. Mussolini Gambles

AT THE OUTBREAK of the conflict in 1939, Hitler had no intention of waging war in the Mediterranean, and asserted his determination not to commit German resources there. It was his fellow dictator Benito Mussolini who yearned to create an Italian lake, and on his own initiative launched the offensives which brought conflict to the region. In the year after the fall of France in June 1940, only in the African and Balkan theatres did Allied and Axis armies clash. Even after Germany invaded Russia in June 1941, the Mediterranean remained for three more years the focus of the Western Allied military contribution to the struggle against Hitler. All this was the consequence of Mussolini's decision to become a protagonist in a struggle for which his nation was pitifully ill-equipped.

Hitler possessed in the Wehrmacht a formidable instrument for pursuing his ambitions. The Duce, by contrast, sought to play the warlord with incompetent commanders, unwilling soldiers and inadequate weapons. Italy was relatively poor, with a GDP less than half the size of Britain's, and barely one-third per capita; it produced only one-sixth as much steel. The nation mobilised its economy less effectively for the Second World War than it had for the First. Even in the sunshine days of Mussolini's relationship with Hitler, such was the Nazis' contempt for their ally that 350,000 Italian workers in Germany were treated little better than slaves; Rome's ambassador in Berlin was obliged to devote most of his energies to pleading for some amelioration of their working conditions. While Hitler cherished an enduring personal loyalty to Mussolini, whom he had once seen as a mentor, most Germans mistrusted and mocked Italy's leader. Berliners claimed that whenever the Duce met the Führer, barrel-organ grinders played the popular tune *"Du Kannst nicht Treue sein"*—"You Cannot Be Faithful." In 1936, when a foolish woman at a party asked Field Marshal Werner von Blomberg who would win the next war, he is alleged to have answered, "Madam, I cannot tell you that. Only one thing I can say: whoever has Italy on his side is bound to lose."

There was a contemptuous joke in Nazi Party circles of Hitler's lackey Wilhelm Keitel reporting, "My Führer, Italy has entered the war!" Hitler answers, "Send two divisions. That should be enough to finish them." Keitel says, "No, my Führer, not against us, but with us." Hitler says, "That's different. Send ten divisions."

In the early months of the war, there was a droll consensus between the Germans and British against initiating Middle Eastern operations. So weak was Britain's global position that its chiefs of staff set their faces against committing forces there. Once Mussolini joined the Axis, the Mediterranean became valueless as a shipping route to the east, in the face of enemy air and naval dominance. The head of the British Army, Gen. Sir John Dill, preferred to dispatch to Asia such men and weapons as could be spared, to strengthen the empire's defences against the looming Japanese threat. Churchill, however, would have none of this: since it was impossible to give battle on the Continent, he determined to do so in Africa. In the summer of 1940 he shipped precious tanks to Britain's Middle East C-in-C, Gen. Sir Archibald Wavell. Other precautionary measures were adopted: 16,000 Gibraltarians—all but 4,000 of the Rock's civilian population—were evacuated first to North Africa, thence to England. It was likely that seizure of the fortress at the gates of the Mediterranean would become an Axis objective, perhaps with the collusion of Spain's dictator, Gen. Francisco Franco.

The Royal Navy had a relatively large Mediterranean fleet, but its C-in-C, Adm. Sir Andrew Cunningham, recognised its vulnerability when almost bereft of air cover—as Churchill did not. For more than two years after Italy entered the war and France left it, Cunningham's forces remained grievously disadvantaged by shortage of both carriers and land bases from which to operate aircraft. Huge expanses of sea were beyond the range of British fighters flying from Gibraltar, Malta, Egypt or Palestine. The Axis, by contrast, could strike at will from an almost unlimited choice of airfields. It was remarkable that between 1940 and 1943 the Royal Navy asserted itself with some success in the Mediterranean, under such handicaps of means and strategic weakness. Cunningham and his warship captains displayed a skill, dash and courage which went far to compensate for the paper superiority of the Italian battlefleet.

Ashore, the war in the North African desert engaged only a handful of British and imperial divisions, while most of Churchill's army stayed at home. This was partly to provide security against invasion, partly for lack of weapons and equipment, partly owing to shortage of shipping to move and supply troops overseas. The clashes between desert armies were little more significant in determining the outcome of the global conflict than the tournaments between bands of French and English knights which provided entr'actes during the Hundred Years' War. But the North African contest caught the imagination of the Western world, and achieved immense symbolic significance in the minds of the British people.

Hostilities were conducted upon a narrow strip of sand along the Mediterranean littoral, seldom more than forty miles wide, which was navigable by tanks. For thirty-two months between September 1940 and May 1943, the rival armies struggled for mastery in a series of seesaw campaigns which eventually traversed more than 2,000 miles of coastal territory. Shifts of advantage were heavily influenced by the distances each side was obliged to move fuel, ammunition, food and water to its fighting units: the British fared best in 1941–42 when closest to their bases in the Nile Delta; Axis forces when nearer to Tripoli. It is foolish to romanticise any aspect of the war, given the universal reality that almost every participant would have preferred to be in his own home; that to die trapped in a blazing tank was no less terrible at Sollum or Benghazi than at Stalingrad. But the emptiness of desert battlefields, where there was neither much slaughter of innocents nor destruction of civilian property, alleviated some of the horrors imposed by collateral damage in populated regions.

While campaigning in the desert was never comfortable, in the protracted intervals between battles it was preferable to winter Russia or monsoon Asia. It is sometimes suggested that in North Africa there was "war without hate." This is an exaggeration, because there was certainly fear, which bred spasms of animosity; most men in the heat of action feel ill-will towards those seeking to kill them. But extremes of brutality, especially the murder of prisoners, were generally avoided by both sides. Italians and Germans, British, Indians, Australians, New Zealanders and South Africans subsisted and fought in a wild and alien environment where none had any emotional stake. They engaged in a common struggle against sand, flies, heat and thirst, even before the enemy entered the reckoning.

In the autumn of 1940, Mussolini was impatient to the point of obsession to achieve some conspicuous Italian success to justify seizing a share of the booty from anticipated Axis victory. Though ignorant of both military and naval affairs, he craved foreign conquests to ennoble fascism and stiffen the frail spirit of his people at home. "The army has need of *glory*," he said. Libya, an Italian colony, adjoined British-controlled Egypt, where Wavell had a small imperial force of one British division, the 7th Armoured, together with an Indian and a New Zealand formation, soon reinforced by two Australian divisions. Britain's presence was anomalous to the verge of absurdity: Egypt was an independent sovereign state ruled by King Farouk, where the British supposedly exercised rights only to defend the Suez Canal. The Cairo government did not formally enter hostilities until February 1945. The sympathies of most Egyptians lay with the Axis, which they believed would liberate them from more than seventy years of British domination. Indeed, such views were widespread among Arab nationalists throughout the Middle East, and were stimulated by Hitler's 1940 successes. That August, the secretary of the grand mufti of Jerusalem visited Berlin to discuss fomenting a revolt in Iraq. In addition, he suggested, prospective rebels in Palestine and Transjordan might be armed with weapons provided by the Vichy French in Syria. The aspiring insurgents' principal demand was that the Nazis should commit themselves to the future independence of the Arab states.

Yet in 1940 Germany's leaders were not much interested in Muslim revolts, less still in Arab freedom. Moreover, at this stage they conceded to Italy the principal diplomatic role in the region. Mussolini's ambitions for extending his African empire were wholly incompatible with local peoples' aspirations: in pursuit of them, his generals had already massacred many thousands of Libyan and Abyssinian tribesmen. Only in 1941 did the Germans engage with Arab nationalists, notably in Iraq and Iran. Their attempted interventions there were late, halfhearted, and easily frustrated by forces dispatched to reassert British hegemony.

In Egypt in September 1939, Britain invoked a clause of its treaty with Farouk which obliged him, in the event of a war, to provide "all the facilities and assistance in his power, including the use of ports, aerodromes and means of communication." Thereafter, the British treated the country as a colonial possession, governed through their ambassador, Sir Miles Lampson. They based their Mediterranean Fleet at Alexandria, and in February 1942 deployed troops in Cairo to stifle a nascent Egyptian rebellion. In the course of the war, desperate hunger among the peasantry caused several food riots; the plight of the Egyptian *felaheen* contrasted starkly with the sybaritic lifestyle of the British military colony centred upon Middle East headquarters, Shepheard's Hotel, the Gezira Sporting Club and a nexus of barracks, supply and repair bases throughout the Nile Delta, where contempt for "the wogs" was almost universal.

American visitors were dismayed by the lassitude and imperial condescension of the British in Egypt, who seemed to regard the conflict being waged in the western wilderness as a mere event in a sporting calendar. This perception was unjust to those doing the fighting and dying: it failed to recognise the British Army's tradition of seeking to make war with a light heart. But a core of truth about the North African campaign was that the British role until late 1942 was characterised by an amateurishness that was occasionally inspired but which more often crippled its endeavours.

So large was the paper strength of Mussolini's armies that in the summer of 1940 it seemed possible they would expel the British from northern and eastern Africa. There were 600,000 Italian and colonial troops in Libya and Abyssinia, confronting fewer than 100,000 men under Wavell's orders in the Middle East, Kenya, Sudan and Somaliland. In August, to Churchill's fury the Italians seized Somaliland almost bloodlessly. Mussolini's people had little stomach for hard fighting but a hearty appetite for victories. During the brief period when cheap African conquests seemed in prospect while the Luftwaffe's efforts against Britain were visibly flagging, an Italian journalist wrote proudly, and with an earnestness that reflected his people's genius for self-delusion: "We want to reach Suez with our own forces alone; perhaps *we* will win the war and not the Germans." But Mussolini's operations were handicapped by his confusion about both means and purposes: at home, he demobilised part of his army to bring in the harvest. Ignoring the vital principle of concentration of force, he prepared to launch an invasion of Yugoslavia and Greece. He failed to exploit a critical window of opportunity to seize Malta. In North Africa, his commanders lacked equipment, skill and resolve. In September 1940, in a gesture symbolic of Italy's generals' insouciance about the struggle, the Ministry of War in Rome reverted to its peacetime practice of closing for business each day at 2:00 p.m.

An Italian diplomat vented his disgust on the mood he encountered during a visit to Milan: "Everyone thinks only of eating, enjoying themselves, making money and relaying witticisms about the great and powerful. Anyone who gets killed is a jerk . . . He who supplies the troops with cardboard shoes is considered a sort of hero." A young Italian officer wrote home from Libya: "We're trying to fight this war as though it were a colonial war in Africa. But this is a European war . . . fought with European weapons against a European enemy. We take too little account of this in building our stone forts and equipping ourselves with such luxury."

Mussolini dismissed Hitler's offer of two armoured divisions for North Africa, which might have been decisive in securing a swift Axis victory: he was determined to keep the Germans out of his own jealously defined sphere of influence. A quarter of Italy's combat aircraft were dispatched to join the Luftwaffe's attack on Britain, leaving Italian troops in Libya almost without air support, while a large army in Albania—occupied by Mussolini in 1939—was held in readiness to attack either Yugoslavia or Greece, as the Duce deemed expedient. The Italians made policy and strategy in the belief that they were participating in the residual military operations of a short war soon to conclude in Axis victory. Mussolini, indeed, was fearful that the British might make terms with Hitler before he had achieved

Poles catch a first glimpse of the Luftwaffe

Poland: the occupiers confront the occupied

Finnish "ghost soldiers"; and (below) a Russian, frozen in death

Norway invaded

Dunkirk evacuated

Parisians watch the Germans march in

Coventry, November 1940

British gunners in North Africa

A German entertains a Frenchwoman who has discovered the virtues of collaboration; and (opposite) a German advances the Final Solution

Wartime food meant different things to different peoples. In America (above) a family celebrates Thanksgiving 1942, in a belligerent nation where hunger remained unknown; and (right) a besieged Leningrader with his bread ration

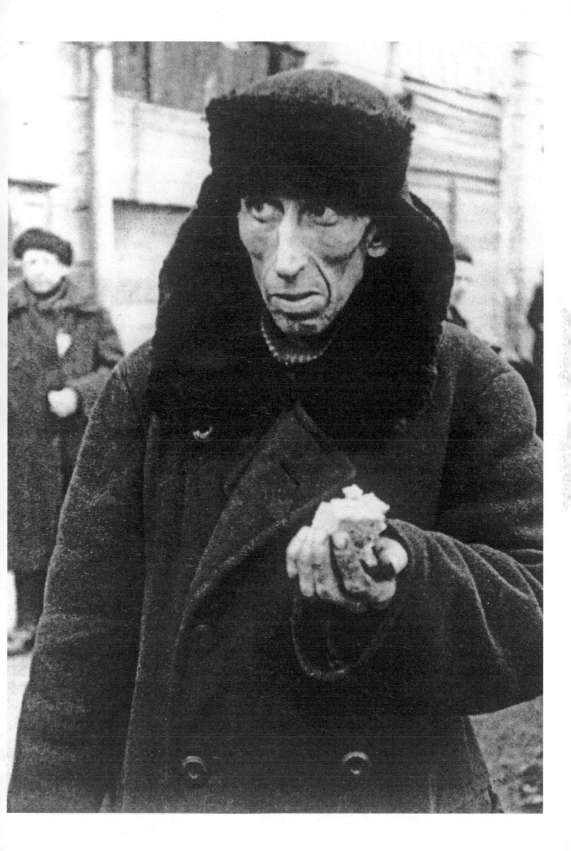

A German discovers Russia's winter

his own conquests. Instead, Italy would become the only nation whose strategic fortunes were decisively affected by events in Africa, where it lost progressively twenty-six divisions, half its air force and its entire tank inventory, together with any vestige of military credibility.

THE BRITISH began operations in the summer of 1940 with a succession of raids across the Libyan border. Marshal Rodolfo Graziani deployed some 250,000 men against 36,000 British in Egypt and a further 27,000—including a division of horsed yeomanry—in Palestine. Mussolini's commander had made his reputation by destroying the Abyssinian army in 1935 with liberal infusions of poison gas. In 1940 he showed himself a resolute defeatist with no stomach for battle. Graziani advanced cautiously into Egypt in September until, unnerved by the British show of aggression and a gross overestimate of Wavell's strength, he halted and dug in south and east of Sidi Barrani. One of his generals, Annibale Bergonzoli, christened "Electric Whiskers" by the British, found some of his artillery officers so craven that during British air attacks he was obliged to hit and kick them back to their guns from the trenches where they had taken refuge. A three-month pause ensued, during which Mussolini chafed, fearful that the Germans might win the war before he had conquered Egypt; Churchill, meanwhile, was equally impatient at the delay before Wavell was ready to launch his counterstrokes.

On 19 January 1941, Maj. Gen. William Platt led a small army from Sudan into Eritrea, seizing the formidable fortress of Keren after heavy fighting on 27 March, at a cost of 536 killed, mostly Indian soldiers, and 3,229 wounded. Meanwhile in February, another British force under Gen. Alan Cunningham, brother of the admiral, advanced from Kenya into Somaliland, marched up the coast to Mogadishu, then turned north for a thrust 774 miles overland to Harar. By 6 April, Cunningham had taken Addis Ababa, Abyssinia's capital, having suffered only 501 battle casualties. Fighting persisted for another six months against pockets of Italian resistance, but the Abyssinian campaign was crowned with British success, after some hard fighting on short commons. Though combat losses were few, 74,550 men succumbed to sickness or accidents and 744 of them died, as did 15,000 camels supporting the British advance. More than 300,000 Italians became prisoners.

But the most dramatic offensive took place in Egypt, where on 6 December 1940 Wavell unleashed Lt. Gen. Sir Richard O'Connor's Operation Compass against Graziani. This began tentatively, with modest objectives, then expanded dramatically amid stunning success. Imperial forces swept into Libya, capturing Italians in tens of thousands. A British gunner described one of O'Connor's racing columns, "loaded with the paraphernalia for making war in the wilderness—rations, ammunition, petrol and that most precious of all requirements, 4-gallon flimsy aluminium containers of water, all carried in three-ton canvas-covered Bedfords. [There were] 5-cwt Morris Scout trucks with the section officer or battery captain standing up in the passenger seat, divisional pennants fluttering in the wind-stream; a couple of RHA 25-pounder guns, cylindrical water bowsers skittering on two wheels behind a 15-cwt. Sometimes a troop of Hussars' light tanks, their tracks screeching and rattling and bouncing over the boulders, their long, slender wireless aerials bobbing and waving. The rolling convoy moved in unison, fanned out in open order, fifty yards separating each vehicle, sand streaming from the wheels like spray in heavy rain."

The Italian defences crumbled with extraordinary speed. "They can't take it," an Australian soldier wrote home contemptuously. "They can't take pain (I saw hundreds of their wounded . . . all in tears), they can't take shells (they flinch when one drops a hundred yards away), the sound of British tanks terrorised them and the sight of our bayonets was enough to make them throw up their hands. Fascism . . . pooh!" Likewise an officer: "All Australians now know that one Aussie is still equal to . . . 50 Italians— almost, anyway." Lt. Tom Bird employed a cricketing metaphor: "One can't help feeling that it is a great bit of luck to have been able to have a practice over or two, so to speak, with the Italians. What more delightful people to fight could there be?" Nothing went right for the Italian war effort. Mussolini's propaganda department in Rome made a film designed to demonstrate the superiority of fascist manhood. To this end, a fight was staged between former world heavyweight champion Primo Carnera and Kay Masaki, a black South African taken prisoner in the desert. Masaki had never entered a boxing ring in his life, and was knocked down when the cameras began to roll. He picked himself up, however, and struck Carnera a blow that rendered him unconscious.

To the outside world, the relative insignificance of Britain's desert triumphs was plain. The Romanian Mihail Sebastian wrote on 7 February 1941: "It goes without saying that the whole of the war in Africa (however interesting and dramatic) is only a sideshow. The struggle is between the British and the Germans; that is where everything will be decided." He was right, of course, but in blitzed London there was rejoicing. By 9 February, O'Connor's force had advanced 500 miles and taken El Agheila; the road west towards Tripoli lay open. Thereafter, to the bewilderment of ordinary soldiers, the advance ended; deep in the sands of Mussolini's colony they halted, and languished. "Every day was the same as the day before," gunner Doug Arthur wrote wearily. "Saturday could have been Monday, Friday could have been Tuesday, even Pancake Tuesday, for all we knew . . . We didn't know what was really going on, where we were going or what faced us when we got there."

They were going no farther in Libya. Four of Wavell's divisions, including the New Zealand division and much of the Australian contingent, were transferred to Greece to meet the anticipated German assault there. It was afterwards claimed that the Greek diversion cost the British a unique opportunity to clear the North African coast and regain control of the southern Mediterranean. This seems doubtful: Lt. Gen. Erwin Rommel's Afrika Korps was already landing at Tripoli, to succour the faltering Italians and thereafter dominate the campaign; the British supply line was stretched to the limits; O'Connor's tanks and vehicles were almost worn out. Fighting the Italians flattered the capabilities of the Western Desert Force, while the simultaneous Abyssinian campaign was a heavy drain on imperial resources. Even if none of Wavell's men had gone to Greece, it is unlikely that the British were strong enough to complete the conquest of North Africa.

DURING THE THREE MONTHS before the British offensive in Libya petered out in February 1941, it achieved an important marginal impact, unrecognised at the time: Operation Compass contributed to keeping Spain out of the war. Franco faced the same dilemmas as Mussolini, but reached different conclusions. He was ideologically enthusiastic towards the Axis and wished to share the spoils of Allied defeat. But he was cautious about exposing his country, ravaged by recent civil war, to the hazards of a new struggle until the British had been reduced to impotence. From 1939 onwards Spain was no neutral, but a belligerent-in-waiting: Spanish foreign minister Serrano Suner, in particular, was wholeheartedly committed to joining the Axis cause. The shrewd Portuguese ambassador in Madrid, Pedro Teotonio Pereira, reported to Lisbon on 27 May 1940: "Beyond doubt Spain continues to hate the Allies . . . German victories are received with joy." Pereira asserted that almost all Spaniards wanted Germany to triumph, and regretted only that the destitution of their country made it inopportune to commit themselves immediately to its cause: "They do not judge the war to be infamous, but themselves in a bad position to take part."

Franco intended to fight, but only if Germany accepted his stiff tariff: "Spain cannot enter *por gusto* [for fun]," he told Hitler during their meeting at Hendaye on the Franco-Spanish border in October 1940. A secret protocol to the Spanish-German accord, finally signed in November, declared Madrid's readiness to join the Axis Tripartite Pact: "In fulfilment of its obligations as an ally, Spain will intervene in the present war of the Axis Powers against England after they have provided it with the military support necessary for its preparedness . . . Germany will grant economic aid to Spain by supplying it with food and raw materials." The Economic Ministry in Madrid drew up a formidable shopping list: 400,000 tons of fuel, half a million tons of coal, 200,000 tons of wheat, 100,000 tons of cotton and vast consignments of fertiliser.

Franco's military planners busied themselves preparing a possible take-over of Portugal as well as Gibraltar. Thereafter, however, relations with Germany soured. The Spanish dictator was galled when Hitler refused to concede to him French colonies in Africa, partly because Germany still hoped to enlist Vichy France as an active ally. Mussolini strongly opposed Spanish belligerence, partly because he was a competitor with Franco for the same French colonies, and also because he sought unreserved personal hegemony over the Mediterranean littoral. Hitler, in his turn, had his own shopping list, wishing to appropriate some of Franco's colonies as German overseas bases: Spanish Equatorial Guinea, Fernando Po and one of the Canary Islands. The most intractable sticking point in negotiations was that the Spanish leader, like Mussolini, was unwilling to allow large numbers of German troops into his country. He admired Hitler vastly, and cherished absurd illusions that the Führer would create a new European polity in which Spain, for so long an abused underdog, would be conceded its rightful place in the sun. But he had no intention of allowing his country to become a Nazi fiefdom.

Hitler's key strategic objective was seizure of Gibraltar. Having scant faith in the Spanish army's ability to accomplish this, he prepared plans for the Wehrmacht to do so. For Franco, however, in the words of historian Stanley Payne, "it was a point of both honor and national interest that Spanish forces carry out the operation." An impasse developed: the Germans would not provide Spain with the weapons and supplies for Franco to make an attempt on Gibraltar, and Franco would not grant the Wehrmacht rights of passage for its own assault. He knew the Spanish people were unwilling to accept the sacrifices of a new war. His generals were hostile, not least because the British were paying them a fortune in secret bribes—$13 million in all—to keep their country neutral. As long as Britain remained undefeated, the Royal Navy could blockade Spain, with devastating economic consequences. Once again, British sea power exercised an important, though invisible, influence upon events.

British successes in Libya and Abyssinia further discouraged Franco from any hasty commitment to fight, at precisely the moment when Hitler was ready to dispatch tanks and troops to take Gibraltar. On 7 December 1940, the Abwehr's chief, Adm. Wilhelm Canaris, met Franco in Madrid, to seek his agreement that German forces should start moving into Spain within a month. Franco refused. Canaris cabled Berlin on 10 December, saying that Spain would not move as long as the British maritime threat persisted. Hitler lost patience, and Operation Felix, the Gibraltar attack, was shelved. By February 1941, his attention had switched irrevocably eastwards. He needed every division for his intended invasion of Russia. His interest in Gibraltar waned, and with it Germany's willingness to pay an extravagant price for Spanish belligerency. Spain remained an active friend of the Axis for almost two years thereafter, until the successful Allied invasion of North Africa made obvious the turn of the tide. Italian aircraft bombing Gibraltar refuelled at Spanish airfields; vital commodities including tungsten continued to flow from Spain to Germany; the country swarmed with Nazi diplomats and spies, who were provided with every facility to impede the Allied war effort. Franco sent a token division to assist Hitler's invasion of Russia; Luftwaffe weather and reconnaissance aircraft flew from Spanish bases until 1945. But Spain sustained nominal neutrality. Gibraltar remained unconquered, and thus the gateway to the Mediterranean stayed open to Allied shipping.

If Franco had joined the war, the inevitable fall of Gibraltar would have doomed Malta. It would have been much harder—perhaps impossible— for the British to hold the Middle East. The damage to their prestige and confidence would have been immense, and Churchill might not have survived as prime minister through 1941. Franco deserved no gratitude from the Allies, because cautious Spanish diplomacy was driven by self-interest; he held back only because he overvalued his own worth to the Axis. But the outcome was much to the advantage of both Britain and Spain.

ROMMEL, WHO HAD MADE his reputation in the 1940 French campaign, arrived in Africa on 12 February 1941. His soldiers, flushed with victory in Europe, were in an exuberant mood, perceiving their deployment as a romantic adventure. "We are all twenty-one years old and crazy," wrote the panzergrenadier lieutenant Ralph Ringer. "Crazy, because we have volunteered of our own free will to go to Africa and have talked about nothing else for weeks . . . tropical nights, palm trees, sea breezes, natives, oases and tropical helmets. Also a little war, but how can we be anything but victorious? . . . Like madmen we jumped around and hugged each other, we really were going to Africa!" Lt. Pietro Ostellino, one of the small minority of dedicated Fascists in the Italian army, wrote exultantly to his wife on 3 March: "Here things are going very well and our reoccupation of Cyrenaica, which has been held by the enemy, is a matter of days or even hours away. We hasten to the front line for the honour of the *Patria*. You must be proud and offer your sufferings to the cause for which your husband is fighting with enthusiasm and passion." He added three days later: "Morale is very high, and in cooperation with our valiant allies we are getting ready to do great things . . . Ours is a holy cause and God is with us."

Rommel launched his first offensive against the British in Libya on 24 March, easily capturing El Agheila, at the base of the Gulf of Sirte. British tanks checked the Afrika Korps at Mersa Brega, but the weak forces now commanded by Lt. Gen. Philip Neame were obliged to withdraw. On 4 April, Rommel attacked again, forcing a new retreat by threatening Neame's supply line. Many British tanks were disabled by mechanical failure, and the Germans had little difficulty in pushing on to Tobruk. The port was left to be defended by an Australian garrison, while the main imperial forces fell back across the Egyptian frontier, almost to the start line of their December offensive.

Wavell had impressed on Neame that it was more important to keep his army intact than to hold ground, but soldiers ignorant of this higher purpose were simply bewildered by their own headlong flight. Gunner Len Tutt described an action in which his 25-pounder battery held off panzers for some hours, then as darkness fell was suddenly ordered to withdraw: "The rot seemed to set in. We dropped into action a little way down the road but had hardly surveyed the position before we were ordered to withdraw again. There seemed no overall direction. Too many units were on the move at the same time, a mistake which contributed to a growing panic. We soon saw the danger signs: men abandoning a stalled truck and running to get on another vehicle, when possibly a few seconds under the bonnet would have kept it going. Others were abandoned because they had run out of petrol, and yet there were three-tonners loaded down with the stuff passing on either side." There was further seesaw fighting in which the Halfaya Pass and Fort Capuzzo changed hands several times, but at the end of May the Germans and Italians occupied the disputed ground.

Pietro Ostellino wrote on 13 May near Tobruk: "We are well advanced now and it is only a question of time. It is quite hot, but bearable, and I am in good health—brown as a salami, partly from the sun and also because we are covered in sand which sticks to our skin and with sweat forms a layer of mud. We have enough water, but fifteen minutes after washing we are back to what we were before." Soon afterwards, hearing news of the Axis advance into Greece, he wrote: "Yesterday I received a letter from Uncle Ottavio from Albania in which he talks of the great victory they have achieved there. We will soon be emulating them and will throw the English out of everywhere." Though the Australians held out in Tobruk even after the Afrika Korps raced past towards Egypt, strategic advantage lay firmly with Rommel. And meanwhile, across the Mediterranean, as Ostellino noted, the British had suffered a further series of disasters.

2. A Greek Tragedy

THE STRUGGLE FOR the Balkans began with a black farce precipitated by Mussolini. Having considered a takeover of Yugoslavia, instead, on 28 October 1940 he launched 162,000 men into Greece from Albania, an operation only revealed to Marshal Graziani in North Africa by Rome Radio's news broadcasts. Even Hitler was kept in the dark: the Duce was so nettled by Germany's takeover of Romania—deemed part of Italy's sphere of influence—without consultation with Rome that he determined to turn the tables by presenting Berlin with his own fait accompli in Greece. The pretext for war was mythical Greek support for British operations in the Mediterranean. A small country of 7 million people was expected to offer no significant resistance; Greece's defences faced Bulgaria, not Albania. The British were committed by treaty to support the Athens government, but initially offered only a few weapons and aircraft. Mussolini told his officers: "If anyone makes any difficulties about beating the Greeks, I shall resign from being an Italian." His foreign minister Ciano, sometimes dovish, favoured the invasion as offering easy pickings. He believed Athens would capitulate in the face of token bombing, and sought to ensure such an outcome by allocating millions of lire to bribe Greek politicians and generals. It remains uncertain whether this money was paid, or merely stolen by fascist intermediaries.

Rome was anyway denied its desired outcome. The Greek people, enraged by an Italian submarine's sinking of the Greek cruiser *Helli* weeks before Mussolini's declaration of war, responded to invasion with resolute defiance. Graffiti appeared: "Death to the spaghetti-eaters who sank our *Helli*." Although grievously impoverished, Greece mobilised 209,000 men and 125,000 horses and mules. Its dictator, Gen. Ioannis Metaxas, whose rule had hitherto been bitterly divisive, wrote in his diary as tensions with Italy mounted: "Now everyone is with me." A peasant named Ahmet Tsapounis sent him a telegram: "Not having any money to contribute to the nation's war effort, I give instead my field at Variko . . . which is

5.5 acres. I humbly ask you to accept this." On predominantly Greek-inhabited Cyprus, popular sentiment had hitherto been pro-Axis, because it was believed that a Nazi victory would free the island from British colonial rule. Now, however, a Cypriot wrote: "The supreme desire was for the defeat of the armies which had invaded Greek soil, to be followed by 'the fruits of victory'—'freedom,' as promised by Churchill."

To the astonishment of the world, not only did the Greek army repel the Italian invasion, but by November its forces had advanced deep into Albania. The Italian general Ubaldo Soddu suggested asking the Greeks for an armistice. In Athens, Maris Markoyianni heard a small boy ask: "When we've beaten the Italians, what shall we do with Mussolini?" Hitler was furious about the Greek fiasco. He had always opposed it, and emphatically so until after the November U.S. elections: he feared that new Axis aggression must aid Roosevelt. He had urged Mussolini to secure Crete before attacking the mainland, to frustrate British intervention. In a letter from Vienna on 20 November, he expressed dismay about Italian blundering. The Duce, replying, blamed his setbacks on bad weather; Bulgarian assurances of neutrality, which allowed the Greeks to shift large forces westwards; and local Albanians' unwillingness to aid the Axis. He told Hitler that he was preparing to launch thirty divisions "with which we shall utterly destroy Greece." Those who supposed him a less brutal tyrant than Germany's Führer were confounded by his directive to Badoglio, his chief of staff: "All [Greek] urban centres of over 10,000 population must be destroyed and razed to the ground. This is a direct order."

He achieved nothing of the kind. Instead, through the months that followed the Greek and Italian armies remained stalemated in the Albanian mountains, amid the worst winter weather for half a century. Sgt. Diamantis Stafilakas, from Chios, wrote in his diary on 18 January 1941: "The door of our shelter will not open because of the snow. The fierce wind drives the snow up against it. Today it is raining again. We are soaked through. There is no chance of lighting a fire because the smoke chokes us. Our nights are spent in excruciating discomfort, so that I get up, go outside and walk around. I tried to build a new shelter, and managed to dig down twenty centimetres before the snow began again and I gave up."

Frostbite inflicted thousands of casualties. Spyros Triantafillos grieved at abandoning his beloved grey horse after it broke down in a snowdrift: "Starving, soaked to the bone, tortured by endless movement on rocky ground, it was doomed to stay there. I emptied my saddlebags to follow the others on foot, then stroked the back of its neck a little and kissed it. It might be an animal, but it had been my comrade in war. We had faced death many times together, had lived through unforgettable days and nights. I saw it looking at me as I walked away. What a look that was, my friends. It revealed so much anguish, so much sadness. I wanted to cry, but the tears did not come. War leaves no time for such things. Momentarily I thought of killing it, but couldn't bear to do so. I left it there, staring after me until I disappeared behind a rock."

Hitler, exasperated, ignored Mussolini's protestations that he could defeat the Greeks unaided. On 13 December, he issued Directive No. 20 for Operation Marita: "In the light of the threatening situation in Albania, it is doubly important to frustrate English efforts to establish, behind the protection of a Balkan front, an air base which would threaten Italy . . . and, incidentally, the Romanian oilfields." Following the installation of General Ion Antonescu as Romania's prime minister on 12 October 1940, that country and its vital oil reserves fell under German control; most Romanians considered Germany an inescapable ally, when their country was threatened by the territorial ambitions of the Soviet Union.

By January, the Luftwaffe was attacking British shipping in the Mediterranean from Sicilian bases. General Metaxas died suddenly on 29 January. In March, German diplomatic pressure persuaded Bulgaria to join the Axis; Yugoslavia likewise acceded, though a palace coup in Belgrade installed a short-lived pro-British regime. The morale of the Italian people slumped, as it became brutally apparent that their own leader's ambitions had suffered humiliating frustration, and that the consequence was that they themselves must share in bowing to German hegemony in the Mediterranean region. A police informant in Milan wrote: "Many, many pessimists see Italy as a protectorate of Germany, and conclude that if we endured three wars, the severe losses of the navy, the sacrifice of our raw materials and gold reserves . . . in order to achieve the loss of our political, economic and military independence, there is nothing to be proud of about the policies followed." The privations of the Italian people had worsened through the winter, with prices soaring. The official ration of pasta and rice was cut to 4.4 pounds per person per month, when the average worker consumed fourteen ounces a day. Italian popular enthusiasm for the war, always brittle, never recovered from its disastrous slump following the 1940–41 defeats. Thereafter, most of Mussolini's soldiers, sailors, airmen and civilians were unhappy prisoners, chained to Hitler's chariot wheels.

On 6 April, thirty-three German divisions, six of them armoured, swept into Yugoslavia, easily overwhelming its army. A Luftwaffe bomber attack on the capital killed 17,000 people, an appalling toll which reflected its citizens' absolute unpreparedness for their fate. Six days later the invaders occupied the city, and on 17 April the Yugoslavs capitulated.

A 56,000-strong British-led force, mostly composed of Australians and New Zealanders, began to land in Greece in March, to deploy in the northeast. Churchill's insistence on committing imperial troops at the discretion of British commanders provoked serious and understandable dismay among the leaders of the white dominions. In theory, Canadian, Australian and New Zealand formations could be deployed only with the express sanction of their home governments. But, especially in 1940–41, before dominion ministers dug in their heels against abuses of their constitutional rights, such approval was often sought only retrospectively. The Australian prime minister, Robert Menzies, attended the 24 February 1941 British War Cabinet meeting at which the decision was made to dispatch an army to Greece; but he and his fellow ministers were wilfully misled about the opinions and fears of commanders in the theatre, including their own most senior officers. Only after the first New Zealand soldiers had been in Greece for some weeks in December 1940 did their government in Wellington learn of the fact. Anzac rather than British forces were called upon to bear the chief burden of the most hazardous Allied military gamble of the Mediterranean campaign, serving under a British commander-in-chief. Australian politicians, in particular, were deeply dismayed.

Anzac soldiers, however, cherished more innocent sensations. The New Zealanders were voyaging towards their first battlefield; like most young men in such circumstances, they revelled in excited anticipation and exotic sensations, oblivious of peril. Lance-Bombardier Morry Cullen wrote home euphorically about the thrill of sailing the Mediterranean: "I have never seen such beautiful shades of blue, from a light sky shade to the deepest blue black and there was hardly a ripple on the water." Pvt. Victor Ball wrote in his diary about Athens: "Best place we have been in and people very friendly. Had a look at the Acropolis, the old ruins of Athens . . . The brothel area is a lot cleaner than Cairo. We got very drunk but got home alright." Lt. Dan Davin reflected later: "We were all absolutely the picture of youth and health . . . There's a sort of natural courage in people who've been fed all their lives on good meat." These dominion troops approached their first experience of war with a confidence and enthusiasm that persisted, in remarkable degree, through the ordeal which now began to unfold. Some of their officers, however, were more cynical: Gen. Sir Thomas Blamey, the seedy old reprobate commanding the Australian corps—"a coward and not a commander," in the words of one of his staff officers—spent 26 March reconnoitring possible evacuation beaches in southern Greece.

·   ·   ·

THE GERMANS INVADED on 6 April 1941, simultaneously with their assault on Yugoslavia. They cited the British presence to justify their action: "The government of the Reich has consequently ordered its armed forces to expel British troops from the soil of Greece. All resistance will be ruthlessly crushed . . . It is emphasised that the German army does not come as an enemy of the Greek people, and it is not the desire of the German people to fight Greeks . . . The blow which Germany is obliged to strike on Greek soil is directed against England." British forces were spread far too thin to check the invaders. Where Germans met resistance—and there were some stubborn little stands—they merely pulled back and probed until they found a gap elsewhere.

New Zealander Victor Ball described the first stage of what became a long, painful withdrawal: "We were followed by shellfire the whole way, wherever we went they shelled us. One chap killed outright just alongside me—hit in the throat—and quite a few hit with bits of shale and stone. Planes coming over one at a time bombing and machine-gunning. Things sure get on your nerves when you can't fight back." Russell Brickell, another New Zealander, reflected on the experience of being dive-bombed: "It's a peculiar feeling, lying on one's tummy in a trench or ditch listening to the scream of an approaching bomb, a second's silence as it hits the ground, then the earth comes up and hits one in the face and there is a tremendous woomph! and bits whistle through the air."

German forces were soon pouring through the Monastir Gap on the Yugoslavian border, threatening the rear of the Greek positions in Albania. Allied forces fell back southwards in increasing disorder, outnumbered, outmanoeuvred, and naked against air attack. An Australian medical officer described how "the patter of feet, human and animal, could be heard all night long" as the Greek retreat became a panic-stricken rout. Everywhere in the path of the Axis advance, communities were visited by scenes of horror. A column of Italian prisoners being marched under escort through a village was suddenly enveloped in mortar and artillery fire, which killed and wounded dozens. An old woman, who had lost her eldest son, Stathi, in Albania, began to sob. A café owner urged her now to check her tears for the Italians: "They were the ones who killed your son." She ignored him, and ran to a soldier torn open by shrapnel, who lay crying, "Bread, mother!" The old woman tried to wash his wounds with a cloth dipped in raki, still sobbing and talking to the man: "Don't cry, Stathi. Yes, I am your mother. Don't cry. I've got both bread and milk."

The Greek army had exhausted itself confronting the Italians through the winter. It lacked transport for rapid manoeuvre. The Germans ruthlessly exploited their dominance of the air, especially effective in a country

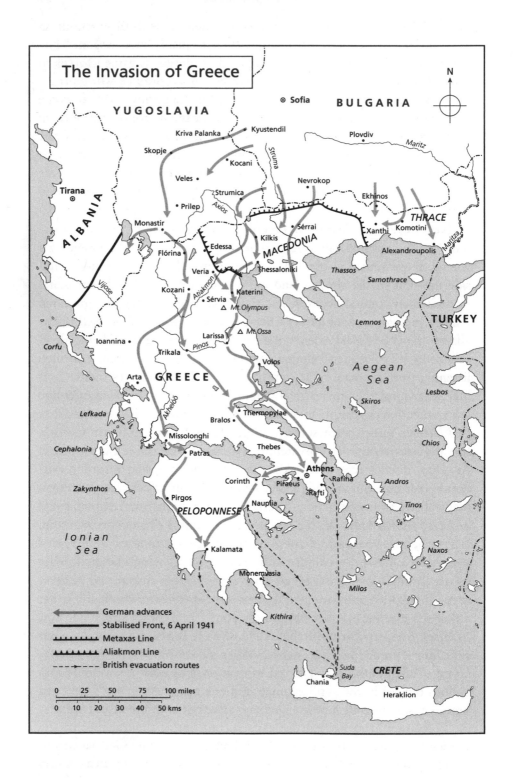

The Invasion of Greece

German advances

Stabilised Front, 6 April 1941

Metaxas Line

Aliakmon Line

British evacuation routes

| 0 | 25 | 50 | 75 | 100 miles |
| 0 | 10 | 20 | 30 | 40 | 50 kms |

BULGARIA

Sofia

Plovdiv

Maritz

Kyustendil

Kriva Palanka

Skopje

Kocani

YUGOSLAVIA

Veles

Nevrokop

Strumica

Ekhinos

Prilep

Struma

Axios

THRACE

Monastir

Komotiní

Xanthi

ALBANIA

Tirana

Flórina

Edessa

Kilkis

Sérrai

Alexandroupolis

Veria

MACEDONIA

Thessaloniki

Maritza

Vijose

Kozani

Katerini

Thassos

Samothrace

Sérvia

Mt. Olympus

TURKEY

Corfu

Ioannina

Larissa

Mt. Ossa

Lemnos

Trikala

Pinos

Volos

Aegean Sea

Arta

GREECE

Lesbos

Lefkada

Skiros

Bralos

Thermopylae

Akhelóo

Chios

Cephalonia

Missolonghi

Thebes

Patras

Zakynthos

Corinth

Athens

Piraeus

Rafína

Andros

Pirgos

Nauplia

Rafti

Tinos

PELOPONNESE

Ionian Sea

Kalamata

Naxos

Monemvasia

Milos

Kithira

Suda Bay

CRETE

Chania

Heraklion

with few roads. "During the afternoon we had our first look at the great Jerry Luftwaffe," wrote the Australian captain Charles Chrystal. "190 bombers came over and bombed . . . till there was not a thing left. They flew in close formation . . . and I can tell you we simply gasped in amazement and were absolutely spellbound to see such numbers." Although the Australians and New Zealanders conducted some determined little rearguard actions, on 28 April the first major naval evacuations began, from Rafina and Porto Rafti. The Germans fanned out across the Peloponnese, where the Royal Navy took off troops from Nauplia and Kalamata.

Citizens in uniform, until with time they grow the skins of soldiers, are shocked by the waste created by war. Among many Anzacs' most vivid memories of the retreat from Greece was the colossal detritus of wrecked and abandoned vehicles, guns, stores, wirelesses, range-finders—millions of pounds' worth of scarcely used equipment, ditched by the roadsides of the Peloponnese. Men boarding the Royal Navy's ships were ordered to discard weapons, especially machine guns and mortars, which they had stubbornly retained through the retreat. This policy had serious consequences for the defence of Crete a few weeks later. Most fugitives suffered a sense of shame about abandoning the local people, who embraced them even in defeat.

By April's end, the Germans held Greece. Some 43,000 of Wavell's troops had been evacuated, leaving behind a further 11,000 who became prisoners, together with all their transport and heavy equipment; Prime Minister Alexandros Koryzis committed suicide. Greek soldiers trickled down from the hills, many having abandoned their arms. "At one moment," wrote an eyewitness, "I saw a captain mount a hillock and address thousands of men who were gathered around it. He shouted: 'Men, alas our country has lost the war!' The audience responded with an eerie, nightmarish, perverse cry of 'Zeto!'—'Hurrah!' 'Zeto!' meant 'We are alive!'"

Such deliverance provided only brief consolation to a nation which thereafter suffered appallingly under Nazi occupation. A Greek general told an air force officer, George Tzannetakis: "George, a black night descends on our country." In the capital on 27 April, a German officer, Georg von Stumme, addressed Greek archbishop Ieronymos: "He began by saying that he had always wanted to visit Athens, of which he had learnt so much at school and Military Academy. At this point the Archbishop interrupted him and said: 'Indeed, before the war Germany had many friends in Greece, among whom I was one.'" Now, all that was over. A Greek wrote: "Von Stumme learnt that in Greece he might meet a few Quislings, but he would not find any friends."

Three weeks later, on 20 May, the Germans launched a paratroop assault on Crete. British and New Zealand defenders along the island's north coast fought staunchly on the first day, inflicting savage losses on the airborne invaders. But on 21 May the Germans secured Máleme airfield, opening the way for follow-up forces. British counterattacks were frustrated, and in the succeeding six days the paratroopers progressively rolled up the defences, relieving their units isolated at Retimo and Heraklion. The British fell back. "Everyone was exhausted . . . and by this time morale was pretty low," said Ian Stewart, a battalion medical officer. "It cannot be said to have been a particularly restful trip . . . up the very high mountains, going mostly at night in a very slow tread and just the jingling of waterbottles and occasionally stumbling over people who had fallen out. Perhaps the most evocative thing was the dew on the flowers . . . the very aromatic scents of Crete are unforgettable." Another officer observed, "It was a journey that showed human nature at its Christian best but also at its ugly, selfish worst." Gen. Bernard Freyberg, the New Zealander commanding the defence, decided that evacuation was the only option. By the night of 30 May, when the Royal Navy was obliged to abandon its costly rescue efforts, 15,000 troops had been taken off; a further 11,370 became prisoners and 1,742 had been killed. A New Zealander heard the order given to those left behind to surrender. "Everything was dead quiet. You could have heard a pin drop. Every man was left to his own thoughts, that is if they could think. Now and again you would hear a shot ring out further down the waadi—some poor chap was taking his own life. Then later on I heard my first German's words: '*Alle man raus, schnell, schnell,*' and I looked up and saw him standing there, rifle at the ready. We were marched back to Canaea like a mob of sheep."

Crete cost Admiral Cunningham three cruisers and six destroyers sunk, and seventeen other ships damaged—the navy's heaviest losses of the war in a single operation. The Germans lost 6,000 killed highly-trained paratroopers, a price which dissuaded Hitler from ever again attempting a large-scale airborne operation. But the immediate outcome was that the invaders had defeated a larger Allied army, provided through Ultra intercepts with detailed foreknowledge of German intentions, plans and timetable.* Freyberg, as commander, bore substantial responsibility for failure, but he was handicapped by lack of transport to shift men, and a dire shortage of radios. Once the battle began, he had neither a clear idea of what was happening nor means to pass orders. The Luftwaffe exercised almost unchallenged command of the skies, taking a heavy toll on morale

---

* In this text, for convenience I have referred to all Axis decrypted messages as Ultra, although the Americans used the code-word Magic to denote Japanese traffic.

as well as men and ships. German energy, skill, tactics, determination and leadership at all levels surpassed those of most of the defenders, despite some fine local stands, especially by New Zealanders.

Hitler would have secured a much greater strategic gain by using his paratroops to seize Malta, as they could probably have done. The Germans profited little from accepting responsibility to sustain an occupation of Crete amid a bitterly hostile population. If Freyberg had held on, the Royal Navy would have faced immense difficulties in supplying the island in the face of enemy air superiority. Once Greece was lost, the outpost could have done the British little good. They lacked adequate aircraft to support the North African campaign, far less to exploit Crete as an air base for offensive operations, and were better without the place.

However, no such consolation was evident to the world and the British people in June 1941. A soldier at home, Len England, wrote on 29 May: "I think . . . the masses have *for the first time* considered the possibility of defeat. A general trend is this: 'Every time we meet the Germans we get driven back. We're even losing on the sea, and we're supposed to have command of that.' The infallibility of the Germans is an idea that is rapidly gaining ground." Churchill had boldly declared Britain's determination to hold Crete, yet its garrison had been defeated by smaller forces. Though the prime minister for years afterwards sustained his enthusiasm for resurrecting a Balkan front against Hitler and bringing Turkey into the war, this remained a fantasy. The Balkans were incorporated wholesale into the Axis empire, much to its own detriment. Italy initially accepted responsibility for occupying the region, committing half a million troops who would eventually suffer heavier losses there than in North Africa. The Germans, in their turn, came to find Greece and Yugoslavia a crushing burden. But all this was far away, in the bleak summer of 1941.

3. Sandstorms

THE BRITISH achieved two modest successes to set against their eviction from the Balkans. Though Iraq had become an independent state in 1932, the British retained treaty and basing privileges there, to protect their important oil interests. Since the outbreak of war, rival factions in Baghdad had contested power and disputed the merits of supporting the Axis. In April 1941 the pro-Nazi nationalist Rashid Ali became prime minister following a military coup. Impressed by Hitler's successes, and insufficiently mindful that Berlin was far away, he abrogated British military-movement rights and sent troops to besiege the RAF base at Habbaniya. Luftwaffe planes began to shuttle aid to the Baghdad government through

Syria. The Vichy French authorities in Damascus provided fighter escorts and some matériel to aid the Germans. Wavell, in Cairo, was reluctant to divert troops to Iraq, but Churchill insisted. An Indian Army relief column landed at Basra and drove inland, joined by 1,500 men of the Arab Legion from Transjordan. The Iraqi army offered only ineffectual resistance. Within a month Habbaniya was relieved and an armistice signed. A pro-British government was installed in Baghdad, which was eventually persuaded to declare war on the Axis.

Vichy's meddling in Iraq, and a growing German presence in Syria, convinced Churchill that Britain could not risk Nazi dominance of the Levant. He ordered Wavell to dispatch another force to occupy Syria, ruled by France since 1920 as a League of Nations "mandated territory" joined with Lebanon. Churchill and his commanders hoped that the defenders, outnumbered and outgunned, would offer only token resistance. Instead, however, in June 1941 Vichy forces fought hard. Their conduct highlighted the division and confusion of French loyalties, which had been apparent since the 1940 surrender and persisted until 1944. During the ill-fated British and Gaullist attempt on Vichy Dakar in September 1940, the submarine *Bévéziers* torpedoed the British battleship *Resolution*, which suffered serious damage. Churchill enraged the French by insisting on the award of a DSO to Commander Bobby Bristowe, who led a volunteer naval party in a launch alongside the brand-new Vichy battleship *Richelieu*, laying four depth charges below its hull. In retaliation for Dakar, Vichy aircraft bombed Gibraltar.

A farcical exchange took place when Hitler met Marshal Pétain at Montoire-sur-le-Loir on 24 October 1940. Germany's Führer said: "I am happy to shake the hand of a Frenchman who is not responsible for this war." His words were not translated, and Pétain supposed that he was being asked a polite question about his journey. He responded: *"Bien, bien, je vous remercie."* Even if the marshal did not intend to sound so slavish, his regime pursued policies and adopted a propaganda line strongly hostile to the British. Adm. René Godfroy, commanding a French squadron interned at Alexandria which resolutely resisted the Royal Navy's blandishments to join its struggle, wrote to the Mediterranean C-in-C on 26 June 1940: "For us Frenchmen the fact is that a government still exists in France, a government supported by a parliament established in non-occupied territory and which in consequence cannot be considered as irregular or deposed. The establishment elsewhere of another government, and all support for this other government, would clearly be rebellion."

Frenchmen everywhere took sides, displaying bitter animosity towards those who made a different choice. Aboard the French mine-laying submarine *Rubis* a vote was held in which all but two of its forty-four crew opted to fight alongside the British. By contrast, in November 1940, 1,700 French naval officers and men exercised the right to repatriation which the British conferred on them. Their new friends the Germans responded uncharitably, torpedoing off the French coast a hospital ship carrying them home under the red cross. Four hundred drowned, but a survivor, Cmdr. Paul Martin, wrote impenitently to a senior officer in Toulon: "Churchill's policy makes me fear for a demagogic disaster. Thinking Englishmen fear for the future, being carried away as they are by democracy, international financiers and Jews. It is undeniable that the French corrective to this is envied."

If this was an extreme view, French anti-Semitism ran deep. Vichy's bureaucracy and enforcement agencies seized Jews and bearers of Free France's symbolic Cross of Lorraine almost as readily as did the Germans. "My God, what is this country doing to me?" the Jewish writer Irène Némirovsky, who would later meet death in Auschwitz, wrote from her precarious French refuge in June 1941. "Since it is rejecting me, let us consider it coldly, let us watch as it loses its honour and its life." The Resistance until June 1944 engaged only a small minority of French people, and incurred the hostility of many more. After the liberation, service with de Gaulle became a badge of pride. Throughout the occupation, however, many French people treated his followers as troublemakers and traitors, and frequently betrayed them to the Vichy authorities or the Germans.

On 8 June 1941, Australian, British and Free French units advanced into Syria and Lebanon. British commandos landing on the coast met fierce resistance at the mouth of the Litani River, and suffered heavy casualties—forty-five dead, including its commanding officer, and seventy-five wounded. Two French heavy destroyers bombarded the British positions, then turned their fire on a British destroyer flotilla, of which one ship was badly damaged. Vichy bombers joined the attack on the warships, and their escorting fighters shot down three Hurricanes. A defiant French NCO prisoner told the war correspondent Alan Moorehead: "You thought we were yellow, didn't you? You thought we couldn't fight in France. You thought we were like the Italians. Well, we've shown you."

It demanded courage for a man to separate himself from his country, home and family, to accept the status of a renegade in the eyes of his own people, in order to serve in the ranks of Free France. But many Poles made such a choice. Why did the French instead oppose Allied forces fighting their conquerors and occupiers? There was deep bitterness about France's predicament, which demanded scapegoats. Many Frenchmen

considered their country betrayed by the British in June 1940, a sentiment intensified by the Royal Navy's destruction of French capital ships
at Mers-el-Kébir. There was self-hatred, which bred anger. Overlaid upon
centuries-old resentment of *perfide Albion*, there was now the fresh grievance that Churchill had fought on after Pétain succumbed. The German
occupiers of France were disliked, but so too were the British across the
Channel, especially by French professional soldiers, sailors and airmen.

"France does not want to be liberated," the former Vichy prime minister and prominent collaborator Pierre Laval told the *New York Times*. "She
wants to settle her fate herself in collaboration with Germany." Many
of his compatriots agreed: the Resistance became a significant force in
France only in 1944, and made a negligible military contribution by comparison with the partisans of Russia and Yugoslavia. Few French defenders
of Syria in 1941 found anything distasteful about killing British, Indian
and Australian invaders. British troops advancing into Syria found graffiti
on the wall of an abandoned fort: "Wait, dirty English bastards, until the
Germans come. We run away now, and so will you soon."

As the Allied forces advanced on Damascus, strafing Vichy fighters
badly wounded one column's senior Free French officer. On 16 June, Fleet
Air Arm Swordfish torpedo bombers sank the superdestroyer *Chevalier-
Paul* off Beirut, and a Vichy submarine was later torpedoed with the loss
of fifty-five lives. At Mezze on 19 June, strong Vichy counterattacks with
armoured support prompted the surrender of two Indian battalions and
a unit of the Royal Fusiliers. British gestures of chivalry and attempts to
parley were treated with contempt. A flight of Hurricanes sent to attack
a French airfield made their first low-level pass without firing when the
pilots glimpsed on the ground Vichy airmen entertaining girlfriends with
aperitifs beside their planes. In consequence, on a second pass heavy
ground fire damaged several Hurricanes including that of Roald Dahl,
later famous as a writer. The French brought in aircraft reinforcements
from their North African colonies. Among the Roman ruins of Palmyra,
a unit of the Foreign Legion halted a British thrust from the east for nine
days, though some Spanish legionnaires in the Vichy camp decided that
the ideological conflict was unacceptable, and surrendered without a fight.

By the time Vichy's high commissioner, Gen. Henri Dentz, bowed to
the inevitable and signed an armistice on 14 July after five weeks' fighting,
his own forces had suffered over a thousand killed. Allied casualties were
somewhat fewer, but the Australians lost 416 dead. Vichy hailed as heroic
the feats of Pierre le Gloan of the French air force, an ace who shot down
seven RAF aircraft during the campaign. There was intense British bitterness about the vigour of resistance, and the callousness and sometimes

brutality with which Allied prisoners were treated. Roald Dahl wrote later: "I for one have never forgiven the Vichy French for the unnecessary slaughter they caused."

Dentz, in a gesture of spite, shipped sixty-three British officer and NCO prisoners to Greece en route to POW camps in Germany, even while he was negotiating the armistice. Only British threats that he and his senior colleagues would be denied repatriation secured the captives' return. Thereafter, 32,032 Vichy and colonial troops chose to sail with their commanders to occupied France, while 5,668 accepted service with de Gaulle. Gen. Georges Catroux, condemned to death in absentia by the Pétain regime for his support of de Gaulle, became Free French plenipotentiary for the Levant. The Syrian people remained unenthusiastic about rule by Frenchmen of any hue, but the region was now safe from German dominance. Churchill's boldness, amid the caution of his generals, was vindicated, even if the clumsy management of the little campaign promoted scant confidence in British military competence.

The Syrian venture ended in a useful strategic success. The achievement of securing Britain's flank in the Middle East was more important than the loss of Crete. But across Europe, oppressed and threatened people struggled to find consolation amid so many conspicuous Allied defeats and failures. Mihail Sebastian wrote in Bucharest on 1 June 1941: "So long as Britain does not surrender, there is room for hope." But with Axis air power now dominant across most of the Mediterranean, the prestige of British arms lay low—and would fall lower yet.

ON 15 JUNE 1941 WAVELL, reinforced by a consignment of tanks dispatched at great risk from Britain through the Mediterranean, launched a new offensive, Operation Battleaxe. Within two days, this foundered after Rommel's 88mm guns inflicted heavy tank losses on the attackers. Failure cost the Middle East C-in-C his job. He was replaced by Gen. Sir Claude Auchinleck, who in turn appointed Alan Cunningham, victor in Abyssinia, to command the newly christened Eighth Army in the desert. To Churchill's frustration, there followed a five-month lull in big battlefield operations. The British Army engaged in only minor actions in North Africa and elsewhere, though much was made of the Australian defence of beleaguered Tobruk.

The next desert offensive, Crusader, was launched on 18 November. Cunningham's forces were much stronger than those of Rommel, who was slow to grasp the weight and identify the focus of the British assault. The Eighth Army swept forward to relieve Tobruk after heavy fighting.

Rommel's counterstrokes failed: he was obliged to withdraw, having suffered 38,000 Italian and German casualties to 18,000 British, and losing 300 tanks to Cunningham's 278. By the last days of 1941, the Axis army was back at El Agheila, some 500 miles from its farthest point of advance into Egypt. The British briefly supposed that they had turned the tide of the desert war; Churchill rejoiced in a rare success.

But most Axis soldiers saw their predicament as readily reversible. Lt. Pietro Ostellino wrote on 7 December: "I can only now take up this letter: before, the English wouldn't let me! We were surrounded for two and a half days by forces who were a hundred times superior, with artillery that really hammered us. But we held out until reinforcements arrived, then put the enemy to flight. We captured prisoners and armoured vehicles. Of course, we too suffered painful losses. Please don't worry if I don't write to you so often at the moment: the post can't operate every day."

The pattern of the desert war was established. The Germans held at least marginal air superiority, because most of the RAF's best aircraft remained in England, obliging its desert pilots to fight the Luftwaffe's Bf-109s with inferior Tomahawks, Kittyhawks and Hurricanes. The British also lagged behind their enemies in developing techniques of air-ground cooperation, using planes in a tactical role as artillery. They had numerical superiority of men and armour, but this advantage was nullified by weaknesses of command, tactics and equipment. German tanks were better. Mechanical failure imposed a battlefield toll even more serious than enemy action, and the British tank recovery and repair system was weak; petrol cans leaked; Cunningham's army did not match the Afrika Korps' skill in mixing panzers, antitank guns and infantry. Again and again, British armour exposed itself unsupported—and was destroyed: during Crusader, for instance, the 7th Armoured Brigade lost 113 of its 141 tanks.

"We can *learn* from the Germans," wrote the Australian John Butler during the siege of Tobruk. "Their battalions are a complete unit—with anti-tank guns, tanks, air force and field workshops and ack-ack defence and artillery—with us if we wanted support from the air force we must give 48 hours notice—a Gilbertian situation like writing a letter to the fire-brigade when one's home catches alight." The institutional weakness of the British Army produced commanders at every level who lacked energy, imagination and flexibility; most units deployed in the desert were poorly led and trained. "In 1941 and early 1942 the morale of the British Army . . . was very low," wrote one of its officers, Lt. Michael Kerr. "The standard of infantry training was really quite terrible. Soldiers were unable to understand what they were meant to be doing and what everything was about."

The scale of operations in North Africa was tiny by comparison with that of the war's decisive confrontation in Russia: at that period, the British seldom deployed more than six divisions against three German and five Italian formations. But the Eighth Army's doings commanded intense attention at home, because this was the only theatre in which Britain's soldiers were fighting Germans. Rommel achieved celebrity on both sides, admired for flair, boldness, and dashing personal leadership; less was known about his neglect of logistics, always a critical factor in North Africa. The British chose to regard the Afrika Korps' commander as a "good German," ignoring the fact that he remained an impassioned supporter of Hitler until it became plain that Germany was losing the war. The Allies usually enjoyed a notable intelligence advantage through their breaking of Axis codes, but in 1941–42 Rommel was uniquely well-informed about British operations, thanks to his interception of the daily reports of the U.S. military attaché in Cairo, Col. Bonner Fellers. Rommel referred affectionately to these signals as his "little Fellers," and they gave him an important edge until Fellers's recall to Washington in July 1942. The chief influence on the battlefield, however, remained the institutional superiority of the German army. This contributed more to Rommel's successes, and his own generalship rather less, than the contemporary British media acknowledged and modern legend sometimes suggests.

THERE WAS A PERCEIVED ROMANCE about combat in the vast spaces of Libya, with headlong advances and retreats. Much anecdotage, sometimes reported in the British press, noted the Afrika Korps' humane treatment of prisoners, and occasional truces between combatants for the recovery of wounded. "One enemy post was approached," wrote an Australian, Private Butler, during the siege of Tobruk, "just in the act of drawing the pin [on a grenade] when a voice was heard from a sangar, 'Stay Aussie—we have two wounded Diggers here' . . . The Aussies said the Germans had shot them and then went out at great personal risk, brought them in and dressed their wounds, gave them hot coffee and then sent for their medical assistance. Thank God there is chivalry." Likewise, a participant recorded a halt in fighting while both sides recovered their wounded: "Men of both armies stood up under an astonished sun. The absolute stillness almost tinkled with tension . . . It was the more incredible in contrast with the fury of the night . . . The truce was as if two armoured combatants had paused and raised their visors, and for a moment one had glimpsed the human faces behind the steel." After one failed German attack an Australian wrote: "We were sitting up on the parapet, waving and singing to them. There

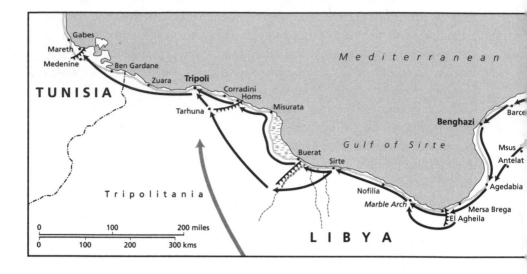

were shouts of 'Heil Hitler.' 'How would a pint of beer go, mate?' 'Have another go tonight,' and many other remarks not so complimentary."

As Sgt. Sam Bradshaw searched for the rest of his tank squadron during the shambles of Crusader, he glimpsed an enemy soldier limping beside the sandy track.

> I drew alongside and called out, "Are you Italian?" He replied, in very good English, "No, I'm not a bloody Italian, I'm a German," obviously annoyed at the suggestion. He was wounded, so I gave him a lift on the tank [and] a drink of water. He gave me a Capstan cigarette. "We got one of your supply columns," he said. We saw some German armoured cars about 1,000 yards away and he rolled off the tank and hobbled towards them. My gunner traversed on to him and I shouted on the intercom "Don't fire—let him go." He turned around and saluted and called out cheekily, "I'll see you in London." I called back, "Make it Berlin."

There were disadvantages, however, to this "civilised" approach to making war. Allied troops who regarded their tactical position as hopeless saw little risk and no shame in surrendering, rather than fight to the death or submit themselves to a waterless desert. British commanders, and their superiors in London, became increasingly dismayed by local capitulations and the allegedly excessive sporting spirit of the campaign.

The Eighth Army was comprised of a remarkable range of national

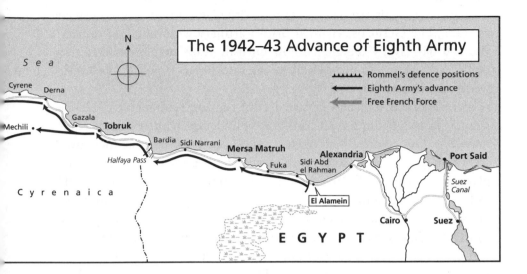

contingents. Its New Zealand division—later a corps—was recognised as outstanding, reflecting all its nation's virtues of resolution and self-reliance. Two Australian divisions were also highly rated, especially after the legend was established of the "Diggers'" stand at Tobruk. A German officer shouted indignantly at a prisoner: "You are an Australian and you come all the way over here to fight for the filthy, bloody English!" War correspondent Alan Moorehead wrote of "men from the dockside of Sydney and the sheep-stations of the Riverina [who] presented such a picture of downright toughness with their gaunt dirty faces, huge boots, revolvers stuffed in their pockets, gripping their rifles with huge, shapeless hands, shouting and grinning—always grinning." Notoriously ill-disciplined out of the line, and sometimes poorly officered, they deserved their formidable reputation, especially for night operations. "The Australians regarded themselves as the best fighters in the world," wrote a British officer. "They were." He added that their units were held together by "mateship," almost always a stronger motivation for successful soldiers than any abstract cause.

Opinions about the South African component of Auchinleck's army were more equivocal. On good days it was good, but on bad ones the division did not impress. The same might be said of Indian units: the Indian Army sometimes displayed remarkable courage and fighting skill, but its performance was uneven. The British justly esteemed the prowess of their beloved Gurkhas, but not every man or battalion excelled. For all its white officers' complacency about their men's loyalty to the king emperor, the

Indian Army was a force of mercenaries. Among the Eighth Army's British formations, the 7th Armoured Division—"the Desert Rats"—was deemed an elite. The Germans regarded British artillery with unfailing respect. But the old cavalry regiments, now uneasily translated from horses to tanks, were prone to displays of mindless courage which evoked their worst traditions.

An important difficulty persisted until the late summer of 1942: the Eighth Army's fighting men had little confidence in their higher commanders. The colonial contingents, especially, believed that their lives were being risked, and sometimes sacrificed, in pursuit of ill-conceived plans and purposes. There was bitter resentment about the huge "tail" of the army, indulging a privileged lifestyle in Egypt while fighting soldiers endured constant privation "up the desert." A British gunner wrote sourly: "I came to realise that, for every man sweating it out in the muck and dust of the Western Desert, there were twenty bludging and skiving in the wine bars and restaurants, night-clubs and brothels and sporting clubs and race-tracks of Cairo." Another cynical soldier wrote the song of this tribe:

> We never went west of Gezira,
> We never went north of the Nile,
> We never went past the Pyramids
> Out of sight of the Sphinx's smile.
> We fought the war in Shepheard's and the Continental Bar,
> We reserved our punch for the Turf Club lunch
> And they gave us the Africa Star.

Britain's prime minister shared that soldier's disgust. An elaborate support system was essential to sustain the Eighth Army in a country lacking its own industrial infrastructure. But Churchill fumed about the extravagant manpower committed to logistical and administrative rather than combat functions.

The men who fought the desert war suffered fewer hardships than those serving in Russia, Burma or the Pacific, but water shortages imposed chronic discomfort. "The flies plague us in millions from the first hour in the morning," wrote an Italian officer. "The sand always seems to be in our mouths, in our hair and in our clothes, and it is impossible to get cool." The armour officer Pietro Ostellino wrote in August: "Even the climate has begun to make us lose hope. All day we suffer an infernal heat while the shade is rendered useless by a constant suffocating wind. It seems as though the valley has become a furnace. After eight in the evening the wind drops, but . . . we suffocate." In their tanks, the temperature often rose above 110 degrees Fahrenheit. Opening hatches merely allowed sand and dust to swirl in.

British soldiers received a water ration of two pints a day, together with copious issues of tea brewed in old fuel tins on fires of mingled petrol and sand. They ate chiefly bully beef, biscuits and canned fruit. The Germans rejoiced in captures of the Eighth Army's rations, which they preferred to their own, especially the generous issues of cigarettes. "We . . . slowly make ourselves become Tommies," wrote Wolfgang Everth wryly during one of Rommel's advances. "Our vehicles, petrol, rations and clothing were all English. I . . . breakfasted off two tins of milk, a tin of pineapple, biscuits and Ceylon tea."

Men learned that the desert was perilously nuanced terrain on which to move and fight. "Smooth yellow sand, attractive to the uninitiated, was deadly," wrote a British officer. "Unless it was of short duration and taken at speed the truck would bog to the axles. Pebbly going was usually good, but sometimes it was a deceptive crust with soft sand underneath which only the experienced eye could detect at a distance. In some places the desert was smooth and firm as a race-track for miles on end and in every direction; in others it was treacherous as treacle." Both sides were sometimes confused by their enemies' use of captured transport. Again and again, British troops received unwelcome surprises from approaching British vehicles and even tanks which proved to be driven by Rommel's men. The Italian Bologna Division was panicked one day by the sight of a column of British trucks in their midst, until they discovered that it carried Germans.

Between offensives, there were long intervals of boredom, training and preparation. "The chief occupation of soldiers in wartime is hanging around doing nothing, though preferably purposefully," wrote a British soldier. Men dug incessantly, laid minefields, patrolled and conducted sniping duels. They suffered from desert sores, jaundice, dysentery. Both sides learned to curse *khamsins*, sandstorms that reduced vision to a few yards and drove yellow grit into every crevice of vehicles, equipment and human bodies. Italians called them *ghibli*. Pietro Ostellino wrote home: "You would think it impossible to take two and a half hours to cover the two hundred metres which separated the mess from my tent but that is the truth. I have never seen a night so dark: you stopped for a moment to clear your eyes and immediately lost your bearings. When finally I got to my tent I found everything under five centimetres of sand. At any moment, the canvas seemed likely to blow away."

Even during long lulls between battles there were few diversions save the arrival of mail, every soldier's obsession. Many men wrote home almost daily, because there was nothing else to do. The act of writing maintained a link with their other lives which became ever more precious as the passage of months extended into years. The Eighth Army's soldiers were granted occasional brief leaves in Cairo, a city they learned to hate. Olivia Manning, who later became famous as author of *The Balkan Trilogy*, arrived there as a refugee from Greece in April 1941: "The unreality had something to do with the light . . . It was too white. It flattened everything. It drained the colour out of everything. It lay on things like dust . . . we were shocked by the colourless summer delta. The squalor of the delta shocked us horribly—not only the squalor, the people's contentment with squalor. For weeks we lived in a state of recoil."

Having been abroad since 1939, Manning gazed curiously at the throng of British soldiers in the streets: "Sweat shining, hair bleached to sameness, the pink burn of English skin disguising differences; much of a size, not tall . . . Their worn, thin, washed-out khaki was wrinkled with heat. Dark patches of sweat showed between their shoulder blades and under their arms." Officers found consolations in the smart rendezvous of Egypt: "Groppi's at Cairo and Pastroudi's at Alexandria stay in the mind," wrote one. "There is a splendid decadence in having morning coffees and éclairs amid gilt mirrors and all the kitsch of afffuence." Other ranks, however, knew only Cairo's sordid bars and brothels, which inflicted alarming disease rates on the Eighth Army.

For Mussolini's soldiers, from the outset the North African campaign was a nightmare. The usual hazards of war were rendered almost unendurable by Italian shortages of food, ammunition, vehicles, medical supplies and belief in their cause. A transport driver, Vittorio Vallicella, kept a diary which is an unflagging tale of woe. The campaign was hopeless, he said, "not because of our incompetence or the enemy's courage, but because the other side was so much better organised." He added bitterly: "This is 'the war of the poor' wished upon us by the Fascist hierarchy, comfortably ensconced in Rome's Palazzo Venezia."

Vallicella claimed to have seen only one Italian ambulance in all his time in Africa; he complained bitterly of lack of leadership at every level, from supreme headquarters in Rome down to his own unit's officers: "How many times have we veterans saved their bacon. Our ally's divisions are much more aggressive, with vastly superior fire power and manoeuvrability, led by officers who really lead. Many of our own officers have been sent home wounded or sick." Italian soldiers resented the disparity between their own meagre rations—soup, bread, a little jam, the occasional lemon—and those of officers, who enjoyed wine and mess dinners with mineral water flown in from Italy. They cherished rare glimpses of home comforts, such as a visit from Red Cross girls bringing parcels sent by well-wishers in central Italy: "After nearly twenty months it is wonderful to see these lovely women bringing useful gifts."

Their best source of decent food, however, was the enemy: "For those lucky enough to return alive from a night patrol there was booty: jars of jam and fruit, packets of biscuits and tea, tins of corned beef, bottles of liqueurs, cigarettes, sugar, coffee, shirts, trousers, casual shoes, towels, lavatory paper, medicines like aspirin and quinine, condensed milk, jerseys made from real wool, compasses and every other kind of equipment under the sun. Such things never featured in our own supplies." When Vallicella caught malaria, he prayed that it might be something worse, to justify his repatriation to Italy—and was disappointed. Where most men thrilled to receive mail from home, he was dismayed to learn from his family letters that those at home knew little about "the hell we were in." He was rash enough to voice aloud the view that without armour and rations it was impossible to fight, which caused him to be threatened with a firing squad. Only the intervention of his colonel saved his life.

WAVELL BEGAN the Middle East war with 80,000 troops under his command. By the time Auchinleck, his successor, launched Operation Crusader in November 1941, he fielded 750,000, albeit most committed to garrison, logistical and support tasks across the theatre. After pushing Rommel back to El Agheila, the British anticipated a lull, and set about refitting their armoured units. But the Axis forces, having escaped destruction, regrouped with remarkable speed. When Pietro Ostellino emerged from the long and bloody Crusader mêlée, "I had the pleasant surprise of finding my kit, which I thought had fallen into English hands. It was aboard a truck which managed to escape the enemy encirclement. I finally got to sleep on my camp bed. I was in tatters after ten days without even washing my hands. I got rid of all the dirt as well as lice—some of these are still with me, but a little petrol should get rid of them. Clean, I feel a new man."

Most of the Axis army shared Ostellino's reinvigoration. On 21 January 1942, the British were rudely surprised when Rommel launched a new offensive, with devastating effect. Within three weeks he advanced almost 300 miles eastwards before familiar logistical problems obliged him to halt. Neil Ritchie, now the Eighth Army's commander, set about creating strong defensive positions—the so-called Gazala Line, based upon brigade "boxes" protected by mines and wire. He intended Rommel to dissipate his strength assaulting these, at which point he would commit British armour, as usual superior in numbers, to press his advantage.

This gambit failed miserably: Ritchie had failed to study his enemy's commitment to deep penetration and flanking operations. When Rommel attacked on 26 May, Ritchie's "boxes" proved too widely separated to provide mutual support. For some days a Free French brigade staunchly defended the southernmost, at Bir Hacheim, but was then forced to withdraw. German armour manoeuvred with its usual skill: "We could never fire more than a couple of shots at any one tank before it was hidden by dust and the Germans were keeping just outside our range," wrote a frustrated British tank officer. Then his squadron was ordered to charge. "Ten to one we don't make it," muttered a tank commander. He noted the look of disgust on his loader's face as the man thrust another round into the smoking breech—he had been married a few weeks before leaving England. "I felt sorry for him." Then they began to fire: "Driver left-halt. Two-pounder traverse right—steady, on. Three hundred, fire!" Within seconds of their own shot, in the words of the tank commander,

> there was a tremendous crash. I felt a sharp pain in my right leg, heard the operator groaning, and said, "Driver, advance." Nothing happened. The shell, an 88mm, had exploded in his stomach . . . At the time I realised only that the engine had stopped, the Tannoy internal communication set had broken down, air was escaping from the high pressure pipes and clouds of acrid smoke were coming up from inside. It all happened in a moment. Then we were out of the tank and running towards another one. It was our squadron leader, who had stopped to rescue us; my gunner was already on the tank, the operator had disappeared on another, but I could only hobble because my leg wobbled uncontrollably beneath my weight. I was terrified they would go without me. The Germans shelled me as I ran. The ground opened up at my feet and I staggered as the blast struck me, but I was not hurt. I hurled myself onto the tank, dizzy and exhausted as we moved off to safety. The gunner was beside me smiling cheerfully though his right arm was smashed to bits below the elbow. Bones gleamed white through the blood and his fingers dangled on shreds of skin. He was bleeding badly so we fixed up a tourniquet and I gave him my syringe of morphia. We talked about going home.

At a field hospital, he recovered consciousness after an operation to hear falling bombs and the terrific din of Tobruk's antiaircraft guns. "There were so many wounded that the floor was covered with patients on stretchers, the reek of anaesthetic filled the air and people were groaning or shouting in delirium as they died. The heat and stuffiness were quite appalling. My right leg was in plaster to the hip, the other was smothered in dried blood. There were no sheets and the blankets scratched."

Both sides suffered heavy tank losses in confused fighting around "the Cauldron" in the centre of the British line, but by 30 May the Germans had gained a decisive advantage. The British were forced into headlong retreat. A South African and Indian force was left to defend Tobruk, while the remainder of the Eighth Army fell back into Egypt. Rommel bypassed Tobruk, then on 20 June turned and assaulted its defences from the rear, where the line was weakest, and soon broke through. The South African commander, Maj. Gen. Hendrik Klopper, surrendered the next morning. By nightfall on 21 June, all resistance had ended. More than 30,000 prisoners fell into Axis hands. Only a few units made good their escape to rejoin the Eighth Army.

Vittorio Vallicella was among the first Axis troops to reach the port of Tobruk. "What a shock to find there hundreds of Senegalese [French colonial troops] who, at the sight of our little band, leap to their feet raising their hands in token of surrender," he wrote in his diary. "How extraordinary that they should do this to poorly armed men far fewer than themselves. With surprise but also respect, we gaze fascinated at these poor black soldiers who serve rich England, who have come from afar to take part in a war, when perhaps they don't even know for whom or for what they are fighting." Exploring the town, the Italians were astonished by the comfort of the English quarters, with their showers, every officer's bed with its mosquito net, and a surfeit of supplies. They delighted in the discovery of luxuries: tinned plums and boxes of what Vallicella at first took for dried grass. His sergeant explained that this was tea, a real treat. Some Arabs found plundering the dead were shot. Several men killed themselves by wandering into minefields. The Germans quickly placed guards on all the British food dumps, which the Italians interpreted as a slight on themselves: "Even here our allies want to lord it over us." For a brief period, victory at Tobruk raised Italian as well as German morale. "We hope this nightmare is at an end," wrote Vallicella. "We have only one thought: Alexandria, Cairo, the Nile, pyramids, palm trees and women."

During early-summer operations, the Germans had suffered just 3,360 casualties, the British 50,000—most of these taken prisoner. Much of Auchinleck's armoured force had been destroyed. Churchill, in Washington to meet Roosevelt, was shocked and humiliated. The end of June 1942 found the British occupying a line at El Alamein, back inside Egypt. One of Auchinleck's soldiers wrote: "The order came to us, 'Last round, last man.' This was chilling. It was curious to see that this legendary phrase of heroic finality could still be used. Presumably it was intended to instil a steely resolve . . . But being interpreted, it meant that there was no hope for Tobruk and that we were being left to our fate—the very reverse of morale building . . . We were a downcast, defeated lot." Britain's fortunes in the Middle East, and the global prestige of its army, had reached their lowest ebb. Churchill's attempt to exploit Africa as a battlefield against the Axis had thus far served only to make Rommel a hero, and grievously to injure the morale and self-respect of the British people at home. It was fortunate indeed that the desert was not the cockpit of the war; that events elsewhere, on the Russian steppe, had drastically diminished the significance of British failure.

CHAPTER SIX

BARBAROSSA

AT 3:15 A.M. BERLIN time on 22 June 1941, Russian border guards on the Bug River bridge at Kolden were summoned by their German counterparts "to discuss important matters," and machine-gunned as they approached. Wehrmacht sappers tore away charges laid on the railway bridge at Brest-Litovsk, then waved forward the assault units at 3:30 a.m. German special forces—"Brandenburgers," who included some Russian-speakers—had been parachuted or smuggled across the lines during the preceding days, and were already at work sabotaging communications behind the front. Some 3.6 million Axis troops began to advance into the Soviet Union on a 900-mile front from the Baltic to the Black Sea, smashing into the defences with devastating effect. A Russian, the poet David Samoilov, said later, "We were all expecting war. But we were not expecting *that* war." Divisions and soon whole armies dissolved in the Germans' path, so that collapses and surrenders characterised the first weeks of the Red Army's campaign. A Soviet officer wrote of an exchange with a comrade: "Kuznetsov informed me, with a tremble in his throat, that the only thing left of the 56th Rifle Div was its number." This was merely one among a thousand such disasters.

Hitler's invasion of the Soviet Union was the defining event of the war, just as the Holocaust was the defining act of Nazism. Germany embarked upon an attempt to fulfil the most ambitious objectives in its history, to push back the frontiers of Slavdom and create a new empire in the east. The Nazis argued that they were merely following the historic example set by other European nations in pursuing *Lebensraum*, living space, by seizing an empire in the territories of savages. The British historian Michael Howard has written: "Many, perhaps most Germans, and certainly most German intellectuals, saw the First World War as a battle for cultural survival against the converging forces of Russian barbarism and, far more subversive, the decadent civilisation of the West, embodied no longer by French aristocrats but by the materialist societies of the Anglo-Saxon world. This belief was taken over in its entirety by the Nazis and provided the bedrock of their own philosophy."

Millions of young Germans had been conditioned since childhood to believe that their nation faced an existential threat from the Soviet Union. "The situation is ideal for the Bolshevists to launch their attack on Europe in furtherance of their general plan for world domination," wrote an ardent Nazi Luftwaffe pilot, Heinz Knoke, in 1941. "Will Western capitalism, with its democratic institutions, enter into an alliance with Russian Bolshevism? If only we had a free hand in the west, we could inflict a shattering defeat on the Bolshevist hordes despite the Red Army. That would save Western civilisation." Imbued with such logic, Knoke was thrilled to find himself participating in the invasion of Russia. So were some more senior officers. Hans Jeschonnek, the Luftwaffe's chief of staff, was chastened by the 1940 failure against Britain, a campaign which he thought ill-suited to his force's capabilities. Now, he exulted, "at last, a proper war again!"

Eighteen-year-old Henry Metelmann, a Hamburg locksmith turned tank driver, wrote later: "I accepted as natural that it was a German duty for the good of humanity to impose our way of life on lower races and nations who, probably because of their limited intelligence, would not quite understand what we were on about." Like many young Germans at that stage of the war, he viewed his deployment to the east without trepidation. "Few of us realised the serious situation we were in. We looked on this journey, if not the whole war, as one great adventure, an opportunity to escape the boredom of Civvy Street, a lesser object being to fulfil a sacred duty to our Führer and Fatherland."

Much of Hitler's strategy, insofar as it was planned rather than the product of opportunism, derived from the knowledge that time favoured his enemies, empowering them to arm and coalesce against him. As part of Stalin's deterrent strategy, before Barbarossa the German military attaché in Moscow was allowed to visit some of the vast new arms factories under construction in Siberia. His reports, however, had the opposite effect to that which was intended. Hitler said to his generals: "Now you see how far these people have already got. We must strike at once." The destruction of Bolshevism and the enslavement of the Soviet Union's vast population were core objectives of Nazism, flagged in Hitler's speeches and writings since the 1920s. Overlaid on them was the desire to appropriate Russia's enormous natural resources.

Stalin probably intended to fight his menacing neighbour at some moment of his choosing. If Germany had become engaged in a protracted attritional struggle against the French and British on the Western Front in 1940, as Moscow hoped, the Russians might have fallen upon Hitler's rear, in return for major territorial concessions from the Allies. Stalin's generals prepared plans for an offensive against Germany—as they did also for many other contingencies—which could conceivably have been launched in 1942. As it was, however, in 1941 his armies were unfit to face the almost undivided attentions of the Wehrmacht. Though progressively mobilising—Russia's active forces doubled in size between 1939 and the German invasion—they had scarcely begun the reequipment programme that would later provide them with some of the best weapons systems in the world.

In Hitler's terms, this made Operation Barbarossa a rational act, enabling Germany to engage the Soviet Union while its own relative advantage was greatest. Hubris lay in its underestimation of the military and industrial capability Stalin had already achieved; reckless insouciance about Russia's almost limitless expanses; and grossly inadequate logistical support for a protracted campaign. Despite the expansion of the Wehrmacht since the previous year and the delivery of several hundred new tanks, many formations were dependent on weapons and vehicles taken from the Czechs in 1938–39 or captured from the French in 1940; only the armoured divisions were adequately provided with transport and equipment. It did not occur to Hitler, after his victories in the west, that it might be more difficult to overcome a brutalised society, inured to suffering, than democracies such as France and Britain, in which moderation and respect for human life were deemed virtues.

The senior officers of the Wehrmacht flattered themselves that they represented a cultured nation, yet they readily acquiesced in the barbarities designed into the Barbarossa plan. These included the starvation of at least 30 million Russians, in order that their food supplies might be diverted to Germany, originally a conception of Nazi agriculture chief Herbert Backe. At a meeting held on 2 May 1941 to discuss the occupation of the Soviet Union, the army's armament-planning secretariat recorded its commitment to a policy noteworthy even in the context of the Third Reich:

1   The war can only be continued, if the entire Wehrmacht is fed from Russia in the third year.
2   If we take what we need out of the country, there can be no doubt that many millions of people will die of starvation.

Barbarossa was therefore not merely a military operation, but also an economic programme expected to encompass the deaths of tens of millions of people, an objective which it partially attained. Some generals protested against orders requiring their men to participate in the systematic murder

of Soviet commissars, and rather more questioned Hitler's invasion strategy. Maj. Gen. Erich Marcks, the brilliant officer responsible for early
planning, proposed that the decisive thrust should be delivered north of
the Pripet Marshes, because Russian deployments anticipated an assault
farther south. Several commanders argued that a conquered population
which was treated mercifully would be more manageable than one which
gained nothing by accepting subjection. Such objections were framed in
pragmatic rather than moral terms; when Berlin rejected them, the critics
lapsed into acquiescence and faithfully executed Hitler's orders.

Industrialised savagery was inherent in Barbarossa. Göring told those
charged with administering the occupied territories: "God knows, you are
not sent out there to work for the welfare of the people in your charge,
but to get the utmost out of them, so that the German people can live."
Col. Gen. Erich Hoepner, the fifty-five-year-old cavalryman commanding Fourth Panzer Group, said: "The war with Russia is a vital part of the
German people's fight for existence. It is the old fight of German against
Slav, the defence of European culture against the Muscovite-Asiatic flood,
and the repulse of Jewish Bolshevism. This war must have as its goal the
destruction of today's Russia—and for this reason it must be conducted
with unprecedented harshness. Every clash, from conception to execution, must be guided by an iron determination to annihilate the enemy
completely and utterly." From June 1941 onwards, few German senior
officers could credibly deny complicity in the crimes of Nazism.

The Soviet Union on the eve of Hitler's invasion was the most rigorously regulated and policed society in the world. Its machinery of domestic repression was much more elaborate, and in 1941 had killed far more
people, than that of Nazism: 6 million peasants perished in the course
of Stalin's programme of enforced industrialisation, and vast numbers of
loyal comrades had fallen victim to his paranoia. Germans, other than
Jews, had greater personal freedom than did any Russian. Yet Stalin's tyranny was less adequately organised to defend itself against foreign enemies than against its own people. The Red Army's formations in the west
were poorly deployed, in a thin forward line. Many of its best commanders had been killed in the 1937–38 purges, and replaced by incompetent
lackeys. Communications were crippled by lack of radios and technical skills; most units lacked modern arms and equipment. No defensive
positions had been created, and Soviet doctrine addressed only offensive
operations. The dead hand of the party crippled efficiency, initiative and
tactical prudence.

Stalin dismissed many warnings from his own generals as well as from

London about the impending invasion. The 10 May parachute descent on Britain by Deputy Führer Rudolf Hess, in pursuit of a lone peace mission, increased Soviet fears of British duplicity, and suspicion that Churchill intended a bilateral deal with Hitler. Stalin also rejected explicit intelligence about Barbarossa from Soviet agents in Berlin and Tokyo, scrawling across one such report from Beria: "You can tell your 'source' from the German Air Headquarters that he can go and fuck his mother. This is not a source, but a disinformant. I.St." The Luftwaffe played its part in Berlin's deception operations by dispatching 500 bombers against London on 10 May, inflicting 3,000 casualties, days before most of its squadrons redeployed eastwards.

The huge troop movements preceding Barbarossa became the stuff of café gossip on the streets of Europe: the writer Mikhail Sebastian was telephoned by a friend in Bucharest on 19 June who said, "The war will begin tomorrow morning if it stops raining." Yet Stalin forbade every movement that might provoke Berlin, overruling repeated pleas from his commanders to alert the front. He ordered antiaircraft defences not to fire on Luftwaffe overflights of Soviet territory, of which ninety-one were reported in May and early June. Himself a warlord of icy purpose, Stalin was confounded by the apparent perversity of Hitler's behaviour. Under the terms of the Nazi-Soviet Pact, Germany was receiving enormous material aid from Russia: supply trains continued to roll west until the very moment of the invasion; the Luftwaffe's aircraft were largely fuelled by Soviet oil; the Kriegsmarine's U-boats had access to Russian port facilities. Britain remained undefeated. Stalin thus refused to believe that Hitler would precipitate a cataclysmic breach with him, and was personally responsible for the fact that the German onslaught, no surprise to his senior commanders, caught the defences unprepared. Georgy Zhukov, chief of the general staff, dispatched an alert order to all commands late on 21 June, but this reached them only an hour before the Germans attacked.

On the Western Front, some 2.5 million of Stalin's 4.7 million active soldiers were deployed—140 divisions and 40 brigades with more than 10,000 tanks and 8,000 aircraft. Hitler launched against them 3.6 million Axis troops, the largest invasion force in European history, with 3,600 tanks and 2,700 aircraft of superior quality to those of the Russians. Under the overall command of Field Marshal Walther von Brauschitsch, the Germans struck in three army groups. Hitler rejected the urgings of his best generals to make a single thrust towards Moscow, insisting upon a simultaneous drive into Ukraine, to secure its vast natural and industrial resources. This is sometimes described as a decisive strategic error.

It seems more plausible, however, to question whether Germany had the economic strength to fulfil Hitler's eastern ambitions, in whichever way these were addressed.

Many German people were shocked, indeed appalled, by news of the invasion. Goebbels wrote: "We must win and win quickly. The public mood is one of slight depression. The nation wants peace, though not at the price of defeat, but every new theatre of operations brings worry and concern." A young translator at the Soviet embassy in Berlin, Valentin Berezhkov, recorded a notable experience during his confinement with the rest of his delegation after the outbreak of war. He was befriended by a middle-aged SS officer named Heinemann, who took him out to a café for a drink, where they were embarrassed to be joined by six other SS men. Heinemann hastily covered himself by saying that his guest was a relation of his wife's, engaged in secret work that he could not discuss.

They talked about the war for a while, until the SS officers declared a toast "To our victory." Berezhkov raised his glass "to *our* victory" without attracting unwelcome attention. Heinemann was desperately anxious that his son, who had just joined the SS, should not perish in Russia, and was also short of cash to fund medical treatment for his wife. Berezhkov gave him a thousand marks from the embassy safe, knowing that the Russians would not be allowed to take large sums with them when they were repatriated. At their parting Heinemann, who helped to organise the mission's eventual evacuation in the exchange of Moscow and Berlin diplomats, gave the Russian a signed photo of himself, saying, "It may so happen that some time or other I'll have to refer to the service I rendered to the Soviet Embassy. I hope it won't be forgotten." The two never heard of each other again, but Berezhkov always wondered if the German, even though an SS officer, secretly apprehended his nation's defeat in Russia.

Such misgivings did not extend to most of Hitler's young soldiers, still flushed with the triumphs of 1940. "We were uncritically enthusiastic, proud to be alive in times we regarded as heroic," wrote twenty-one-year-old paratrooper Martin Poppel. He thrilled to the prospect of fighting in the east: "Our destination is Russia, our objective is war and victory . . . We're desperate to be involved in the great struggle . . . There's no country on earth that exerts such magnetic attraction on me as Bolshevist Russia." The Germans struck from East Prussia into Lithuania, from Poland towards Minsk and Kiev, from Hungary into Ukraine. Almost everywhere, they smashed contemptuously through Soviet formations, destroying planes wholesale on the ground—1,200 in the first twenty-four hours.

In the Baltic republics, the invaders were bewildered to be greeted as liberators, with offerings of flowers and food. During the preceding weeks, Beria's NKVD had made tens of thousands of arrests and consequently millions of enemies among Estonians, Latvians and Lithuanians. Retreating Russian troops faced harassment and sniper fire from local inhabitants. Many civilians fled into the wilds until Stalin's forces were expelled. "These days bogs and forests are more populated than farms and fields," wrote the Estonian Juhan Jaik. "The forests and bogs are our territory while the fields and farms are occupied by the enemy." He meant the Russians, and they were soon gone.

Latvians seized three towns from their Soviet occupiers before the Germans arrived; by the end of 1941 Estonian partisans claimed to have captured 26,000 Soviet troops. In Ukraine likewise, the Red Army suffered at the hands of local guerrillas as well as the Germans. A Ukrainian Polish teenager, Stefan Kurylak, was among a host of his countrymen who welcomed the expulsion of the Russians. One of their last acts in his riverside village was casually to hack down his best friend, Stasha, fifteen years old, who had incurred their suspicion. The Germans' arrival prompted widespread celebration among Ukrainians on both sides of the Soviet border. "As there seemed no doubt as to who the victors would be," wrote Kurylak, "our people . . . began to cooperate in every possible way with the German 'liberators' . . . Some . . . even raised right arms to them smartly in the Nazi salute."

In the first weeks of Barbarossa, the Wehrmacht achieved some of the greatest victories in the annals of war. Entire armies were enveloped and destroyed, notably at Bialystok-Minsk and Smolensk. Stalin's soldiers surrendered in tens and hundreds of thousands. Russian aircraft losses mounted daily. Twenty-year-old pilot Heinz Knoke, a dedicated Nazi, described the exhilaration of strafing: "I never shot as well as this before. My Ivans lie flat on the ground. One of them leaps to his feet and dashes into the trees. The remainder forget to get up again . . . Smiling faces all around when the pilots report. We have dreamed for a long time of doing something like this to the Bolshevists. Our feeling is not exactly one of hatred, so much as utter contempt. It is a genuine satisfaction for us to be able to trample the Bolshevists in the mud where they belong."

Ivan Konovalov, one of thousands of Stalin's pilots surprised by dive-bombers on his airfield, wrote: "All of a sudden there was an incredible roaring sound. Someone yelled 'Take cover!' and I dived under a wing of my plane. Everything was burning—a terrible, raging fire." Alexander Andrievich, a supply officer, came upon the remains of a Soviet unit shattered by air attack: "There were hundreds upon hundreds of dead . . . I saw one of our generals standing by a crossroads. He had come to review his troops and was wearing his best parade uniform. But his soldiers were fleeing in the opposite direction. He stood there forlorn and alone, while the troops flooded past. Behind him was an obelisk, marking the route of Napoleon's invasion in 1812." The deputy political officer of the 5/147th Rifles led his men into action shouting, "For the Motherland and Stalin!" and was among the first to fall.

In brilliant sunshine, German troops in shirtsleeves rode their tanks and trucks in triumphant dusty columns across hundreds of miles of plains, swamps, forests. "We were following Napoleon's invasion route," Maj. Gen. Hans von Griffenberg wrote later, "but we did not think that the lessons of the 1812 campaign applied to us. We were fighting with modern means of transport and communication—we thought that the vastness of Russia could be overcome by rail and motor engine, telegraph wire and radio. We had absolute faith in the infallibility of Blitzkrieg." A panzer gunner wrote to his father, a World War I veteran, in August 1941: "The pitiful hordes on the other side are nothing but felons who are driven by alcohol and the threat of pistols at their heads . . . a bunch of arseholes . . . Having encountered these Bolshevik hordes and seen how they live has made a lasting impression on me. Everyone, even the last doubter, knows today that the battle against these sub-humans, who've been whipped into frenzy by the Jews, was not only necessary but came in the nick of time. Our Führer has saved Europe from certain chaos." An artillery battery commander wrote on 8 July: "We launch wonderful attacks. There's only one country one's got to love because it is so marvellously beautiful—Germany. What in the world could compare with it?" This officer was killed soon afterwards, but his enthusiasm no doubt cheered his final days.

The advancing armies streamed through towns and cities reduced to flaming desolation either by German guns or by the retreating Soviets. Thousands of casualties overwhelmed Russian field hospitals, arriving in trucks or carts, "some even crawling on their hands and knees, covered in blood," in the words of medical orderly Vera Yukina. "We dressed their wounds, and surgeons removed shell fragments and bullets—and with little anaesthetic remaining, the operating theatre resounded to men's groans, cries and calls for help." After the first five days of war, 5,000 casualties were crammed into one Tarnopol hospital intended for 200. Along the length of the front, stricken soldiers for whom there were no beds lay in rows on bare earth outside medical tents. Columns of prisoners tramped in bewildered thousands towards improvised cages, their numbers astounding their captors—and the audience in the Kremlin's private cinema, when Stalin and his acolytes viewed captured German newsreels.

A twenty-one-year-old translator, Zarubina Zoya, wrote: "When the commentator announced the number of Soviet troops killed or captured there was an audible gasp in the room, and one army commander close to me gripped the seat in front of him, rigid with shock. Stalin sat in stunned silence. I will always remember what appeared next on the screen—a close-up of our soldiers' faces. They were just young kids, and they looked so helpless, so utterly lost."

The world watched the unfolding drama with fascination and profoundly confused sentiments. In America, the archisolationist Charles Lindbergh proclaimed: "I would a hundred times rather see my country ally herself with Britain, or even with Germany with all her faults, than the cruelty, the Godlessness and the barbarism that exist in Soviet Russia." Warwickshire housewife Clara Milburn found herself prey to bewilderment, writing on 22 June: "So now Russia will get a bit of what she gave Finland—and perhaps a lot more. Mr. Churchill broadcast tonight and said we must stand by Russia. I suppose we must, as she is now against the enemy of mankind. But I wish we need not when I think of her ways, which are not our ways." On 1 July a Bucharest streetcar driver, seeing Mihail Sebastian with a newspaper in his hand, asked about the German advance. "Have they entered Moscow?" "Not yet. But they will for sure—today or tomorrow." "Well, let them. Then we can make mincemeat of the yids."

Euphoria overtook Berlin. Halder, the Wehrmacht's chief of staff, declared on 3 July: "I think I am not exaggerating when I say that the campaign . . . has been won in fourteen days"; Hitler spoke of a victory parade in Moscow by the end of August. Former doubters in high places felt themselves confounded by Soviet command incompetence, the ease with which thousands of Russian aircraft had been destroyed, the effortless tactical superiority of the invaders. At the front Karl Fuchs, a tank gunner, exulted: "The war against these subhuman beings is almost over . . . We really let them have it! They are scoundrels, the mere scum of the earth—and they are no match for the German soldier." By 9 July Army Group Centre had completed the isolation of huge Soviet forces in Belorussia, which lost 300,000 prisoners and 2,500 tanks. Russian counterattacks delayed the capture of Smolensk until early August—a setback that afterwards proved significant, because it cost the Wehrmacht precious summer days—and the Red Army sustained strong resistance in the south. But when the forces of Bock and Rundstedt met at Lokhvitsa, east of Kiev, on 15 September, two entire Russian armies were trapped and destroyed, with the loss of half a million men. Leningrad was besieged, Moscow threatened.

The ruthlessness of the invaders was swiftly revealed. In France in 1940, more than a million French prisoners were caged and fed; in Russia, by contrast, prisoners were caged only to perish. First in hundreds of thousands, soon in millions, they starved to death in accordance with their captors' design, and inability to cope with such numbers even had they wished to do so—the Reich's camps had capacity for only 790,000. Some prisoners resorted to cannibalism. Many German units killed POWs merely to escape the inconvenience of supervising their more protracted end. Gen. Joachim Lemelsen protested to the high command: "I am repeatedly finding out about the shooting of prisoners, defectors or deserters, carried out in an irresponsible, senseless and criminal manner. This is murder. Soon the Russians will get to hear about the countless corpses lying along the routes taken by our soldiers, without weapons and with hands raised, dispatched at close range by shots to the head. The result will be that the enemy will hide in the woods and fields and continue to fight—and we shall lose countless comrades."

Berlin was indifferent. Hitler sought to conquer as much land, and to inherit as few people, as his armies could contrive. He often cited the precedent of the nineteenth-century American frontier, where the native inhabitants were almost extinguished to make way for settlers. On 25 June Police General Walter Stahlecker led Einsatzgruppe A into the Lithuanian city of Kaunas behind the panzers. A thousand Jews were rounded up and clubbed to death by Lithuanian collaborators at the Lietukis garage, less than 200 yards from army headquarters. Stahlecker reported: "These self-cleansing operations went smoothly because the army authorities, who had been informed beforehand, showed understanding for this procedure."

The Soviets, for their part, shot many POWs as well as their own political prisoners; when their retreating forces abandoned a hospital where 160 German wounded were held, these were killed either by smashing in their heads or throwing them from windows. A German platoon which surrendered after a Soviet counterattack on the Dubyssa River on 23 June was found next day when the Russians were again driven back. They were not only dead, but mutilated. "Eyes had been put out, genitals cut off and other cruelties inflicted," wrote a shocked German staff officer. "This was our first such experience, but not the last. On the evening [after] these first two days I said to my general, 'Sir, this will be a very different war from the one in Poland and France.'" Whether or not the Germans' atrocity story was true, a culture of massacre would characterise the eastern struggle.

Stalin delegated to Molotov, who strove to overcome his stutter, the task of informing the Russian people that they were at war, in a national broadcast at 12:15 p.m. on 22 June. In the days that followed, the Soviet warlord met repeatedly with his key commanders—there were twenty-nine sessions on the day of the invasion—and made some critical decisions, notably for an evacuation eastwards of industrial plant. The NKVD embarked on wholesale executions and deportations of "unreliable elements," which included many people who merely bore German names. All privately owned radios were confiscated, so that Russians became dependent on broadcast news relayed into factories and offices "at strictly determined times." For some days, Stalin clung to an absurd, self-justificatory flicker of hope that the invasion represented a misunderstanding; there is fragmentary evidence that NKVD agents in neutral countries sought to explore with German interlocutors the possibility of further negotiations, which were spurned.

By 28 June, when Minsk fell, such fantasies were dispelled. Stalin suffered a collapse of nerve which caused him to retreat to his dacha outside Moscow. When a Kremlin delegation headed by Anastas Mikoyan visited him on 30 June, he greeted them with obvious unease, asking sullenly, "Why have you come?" He appears to have anticipated his own overthrow by the minions whom his vast misjudgement had betrayed. Instead, those irredeemably cowed and subservient men besought their ruler to lead them. This, at last, Stalin roused himself to do; on 3 July, he broadcast to the Russian people. In a notable break with the uncompromising authoritarianism that defined his rule, he began with an emotional appeal: "Comrades! Brothers and sisters! Fighters of our army and fleet! I address you, my friends!" He called for a "Patriotic War," the preemptive destruction of everything useful in the enemy's path, and partisan warfare behind the front. Implicitly recognising the British as allies, without irony he declared the war to be part of "a united front of peoples standing for freedom." Then he threw himself into personal direction of every detail of the Soviet Union's defence as chairman of the Stavka, the State Committee for Defence, the People's Commissariat for Defence and the Transport Commission. On 8 August, he also appointed himself supreme commander of the Red Army.

Stalin would ultimately prove the most successful warlord of the conflict, yet no more than Hitler, Churchill or Roosevelt was he qualified to direct vast military operations. Ignorant of the concept of defence in depth, he rejected strategic retreat. His insistence that ground should be held to the last, even when armies faced encirclement, precipitated their destruction. Following the early battles, thousands of officers and men deemed guilty of incompetence or cowardice were shot, including Western Front commander Dmitry Pavlov. Stalin responded to reports of mass surrenders and desertions with draconian sanctions. His Order No. 270 of 16 August 1941 called for the execution of "malicious deserters," and the arrest of their families: "Those falling into encirclements are to fight to the last . . . Those who prefer to surrender are to be destroyed by all available means." Order No. 270 was read aloud by commissars at thousands of soldiers' assemblies.

In the course of the war, 168,000 Soviet citizens were formally sentenced to death and executed for alleged cowardice or desertion; many more were shot out of hand, without a pretence of due process. A total of around 300,000 Russian soldiers are believed to have been killed by their own commanders—more than the entire toll of British troops who perished at enemy hands in the course of the war. Even Russians who escaped from captivity and returned to the Soviet lines were seized by the NKVD and dispatched to Siberia or to staff battalions—suicide units—which became institutionalised a few months later, in the proportion of one to each Soviet army—the equivalent of a Western Allied corps. As Hitler's spearheads approached Moscow, more than 47,000 suspected deserters were detained in the city; hundreds of people were executed for alleged espionage, desertion or "fascist agitation." Political officers at every level were granted powers matching those of operational commanders, a grievous impediment to decision making on the battlefield. Stalin sought to manage personally the movements not merely of armies, but of single divisions.

The German invasion prompted a modest surge of popular enthusiasm for Mother Russia: some 3,500 Muscovites volunteered for military service within thirty-six hours, as did 7,200 men in Kursk Province in the first month. But many Russians were merely appalled by their nation's predicament. The NKVD reported a Moscow legal adviser named Izraelit saying that the government had "missed the German offensive on the first day of the war, and this led to the subsequent destruction and colossal losses of aircraft and personnel. The partisan movement which Stalin called for—that's a completely ineffective form of warfare. It is a gust of despair. As for hoping for help from Britain and the United States, that's mad. The USSR is in a ring, and we can't see a way out."

Correspondent Vasily Grossman described an encounter with a cluster of peasants behind the front: "They are crying. Whether they are riding somewhere, or standing by their fences, they begin to cry as soon as they begin to speak, and one feels an involuntary desire to cry too. There's so much grief! . . . An old woman thought she might see her son in the column that was trudging through the dust. She stood there until evening and then came to us. 'Soldiers, take some cucumbers, eat, you are welcome.' 'Soldiers, drink this milk.' 'Soldiers, apples.' 'Soldiers, curds.' 'Soldiers, please take this.' And they cry (these women), they cry, looking at the men marching past them." Yevgeni Anufriev was one of a host of messengers delivering call-up orders to the homes of reservists: "We were surprised how many of the recipients tried to hide so that they wouldn't have to accept the papers. There was no enthusiasm for the war at that stage."

The overwhelming majority of the Red Army's soldiers were conscripts, no more eager for martyrdom than their British or American counterparts. Some arrived drunk at mobilisation centres, after long trudges from their villages. Soviet educational standards had risen since the revolution, but many recruits were illiterate. The best human material was drafted to units of the NKVD, directed by Lavrenty Beria, which eventually grew into an elite enforcement arm 600,000 strong. Men from Ukraine, Belorussia and the Baltic republics were deemed too politically unreliable to serve in tank crews. As a consequence of Stalin's purges the Red Army suffered a critical lack of competent officers and NCOs.

Infantrymen in the first months of war were taught only how to march, wearing *portyanki*—foot cloths—to compensate for the shortage of boots; to take cover on command; to dig; and to perform simple drills with wooden rifles. There were insufficient weapons, no barracks or transport. Each man learned to cherish a spoon as his most useful possession— veterans said they might throw away their rifles, but never the spoons tucked into their boots. Only officers had watches. In the desperate days of 1941, many recruits were herded into action within a week or two of being drafted. A regimental commissar named Nikolai Moskvin wrote despairingly in his diary on 23 July: "What am I to say to the boys? We keep retreating. How can I get their approval? How? Am I to say that comrade Stalin is with us? That Napoleon was ruined and that Hitler and his generals will find their graves with us?"

Moskvin did his best in a harangue to his unit, but next day acknowledged its failure: thirteen men had deserted during the night. A Jewish refugee, Gabriel Temkin, watched Russian troops advancing to the front near Bialystok, "some in trucks, many on foot, their outdated rifles hanging loosely over their shoulders. Their uniforms worn out, covered with dust, not a smile on their mostly despondent, emaciated faces with sunken cheeks." Self-inflicted wounds were commonplace. When a war correspondent sought to flatter a Soviet commander by asserting that casualties looked astonishingly cheerful as they arrived at hospitals from the battlefield, the general responded cynically, "Especially those wounded in the left hand." Self-mutilation declined sharply after suspects began to be shot. Beyond sanctions for failure, on 1 September the Stavka introduced the only comfort ever provided to its soldiers: the legendary "hundred grams" or "product 61," a daily allowance of vodka. This proved important in sustaining men's will to resist, but reinforced the Red Army's pervasive, self-immolatory culture of drunkenness.

A critical strand in the Soviet Union's response to Barbarossa was a commitment to the doctrine of total mobilisation, first articulated by Mikhail Frunze, the brilliant war minister under Lenin. Michael Howard has observed that, while the Russians suffered a stunning tactical surprise in June 1941, strategically and psychologically they had been preparing themselves since 1917 to fight a big war against Western capitalism. It is hard to exaggerate the magnitude of the eastward evacuation of key factories and workers, the fortitude of those who carried it out, and the importance of its success. Russia's industrial migration eventually embraced 1,523 undertakings, including 1,360 major plants. Fifteen percent were transferred to the Volga, 44 percent to the Urals, 21 percent to Siberia and 20 percent to Soviet Central Asia, in 1.5 million railway wagon loads. Some 16.5 million workers embarked on new lives in conditions of appalling privation, labouring eleven hours a day, six days a week, initially often under open skies. It is hard to imagine that British or American workers could have established and operated production lines under such handicaps.

Stalin could justly claim that his enforced industrialisation of the Soviet Union in the 1930s, at the cost of imposing misery and death on millions of dispossessed peasants, alone made it possible for the country now to build the tanks and planes needed to resist Hitler. His prioritisation of heavy industries capable of undertaking weapons manufacture reflected his acceptance of Frunze's total war concept. An American diplomat evacuated to Kuibyshev on the Volga was one day astonished to find himself in the midst of a vast, unidentified industrial area a few miles from the city, which the Russians had ironically christened Bezymyanny—"Nameless." On a nearby airfield stood hundreds of newly completed aircraft, produced in its plants. The 1941 industrial evacuation proved one of the crucial achievements of Russia's war. Every Soviet citizen over fourteen was declared eligible for mobilisation for industrial labour. With civilian rations cut to starvation levels, only the produce of private vegetable gardens enabled millions to survive. The nation was officially informed that squirrel meat contained more calories than pork, and those who could catch such prey ate it.

Though astonishing industrial output was achieved amid chronic hunger, it would be mistaken to idealise this: production of a Soviet aero

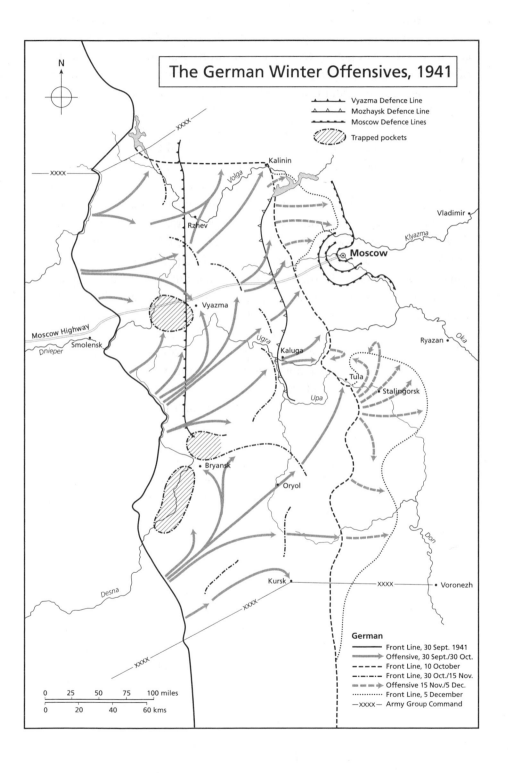

N

The German Winter Offensives, 1941

⊥▲⊥▲⊥ Vyazma Defence Line
⊥▲⊥▲⊥ Mozhaysk Defence Line
⊥▪⊥▪⊥ Moscow Defence Lines
◌ Trapped pockets

XXXX

XXXX

Volga

Kalinin

Vladimir •

Rzhev

Klyazma

Moscow

Moscow Highway

Vyazma

Smolensk

Dnieper

Ugra

Kaluga

Ryazan •

Oka

Upa

Tula •

Stalingorsk •

Bryansk •

Oryol •

Don

Desna

Kursk •

XXXX • Voronezh

XXXX

XXXX

German

━━━ Front Line, 30 Sept. 1941
━━➤ Offensive, 30 Sept./30 Oct.
╌╌╌ Front Line, 10 October
╍╸╍╸ Front Line, 30 Oct./15 Nov.
╍╍➤ Offensive 15 Nov./5 Dec.
·········· Front Line, 5 December
—XXXX— Army Group Command

0   25   50   75   100 miles
0   20   40   60 kms

engine required five times as many man hours as its U.S. counterpart. Yet the evacuation represented part of what a British intelligence officer once called "the Russian genius for piecemeal improvisation." Another feature of total war was the wholesale deportation of minorities whose loyalty was deemed suspect. Stalin accepted the drain on vital transport resources needed to remove—for instance—74,225 "Volga Germans" from their own little republic to remote Kazakhstan. Later, they would be followed by many more such outcasts, notably Chechens and Crimean Tatars.

In western Russia, the invaders' juggernaut still rolled forward, sustaining complacency in Berlin. Hitler busied himself with detailed planning for his new empire. He decreed the permanence of occupation, guided by three principles: "first to rule, second to administer, third to exploit"; all dissent was to be rewarded by death. As early as 31 July, Göring ordered preparations for a "total solution to the Jewish question in the German sphere of influence in Europe." Tens of thousands of Russian Jews were slaughtered where they were found by the Einsatzgruppen killing squads which followed the Wehrmacht's spearheads. Nazi officials began drafting plans for a transfer east of 30 million Germanic colonists. Hundreds of thousands of young women were shipped to the Reich from Ukraine and the Baltic states to become domestic servants and farm labourers. Some went not unwillingly: amid the ruin of their own shattered homes and communities, they faced destitution. On 19 August, in his diary Goebbels expressed surprise that Hitler thought the war might end soon and suddenly: "The Führer believes a moment may come when Stalin will sue for peace . . . I asked him what he would do if that happened. The Führer replied that he would agree to peace. What then happened to Bolshevism would not matter to us. Bolshevism without the Red Army does not represent a threat."

SINCE THE 1917 REVOLUTION, the population of the Soviet Union had endured the horrors of civil war, famine, oppression, enforced migration and summary injustice. But Barbarossa transcended them all in the absolute human catastrophe that unfolded in its wake, and eventually became responsible for the deaths of 27 million of Stalin's people, of whom 16 million were civilians. A soldier named Vasilii Slesarev received a letter, carried to the Soviet lines by partisans, from his twelve-year-old daughter, Manya, in their home village near Smolensk: "Papa, our Valik died and is in the graveyard . . . Papa, the German monsters set fire to us." The family home was burnt, and Slesarev's son Valerii died of pneumonia while hiding from the invaders. Manya continued: "Many people have been killed in the villages round here. And all they think about is the blood-thirsty monsters, you can't even call them humans, they're just robbers and drinkers of blood. Papa, kill the enemy!" If such missives were cynically exploited by the Soviet propaganda machine, they reflected real circumstances and genuine sentiments in thousands of communities across vast expanses of Russia.

Sgt. Victor Kononov wrote to his family on 30 November, describing his experiences after being taken prisoner by the Germans: "The fascists drove us on foot to the rear for six days during which they gave us neither water nor bread . . . After these six days we escaped. We saw so much . . . The Germans were robbing our collective farmers, taking their bread, potatoes, geese, pigs, cattle and even their rags. We saw farmers hanging on gallows, corpses of partisans who had been tortured and shot . . . The Germans fear every bush, every little noise. In every collective farmer, old or young, they see a partisan."

The partisan movement, sustaining armed resistance behind the German lines, began in June 1941 and became one of the most notable features of Russia's war. By the end of September the NKVD claimed that 30,000 guerrilla fighters were operating in Ukraine alone. It was impossible for the invaders to secure the huge wildernesses behind the front. But bands of desperate men, conducting a campaign dependent on starving civilians for food, were by no means acclaimed by them as heroes. One of their commissars, Nikolai Moskvin, wrote: "It's not surprising that local people run off and complain to the Germans. A lot of the time we're just robbing them like bandits." Later in the campaign he added an emotional postscript: "I am writing for posterity that partisans undergo inhuman sufferings." So did civilians. The struggle for survival, in a universe in which the occupiers controlled most of the food, caused many women to sell their bodies to Germans, and many men to enlist as auxiliaries of the Wehrmacht—"Hiwis," as they became known: 215,000 Soviet citizens died wearing German uniforms. But partisan operations achieved a strategic importance in Russia, harassing the German rear and disrupting lines of communication to a degree unmatched anywhere else in the Nazi empire save Yugoslavia.

Moreover, for all the Wehrmacht's dramatic successes and advances, the Red Army remained unbroken. If many of Stalin's soldiers readily surrendered, others fought on, even in hopeless circumstances. They astonished the Germans by their weeklong defence of the frontier fortress of Brest in June; a divisional report asserted that its attackers were obliged to overcome "a courageous garrison that cost us a lot of blood . . . The Russians fought with exceptional stubbornness . . . They displayed superb infantry training and a splendid will to resist." The Soviets had some good heavy tanks. As Hitler's commanders smashed one Soviet army, they were bemused to find another taking its place. On 8 July German intelligence reported that, out of 164 Soviet formations identified at the front, 89 had been destroyed. Yet by 11 August the mood of Halder in Berlin was much sobered: "It is increasingly clear that we underestimated the Russian colossus . . . We believed that the enemy had about 200 divisions. Now we are counting 360. These forces are not always well-armed and equipped and they are often poorly led. But they are there."

Helmuth von Moltke, an anti-Nazi working in the German Abwehr, wrote to his wife, expressing regret that he had been foolish enough "in my heart of hearts" to approve the invasion. Like many of his fellow aristocrats in France and Britain, his loathing for communism had exceeded his antipathy to Hitler: "I believed that Russia would collapse from within and that we could then create an order in that region which would present no danger to us. But nothing of this is to be noticed: far behind the front Russian soldiers are fighting on, and so are peasants and workers; it is exactly as in China. We have touched something terrible and it will cost many victims." He added a week later: "One thing seems certain to me in any case: between now and 1st April next year more people will perish miserably between the Urals and Portugal than ever before in the history of the world. And this seed will sprout. Who sows the wind reaps the whirlwind, but after such a wind as this what will the whirlwind be like?"

Initial bewilderment among the Russian people following the invasion was rapidly supplanted by hatred for the invaders. A Soviet fighter landed back at its field with human flesh adhering to its radiator grille, after a German ammunition truck exploded beneath it. The squadron commander curiously picked off fragments, and summoned the unit doctor to examine them. He pronounced: "Aryan meat!" A war correspondent wrote in his diary: "Everyone laughs. Yes, a pitiless time—a time of iron—has come!"

Hitler repeatedly switched objectives: at his personal insistence, in July Army Group Centre, driving for Moscow, halted in the face of strong Russian resistance. This enabled German forces farther north to push forward to Leningrad, while those in the south thrust onwards across Ukraine. At Kiev, they achieved another spectacular encirclement, and the spirits of the victorious panzer crews rose again. "I felt an incredible sense of triumph," wrote Hans-Erdmann Schonbeck. Once more, vast columns of dejected prisoners, 665,000 of them, tramped westwards towards cages in which they starved. In a hostel at Orel, 300 miles south of Moscow, on 2 October Vasily Grossman and some correspondent colleagues came upon a school map of Europe: "We go to look at it. We are terrified at how far we have retreated." Two days later, he described a scene on the battlefield:

> I thought I'd seen retreat, but I've never seen anything like what I'm seeing now . . . Exodus! Biblical exodus! Vehicles are moving in eight columns, there's the violent roaring of dozens of trucks trying simultaneously to tear their wheels out of the mud. Huge herds of sheep and cows are driven through the fields. They are followed by trains of horse-drawn carts, there are thousands of wagons covered with coloured sackcloth, veneer, tin . . . there are also crowds of pedestrians with sacks, bundles, suitcases. This isn't a flood, this isn't a river, it's the slow movement of a flowing ocean . . . hundreds of metres wide.

The rout described by Grossman was a consequence of the success of the German southern thrust. Meanwhile in the north, Leningrad was encircled and besieged. Russian morale was at its lowest ebb, organisation and leadership pitifully weak. Operations were chronically handicapped by the paucity of radios and telephone links. The Red Army had lost nearly 3 million men—44,000 a day—many of them in the great encirclements at Kiev and Vyaz'ma. Stalin started the war with almost 5 million soldiers under arms; now, this number was temporarily reduced to 2.3 million. By October 90 million people, 45 percent of Russia's prewar population, inhabited territory controlled by the Germans; two-thirds of the country's prewar manufacturing plant had been overrun.

Foreign observers in Moscow, especially the British, assumed the inevitability of Russian defeat, and merely sought to predict the duration of residual resistance. But on the battlefield, Stalin's soldiers fought doggedly on. They were half starved, short of ammunition, sometimes deployed without arms and dependent on seizing those of the dead. Even Molotov cocktails, the most primitive of antitank weapons, were in short supply until factory women began filling 120,000 a day. The Russians lost twenty casualties for every German, six tanks for every panzer; in October their losses were even worse than those of the summer, with sixty-four divisions written off. But other formations survived, and clung to their positions. On the southern front a Captain Kozlov, the Jewish commander of a Soviet motorised rifle battalion, said to Vasily Grossman: "I have told myself that I will be killed whatever happens, today or tomorrow. And once I realised this, it became so easy for me to live, so simple, and even somehow so clear and pure. I go into battle without any fear, because I have no expectations." Kozlov may even have been telling the truth.

· · ·

RUSSIA WAS SAVED from absolute defeat chiefly by the size of the country and of its armies. The Germans seized great tracts of territory, but larger ones remained; the 900-mile initial front broadened to 1,400 miles when the invaders reached the Leningrad–Odessa line. They destroyed hundreds of Soviet divisions, yet there were always more. Moscow was shocked by the readiness of its units to surrender, and of subject populations—notably in Ukraine and the Baltic republics—to embrace the Germans. But the dogged animal stubbornness of some Red Army soldiers, which had initially bewildered the Germans, now began to alarm them; every Russian who died cost the Wehrmacht effort, ammunition and precious time to kill. Hitler's young crusaders found it intoxicating to ride their bucketing tanks across hundreds of miles of enemy territory, but the strain on machinery was relentless; as men grew tired, so too did their vehicles: tracks wore out, cables frayed, springs broke. The strength of many formations was badly reduced: by autumn, 20 percent of the original invasion force was gone, and two-thirds of its armour and vehicles; only thirty-eight tanks remained in one panzer formation, and barely sixty in another. A division commander wrote of the importance of reducing losses "if we do not intend to win ourselves to death."

By September, Moscow was tantalisingly close. But if Russian counter-attacks were clumsy, as at Smolensk between 30 August and 8 September, they remained amazingly persistent. Between June 1941 and May 1944, each month Germany suffered an average of 60,000 men killed in the east; though the enemy's losses were far greater, this was a shocking statistic. One of its symbolic components was Lt. Walter Rubarth, killed on 26 October fighting for the Minsk–Moscow road; this was the man who, as a sergeant seventeen months earlier, led the triumphant German crossing of the Meuse. A worm of apprehension gnawed at his comrades: "Perhaps it is only 'talk' that the enemy is broken and will never rise again," wrote Hans-Jürgen Hartmann. "I cannot help myself—I am totally bewildered. Will the whole war still be over before winter?"

Yet Hitler's confidence was unimpaired. With Leningrad encircled and his armies triumphant in Ukraine, he had secured his flanks and was ready to resume the assault on Moscow. In an address on 2 October, he described the Wehrmacht's drive on the capital as "the last large-scale decisive battle of this year," which would "shatter the USSR." Helmuth von Moltke of the Abwehr wrote: "If we don't succeed this month we'll never succeed." But it was perilously late in the season. The price of Germany's advances elsewhere was that the Russians were granted time to strengthen their line before Moscow. Zhukov, Stalin's ablest commander, had been sacked as chief of the General Staff on 29 July for insisting upon the evacuation of Kiev; he then became commander of the Reserve Front, in which role he quickly made himself indispensable, and secured credit for organising the defence of Leningrad. Now, he was recalled to direct the salvation of the capital.

Six German armies—1.9 million men, 14,000 guns, 1,000 tanks and 1,390 aircraft—participated in Hitler's Operation Typhoon, the "decisive" assault on Moscow. Once more they swept forward, and once more the Russians suffered vast losses: eight Soviet armies reeled in the path of the offensive, many units broke, many more were cut off. Maj. Ivan Shabalin, a political officer struggling to lead a mass of stragglers out of an encircled pocket, wrote in his diary on 13 October, a few days before his death: "It is wet and cold and we are moving terribly slowly—all our vehicles are bogged down on the muddy roads . . . More than fifty had to be abandoned in ground that resembled a quagmire; about the same number are stuck fast in a nearby field. At 0600 the Germans opened fire on us—a continuous bombardment of artillery, mortars and heavy machine-guns—and it went on all day . . . I cannot remember when I last slept properly." On 15 October the German tank gunner Karl Fuchs exulted: "From now on, Russian resistance will be minor—all we have to do is keep rolling forward . . . Our duty has been to fight and free the world from this communist disease. One day, many years hence, the world will thank the Germans and our beloved Führer for our victories here in Russia."

Yet the mud Ivan Shabalin complained of was already proving more dangerous to the Germans, as they struggled to advance, than to the defenders holding their ground. Autumn rains were part of Russia's natural cycle, but those that began on 8 October 1941 astonished the commanders of the all-conquering Wehrmacht, which was strange, since several of them had fought there between 1914 and 1917. In a vast country with few and poor roads—only 40,000 miles of tarmac, less than 50,000 of rail track—they failed to anticipate the impact of weather upon mobility. Suddenly, the racing panzer spearheads found themselves checked, tank tracks thrashing ineffectually in a morass. The German supply system floundered under the strain of shifting food and ammunition across hundreds of miles in weather that deteriorated daily.

Soviet reinforcements were arriving from the east, for Stalin's Tokyo agent Richard Sorge had convinced him that the Japanese would not attack in Siberia. The rains became heavier, and soon it grew cold. "We have had continuous sleet and snow," lamented the German chaplain Ernst Tewes. "Our men are suffering—the vehicles are not properly covered and winter clothing has not yet arrived. We are struggling to move along terrible roads." Soldier Heinrich Haape bemoaned the difficulties of keeping supply wagons moving: "The men hauled and pushed, the horses sweated and strained—at times we had to take a brief ten-minute rest from sheer exhaustion. Then, back to the transport, our legs in black mud up to the knees—anything to keep the wheels moving."

Almost every man engaged on both sides in the battles of those days endured extraordinary experiences. Nikolai Redkin, a thirty-five-year-old infantryman, wrote to his wife on 23 October: "Hello, Zoya! I barely escaped death in the last battle. My chances of survival were one in a hundred, but I made it . . . Imagine a party of soldiers surrounded on all sides by enemy tanks and forced against a 70-metre-wide stretch of riverbank. There was only one way out—jump in the river, or die. I jumped and swam. But the bank remained under heavy enemy fire. I had to sit in ice-cold autumn water for three hours, completely numb. When darkness fell the German tanks pulled back and I was picked up by collective farmers. They thawed me and cared for me. It took all of ten days for me to get back from the enemy's rear areas to our lines. Now I am back with my unit and ready to fight. We shall have a brief rest now, then return to the battle. Damn us if we don't make the Germans take the same bath as we had. We shall make them bath in snow until they die." Redkin's wish was eventually fulfilled, but he himself did not live to see it: he was still fighting thirty months later when killed in action near Smolensk.

The Germans were weather-bound. Army surgeon Dr. Curt Emmerich wrote: "The back wheel of some horse-drawn vehicle in the mile-long column slips into a deep shell crater concealed by a puddle of water. The wheel breaks. The shaft rises in the air. The horses, wrenched upwards, shy and kick. One of the traces parts. The vehicle behind tries to overtake on the left, but is unable to drive quite clear of the deep ruts. The right-hand back wheel of the second vehicle catches in the left-hand back wheel of the first. The horses rear and start kicking in all directions. There is no going forwards or backwards. An ammunition lorry returning empty from the front tries to pass the hopeless tangle. It slowly subsides into the ditch and sticks fast. Everyone becomes infected with uncontrollable fury. Everyone shouts at everyone else. Sweating, swearing, mud-spattered men start laying into sweating, shivering, mud-caked horses that are already frothing . . . This scene is repeated a hundred times a day."

On 30 October, panzer commander Col. Gen. Erich Hoepner wrote despairingly: "The roads have become quagmires—everything has come to a halt. Our tanks cannot move. No fuel can get through to us, the heavy rain and fog make air drops almost impossible." He added: "Dear God, give us fourteen days of frost. Then we will surround Moscow!" Hoepner got his weather wish soon enough—far more than fourteen days of frost. But the descent of subzero temperatures and heavy snow did nothing for the Wehrmacht, and much for its enemies. German vehicle and weapon lubricant froze, and soon likewise soldiers. The Russians, by contrast, were equipped to fight on.

The second week of October 1941 was afterwards identified as the decisive period of the crisis. Zhukov was summoned to the Kremlin; he found Stalin ailing with "flu, standing before a map of the front, complaining bitterly about a lack of reliable information." The general drove forward to the so-called Mozhaisk defence line, where he was appalled to find yawning gaps, wide open to German assault. "In essence," he said later, "all the approaches to Moscow were open. Our troops could not have stopped the enemy." Zhukov telephoned Stalin to report. He recognised that if the Germans attacked in strength, the capital was doomed. Much of the bureaucracy of Stalin's government, together with diplomatic missions, was evacuated from Moscow to Kuibyshev, 500 miles east on the Volga. Beria conducted a frenzy of shootings of "dissident elements" in his prisons. One batch of 157 executed on 3 October included several women: Trotsky's sister, Olga Kameneva, the widow of prominent purge victim Lev Kamenev; a thirty-one-year-old air force major named Mariya Nesterenko; forty-year-old Aleksandra Fibikh-Savencho, wife of a senior ordnance officer. Moscow's key installations and industrial plants were prepared for demolition. A quarter of a million people, mostly women, were set to work digging antitank ditches in the suburbs. Panic was reflected in widespread looting of shops. Beria found it convenient to depart for a visit to the safety of the Caucasus. The dictator himself was about to quit the capital.

Suddenly, however, on the evening of 18 October Stalin changed his mind. He stayed, temporarily moved his office to air defence headquarters in Kirov Street, and declared Moscow a fortress. Order on the streets was restored by a curfew and imposition of the usual brutal sanctions. On 7 November, by a brilliant propaganda stroke, units en route to the front were diverted to stage the traditional parade through the capital celebrating the anniversary of the Bolshevik Revolution. That night came the first heavy snowfall of the year. The Germans, their operations crippled by the weather, lacked sufficient mass to make the final breakthrough; they languished outside the city, suffering rapidly increasing privations. Halder and Bock insisted that a further thrust should be made. More ground was gained: the advancing spearheads occupied some of Moscow's outlying tram stations while aircraft and artillery bombarded the city.

Some Russians were sincerely moved by Stalin's appeals for desperate measures in desperate circumstances. A Moscow plastics worker said: "The leader did not remain silent about the fact that our troops have had to retreat. He does not hide the difficulties that lie ahead for his people. After this speech I want to work even harder. It has mobilised me for great deeds." But sceptics were not lacking—it would be mistaken to exaggerate Russian unity and confidence in the winter of 1941. A Moscow engineer said: "All this talk about mobilising the people and organising civil defence just goes to show that the situation at the front is absolutely hopeless. It's clear that the Germans will take Moscow soon and Soviet power will not hold out." Here was an echo of the despair that overtook some informed British people in 1940. Farther south in Kursk Province a woman said: "Shoot me if you like, but I'm not digging any trenches. The only people who need trenches are the communists and Jews. Let them dig for themselves. Your power is coming to an end and we're not going to work for you."

But amid such reluctant comrades, a bare sufficiency of patriots and fighters held the line and repulsed the invaders. By the end of November, the German advance had exhausted itself. "The Führer himself has taken charge," wrote Kurt Grumann, "but our troops walk around as if they were doomed. Our soldiers hack at the frozen ground, but the heaviest blows yield only enough earth to fill one's fingernails. Our strength is decreasing every day." Quartermaster-General Edward Wagner said: "We are at the end of our personnel and materiel strength." Germany's fuel situation was so critical that its navy was virtually immobilised. The army's supply system struggled to support spearheads 300 miles beyond the forward dumps at Smolensk. A gallows joke circulated in German official circles: "Eastern campaign extended by a month owing to great success."

IN BERLIN on 28 November, a conference of industrialists chaired by armaments supremo Fritz Todt reached a devastating conclusion: the war against Russia was no longer winnable. Having failed to achieve a quick victory, Germany lacked resources to prevail in a sustained struggle. Next day, Todt and tank-production chief Walter Rohland met Hitler. Rohland argued that, once the United States became a belligerent, it would be impossible to match Allied industrial strength. Todt, though an ardent Nazi, said, "This war can no longer be won by military means." Hitler demanded, "How then shall I end this war?" Todt replied that only a political outcome was feasible. Hitler dismissed such logic. He chose to convince himself that the imminent accession of Japan to the Axis would transform the balance of strength in Germany's favour. But the November diary of army chief of staff Franz Halder records other remarks by Hitler that acknowledged the implausibility of absolute triumph. For the rest of the war, those responsible for Germany's economic and industrial planning fulfilled their roles in the knowledge that strategic success was unattainable. They drafted a planning paper in December 1941 entitled "The Requirements for Victory." This concluded that the Reich needed to commit the equivalent of $150 billion to arms manufacture in the succeeding two years; yet such a sum exceeded German weapons expenditure for the entire conflict. Whatever the prowess of the Wehrmacht, the nation lacked means to win; it could aspire only to force its enemies to parley, together or severally.

Many more months elapsed before the Allies saw that the tide of war had turned. In 1942, the Axis would enjoy spectacular successes. But it is a critical historical reality that senior functionaries of the Third Reich realised as early as December 1941 that military victory had become unattainable, because Russia remained undefeated. Some thereafter sustained hopes that Germany might negotiate an acceptable peace. But they, and perhaps Hitler also in the innermost recesses of his brain, knew the decisive strategic moment had passed. Gen. Alfred Jodl, the Führer's closest and most loyal military adviser, asserted in 1945 that his master understood in December 1941 that "victory could no longer be achieved." This did not mean, of course, that Hitler reconciled himself to Germany's defeat: instead, he now anticipated a long war, which would eventually expose the fundamental divisions between the Soviet Union and the Western democracies. He aspired to achieve sufficient battlefield success to force his enemies to make terms, and he clung to this hope until April 1945. Since the Western Allies and the Russians shared morbid and persistent fears of each other seeking a separate peace, Hitler's speculation was at least a little less fanciful than it might now appear. Only time would show that the struggle was destined to be fought out to the end; that the rupture he anticipated between the West and the Soviet Union would indeed take place, but too late to save the Third Reich.

CHAPTER SEVEN

MOSCOW SAVED, LENINGRAD STARVED

THOSE WHO FOUGHT the war saw its turning point in late 1942, when Japanese advances in the Pacific were checked and the Germans eclipsed at Stalingrad and in North Africa. For months before those events, the Allied nations endured a diet of almost unbroken ill tidings, which the United States' entry into the conflict could not deflect. Konstantin Rokossovsky, the most glamorous as well as one of the most formidable of Stalin's generals, was commanding the Sixteenth Army north of Moscow. In mid-November he told a reporter, "Soon the Germans will start to get washed out and the time will come—we'll be in Berlin." His words later seemed prescient, but at the time few people around the world grasped the gravity of the Wehrmacht's predicament in Russia, the fact that some of Hitler's closest advisers already believed his bid for global domination doomed.

German forces were still thrusting forward north and south of Moscow, but losing momentum. On 17 November, a Wehrmacht division broke and fled in the face of an attack by new Soviet T-34 tanks. Fresh Russian armies were taking the field; the invaders were running out of armour, fuel, men and faith. A young SS officer wrote: "Thus we are approaching our final goal, Moscow, step by step. It is icy cold . . . To start the [vehicle] engines, they must be warmed by lighting fires under the oil pan. The fuel is partially frozen, the motor oil is thick and we lack antifreeze . . . The remaining limited combat strength of the troops diminishes further due to the continuous exposure to the cold . . . The automatic weapons . . . often fail to operate because the breechblocks can no longer move." If a man spat, the moisture froze before reaching the ground. A single regiment reported 315 frostbite cases. On 3 December Hoepner, commanding Fourth Panzer Group, reported: "The offensive combat power of the Corps *has run out*. Reasons: physical and moral over-exertion, loss of a large number of commanders, inadequate winter equipment . . . The High Command should decide whether a withdrawal should be undertaken."

Again and again the Germans threw themselves at the Russian positions—and again and again they were repulsed. Georgi Osadchinsky saw a group of German tanks and supporting infantry mill in confusion before a railway embankment they could not pass, as Soviet guns wreaked havoc. Tank after tank caught fire, and the survivors began to retreat. He watched a German soldier flounder helpless in the snow on all fours, while others scrambled clumsily back towards their own line. "Relief and happiness swept through our ranks," wrote Osadchinsky. "The Germans did not seem so terrible now—they could be beaten." Russian tactics were still murderously clumsy, based upon frontal assaults often launched at Stalin's personal behest: one such, against the flank of the German Ninth Army, caused the slaughter of 2,000 men and horses of a cavalry division. Tactical leadership was poor, troops ill-trained; Rokossovsky railed against Zhukov's insistence on the doctrine of "no retreat" imposed by the Kremlin. Russian blood leeched into the snow in unimaginable volume.

But German commanders still underrated their foes. An army intelligence report on 4 December concluded that "at present the enemy in front of Army Group Centre are not capable of conducting a counter-offensive without significant reserves." They had no notion that Zhukov had been reinforced by nine new armies consisting of twenty-seven divisions; more horsed cavalry units had been raised, which could move through snow where vehicles could not go. The invaders stood just twenty-five miles from the Kremlin, with spearheads nine miles from the capital's outskirts. But, after suffering 200,000 dead since the start of Typhoon, they had shot their bolt.

On 5 December, the Russians launched a massive assault which caught the Germans almost literally frozen in their positions. The Stavka had awaited the assistance of General Winter. The thermometer fell to 22 degrees below zero Fahrenheit, so that German lubricants hardened while Russian weapons and tanks still worked—the T-34 had a compressed-air starter, immune to frost. A stunned infantryman named Albrecht Linsen described the response of his unit to the Soviet assault: "Out of the snowstorm soldiers were running back, scattering in all directions like a panic-stricken herd of animals. A lone officer stood against this desperate mass; he gesticulated, tried to pull out his pistol and then simply let it pass. Our platoon commander made no attempt at all to stop people. I paused, wondering what to do, and there was an explosion right next to me and I felt a searing pain in my right thigh . . . I thought: 'I am going to die here, 21 years old, in the snow before Moscow.'"

The Russian offensive smashed into the two exposed German salients north and south of Moscow, then exploited westward. The unthinkable became reality: the invincible Wehrmacht began to retreat. "Each time we leave a village, we set it alight," wrote the panzer lieutenant Gustav Schrodek. "It is a primitive form of self-defence, and the Russians hate us for it. Yet its grim military logic is clear—to deny our pursuing opponents shelter in the terrible cold." Lt. Kurt Grumann wrote from a field dressing station: "Eighty men were brought in here today, half of whom have second- or third-degree frostbite. Their swollen legs are covered in blisters, and they no longer resemble limbs but rather some formless mass. In some cases gangrene has already set in. What is it all for?" Many tanks and vehicles were abandoned, immured in snow and ice. "The ghost of the Napoleonic *Grande Armée* hovers ever more strongly above us like a malignant spirit," wrote gunner Josef Deck.

For ten days the Wehrmacht staggered back through a white wilderness landmarked with huddled corpses and the blackened carcasses of abandoned vehicles. Most German commanders favoured a major withdrawal. Hitler, displaying an obstinacy which mirrored that of Stalin, called instead for "fanatical resistance." The ardent Nazi general Walther Model played a hero's part in stabilising the line. Stalin, against Zhukov's strong advice, insisted upon extending operations. On 5 January he ordered a counteroffensive along the length of the front. Once more following Hitler's example, by spurning an opportunity to concentrate forces against the weak point in the German line Stalin threw away the possibility of a great victory; Rokossovsky later offered a scornful catalogue of the blunders made, chances missed. The Germans still resisted fiercely, mowing down attackers in tens of thousands. Soviet reserves were soon exhausted, and their advance ran out of steam. Model recovered some lost ground, and Zhukov's hopes of encircling Army Group Centre were frustrated. But the decisive reality persisted: the invaders had been pushed back between 60 and 150 miles. The Russians held Moscow.

EVEN AS THE FATE of Russia's capital was decided, farther west a parallel drama unfolded, of almost equal magnitude and embracing even greater human suffering. From the northwest and south, in the autumn of 1941 Axis forces closed upon Russia's old capital, Leningrad. Barbarossa persuaded the Finns to avenge their 1940 defeat: in June 1941 Finland's army, reequipped by Hitler, joined the assault on the Soviet Union. German troops thrust from northern Norway to reach positions within thirty miles of Murmansk. The Finns showed no enthusiasm for advancing much beyond their 1939 frontier, but on 15 September, with their aid the Germans completed the encirclement of Leningrad. The ensuing siege of the city—the tsars' St. Petersburg, with its elegant avenues, baroque palaces and seaside quays—became an epic that continued for more than two years. It assumed a character unique in its horror, and cost its defenders and citizens more lives than Britain and America together lost in the entire war.

Before the battle began, Soviet commanders had anticipated a direct assault. Tens of thousands of civilians dug defensive works under incoming artillery fire; shells fell on them "methodically, precisely," in the words of a veteran. "Our soldiers dashed from their dugouts, grabbing youngsters and women, pulling them off the road and out of the line of fire . . . An incendiary shell landed. A herd of cattle, frightened by the flaming asphalt, began a stampede, kicking up a huge cloud of dust. Then the terrified animals charged straight into a minefield." Some children were belatedly evacuated from the city—into the path of the advancing Germans: more than 2,000 perished in a Luftwaffe attack on a trainload of fugitives at Lychkovo.

The credentials of the hoary old Bolshevik general Kliment Voroshilov, charged with the defence of Leningrad, rested solely upon his loyalty to Stalin; he despised professional soldiers and understood nothing of military science. Moscow dispatched a large food convoy to the city, but Voroshilov decided that to acknowledge a need for it would represent defeatism. He diverted the supplies elsewhere, and launched impromptu assaults on the Germans which yielded only slaughter. A despairing Lieutenant Yushkevich wrote in his last diary entry before being killed: "Our soldiers are only issued with old rifles and we have pathetically few machine-guns. We haven't any grenades either. There are no medics! This is not a military unit—we are simply cannon fodder." He described his men "being hunted through the woods like animals . . . Constant shooting—panzers everywhere."

On 8 September the encirclement of Leningrad became complete, its siege formally commenced. Next day, Stalin dispatched Zhukov to relieve Voroshilov. His unexpected arrival by light aircraft prompted a petty farce: for fifteen minutes guards at the city's *front** headquarters beside the Smolny Institute declined to admit him, for lack of a pass. "Well, that's the army for you," shrugged Zhukov later, but at the time he was probably less philosophical. Voroshilov, flown back to Moscow, dared to denounce Stalin to his face, shouting: "You have yourself to blame for all this! You're the one who annihilated the Old Guard of the army; you had our best generals killed!" When Stalin demurred, the old revolutionary seized a salver bearing a roast suckling pig and smashed it down on the table. Voroshilov was fortunate to escape a firing squad.

---

* In this text the italicised word *front* is used as the Red Army did, to denote an army group.

Zhukov reorganised Leningrad's defence, countermanding Voroshilov's order to scuttle what was left of the Baltic Fleet in the harbour; through the years ahead, the warships' guns provided critical support for the land forces. The general launched a series of thrusts against the Germans which climaxed on 17 September, cost thousands of lives, and foundered amid devastating artillery fire. A marine officer, Nikolai Vavin, described an attempt to reinforce the island fortress of Oreshek on Lake Ladoga: "Our guys just didn't have a chance. The Germans quickly spotted us from the air—and it became a mass execution. The enemy's planes first bombed and then machine-gunned us. Out of my own landing group of two hundred men, only fourteen reached the shoreline." Faced with protests from his officers about the futility of such attempts, especially from the Nevsky bridgehead on the east bank of the Neva, Zhukov remained implacable: "I said attack!" Casualties soared, while medical facilities for the wounded were almost nonexistent. Zhukov placed blocking units—*zagradotryady*—behind the front, to shoot down his own men who attempted to flee, a practice that became institutionalised in the Red Army. German propaganda loudspeakers taunted the doomed assailants on the battlefield: "It's time to assemble at your extermination points again—we shall bury you on the banks of the Neva." Then the next barrage fell upon Soviet troops milling helplessly in their positions.

For weeks, the Russians remained oblivious of the fact that the Germans had no intention of launching a ground attack on Leningrad, nor even of accepting its surrender. Zhukov acquired a prestige in Stalin's eyes as saviour of the city, rooted in failure to understand that it had not been seriously assaulted. In a moment of fantasy, German staff officers in Berlin discussed the possibility of making a propaganda gesture by inviting the United States to accept the 2.5 million inhabitants of Peter the Great's capital as refugees. Hitler, instead, set out to starve them to death. Professor Ernst Zigelemeyer of Munich's Institute of Nutrition—one of many scientists who provided satanic counsel to the Nazis—was consulted about practicalities. He agreed that no battle was necessary; it would be impossible for the Russians to provide their beleaguered citizens with more than 8.8 ounces of bread a day, which could not sustain human life on a protracted basis: "It is not worth risking the lives of our troops. The Leningraders will die anyway. It is essential not to let a single person through our front line. The more of them that stay there, the sooner they will die, and then we will enter the city without trouble, without losing a single German soldier."

Hitler declared: "Petersburg—the poisonous nest from which, for so long, Asiatic venom has spewed forth into the Baltic—must vanish from the earth's surface. The city is already cut off. It only remains for us to bomb and bombard it, destroy its sources of water and power and then deny the population everything it needs to survive." The first major Luftwaffe attack on Leningrad destroyed the waterside Badaev warehouses, holding most of the city's food stocks; melted sugar ran along a neighbouring road, and fires burned for days. The citizens quickly understood their plight. A woman named Elena Skryabina wrote in her diary: "We are approaching the greatest horror . . . Everyone is preoccupied with only one thought: where to get something edible so as not to starve to death. We have returned to prehistoric times. Life has been reduced to one thing—the hunt for food."

Pravda correspondent Lazar Brontman described in his diary how citizens made soup and bread with grass. Once such fare was accepted as a norm, he said, "grass cakes found their own price in the market." A single match cost a rouble, which caused many people to ignite their kindling with magnifying glasses under the sun. One of Brontman's writer friends was eccentric enough to cling to his household pet, "probably the only surviving dog in Leningrad." Bicycles provided the sole means of civilian transport. Since water supplies now depended on hydrants, women washed clothes in the street while passing military vehicles weaved between them. Every vestige of vacant soil was tilled for vegetables, each plot marked with its owner's name. Fuel was desperately short, because the city was invested before the inhabitants could make their annual pilgrimages to collect firewood from outlying forests.

The Germans removed their tanks to reinforce operations farther south. The besiegers, less numerous than the defending Russian troops, dug themselves into bunkers and gun emplacements for the winter. Every movement towards their lines by either attacking soldiers or fleeing civilians was met with annihilating artillery, mortar and machine-gun fire. Capt. Vasily Khoroshavin, a thirty-six-year-old Soviet battery commander, wrote to his wife on 25 October: "I have received a letter from you and I cannot describe the pleasure it gave. Today is the sixth that I am spending in the cellar of a mason's shop only accessible by crawling. I sit here directing fire while mines and shells explode around me, shaking the earth. It is impossible to get out for water. Hot tea is our greatest luxury, and rations are brought to us by night. Yesterday a shell exploded between me and a reconnaissance man, shredding the tails of my greatcoat. I was unhurt, except that my gas mask case hit me on the head." Khoroshavin was less fortunate three months later, when another German salvo killed him.

"All our soldiers on the front look like ghouls—emaciated by hunger and cold," wrote one of them, Stepan Kuznetsov. "They are in rags, filthy, and very, very hungry." Thereafter, the saga of Leningrad focused not on the battlefield, but on the struggle for survival among its inhabitants, which many lost. German artillery shelled the city daily, at hours most likely to catch victims in the open: 8 to 9 and 11 to 12 in the morning, and 5 to 6 and 8 to 9 in the evening. The bread ration for civilians fell below the level the murderous Professor Zigelemeyer deemed necessary for existence: a daily minimum of a hundred tons of supplies a day had to reach the city across Lake Ladoga, and there was often a shortfall: on 30 November, for instance, only sixty-one tons got through. Loaves were baked with mouldy grain salvaged from a ship sunk in the harbour, from cottonseed oilcake, "edible" cellulose, flour-sack and floor sweepings, and horse oats.

Through October and November, conditions worsened steadily: German guns and bombers pounded streets, schools, civic buildings, and hospitals. For countless citizens, starvation beckoned: they began to boil wallpaper to extract its paste, to cook and chew leather. As scurvy became endemic, an extract was produced from pine needles to provide vitamin C. There was a plague of thefts of ration cards—mere money had become redundant. Pigeons vanished from the city squares as they were caught and eaten, as too were crows, gulls, then rats and household pets. At an art academy, old Professor Yan Shabolsky sent for his star pupil, eighteen-year-old Elena Martilla. "Lena," he said, "things are getting very bad here. I don't expect to survive this. But someone must make a record of what is happening. You are a portrait artist—so draw pictures of Leningrad's people under siege—honest pictures, showing how they are suffering in these diabolical circumstances. We must preserve this for humanity. Future generations must be warned of the absolute horror of war."

Thereafter Elena Martilla roamed the streets, making such quick sketches as cold and weakness allowed of faces stretched, drawn, sunken, hollowed by deprivation no other modern European civilisation had experienced on such a scale. She noticed that many adults responded to their desperation by closing down emotionally, becoming passive and withdrawn, apparently sleepwalking. Children, however, became unnaturally alert: a small boy delivered a vivid, witty running commentary on a Luftwaffe attack to his terrified adult companions in a shelter. She wrote: "It was as if that boy had aged fifty years in as many days—his face looked so old, and through this unnatural ageing I felt that he had been robbed of the innocence of childhood. It was horrifying to hear his natural curiosity welded to the ghastly machinery of war . . . I looked more closely into his face—and saw an uncanny wisdom in it. What I glimpsed in that moment shook me: I realised that a little child could look like a sage old man. Amid the agony we were suffering, something extraordinary had briefly come to life."

Most Leningraders, deprived of power, heat, light and employment, eked out a hibernatory existence amid mounting snow and rubble; their lives and metabolic processes slowed like the fading of an old clockwork gramophone. In Svetlana Magaeva's apartment building, an old woman named Kamilla grew steadily more enfeebled, though neighbours burned furniture in her stove to preserve a flicker of life. One morning, she suddenly rose from her bed and embarked upon a frenzied search of every cupboard and crevice for food. Frustrated, she took plates and dishes from her cabinet and dropped them one by one on the floor. Then she fell on her hands and knees, and searched the fragments for breadcrumbs. Soon afterwards, Kamilla died.

By December, the temperature had dropped to minus 22 degrees Fahrenheit, and starvation was killing tens of thousands. The bread ration shrank to 4.5 ounces. Some people mechanically continued their work: at the city's Zoological Institute, fifty-year-old beetle expert Axel Reichardt worked on his magnum opus, *The Fauna of the Soviet Union*, until one day he was found lying dead on a mattress in his office. Sasha Abramov, an actor at the Musical Comedy Theatre, where the cast were almost too weak to walk to performances, expired during an interval, wearing his costume as one of Dumas's three musketeers. Elena Skrjabina wrote: "People are so weak with hunger that they are completely indifferent to death; they perish as if they are falling asleep. Those half-dead people who are still around do not even pay any attention to them." Stiffened corpses lay in the streets until they were piled onto sledges for disposal in shell craters. German intelligence, monitoring the city's agony with clinical fascination, calculated that 200,000 people had died in three months.

Yet the privileged escaped most of the suffering. Zhukov was recalled to Moscow when it became plain that there would be no battle, leaving Leningrad in the hands of party officials who ate prodigiously throughout the siege. It became a characteristic of Russia's war that corruption and privilege persisted, even as tens of millions starved and died. Some functionaries were evacuated by air, as was the city's most famous resident, the composer Dmitry Shostakovich, who completed elsewhere his Seventh *Leningrad* Symphony, which became a symbol of the experience. For the dignitaries who stayed, bread, sugar, meatballs and other cooked food remained readily available at a canteen in the Smolny Institute; they also had access to a private heated cinema. Rumours circulated about the party's shameless cynicism and privileges: an anonymous pamphleteer signing himself "the Rebel" printed a leaflet that was found in the streets:

"Citizens, down with the regime that lets us die of starvation! We are being robbed by scoundrels who deceive us, who stockpile food and leave us to go hungry. Let us go to the district authorities and demand more bread. Down with our leaders!" The NKVD devoted immense effort to identifying "the Rebel," and in December 1942 extracted a confession from a fifty-year-old factory worker named Sergei Luzhkov, who was dispatched to his inevitable fate before a firing squad.

At the end of 1941, the freezing of Lake Ladoga opened a more resilient link to the outside world: the legendary six-lane ice highway created by 30,000 civilian workers. Four thousand lorries were soon shuttling along this "Road of Life," but few of the incoming supplies—initially 700 tons a day—reached ordinary citizens. On Stalin's orders, a renewed attack was launched to break the German encirclement, which failed with the usual heavy losses. A radio operator on the Volkhov Front east of the city, Nikolai Nikulin, wrote: "I learned what war was really like. One quiet night I was sitting in my icy hole, unable to sleep because of the cold, scratching my lice-infested body, crying from weakness and misery . . . In an empty German dugout I found some potatoes, frozen hard as stones, made a fire and boiled them in my helmet. With food in my stomach, I gained spirit. I started to change after that night, developing defence mechanisms, an instinct for self-preservation, staying power. I learned how to find grub . . . Once a horse that was pulling a sledge near us was killed by a shell. Twenty minutes later, little was left of it save the mane and guts, because smart guys like me dismembered it. The driver hadn't even recovered from the shock—he just sat on his sledge clutching the reins." Twenty Soviet divisions were destroyed in attempts to relieve Leningrad; their only significant success was recapture of the northeastern junction at Tikhvin on 9 December, which made it possible to move supplies to a railhead within distant reach of the city.

Extreme hunger persisted: on 13 January, after hours of queuing in the snow, Elena Kochina had just collected her pitiful ration when a man behind her seized the bread, thrust it into his mouth and sought to gobble it down. In blind fury, the desperate mother turned and threw herself upon him: "He fell to the ground—I fell with him. Lying on his back, he tried to cram the whole piece of bread into his mouth at once. With one hand I grabbed him by the nose, turning it aside. With the other I tried to tear the roll out of his mouth. The man resisted, but more and more weakly. Finally, I succeeded in retrieving everything he hadn't managed to swallow. People watched our struggle in silence."

Lidya Okhapkina had her ration cards stolen, a misfortune that threatened her little family with imminent death, so narrow was the margin of survival. That night, for the first time in her life the despairing woman fell on her knees and prayed to the deity whose existence Stalin's regime denied: "Have mercy O God on my innocent children." Next morning came a knock on her door. She opened it to find a Red Army soldier she had never seen, bearing a parcel from her husband, fighting hundreds of miles away, containing two pounds of semolina, two pounds of rice and two packets of biscuits. These proved to represent the difference between life and death for her family. Others were less fortunate. In the first ten days of January, the NKVD reported forty-two cases of cannibalism: corpses were found with thighs and breasts hacked off. Worse, the weak became vulnerable to murder not for their meaningless property, but for their flesh. On 4 February a man visiting a militia office reported seeing twelve women arrested for cannibalism, which they did not deny. "One woman, utterly worn out and desperate, said that when her husband fainted through exhaustion and lack of food, she hacked off part of his leg to feed herself and her children." The prisoners sobbed, knowing that they faced execution.

In February, by far the worst month of the siege, 20,000 people a day were reported to be dying; amid the weakened population, dysentery became a killer. There were queues at street taps for water, and fires burned unchecked for lack of means to put them out. The Musical Comedy Theatre closed, and supplies of coffins ran out. Many of those with energy to read turned to *War and Peace*, the only book that seemed capable of explaining their agony. Those who survived had not merely exceptional will, but also commitment to a routine: washing themselves, eating off plates, even continuing academic studies. The authorities considered transporting civilians to safety on trucks returning empty across Lake Ladoga. Some mothers and babies indeed travelled, and often died en route; but Stalin rejected a wholesale evacuation, for prestige reasons. Leningrad's ordeal became a display of fortitude such as only a tyranny could have enforced, and probably only Russians could have endured.

THE BRITISH AND AMERICANS continued to fear Soviet defeat until the end of 1942: they were slow to comprehend the losses and miseries of the invaders. As 1941 drew to a close, 2 million German soldiers, their tunics lined with newspaper and straw to compensate for the clothing they lacked, were in straits almost as dire as those of Russia's people. Hans-Jürgen Hartmann wrote from Kharkov: "I have often wondered what this Christmas might be like. I always cast out the war from my imaginary picture, or at least push it to the very edges. I conjured up special words for the occasion. Christmas, homeland, longing, joy and hope. Yet these words, always sincere and heartfelt, became increasingly strange and precious to me. They evoked something timeless, precious—and yet, in the conditions of the Eastern Front, seemed scarcely believable any more . . . How brutal this war is becoming. It is now a total war, a war against women, children and old people—and that is the greatest horror."

Franz Peters and some comrades wandered into a church in a little town; the communists had ripped out its altar, but the Germans clustered around the hole where this had stood, and began carolling. "I have never heard 'Silent Night' sung with such fervour . . . Many of us were moved to tears." Karl-Gottfried Vierkom read aloud to his comrades a card which accompanied a marble cake sent by his mother from Germany: "When I finished, there was complete silence. Far away from this terrible disaster—which no one imagined possible when we first entered Russia—something else still existed. Was there still a Christmas somewhere, where people peacefully exchanged gifts, gathered around the tree and went to Midnight Mass?"

In Berlin there was no place for such sentimentality, which was anyway grotesque at a time when systemic barbarism was being perpetrated by the same German soldiers in Russia who sang carols and nursed self-pity. Hitler, enraged by the repulse before Moscow, appointed himself to replace Walther von Brauchitsch as army C-in-C. He repeated to Model his draconian injunctions against yielding ground. General Hoepner, one of many advocates of a strategic disengagement, wrote: "There is a serious cost to one's nerves fighting against the enemy and one's own supreme commander at the same time." A few days later Hoepner joined a long list of commanders in the east, including von Rundstedt and Guderian, sacked for alleged lack of steel.

Model, a blunt soldier's general and dedicated Nazi, addressed the threat of disaster with energy and success. By mid-January, the Soviets had ceased to win ground; on the twenty-first, to the amazement of his demoralised officers Model launched a counterblow at the Russian flank west of Moscow. His staff asked what reinforcements he could deploy. "Myself!" he declared irrepressibly—and this sufficed. Everywhere he improvised, dashing from unit to unit, often under fire, urging local commanders first to stand, then to strike back. Desperate expedients were employed to enable men to keep fighting in temperatures of minus 40 degrees Fahrenheit: heated shelters were established, for recuperation between the few hours of exposed activity that were all a soldier could endure; "snow shacks" were built around aircraft engines, to warm them through the night so the Luftwaffe could fly once more. In the last days of January and the first of

February, Model's troops inflicted repeated repulses and heavy casualties on the Russians, still seeking to push forward in the Rzhev salient.

Horrors afflicted both sides. War correspondent Vasily Grossman met a peasant carrying a sack of frozen human legs, which he proposed to thaw on a stove in order to remove their boots. Fritz Langkanke of the SS Das Reich Division described how a dead Russian, frozen stiff, became wedged between the wheels of his armoured car: "I grabbed a saw, wriggled underneath and began cutting away his arms. As I did this, our two faces came close together and with the sawing motion he suddenly began to move. I froze in horror. It was only in response to the saw's action, but it seemed for a moment he was shaking his head at me."

Wolf Dose, a German soldier supervising a POW work detail outside Leningrad, described with bleak detachment the fate of a Russian who collapsed while gathering wood outside a dugout: "He lay for a while in the frozen snow, at –20 degrees Celsius. He recovered somewhat . . . lifted himself up. But the cold had a strange effect on him. He threw himself forward [into the dugout] with such sudden vigour that he landed right on top of the stove. He just lay there, stunned, his skin burning away. Someone managed to pull him off and laid him on the ground. His head was resting on some of the wood he had gathered; his charred hand was soldered onto one of the pieces. He groaned quietly." Then someone hauled the man to his feet. "Because of the shock of the sudden movement, he emptied the contents of his intestines into his trousers, which swelled up and burst. I saw his thin, distended abdomen covered in blood, excrement and remains of clothing . . . His eyes stared into empty space. His face had a strange blue-green hue . . . One only hopes that a quick shot will bring his misery to an end."

Men on both sides became inured to such sights, for each was overwhelmingly preoccupied with his own salvation. Dose shrugged: "Russia, a country full of cruelty, must be cruelly treated." The Red Army struggled to regain the initiative, but again and again was thrown back. The Wehrmacht's iron professionalism was unbroken. Gen. Gotthard Heinrici asserted that the Russians had repeated the earlier German mistake of seeking to advance on too wide a front, and Zhukov was of the same opinion. It is unlikely that the Russians had the strength or skill required to inflict absolute defeat on the Germans that winter, whatever course they had adopted. But Stalin's clumsy interventions, matching those of Hitler, removed even such a possibility. The Soviet Twenty-ninth Army, cut off west of Rzhev, fought almost to the last man. There was no repeat of the mass surrenders of the previous summer, not least because Zhukov's soldiers now knew the fate awaiting them if they accepted captivity. The

Germans claimed that 26,000 Russians died in the Rzhev battle, about as many men as Britain's army lost in three years of North African campaigning. Evidence of the human cost lay everywhere. "As we picked our way through the carnage, the hard frozen bodies clinked like porcelain," wrote a German officer, Max Kuhnert. But the Russians never grudged losses; what mattered to them was that the front had been pushed back 175 miles from Moscow. Between 22 June 1941 and 31 January 1942, Germany suffered almost a million casualties, more than a quarter of all the soldiers originally committed to Barbarossa. For the rest of the winter, the invaders dug in to hold their ground and rebuild their armoured formations.

The doctrine of blitzkreig evolved progressively, in the course of Germany's 1939–40 campaigns in Poland and France. But in 1941, Hitler explicitly committed himself to destroy Russia by waging a "lightning war." His armed forces, and Germany's economy, lacked the fundamental strength to accomplish anything else. The Wehrmacht's plan for Barbarossa was overwhelmingly dependent for success on accomplishing the defeat of Stalin's armies west of the Dnieper-Dvina river line. The deeper within the country heavy fighting took place, the graver became the logistical difficulties of supplying Hitler's troops, with few railways and inadequate numbers of trucks, which consumed precious fuel merely to deliver loads. The key battles of the 1940 French campaign took place within a few hours' drive of the German border; now, instead, the Wehrmacht was committed to a struggle thousands of miles from its bases.

Few soldiers of the German army who survived the winter of 1941 ever regained the faith in their leadership that was forfeited by that experience. They saw Russian soldiers advancing to attack on skis, clad in quilted snowsuits such as they themselves lacked. German weapons and vehicles froze, while those of their enemies worked. Stalin's soldiers never matched the tactical proficiency of the Germans: their attacks relied on the exploitation of mass and a willingness to sacrifice lives. But Soviet artillery was formidable, and their aircraft increasingly effective. The new Katyusha multiple rocket launcher and the T-34, probably the best tank of the war, shocked the Germans and heartened the Russians, though the first time Katyushas were used men of both sides fled in terror. A Wehrmacht officer, Helmut von Harnack, wrote: "The fact that we did not bring this campaign to a finish, and go on to take Moscow, is a massive blow for us. The lack of foresight about the weather . . . is of course an important reason. But the truth is we totally underestimated our opponent. He showed a strength and resilience we did not believe him capable of—indeed, resilience greater than most of us imagined humanly possible."

Stalin's personal direction of Russia's 1941 campaigns inflicted disasters which at times threatened to become irretrievable. His refusal to yield ground was responsible for the loss of many of the 3.35 million Russian soldiers who passed into German captivity that year. But his people revealed a will to fight, and a willingness to die, that owed little to ideology and much to peasant virtues, a visceral devotion to Mother Russia, and the fruits of compulsion. A soldier, Boris Baromykin, described the execution of a comrade from a Central Asian republic, charged with unauthorised withdrawal from his position: "The poor fellow was standing just a couple of metres from me, peacefully chewing a piece of bread; he could only speak a few words of Russian and had no idea what was going on. Abruptly the major heading the military tribunal read out an order: 'Desertion from the front line—immediate execution,' and shot him in the head. The guy collapsed in front of me—it was horrible. Something inside of me died when I saw that."

But Baromykin, acknowledging the chaos of one of their retreats, "like a herd of desperate cattle," added: "The only thing holding us together was fear that our commanders would shoot us if we tried to run away." A soldier shot by his comrades as he attempted to desert swore at them as he lay dying in the dust: "They'll kill the lot of you." He glimpsed Nikolai Moskvin, the unit's political officer. "And you, you bloodstained commissar, they'll hang you first." Moskvin drew his revolver and finished the man off. He wrote in his diary: "The boys understood; a dog's death for a dog." To discourage desertion, the Red Army adopted a new tactic: dispatching groups of men towards the German lines with their hands in the air, who then tossed a shower of grenades. This was designed to provoke the Germans to fire on others who attempted to surrender in earnest.

The ruthlessness of the Soviet state was indispensable to confound Hitler. No democracy could have established as icily rational a hierarchy of need as did Stalin, whereby soldiers received the most food; civilian workers less; and "useless mouths," including the old, only a starvation quota. More than 2 million Russians died of hunger during the war in territories controlled by their own government. The Soviet achievement in 1941–42 contrasted dramatically with the feeble performance of the Western Allies in France in 1940. Whatever the limitations of the Red Army's weapons, training, tactics and commanders, Soviet culture armoured its forces to meet the Wehrmacht with a resolution the softer citizens of the democracies could not match.

"This is no gentleman's war," admitted Wehrmacht Lt. von Heyl in a letter to his family. "One becomes totally numb. Human life is so cheap, cheaper than the shovels we use to clear the roads of snow. The state we have reached will seem quite unbelievable to you back home. We do not kill humans but 'the enemy,' who are rendered impersonal—animals at best. They behave the same towards us." The spectacle of starving prisoners dehumanised Russians in the eyes of many Germans, in a fashion that destroyed any instinct towards pity. A Wehrmacht soldier wrote: "They whined and grovelled before us. They were human beings in whom there was no longer a trace of anything human."

German savagery reconciled Stalin's nation to the savagery of its own leaders: Hitler's invasion united tens of millions of Russians who had hitherto been alienated by ideological and racial differences, purges, famines, institutionalised injustice and incompetence. The "Great Patriotic War" Stalin had declared became a reality that accomplished more for the cohesion and motivation of his peoples than any other event since the 1917 revolution. Even Hitler's SS became reluctantly impressed with the Soviets' indoctrination of their own soldiers. Whatever delusions persisted in Berlin, on the battlefield almost every German soldier now recognised the magnitude, perhaps the impossibility, of the task to which his nation was committed. The panzer officer Wolfgang Paul acknowledged: "We have blundered, mistakenly, into an alien landscape with which we can never be properly acquainted. Everything is cold, hostile and working against us." Another soldier wrote home: "Even if we capture Moscow, I doubt whether this will finish the war in the east. The Russians are capable of fighting to the very last man, the very last square metre of their vast country. Their stubbornness and resolve are quite astonishing. We are entering a war of attrition—and I only hope in the long run Germany can win it."

The last letter from Russia received by gunner lieutenant Jasper Monckeburg's family in Hamburg was dated 21 January 1942: "Forty per cent of our men have got oozing eczema and boils all over their bodies, particularly on their legs . . . Our duty periods stretch over forty-eight hours, with two or three hours' sleep, often interrupted. Our lines are so weak, twenty to thirty-five men per company over two kilometres, that we would be completely overrun if we, the artillery, did not stem the onslaught of the enemy, who are ten or twelve times stronger." After repulsing one Russian attack, infantrymen carried the lieutenant into his bunker: "Since I had been lying for 4½ hours in the snow—35 degrees of frost—I could no longer feel hands or legs and was completely unable to stand . . . If it weren't for this swinish cold!" Monckeburg was killed a few days later.

Gen. Gotthard Heinrici, visiting Berlin in February, was struck by Hitler's indifference to eyewitness accounts of the enormous tragedy unfolding in the east. The Führer chose to discuss only technical issues such as the design of antitank defences. When once he spoke of the Russian winter, it was with flippancy: "Luckily nothing lasts for ever, and that is a consoling thought. If, at this present moment, men are being turned into blocks of ice, that won't prevent the April sun from shining and restoring life to these desolate places." A German soldier named Wolfgang Huff wrote on 10 February 1942, at Sinyavino, in Russia: "Dusk is falling. The crack of artillery fire—and white smoke rises above the forest. The harsh reality of war: gruff cries of command, struggling with ammunition through the snow. And then a surprising question—'Did you see the sunset?' Suddenly I thought: how grievously we have broken the peace and tranquillity of this land."

Throughout February, at Stalin's orders his armies threw themselves again and again at the German positions—and were repulsed with huge losses. The Soviet supply system tottered close to collapse, and many soldiers existed at the extremities of privation. Some 2.66 million Russians had already been killed in action. But the campaign had cost the German army almost a million casualties, together with 207,000 horses, 41,000 trucks and 13,600 guns. On 1 April, its high command judged only 8 of 162 divisions in Russia to be "attack ready." Just 160 tanks were serviceable among 16 panzer formations. As Hitler anticipated, once spring came his armies would once more roll forward, and once more win victories. But the critical reality of the first year of war in the east was that Russia remained undefeated.

Near Tula, an old woman gave Vasily Grossman and his little party potatoes, salt and some firewood. Her son Vanya was fighting. She said to Grossman, "Oh, I used to be so healthy, like a stallion. The Devil came to me last night and gripped my palm with his fingernails. I began to pray: 'May God rise again and may his enemies be scattered' . . . My Vanya came to me last night. He sat down on a chair and looked at the window. I said to him, 'Vanya, Vanya!' but he didn't reply." Grossman wrote: "If we do win this terrible, cruel war, it will be because there are such noble hearts in our nation, such righteous people, souls of immense generosity, such old women, mothers of sons who, from their noble simplicity, are now losing their lives for the sake of their nation with the same generosity with which this old woman from Tula has given us all that she had. There is only a handful of them in our land, but they will win."

THE BRITISH PEOPLE, awed by Russian resistance, embraced the Soviet Union as an ally with an enthusiasm that dismayed and even frightened their own ruling caste. At a humble level, such sentiment was manifested by an elderly London cockney who said in an East End pub, "I never believed them Roosians was 'arf as black as they was painted. Seems to me a lot of them is better off than some of us. Here's to 'em, anyway." In loftier circles, and assisted by exclusion from the media of all discussion of Soviet barbarities, intellectual apologists extolled the virtues of Stalin's society. In the United States, the Republicans' 1940 presidential candidate Wendell Willkie wrote in his contemporary book *One World*: "First, Russia is an effective society. It works. It has survival value . . . Second, Russia is our ally in this war. The Russians, more sorely tested by Hitler's might even than the British, have met the test magnificently . . . Third, we must work with Russia after the war . . . There can be no continued peace unless we learn to do so." British academic Sir Bernard Pares wrote in the *Spectator* about his nation's "grateful recognition of the immense burden shouldered by a great and gallant people in our common struggle against the forces of evil, together with the earnest wish that after the war there should be a continuation of this close friendship, without which no peace in Europe is possible."

Pares applauded a new account of Soviet society published by an American admirer: "It is a picture of . . . fallible human beings, ready to learn from their mistakes, amidst enormous difficulties . . . trying to build up in one of the most backward countries in Europe a new human society in which the chief consideration of the State goes to . . . the great mass of the population." Many people happily swallowed such nonsense, nodding that the war proved the superiority of the Soviet system. A friend told the British soldier Henry Novy, "It hasn't half shown up Communism . . . no other country could have done it, only a Communist country, with the people really behind it."

It was probably true that only Russians could have borne and achieved what they did in the face of the 1941 catastrophe. It was less plausible to attribute this to the nobility of communist society. Until Barbarossa, Stalin sought to make common cause with Hitler, albeit to attain different objectives. Even when Russia became joined with the democracies to achieve the defeat of Nazism, Stalin pursued his quest for a Soviet empire, and the domination and oppression of hundreds of millions of people, with absolute single-mindedness and ultimate success. Whatever the merits of the Russian people's struggle to expel the invaders from their country, Stalin's war aims were as selfish and inimical to human liberty as those of Hitler. Soviet conduct could be deemed less barbaric than that of the Nazis only because it embraced no single enormity to match the Holocaust. Nonetheless, the Western Allies were obliged to declare their gratitude, because

Russia's suffering and sacrifice saved the lives of hundreds of thousands of young British and American soldiers. Even if no exalted assertion of principle—instead, only a grapple between rival monsters—caused Russia to become the principal battleground of the war, it was there that the Third Reich encountered the forces that would contrive its nemesis.

CHAPTER EIGHT

AMERICA EMBATTLED

THE PEOPLE OF the United States observed the first twenty-seven months of the struggle in Europe with mingled fascination, horror and disdain. The chief character in J. P. Marquand's contemporary novel *So Little Time* says: "You could get away from the war for a little while, but not for long, because it was everywhere, even in the sunlight. It lay behind everything you said or did. You could taste it in your food, you could hear it in music." Many saw the conflict, and the triumphs of Nazism, as reflecting a collective European degeneracy. There was limited animosity towards the Axis, and some active support for Hitler in German ethnic communities. A Princeton poll on 30 August 1939 found that while 68 percent of Americans thought that U.S. citizens should not be permitted to enlist in the Wehrmacht, 26 percent believed they should retain that option. Very few wanted to see their own nation join either side in a bloodbath an ocean apart from their own continent. A Roper poll in September 1939 asked how the U.S. should frame policy towards the warring nations. Among respondents, 37.5 percent favoured eschewing partisanship, but continuing to sell goods to all parties on a cash-and-carry basis; some 23.6 percent opposed any commercial traffic with any combatant; just 16.1 percent favoured a modification of neutrality to offer aid to Britain and France if they were threatened with defeat. Interventionism enjoyed most support in the southern and western states.

For half the previous decade, President Franklin Roosevelt had been expressing dismay about his people's reluctance to acknowledge their own peril. On 30 October 1939, he wrote to U.S. London ambassador Joseph Kennedy: "We over here, in spite of the great strides towards national unity during the past six years, still have much to learn of the 'relativity' of world geography and the rapid annihilation of distance and purely local economics." Given the strength of isolationism, however, between 1939 and 1941 he felt obliged to act with circumspection in aiding Britain. In many respects a cautious politician, he had to manage what one of his supporters called "the most volatile public opinion in the world." The White House familiar Robert Sherwood wrote: "Before the advent of calamity in

Western Europe and of Winston Churchill, the Allied cause did not have a good smell even in the nostrils of those who hated Fascism and all its evil works."

The writer John Steinbeck spent some weeks in the spring of 1940 sailing down the Pacific coast of South America, from whence he wrote to a friend on 26 March: "We haven't heard any news of Europe since we left and don't much want to. And the people we meet on the shore have never heard of Europe and they seem to be the better for it. This whóle trip is doing what we had hoped it might, given us a world picture not dominated by Hitler and Moscow, but something more vital and surviving than either." Like many liberals, Steinbeck was convinced America would eventually have to fight, but viewed the prospect without enthusiasm. "If it weren't for the coming war, I could look forward to a good quiet life for a few years," he wrote on 9 July.

The morning after Hitler invaded Norway in April 1940, reporters crowded into FDR's office and asked if this brought the United States closer to belligerence. The president chose his words as carefully as ever: "You can put it this way: that the events of the past forty-eight hours will undoubtedly cause a great many more Americans to think about the potentialities of war." Roosevelt avowed reluctance to run for a third presidential term in 1940, and intimated that only world crisis, and explicitly the fall of France, persuaded him to do so. "The question of whether Roosevelt would run," wrote Adolf Berle, one of the president's intimates, on 15 May that year, "is being settled somewhere on the banks of the Meuse River." The president's equivocation was probably disingenuous since, like most national leaders, he loved power. Posterity is assured that no American was better qualified to direct the nation through the greatest emergency in world history, but an insistent minority of Roosevelt's countrymen, notably including the business community, rejected this proposition at the time. Donald Nelson, who later became overlord of America's industrial mobilisation, wrote: "Who among us except the President of the United States really saw the magnitude of the job ahead? . . . All the people I met and talked to, including members of the General Staff, the Army and Navy's highest ranking officers, distinguished statesmen and legislators, thought of the defensive program only as a means of equipping ourselves to keep the enemy away from the shores of the United States."

Rearmament had begun in May 1938, with Roosevelt's $1.15 billion Naval Expansion Bill, followed by the November 1939 Cash-and-Carry Bill, modifying the Neutrality Act to allow belligerents—effectively, the French and British—to purchase American weapons. Roosevelt presided at a meeting of service chiefs at the White House, during which he instructed them to prepare for war and a large expansion of the armed forces. In 1940 he pushed through Congress a Selective Service Act imposing military conscription, and a $15 billion domestic rearmament programme. He delivered a personal message to the legislature declaring that he wanted the United States to build 50,000 planes a year. This prompted a terse note from his chiefs of staff signed by the navy's Adm. Harold "Betty" Stark: "Dear Mr. President,—GREAT—Betty (for all of us)." The U.S. Army expanded from 140,000 men in September 1939 to 1.25 million two years later, but all three chiefs of staff knew that their services remained lamentably ill-prepared to fight a big war. Many members of the armed forces as well as of the civilian community remained unconvinced either that their nation should engage, or that it would.

Young Americans conscripted under the Selective Service Act sulked in their camps: "An army post in peacetime is a dull place," wrote Carson McCullers in a 1941 novel. "Things happen, but then they happen over and over again . . . Perhaps the dullness of a post is caused most of all by insularity and by a surfeit of leisure and safety, for once a man enters the Army, he is expected only to follow the heels ahead of him." Journalist Eric Sevareid described how Roosevelt was "slowly gathering together a reluctant, bewildered and resentful army. No civil leaders dared call them 'soldiers'—as though there were something shameful in the word . . . Few made so bold as to suggest that their job was to learn to kill."

The hesitant military buildup included purchase of an additional 20,000 horses. "The U.S. Army started far too late to prepare seriously for World War II," wrote Martin Blumenson. "As a result, the training program, the procurement of weapons, and virtually all else were hasty, largely improvised, almost chaotic, and painfully inadequate throughout the intensely short period of mobilization and organization before and after Pearl Harbor." Lt. Col. Dwight Eisenhower, commanding an infantry battalion at Fort Lewis, Washington, told his men: "We're going to war. This country is going to war, and I want people who are prepared to fight that war." But such rhetoric merely earned him the derisive nickname "Alarmist Ike."

Many intellectuals disdained Europe's war because they perceived it as a struggle between rival imperialisms, a view reflected in Quincy Howe's 1937 tract *England Expects Every American to Do His Duty*. They found it easier to contemplate an explicitly American crusade against fascism than one that allied them with the old European nations, recoiling from association with the preservation of the British, and for that matter French and Dutch, empires. They disliked the notion that the honour and virtue of the United States should be contaminated by association. They questioned whether a war fought in harness with old Tories could be dignified as a moral undertaking. The left-wing *Partisan Review* asserted: "Our entry into the war, under the slogan of 'Stop Hitler!' would actually result in the immediate introduction of totalitarianism over here."

The treasurer of Harvard, William Claflin, told the university's president: "Hitler's going to win. Let's be friends with him." Robert Sherwood noted the number of businessmen such as Gen. Robert Wood, Jay Hormel and James Mooney likewise convinced of Hitler's impending triumph, and thus "that the United States had better plan to 'do business' with him." At a meeting at the U.S. embassy in London on 22 July, senior diplomats agreed there was an even chance that Britain might still be unconquered by 30 September, but this tepid vote of confidence implicitly acknowledged a similarly plausible prospect that Churchill's island might by that date be occupied. In the September 1940 *Atlantic Monthly*, Kingman Brewster and Spencer Klaw, editors respectively of the Yale and Harvard student papers, published a manifesto asserting students' determination not to save Europe from Hitler.

The British read such declarations with understandable dismay. While their prime minister pinned all his hopes of ultimate victory on U.S. belligerence, in the summer of 1940 his exasperation at the paucity of American aid was matched by scepticism about whether some Washington decision makers could even be entrusted with British confidences. Churchill wrote on 17 July, opposing disclosure of sensitive defence information: "I am not in a hurry to give our secrets until the United States is much nearer to the war than she is now. I expect that anything given to the United States Services, in which there are necessarily so many Germans, goes pretty quickly to Berlin." He modified this view only when it became plain that frankness was indispensable to secure American supplies.

Roosevelt gained domestic support for both aid to Britain and U.S. rearmament by adopting the argument advanced by Gen. John Pershing, his nation's most famous soldier of World War I: his policies would not hasten engagement in the conflict, but instead push it away from America's shores. The British were obliged to pay cash on the nail for every weapon shipped to them until their cash and gold reserves were exhausted, and Lend-Lease became effective, late in 1941. It was as a defensive measure that Roosevelt reconciled the American people to the September 1940 destroyers-for-bases deal with Britain, which even the isolationist *Chicago Tribune* welcomed: "Any arrangement which gives the U.S. naval and air bases in regions which must be brought within the American defense zone is to be accepted as a triumph." Churchill heeded urgent and frequent warnings from Washington that he should say nothing publicly before the 1940 U.S. election that suggested an expectation that America would fight in Europe.

The Luftwaffe's defeat in the Battle of Britain significantly shifted American sentiment not in favour of joining the fight, but towards a belief that Churchill's people might hold out. That September, Secretary of War Henry Stimson wrote in his diary: "It is very interesting to see how the tide of opinion has swung in favour of the eventual victory of G[reat] B[ritain]. The air of pessimism which prevailed two months ago has gone. The reports of our observers on the other side have changed and are now quite optimistic." Meanwhile, the Tripartite Pact signed by Germany, Italy and Japan strengthened American public perceptions of a common evil threatening the world: the United States and Britain now found themselves two among only a dozen surviving democracies. An October opinion poll showed 59 percent American support for material aid to Churchill's people, even at the risk of war.

But isolationism remained a critical force in the 1940 presidential race. Though Republican candidate Wendell Willkie was at heart an interventionist, during the campaign his rhetoric was stridently hostile to belligerence. Roosevelt became alarmed that, as a supposed advocate of war, he was threatened with defeat. Gen. Hugh Johnson, a Scripps-Howard syndicated columnist, wrote: "I know of no well-informed Washington observer who isn't convinced that if Mr. R is elected he will drag us into war at the first opportunity, and that if none presents itself he will make one." A *Fortune* poll on 4 November 1940 showed that 70 percent of Americans saw at least an even chance of their country getting into the war; but while 41 percent favoured giving Britain all possible material aid, only 15.9 percent advocated sending Americans to fight. Lyndon Johnson, a Democratic congressman close to the administration on almost all domestic issues, secured big pork-barrel funding for Texas from the surge in defence spending. Johnson nonetheless spoke out against U.S. involvement in Europe, telling his constituents in June 1940: "The ability of the American people to think calmly and act wisely during a crisis is going to keep us out of a war." He changed his mind only in the summer of 1941, when British defeats in the Mediterranean persuaded him that the threat of an Axis triumph was unacceptable to the United States.

The strength of isolationism caused FDR to make a declaration during a 1940 campaign broadcast which became one of the most controversial of his life: "And while I am talking to you mothers and fathers, I give you one more assurance. I have said this before, but I shall say it again and again and again. Your boys are not going to be sent into any foreign wars." The president's wife, Eleanor, was among those dismayed by this remark. In her newspaper column "My Day," she qualified it importantly: "No one can honestly promise you today peace at home or abroad. All any human being can do is to promise that he will do his utmost to prevent this country being involved in war." The president's penchant for opacity, indeed deceit, was well recognised. But the enigma which so troubled Winston Churchill as well as the American people in 1940–41 will never be susceptible to resolution: whether Roosevelt could ever have made the United States a full fighting partner in the war had not the Axis precipitated such an outcome.

On polling day, 5 November 1940, the president secured 55 percent support for his reelection, 27.2 million votes to 22.3 million. The U.S. minister to Ireland, who was Roosevelt's uncle, described British reaction to the result: "The gentlemanly announcer on the BBC this morning at eight o'clock began 'Roosevelt is in!' His voice betrayed relief and some exultation." But the election outcome emphasised the strength of continuing opposition to the president. Many millions shared the views of George Fisk of Cornell University, who argued that "no war ever accomplished what it was intended to." In December, Roosevelt emphasised to the British government the need for absolute secrecy about the details of arms purchases—for his own domestic political reasons, not those of security.

The American writer Joe Dees wrote to a British friend from New York in January 1941: "All talk centers around aid to England. Americans are proud of the way England is sticking it out, excited by the successes in Albania and Libya, worried over Ireland's suicidal obstinacy [in remaining neutral], fearful of entry ourselves, yet wanting to help out as much as possible." But Dees displayed a shrewd understanding of the range of sentiment in his own country when he wrote later in the year: "Some of my friends hold the opinion that Roosevelt should take stronger measures, full-out convoying with American war vessels etc. They think FDR is behind the national tempo instead of ahead of it. But I think he's driving us as fast as we'll allow. 'We' means 130 million people, includes a mass of corn and wheat-growing, cattle-raising mid-westerners who are sentimentally anti-Nazi but can't see how the Germans could come all the way across the ocean and do anything when they get here. I couldn't call the American public unaware. It is aware all right. But it hasn't that driving conviction that made men die in Spain and other men join the Free French."

The arguments advanced by Roosevelt for supporting Britain mirrored those later deployed by the Western Allies to justify assistance to the Soviet Union: material aid saved American blood, just as Russian blood spared many British and American lives. The March 1941 Lend-Lease Act authorised credit deliveries: only 1 percent of munitions used by Churchill's forces that year was Lend-Lease material, but thereafter the programme provided most of the island's food and fuel, together with a large part of its armed forces' tanks, transport aircraft and amphibious operations equipment. The British focused their own industrial production on combat aircraft, warships, army weapons and vehicles. From 1941 onwards, they were almost wholly dependent upon American credit to pay for their war effort.

Though Winston Churchill strained every sinew to induce the U.S. president to lead his nation into belligerence before Pearl Harbor, it was fortunate that his efforts failed. In the unlikely event that Roosevelt could have forced a declaration of war on Germany through the U.S. Congress, thereafter he would have led a divided nation. Until December 1941, public opinion remained stubbornly opposed to fighting Hitler. A much higher proportion of people favoured stern action against the Japanese, a policy most conspicuously manifested in the July 1941 freeze on Japanese assets and embargo on all exports, which was decisive in committing Tokyo to fight, since 80 percent of its oil supplies came from the United States and the Dutch East Indies. The embargo was far more popular at home than Roosevelt's escalation of the U.S. Navy's role in the Battle of the Atlantic—escorting convoys to Britain progressively farther east, and sporadically exchanging fire with U-boats.

Whatever the president's personal wishes, Congress remained a critical check upon American policy until Tokyo and Berlin put an end to argument. Historian David Kennedy has suggested that, since Germany was always the principal enemy of the democracies, Roosevelt would have better served his nation's interests by averting war with Japan in order to concentrate upon the destruction of Nazism: "a little appeasement—another name for diplomacy—might have yielded rich rewards." Once Hitler was beaten, Kennedy argues, the ambitions of Japan's militarists could have been frustrated with vastly less expenditure of life and treasure, by the threat or application of irresistible Allied power. But this argument raises a larger question: whether Roosevelt could ever have persuaded his people to fight the Germans, in the absence of overwhelming aggression such as Hitler refused to initiate.

Even after war was declared in December 1941, and indeed until the end of hostilities, few Americans felt anything like the animosity towards Germans that they displayed against the Japanese. This was not merely a matter of racial sentiment. There was also passionate sympathy for the horrors China had experienced, and continued to experience, at Japanese hands. Most Americans deplored what the Nazis were doing to the world, but would have remained unenthusiastic or indeed implacably hostile about sending armies to Europe, had not Hitler forced the issue.

On 27 May 1941, following the fall of Greece and Crete, 85 million Americans listened to Roosevelt's national radio broadcast, in which he warned of the perils of Nazi victory. The nation was, in one historian's words, "afraid, unhappy and bewildered." The president concluded by declaring a "state of unlimited national emergency." No one was sure what this meant, save that it brought war closer and increased the powers of the executive. Many towns, especially in the South, began to experience economic booms on the back of military and naval construction programmes. Yet labour disputes dogged the nation: some industrial workers felt as alienated from America's national purposes, and from their employers, as their counterparts in Britain did. Unregulated mining killed nearly 1,300 U.S. underground workers in 1940 and maimed many more; passions ran so high that strikes were often violent. Four men died and twelve more were badly injured during a 1941 dispute in Harlan County, Kentucky.

Popular sentiment strongly resisted admitting foreign refugees, victims of Nazi persecution: in June 1941 it was decreed that no one with relatives in Germany could enter the United States. The isolationists never quit. There was a powerful Irish lobby, most stridently represented by Father Charles Coughlin, a pamphleteer and radio star. Roosevelt wrote on 19 May 1941 to one of Coughlin's supporters, Representative James O'Connor of Montana, an extreme isolationist: "Dear Jim, When will you Irishmen ever get over hating England? Remember that if England goes down, Ireland goes down too. Ireland has a better chance for complete independence if democracy survives in the world than if Hitlerism supersedes it. Come down and talk to me about it some day—but do stop thinking in terms of ancient hatreds and think of the future. Always sincerely."

Senator D. Worth Clarke of Idaho, another isolationist, suggested in July 1941 that the United States should draw a line across the ocean behind which Americans would stand, taking peaceful control of their entire hemisphere, South America and Canada included: "We could make some kind of an arrangement to set up puppet governments which we could trust to put American interests ahead of those of Germany or any other nation of the world." His remarks were gleefully reported in the Axis media as evidence of Yankee imperialism. Informed Germans assumed U.S. participation in the war much more confidently than did the British, or indeed many Americans. Back in 1938, Reich Finance Minister Schwerin von Krosigk anticipated a struggle that "will be fought not only with military means but also will be an economic war of the greatest scope." Von Krosigk was deeply troubled by the contrast between Germany's economic weakness and the enormous resources available to its prospective enemies. Hitler believed that these would include America from 1942. He preferred not to hasten U.S. belligerency, but was untroubled by its prospect, partly because his own grasp of economics was so weak. Amid so many American domestic divisions, so much equivocation and hesitation, it was fortunate for the Allied cause that the decisions which brought the United States into the war were made in Tokyo rather than Washington, D.C.

JAPAN'S MILITARY LEADERS made their critical commitment in 1937, when they embarked upon the conquest of China. This provoked widespread international hostility, and proved a strategic error of the first magnitude. Amid the vastness of the country, their military successes and seizures of territory were meaningless. A despairing Japanese soldier scrawled on the wall of a wrecked building: "Fighting and death everywhere and now I am also wounded. China is limitless and we are like drops of water in an ocean. There is no purpose in this war. I shall never see my home again." Though the Japanese dominated the China war against the corrupt regime and ill-equipped armies of Generalissimo Chiang Kai-shek, they suffered debilitating attrition, including 185,000 dead by the end of 1941. Even a huge deployment of manpower—a million Japanese soldiers remained in China until 1945—proved unable to force a decisive outcome upon either Chiang's Nationalists or the communists of Mao Tse-tung, whose forces they confronted and sometimes engaged across a front of 2,000 miles.

Western perceptions of the war with Japan are dominated by the Pacific and Southeast Asian campaigns. Yet China, and Tokyo's refusal to abandon its ambitions there, were central to Japan's ultimate failure. Between 1937 and 1939, major war fighting took place, largely unrecognized in the West, in which Japanese forces prevailed, but at the cost of heavy losses. Its withdrawal from the mainland could probably have averted war with the United States, since Japanese aggression there, and the culture of massacre symbolised by the deaths of at least 60,000 and perhaps many more civilians in Nanjing, were the principal sources of American animosity, indeed outrage. Moreover, even if China's own armies were ineffectual, Japan's commitment imposed a massive haemorrhage of resources. The curse upon the Tokyo government was its dominance by soldiers committed to the perceived virtue of making war for its own sake. Intoxicated by a belief in their warrior virility, they failed to grasp the difficulty, even impossibility, of successfully making war upon the United States, the world's greatest industrial power, impregnable to assault.

Japan's 1941–42 military triumphs caused the Western Allies to overrate its army, as they might not have done had they known of a significant earlier clash, which it had suited both parties to cloak in secrecy. In the summer of 1939, skirmishes between the Japanese and Russian armies on their common border dividing Manchuria from Mongolia erupted into full-scale war, commonly known as the Nomonhan Incident. Since the beginning of the century, powerful voices in Japan had urged imperialist expansion into Siberia. In the aftermath of the 1917 Bolshevik Revolution, for some time Japanese forces deployed there, hoping to stake claims which could later be formalised. Only the belated decision of the Western powers to support a stabilised, unified Soviet Union caused them to withdraw. In 1939, Tokyo judged the Russians weak and vulnerable, and committed an army to test their resolve.

The outcome was a disaster for the Japanese. Gen. Georgy Zhukov launched a counteroffensive, supported by powerful armoured and air forces, which achieved a comprehensive victory. Published casualty figures are unreliable, but probably totalled at least 25,000 on each side. Peace was restored in October, on Moscow's terms. The strategic consequences were important to the course of the Second World War: the Japanese army set its face against the "strike north" policy, flinching from renewed conflict with the Soviet Union. In 1941 Tokyo signed a neutrality pact with Moscow. Most of Japan's leaders favoured honouring this, believing that the Western empires in Southeast Asia offered softer targets for national expansion. They expected Germany to win the war in Europe. Japanese military attachés in London and Stockholm who reported that the Germans were ill-equipped to launch an invasion of Britain were rebuked by their superiors in Tokyo, to whom such views were unacceptable. Germany's war in Europe was overwhelmingly responsible for precipitating Japan's war in Asia: Tokyo would never have dared to attack but for its conviction that a Hitlerian triumph in the west was imminent.

On 27 September 1940, the Tripartite Pact was signed in Berlin between Germany, Italy and Japan, which promised mutual assistance if any of the parties was attacked by a nation not engaged in the European war. This was a move designed to deter the United States from exerting further pressure on Japan, and it failed. The United States, implacably hostile to Japanese imperialism in China, imposed further sanctions.

In response, the Japanese committed themselves to execute the "strike south" strategy. They prepared to seize the West's ill-defended Southeast Asian possessions in a series of lightning operations, bludgeoning America into acquiescence by evicting its forces from the western Pacific.

In the middle of 1941, the Japanese military drafted their optimistically titled "Operational Plan for Ending the War with the U.S., Britain, the Netherlands and Chiang Kai-shek." Initially, they intended to "await a good opportunity in the European war situation, notably collapse of mainland England, ending of the German-Soviet war and success of our policies towards India." Emperor Hirohito said, after studying the plan: "I understand you are going to do Hong Kong after Malaya starts. Well, what about the foreign concessions in China?" His Majesty was assured that such European properties would indeed be seized. Tokyo was disappointed, however, in its hopes of delaying a declaration of war until Germany's victory in the west became complete. This miscalculation was almost as fundamental as the Japanese misreading of the enemy's character. With the notable exceptions of a few enlightened officers such as Adm. Isoroku Yamamoto, the naval commander-in-chief, Japanese regarded Americans as an unwarlike and frankly degenerate people, whom a series of devastating blows would reconcile to a negotiated peace.

Hesitation and incoherence characterised Japan's pre–Pearl Harbor strategy. In 1940, Tokyo committed troops and aircraft in French Indochina, with Vichy's assent under duress. The Indochinese supply route to China was closed, increasing pressure on Chiang Kai-shek. Japan's foremost objective in Southeast Asia was the oil of the East Indies, to which the Dutch exile government in London continued to refuse access. For a time, Japan's generals cherished hopes of confining an assault to the European colonies, sparing America's Philippines dependency. But in the early months of 1941, Japanese naval commanders convinced their army counterparts that U.S. belligerence was inevitable in the event of any "strike south." Tokyo's planners thereupon set about devising plans for a series of swift thrusts that would overrun the weak defences of Malaya, Burma, the Philippines and the Dutch East Indies, creating new realities which the United States would deem it too costly to try to undo.

The calculations of Japan's militarists were rooted in conceit, fatalism—a belief in *shikata ga nai*, "it cannot be helped"—and ignorance of the world outside Asia. Japan's soldiers had remarkable powers of physical endurance, matched by willingness for sacrifice. The army had good air support, but was seriously deficient in tanks and artillery. The country's industrial and scientific base was much too weak to support a sustained conflict against the United States. Germany and Japan never seriously coordinated strategy or objectives, partly because they had few in common beyond defeat of the Allies, and partly because they were geographically remote from each other. Hitler's racial principles caused him to recoil from association with the Japanese, and only grudgingly to acknowledge them as his cobelligerents. It is just possible that, if Japan had struck west into Russia soon after the German invasion of June 1941, such a blow would have turned the scale against Stalin, making possible Axis victory, and delaying if not averting a showdown with the United States. Foreign Minister Yosuke Matsuoka resigned from the Tokyo government when this option, which he favoured, was rejected by his colleagues.

As it was, though Japan's 1941–42 Asian conquests shocked and appalled the Western powers, they were assuredly reversible if Germany could be beaten. No one in London or Washington doubted that Japan's defeat would be a lengthy and difficult task, partly because of the distances involved. But few thoughtful strategists, and certainly not Admiral Yamamoto, doubted the inevitability of America's eventual triumph, unless its national will collapsed in the face of early defeats. Given that Japan could not invade the United States, American power must ultimately prove irresistible by a nation with only 10 percent of U.S. industrial capacity and dependent on imports for its existence.

Japan made an essential preliminary move for its descent on Malaya by occupying all of neighbouring Indochina at the end of July, without incurring Vichy French resistance. On 9 August, Tokyo made a final decision against launching an attack on Russia, in 1941 anyway. By September, Japanese thinking was dominated by the new reality of the U.S. oil embargo, an earnest of Roosevelt's resolve, though there is evidence that his subordinates misinterpreted a presidential desire to limit Japanese oil supplies and thus promote strategic restraint into an absolute cut off that accelerated the slide to war. Tokyo concluded that its only options were to bow to U.S. demands, the least palatable of which was to quit China, or to strike swiftly. Emperor Hirohito pressed his government for further diplomacy, and Prime Minister Prince Konoe accordingly proposed a summit between himself and Roosevelt. Washington, recognising an attempt at prevarication, rebuffed this initiative. On 1 December an imperial conference in Tokyo confirmed the decision to fight. War Minister Gen. Hideki Tojo, who assumed the premiership on 17 October, said: "Our empire stands at the threshold of glory or oblivion." Thus starkly did Japan's militarists view their choices, founded in a grandiose vision of their rightful dominance of Asia. Yet even Tojo recognised the impossibility of achieving outright victory over the United States. He and his colleagues instead sought to empower themselves by battlefield triumphs to achieve a negotiated settlement.

JAPAN LAUNCHED its strike against Pearl Harbor and its assault on Southeast Asia on 7 December 1941, just twenty-four hours after the Russians began the counteroffensive that saved Moscow. It would be many months before the Western Allies recognised that the Soviet Union would survive. But if Japan's emissaries had better understood the mood in Berlin, had they been less blinded by their admiration for the Nazis and thus capable of grasping the gravity of Germany's predicament in the east, Tojo's government might yet have hesitated before unleashing its whirlwind. With hindsight, Japan's timing was lamentable: its best chance of exploiting its victims' weakness was already past. A cardinal Japanese error was to suppose that Tokyo could set limits for the war it started, notably by staying out of the German-Soviet struggle. In reality, once Japan had transformed the European war into a global conflict, inflicting humiliation upon its Western enemies, the only possible outcomes were either absolute victory or absolute defeat. Japan attacked on the basis of calculations which were introspective—indeed, self-obsessed even by the normal standards of nation-states—and matched by stunning geopolitical ignorance.

The nakedness of America's Pacific bases continues to puzzle posterity. Overwhelming evidence of Tokyo's intentions was available throughout November, chiefly through decrypted diplomatic traffic; in Washington as in London, there was uncertainty only about Japanese objectives. The thesis advanced by extreme conspiracists, that President Roosevelt chose to permit Pearl Harbor to be surprised, is rejected as absurd by all serious historians. It remains nonetheless extraordinary that his government and chiefs of staff failed to ensure that Hawaii, as well as other bases closer to Japan, were on a full precautionary footing. On 27 November 1941, Washington cabled all Pacific headquarters: "This dispatch is to be considered a war warning. An aggressive move by Japan is expected within the next few days . . . Execute appropriate defensive deployment." The failure of local commanders to act effectively in response to this message was egregious: at Pearl Harbor on 7 December, antiaircraft ammunition boxes were still locked, their keys held by duty officers.

But it was a conspicuous feature of the war that again and again, dramatic changes of circumstance unmanned the victims of assault. The British and French in May 1940, the Russians in June 1941, even the Germans in Normandy in June 1944, had every reason to anticipate enemy action, yet responded inadequately when this came, and there were many lesser examples. Senior commanders, never mind humble subordinates, found it hard to adjust their mind-set and behaviour to the din of battle until this was thrust upon them, until bombardment became a reality rather than a mere prospect. Adm. Husband Kimmel and Lt. Gen. Walter Short, respectively navy and army commanders at Pearl Harbor, were unquestionably negligent. But their conduct reflected an institutional failure of imagination which extended up the entire U.S. command chain to the White House, and inflicted a trauma on the American people.

"We were flabbergasted by the devastation," wrote a sailor aboard the carrier *Enterprise*, which entered Pearl late on the afternoon of 8 December, having been mercifully absent when the Japanese struck. "One battleship, the *Nevada*, was lying athwart the narrow entrance channel, beached bow first, allowing barely enough room for the carrier to squeeze by . . . The water was covered with oil, fires were burning still, ships were resting on the bottom mud, superstructures had broken and fallen. Great gaps loomed where magazines had exploded, and smoke was roiling up everywhere. For sailors who had considered these massive ships invincible, it was a sight to be seen but not comprehended . . . We seemed to be mourners at a spectacular funeral."

The assault on Pearl Harbor prompted rejoicing throughout the Axis nations. Japanese lieutenant Izumiya Tatsuro wrote exultantly of "the glorious news of the air attack on Hawaii." Mussolini, with his accustomed paucity of judgement, was delighted: he thought Americans stupid, and the United States "a country of Negroes and Jews," as did Hitler. Yet fortunately for the Allied cause, American vulnerability at Hawaii was matched by a Japanese timidity which would become an astonishingly familiar phenomenon of the Pacific conflict. Again and again, Japanese fleets fought their way to the brink of important victories, then lacked either the will or the means to follow through. Adm. Chuichi Nagumo was stunned by the success of his own aircraft in wrecking five U.S. battleships in their Sunday-morning attacks. For many years, it was argued that he wilfully missed the opportunity to follow through with a second strike against Pearl Harbor's oil storage tanks and repair facilities, which might have forced the Pacific Fleet to withdraw to the U.S. west coast. Recent research shows, however, that this was not feasible. The winter day was too short to launch and recover a second strike, and in any event Japanese bombloads were too small to plausibly wreck Pearl's repair bases. Even the problem created by destruction of shore oil tanks could have been solved by diverting tankers from the Atlantic. The core reality was that Nagumo's attack sufficed to shock, maul and enrage the Americans, but not to

decisively cripple their war-fighting capability. It was thus a grossly mis-
conceived operation. From 7 December 1941 the United States became
unshakeably committed to total war, total victory. The legend of the "Day
of Infamy" united the American people as belligerents in a fashion no
lesser provocation could have achieved.

For many months, Winston Churchill had been haunted by apprehension that Japan might attack only the European empires in Asia, so that
Britain would confront a new enemy without gaining the United States
as an ally. Hitler meanwhile contemplated a mirror image of this spectre, fearing that America might enter the war against Germany, while
Japan stayed neutral. He had always expected to fight Roosevelt's people
once he had completed the destruction of Russia. In December 1941 he
considered it a matter of course to follow Japan's lead, and entertained
extravagant hopes that Hirohito's fleet would crush the U.S. Navy. Four
days after Pearl Harbor, he made the folly of the strike comprehensive
by declaring war on the United States, relieving Roosevelt from a serious
uncertainty about whether Congress would agree to fight Germany. John
Steinbeck wrote to a friend: "The attack, whatever it may have gained
from a tactical point of view, was a failure in that it solidified the country.
But we'll lose lots of ships for a while."

In the course of 1941, the *Ladies' Home Journal* had published a fascinating series of domestic profiles of Americans of all social classes, under
the heading "How America Lives." Until December, the threat of war
scarcely impinged on the existences of those depicted. Some struggled
financially, and a few acknowledged poverty, but most asserted a real satisfaction with their lot, which explains their dismay, following Pearl Harbor,
at beholding familiar patterns broken, dreams confounded, and families
sundered. The magazine's editor, Mary Carson Cookman, wrote a postscript, reflecting on the profiles published earlier in the year, and the new
circumstances of Americans: "War is changing the condition of life everywhere. But . . . the people of the United States are good people; they are
almost surprisingly modest in their demands upon life. What they have is
precious to them . . . What they hope to achieve, they are willing to work
for—they don't want or expect it to be given them . . . What we have now
will do. But it ought to be better, it must be better, and it *will* be better."

If this was a trite assertion of the American Dream as the nation
embarked upon hostilities, it seems nonetheless to reflect its dominant
mood. The struggle would cost the United States less than any other
combatant—indeed, it generated an economic boom which enabled
Americans to emerge from the war much richer than they started. But

many suffered a lasting sense of unfairness, that the wickedness of others had invaded and ravaged their decent lives. Like hundreds of millions of Europeans before them, they began to discover the sorrow of seeing their nearest and dearest leave home to face mortal risk. Mrs. Elizabeth Schlesinger wrote about the departure of her son Tom for the army: "I knew after Pearl Harbor that his going was inevitable. I won't let myself think personally about it. I am only one of millions of mothers who love their sons and see them go off to war and my feelings are universal and not mine alone. I have accepted what I must face and live with for many future months and perhaps years. Tom said, 'Why, I thought you would be much more upset by my going.' Little does he know the depths of what it means to me and the countless anxieties that clamor for my thoughts."

In the absence of Pearl Harbor, it remains highly speculative when, if ever, the United States would have fought. In John Morton Blum's words, "The war was neither a threat nor a crusade. It seemed, as *Fortune* put it, 'only a painful necessity' . . . Within the United States, Americans never saw the enemy. The nation did not share or want to share in the disasters that visited Europe and Asia." For all the exuberant declarations of patriotism that followed the "Day of Infamy," many Americans remained resentful about the need to accept even a modest share of the privations thrust upon most of the world's peoples. Early in 1942, Arthur Schlesinger visited the Midwest on a tour of army bases for the Office of War Information: "We arrived in the midst of the whining about gas rationing, and it was pretty depressing. The anti-administration feeling is strong and open."

Fortunately for the Allied cause, however, the leadership of the United States showed itself in this supreme crisis both strong and wise. At Roosevelt's Washington summit with Churchill at the end of December 1941, the United States confirmed its provisional commitment, made during earlier staff talks, to prioritise war with Germany. Since 1939, American military and naval preparations—notably Plan Orange, eventually translated into Rainbow 5—had assumed the likelihood of a two-front struggle. The army correctly judged that this could not be won "primarily by naval action"; that the creation and deployment overseas of large land forces would be indispensable. Adm. Harold Stark wrote to the secretary of the navy on 12 November 1940: "Alone, the British Empire lacks the manpower and the material means to master Germany. Assistance by powerful allies is necessary both with respect to men and with respect to munitions and supplies." Stark anticipated the likelihood that, if the Japanese struck, the British would lose Malaya. He proposed a blockade of Japan, to which its absolute dependence on imports rendered it exceptionally vulnerable, then envisaged fighting a limited war in the East, while sending large land and air forces to Europe.

The U.S. chiefs of staff recognised that Germany represented by far the more dangerous menace. The Japanese, for all their impressive frontline military and naval capability, could not threaten the American or British homelands. Of the white Anglo-Saxon nations, only Australia lay within plausible reach of Tokyo's forces, which prompted intense bitterness among Australian politicians about Britain's unwillingness to dispatch substantial forces to its defence. In the event, while the broad principles established by Stark were sustained, the dominance of Russia in defeating the Wehrmacht—wholly unanticipated in December 1941—somewhat altered the balance of America's wartime commitments. While the army the United States eventually dispatched to Europe was large, it was nothing like as powerful as would have been necessary had the Western Allies been obliged to fulfil the principal role in defeating Germany. As a corollary of this, once Russia's survival and fighting power became plain in 1943, the American chiefs of staff felt able to divert significant strength to the Pacific sooner than expected; popular sentiment, so much more hostile to Japan than Germany, made this politically expedient as well as strategically acceptable.

Geoffrey Perrett has observed that the United States was not ready for Pearl Harbor, but was ready for war. This was true only insofar as a large naval building programme was in progress. In the week following the attack, American yards launched 13 new warships and 9 merchantmen, harbingers of a vast armada that was already on the stocks and would be launched during the next two years. The nation had under construction 15 battleships, 11 carriers, 54 cruisers, 193 destroyers and 73 submarines. Nonetheless, it was plain to the governments of Britain and America, if not to their peoples, that a long delay was in prospect before Western land forces could engage Germany on the Continent. For years to come, Russia must bear the chief burden of fighting the Wehrmacht. Even if, as the U.S. chiefs of staff wished, the Western Allies launched an early diversionary landing in France, their armies would remain relatively small until 1944.

Roosevelt and Churchill consequently accepted, as some of their commanders did not, the necessity to undertake secondary operations, plausible only in the Mediterranean theatre, to sustain a sense of momentum in the minds of their peoples. The bomber offensive against Germany would grow as fast as the necessary aircraft could be built. But as long as the Eastern Front remained the decisive ground theatre, aid to Russia was a priority. Even if quantities of material available for shipment remained relatively small until 1943, both Washington and London acknowledged the importance of making every possible gesture to deter Stalin from negotiating a separate peace. Anglo-American fears that the Russians would be beaten, or at least driven to parley with Hitler, remained a constant spectre in alliance relations until the end of 1942.

Meanwhile in the east, Japan held the initiative, and deployed formidable forces on land, at sea and in the air. "We Japanese," asserted the field manual distributed to all Hirohito's soldiers as they embarked for their assault on the Western empires, "heirs to 2,600 years of a glorious past, have now, in response to the trust placed in us by His Majesty the Commander-in-Chief, risen in the cause of the peoples of Asia, and embarked upon a noble and solemn undertaking which will change the course of world history . . . The Task of the Showa Restoration, which is to realise his Imperial Majesty's desire for peace in the Far East, and to set Asia free, rests squarely on our shoulders." Having devastated the battleships of the U.S. Pacific Fleet, the Japanese now fulfilled their longstanding ambition to seize the American dependency of the Philippines, together with the vast natural resources of the Dutch East Indies—modern Indonesia—and British Hong Kong, Malaya and Burma. Within the space of five months, against feeble resistance, they created an empire. Even though this would prove the most short-lived in history, for a season Japan gained dominance over vast expanses of the Asian landmass and Pacific seascape.

CHAPTER NINE

JAPAN'S SEASON OF TRIUMPH

1. "I Suppose You'll Shove the Little Men Off"

MANY JAPANESE welcomed the war, which they believed offered their country its only honourable escape from beleaguerment. The novelist Dazai Osamu, for instance, was "itching to beat the bestial, insensitive Americans to a pulp." But it would be mistaken to imagine Osamu's society as a monolith. Lt. Gen. Kuribayashi Tadimichi, who had spent two years in the United States, wrote to his wife asserting his strong opposition to challenging so mighty a foe on the battlefield: "Its industrial potential is huge, and its people are energetic and versatile. One must never underestimate the Americans' fighting ability." Eighteen-year-old Sasaki Hachiro mused to his diary: "How many really die 'tragic deaths' in this war? I am sure there are more comical deaths under the disguise of tragic deaths . . . Comical deaths involve no joy of life, but are filled with agony without any meaning or value." Hachiro at an early stage resigned himself to his own extinction, and volunteered as a pilot with an almost explicit determination to satisfy fate, as indeed he did—*shikata ga nai*. His disdain for Japan's militarists never faded: he persuaded his younger brother to become a science student with immunity from conscription, so that he, at least, might survive.

Hachiro's contemporary Hayashi Tadao was another fatalist, strongly opposed to the war. His diary repeatedly expressed disgust towards his own country. He asked himself: "Japan, why don't I love and respect you? . . . I feel that I have to accept the fate of my generation to fight in the war and die . . . We have to go to the battlefield without being able to express our opinions, criticise and argue pros and cons of issues . . . it is a great tragedy." Japan's 1941–42 successes against feeble Western resistance caused both sides to overrate the power of Hirohito's nation. Just as Germany was not strong enough to defeat the Soviet Union, Japan was too weak to sustain its Asian conquests unless the West chose to acquiesce in early defeats. But this, like so much else, is more readily apparent today than it was seventy years ago, in the midst of Japanese triumphs.

Until December 1941, the sluggish, humid, pampered rhythm of colonial life in Asia was scarcely interrupted by events in Europe. In America's

Philippines dependency, army nurse Lt. Earlyn Black was one of thousands of expatriates who revelled in a life of comfort and elegance, cushioned by submissive servants: "Each evening we dressed for dinner in long dresses, the men in tuxedos, dinner jackets with cummerbunds. It was very formal-type living. Even to go the movies, we'd put on a long dress." Another nurse, twenty-five-year-old Lt. Hattie Brantly from Jefferson, Texas, found the notion of war with Japan inconceivable: "It was a joke and our Chief Nurse would say in the mess, 'Have another biscuit, girls. You're going to need this when the Japs get us' . . . We just sort of rocked along and were happy, and didn't give it too much thought."

Likewise in British Singapore, a Czech motor engineer, Val Kabouky, described the white residents as "modern Pompeiians." Even after more than two years of war, 31,000 Europeans among a population of 5 million Malays and Chinese sustained a parody of imperial privilege. New Western arrivals in the colony who sought to learn as much as was necessary of the local language could purchase a phrase book entitled *Malay for Mems*—short for "Memsahibs." It was couched in the language of command: "Put up the tennis net," "You must follow the Mem," "Shoot that man." In 1941 arriving troops, especially Australians, were disgusted to find themselves excluded from the colonists' social bastions. Indians were not permitted to ride in the same rail carriages as the British, nor to enter their clubs. There was a mutiny in the Hyderabad Regiment when an Indian officer was ordered home for having sexual relations with a white woman; he was reinstated and the affair hushed up, but bitterness persisted. Lady Diana, wife of the British minister Duff Cooper, wrote with aristocratic scorn for the pretensions of the British expatriates: "most frail, tarty and peasant-pompous." Her own enthusiasm for Singapore's tourist charms struck a bizarre note as catastrophe unfolded farther north: "There is the working life of the Chinks going on before your eyes down every street—coffin-making, lantern-painting, and a tremendous lot of shaving. I never tire of strolling and savouring."

In Malaya, Britain's military commanders and rulers alike reflected a paucity of talent. The empire seemed to have an inexhaustible supply of unwarlike warrior chieftains. Air Marshal Sir Robert Brooke-Popham, commander-in-chief Far East until the end of 1941, was a sixty-three-year-old former governor of Kenya. Lt. Gen. Arthur Percival, the army commander, was a long-serving staff officer whose meagre operational experience had been gained against the Sinn Féin insurgency in Ireland. Sir Shenton Thomas, the colony's governor, said to the generals as the Japanese began to land in the north early on 8 December: "I suppose you'll shove the little men off." His contempt might have been enhanced by reading the orders issued to Japan's soldiers committed to the assault on Malaya, which included homely injunctions to avoid constipation and heartburn, and to employ deep-breathing exercises to escape seasickness: "Remember that in the dark and steaming lowest decks of the ship, with no murmur of complaint of their treatment, the Army horses are suffering patiently." Men were urged: "When you encounter the enemy after landing, regard yourself as an avenger come at last face to face with your father's murderer."

Although British and imperial troops were deployed in northern Malaya in expectation of a Japanese amphibious assault from Siam, the onset of war inflicted a cultural shock as devastating as the attack on Pearl Harbor. Each society around the world which found itself overtaken by the contagion of violence responded with initial disbelief, even if logic had been proclaiming its inevitability from the rooftops. When the first Japanese bombs fell on Singapore in the early hours of 8 December, Australian engine-room artificer Bill Reeve was asleep in his bunk in the harbour aboard the destroyer *Vendetta*, fresh from months of heavy action in the Mediterranean. On hearing explosions, Reeve thought he was having a bad dream of battles past: "I said to myself, 'You silly bastard, roll over.'" A heavy concussion close at hand caused him to acknowledge reality, yet even as successive sticks of bombs fell, the city's street lights blazed on.

Churchill had made a brutal and probably inescapable decision to concentrate the best of the empire's forces in the Middle East. The air defence of Malaya mustered just 145 aircraft, of which 66 were Buffaloes, 57 Blenheims and 22 Hudsons. The obsolesence of most of these aircraft was less significant than the overwhelming superiority of Japanese pilots in experience and proficiency to those of the Allies. When invaders began to land at Kota Baharu, the defenders' response was pitifully limp: it was some hours before local RAF commanders bestirred themselves to launch strikes against the invasion fleet. When they did so, British and Australian planes, along with the shoreline defenders, inflicted over a thousand casualties. Not all the invading troops showed themselves heroes: a Japanese officer described how "one section of non-commissioned officers of the Independent Engineers had . . . become panic-stricken at the enemy's bombing. Without orders from the troop leader, they boarded the large motor boats . . . and retreated to the open sea off Saigon."

Yet by the end of the first day, British air strength in northern Malaya had been halved, to around fifty serviceable planes. Many senior officers and ground crews failed to act effectively: the pilots of a section of Buffalo fighters which took off to intercept attacking Japanese were disgusted to discover that armourers had failed to load their guns. At Kuantan airfield, hundreds of ground personnel fled in panic. "How is this possible? They are all sahibs," a bemused Indian driver of the Royal Garwhal Rifles asked his officer as the two contemplated a chaos of equipment, personal baggage, tennis rackets and debris strewn around airfield buildings. The young lieutenant snapped back crossly: "They are not sahibs, they're Australians." But British soldiers and airmen were also fleeing. Some Indian units collapsed in panic; the British commander of a Sikh battalion was believed to have been shot by his own men before they bolted. "We now understood the capacity of the enemy," wrote a Japanese officer contemptuously. "The only things we had to fear were the quantity of munitions he had and the thoroughness of his demolitions."

The first of countless atrocities took place. Three British airmen who crash-landed in Siam were arrested by its gendarmerie, who handed them over to the Japanese. Tokyo's local vice-consul told a Siamese judge that they were "guilty of taking Japanese lives and destroying Japanese property," and the men were beheaded on a nearby beach. Historically, and notably in the 1905 Russo-Japanese war, the Japanese army's conduct towards defeated enemies had been characterised by mercy. The ruling Tokyo "control group" changed all that, instilling a culture of ruthlessness indistinguishable from barbarism into its armed forces; in 1934 the Ministry of War published a pamphlet which ennobled conflict as "the father of creation and mother of culture. Rivalry for supremacy does for the state what struggle against adversity does for the individual." The Allies now began to discover the significance of this merciless vision for those who fell into enemy hands.

Before the battle cruiser *Repulse* left Singapore with the battleship *Prince of Wales*, to seek Japanese amphibious shipping, there was a dance on the great ship's after-deck. This roused in Diana Cooper's breast ghosts of the Duchess of Richmond's legendary soirée before the Battle of Waterloo: "Brussels ball once again." Off eastern Malaya, Captain William Tennant told his crew: "We are going to carry out a sweep to the northwards to see what we can pick up and what we can roar up. We must all be on our toes . . . I know the old ship will give a good account of itself . . . Life-saving gear is to be worn or carried . . . not because I think anything is going to happen to the ship—she is much too lucky." Yet just before midday on 10 December, *Repulse* and *Prince of Wales* were sunk by Japanese aircraft, a devastating blow to British prestige throughout Asia. Consolation could be sought only in the heroism of some doomed men such as Wilfred Parker, the New Zealand chaplain of *Prince of Wales* who stayed with the dying rather than save himself. A British fighter pilot who flew over the scene as hundreds of sailors clung to wreckage in the oil-

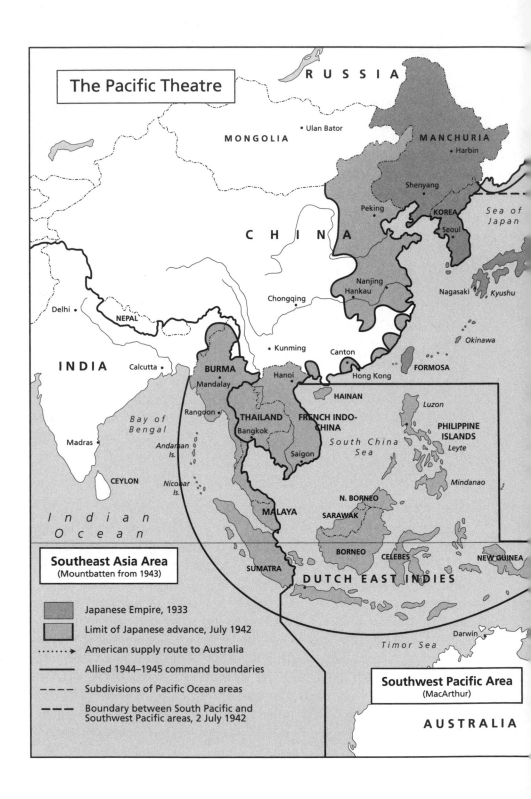

The Pacific Theatre

RUSSIA

MONGOLIA
• Ulan Bator

MANCHURIA
• Harbin

Shenyang •

Peking •

KOREA

Sea of Japan

CHINA

Seoul •

Nanjing
Hankau

Nagasaki   Kyushu

Chongqing •

• Delhi

NEPAL

• Kunming   Canton •

Okinawa

INDIA   Calcutta •

BURMA
Mandalay •

Hanoi •

Hong Kong

FORMOSA

HAINAN

Luzon

Bay of
Bengal

Rangoon •

THAILAND

FRENCH INDO-
CHINA

PHILIPPINE
ISLANDS

Madras •

Bangkok •

Andaman
Is.

South China
Sea

Leyte

CEYLON

Nicobar
Is.

Saigon •

Mindanao

N. BORNEO

MALAYA

SARAWAK

Indian
Ocean

BORNEO   CELEBES   NEW GUINEA

Southeast Asia Area
(Mountbatten from 1943)

SUMATRA

DUTCH EAST INDIES

Japanese Empire, 1933

Limit of Japanese advance, July 1942

Darwin •

American supply route to Australia

Timor Sea

Allied 1944–1945 command boundaries

Subdivisions of Pacific Ocean areas

Southwest Pacific Area
(MacArthur)

Boundary between South Pacific and
Southwest Pacific areas, 2 July 1942

AUSTRALIA

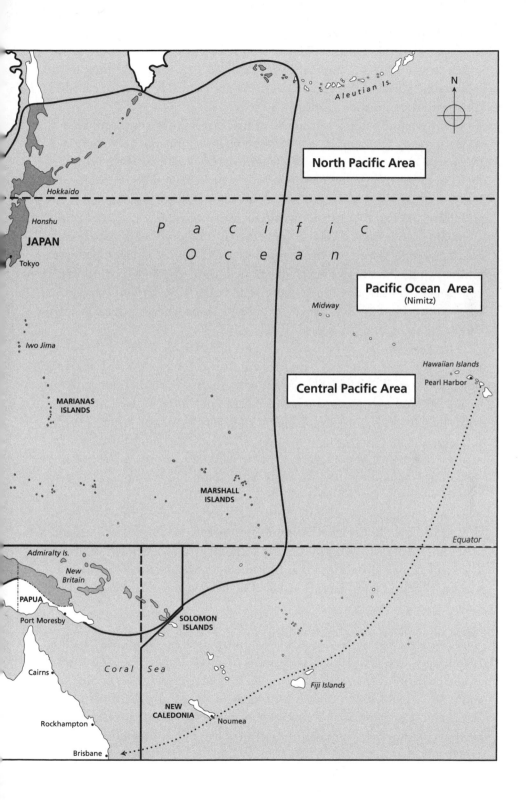

soaked water wrote admiringly: "Every man waved and put his thumb up to me . . . as if they were holidaymakers at Brighton . . . I saw the spirit which wins wars." Yet survivors later asserted that, in truth, they were shaking their fists at the airmen overhead and shouting derisive catcalls: "RAF—Rare as Fucking Fairies!"

In the northern jungle, again and again British units were confounded by fast-moving Japanese. The 1st Battalion 14th Punjabis were surprised by enemy tanks while sheltering from torrential rain in their vehicles; their accompanying antitank guns had no time to unlimber. "Suddenly I saw some of my trucks and a carrier screaming down the flooded road and heard the hell of a battle," wrote their commander, Lt. Peter Greer. "The din was terrific . . . almost immediately a medium tank roared past me. I dived for cover . . . within the next two minutes a dozen medium tanks . . . passed me . . . They had crashed right through our forward companies . . . I saw one of my carriers; its tail was on fire and the Number Two was facing back firing his light machine-gun at a tank twenty yards behind me. Poor beggar."

The Punjabis' survivors scattered and never reassembled. The same fate befell a green Gurkha battalion: 30 of its men were killed in their first action, while only 200 escaped with their weapons, leaving most to be captured. An officer recorded "scenes of indescribable confusion, with small leaderless parties of Indian and Gurkha troops firing in every direction . . . no one appeared to know what was happening . . . their own artillery was falling short among the British troops." Some units, notably including a battalion of the Argyll & Sutherland Highlanders, acquitted themselves well. But isolated stands were of little value when Japanese who met resistance repeatedly outflanked the defenders by infiltration through jungle the British had deemed impassable.

Duff Cooper, the British resident minister in the Far East, wrote to Churchill about Britain's military commander in Malaya, Gen. Arthur Percival: "A nice, good man . . . calm, clear-headed and even clever. But he cannot take a large view; it is all a field day at Aldershot to him. He knows the rules so well and follows them so closely and is always waiting for the umpire's whistle to signal ceasefire and hopes that when the moment comes his military dispositions will be such as to receive approval." The British defence of Malaya was hampered by Percival's limitations, poor communications, and the familiar institutional weakness of the British Army. Some units resorted to communication by bugle call when radio failed and field telephone lines were cut. The Japanese could exploit almost absolute command of sea and air. When Gen. Tomoyuki Yamashita's forces met stubborn resistance at Kampar, in central Malaya, he simply launched a new amphibious landing to outflank the defenders. The British were confounded by bold Japanese use of tanks, against which the defenders lacked even Molotov cocktails. Yamashita's three divisions, though heavily outnumbered, displayed an aggression and energy of which their opponents were bereft. Their commander penned a poem:

> On the day the sun shines with the moon
> The arrow leaves the bow
> It carries my spirit towards the enemy
> With me are a hundred million souls
> My people of the East
> On this day when the moon shines
> And the sun also shines.

Churchill asserted that the Japanese army was expert in jungle warfare. Yamashita's three divisions had indeed gained combat experience in China, but their men entered jungle for the first time when they landed in Malaya. In China, they had used horses for transport, but now bicycles were substituted—6,000 were issued to each division, in addition to 500 motor vehicles. In the intense heat the bikes suffered frequent punctures, and two-man repair teams attached to each company mended an average of twenty tyres a day. Infantrymen meeting resistance on roads merely sought a bypass, humping their machines across rivers and through jungle, pedalling up to twenty hours a day, carrying a sixty-pound pack behind their saddles. Even old Lt. Col. Yosuke Yokoyama, commanding an engineer regiment, rode a bicycle. Short, chunky, dripping with sweat, he followed close behind the leading infantry inspecting British demolitions and directing bridge repairs, effected by raiding local sawmills for lumber. The Japanese referred to the huge ration dumps they captured, and exploited for their own units, as "Churchill supplies."

"The Jitra line was penetrated in about fifteen hours by barely five hundred men," Col. Manasonbu Tsuji wrote contemptuously. In that action, he reported Japanese casualties of only twenty-seven killed and eighty-three wounded. "The enemy retreated leaving behind as souvenirs about fifty field guns, fifty heavy machine-guns, three hundred trucks and armoured cars, and provisions for a division for three months. Over 3,000 men surrendered having thrown away their arms in panic and taken refuge in the jungle . . . The majority of these were Indian soldiers."

Some such units crumbled swiftly, especially when their British officers fell, as many did. The reputation of the Indian Army suffered severely in Malaya, where the lack of motivation of many of its mercenaries was laid bare. The Japanese used "jitter" tactics to formidable effect, panicking defenders into retreat and sometimes headlong flight by noisy demonstrations behind their front. The huge wartime expansion of the Indian Army had resulted in some British officers being deployed with only six months training in place of the usual thirty, and unable to speak Urdu, thus incapable of communicating with their men. The cultural chasm between foes was exposed when British troops surrendered. They expected the mercy customarily offered by European armies, even those of the Nazis; instead, they were stunned to see their captors killing casualties incapable of walking, often also unwounded men and civilians. The teenage daughter of a Chinese teacher who brought food to an Argyll officer in his jungle hiding place one day left a note in English for him about the Japanese: "They took my father and cut off his head. I will continue to feed you as long as I can." At an early stage, discipline collapsed in parts of Percival's army, in a fashion evidenced by fleeing soldiers' looting of Kuala Lumpur. Counterattacks, a vital element of any successful defence, were seldom pressed. Most Indian units were composed of young and poorly trained soldiers. Whatever else Percival's subordinates lacked, they displayed considerable courage, reflected in a high loss rate among British officers striving by example to keep Indian troops fighting. In this, they were seldom successful: one entire Indian brigade simply melted away under attack.

Some British units performed no better: the 18th Division arrived at Singapore as a belated reinforcement, and suffered swift humiliation. One of its battalions, the 6th Norfolks, lost six subalterns and a captain in its first seventy-two hours of action. The attacking force may have been small, but Yamashita's three divisions were among the best in the Japanese army; they moved fast, and losses seldom deterred them from sustaining attacks. The code of Bushido caused them to treat themselves as mercilessly as they did their foes. A Japanese fighter pilot crash-landing in Johore fired a pistol at curious Malays who surrounded him, then used his last bullet to shoot himself.

From the outset, fleeing British clung to the racial conventions of empire and shamelessly abandoned their native subjects. The commissioner in Penang refused to allow Malay firefighters to enter the European quarter after bombing raids, and rejected pleas to demolish some European houses to create a firebreak. When Penang Island was evacuated, non-Europeans were denied access to shipping. A Chinese judge was evicted after boarding, though the fortress commander's car was embarked. A refugee from the island said later that the manner of the British evacuation was "a thing which I am sure will never be forgotten or forgiven." Sikh police in Singapore were assured by their British chief that he would stay with them to the end; instead, he fled. In the Cameron Highlands, departing settlers appealed to Asian members of the local defence force to stick with their units; unsurprisingly, they resigned en bloc. In Kuala Lumpur, British doctors abandoned hospital wards to the care of their Asian counterparts. A young actor with a Chinese theatre troupe told his audience in the mining centre of Ipoh: "The British are treating their empire as property and handling the whole thing as if it was a business transaction."

The behaviour of British communities in Malaya and later Burma was rational enough: word had reached Southeast Asia about the orgy of rape and massacre which accompanied the fall of Hong Kong at the end of December. But the spectacle of white rulers succumbing to panic mocked the myth of benign imperial paternalism. Racism and self-interest were almost absolutes: when Chinese stewards aboard the light cruiser *Durban* mutinied, Capt. Peter Cazalet wrote ruefully, "We have not treated the Chinese well in peacetime . . . they have no real loyalty towards us and why should they have?" He noted that one mutineer expressed a desire to join the Japanese army. An eyewitness at Singapore noticed that as civilian bombing victims were thrown into mass graves, in death as in life European and Asian bodies were segregated. The condescension of the rulers was exemplified by the reaction of Malaya's governor when his manservant was killed by a Japanese bomb behind Government House. Shenton Thomas wrote in his diary: "Terribly sad about my boy. He was such a faithful soul." Other nations of the British Empire "family" showed scant enthusiasm for receiving refugees from Southeast Asia. Australia at first agreed to grant entry to just 50 Europeans and the same number of Chinese; Ceylon set an initial limit of 500, with priority for its own citizens. Immigration barriers were lifted only belatedly, in the face of catastrophe.

On 31 January, the causeway linking Malaya to Singapore Island was blown up. The British principal of Raffles College, hearing the explosion, asked what it signified. A young Chinese, Lee Kuan Yew, claims to have responded: "That is the end of the British Empire." For fifty-five days, the Japanese had maintained a daily average advance of twelve miles, fighting ninety-five engagements and repairing 250 bridges. They were now almost out of ammunition, and Percival's remaining 70,000 combatants were more than double Yamashita's strength. But the British general made the cardinal error of dispersing his strength to defend Singapore's seventy-two miles of coastline. Morale was wretchedly low, and fell further as engineers began demolitions in the naval dockyard. Belated efforts were made to evacuate dependents to the Dutch East Indies. More than 5,000 people sailed amid scenes of chaos, panic and sometimes violence at the dockside, as military deserters sought to force a passage. Barely 1,500 of the refugees eventually reached the safety of India or Australia. Almost every ship approaching or leaving Singapore faced an ordeal by Japanese air attack. A Northumberland Fusilier described the experience of running the gauntlet on a transport under fire: "It was as if you were locked inside a tin can which people were beating with sticks."

Yamashita's forces began landing on Singapore Island in darkness on 8 February, employing a makeshift armada of 150 boats which carried 4,000 men in the first wave, followed by the rest of two divisions. The British mounted no searchlights, and their artillery scarcely troubled the assault troops. Shellfire quickly severed most phone communications in forward areas, and heavy rain left sodden defenders huddled in their trenches. The Japanese pushed rapidly forward, while demoralised Australian units fell back. As it became plain that Singapore would be lost, the commanding officer of the naval base, Rear Adm. Jack Spooner, wrote bitterly: "The present state of affairs was started by the AIF [Australian Imperial Forces] who just turned tail, became a rabble, and let the Japs walk in unopposed."

A disconsolate Maj. Gen. Gordon Bennett, commanding the 8th Australian Division, told one of his officers: "I don't think the men want to fight." He himself anyway did not, catching a plane which took him home in twelve days. And if the Australians performed poorly, so did British units, reflecting a collapse of will throughout Percival's command. Capt. Norman Thorpe, a Derbyshire Territorial serving in the Sherwood Foresters, described his curious sense of detachment from the catastrophe unfolding around him: "I myself only feel mildly excited and hardly feel it concerns me." When Thorpe led a counterattack, he found that only a handful of his men followed him forward; the little party's advance was soon crushed. The commanding officer of an Australian unit spoke of fugitives from the forward positions who were "quite out of control and stated they had had enough." The Japanese were no more merciful to those who quit than to those who resisted. Corp. Tominosuke Tsuchikane described his bewilderment at encountering enemies who hoped to save themselves by mere inertia: "Having lost their nerve, some soldiers were simply cowering in terror, squatting down and avoiding hand-to-hand combat in a wait-and-see position. They, too, were bayoneted or shot without mercy."

Churchill dispatched a histrionic signal to Wavell, the newly appointed Allied supreme commander, urging a last-ditch resistance in Singapore: "There must at this stage be no thought of saving the troops or sparing the population. The battle must be fought to the bitter end at all costs . . . Commanders and senior officers should die with their troops.

The honour of the British Empire and of the British Army is at stake. I rely on you to show no weakness or mercy in any form. With the Russians fighting as they are and the Americans so stubborn at Luzon the whole reputation of our country and our race is involved."

Churchill's message is important, in emphasising the contrast between rival combatants' conduct of the war. He demanded from Singapore's garrison no more and no less grit and will for sacrifice than Germans, Japanese and Russians routinely displayed, albeit under threat of draconian sanctions. Even if Malaya was lost, the prime minister sought to salvage some redeeming legend of its defenders resisting to the last. But the concept of self-immolation was beyond the bounds of Western democratic culture. On the evening of 9 February an Australian brigade commander told Percival, "In civil life I am a doctor. If the patient's arm is bad I cut it off, but if the whole body goes bad then no operation can save the patient—he must die. So it is with Singapore—there is no use fighting to prolong its life." A small number of British, Indian and Australian soldiers displayed courage during the defence of Malaya, but this was futile amid a general collapse. Few Allied officers appealed to their men for sacrifices they knew would be denied.

At Singapore more than any other British battlefield, a chasm was revealed between the prime minister's heroic vision of the empire at war and the response of its fighting men. Percival's soldiers had lost confidence in their leaders and in themselves. If confronted face-to-face by Churchill, they might have told him that if he wanted Malaya staunchly defended, he should have given them competent officers, better weapons and some of the hundreds of modern fighters idling at English airfields. They lacked any appetite for the fight to the death he wanted. There was a matching unwillingness among their superiors to use extreme measures to enforce discipline. Some Australian deserters forced their way at gunpoint aboard a refugee ship. When these men were arrested and imprisoned on Batavia, British officers wished to shoot them. Australian prime minister John Curtin signalled Wavell, insisting that any death sentence imposed on his citizens must be authorised by Canberra, as of course it would not be. Even at this dire moment of the empire's fortunes, a squeamishness persisted which reflected "civilised" Western values, but did scant service to the Allied cause.

In Singapore, emotional British civilians queued outside veterinary surgeries to have their pets humanely destroyed. A pall of smoke from burning oil tanks hung over the city, while military police used their rifles as clubs to drive back panic-stricken men, often drunk, from the last departing ships. A subsequent British report lambasted the Australians: "Their conduct was bestial." By that stage, such remarks merely reflected a search for scapegoats. At Wavell's last meeting with Malaya's governor before flying out to Batavia, he said again and again, thumping his knee with his fist, "It shouldn't have happened. It shouldn't have happened." As the Japanese drove forward into the city, atrocities became commonplace. At the Alexandra hospital, a twenty-three-year-old patient hearing the Japanese approach the ward, shooting and bayoneting as they came, thought sadly, "I'll never be twenty-four. Poor Mum." In the event, he proved one of only four survivors in the ward, because his blood-soaked body persuaded the Japanese he was dead. At the Alexandra, 320 men and 1 woman were killed, and many nurses raped. One group of 22 Australian nurses escaped from the city, only to fall into Japanese hands on a Dutch island. As they were driven into the sea to be machine-gunned, the last words of their matron Irene Drummond were recorded by the sole survivor: "Chin up, girls. I'm proud of you and I love you all."

Percival surrendered Singapore to Yamashita on 15 February. The photograph of a British officer named Major Wylde, in baggy shorts and helmet askew, beside his general as they carried the union flag to the Japanese lines became one of the most wretchedly memorable images of the war. It seemed to symbolise the bungling, blimpish ineffectuality of the men who had been entrusted with the defence of Britain's eastern empire. Along with Singapore, Percival signed away a significant portion of the honour of the British and Indian armies, as Churchill and his people well understood. The Japanese had gained their victory in barely seventy days, at a cost of only 3,506 dead, half of those in the battle for Singapore. Imperial forces lost around 7,500 killed, while the victors counted 138,000 prisoners, half of them Indians. One such officer, Capt. Prem K. Saghal, saw his unit's British second-in-command beheaded before his eyes and said later: "The fall of Singapore finally convinced me of the degeneration of the British people." Saghal concluded that by their conduct the imperial rulers had forfeited their claim upon the loyalty of Indians. Likewise another officer, Shahnawaz Khan, who felt he and his men "had been handed over like cattle by the British to the Japs." The Japanese began immediately to recruit among the POWs for their "Indian National Army" to fight against the British, and achieved some success. The prestige of the Raj hinged upon the myth of its invincibility, which was now shattered.

Another prisoner, Lt. Stephen Abbott, recorded the scene as he and his companions began the long trek through Singapore to improvised prison camps: "The area presented a picture of appalling destruction.

Overturned lorries, bicycles, prams, furniture lay in huge bomb craters, or were scattered over roads and pavements. Buildings with gaping holes displayed their pathetic interiors to the world. Naked bodies and grotesque human limbs rested where they had been flung. A repulsive stench rose in the humid atmosphere. The local population—Chinese, Malay and Indian—stood by the wreckage of their former homes in stunned misery, tiny children clinging in fear to their mothers' clothing. From every building which remained standing in any shape or form, the red ball of the Japanese flag was hung . . . I stared at the Japanese soldiers in the streets as we passed. Were these the men we had been fighting, and who were now to be our masters? They were like unkempt children in their ragged uniforms, but children triumphant, and more than ready to mock their victims."

For Singaporeans, after more than a century of colonial rule the revelation of its frailty changed everything. Lim Kean Siew, the eighteen-year-old son of a Chinese notable, wrote: "The heavens had indeed opened for us. From a languid, lazy and lackadaisical world, we were catapulted into a world of somersaults and frenzy from which we would never recover." Likewise Lee Kuan Yew, who as an eighteen-year-old student at Raffles College watched the British enter captivity: "I saw them tramping along the road in front of my house for three solid days, an endless stream of bewildered men who did not know what had happened, why it had happened or what they were doing here in Singapore in any case."

Savouring Japanese victory, Major General Imai, chief of staff of the Imperial Guards Division, said to captive Indian Army maj. gen. Billy Key: "We Japanese have captured Malaya and Singapore. Soon we will have Sumatra, Java and the Philippines. We do not want Australia. I think it is time for your British Empire to compromise. What else can you do?" Key replied defiantly, "We can drive you back. We will eventually occupy your country. This is what we can do." The Japanese seemed unconvinced, because the battlefield performance of Britain's forces in Malaya had been so pitiful. Yamashita and his officers celebrated victory with dried cuttlefish, chestnuts and wine, gifts of the emperor, set out upon a white tablecloth.

Col. Manasobe Tsuji, one of the Japanese army's foremost and most brutal militarists, gazed with contempt upon British and Australian prisoners, who had so easily allowed themselves to be defeated: "Groups of them were squatting on the road smoking, talking and shouting in rather loud voices. Strangely enough, however, there was no sign whatever of hostility in their faces. Rather was there an expression of resignation such as is shown by the losers in fierce sporting contests . . . The British soldiers looked like men who had finished their work by contract at a suitable salary, and were now taking a rest free from the anxiety of the battlefield."

MP Harold Nicolson wrote in his diary that Singapore's surrender "has been a terrific blow to all of us. It is not only the immediate dangers . . . It is dread that we are only half-hearted in fighting the whole-hearted." Churchill agreed. He was disgusted by the poor British showing in Malaya not merely because defeat was bitter, but because the Japanese won so much at such small cost. In a 20 December 1941 strategy paper for the Anglo-American leaderships, he had asserted: "It is of the utmost importance that the enemy should not acquire large gains cheaply; that he should be compelled to nourish his conquests and be kept extended—and kept burning his resources." British forces' conspicuous failure to fulfil this objective was gall and wormwood to the prime minister. "We had cause on many previous occasions to be uneasy about the fighting qualities of our men," wrote Gen. Sir John Kennedy, director of military operations at the War Office. "They had not fought as toughly as the Germans or Russians, and now they were being outclassed by the Japanese . . . We were undoubtedly softer, as a nation, than any of our enemies, except the Italians . . . Modern civilization on the democratic model does not produce a hardy race, and our civilization . . . was a little further removed from the stage of barbarity than were the civilizations of Germany, Russia and Japan."

Masanobu Tsuji, who later wrote several books celebrating the Japanese army's achievements, was a prime mover in its Malayan atrocities. It was sometimes asserted that Yamashita's postwar execution for war crimes was unjustified, but the general was never even indicted for the systematic massacres of Chinese which took place at Singapore under his command. Yamashita once delivered a speech in which he asserted that, while his own people were descended from gods, Europeans were descended from monkeys. British racism in Southeast Asia was now eclipsed by that of the Japanese. Tokyo's new regime was characterised by a brutality such as the evicted imperialists, whatever their shortcomings, had never displayed.

The Japanese began their treatment of Allied prisoners as they intended to continue. After the fall of Hong Kong on Christmas Day 1941, the invaders launched an orgy of rape and massacre which embraced nuns and nurses, hospital patients bayoneted in their beds. Similar scenes took place on Java and Sumatra, the largest islands of the Dutch East Indies, which were easily overrun after the fall of Singapore. The Japanese army in its new conquests sustained the tradition of savagery it had established in China, a perversion of virility and warrior spirit which was the more shocking for being institutionalised. Soldiers of all nations, in all wars, are sometimes guilty of atrocities. An important distinction can be made, however, between armies in which acts of barbarism represent a break with regulations and the norm, and those in which they are indulged or even incited by commanders. The Japanese were prominent among the latter.

On Java, Lt. Col. Edward "Weary" Dunlop, an Australian surgeon, dismissed a parade of his men after they had been inspected and addressed by a certain Lieutenant Sumiya on 19 April:

> I moved to the Nipponese officer, saluting. To my astonishment, he swung a "haymaker" which hit me heavily on the jaw. I narrowly avoided being felled by moving my head back a little . . . Lt. Sumiya ripped out his sword and lunged at my throat with a deadly tigerish thrust. I avoided the point with a boxer's reflexes, but the haft hit my larynx with a sickening thud and I could not temporarily breathe or speak.
>
> The troops muttered angrily and began moving forward. The guards levelled their rifles and thrust their bayonets menacingly towards them. The scene was tense with the impending massacre. I put my left hand towards my troops, motioning "Don't move!," and then turned to the officer, gave a coldly formal bow . . . I stood to attention too coldly furious to flinch, whilst he swung the sword about my head, fanning my ears and bellowing loudly.

In the years that followed, Dunlop and his comrades suffered many worse beatings, and thousands died of disease and starvation. The Australian surgeon became an acknowledged hero of the terrible experience of Japanese captivity, a secular saint. The battle for Malaya might have taken a different course had its defenders foreseen the price they would pay for their ready submission to defeat.

WITHIN DAYS of the fall of Singapore, the Japanese struck out for the East Indies and its precious oil, their foremost strategic objective. From bases in the Palau islands, invasion convoys sailed for Sarawak, Borneo and Java, supported by overwhelmingly powerful naval forces. The Allied defenders were weak, demoralised and ill-coordinated. In a series of dogfights over Java on 19 February, Japanese aircraft destroyed fifteen fighters. On the twenty-seventh an Allied squadron commanded by the Dutch admiral Karel Doorman, and composed of two heavy and three light cruisers escorted by nine destroyers, attempted to attack the amphibious convoy approaching Java, covered by two Japanese heavy cruisers, two light cruisers and fourteen destroyers. The rival fleets sighted each other at 4:00 p.m., and opened fire a few minutes later. The first exchanges did little damage, for both sides' shooting was poor: of ninety-two Japanese torpedoes fired, only one achieved a hit, sinking a Dutch destroyer. The cruiser *Exeter* suffered serious damage from a shell which struck in its boiler room, and limped towards the safety of Surabaya. At 6:00 p.m., the American destroyer contingent quit the squadron on its own initiative, having expended all its torpedoes.

The next encounter, after darkness fell, proved disastrous for the Allies: the Dutch cruisers *De Ruyter* and *Java* were sunk by torpedoes, and Admiral Doorman perished with many of his sailors. The *Perth* and the *Houston* escaped, only to meet the main Japanese invasion fleet the next night in the Sunda Strait, where both were sunk. On 1 March, *Exeter* and two escorting destroyers were caught and sunk attempting to make a break for Ceylon, while one Dutch and two more American destroyers were lost on passage to Australia. Ten ships and more than 2,000 men had thus vanished to the bottom in less than a week, almost eliminating the Allied naval presence in the East Indies. Dutch and residual British forces ashore sustained a desultory resistance for a week, before the Japanese secured mastery of the East Indies. No other outcome of the campaign was plausible, given the overwhelming Japanese strength deployed in the region.

2. The "White Route" from Burma

THE CONQUERORS, emboldened by their Malayan triumph, seized the opportunity also to occupy British Burma, partly to secure its oil and natural resources, partly to close the "Burma Road" to China. The first bombs fell on its capital, Rangoon, on 23 December. In a little house on Sparks Street, one of the Indian railway engine driver Casmir Rego's sons was practising "Silent Night" on his violin. Lena, his little sister, was making paper chains, while their parents were out Christmas shopping. Suddenly, the sounds of aircraft and machine-gun fire burst upon the seasonal idyll. Bombs exploded, fires broke out, wholesale panic spread.

A Burman midwife, Daw Sein, recalled later that though she had heard vaguely about a war, at first she was uncertain who was fighting whom. Now, her husband burst into the kitchen and yelled: "Out! Quick! We must get away!" They fled their house and were halfway to the railway station when she realised that she was half naked. Her husband tore his own *longyi* in half and gave her the rent cloth to cover her breasts. Thus clad, they tumbled aboard the first departing train, for Moulmein. Packed to the doors with fugitives like themselves, after some miles it halted, then stood immobile for hours with its cargo of foetid, hungry, thirsty, desperate humanity. Finally a man walked along the track beside the coaches shouting, "Moulmein has been destroyed! Bombs are falling everywhere! The train isn't going any further!" After fevered consultation, Daw Sein and her husband set off on foot towards Mandalay, far to the north.

In the days that followed, as air raids continued, food distribution broke down. Many Rangoon inhabitants became scavengers, breaking into abandoned homes in search of anything edible. After one raid, to the horror of the Rego family, their youngest son, Patrick, vanished. As his brothers scoured the streets for him, they came upon a van laden with corpses and severed limbs. They glimpsed a woman who cried out from under the heap of bodies, "I'm not dead! Please take me out!" Then more dead were thrown on top of her, and the van was driven away. Patrick reappeared unharmed, but the children never forgot the woman trapped among corpses.

Colonial mastery crumbled as swiftly and ignominiously in Burma as in Malaya. A host of Indian fugitives took to the jungle or set out westwards, including the low-caste "sweepers" who emptied their rulers' "thunderboxes" and cleaned the streets. Sir Reginald Dorman-Smith, the governor, reflected ruefully on the revelation that such people were indispensable to sahibs' lives: "Life begins with the sweeper. That lowest of all human beings, who holds in his hands the difference between health and disease, cleanliness and filth." The civilian administration rapidly collapsed, and so too did the defence: through February and March, the Japanese swept across the country. When soldier Robert Morris of the 7th Hussars landed at Rangoon, he found chaos: "All we saw were blazing fires and oil dumps set alight. Mounds of equipment such as aircraft marked 'Lease-Lend to China from U.S.A.' lay in crates awaiting assembly. The number of lorries lined up ready for shipment to China amazed us. The port had been deserted and ransacked."

Dorman-Smith was yet another poor specimen of proconsulship. He professed himself baffled as to why, after a century of British rule, there was no Burmese loyalty to the empire such as appeared to exist "among other subject nations." A civil servant, John Clague, provided an easy answer: "We Europeans lived in a world where very often the people hardly counted in our human or intimate thoughts. No Burman belonged to the Moulmein Gymkhana. No Burman came to dinner and breakfast."

Now, orders were issued that no Burmese or Indians should be accommodated on refugee transports.

The Far East C-in-C, Sir Robert Brooke-Popham, matched Dorman-Smith's gloom. He reported, accurately enough, that many local people openly favoured a Japanese victory: "It is rather disheartening, after all the years we have been in Burma and the apparent progress that has taken place under our rule, to find that the majority of the population want to be rid of us . . . I can only suggest the three things that are, at any rate, worthy of investigation. First a tendancy [sic] among Englishmen to regard themselves as naturally superior in every way to any coloured race, without taking steps to ensure that this is always a fact. Secondly, a failure to develop a sympathetic understanding with the Burmese . . . Thirdly, the fact that the majority of non-official Englishmen in Burma were more concerned with making money . . . than benefiting the native population."

A Burmese could not have expressed the matter better. Two out of three national prime ministers since separation from India had been detained by the British for making advances to Tokyo, as was a group of student nationalists receiving Japanese training in preparation for collaboration. In the unlikely event that a referendum had been held in Burma, offering the population a choice of wartime allegiances, pro-Japanese sentiment would assuredly have prevailed. Maj. Gen. Sir John Smyth, newly appointed commander of the 17th Indian Division, which was deployed in the south beyond Moulmein, wrote later that the Burmese provided the invaders with eager assistance: "[The Japanese] not only got information of our every movement, but they got guides, rafts, ponies, elephants and all the things which we could not get for love, and only with great difficulty for money."

Mi Mi Khaing, a twenty-five-year-old Burmese woman who had studied at Rangoon University, wrote bitterly about the fashion in which her people were thrust into the war with no pretence of popular consultation. Hers was, she said, "a country which had lost proud sovereignty fifty-years before, which had not yet gained a modern replacement for it, and which felt itself to be only incidentally in the path of the war monster's appetite." By chance, Burmese prime minister U Saw was passing through the United States at the moment of Pearl Harbor. Impressions of American disarray and hysteria enhanced his contempt for the white races. Back in Burma shortly afterwards, Ultra decrypts revealed U Saw making overtures to the Japanese, which caused him to be exiled to East Africa. In such circumstances, British claims to be upholding the cause of democratic freedom by fighting in Burma seemed less than wholly convincing.

The invaders, meanwhile, were astonished by the warmth of the welcome they received, especially from Burmese youths. One of their liaison officers wrote: "It came to us how strong was their passion for independence." Burmese villagers crowded around Japanese soldiers, offering them water and *saybawleit* cheroots. Soldiers were bewildered to be questioned in English, the only foreign language local people spoke. The commonest question was: "Has Singapore fallen?" Lt. Izura Tatsuro said: "I answered proudly, 'Yes, Singapore has fallen.'"

Some of the first bombs to fall on Mandalay wrecked the colonists' Upper Burma Club. A guest at a lunch party there said, "We didn't know what hit us. One minute we were seated at table, the next the roof caved in, tables, chairs, food and ourselves were scattered all over the room." The attacks started fires which burned down much of the city. Bodies lay unburied for days, intensifying popular contempt for British incompetence. With a symbolism that did not go unnoticed, flowers in the colonists' gardens began to die, because the servants who watered them had abandoned their posts. The British bosses of the Burma Corporation washed their hands of their local staff, shrugging and saying that they could do nothing for them.

In reply to a plea for reinforcements for Burma, Wavell, in Java, signalled Rangoon on 22 January: "I have no resources with which I can assist you . . . Cannot understand why with troops at your disposal you should be unable to hold Moulmein and trust you will do so. Nature of country and resources must limit Japanese effort." When the modest Japanese invasion force of two divisions launched its attack from Siam in the last days of January, some Indian units mounted a stalwart defence, but the locally recruited Burma Rifles crumbled quickly. The British had no significant air or artillery support, and John Smyth was furious that his superiors insisted on an attempt to hold exposed Moulmein. The first crisis of the campaign came in the early hours of 23 February, at a bridge across the Sittang eighty miles north of the town. As the Japanese approached, in darkness British engineers fired demolition charges. Two of Smyth's brigades were cut off east of the river. All but a handful of men were obliged to surrender, a crippling moral and strategic blow.

Lt. John Randle of the Baluch Regiment was holding a position west of the Salween River when he realised Japanese troops were behind him. "I sent my runner, the company bugler, with a message to my CO to tell him there were a lot of Japs about. They cut in behind us and we could hear the runner screaming as they killed him with swords and bayonets . . . The Japs butchered all our wounded." His battalion lost 289 men killed and

229 taken prisoner in its first engagement. Randle said: "We were arrogant about the Japs, we regarded them as coolies. We thought of them as third rate. My goodness me, we soon changed our tune. The Japs fought with great ferocity and courage. We had no idea about jungle fighting, no pamphlets, doctrine etc. Not only were we raw troops, we were trying to do something entirely new."

By early March Rangoon was a ghost city, where the remaining policemen and a small British garrison skirmished with mobs of looters. Fighter pilots of Claire Chennault's American Volunteer Group, transferred to Burma from China, sustained the only significant resistance to Japanese air attacks. The defence was collapsing. British liaison officer W. E. Abraham reported from Rangoon: "The general atmosphere of gloom was almost impossible to describe. GHQ at Athens when getting out of Greece was almost light-hearted by comparison." Wavell, raging against the alleged defeatism of his subordinates, sacked both his Burma C-in-C and Smyth, a sick man struggling to direct the remains of his division in a battle he never thought winnable. The British government pleaded with Australia's prime minister, John Curtin, to allow two Australian formations then in transit between the Middle East and their threatened homeland to be diverted to Burma. Curtin refused, and was surely right: the Australians, fine and experienced soldiers though they were, could not have turned the tide in a doomed campaign.

Wavell was haunted by memories of the allegations of pessimism and defeatism thrown at him by Churchill before his 1941 sacking as Middle East C-in-C. In Southeast Asia, he strove to show himself a man of steel, to put spine into his subordinates. "Our troops in Burma are not fighting with proper spirit," he signalled London. "I have not the least doubt that this is in great part due to lack of drive and inspiration from the top." In truth, so much was wrong with Britain's Far East forces that the rot was unstoppable in the midst of a Japanese offensive. Wavell seemed to acknowledge this in another signal to London: "I am very disturbed at lack of real fighting spirit in our troops shown in Malaya and so far in Burma. Neither British, Australians or Indians have shown real toughness of mind or body . . . Causes go deep, softness of last twenty years, lack of vigour in peace training, effects of climate and atmosphere of East." Wavell became a regular visitor to Rangoon, likened by one historian to "a Harley Street specialist, complete with a black bag, coming to see a very sick patient."

On 5 March Lt. Gen. Sir Harold Alexander arrived to take command. The impeccable "Alex," Churchill's favourite general, could only contribute his unfailing personal grace and serenity to what now became a rout.

Initially he ordered a halt to the British retreat, then within twenty-four hours accepted that Rangoon could not be held and endorsed its evacuation. The invaders missed a priceless opportunity to trap the entire British army in Burma when a local Japanese commander withdrew a strong roadblock closing the road north. Misinterpreting his orders, he supposed that all the attacking forces were intended to close on Rangoon for a big battle. This fumbled pass allowed Alexander's force to retreat northwards—and the general himself to escape captivity.

In desperation, Wavell accepted Chiang Kai-shek's offer of two Chinese Nationalist divisions. Chinese willingness to join the campaign was not altruistic. The Japanese advance in the north had closed the Burma Road, by which American supplies reached China. Reopening it was a vital Chinese interest. Wavell's caution about acceptance of assistance from Chiang's troops was prompted by knowledge that they lacked their own supply system and aspired to live off the land. There were also doubts about who gave their orders: U.S. general Joseph Stilwell claimed that he did, only to be contradicted by Chinese general Tu Lu Ming, who told Burma's governor, Dorman-Smith: "The American General only thinks he is commanding. In fact he is doing no such thing. You see, we Chinese think that the only way to keep the Americans in the war is to give them a few commands on paper. They will not do much harm as long as we do the work!"

Stilwell, an inveterate anglophobe, was underwhelmed by his first meeting with Alexander on 13 March. He wrote in his diary with accustomed sourness: "Astonished to find me—mere me, a goddam American—in command of Chinese troops. 'Extrawdinery!' Looked me over as if I had just crawled out from under a rock!" Stilwell was given the assistance of a British-led Frontier Force mounted unit, for reconnaissance duties. Its leader, Capt. Arthur Sandeman of the Central India Horse, achieved the doubtful distinction of becoming the last British officer to die leading a cavalry charge. Blundering into the path of Japanese machine gunners, he drew his sabre, ordered his bugler to signal the attack, and advanced on the enemy until he and his companions met their inevitable fate.

The Chinese intervention provoked the Japanese to reinforce their two-division invasion army, sending two more formations to Rangoon by sea. The British were reorganised into a corps commanded by William Slim, a shrewd, rugged Gurkha officer who would eventually show himself to be Britain's ablest general of the war. On 24 March the Japanese struck hard at the Chinese in the north. The British counterattacked to relieve pressure on their allies, but the enemy prevailed on both fronts.

Slim's Burcorps, struggling to avert complete collapse on the east bank of the Irrawaddy, called for Chinese assistance. Stilwell was predictably contemptuous, writing on 28 March: "Riot among British soldiers at Yenangyaung. British destroying the oil fields. GOOD GOD. What are we fighting for?" Yet to the astonishment of Stilwell as well as the British, a Chinese division, led by one of Chiang's ablest officers, Gen. Sun Li-Jen, pushed back the Japanese and achieved a notable little victory. Although an imperial formation was almost wiped out in the fighting around the Irrawaddy, Slim emerged from the battle full of respect for General Sun's men, whose intervention was decisive in enabling the British to avert the annihilation of the Burcorps.

But the Allied position in Burma had become untenable. Chinese troops matched Sun's. The Japanese considered that the Chinese formations fought more bravely and energetically than the Commonwealth forces, but within days they were falling back northwards, eventually into China. The pursuing Japanese were content to halt at the border. Stilwell and a motley party of Americans, Chinese and press correspondents walked through the jungle for two weeks before reaching the safety of Imphal, in British-ruled Assam, on 20 May. The American wrote: "We got a hell of a beating. It was as humiliating as hell. We ought to find out why it happened and go back!" He himself bore substantial responsibility for mishandling the Chinese troops under his command, whom he abandoned to make his own escape. By 30 April, Slim's men were safely across the Irrawaddy. They then retreated westwards preceded by a rabble of deserters and looters, who behaved with predictable savagery towards the civilian population. On 3 May, the Burcorps began its withdrawal across the Chindwin River boundary between Burma and India under Japanese fire. The Burma Rifles platoon defending Slim's own headquarters melted away into the night. Most of his men made good their escape, but almost all transport and heavy equipment—some 2,000 vehicles, 110 tanks and 40 guns—had to be abandoned on the east bank of the river. Even when the fugitives reached safety, they found no warm welcome. "The attitude of the army [in India] to those of us back from Burma was appalling," said Corp. William Norman. "They blamed us for the defeat."

The Japanese had advanced across Burma for 127 days, covering 1,500 miles at an average speed of almost 30 miles a day, while fighting 34 actions. The British had lost 13,000 men killed, wounded and captured, while the Japanese suffered only 4,000 casualties. This was not a disaster of the same magnitude as Malaya, and Slim conducted his retreat with some skill. But the Japanese now occupied Britain's entire Southeast Asian empire, to the gates of India. An Asian wrote of the spectacle of Western POWs driven to hard labour alongside the native peoples: "We always felt that they were superior to us. The Japanese opened our eyes; because [the white men] were sweeping the floor with me . . . walking without shoes." This proved an enduring revelation. Meanwhile, the Burma Road to China would remain closed for almost three years.

ENFORCED CIVILIAN MIGRATIONS were a major feature of the war almost everywhere around the globe where armies struggled for mastery. Few Burmese attempted to flee before the Japanese, because they believed they had nothing to fear from their victory, and much to hope for. When members of the newly mobilised Burma Independence Army marched through Rangoon for the first time under the eyes of its Japanese sponsors, an enthusiastic citizen wrote: "How thrilling it was to see Burmese soldiers and officers wearing assorted uniforms, bearing assorted arms, tricolour armbands on the shirtsleeve, seriousness on the face."

But almost a million Indians also lived in the country, some dominating commercial life and others performing menial functions indispensable to the welfare of sahibs, but disdained by their Burmese subjects. The Indians were unloved, and fearful of local nationalism. As the invasion tide swept forward, the British did nothing to assist the flight of some 600,000 of these, their dependents. It was argued that the rulers had trouble enough saving themselves. But here, once again, British conduct highlighted the breakdown of the supposed imperial compact, whereby native peoples received protection as the price of accepting subjection. Rich fugitives bought airline tickets or cabins aboard ships bound for India. Indians bitterly dubbed the ferry up the Chindwin "the white route," because access was almost the exclusive privilege of the British and Eurasians. As paddle steamers thrashed upriver, they passed corpses floating down, victims of hapless Indians' overland "black route."

Throngs of people too poor to purchase tickets to salvation were obliged to take to the roads and tracks north and westwards, towards Assam. The monsoon broke in May; thereafter, rain and mud clogged the passage alike of the fortunate in cars and the impoverished afoot. They were robbed and sometimes raped; they paid exorbitantly for scraps of food; they succumbed to dysentery, malaria and fever. At ferries and roadblocks, their last rupees were extracted by avaricious policemen and villagers. No one knows exactly how many Indians died in the spring and summer of 1942 on the road to Assam, but it was at least 50,000, and perhaps more. Their skeletons littered the roadside for years, to shame British passers-by when they later went that way again. An officer searching for stragglers at Tagun Hill on the way to Ledo came upon a village of the dead:

> The clearing was littered with tumbledown huts, where often whole families stayed and died together. I found the bodies of a mother and child locked in each other's arms. In another hut were the remains of another mother who had died in childbirth, with the child only half-born. In this one [clearing] more than fifty people had died. Sometimes pious Christians placed little wooden crucifixes in the ground before they died. Others had figures of the Virgin Mary still clutched in their skeleton hands. A soldier had expired wearing his sidecap, all his cotton clothing had rotted away, but the woollen cap sat smartly on the grinning skull. Already the ever-destroying jungle had overgrown some of the older huts, covering up the skeletons and reducing them to dust and mould.

Among the fugitives were many mixed-raced Catholics, who had originated in Portuguese Goa. Customs officer Jose Saldhana walked for days through the jungle with his seventeen-year-old son, George, having dispatched the rest of his family on a ship overladen with panic-stricken people. The walkers endured ghastly privations, relieved by a surreal moment in a camp in the jungle where a girl named Emily D'Cruz serenaded them: "Her voice soared clear and beautiful in the still of the night," singing "Alice Blue Gown." Then George succumbed to dysentery. He persuaded his father to leave him, sitting against a tree deep in the jungle. After some hours, the teenager saw a Naga woman, from a tribe of notorious head-hunters. Terror overcame his weakness, and he began to walk again. For days he stumbled northwestwards, living off berries which he saw monkeys eating, and thus assumed must be safe for humans. One day he came upon a flock of butterflies, of fabulous beauty. Fascinated, he approached them—only to recoil when he found them feasting off juices oozing from a decaying corpse. He fled onwards, and at last reached safety and a family reunion. Others were less fortunate. In the Hukawng Valley, boys from a Catholic school in Tavoy came upon the body of their headmaster, Leo Menenzes. His weak heart had collapsed under the strain of the trek.

Even when surviving refugees reached British-controlled Imphal, there were no better facilities and medical aid for Indian civilians than for Indian soldiers. With all the resources of the subcontinent at its disposal, the Raj proved incapable of organising basic humanitarian support for the flotsam of its war. Kachin and Naga villagers gave more help to refugees than did the British. An Anglo-Indian manager of the Irrawaddy Steamship Company who reached a rescue station in Assam after a struggle across the mountains was met by a British officer who insisted that he could be fed only at the Indian canteen. Conditions were appalling in hospitals receiving stricken fugitives. A British woman wrote bitterly to a friend in England, the wife of government minister R. A. Butler, describing what she had seen in Ranchi: "The medical wards are like *Gone with the Wind*— pallets touching each other, people moaning for water and sicking up and so on everywhere. It's all a shocking crime and may God forever damn the Eastern Command staff." Cholera broke out in some refugee camps.

Alexander's beaten army was rebuilt only sluggishly and unconvincingly: two long years would elapse before it was able to meet the Japanese with success. In August 1942, the general himself was transferred to command Britain's forces in the Middle East. The memory of that terrible Burma spring, and of its victims, remained imprinted upon the minds of all who witnessed it. The Indian National Congress party leader, Jawaharlal Nehru, from the Indian prison cell to which he had been consigned by the British, commented with just disdain on the collapse of government in Burma and the flight of colonial officials, who abandoned hundreds of thousands of his compatriots to their fate: "It is the misfortune of India at this crisis in her history not only to have a foreign government, but a government which is incompetent and incapable of organising her defence properly or of providing for the safety and essential needs of her people." This was just. The loss of Britain's empire in Southeast Asia brought disgrace as well as defeat upon its rulers, as Winston Churchill readily recognised.

CHAPTER TEN

SWINGS OF FORTUNE

1. Bataan

WE CANNOT WIN this war until it . . . becomes a national crusade for America and the American Dream," wrote *New York Times* reporter James Reston in his 1942 book *Prelude to Victory*, which attained best-sellerdom. This was now, indeed, a global conflict. The American people's initial response to finding themselves engaged in it was as muddled and well-meaning as had been that of the British in September 1939. There was a surge of enthusiasm for first-aid instruction—the most popular handbook sold 8 million copies; thousands of high school students carved and glued wooden models of enemy aircraft for military trainers. Millions of citizens donated blood and collected scrap metal; resort hotels in Miami Beach and Atlantic City were turned over to army recruits. Bowing to the gravity of the new national circumstances, sport hunting and fishing, together with manufacture of golf and tennis balls, were temporarily banned. There was a boom in fortune-telling, checkers, sales of world maps and cookery books. Movies attained extraordinary popularity, partly because many people found more cash in their pockets: 1942 cinema audiences were double those of 1940. Prisoners in San Quentin volunteered for war-production duty, and began making antisubmarine nets.

From the outset, and aided by the fact that some big industrial commitments had already been made, America's economic mobilisation awed visitors from poorer and less ambitious societies who witnessed it. Even intelligent and informed British people failed to recognise the almost limitless scale of the nation's resources: "The Army . . . are aiming at a vast programme," British air marshal John Slessor wrote to Sir Charles Portal, chief of the Air Staff, from Washington back in April 1941, assessing the buildup of the U.S. armed forces, "their present target being two million men, and they are now considering another 2 million on top of that. Who they are going to fight with an army of this size or how they are going to transport it overseas I do not know and very much doubt whether they would have aimed at anything like this if they had a really thorough joint strategic examination of their defence commitments and requirements."

Such scepticism was dramatically confounded between 1942 and 1945.

"After Pearl Harbor," Lt. Gen. Frederick Morgan, the British chief planner for D-Day, said of the Americans, "they decided to make the biggest and best war ever seen." The secretary of the American Asiatic Association wrote to a friend in the State Department, "It will be a long, hard war, but after it is over Uncle Sam will do the talking in the world." The federal budget soared from $9 billion in 1939 to $100 billion in 1945, and in the same period America's GNP grew from $91 to $166 billion. The index of industrial production rose 96 percent, and 17 million new jobs were created. Some 6.5 million additional women entered the U.S. labour force between 1942 and 1945, and their wages grew by over 50 percent; sales of women's clothing doubled. The imperatives of America's vast industrial mobilisation favoured tycoons and conglomerates, which flourished mightily. Antitrust legislation was thrust aside by the pressures of war demand: America's hundred largest companies, which in 1941 were responsible for 30 percent of national manufacturing output, generated 70 percent by 1943. The administration overcame its scruples about monopolists who could deliver tanks, planes, and ships.

Everything grew in scale to match the largest war in history: in 1939 America had only 4,900 supermarkets, but by 1944 there were 16,000. Between December 1941 and the end of 1944, the average American's liquid personal assets almost doubled. With luxuries scarce, consumers were desperate to find goods on which to spend their rising earnings: "People are crazy with money," said a Philadelphia jeweller. "They don't care what they buy. They purchase things just for the fun of spending." By 1944, while British domestic production of consumer goods had fallen by 45 percent from its prewar levels, that of the United States had risen by 15 percent. Many regions experienced severe housing shortages and rents soared, as millions of people sought temporary accommodation to fit their wartime job relocations. "The Good War myth," wrote Arthur Schlesinger, who then worked for the Office of War Information,

> envisages a blissful time of national unity in support of noble objectives. Most Americans indeed accepted the necessity of the war, but that hardly meant the suppression of baser motives. In Washington we saw the seamy side of the Good War. We saw greedy business executives opposing conversion to defense production, then joining the government to maneuver for post-war advantage ... We were informed that one in eight business establishments was in violation of the price ceilings. We saw what a little-known senator from Missouri [Harry Truman] called "rapacity, greed, fraud and negligence" ... The war called for equality of sacrifice. But everywhere one looked was the

miasma of "chiseling" . . . The home front was not a pretty sight at a time when young Americans were dying around the world.

Among the worst rackets uncovered was that of a primary war contractor, National Bronze and Aluminum Foundry Company of Cleveland, which knowingly sold scrap metal as parts for fighter engines; four of its executives were jailed. The U.S. Cartridge Company of St. Louis issued millions of rounds of defective ammunition, though such chicanery could cost lives. Citizens sought otherwise unavailable commodities through the black market, and many businesses evaded price controls. An American observed ruefully that Europe had been occupied, Russia and China invaded, Britain bombed; but the United States was "fighting this war on imagination alone." Pearl Harbor, together with racism soon fuelled by tidings of Japanese savagery, ensured that Americans found it easy to hate their Asian enemy. But from beginning to end, few felt anything like the animosity towards the Germans that came readily to Europeans; it proved hard even to rouse American anger about Hitler's reported persecution of the Jews. Combat historian Forrest Pogue later observed wonderingly of Bradley's army in France: "The men have no great interest in the war. You can't work them up unless the Germans hit some of their friends." A behaviourist noted for his work with rats, Professor Norman Maier of Michigan University, suggested that Americans could be more effectively galvanised into a fighting mood by cutting off their gasoline, tyres and civil liberties than by appealing to their ideals. This was an overly cynical view, for some people displayed real patriotism, and on the battlefield many Americans would display much courage. But it was true that the remoteness of the United States from the fighting fronts, and its security from direct attack or even serious hardship, militated against the passion that moved civilians of nations suffering occupation or bombardment.

After Pearl Harbor, America's political and military leaders knew that they, like the British, must suffer defeats and humiliations before forces could be mobilised to roll back the advancing Japanese. There was much ignorance and innocence about the enemy, even among those who would have to fight them. "Suddenly we realized that nobody knew anything about the Japs," said carrier pilot Fred Mears. "We had never heard of a Zero then. What was the caliber of Jap planes and airmen? What was the strength of the Japanese Navy? What kind of battles would be fought and where? We were woefully unprepared." Many Americans had acknowledged for months the logic of their nation's belligerence. Yet it is characteristic of all conflicts that until enemies begin to shoot, ships to sink and loved ones—or at least comrades—to die, even professional warriors often lack urgency and ruthlessness. "It was amazing how long it took to get the hang of it and to react instantly in the right way," an American sailor, Alvin Kernan, observed. "War, we gradually learned, is a state of mind before it can be anything else." Ernie Pyle wrote: "Apparently it takes a country like America about two years to become wholly at war. We had to go through that transition period of letting loose of life as it was, and then live the new war life so long that it finally became the normal life to us."

All this makes it remarkable that, within a mere seven months of Pearl Harbor, American fleets had gained victories which turned the tide of the Asian war. Germany dominated western Europe for four years, but by autumn 1942 the Japanese perimeter was already beginning to shrink; the speed of the American resurgence in the Pacific reflected the fundamental weakness of the Asian enemy. First, however, came the pain. In the weeks following 7 December 1941, the Japanese seized Guam, Wake, and other U.S. island outposts. Gen. Douglas MacArthur, commanding the defence of the Philippines, rejected his air commander's plea to strike back during the ten hours which elapsed between news of Pearl Harbor and a devastating Japanese air assault that destroyed almost 80 U.S. aircraft undispersed on the ground.

Next day, MacArthur began to make belated preparations to withdraw his Filipino and American troops to Luzon's Bataan Peninsula, which alone might be defensible. But it was a huge task to quickly shift supplies there: the general had dismissed proposals to do so before war came, scorning "passivity." The army hastily bought rice from Chinese merchants and all the beef, meat and fruit it could get from local canneries. On 12 December, MacArthur belatedly informed Manuel Quezon, the president of the Philippines, of the mooted withdrawal, which he began to implement on the twenty-third. Doctors warned that Bataan was notoriously malaria-ridden, because of the prevalence there of the anopheles mosquito, but little was done to secure stocks of prophylactics. Meanwhile, Manila was bombed every day between noon and 1:00 p.m., causing American officers to advance their lunch to 11:00 a.m.

MacArthur expected a Japanese landing at the south end of the Lingayen Gulf, and deployed some troops accordingly. Yet the Japanese invasion force got ashore after easily brushing aside a challenge by ill-trained and poorly equipped Filipino troops. By 22 December, 43,110 men of Lt. Gen. Masaharu Homma's Fourteenth Army had established a beachhead with few casualties. Faulty American torpedoes caused the failure of all but one submarine attack on the troopships. A further 7,000 Japanese landed unopposed at Lamon Bay, 200 miles southeastwards. The army in the Philippines crumbled quickly; U.S. air commander Gen. Lewis

Brereton, with most of his planes gone, prudently decamped to Australia. MacArthur issued a bombastic communiqué: "My gallant divisions are holding ground and denying the foe the sacred soil of the Philippines. We have inflicted heavy casualties on his troops, and nowhere is his bridge-head secure. Tomorrow we will drive him into the sea."

In reality, the Japanese advanced on Manila against negligible resis-tance. In Washington, the U.S. chiefs of staff wisely forswore any notion of reinforcing the defence. MacArthur enjoyed just one piece of good for-tune: the invaders focused on occupying the capital, and made no attempt to frustrate his retreat to Bataan. The *Life* photographer Carl Mydans watched from the Bay View Hotel as the first Japanese entered Manila on 2 January: "They came up the boulevards in the predawn glow from the bay riding on bicycles and on tiny motorcycles. They came without talk and in good order, the ridiculous pop-popping of their one-cylinder cycles sounding loud in the silent city."

A week later, Homma launched his first attack on the American-Filipino line across the Bataan Peninsula. In the days that followed, the defenders had little difficulty in repulsing successive assaults, though they suffered steady losses from air attack. From the outset, they were also hot and hungry, with 110,000 people to be fed—85,000 U.S. and Filipino troops and 25,000 civilian refugees. The Corps of Engineers set about gathering and threshing rice in the fields. Fish traps operated along the coast until destroyed by enemy fighters, and farm animals were slaugh-tered. Malaria swiftly reached epidemic proportions. Nurse Ruth Straub wrote in her diary: "I guess we are all self-imposed prisoners-of-war. All we're doing is protecting our own lives."

But the defenders of Bataan displayed more energy and initiative than the British in Malaya: several Japanese attempts to turn the Americans' flank by landing troops on the coast behind the front resulted in their annihilation. One unit was forced back to the sheer cliffs of Quinauan Point. "Scores of Japs ripped off their uniforms and leaped, shrieking, to the beach below," wrote Capt. William Dyess. "Machine-gunfire raked the sand and surf for anything that moved." When Japanese infantry punched through the perimeter and seized two salients at Tuol and Cotar on 26 January, after bloody fighting the line was restored by counterat-tack. Bombing inflicted remarkably little damage on American artillery positions. When fodder ran out for the cavalry's horses, the garrison ate them. Almost every wild animal on Bataan was hunted down and thrown into the pot, while men picked mangoes, bananas, coconuts, and papayas, and fished at sea with dynamite.

Through February and March the Japanese made no headway, but the defenders were fast weakening from hunger, and antimalarial quinine was running out. MacArthur escaped to Australia by PT boat with his family and personal retainers, in obedience to an order from Roosevelt, leaving Gen. Jonathan Wainwright to direct the defence through its last weeks. By late March, a thousand malaria cases a week were being admitted to hospital. In civilian refugee camps behind the perimeter, according to Lt. Walter Waterous, conditions were "the most deplorable I have ever seen and the death rate was appalling." Bombing wrecked almost every facility above ground on the fortress island of Corregidor; thousands of sick and wounded were crowded into its Malinta Tunnel.

Thirty-year-old Texan nurse Lt. Bertha Dworsky found that one of the worst aspects of her work was personal acquaintance with many of the terribly wounded men brought in: "They were usually people that we'd been with at the Officers' Club, or they were our friends. It was a tremendously emotional experience. We just never knew who they were going to bring in next." The wounded often asked if they were going to survive, and doctors disputed whether it was best to tell them the truth. Dr. Alfred Weinstein wrote: "The argument raged back and forth with nobody knowing the correct answer. Most of us followed a middle course, ducking the question . . . If a patient looked as if he might kick the bucket, we called in the chaplain to give him last rites, collect personal mementoes and write last messages . . . More often than not they didn't have to be told."

The condition of the besiegers was little better than that of the besieged: the Japanese, too, suffered heavy losses to malaria, beriberi and dysentery—more than 10,000 sick by February. Tokyo was increasingly exasperated by American defiance, and by the triumphalist propaganda which the saga of Bataan promoted in the United States. On 3 April, Homma's reinforced army launched a major offensive preceded by a massive bombardment. Filipino units broke in panic before Japanese tanks; every movement by the defenders provoked strafing from the air; many men were so weakened by hunger that they could scarcely move from their foxholes. The Japanese pushed steadily forward, breaching successive American lines. On the evening of 8 April, Maj. Gen. Edward King on his own initiative decided he must surrender the peninsula, and sent forward an officer bearing a white flag to the Japanese lines. From jungle refuges all over Bataan, groups of defenders emerged, seeking paths towards Corregidor Island, where Wainwright still held out.

On the morning of April 9, King met Col. Motoo Nakayama, Homma's operations officer, to sign a surrender. "Will our troops be well treated?" King asked. The Japanese answered blandly, "We are not barbarians."

Some 11,500 Americans and 64,000 Filipinos fell into enemy hands. The transfer of these debilitated men to cages became known to history as the Bataan Death March. Scores of Filipinos were casually killed, some used for bayonet practice. An American private soldier saw a weakened compatriot pushed under an advancing tank. Blair Robinett said: "Now we knew, if there had been any doubts before, we were in for a bad time." Sgt. Charles Cook described seeing captives bayoneted if they tried to get water. Staff Sgt. Harold Feiner said: "If you fell, bingo, you were dead." More than 300 Filipino prisoners were butchered in a ravine near the Pantingan River. Their killers explained that if the garrison had surrendered sooner they might have been treated mercifully, but as it was, "we suffered heavy casualties. So just pardon us." An estimated 1,100 Americans and more than 5,000 Filipinos perished on the Death March.

The Japanese now concentrated artillery fire on Corregidor, little larger than New York's Central Park; on 3 May Wainwright reported to MacArthur in Australia that every structure above ground had been levelled, the island denuded of vegetation. Conditions became unspeakable in the hot, stinking Malinta Tunnel, packed with fearful humanity. That night the submarine *Spearfish* evacuated the last party to escape safely to Australia, twenty-five strong, including thirteen women. A few hours later, the Japanese landed amphibious forces to storm Corregidor. At noon on 6 May, after two days of fighting, Wainwright surrendered all remaining U.S. forces in the Philippines, first signalling to Washington: "With profound regret and with continued pride in my gallant troops I go to meet the Japanese commander . . . Goodbye, Mr. President." An American navy doctor among the garrison, George Ferguson, sat down and wept, "just so disappointed in the good old U.S.A.." Amid emotional and physical exhaustion, however, many men were simply glad the battle had ended. Only later did they discover that the ordeal had scarcely begun for 11,500 Americans who became prisoners of the Japanese.

The four-month defence of Bataan and Corregidor, which cost 2,000 American dead and 4,000 casualties among the invaders, was made possible in part by Japanese incompetence. The initial invasion force was weak, and composed of troops with nothing like the training and experience of Yamashita's army in Malaya. If Homma and his officers had displayed more energy, the Philippines saga would have ended sooner, as Tokyo's angry high command asserted. But nothing can detract from the gallantry of Wainwright, who did his duty more impressively than MacArthur, and of his garrison. They created a legend in which Americans could take pride—and of which Churchill was envious. To put the matter bluntly, U.S. soldiers on Bataan and Corregidor showed themselves more stalwart than British imperial forces in Malaya and at Singapore, albeit likewise in a doomed cause.

Brigadier Dwight Eisenhower, who had served unhappily under MacArthur a few years earlier, wrote in his diary: "Poor Wainwright! He did the fighting . . . [MacArthur] got such glory as the public could find . . . MacArthur's tirades, to which . . . I so often listened in Manila . . . would now sound as silly to the public as they then did to us. But he's a hero! Yah." At home in the United States, news commentators squeezed every ounce of glory from Bataan, from skirmishes at sea and manifestations of America's embryo mobilisation. But in the Pacific, no one was fooled. Every Allied soldier, sailor and airman knew that the enemy was making the weather in every corner of the theatre. Lt. Robert Kelly of Motor Torpedo Boat Squadron 3, which evacuated MacArthur from Corregidor, said: "The news commentators had us all winning the war. It made us very sore. We were out here where we could see these victories. There were plenty of them. They were all Japanese. Yet if even at one point we are able to check an attack, the silly headlines chatter of a 'victory.' "

Kelly, like Eisenhower, failed to grasp the importance of legends, indeed myths, to sustain the spirit of nations in adversity. American dismay in the face of those early defeats was assuaged by skilful propaganda. The United States had much less to lose in the East than did the British Empire. The epic of Bataan and MacArthur forged by Roosevelt and the U.S. media was serviceable, even precious to the American people. The general was a vainglorious windbag rather than a notable commander, whose personality was repugnant. But his flight from Corregidor was no more discreditable than those of many wartime British commanders from stricken fields, including Wavell's from Singapore. During the years that followed, MacArthur's status as a figurehead for American endeavours in the southwest Pacific did much for morale at home, if less for the defeat of Japan. The 1942 Philippines campaign served no useful strategic purpose: the islands were indefensible by the small forces available, and far from friendly bases. If the garrison had held out longer, domestic public opinion might have forced some doomed venture to relieve the siege of Bataan. The U.S. Navy would have suffered a catastrophe had it attempted to assist Wainwright in the face of overwhelming Japanese air and naval strength; Corregidor's surrender relieved Washington of an embarrassment.

Throughout the war in the Pacific, few ground actions came close to matching the scale of those waged against Germany. The struggle engaged relatively few men, though it was conducted over vast distances and involved large naval commitments. Most of the Japanese army stayed in China. Tokyo's Asian and Pacific conquests were achieved by small forces, dispersed across the hemisphere. The United States, Australia and Britain, in their turn, contested mastery of islands and densely forested wildernesses with modest ground contingents of two or three divisions, while on Russian battlefields hundreds of formations clashed. The critical factors in each successive Pacific encounter were the supporting naval and air forces. Both sides' soldiers and marines knew that their blood and sweat must go for nothing unless sea supply routes could be held open and dominance of the sky denied to the enemy. The United States Navy became the decisive force in the war against Japan.

2. The Coral Sea and Midway

IN JANUARY 1942, the Japanese seized Rabaul, on New Britain, and transformed it into a major air and naval hub. In the full flight of euphoria following their triumphs—"victory disease," as sceptics among Hirohito's people came to call it—they determined to extend their South Pacific holdings to embrace Papua, the Solomons, Fiji, New Caledonia and Samoa. The navy persuaded the army to agree to an advance to a new imperial outer perimeter with Midway Atoll in the centre and the Aleutians in the north, both of which should be seized from the Americans. They would then have bases from which they could interdict supply routes to Australia, now the Allies' main staging post for the Asian war.

Even before Corregidor fell, the Americans made a gesture which dismayed and provoked their enemies, because it provided an early hint of Japan's vulnerability and lent urgency to their further endeavours. Lt. Col. James Doolittle's 18 April air strike against Tokyo by sixteen B-25 bombers, launched from the carrier *Hornet* 650 miles from Japan, was materially insignificant but morally important. Heartening the Allied peoples in a season of defeats, it was an imaginative act of military theatre, of the kind Churchill often indulged. It persuaded the Japanese that they must seize Midway, America's westernmost Pacific foothold, held since 1867. Once Adm. Isokoku Yamamoto had aircraft based on Midway, these could frustrate further Doolittle-style adventures.

Japan's objectives would prove disastrously overambitious; but the alternative, from Tokyo's perspective, was to concede to the Americans freedom to mass forces for a counterstroke. Yamamoto and his colleagues knew that, unless the United States could be kept under relentless pressure, Japanese defeat was inevitable. Their only credible strategy, they believed, was to strike at the Allies again and again, until Washington bowed to the logic of Japanese dominance and negotiated a settlement.

Above all, the Imperial Navy sought to engage and destroy U.S. warships at sea.

Before addressing Midway, the Japanese moved against Papua and the Solomons. At the beginning of May 1942, three invasion convoys set sail for Port Moresby, protected by powerful strike and covering forces including three carriers. Vice Adm. Shigeyoshi Inoue, directing operations, hoped that an American fleet would seek to intervene, for he expected to destroy it. The amphibious force destined for Tulagi Island, in the south Solomons a few miles off Guadalcanal, landed unopposed on 3 May. Next day, aircraft from the carrier *Yorktown* struck Japanese ships offshore, sinking a destroyer and two smaller vessels, but the destruction was disappointing because the attackers enjoyed almost ideal conditions.

On 5 May a U.S. fleet with a small Australian contingent, led by Rear Adm. Frank Fletcher and forewarned by Ultra intelligence of Japanese intentions, steamed to intercept Inoue's main force. At dawn on 7 May in the Coral Sea, Fletcher dispatched his cruisers, led by British rear admiral Jack Crace, to attack the enemy's transports. Fletcher was misinformed about enemy locations. U.S. air squadrons, instead of finding the Japanese carriers, chanced upon Inoue's amphibious force. Its transports promptly turned away, to await the outcome of the fleet encounter. Crace withdrew, on learning that he was advancing into empty ocean. Planes from the *Lexington* scored an early success, sinking the small carrier *Shoho*. Meanwhile Fletcher's carrier group had an extraordinarily lucky escape. The Japanese fleet was 175 miles astern of him; his own planes were absent when enemy aircraft sank and destroyed an American tanker and escorting destroyer which were trailing his task groups. If Inoue's bombers had flown farther and found the U.S. carriers, these would have been exposed to disaster. As it was, on that first day both rival admirals groped ineffectually.

Next morning, 8 May, as sunrise came at 6:55, sailors in foetid confinement below took turns to snatch breaths of clean air from vents or scuttles, as waves of American and Japanese aircraft lifted off from their respective flight decks. Lt. Cmdr. Bob Dixon, who had led the previous day's air attack on *Shoho*, again distinguished himself by locating the Japanese fleet. He lingered overhead to maintain surveillance, nursing his engine to save fuel—a constant preoccupation of naval fliers.

The first wave of U.S. aircraft located and attacked the carrier *Shokaku*, inflicting significant but not fatal damage—most of the torpedo carriers and dive-bombers missed. The strikes were poorly coordinated. Dive-bomber crews suffered severe problems when their sighting telescopes and windshields misted up during the steep descent from "pushover" at 17,000 feet to "pull-up" at 1,500. Pilots fumed at their own lack of speed and defensive firepower against Japanese fighters. Cmdr. Bill Ault got lost on his way home, a frequent and fatal error in that vast ocean. He sent a laconic farewell message before ditching and vanishing forever: "Okay, so long people. Remember we got a thousand-pound hit on the flat top." But *Shokaku* survived. Lt. Cmdr. Paul Stroop, a staff officer aboard the *Lexington*, acknowledged ruefully, "We should have been more effective."

And even as the Americans were diving on Inoue's fleet, the Japanese struck Fletcher's ships much harder. When radar reported enemy aircraft closing, the U.S. carrier captains called for twenty-five-knot flank speed and began evasive action before meeting shoals of incoming torpedoes and a rain of bombs. The *Yorktown* suffered a single hit which killed more than forty men, and a near miss which momentarily blasted the ship's racing screws clear of the water. Her captain asked the engine room if he should reduce speed, to receive the defiant answer: "Hell no, we'll make it." But the *Lexington*'s full-helm turn as torpedoes approached failed to save her: the 40,000-ton carrier was struck with devastating effect. "It was pretty discouraging to see these Japanese launch their torpedoes then fly very close to the ship to get a look at us," said Paul Stroop. "They were curious and sort of thumbed their noses at us. We were shooting at them with our new 20mms and not hitting them at all." Blazes broke out which found plentiful tinder—inflammable bulkhead paint and wooden furniture such as no U.S. warship would carry again. Half-naked sailors suffered terrible burns—"the skin was literally dripping from their bodies." This was the last time American crews willingly exposed flesh in action. After just thirteen minutes the Japanese planes turned away, leaving a shambles which greeted Fletcher's airmen returning from their own strike.

Heroic efforts were made to control the *Lexington*'s fires: Lt. Milton Ricketts, sole survivor of a damage-control team wiped out by a bomb, was himself mortally wounded, but ran out a hose and began playing water on the flames before collapsing dead. Soon, however, in Stroop's words "fires had gotten increasingly violent and we were beginning to get explosions . . . that sounded like a freight train rumbling up the hangar deck . . . A rushing wall of flame . . . would erupt around the perimeter of the elevator." Leaking gasoline fumes triggered a massive blast belowdecks and ammunition began to cook off; the decision was made to abandon the ship. Its senior officer, Admiral Fitch, walked calmly across the flight deck accompanied by a marine orderly clutching his jacket and dispatches, to be picked up by a destroyer's boat below. Men in their hundreds began to leap into the water. The rescuers were so effective that only 216 of the *Lexington*'s crew were lost out of 2,735, but a precious carrier was gone. *Yorktown* was severely damaged, though she was able to

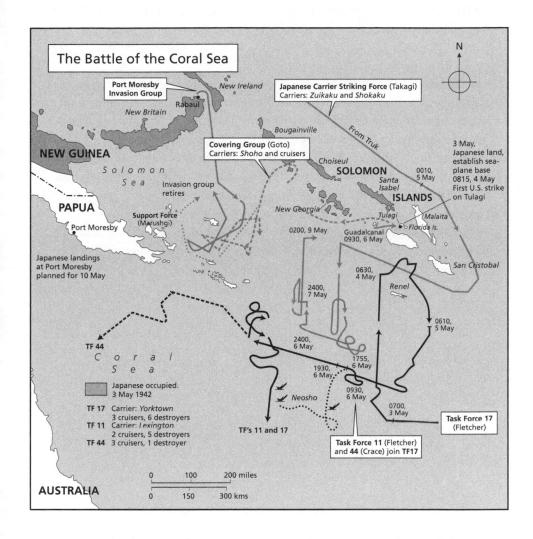

The Battle of the Coral Sea

complete landing on planes two minutes after sunset. In the small hours of darkness, the dead were buried over the side, in expectation of renewed action the next day.

But the battle was done: both fleets turned away. Fletcher's task groups had lost 543 lives, 60 aircraft and 3 ships, including the *Lexington*. Inoue lost over 1,000 men and 77 aircraft—the carrier *Zuikaku*'s air group suffered heavy attrition. The balance of destruction nonetheless favoured the Japanese, who had better planes than the Americans and handled them more effectively. Amazingly, however, Inoue abandoned the operation against Port Moresby and retired, conceding strategic success to the U.S. Navy. Here, once again, was a manifestation of Japanese timidity: at the Coral Sea, victory was within their grasp, but they failed to press their advantage. Never again would they enjoy such a favourable opportunity to establish dominance of the Pacific.

IN THE COURSE of the war, the U.S. Navy would show itself the most impressive of its nation's fighting services, but it faced a long, harsh learning process. Several early commanders were found wanting, because they were slow to grasp the principles of carrier operations, which would dominate the Pacific campaign. American fliers' courage was never in doubt, but at the outset their performance lagged that of their enemies. At Pearl Harbor, albeit against an unprepared and static enemy, Japanese planes achieved the remarkable record of nineteen hits and detonations out of forty torpedo launches, a level of accuracy no other navy matched. When U.S. carrier planes attacked the Tulagi anchorage on 3 May 1942 against slight opposition, twenty-two Douglas Devastator torpedo bombers achieved just one hit. Attacking *Shokaku* two days later, twenty-one Devastators scored no hits at all. Most American torpedoes, the Japanese said later, were launched too far out, and ran so slowly that they were easily avoidable.

Among U.S. naval aircraft, the Coral Sea battle showed that the Dauntless dive-bomber was alone up to its job, not least in having adequate endurance. The Devastator was "a real turkey," in the words of a flier, further handicapped by high fuel consumption. Worst of all, the Mk 13 aerial and Mk 14 sea-launched torpedoes were wildly unreliable, unlikely to explode even if they hit a target. A most un-American reluctance to learn from experience meant that this fault, afflicting submarine as much as air operations, was not fully corrected until 1943.

War at sea was statistically much less dangerous than it was ashore for all participants, save for such specialists as aviators and submariners. Conflict was impersonal: sailors seldom glimpsed the faces of their enemies. The fate of every ship's crew was overwhelmingly at the mercy of its captain's competence, judgement—and luck. Seamen of all nations suffered crampled living conditions and much boredom, but peril intervened only in spasms. Individuals were called upon to display fortitude and commitment, but seldom enjoyed the opportunity to choose whether or not to be brave. That was a privilege reserved for their commanders, who issued the orders determining the movements of ships and fleets. The overwhelming majority of sailors, performing technical functions aboard huge seagoing war machines, made only tiny, indirect personal contributions to killing their enemies.

Carrier operations represented the highest and most complex refinement of naval warfare. "The flight deck looked like a big war dance of different colors," wrote a sailor aboard the *Enterprise*. "The ordnance gang wore red cloth helmets and a red T-shirt when they went about their work of loading machine-guns, fusing bombs, and hoisting torpedoes . . . Other specialties wore different colors. Brown for the plane captains—one attached to each plane—green for the hydraulic men who manned the arresting gear and the catapults, yellow for the landing signal officer and deck control people, purple for the oil and gas kings . . . Everything was 'on the double' and took place with whirling propellers everywhere, waiting to mangle the unwary." The U.S. Navy would refine carrier assault to a supreme art, but in 1942 it was still near the bottom of the curve: not only were its planes inferior to those of the Japanese, but commanders had not yet evolved the right mix of fighters, dive-bombers and torpedo carriers for each "flattop"—after the Coral Sea, captains deplored their inadequate proportion of Wildcat fighters. U.S. antiaircraft gunnery was no more effective than that of the Royal Navy. Radar sets were unreliable and of inadequate range in comparison with those of the later war years. Damage control, which became an outstanding American skill, was poor.

The U.S. Navy boasted a fine fighting tradition, but its crews were still dominated by men enlisted in peacetime, often because they could find nothing else to do. Naval airman Alvin Kernan wrote:

> Many of the sailors were there, as I was, because there were few jobs in Depression America . . . We would have denied that we were an underclass . . . There wasn't such a thing in America, we thought— conveniently forgetting that blacks and Asians were allowed to serve in the navy only as officers' cooks and mess attendants. Our teeth were terrible from Depression neglect, we had not always graduated from high school, none had gone to college, our complexions tended to acne, and we were for the most part foul-mouthed, and drunkenly rowdy when on liberty . . . I used to wonder why so many of us were skinny, bepimpled, sallow, short and hairy.

Cecil King, the chief ship's clerk on the *Hornet*, recalled: "We had a small group of real no-goodniks. I mean these kids were not necessarily honest-to-God gangsters, but they were involved in anything that was seriously wrong on the ship—heavy gambling and extortion. One night one of them was thrown over the side." For most men, naval service required years of monotony and hard labour, interrupted by brief passages of violent action. A few, including King, actively enjoyed carrier life: "I just felt at home at sea. I felt like that's what the Navy's all about. Many times I would wander around the ship, particularly in the late afternoon, just enjoying being there. I would go over to the deck edge elevator and stand and watch the ocean going by. I feel like I'm probably one of the luckiest people in the entire world . . . for having been born in the year that I was, to be able to fight for my country in World War II; this whole era . . . is something that I feel real privileged for having gone through."

The expansion of the U.S. Navy's officer corps made a dramatic and brilliant contribution to the service's later success, and some learned to love the sea service and the responsibilities it conferred on them. Most ordinary sailors, however—especially as ships began to fill with wartime recruits—did their duty honourably enough, but found little to enjoy. Some found it all too much for them: a sailor on the *Hornet* climbed out on the mast yardarm, and hung 160 feet over the sea trying to muster nerve to jump and kill himself until dissuaded by the chaplain and the ship's doctor. He was sent home for psychiatric evaluation—and eventually returned to the *Hornet* in time to share the ship's sinking, the fate of which he had been so fearful.

Those who experienced the U.S. Navy's early Pacific battles saw much of failure, loss and defeat. The horrors of ships' sinkings were often increased by fatal delays before survivors were located and rescued. The Pacific is a vast ocean, and many of those who fell into it, even from large warships, were never seen again. When the damaged light cruiser *Juneau* blew up after a magazine explosion on passage to the repair base at Espíritu Santu, gunner's mate Allen Heyn was one of those who suddenly found himself struggling for his life: "There was oil very thick on the water, it was at least two inches thick, and all kinds of blueprints and documents floating around, roll after roll of toilet paper. I couldn't see anybody. I thought: 'Gee, am I the only one here' . . . Then I heard a man cry and I looked around it was this boatswain's mate . . . He said he couldn't swim and he had his whole leg torn off . . . I helped him on the raft . . . It was a very hard night because most of the fellows were wounded badly, and they were in agony. You couldn't recognize each other unless you knew a man very well before the ship went down." After three days, their party had shrunk from 140 men to 50; on the ninth day after *Juneau*'s loss, the ship's 10 remaining survivors were picked up by a destroyer and a Catalina flying boat. Sometimes, vessels vanished with the loss of every man aboard, as was almost always the case with submarines.

The Japanese began the war at sea with a corps of highly experienced seamen armed with the Long Lance torpedo, the most effective weapon of its kind in the world. Their radar sets were poor, and many ships lacked them altogether. They lagged woefully in intelligence gathering, but excelled at night operations, and in early gunnery duels often shot straighter than Americans. Their superb Zero fighters increased combat endurance and speed by forgoing cockpit armour and self-sealing fuel tanks. The superiority of Japanese naval air in 1942 makes all the more astonishing the outcome of the next phase of the war in the Pacific.

ADMIRAL YAMAMOTO strove with all the urgency that characterised his strategic vision to force a big engagement. Less than a month after the bungled Coral Sea action, he launched his strike against Midway Atoll, committing 145 warships to an ambitious, complex operation intended to split U.S. forces. A Japanese fleet would advance north against the Aleutians, while the main thrust was made at Midway: Adm. Chuichi Nagumo's four fleet carriers—*Zuikaku* and *Shokaku* were left behind after their Coral Sea mauling—would approach the island from the northwest, with Yamamoto's fast battleships 300 miles behind; a flotilla of transports, carrying 5,000 troops to execute the landing, would close from the southwest.

Yamamoto may have been a clever and sympathetic personality, but the epic clumsiness of the Midway plan emphasised his shortcomings. It required him to divide his strength; worse, it reflected characteristic Japanese hubris, by discounting even the possibility of American foreknowledge. As it was, Adm. Chester Nimitz, the U.S. Navy's Pacific commander-in-chief, knew the enemy was coming. By one of the war's most brilliant feats of intelligence work, Cmdr. Joseph Rochefort at Pearl Harbor used fragmentary Ultra decrypts to identify Midway as Nagumo's objective. On 28 May the Japanese switched their naval codes, which thereafter defied Rochefort's cryptographers for weeks. By miraculous luck, however, this happened just too late to frustrate the breakthrough that betrayed Yamamoto's Midway plan.

Nimitz made a wonderfully bold call: to stake everything upon the accuracy of Rochefort's interpretation. Japanese intelligence, always weak, believed that the *Yorktown* had been sunk at the Coral Sea, and that the other two U.S. carriers, the *Hornet* and the *Enterprise*, were far away in the Solomons. But heroic efforts by 1,400 dockyard workers at Pearl Harbor made *Yorktown* fit for sea, albeit with a makeshift air component. Nimitz was therefore able to deploy two task groups to cover Midway, one led by Fletcher—in overall command—and the other by Raymond Spruance.

This would be a carrier action, with Nagumo's flattops its objectives; the slow old American battleships were left in Californian harbours. The navy's planes were recognised as the critical weapons.

Almost a century earlier, Herman Melville, America's greatest novelist of the sea, wrote: "There is something in a naval engagement which radically distinguishes it from one on land. The ocean . . . has neither rivers, woods, banks, towns, nor mountains. In mild weather, it is one hammered plain. Stratagems, like those of disciplined armies, ambuscades—like those of Indians—are impossible. All is clear, open, fluent. The very element which sustains the combatants yields at the stroke of a feather . . . This simplicity renders a battle between two men-of-war . . . more akin to the Miltonic contests of archangels than to the comparatively squalid tussles of earth."

In 1942, Melville's lyrical vision of the sea remained recognisable to another century's sailors, but two factors had transformed his image of naval battle. First, radio communication and interception made possible "ambuscades and stratagems," such as that which took place at Midway— the location and preemption of the enemy before his figurative sails were sighted. Superior American radar conferred another important advantage over the Japanese. Meanwhile, the advent of air power meant that all was no longer "clear, open, fluent": rival fleets became vulnerable to surprise while hundreds of miles apart. But exactitude of knowledge was still lacking. In a vast ocean, it remained hard to pinpoint ships, or even fleets. Rear Adm. Frank Fletcher said: "After a battle is over, people talk a lot about how the decisions were methodically reached, but actually there's always a hell of a lot of groping around." This had been vividly demonstrated by the Coral Sea engagement; despite Commander Rochefort's magnificent achievement, uncertainty and chance also characterised Midway.

The engagement was fought only six months after Pearl Harbor, when the U.S. Navy still had fewer carriers than the British, though they carried many more planes. The two American task groups were deployed too far apart to provide mutual support or to effectively coordinate their air operations. On 3 June, the first skirmish took place: at 2:00 p.m., nine land-based B-17 Flying Fortresses delivered an ineffectual attack on the Japanese amphibious force. Early that morning, Japanese aircraft also launched a heavy attack on the Aleutians. For tens of thousands of men on both sides, a tense night followed. The garrison of Midway prepared to sell their lives dearly, knowing the fate that had already befallen many other island defenders at Japanese hands. On the U.S. carriers 300 miles to the northeast, airmen readied themselves to fight what they knew would

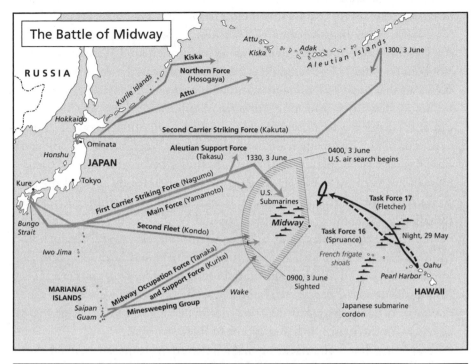

The Battle of Midway

RUSSIA

Attu
Kiska
Kiska
Adak
Aleutian Islands
1300, 3 June

Kurile Islands

Kiska

Northern Force
(Hosogaya)

Attu

Hokkaido

Second Carrier Striking Force (Kakuta)

Ominata

Honshu
JAPAN

Aleutian Support Force
(Takasu)
1330, 3 June

0400, 3 June
U.S. air search begins

Kure
Tokyo

First Carrier Striking Force (Nagumo)

Main Force (Yamamoto)

Task Force 17
(Fletcher)

U.S.
Submarines

Midway

Bungo
Strait

Second Fleet (Kondo)

Task Force 16
(Spruance)

Night, 29 May

Iwo Jima

*French frigate
shoals*

Oahu

0900, 3 June
Sighted

Pearl Harbor

Midway Occupation Force (Tanaka)
and Support Force (Kurita)

Wake

HAWAII

MARIANAS
ISLANDS

Saipan
Guam

Minesweeping Group

Japanese submarine
cordon

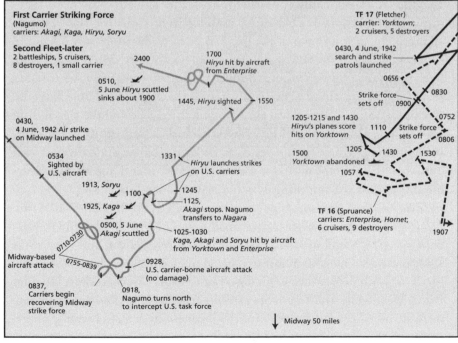

First Carrier Striking Force
(Nagumo)
carriers: *Akagi, Kaga, Hiryu, Soryu*

Second Fleet-later
2 battleships, 5 cruisers,
8 destroyers, 1 small carrier

TF 17 (Fletcher)
carrier: *Yorktown*;
2 cruisers, 5 destroyers

2400

1700
Hiryu hit by aircraft
from *Enterprise*

0430, 4 June, 1942
search and strike
patrols launched

0656

0510,
5 June *Hiryu* scuttled
sinks about 1900

Strike force
sets off

0830

0900

1445, *Hiryu* sighted

1550

0752

0430,
4 June, 1942 Air strike
on Midway launched

1205-1215 and 1430
Hiryu's planes score
hits on *Yorktown*

1110

Strike force
sets off

0806

0534
Sighted by
U.S. aircraft

1331
Hiryu launches strikes
on U.S. carriers

1500
Yorktown abandoned

1205

1430

1530

1057

1913, *Soryu*

1100

1245

1925, *Kaga*

1125,
Akagi stops. Nagumo
transfers to *Nagara*

TF 16 (Spruance)
carriers: *Enterprise, Hornet*;
6 cruisers, 9 destroyers

0500, 5 June
Akagi scuttled

1025-1030
Kaga, Akagi and *Soryu* hit by aircraft
from *Yorktown* and *Enterprise*

1907

0710-0730

Midway-based
aircraft attack

0755-0839

0928,
U.S. carrier-borne aircraft attack
(no damage)

0837,
Carriers begin
recovering Midway
strike force

0918,
Nagumo turns north
to intercept U.S. task force

↓ Midway 50 miles

be a critical action. One of them, Lt. Dick Crowell, said soberly as they broke up a late-night craps game on the *Yorktown*: "The fate of the United States now rests in the hands of 240 pilots." Nimitz was satisfied that the scenario was unfolding exactly as he had anticipated. Yamamoto was troubled that the U.S. Pacific Fleet remained unlocated, but he remained oblivious that any carriers might close within range of Nagumo.

Before dawn next morning, "a warm, damp, rather hazy day," American and Japanese pilots breakfasted. The *Yorktown*'s men favoured "one-eyed sandwiches"—an egg fried in a hole in toast. Nagumo's fliers enjoyed rice, soybean soup, pickles and dried chestnuts before drinking a battle toast of hot sake. At 4:30 a.m. seventy-two Japanese bombers and thirty-six fighters took off to attack Midway Island. At 5:45, a patrolling Catalina signalled the incoming attack, then spotted Nagumo's carriers. Fletcher needed three hours' steaming to close within attack range. Meanwhile, Midway-based marine and army torpedo bombers and bombers took off immediately, as did Wildcat and Buffalo fighters. The latter suffered terribly at the hands of Zeroes. All but three of twenty-seven were either shot down or so badly damaged that they never flew again. But the Japanese attackers, in their turn, lost 30 percent of their strength.

Nagumo's bomber attack, at 6:35, inflicted widespread damage but failed to knock out Midway's airfields. Its leader signalled the fleet: "Second strike necessary." Thereafter, nothing went right for the Japanese admiral. His first mistake of the day had been to dispatch only a handful of reconnaissance aircraft to search for American warships; one seaplane, from the heavy cruiser *Tone*, was delayed taking off—and it was vectored to search the sector where Fletcher's carriers were steaming. Thus, Nagumo was still ignorant of any naval air threat when he received the signal from his Midway planes. At 7:15 he ordered ninety-three Kate strike aircraft, ready with torpedoes on his decks, to be struck below and rearmed with high-explosive bombs to renew the attack on the island, meanwhile clearing the way for the returning Midway planes to land on.

Even as they did so, ships' buglers sounded another air-raid alarm. Between 7:55 and 8:20, successive small waves of Midway-based U.S. aircraft attacked Nagumo's fleet. They had no fighter cover, and were ruthlessly destroyed by antiaircraft fire and Zeroes without achieving a single hit. The gunfire died away, the drone of the surviving attackers' engines faded. Meanwhile, the first of Spruance's torpedo planes and dive-bombers were already airborne, heading for the Japanese fleet from extreme range. Although the *Tone*'s scout plane belatedly spotted the American ships, only at 8:10 did its pilot report that they seemed to include a carrier. Among

Nagumo's staff, this news prompted a fierce argument about how to respond, which continued even as the last of the U.S. land-based attacks was repulsed.

The only achievement of the strikes from Midway, purchased at shocking cost, was to impede flight operations aboard the Japanese carriers. Nagumo was hamstrung by the need to recover his attack force, which was short of fuel, before he could launch a strike against Fletcher's fleet; meanwhile, he ordered the Kates in the hangars once more to be armed with torpedoes. By far his wisest course, at this stage, would have been to turn away and open the range with the enemy, until he had reorganised his air groups and was ready to fight. As it was, however, with characteristic lack of initiative he held his course. At 9:18, the Japanese flight decks were still in chaos as aircraft completed refuelling. Picket destroyers now signalled another warning, and began to make protective smoke. The first of Fletcher's planes were closing fast, and Zeroes scrambled to meet them.

Before the American planes were launched, Lt. Cmdr. John Waldron, a rough, tough, much-respected South Dakotan who led Torpedo Squadron 8 from the *Hornet*, told his pilots that the coming battle "will be a historic and, I hope, a glorious event." Wildcat squadron commander Jimmy Gray wrote: "All of us knew we were 'on' in the world's center ring." Lt. Cmdr. Eugene Lindsey, commanding Torpedo 6, had been badly injured only a few days earlier when he ditched his plane after making a botched landing; his face was so bruised that it was painful for him to wear goggles. But on the morning of the Midway strike he insisted on flying: "This is what I have been trained to do," he said stubbornly, before taking off to his death.

The American attackers approached the Japanese in successive waves. Jimmy Gray wrote: "Seeing the white feathers of ships' wakes at high speed at the far edge of the overcast, and realising that there for the first time in plain sight were the Japanese who had been knocking hell out of us for seven months was a sensation not many men know in a lifetime." The twenty escorting Wildcats flew high, while the Devastators necessarily attacked low. Over the radio, crackling disputes about tactics between fighters and torpedo carriers persisted even as they approached the enemy; the Wildcats maintained altitude, and anyway lacked endurance to linger over the enemy fleet. The consequence was that when fifty Japanese Zeroes fell on the Devastators, these suffered a massacre. The twelve planes of Torpedo 3 were flying in formation at 2,600 feet and still fifteen miles from their targets when they met the first Japanese. Slashing attacks persisted throughout their attack run. One of the few surviving

American pilots, Wilhelm "Doc" Esders, wrote: "When approximately one mile from the carrier our leader apparently expected to attack, his plane was hit and it crashed into the sea in flames . . . I saw only five planes drop their torpedoes." Esders's own Devastator was hit, his radio-man fatally wounded; the CO_2 fire extinguisher in the cockpit exploded; flak shells burst below them, while the Zeroes kept firing. The crew was extraordinarily lucky that the enemy planes turned away after following them homewards for twenty miles.

The Devastators ploughed doggedly towards their targets at their best speed of 100 knots, until each wave in turn was shot to pieces and plunged into the sea. A bomber gunner heard Waldron talking over the radio as he led his planes in: "Johnny One to Johnny Two . . . How'm I doing Dobbs? . . . Attack immediately . . . There's two fighters in the water . . . My two wingmen are going in the water." Waldron himself was last seen attempting to escape from his flaming plane. After the first wave had attacked, the Zeroes' group leader reported laconically: "All fifteen enemy torpedo-bombers shot down." Many of the next wave were destroyed while manoeuvring to achieve an attack angle as the Japanese carriers swung wildly to avoid them. A despairing American gunner whose weapon jammed fired his .45-calibre automatic pistol at a pursuing Zero.

George Gay, who flew from the *Hornet* at the controls of a Devastator, had a reputation in his squadron as a Texas loudmouth, but proved to be its only survivor. Shot down in the sea with a bullet wound and two dead crewmen, he trod water all day watching the battle, because he had heard many stories about the Japanese shooting downed airmen. At nightfall, he cautiously inflated his dinghy and had the fantastic good fortune to be picked up the next morning by a patrolling American amphibian.

On the flight decks of Nagumo's carriers, the Japanese experienced an hour of acute tension as the Devastators approached through a storm of antiaircraft fire. But most of the torpedoes were dropped beyond effective range, and the Mk 13s ran so slowly that the Japanese ships had ample time to comb their tracks. "I was not aware or did not feel the torpedo drop," said a Devastator gunner afterwards, adding that this was probably because his pilot was trying to jink. "A few days later I asked him when he dropped. He said when he realized that we seemed to be the only TBD still flying and that we didn't have a chance of carrying the torpedo to normal drop range. I couldn't figure out what he was trying to do and the flak was really bad, so I yelled into the intercom, 'Let's get the hell out of here!' It is possible that my yell helped him make his decision."

Just after 10:00 a.m., the attackers had shot their bolt, having achieved no hits. Of 41 American torpedo bombers which took off that day, only 6 returned, and 14 of 82 airmen survived. Most of the survivors' planes were shot full of holes. Lloyd Childers, a wounded gunner, heard his pilot say, "We're not going to make it." The Devastator reached the fleet, but was prevented from landing back on the *Yorktown* by a gaping bomb crater in its flight deck. The pilot ditched safely in the sea alongside, and Childers patted his plane's tail as it sank, in gratitude for getting him back. Many survivors, however, were enraged by the futility of their sacrifice, and embittered by the lack of protection from their own fighters. A Devastator gunner who landed back on the *Enterprise* had to be forcibly restrained as he threw himself at a Wildcat pilot.

American fighters had few successes that day. One of them was achieved by Jimmy Thach, who went on to become one of the foremost naval aviation tacticians of the war. Thach said he lost his temper when he saw Japanese aircraft boring into his neighbour: "I was mad because here was this poor little wingman who'd never been in combat before, had had very little gunnery training, the first time aboard a carrier and a Zero was about to chew him to pieces . . . I decided to keep my fire going into him and he's going to pull out, which he did, and he just missed me by a few feet; I saw flames coming out of the bottom of his airplane. This is like playing 'chicken' with two automobiles on the highway headed for each other except we were both shooting as well."

The Americans had suffered a shocking succession of disasters, which could easily have been fatal to the battle's outcome. Instead, however, fortune changed with startling abruptness. Nagumo paid the price for his enforced failure to strike at Spruance's task force even when he learned it was near at hand. Moreover, his Zeroes were at low level and running out of fuel when more American aircraft appeared high overhead, a few minutes after the last torpedo bombers attacked.

The Dauntless dive-bomber was the only effective U.S. naval aircraft in 1942; what followed changed the course of the Pacific war in the space of minutes. Dauntlesses fell on Nagumo's carriers, wreaking havoc. "I saw this glint in the sun," said Jimmy Thach, "and it just looked like a beautiful silver waterfall, these dive-bombers coming down. It looked to me like almost every bomb hit." In reality, the first three bombs aimed at the *Kaga* missed, but the fourth achieved a direct hit, setting off sympathetic detonations among munitions scattered across the carrier's decks and in its hangars. The *Soryu* and *Akagi* suffered similar fates. Flier Tom Cheek was another fascinated spectator as the dive-bombers pulled out. "As I looked back to *Akagi* hell literally broke loose. First the orange-colored flash of a bomb burst appeared on the flight deck midway between the island structure and the stern. Then in rapid succession followed a bomb burst amidships, and the water founts of near-misses plumed up near the stern. Almost in unison *Kaga*'s flight deck erupted with bomb bursts and flames. My gaze remained on *Akagi* as an explosion at the midship waterline seemed to open the bowels of the ship in a rolling, greenish-yellow ball of flame . . . *Soryu* . . . too was being heavily hit. All three ships had lost their foaming white bow waves and appeared to be losing way. I circled slowly to the right, awe-struck."

Equally fascinated—and appalled—was Cmdr. Mitsuo Fuchida, the hero of the Pearl Harbor strike, now an impotent spectator on the deck of the *Akagi*: "I was horrified at the destruction that had been wrought in a matter of seconds. There was a huge hole in the flight deck just behind the midship elevator . . . Deck plates reeled in grotesque configurations. Planes stood tail up belching livid flames and jet-black smoke. Reluctant tears streamed down my cheeks."

The dive-bomber attack sank two Japanese carriers immediately, and the third flaming hulk was scuttled that evening. It was an extraordinary achievement, not least because two American squadrons of dive-bombers and their Wildcat escort, from the *Hornet*, had been dispatched on the wrong course and failed to engage. All ten Wildcat pilots in the *Hornet*'s Fighting Squadron 8 ran out of fuel and splashed into the sea without sighting an enemy; most of the ship's Dauntlesses landed on Midway, having missed the battle.

The Japanese were enraged by the loss of their carriers, and vented their spleen on every American within reach. Wesley Osmus, a twenty-three-year-old torpedo-bomber pilot from Chicago, was spotted in the sea by a destroyer lookout, retrieved from the water and interrogated on the bridge by an emotional officer waving a sword. Towards sunset the Japanese, losing interest in their captive, took Osmus to the fantail of the ship and set about him with a fire axe. He was slow to die, clinging to the rail until his fingers were smashed and he fell away into the sea. The Imperial Japanese Navy was as profoundly and institutionally brutalised as Hirohito's army.

At midmorning Nagumo's sole surviving carrier, the *Hiryu*, at last launched its own attack, which fell on Fletcher's *Yorktown*. American radar detected the incoming dive-bombers fifty miles out, and fighters began to scramble. Eleven Val bombers and three Zeros were shot down by Wildcats, two more Vals by antiaircraft fire; three Japanese bombs hit the *Yorktown*, but energetic damage control enabled the carrier to continue landing its dive-bombers, even as the crew fought huge fires. Admiral

Fletcher transferred his flag to the cruiser *Astoria*, and surrendered overall command to Spruance.

At 2:30 p.m., a wave of Japanese torpedo bombers from the *Hiryu* closed on the *Yorktown*, which again flew off fighters. Ensign Milton Tootle had just cleared the deck of the carrier in his Wildcat when the attackers closed in. Tootle turned through the American antiaircraft barrage, shot down an enemy plane, then was himself downed by a Zero after a flight lasting barely sixty seconds; he was lucky enough to be rescued from the water. Several attackers were shot down, but four launched their torpedoes, two of which struck the carrier. The ocean flooded in, and the ship took on a heavy list. Just before 3:00 p.m., the captain ordered the *Yorktown* abandoned. The decision was possibly premature, and the ship might have been saved, but in 1942 less was known about damage control than the U.S. Navy had learned two years later. Destroyers rescued the entire crew, save those who had perished during the attacks.

At 3:30 p.m., at Fletcher's behest Spruance launched another strike, by twenty-seven dive-bombers, including ten *Yorktown* planes which had landed on his flattops while their own ship was being attacked. Just before 5:00, these reached the *Hiryu* while its crew were eating riceballs in their mess decks. The ship had sixteen aircraft left, ten of them fighters, but only a reconnaissance plane was airborne, and the Japanese now lacked radar to warn of the Americans' coming. Four bombs struck the carrier, starting huge fires. Little Adm. Tamon Yamaguchi, the senior officer aboard, mounted a biscuit box to deliver a farewell address to the crew. Then he and the captain disappeared to their cabins to commit ritual suicide, while the remaining seamen were taken off. The stricken ship was scuttled with torpedoes: four of the six carriers that had attacked Pearl Harbor were now at the bottom of the Pacific. On the American side, the *Hornet*'s ill-fortune persisted when a pilot, returning wounded, accidentally nudged his gun button as he bumped down heavily onto the flight deck. A burst of fire killed five men on the superstructure. The returning airmen were shocked by their losses, but in Jimmy Gray's words, "We were too tired and too busy to do more than feel the pain of an aching heart."

The American sacrifice had been heavy, but victory was the reward. Admiral Nagumo opted for withdrawal, only to have his order countermanded by Yamamoto, who demanded a night surface attack on the Americans. This was frustrated when Spruance turned away, recognising that his fleet had accomplished everything possible. The disengagement was finely judged: Yamamoto's battleships, of which the Americans knew nothing, were closing fast from the north. Spruance had achieved an overwhelming balance of advantage. His foremost priority now was to

maintain this, protecting his two surviving carriers. Yamamoto acknowledged failure, and ordered a Japanese retreat. Spruance again turned and
followed, launching a further air strike which sank one heavy cruiser and
crippled another. This was almost the end of the battle, save that on
7 June a Japanese submarine met the burnt-out *Yorktown* under tow, and
dispatched her to the bottom. This blow was acceptable, however, set
against the massive Japanese losses.

Both Nimitz and Spruance had displayed consummate judgement,
contrasted with Yamamoto's and Nagumo's errors. The courage and skill
of America's dive-bomber pilots overbore every other disappointment and
failure. The U.S. Navy had achieved a triumph. Nimitz, with characteristic
graciousness, sent his car to bring Commander Rochefort to a celebration
party at Pearl Harbor. Before his assembled staff, the commander-in-chief
said: "This officer deserves a major share of the credit for the victory at
Midway." Luck, which favoured the Japanese in the war's first months,
turned dramatically in favour of the Americans during the decisive naval
battle of the Pacific war. But this does not diminish the achievement of
Nimitz and his subordinates.

The Japanese fleet remained a formidable fighting force: in the months
that followed, it inflicted some severe local reverses on the Americans in
the Pacific. But the U.S. Navy had displayed the highest qualities at a
critical moment. Japanese industrial weakness made it hard to replace the
carrier losses of Midway, and one of the cardinal misjudgements of the
Axis war effort was failure to sustain a flow of trained pilots to replace
casualties. The Americans, by contrast, soon began to deploy thousands of
superbly trained airmen, flying the new Hellcat fighter. Nimitz remained
short of carriers until well into 1943, but thereafter America's building
programme delivered an awesome array of new warships. The pattern
of the Pacific war was set, wherein the critical naval actions were fought
between rival fleets whose major surface elements seldom engaged each
other. Carrier-borne aircraft had shown themselves the decisive weapons,
and the United States would soon employ these more effectively and in
much larger numbers than any other nation in the world. Marc Mitscher,
captain of *Hornet*, feared that his career was finished, so poorly had his
ship's air group performed at Midway; it is widely believed that he falsi-
fied the log record of his squadrons' designated attack course to conceal
his own blunder, which kept them out of the battle. Nimitz and Spruance,
together with the airmen of the *Yorktown* and *Enterprise*, were the heroes
of Midway, but Mitscher went on to become the supreme American carrier leader of the war.

3. Guadalcanal and New Guinea

THE NEXT PHASE of the Pacific campaign was driven by expediency and characterised by improvisation. The United States, committed to "Germany first," planned to dispatch most of its available troop strength to fight in North Africa. MacArthur, in Australia, lacked men to launch the assault on Rabaul which he favoured. Instead, Australian troops, slowly reinforced by Americans, were committed to frustrate Japanese designs on the vast jungle island of Papua New Guinea. Separated from the northern tip of Australia by only 200 miles of sea, this became the scene of one of the grimmest struggles of the war.

Meanwhile, 600 miles eastwards, in the Solomons, Japanese who had occupied Tulagi Island moved on to neighbouring Guadalcanal, where they began to construct an airfield. If allowed to complete and exploit this, their planes could dominate the region. An abrupt American decision was made to preempt them, by landing the 1st Marine Division. Such a stroke fulfilled the U.S. Navy's driving desire, promoted by Adm. Ernest King, the commander-in-chief of the U.S. Fleet, in Washington, to engage the enemy wherever opportunity allowed. The marines were staging through Wellington, New Zealand, en route to an undecided objective; they found themselves ordered to restow their ships for an immediate assault landing; when the local dock labour force refused to work in prevailing heavy rain, marines did the job themselves. Then, in the first days of August 1942, they sailed for Guadalcanal. In their innocence, many supposed that they were destined to wage war in a tropical paradise.

On 7 August, 19,000 Americans began to land, first on the outlying islands, then on Guadalcanal proper, in the face of slight opposition following a heavy naval bombardment. "In the dirty dawn . . . there were only a few fires flickering, like the city dumps, to light our path to history," wrote a marine, Robert Leckie. The Australian coast watcher Captain Martin Clements watched exultantly from his jungle hideout as the Americans came ashore, writing in his diary, "Wizard!!!—Caloo, Callay, Oh! What a day!" On the beach, men vastly relieved to find themselves alive split coconuts and gorged on the milk, heedless of implausible warnings that the Japanese might have poisoned them. Then they began to march inland, soon parched and sweating prodigiously. The Japanese, following another huge intelligence failure, had not anticipated the Americans' arrival. In what would prove a critical action of the Pacific war, the landing force quickly seized the airstrip, christened Henderson Field in honour of a marine pilot hero of Midway. Some men liberated caches of enemy supplies, including sake, which allowed them to become gloriously drunk during the nights that followed. Thus ended the last easy part; what followed became one of the most desperate campaigns of the Far Eastern war, characterised by small but bloody battles ashore, repeated clashes of warships afloat.

TWO DAYS after the initial assault, at sea off Guadalcanal the U.S. Navy endured a humiliation. Admiral Fletcher had signalled Nimitz that he believed local Japanese air power presented an unacceptable threat to his three aircraft carriers, and recommended their withdrawal. Without waiting for approval, he set course northeastwards. Rear Adm. Kelly Turner, commanding the transports inshore, made plain his belief that the carrier commander had deserted his post of duty: Fletcher's reputation suffered lasting harm. But modern historians, Richard Frank notable among them, believe that Fletcher made an entirely correct decision to treat the safety of his carriers as the foremost strategic priority.

In the early hours of the following morning, 9 August, Allied naval forces suffered a surprise which revealed both command incompetence and a fatal paucity of night-fighting skills. Japanese vice admiral Gunichi Mikawa led a heavy cruiser squadron into an attack on the offshore anchorage, which was protected by one Australian and four American heavy cruisers, together with six destroyers. The enemy ships had been spotted the previous afternoon by a Royal Australian Air Force (RAAF) Hudson, but its sighting report was not picked up at its base at Fall River on New Guinea because the radio station was shut down during an air raid. Even when the Hudson landed, there was an inexcusable delay of several hours before word was passed to the warships at sea.

The Americans were deployed off Savo Island in anticipation of a Japanese strike, but in the darkness Mikawa's cruiser column steamed undetected through the U.S. destroyer radar-picket line. Within three minutes of the Americans belatedly spotting the *Chokai*, the leading Japanese ship, at 1:43 a.m. the Australian cruiser *Canberra* was struck by at least 24 shells which detonated, in the words of a survivor, with "a terrific orange-greenish flash." Every man in the boiler rooms was killed and all power lost; the *Canberra* was unable to fire a shot during the subsequent hours before being abandoned. There is also disputed evidence of a torpedo hit by the American destroyer *Bagley*, aiming at the Japanese.

The destroyer *Patterson* found itself in a perfect firing position, but amid the deafening concussion of its guns, the ship's torpedo officer failed to hear his captain's order to trigger the tubes. At 1:47 two Japanese torpedoes hit the *Chicago*. Only one of these exploded, in the bow, but the ship's fire-control system was crippled. The *Astoria* fired thirteen salvoes without effect because she too failed to see Mikawa's ships, and her gunnery radar was defective. The cruiser was wrecked by Japanese gunfire at a range of three miles, and abandoned the next day with heavy loss of life.

The *Vincennes* was likewise devastated, and already on fire when its own armament began to explode. Her commanding officer, Capt. Frederick Riefkohl, had no notion the enemy was attacking, and supposed himself a victim of friendly fire. As Mikawa's huge searchlights illuminated the American cruiser, Riefkohl broadcast angrily over his voice radio, demanding that they should be switched off. Thereafter, he concentrated on trying to save his ship, hit by three torpedoes and seventy-four shells which reduced it to a flaming hulk. Only belatedly did the American captain acknowledge that the Japanese were responsible, and order destroyers to attack them—without success. The *Quincy* fired starshells which proved ineffective because they burst above low cloud, while a Japanese seaplane dropped illumination flares beyond the American squadron, silhouetting its ships for Mikawa's gunnery directors. The hapless *Quincy*'s captain was killed a few moments after ordering an attempt to beach the ship, which sank with the loss of 370 officers and men. *Chokai* suffered only one hit, in its staff chartroom.

At 2:16 a.m., the Japanese ceased fire, having achieved a crushing victory inside half an hour. There was a heated debate on the bridge of the flagship about whether to press on and attack the now defenceless American transports beyond, off Guadalcanal. Mikawa decided that it was too late to regroup his squadron, make such an assault, then before daylight withdraw out of range of American carrier aircraft, which he wrongly supposed were at hand. Amid a sky dancing with lightning in a tropical rainstorm, the Japanese turned for home. Chaos among the stricken Allied warships persisted to the end: at dawn, an American destroyer fired 106 5-inch shells at a cruiser before discovering that its target was the crippled *Canberra*. When it was decided that the Australian warship must be sunk, U.S. destroyers fired a further 370 rounds into the hulk before being obliged to use torpedoes to end its agony. The only consolation for the Allies was that an American submarine torpedoed and sank the *Kako*, one of Mikawa's heavy cruisers, during its withdrawal after the action.

In the Guadalcanal anchorage, Admiral Turner continued offloading supplies for the marines until noon on 9 August, when to the deep dismay of the men ashore he removed his transports until more air cover became available. Reviewing the disaster off Savo, he wrote: "The navy was still obsessed with a strong feeling of technical and mental superiority over the enemy. In spite of ample evidence as to enemy capabilities, most of our officers and men despised the enemy and felt themselves sure victors in all encounters under any circumstances . . . The net result of all of this was a fatal lethargy of mind . . . We were not mentally ready for hard battle. I believe that this psychological factor as a cause of our defeat was even more important than the element of surprise." The U.S. Navy learned its lessons: never again in the war did it suffer such a severe humiliation. And the critical reality, which soon dawned on the Japanese, was that yet again one of their admirals had allowed caution to deprive him of a chance to convert success into a decisive strategic achievement. The lost Allied cruisers could be replaced; the landing force was able to hold on at Henderson Field because its supporting amphibious shipping remained unscathed, and soon returned to Lunga Bay. Savo would be redeemed.

The Japanese were slow to grasp the importance of the American commitment to Guadalcanal. They drip fed a trickle of reinforcements to the island, who were thrown into repeated frontal attacks, each one insufficiently powerful to overwhelm the precarious marine perimeter. The Americans holding Henderson Field and the surrounding tropical rain forests found themselves locked in an epic ordeal. Visibility amid an almost impenetrable tangle of vines and ferns, giant hardwoods and creepers, was seldom more than a few yards. Even when gunfire was temporarily stilled, leeches, wasps, giant ants and malarial mosquitoes inflicted their own miseries. The intense humidity made fungal and skin infections endemic. Marines encountering the jungle for the first time were alarmed by its constant noises, especially those of the night. "Whether these were birds squawking . . . or some strange reptiles or frogs, I don't know," said one man, "but we were terrified by any noise because we'd been told that the Japanese signaled each other in the jungle by imitating bird calls."

Amid incessant rainstorms, they bivouacked in mud, which became a curse of the campaign, and endured short rations and dysentery. Nervous men not infrequently shot one another. There was a steady stream of combat-fatigue evacuees. A platoon commander who lost four men to hysteria, 15 percent of his strength, reckoned that this was typical. Experience of Japanese barbarism bred matching American savagery. A marine, Ore Marion, described a scene after a bitter night action: "At daybreak a couple of our kids, bearded, dirty, skinny from hunger, slightly wounded by bayonets, clothes worn and torn, whack off three Jap heads and jam them on poles facing the 'Jap side' of the river." The regimental commander remonstrated fiercely that this was the conduct of animals. "A dirty, stinking young kid says, 'That's right Colonel, we are animals. We live like animals, we eat and are treated like animals, what the fuck do you expect?' "

Some of the fiercest fighting took place on the Tenaru River, where both sides suffered heavily as the Japanese attacked again and again with suicidal courage and tactical clumsiness. As a green Japanese flare burst overhead, Robert Leckie described the scene: "Here was cacophony; here was dissonance; here was wildness . . . booming, sounding, shrieking, wailing, hissing, crashing, shaking, gibbering noise. Here was hell . . . The plop of the outgoing mortar with the crunch of its fall, the clatter of the machine guns and the lighter, faster rasp of the Browning automatic rifles, the hammering of fifty-caliber machine-guns, the crash of 75-millimetre anti-tank guns firing point-blank canister at the enemy—each of these conveys a definite message to the understanding ear." After hours of this, dawn revealed heaped enemy bodies and a few survivors in flight. But as night succeeded night of such clashes and counterattacks, the strain told on the Americans.

"Morale was very bad," said marine lieutenant Paul Moore, who won a Navy Cross. "But there was something about Marines—once we were ordered to attack we decided we damn well were going to do it." Swimming the Matanikau River with his platoon, the young officer glanced up and saw mortar bombs and grenades arching through the air above him, "as if it were raining, with bullets striking all around us." Moore, a few months out of Yale, was shot as he threw a grenade to knock out a Japanese machine gun. The bullet hit him in the chest: "The air was going in and out of a hole in my lungs. I thought I was dead, going to die right then. I wasn't breathing through my mouth, but through this hole. I felt like a balloon going in and out, going pshhhh. I was thinking to myself: now I'm going to die. And first of all it's rather absurd for me, considering where I came from, my early expectations of a comfortable life and all the rest, for me to be dying on a jungle island in combat as a Marine. That's not me . . . Shortly, a wonderful corpsman crawled up and gave me a shot of morphine, and then a couple of other people got a stretcher and started evacuating me."

Guadalcanal set the pattern for the Pacific campaign, a three-year contest for a succession of harbours and airfields, refuges for ships and platforms for planes amid an otherwise featureless watery vastness. The Japanese were never able to reverse their early mistakes, rooted in an underestimate of American strength and will. Each island action was tiny in scale by the standards of the European theatre: at the peak of the Guadalcanal battle, no more than 65,000 Americans and Japanese were engaged with each other ashore, while 40,000 more men served on warships and transports at sea. But the intensity of the struggle, and the conditions in which the combatants were obliged to subsist amid swamps, rain, heat, disease, insects, crocodiles, snakes and short rations caused the Pacific battlefield experience to become one of the worst of the war. Island fighting evolved into a bizarre and terrible routine: "Everything was so organized, and handled with such matter-of-fact dispatch," Corp. James Jones, one of the army men who eventually landed on Guadalcanal to reinforce the marines, observed with fascinated revulsion.

> Like a business. Like a regular business. And yet at the bottom of it was blood: blood, mutilation and death . . . The beach was literally alive with men, all moving somewhere, and seeming to undulate with a life of its own under their mass as beaches sometimes appear to do when invaded by armies of fiddler crabs. Lines, strings and streams of men crossed and recrossed it with hot-footed and apparently unregulated alacrity. They were in all stages of dress and undress . . . They wore all sorts of fantastic headgear, issue, civilian, and homemade, so that one might see a man working in the water totally naked with nothing adorning his person except his identity tags.

Between August and October, the Japanese on Guadalcanal outnumbered their enemies, but thereafter American reinforcements and Japanese casualties progressively shifted the balance against the latter. Their repeated headlong assaults failed against a stubborn defence: they were unable to wrest control of Henderson Field from the Americans, who had superior artillery and air support. This was small consolation to the defenders, however, when the Japanese navy intervened. Seldom in the course of the war did Allied troops have to endure naval bombardments of the kind the Royal Navy and U.S. Navy routinely administered to the Axis, but the Americans on Guadalcanal suffered severely from the guns of Japanese warships. Hour after hour during four nights in October, enemy heavy ships delivered some 900 rounds of 14-inch fire, followed by 2,000 rounds from heavy cruisers. "[It] was the most tremendous thing I've been through in all my life," said a marine afterwards. "There was one big bunker near our galley . . . a shell dropped right in the middle of it and practically everybody in the hole was killed. We tried to dig the men out but we saw it wasn't any use." A correspondent wrote: "It is almost beyond belief that we are still here, still alive, still waiting and still ready." Many aircraft on Henderson Field were wrecked; the strip was rendered unserviceable for a week.

The Japanese were belatedly growing to understand the importance of the battle as a test of wills: "We must be aware," wrote an officer at Imperial General Headquarters, "of the possibility that the struggle for Guadalcanal . . . may develop into the decisive struggle between America and Japan." To the defenders, however, it sometimes seemed that they were a forgotten little army. "It was so lonely," wrote Robert Leckie. ". . . In an almost mawkish sense, we had gotten hold of the notion that we were orphans. No one cared, we thought. All of America's millions doing the same things each day: going to movies, getting married, attending college commencements, sales meetings, café fires, newspaper drives against vivisection, political oratory, Broadway hits and Broadway flops, horrible revelations in high places and murders in tenements making tabloid headlines, vandalism in cemeteries and celebrities getting religion; all of the same, all, all, all, the changeless, daily America—all of this was going on without a single thought for us."

Yet the myth of the invincibility of the Japanese army was shattered on this island, just sixty miles by thirty, where the U.S. Marine Corps, which expanded from its prewar strength of 28,000 to an eventual 485,000 men, first staked a claim to be considered the outstanding American ground force of the war. The Japanese, by contrast, laid bare their limitations, especially a shortage of competent commanders. Even during Japan's victory season, while Yamashita conducted operations in Malaya with verve and skill, the campaigns in Burma and the Philippines suggested that his peers lacked initiative. When defending a position, their ethic of absolute conformity to orders had its uses; but in attack, commanders often acted unimaginatively. Man for man, the Japanese soldier was more aggressive and conditioned to hardship than his Allied counterpart: British general Bill Slim characterised the enemy condescendingly as "the greatest fighting insect in the world." Until 1945, Hirohito's men displayed exceptional night-fighting skills. Collectively, however, the Japanese army had nothing like the combat power of the Wehrmacht, the Red Army—or the U.S. Marine Corps.

It was a reflection of the fantastic Japanese capacity for self-delusion that, after their first stunning wave of conquests, their army commanders proposed establishing small garrisons to hold their island bases, while redeploying most of their troops to China—which they regarded as their nation's main theatre of war. Short of trained manpower, they had scraped the barrel for forces to conduct the Southeast Asia and Pacific island offensives; the long China campaign had weakened and demoralised the army even before Pearl Harbor took place. Thereafter, Japan's generals were obliged to find soldiers from a shrinking pool, then dispatch them into battle with barely three months' training. Japanese strategy had been rooted in a conviction that the United States would treat for peace after a brisk battlefield drubbing. When this hope was disappointed, the army spent the rest of the war struggling to defend Nippon's overblown empire with inadequate means and inferior technology. The important reality of the Pacific war was that the Americans and Australians eventually prevailed on every island they assaulted. Only in Burma and China did the Japanese army maintain dominance until the last phase of the war.

THROUGHOUT THE CAMPAIGN on Guadalcanal, an equally relentless and bloody struggle was conducted at sea. The Savo battle was only the first of a series of dramatic naval encounters, almost all precipitated by Japanese attempts to reinforce and supply their troops ashore, and to impede the matching American buildup. Destroyers of the "Tokyo Express" sought to run men and stores by night through "the Slot," the narrow approach to Guadalcanal. Australian coast watchers manning radios in jungle hideouts on Japanese-held islands played a critical role in alerting the air force to enemy shipping movements. In addition to two fierce carrier battles in open waters offshore, in "the Slot," opposing squadrons of battleships, cruisers, and destroyers manoeuvred for advantage like boxers circling each other in darkness in a giant ring. The challenge was almost always to locate the enemy, then to fire first. Attrition was awesome: the 24 August Battle of the Eastern Solomons cost the Japanese a carrier and heavy aircraft losses in exchange for damage to the *Enterprise*; a week later, the carrier *Saratoga* suffered such severe torpedo damage that it was obliged to quit the theatre for a U.S. dockyard. On 15 September Japanese submarines sank the carrier *Wasp* and damaged the new battleship *North Carolina*, but the Americans inflicted heavy losses on the enemy off Cape Esperance on the night of 11–12 October.

Vice Adm. William "Bull" Halsey, who assumed command of regional naval operations on 18 October, found himself committed to some of the heaviest fleet actions of the war. At the Battle of the Santa Cruz Islands on 26 October, the Japanese lost over a hundred aircraft and the Americans seventy-four, more than the rival air forces on any day of the Battle of Britain. Destruction of the carrier *Hornet* left the Americans for some weeks solely dependent on the damaged *Enterprise* for naval air operations. On the night of 12 November Vice Adm. Hiroake Abe, leading a squadron dominated by two battleships to bombard the Americans ashore on Guadalcanal, met an American cruiser force. Though he inflicted heavy damage, sinking six ships for the loss of three, with familiar caution he chose to retreat after a twenty-four-minute action, only to lose one of his battleships to American aircraft next morning.

Two days later, marine pilots of the "Cactus Air Force"—as the Henderson Field squadrons were known—caught a Japanese troop convoy en route to Guadalcanal and almost annihilated it, sinking seven transports and a cruiser, and damaging three more cruisers. That night there was a dramatic clash between American and Japanese capital ships in which Adm. "Ching" Lee's *Washington* landed nine 16-inch shells on the battleship *Kirishima*, which foundered soon after, an acceptable exchange for damage to the U.S. Navy's battleship *South Dakota*. Only remnants of the Japanese landing force stumbled ashore at dawn, shorn of their heavy equipment, from the last four beached transports of the annihilated convoy. Off Tassafaronga Point on the night of 30 November, five American cruisers and six destroyers attacking eight Japanese destroyers on a supply run suffered one cruiser sunk and three more damaged by torpedoes. The Japanese lost only a single destroyer.

These were epic encounters, reflecting both sides' massive commitment of naval surface forces—and losses: in the course of the Solomons campaign, around fifty major Japanese and U.S. warships were sunk. The men who fought became grimly familiar with long, tense waits, often in darkness, while sweat-soaked radar operators peered at their screens for a first glimpse of the enemy. Thereafter, many sailors learned the terror of finding their ships suddenly caught in the dazzling glare of enemy searchlights, presaging a storm of shell. They witnessed the chaos of repeated encounters in which ships exchanged gunfire and torpedoes at close range, causing ordered decks, turrets, superstructures, and machinery spaces to be transformed within seconds into flaming tangles of twisted steel.

They saw sailors leap in scores and hundreds from sinking vessels. Some were saved, many were not: when the cruiser *Juneau* blew up, Mr. and Mrs. Thomas Sullivan of Waterloo, Iowa, lost five sons. Pilots often took off from heaving flight decks knowing that perhaps a hundred miles away, their enemy counterparts were doing the same. Thus, they were never assured that when they returned from a mission they would find a flight deck intact to land on. Only the Americans' possession of Henderson Field enabled them to deploy sufficient air power to compensate for their depleted carrier force. The men who fought at sea and in the air off Guadalcanal in the latter months of 1942 experienced a sustained intensity of naval surface warfare unmatched at any other period of the struggle.

The Americans prevailed. After the battles of November, despite his squadrons' successes Admiral Yamamoto concluded that Japan's Combined Fleet could no longer endure such attrition. He informed the Imperial Army that his ships must withdraw support from the land force on Guadalcanal. It was a critical victory for the U.S. Navy, and was hailed back home as a personal triumph for Bull Halsey. The achievement of the American shore contingent was to hold out and defend its perimeter through months of desperate assaults. In December, some of the exhausted marines were at last relieved by U.S. Army formations. The Japanese were reduced to supplying their shrinking ground force by submarine. At the end of January 1943, after an American offensive had driven them back into a narrow western perimeter, 10,652 Japanese survivors were evacuated by night in destroyers.

To take and hold Guadalcanal, the U.S. Army, Navy and Marine Corps lost 6,700 killed, a small price for a critical achievement. The Japanese suffered 29,000 ground, naval and air casualties, most of them fatal, including 9,000 men killed by tropical diseases, a reflection of their pitifully inadequate medical services. Every element of the American forces shared undoubted glory. The Cactus Air Force, infantry manning the perimeter, and warship crews afloat displayed a resolve the Japanese had not believed Americans to possess. The U.S. Navy's heavy losses were soon replaced, as those of the Japanese were not. For the rest of the war, the performance of Admiral Yamamoto's squadrons progressively deteriorated, while the U.S. Pacific Fleet grew in proficiency as well as might. In the latter months of 1942, American airmen noted a rapid decline in the skill and resolve of enemy pilots. A Japanese staff officer asserted bleakly that the battle for Guadalcanal had been "the fork in the road which leads to victory." Like Admiral Yamamoto, he knew that his nation was thereafter marching with ever-quickening step towards defeat.

EVEN AS THE MARINES were fighting on Guadalcanal, the most protracted land campaign of the Far Eastern war was unfolding on Papua New Guinea—after Greenland, the largest island in the world. The Japanese began establishing small forces on the eastern coast in March 1942, with the intention of seizing Port Moresby, the capital of Australian-ruled Papua, 200 miles distant on the southwest shore. Initially the Japanese intended an amphibious descent on Moresby, but this was frustrated by the Coral Sea actions. American success at Midway a month later denied the Japanese any prospect of a swift capture of New Guinea through seaborne landings. Tokyo's local commander Colonel Tsugi made a personal decision instead to secure the island the hard way, by an overland advance, and forged an order supposedly from Imperial headquarters to authorize his operations. MacArthur, Allied commander-in-chief for the southwest Pacific, deployed his limited strength to frustrate this.

Australian units began moving towards Papua's north coast in July 1942, but the Japanese secured footholds there first, and began to build up forces for an advance over the Owen Stanley Mountains to Port Moresby. The ensuing battles along its only practicable passage, the Kokoda Trail, were small in scale, but a dreadful experience for every participant. Amid dense rain forest, men struggled for footholds, scrambling through deep mud on near-vertical tracks, bent under crippling weights of equipment and supplies; rations arrived erratically and rain almost daily; disease and insects intensified misery.

"I have seen men standing knee-deep in the mud of a narrow mountain track, looking with complete despair at yet another seemingly unsurmountable ridge," an Australian officer wrote to his former school headmaster. "Ridge after ridge, ridge after ridge, heart-breaking, hopeless, futile country." The need to manpack all supplies and ammunition rendered the Kokoda Trail campaign a colossal undertaking: every soldier bore sixty pounds, some a hundred. "What a hell of a load to lump uphill all the way through mud and slush," wrote Australian corporal Jack Craig. "Some of us lose our footing and finish up flat out. One feels like just lying there for ever. I don't think I have been so exhausted in all my life." Many men suffered agonies from bleeding haemorrhoids as well as more deadly tropical diseases.

As for the Japanese, an Australian said, with a shrug: "This is not murder, killing such repulsive-looking animals." But one of his comrades, detailed by an officer to finish off a hideously wounded enemy soldier, wrote afterwards: "Then came the beginning of some of the terrible things that happen in combat . . . I have lived to this day with those terrified eyes staring at me." A young chaplain wrote from the rear areas of the Papuan front:

> I do not believe there has ever been a campaign when men have suffered hardship, privation and incredible difficulties as in this one. To see these men arrive here wounded and ill from terrible tropical diseases, absolutely exhausted, clothes in tatters and filthy, long matted hair and beards, without a wash for days, having lain in mud and slush, fighting a desperate cruel foe they could not see, emaciated through having been weeks in the jungle, wracked with malaria and prostrated by scrub typhus, has made me feel that nothing is too good for them . . . I have seen so much suffering and sorrow here that more than ever I have realised the tragedy of war and the heroism of our men.

Observations such as this came from the heart, and were characteristic of a witness who, in the nature of things, could make no comparison with the plight of combatants fighting in Russia, the central Pacific, or Burma— the other notably dreadful theatres of war. Conflict in a hostile natural environment, where amenities and comforts were wholly absent, imposed greater miseries than fighting in North Africa or northwest Europe. But the experience of combat for months on end, prey to fear, chronic exhaustion and discomfort, loss of comrades, separation from domestic life and loved ones, bore down upon every frontline fighter, wherever he was. Many, especially in the Pacific theatre, deluded themselves that their enemies found the experience more acceptable. Allied troops believed the Japanese to be natural jungle warriors in a way they themselves were not. Yet many of Hirohito's soldiers used language to describe their experiences and sufferings little different from that employed by their Australian, British and American foes.

The Japanese repulsed the Australians on the Kokoda Trail, then harassed them relentlessly as they retreated with ambushes and outflanking movements. Many stragglers died: "Confusion was the keynote," wrote Sgt. Clive Edwards. "No one knew exactly what was happening, but when the sounds of battle came from in front we were told that the others were trying to fight their way through . . . It was pitiful—the rain was coming down, and there was a long string of dog-tired men straining the last nerve to get wounded men down and yet save their own lives too. Bewilderment . . . showed on every face and as the long line faltered and halted those at the back became affected and sent messages . . . to 'Keep moving, the Jap is on us.' " The Australians were eventually pushed back to within a few miles of Port Moresby.

A new threat to the Allied position in Papua was fortunately pre-empted: Ultra decrypts revealed a Japanese plan to land at Milne Bay, on the southeastern tip of the island. An Australian brigade was hastily shipped there and deployed. When the Japanese landed on the night of 25 August, they met fierce resistance, and on 4 September their survivors were evacuated. But the situation on the Port Moresby front remained critical. MacArthur displayed a contempt for the Australian showing which reflected his ignorance of conditions on the Kokoda Trail. The Japanese battered the Allied perimeter relentlessly, and a disaster beckoned. This was averted chiefly by air power: USAAF bombing of the enemy's over-extended supply line created a crisis for the attackers which worsened when some troops were diverted from New Guinea to Guadalcanal.

The local Japanese commander was ordered to pull back to the north shore of Papua. The Australians found themselves once more struggling up the Kokoda Trail and across the Owen Stanleys, this time pressing a retreating enemy in conditions no less appalling than during the earlier march. "Our troops are fighting in the cold mists of an altitude of 6,700 feet," wrote the Australian correspondent George Johnston, "fighting viciously because they have only a mile or two to go before they reach the peak of the pass and will be able to attack downhill. This means a lot to troops who have climbed every inch of that agonizing track, who have buried so many of their cobbers, and who have seen so many more going back weak with sickness or mauled by the mortar bombs and the bullets and grenades of the enemy, men gone from their ranks simply to win back a few hundred yards of this wild, unfriendly and utterly untamed mountain . . . The men are bearded to the eyes. Their uniforms are hotch-potches of anything that fits or is warm or affords some protection from the insects . . . In the green half-light, amid the stink of rotten mud and rotting corpses, with the long line of green-clad Australians climbing wearily along the tunnel of the track, you have a noisome, unforgettable picture of the awful horror of this jungle war."

In November, MacArthur launched coastal landings by two U.S. regiments to take Buna. The green Americans, shocked by their first encounter with the combat environment of Papua, performed poorly. Meanwhile, the Australians were exhausted by their efforts on the Kokoda Trail. Thousands of soldiers on both sides were weakened by malaria. But Buna was finally taken at the beginning of January 1943, and residual enemy forces in the area were mopped up three weeks later. The Japanese had lost almost two-thirds of their 20,000 men committed, while 2,165 Australians and 930 Americans died. Lt. Gen. Robert Eichelberger, a U.S. divisional commander, wrote: "It was a sly and sneaky kind of combat, which never resembled the massive and thunderous operations in Europe, where tank battalions were pitted against tank battalions and armies the size of city populations ponderously moved and maneuvered . . . In New Guinea, when the rains came, wounded men might drown before the litter-bearers found them. Many did. No war is good war and death ignores geography. But out here I was convinced, as were my soldiers, that death was pleasanter in the Temperate Zone."

The Papua operations were characterised by Allied dissentions and heavy-handed interventions by MacArthur. Disdain and mistrust between Australians and Americans caused bitterness, and belated success at Buna brought little joy. Hard fighting persisted throughout 1943, the battlefields slowly shifting northwards up the huge island. The Japanese, defeated on Guadalcanal, exerted themselves to their utmost to hold a line on New Guinea, feeding in reinforcements. But in March they suffered a crippling blow, during the Battle of the Bismarck Sea. George Kenney's Fifth Air Force, alerted by Ultra, launched a succession of attacks on a Japanese convoy which sank eight transports and four escorting destroyers en route from Rabaul, destroying most of a division intended for Papua New Guinea.

After months of seesaw ground fighting, a decisive breakthrough came when Kenney secretly constructed a forward airstrip from which his fighters could strike at the main enemy airbases at Wewak. This they did to devastating effect in August 1943, almost destroying Japanese air power in the region. Thereafter, a force that eventually comprised one U.S. and five Australian divisions launched a major offensive. By September 1943, the major enemy strongholds had been overrun, and 8,000 Japanese survivors were straggling away northwards. The Huon Peninsula was cleared in December, and Allied dominance of the campaign became explicit. Ultra revealed the location of the remaining Japanese concentrations, enabling MacArthur to launch a dramatic operation to bypass them and cut off their escape by landing at Hollandia in Dutch New Guinea on 22 April 1944. Fighting on the island persisted until the end of the war, Australians providing the main Allied effort. Some 13,500 Japanese emerged from the jungle to surrender there in August 1945.

The New Guinea campaign remains a focus of controversy. It inflicted misery on all its participants, many of whom doubted its usefulness, especially in the later stages. For a few brief weeks before the Coral Sea and Midway, it seemed a possible Japanese stepping stone to Australia, but by June 1942 this prospect was already dead. In some respects, the campaign became thereafter an Asian counterpart of Britain's North African and 1942–44 Burma operations. Once the U.S. Navy and USAAF had gained strategic dominance, the Japanese faced insuperable difficulties in sustaining and supporting their New Guinea operations at the end of a long line of maritime communications. From an Allied viewpoint, the campaign's principal strategic merit was that it provided a theatre in which the enemy could be engaged on a limited scale, when Allied land forces were too small to strike a decisive blow.

But the critical operations against Japan remained those of the U.S. Navy, committed to its own thrust across the central Pacific. Month by month across a battlefield of several hundred thousand square miles, American planes, surface ships and submarines inflicted crippling attrition on Japanese naval power—vital to the maintenance of their long, long supply chains. In 1942–43 the Allies needed airfields on Papua New Guinea, which had to be fought for and won. In 1943–44, however, it was probably unnecessary to launch the costly operations to clear the Japanese from the north coast, once their offensive and air capabilities had been destroyed. The Papua New Guinea campaign, like so many others in the course of the war, gained a momentum and logic of its own. Once thousands of troops were committed, lives lost and generals' reputations staked, it became progressively more difficult to accept anything less than victory. The only senior officer to emerge with an enhanced reputation from the New Guinea operations was the U.S. air chief, Kenney, one of his service's outstanding commanders.

Within a year of Pearl Harbor, the arrest of Japan's Asian and Pacific advances, and the beginnings of their reversal, made its doom inevitable. It is remarkable that, once Tokyo's hopes of quick victory were confounded and American resolve had been amply demonstrated, Hirohito's nation fought blindly on. Japanese strategy hinged upon a belief in German victory in the west, yet by the end of 1942 this had become entirely unrealistic. Thereafter, peace on any terms or even none should have seemed to Tokyo preferable to looming American retribution. But no more in Japan than in Germany did any faction display the will and power to deflect the country from its march towards immolation. *Shikata ga nai*: it could not be helped. If this was a monumentally inadequate excuse for condemning millions to death without hope of securing any redemptive compensation, it is a constant of history that nations which start wars find it very hard to stop them.

CHAPTER ELEVEN

THE BRITISH AT SEA

1. The Atlantic

THE BRITISH ARMY'S part in the struggle against Nazism was vastly smaller than that of the Russians, as would also be the U.S. Army's contribution. Beyond Britain's symbolic role in holding aloft the standard of resistance to Hitler, from 1940 onwards its principal strategic importance became that of a giant aircraft carrier and naval base, from which the bomber offensive and return to the Continent were launched. It fell to the Royal Navy to conduct the critical struggles of 1940–43 to keep the British people fed, to hold open the sea-lanes to the empire and overseas battlefields, and to convoy munitions to Russia. Naval might could not bring about the defeat of Germany, nor even protect Britain's eastern empire from the Japanese. It was a fundamental problem for the two Western Allies that they were sea powers seeking to defeat a great land power, which required a predominantly Russian solution. But if German efforts to interdict shipments to Britain were successful, Churchill's people would starve. A minimum of 23 million tons of supplies a year—half the prewar import total—had to be transported across the Atlantic in the face of surface raiders and U-boats.

Protecting this commerce was a huge endeavour. The navy had suffered as severely as Britain's other services from interwar retrenchment. The construction of big ships required years, and even a small convoy escort took months to build. Britain's shipyards were indifferently managed and manned by an intransigent labour force, which began to work only a little harder when the Soviet Union was obliged to change sides and communists of all nationalities endorsed the war effort. Britain built and repaired ships more slowly, if much more cheaply, than the United States, and could never match American capacity. For the Royal Navy, shortage of escorts was a pervasive reality of the early war years.

It was also hard to concentrate superior strength against enemy capital ships which might be few in number but posed a formidable threat and were deployed many hundreds of miles apart. In the first war years, Germany's surface raiders imposed as many difficulties as U-boats: the need to divert convoys from their danger zones increased the strain on British merchant shipping resources. German sorties between 1939 and 1943 precipitated dramas which seized the attention of the world: the pocket battleship *Graf Spee* sank nine merchantmen before being scuttled after its encounter with three British cruisers off the river Plate in December 1939. The 56,000-ton *Bismarck* destroyed the battle cruiser *Hood* before being somewhat clumsily dispatched by converging British squadrons on 27 May 1941. The British public was outraged when the *Scharnhorst* and *Gneisenau* made a dash to Wilhelmshaven from Brest through the Channel Narrows on 21–22 February 1942, suffering only mine damage amid fumbling efforts by the navy and RAF to intercept them. The presence of the battleship *Tirpitz* in the fjords of northern Norway menaced British Arctic convoys and strongly influenced Home Fleet deployments until 1944. Further afield, the Italian navy had formidable numerical strength, and when the Japanese entered the war the Royal Navy suffered severely at their hands.

Most British battleships were old, slow and could not be adapted for bulky modern fire-control equipment. The Dutch navy's triaxially stabilised Hazemeyer system represented the most advanced antiaircraft gunnery technology in the world, to which the Royal Navy gained access in 1940. It was fragile and unreliable, however, and a British version entered general service only in 1945; antiaircraft fire-control remained sadly ineffective meanwhile. Britain had more carriers than the U.S. Navy until 1943, but there were never enough to meet global demand, and they were too small to carry powerful air groups. Fleet Air Arm pilots displayed notable courage, but their performance was indifferent in both air combat and antishipping operations. The RAF, doctrinally committed to a strategic bomber offensive, resisted the diversion of resources to support operations at sea. Throughout the conflict, the Royal Navy displayed the highest standards of courage, commitment and seamanship. But until 1943, it struggled against odds to fulfil too many responsibilities with too few ships, all vulnerable to air attack.

Churchill's decision to make a major British military effort in North Africa obliged the navy to conduct operations in the Mediterranean with negligible air cover, and in the face of strong Axis air forces operating from fields in Italy, Sicily, Libya, Rhodes, Greece and Crete. Able Seaman Charles Hutchinson described an attack on the cruiser *Carlisle* in May 1941:

> The bombers came and attacked us wave after wave. They seemed to single a ship out and deliver a mass attack on it, diving vertically and from all angles. A huge bomb exploded in the water near our gun. Tons

of water crashed down on us, tearing us away from the gun and tossing us around like straw—I was certain we would be swept over the side. One thought flashed through my mind: "My God, this is the end." After what seemed an eternity, we picked ourselves up, blew up our lifebelts and kicked away our shoes, as I for one expected to abandon ship. But in a short time we were firing again, as we were still being attacked. Huge pieces of shrapnel lay around. There was a huge column of black smoke amidships and a direct hit on number two gun. There isn't a gun now, just a piece of charred metal . . . Nearly all the gun's crew were wiped out, most of the lads trapped underneath the gun or blown against the splinter shield. It was a ghastly sight. We've lived and slept all as a family for a year and a half: laughed, quarrelled, joked, all gone ashore together, discussed our private lives . . . Poor old Bob Silvey is still under the gun—I've seen him, but it's impossible to get him out.

Malta, the only offshore outpost in the central Mediterranean from which Axis supply routes to North Africa could be interdicted, faced three years of siege. Under almost continuous bombardment from nearby Sicily, at times the island became unserviceable as an offensive base for submarines and surface ships, but it remained a vital earnest of Britain's will to fight. Hitler blundered by failing to seize Malta in 1941, and huge efforts and sacrifices were made to sustain it thereafter. Between June 1940 and early 1943, the Mediterranean was largely unusable as an Allied supply route, but Churchillian war making emphasised assertion of the navy's presence and engagements of opportunity, especially against the Italian fleet. Some of the fiercest naval fighting of the war, which resulted in heavy British losses, took place in those limpid waters. The Axis faced increasing pressure on its own sea link to North Africa, but the passage between southern Italy and Tripoli was short; only in mid-1942 did shipping losses and fuel shortages begin to exert an important influence on Rommel's fortunes.

The Atlantic was the dominant naval battlefield, forever the cruel sea. Signalman Richard Butler described a typical Atlantic storm: "I couldn't see anything for the swirling spray. The wind shrieked through the rigging and superstructure. It looked as though we were sailing through boiling water as the wind whipped the wave tops into horizontal spume, white and fuming, which stung my eyes and face. Now and again I caught a glimpse of one of the big merchant-ships being rolled on its beam ends by the huge swells sweeping up under rain-laden skies." Butler's destroyer, *Matchless*, hove to near a struggling merchantman with a twelve-foot split in its upper deck. Soon afterwards, one of their own men was washed overboard. The captain took the brave, futile decision to turn in search of him. Butler thought: "The captain's gone crazy, he's going to risk the lives of two hundred men to look for some silly bastard that hadn't the sense to keep off the upper deck." After a few anxious moments, the hopeless quest was abandoned. Then Butler learned that the lost man was one of his own popular messmates. "I was saddened and shocked, filled with remorse about my selfish attitude . . . 'Snowy' was well liked and had the reputation of being a 'gannet' who never stopped eating. Never again would we hear him ask cheerfully at mealtimes, 'Any gash left?' "

Aboard corvettes, the workhorses of convoy escort groups, conditions were much worse, "sheer unmitigated hell," in the words of a seaman. "Even getting hot food from the galley to fo'c'sle was a tremendous job. The mess decks were usually a shambles and the wear and tear on bodies and tempers something I shall never forget. But we were young and tough and, in a sense, we gloried in our misery and made light of it all. What possible connection it had with defeating Hitler none of us bothered to ask. It was enough to find ourselves more or less afloat the next day with the hope of duff for pudding and a boiler-clean when we reached port."

And then there was the enemy. While Germany's capital ships commanded headlines and their sorties inflicted some injuries, Axis submarine and air forces represented a much graver long-term threat, and the men of both arms displayed courage and skill. U-boats achieved striking early successes, such as sinking the old battleship *Royal Oak* in Scapa Flow, and wreaked havoc upon vulnerable merchantmen. Churchill as first sea lord estimated that the introduction of convoying in 1939 was responsible for a 30 percent fall in Britain's imports. Merchant ships were obliged to waste weeks waiting for convoys to assemble. Once ocean-bound, they travelled painfully slowly, and were offloaded on arrival by a lethargic and sometimes obstructive British dock labour force. Many ships that carried commodities in peacetime had to be diverted to move troops and munitions across huge distances by circuitous routes to avoid Axis air and submarine concentrations—for instance, almost all Egypt-bound cargoes travelled via the Cape of Good Hope. The voyage to Suez lengthened from 3,000 miles to 13,000, while a Bombay-bound ship made a passage of 11,000 miles against the prewar 6,000.

Until 1943, the Royal Navy was desperately short of escorts and effective technology to hunt U-boats. The British sank twelve German submarines in 1940, and just three in the six months between September that year and March 1941; intelligence and skilful convoy routing did more to frustrate Adm. Karl Dönitz, the U-boat C-in-C, than did antisubmarine escorts. The Royal Navy was slow to realise the vulnerability of merchant-men off the African coast, where in 1941–42 just two long-range Type IX U-boats achieved some spectacular destruction, partly because they maintained wireless silence and partly because few defensive resources were available. The British were grievously hampered by lack of air support. The RAF's Coastal Command was short of planes; its long-range Sunderland flying boats suffered from crews' poor navigational and depth-charging skills, together with technical problems that reduced their effort in 1941 to an average of two sorties per aircraft a month. Meanwhile, until 1942 many of the Royal Navy's destroyers remained committed to coastal defence of Britain.

In the course of the entire war, while 6.1 percent of Allied shipping losses were inflicted by surface raiders and 6.5 percent by mines, 13.4 percent were caused by air attack and 70 percent by U-boats. The British suffered their first severe blow in the autumn of 1940, when the slow eastbound Atlantic convoy SC7 lost 21 out of 30 ships, and 12 out of 49 were sunk in the fast HX79. Thereafter, the tempo of the undersea war rose steadily: during 1941, 3.6 million tons of British shipping were lost, 2.1 million of these to submarines. Churchill became deeply alarmed. His postwar assertion that the U-boats caused him greater anxiety than any other threat to Britain's survival has powerfully influenced the historiography of the war. It is scarcely surprising that the prime minister was so troubled, when almost every week until May 1943 he received loss statistics that represented a shockingly steady, debilitating depletion of British transport capabilities.

But the submarine force commanded by Dönitz was weak. Germany's prewar industrial planning envisaged a fleet which achieved full war-fighting capability only in 1944. Naval construction was skewed by a focus on big ships: a hundred U-boats could have been built with the steel lavished on the *Bismarck*. On the eve of war, Adm. Erich Raeder, German naval C-in-C, wrote: "We are not in a position to play anything like an important part in the war against Britain's commerce." Until June 1940, Dönitz did not anticipate waging a major campaign in the Atlantic, because he was denied means to do so; the small, short-range Type VII U-boats that dominated his armoury were designed to operate from German bases. Even when the strategic picture radically changed with Hitler's seizure of Norway and of France's Atlantic ports, the Kriegsmarine continued to build Type VIIs. Productivity in German shipyards, hampered by shortages of steel and skilled labour, and later by bombing, fell below British levels. U-boats remained technically primitive. Innovation—for instance, the 1944–45 snorkel underwater air-replenishment system—was not matched by reliability: the revolutionary Type XXI sailed on its first war patrol only on 30 April 1945.

Thus, Dönitz's force lacked mass, range and quality. Just as the Luftwaffe in 1940–41 attempted to deal a knockout blow to Britain with wholly inadequate resources, so the U-boat arm lacked strength to accomplish the severance of the Atlantic link. Germany never built anything like enough submarines to make them a war-winning weapon. Dönitz calculated that he needed to sink 600,000 tons of British shipping a month to achieve a decisive victory, for which he required 300 U-boats in commission to sustain a third of that number in operational areas. Yet only 13 U-boats were on station in August 1940, falling to 8 in January 1941, rising to 21 the following month. This small force inflicted impressive destruction: 2 million tons of British shipping were sunk between June 1940 and March 1941. But in the same period just 72 new U-boats were delivered, far short of the number Dönitz needed. They achieved their highest rate of productivity—measured by tonnage sunk per submarine at sea—in October 1940; thereafter, while many more boats were deployed, their pro-rata achievements diminished.

As the war developed, while the Allied navies grew apace in skill and professionalism, the quality and determination of U-boat crews declined. One by one Dönitz's aces were killed or captured, and the men who replaced them were of lesser calibre. German torpedo technology was almost as flawed as that of the 1942–43 U.S. Navy. Direction of the U-boat campaign was hampered by changing strategies and impulsive interventions by Hitler. German naval intelligence and grasp of Allied strategy, tactics and technology were chronically weak.

It is a remarkable and important statistic that 99 percent of all ships which sailed from North America to Britain during the war years arrived safely. Even in the bad days of April 1941, for instance, 307 merchantmen sailed in convoy, of which only 16 were sunk, together with a further 11 unescorted vessels. In June that year, 383 ships made the Atlantic passage, in convoys of which submarines attacked only one, sinking 6 ships, along with a further 22 unescorted merchantmen. In 1942, by far the most alarming year of the U-boat war, 609 ships were sunk in the North Atlantic, a total of some 6 million tons. So prodigious was American shipbuilding capacity, however, that in the same period the Allies launched 7.1 million tons of ships, increasing their available pool of 30 million tons.

Yet, as is the way of mankind, the Allies perceived most of the difficulties on their own side. While posterity knows that in 1942 the U-boats inflicted the utmost damage of which they were capable, and that there-after the tide of the convoy war turned steadily against them, at the time Churchill and Roosevelt saw only a steeply rising graph of losses which, if it had continued, would have crippled the war effort. In 1942 British imports fell by 5 million tons, imposing severe strains on food and oil supplies—the latter were reduced by about 15 percent, requiring the government to dip into its admittedly large strategic stockpiles. This was attributable less to Dönitz than to the diversion of 200 ships from the Atlantic shuttle to open an Arctic supply line to Russia. Whatever the causes, however, Britain's shrunken deliveries alarmed a nation with its back to the wall in many theatres and in three dimensions.

Even when the United States supplied Britain with a few B-24 Liberators—suitable for very-long-range conversion and thus ideal for Atlantic convoy support—initially the RAF chose to use most of them elsewhere. Sir Arthur Harris, 1942–45 C-in-C of Bomber Command, fiercely resisted the diversion of heavy aircraft to the convoy war: "It was a continual fight against the navy to stop them as usual pinching every-thing," said Harris, who disliked British sailors almost as much as he abhorred the Germans. "Half my energies were given to saving Bomber Command from the other services. The navy and army were always trying to belittle the work of the air force." The Atlantic "air gap"—the area of ocean beyond range of land-based cover—remained the focus of U-boat activity until late 1943.

An average of just over one convoy a week each way made the North Atlantic passage. Many crossed without suffering attack, because the Ger-mans did not locate them. Ultra intercepts of U-boat position reports, together with "Huff-Duff"—high frequency direction finding equipment on warships—often made it possible to divert convoys away from enemy concentrations: one statistical calculation suggests that in the second six months of 1941 alone, Ultra saved between 1.5 and 2 million tons of Allied shipping from destruction. For a few months in 1941 American escorts protected convoys east of Iceland, but after Pearl Harbor these were withdrawn; Canadian corvettes took up the strain, and the Royal Navy assumed responsibility once ships entered the Western Approaches. Throughout 1941–43, the key period of the Battle of the Atlantic, the Admiralty supplied 50 percent of all escorts, the Royal Canadian Navy (RCN) 46 percent, and American vessels made up the balance.

Yet if the German offensive was mismanaged, especially in 1941–42 Allied merchant seamen suffered grievously from its consequences. Crews were drawn from many nationalities; though some young British men chose the merchant service in preference to conscription into the armed forces, it would be hard to argue that this represented a soft option: some seamen were obliged to abandon ship two or three times. Michael Page described one such experience in Atlantic darkness:

> One minute we had been on watch on deck or in the engine-room, or sleeping snugly in our bunks; the next we were engaged in a frenzied scramble through the dense, shrieking blackness which assailed us with squalls of freezing spray, and slipped and fell on the wet iron decks which canted faster and faster into the hungry sea with every passing second . . . "What's happening? What's happening?" someone kept demanding in a high-pitched wailing cry, full of agonized bewilderment . . . We struggled with stiff reluctant ropes and the bulky gear of the boat in a kind of automatic frenzy . . . The boat was lowered somehow, and we scrambled down towards it. Some of us got there, some did not—misjudging the distance as they jumped. "Cast off!" bawled someone when the boat seemed crowded; a cry echoed by several others, but answered at once by yells and screams above us—"No, no wait! Wait a second!" A darker body hurtled through the darkness and hit the waves with a tremendous splash, reappearing to splash towards the boat and grab at her gunwale . . . A wave broke fully into the boat, drenching and swamping us completely; we gasped and spluttered with the icy shock . . . Someone immediately slipped the painter . . . Whether everyone who could be was in the boat, God knows; we were swirled away in an instant.

Even those fortunate enough to survive a sinking often faced terrible ordeals in open lifeboats, such as that suffered by survivors of the British coal carrier *Anglo-Saxon*. The German auxiliary cruiser *Widder* sank the *Anglo-Saxon* 810 miles west of the Canaries on the night of 21 August 1940, then machine-gunned most of the survivors in the water. Only a tiny jolly boat escaped, carrying Chief Officer C. B. Denny and six others. Taking stock at dawn, they found that the boat carried a small supply of water, some biscuits and a few tins of food. Several men had been hit by German fire. Pilcher, the radio officer, had a foot reduced to pulp. Penny, a middle-aged gunner, was nursing wounds in the hip and wrist.

For the first few days, sailing westwards, spirits in the boat were high. But by 26 August the men's skin was burning, and they were suffering acutely from thirst. Pilcher's foot was gangrenous—he apologised for the stench. Denny wrote in the log: "Trusting to make a landfall . . . with

God's will and British determination." Thereafter, however, their condition deteriorated rapidly. Pilcher died on the twenty-seventh. Denny broke down. Penny, weakened by his wounds, slipped overboard while at the helm one night. Two young seamen who disliked each other began squabbling. On their thirteenth day at sea, the rudder carried away. This proved the final straw for Denny, who said he proposed to end it all. Giving a signet ring to one of the others to pass to his mother, he and the Third Engineer dropped together into the sea, and eventually drifted away.

On the evening of 9 September, a ship's cook named Morgan suddenly stood up and said, "I'll go down the street for a drink." He stepped over the side, leaving behind just two young seamen. It fell to twenty-one-year-old Wilbert Widdicombe to write laconically in the log: "Cook goes mad; dies." Once during the days that followed, both young men jumped into the water. After an argument, however, they thought better of this, and clambered back on board. Soon afterwards, a tropical rainstorm relieved them from thirst; they ate drifting seaweed, and some crabs they found attached to it. After surviving several spells of heavy weather and many quarrels, on 27 October they glimpsed a glittering beach. The two survivors staggered ashore on Eleuthera in the Bahamas, after a passage of 2,275 miles.

Following months of hospital treatment and convalescence, in February 1941 Widdicombe set off homewards—to die as a passenger on the cargo liner *Siamese Prince*, sunk by a U-boat torpedo. His companion in adversity, nineteen-year-old Robert Tapscott, survived later service in the Canadian Army to give evidence at the postwar trial of the *Widder*'s captain for slaughtering survivors of the *Anglo-Saxon* and other ships, for which the German was sentenced to seven years' imprisonment. The horrors suffered by Tapscott and his companions were repeated hundreds of times in the course of the war at sea, often ending without survivors to tell the tale.

As with men in every circumstance of conflict, merchant seamen's performance was uneven: drawn from many nations and lacking the armed forces' discipline, they were often careless of convoy routines, courses and signal procedures. Crews sometimes panicked and abandoned ships that might have been saved. But there were many examples of heroic endeavour, such as that of the 10,350-ton diesel cargo liner *Otari*. On 13 December 1940, 450 miles west of the British coast homeward-bound from Australia, she was hit by a torpedo, causing the sea to rush into her after holds. Frozen sheep carcasses and cases of butter were soon bobbing in the ship's wake. The *Otari*'s propeller shafts were leaking, and the engine-room bulkhead threatened to collapse. But Captain Rice, her master, decided she might be saved: alone on the ocean, mercifully shrouded by mist from further enemy attentions, for three days he and his crew patiently coaxed the *Otari* onward, her pumps just sufficing to sustain buoyancy. The ship at last reached the mouth of the Clyde in darkness, to find the port's defensive boom closed. Only at dawn on 17 December was Rice finally able to bring his ship, decks almost awash, into the anchorage, where most of its precious cargo was salvaged by lighters. By such stubborn determination and courage was Britain's Atlantic lifeline held open.

In 1941, Britain launched 1.2 million tons of new vessels, and achieved dramatic economies of transport usage. Though few U-boats were sunk by naval escorts, which were slowly being equipped with improved radar and Asdic underwater detection systems, the Germans failed to force a crisis upon Churchill's besieged island. By late summer of that year, the British were reading German U-boat signal traffic with reasonable regularity. Some of Dönitz's submarines were transferred to the Mediterranean, or to northern Norway to screen the flank of Germany's assault on the Soviet Union. By Christmas 1941, Hitler had already lost his best chance of starving Britain; once the United States entered the war, the consequent enormous accession of shipping and construction capability transformed the struggle.

But the U-boats enjoyed a surge of success in the months following Pearl Harbor, chiefly because the U.S. Navy was slow to introduce effective convoy and escort procedures. In those days, before attrition diluted the quality of the Kriegsmarine's personnel, the Freikorps Dönitz, as its members proudly called themselves, was an elite. The U-boat captain Erich Topp wrote: "Living and working in a submarine, one has to develop and intensify the ability to cooperate with other members of the crew, because you could need each other simply to survive . . . When you are leaving harbour, closing the hatch, diving, you and your crew are bidding farewell to a colourful world, to the sun and stars, wind and waves, the smell of the sea. All are living under constant tension, produced by living in a steel tube—a very small, cramped and confined space with congested compartments, monotony and an unhealthy lifestyle, caused by bad air, lack of normal rhythms of day and night and physical exercise." Topp took immense pains to massage morale. Once, a few hours after leaving port, he found his navigator looking morose. The man revealed that he had inadvertently left behind a myrtle wreath, the German symbol of marriage which was also his operational talisman. He was convinced that U-552 was thus doomed. Topp reversed course and returned to Bergen to let the navigator fetch his wreath before sailing again, a happy man.

Many of Dönitz's officers were fanatical Nazis; by 1943 their average age had fallen to twenty-three, while that of their men was two years lower: they were finished products of Goebbels's educational system. U-181's Wolfgang Luth regularly harangued his crew about "race and other population policy issues . . . Germany, the Führer and his National Socialist movement." The notion of holding indoctrination sessions in a stinking, sweating steel tube a hundred feet beneath the Atlantic seems surreal; not all Luth's crew can have applauded his refusal to allow pin-up pictures anywhere near the Führer's portrait, and his ban on "corrupt" Anglo-American jazz music. "Whether you like it or not," he told his officers, "is not up for discussion. You quite simply are not to like it. Any more than a German man should like a Jewess. In a hard war, everyone must have learned to hate his enemy unreservedly." In 1944 an experienced U-boat captain ordered his officers to remove a picture of Hitler from a bulkhead, saying, "There will be no idolatory here." He was denounced, accused of undermining the crew's fighting spirit, arrested and executed.

In May and June 1942, a million tons of shipping were sunk in United States eastern coastal waters, often by submarines firing torpedoes at vessels silhouetted against the blaze of shore lights. In the year as a whole, 6 million tons went to the bottom. America's merchant fleet paid dearly for the U.S. Navy's refusal to join the established Canadian convoy network, and to heed British experience. The Germans began to concentrate "wolf packs" of up to a dozen U-boats to swamp convoy escort groups. Changes of Kriegsmarine ciphers caused periodic "blackouts" of Allied signal interception, with severe consequences for convoys unable to avoid submarine lines. But the Allies progressively raised their game: antisubmarine warfare techniques improved and escort numbers grew; naval radar sets profited from the introduction of cavity magnetron technology; escort groups gained from TBS—Talk Between Ships—voice communication, and even more from experience.

To hunt and sink U-boats, close collaboration between two or three warships was vital: a single ship could seldom drop depth charges with sufficient accuracy to achieve a "kill." It became difficult for the Germans to operate close to the U.S. or British coasts, within range of air patrols. U-boats could travel fast only on the surface; submerged craft struggled to intercept a convoy. Overhead aircraft forced them to dive, a more effective countermeasure than bomber attacks on the concrete-encased U-boat pens of Brest and Lorient, which cost the RAF much wasted effort. In

1942, the Battle of the Atlantic focused increasingly on a thousand-mile width of sea beyond reach of most shore-based planes. There Dönitz concentrated his forces, and convoys ran the gauntlet for four to six days of peril.

SC104, a typical convoy of thirty-six merchantmen arrayed in six columns, sailed eastward in October 1942 at seven knots—barely eight miles per hour—with an escort of the destroyers *Fame* and *Viscount* and the corvettes *Acanathus*, *Eglantine*, *Montbretia* and *Potentilla*. The first hint of a looming threat came four days after leaving Newfoundland, at 4:24 p.m. on 12 October, when Huff-Duff detected a U-boat radio transmission to starboard; soon afterwards, a second submarine was identified. As night fell, in heavy seas the escorts took up stations ahead and on the flanks of the merchantmen. Conditions were appalling, especially aboard the corvettes, which rolled continuously. Half-drowned bridge crews struggled to keep awake and alert, knowing that even when their four-hour watches ended they were unlikely to find hot food or dry clothing in waterlogged mess decks. If engineers and stokers in machinery spaces were warmer below, they were unfailingly conscious of their diminished prospects of escape if a ship was hit—42 percent of such victims perished, against 25 percent of deck ratings. For weeks on end, strain and discomfort were constants, even before the enemy struck.

That night of 12 October, visibility for convoy SC104 was four miles between snow showers. Just before midnight, a U-boat was detected four miles astern: the *Fame* turned and raced to launch a radar-guided attack. Just before it reached the U-boat's position, the pounding of the seas disabled the radar, blinding the destroyer. After a fruitless thirty-minute visual and Asdic search, the *Fame* returned to its station. Soon afterwards the *Eglantine* conducted another unsuccessful hunt for a U-boat to starboard. At 5:08 a.m. the escorts heard a heavy explosion, and fired "Snowflake" illuminants. Amid crashing waves which rendered both radar and Asdic almost useless, nothing was seen. An hour later, the escort commander learned that during the night three ships had been sunk without showing sight or sound of distress; a corvette was sent back to search for survivors.

Throughout the daylight hours of 13 October the convoy struggled through mountainous seas, occasionally glimpsing U-boats which submerged before they could be attacked. That night, two more merchantmen were torpedoed. At 8:43 p.m. the *Viscount* spotted a submarine on the surface at a range of 800 yards. Spray blinded her gunners; the enemy dived as the destroyer closed to ram, the bridge crew catching a last glimpse of the U-boat's conning tower thirty yards distant. Again and again through the night, escorts pursued contacts without success. The senior officer's feelings, in his own words, "amounted almost to despair." At dawn he found that half the convoy had lost formation during the night's terrible weather; nine of the stragglers were rounded up, but six ships had been sunk, and the passage was only half over.

The struggle continued through 14 October, with four U-boats identified around the convoy. At nightfall, to the captains' relief visibility worsened, making submarine attacks more difficult. The convoy changed course repeatedly to throw off its pursuers. During the following night, escorts attacked six successive radar contacts. One of these took place at 11:31 p.m., when the *Viscount* picked up a U-boat at 6,200 yards. Her captain closed to ram at twenty-six knots; the U-boat commander took evasive action, but made a disastrous misjudgement which swung his craft across the *Viscount*'s bows. The destroyer smashed into the submarine twenty feet aft of its conning tower, then rode up onto the stricken enemy's hull. The U-boat swung clear, under fire from every calibre of British gun, and finally received a depth charge at point-blank range. U-619 sank stern-first at 11:47. Yet success was dearly bought: the damaged *Viscount* was obliged to set immediate course for Liverpool, where it arrived safely two nights later, needing months of dockyard repairs.

At sunrise on 16 October came the welcome sight of a long-range Liberator, the first covering aircraft to reach the convoy: SC104 had passed through the mid-Atlantic "air gap." The Norwegian navy's *Potentilla* transferred a hundred survivors from her packed mess decks to a merchantman. The morning was uneventful, but at 2:07 p.m. the *Fame*'s Asdic detected a U-boat at 2,000 yards, and she attacked with depth charges five minutes later. The subsequent drama was played out in the midst of the convoy, with merchantmen steaming past on both sides. A large bubble exploded onto the surface, followed by the dramatic spectacle of a U-boat bursting forth with water cascading off its hull, to meet a hail of gunfire. The *Fame* ran alongside, scraping her bottom, and launched a whaler as German crewmen dived over the side. A courageous British officer scrambled into the conning tower, seized an armful of documents from the submarine's control room, then made his escape seconds before U-253 sank.

But the *Fame*, like the *Viscount*, suffered heavily in the collision. Her captain repented his decision to ram, as crewmen struggled for hours to close great gashes in the ship's hull with collision mats and baulks of timber. With pumps straining to keep ahead of seawater gushing into the engine room, the *Fame* followed the *Viscount* towards Liverpool, and thence into dockyard hands. Four slow corvettes now remained to escort twenty-eight ships. At 9:40 that night of 16 October, yet another U-boat was detected by the *Potentilla*. The two approached each other at full speed before the *Potentilla*'s captain swerved at the last moment, to avoid a thirty-two-knot collision which must have been fatal to his own small vessel. The corvette's 4-inch gun, pom-poms and Oerlikons blazed at the submarine, but it escaped almost unscathed. This was SC104's last serious action: despite some false alarms, 17 October passed in thick fog without significant incident. Two days later, the merchantmen entered the Mersey, cheered by news that a VLR Liberator had sunk a third submarine, U-661, close to their track.

This convoy's experiences, each one sufficiently harrowing to represent the drama of a lifetime save in the circumstances of a world at war, were repeated again and again by merchantmen and escorts on the Atlantic run. Moreover, such losses were relatively light for the period. Later that October fifteen ships of SC107 were sunk, while SC125 lost thirteen in a seven-day battle, without destroying a single U-boat. In 1942 as a whole, 1,160 Allied merchantmen were sunk by submarines. Just as the tide of the war was turning dramatically against the Axis, Britain was confronted with its most serious import shortfall. In the winter of 1942 Dönitz's wolf packs reached their greatest strength, with over a hundred U-boats at sea. The North African campaign, and especially the November Torch landings, obliged the Royal Navy to divert substantial resources to the Mediterranean.

Canadian corvettes, which had assumed much of the burden of western Atlantic escort duties, proved to lack both equipment and expertise to match Dönitz's wolf packs: some 80 percent of mid-Atlantic losses between July and September were suffered by Canadian-escorted convoys. Contemporary reports highlighted a critical shortage of competent captains with adequate training and of skills in using Asdic. The Royal Canadian Navy had expanded much faster than its small nucleus of professional seamen could handle—three and a half times more than the Royal Navy or the U.S. Navy. Of one RCN warship arriving in Britain, a reporting officer concluded: "This low state of efficiency appears to be evident generally in all Canadian-manned corvettes." A historian has noted: "These problems often resulted in poor performance against U-boat packs." The Canadians had to be relieved of midocean responsibilities for some months early in 1943, as soon as the Royal Navy could spare its own ships to replace them.

In March that year there was another breakdown of U-boat radio traffic decryption at Bletchley Park. In consequence, for two months half of all Atlantic convoys suffered attack, and one in five of their merchantmen were sunk. Yet this was the last crisis of the campaign. That spring, at last the Western Allies committed resources which overwhelmed the U-boats. Escort groups equipped with 10cm radar, VLR aircraft with improved depth charges, small carriers and renewed penetration of Dönitz's ciphers combined to transform the struggle. Adm. Sir Max Horton, who became C-in-C Western Approaches in November 1942, was a former World War I submariner of the highest gifts, who made a critical contribution to victory, directing the Atlantic campaign from his headquarters in Liverpool.

In May 1943 47 U-boats were sunk, and almost a hundred in the year as a whole. Sinkings of German submarines by aircraft alone rose from 5 between October 1941 and March 1942, to 15 between April and September 1942, to 38 between October 1942 and March 1943. Dönitz found himself losing a U-boat a day, 20 percent of his submarine strength gone in a month. He was obliged to drastically curtail operations. There was a steep fall in merchant ship sinkings, so that by the last quarter of 1943 only 6 percent of British imports were lost to enemy action. The wartime Atlantic passage was seldom less than a gruelling experience, but for the rest of the war British and American forces dominated the ocean, challenged by a shrinking U-boat force with crews whose inexperience and waning morale were often manifest.

Britain's merchant fleet was devastated to a degree which contributed to the nation's postwar economic woes: almost all the 14 million tons of new Allied shipping launched in 1943 were American. But the immediate reality was that Germany had lost its war against Atlantic commerce. In the last seven months of 1943 sinkings of Allied shipping fell to 200,000 tons, around a quarter of this total by submarines. Though shortage of tonnage never ceased to be a constraint on strategy, no important Allied interest was thereafter imperilled by enemy naval action. Before the war, Britain's annual imports totalled 68 million tons. While this figure fell to 24.48 million tons in 1943, in 1944 it rose again to 56.9 million tons.

Perhaps the most vivid statistic of the Battle of the Atlantic is that between 1939 and 1943 only 8 percent of slow and 4 percent of fast convoys suffered attack. Much has been written about the inadequacy of Allied means to respond to the U-boat threat in the early war years. This was real enough, but German resource problems were much greater. Hitler never understood the sea. In the early war period, he dispersed industrial effort and steel allocations among a range of weapons systems. He did not recognise a strategic opportunity to wage a major campaign against British Atlantic commerce until the fall of France in June 1940. U-boat construction was prioritised only in 1942–43, when Allied naval strength was growing fast and the tide of the war had already turned. Germany never gained the capability to sever Britain's Atlantic lifeline, though amid grievous shipping losses it was hard to recognise this at the time.

2. Arctic Convoys

WHEN HITLER invaded Russia, the British and American chiefs of staff alike opposed the dispatch of military aid, on the grounds that their own nations' resources were too straitened to spare arms for others. The Royal Navy saw a further strategic objection: any matériel shipped to the Soviets must be transported through their Arctic ports, Murmansk and Archangel, the latter accessible only in the ice-free summer months. This would require convoys travelling at a speed of eight or nine knots to endure at least a weeklong passage under threat or attack from German U-boats, surface warships and aircraft based in nearby northern Norway. Britain's prime minister and America's president overruled these objections, asserting— surely rightly—that support for the Soviet war effort was an absolute priority. Hitler at first took little heed of the significance of the Arctic link to Russia, though his obsession with a possible British landing in Norway caused him to fortify its coastline. Churchill remained a strong advocate of such an assault until as late as 1944, though he was thwarted by the implacable opposition of his service chiefs. What mattered in 1942, however, was the strong German naval and air presence in the far north, which threatened Arctic convoys.

The First Lord, Adm. Sir Dudley Pound, deplored the diversion of resources from the Battle of the Atlantic to open a hazardous new front merely to aid the repugnant Soviets, who seemed likely to soon succumb to the Germans. Pound was especially uneasy about the prospect of outgunned elements of the Home Fleet meeting one of Hitler's capital ships, most likely the *Tirpitz*; the navy was scarred by memories of its difficulties and losses before the *Bismarck* succumbed. Apprehension was heightened by an unsuccessful carrier air strike against German coastal shipping off northern Norway on 30 July 1941, which cost eleven of twenty Swordfish torpedo bombers dispatched—one of the Royal Navy's notable strategic failures was interdiction of the vital German iron-ore traffic.

Churchill remained implacable: he insisted that the navy must brave the passage, whatever its perils, carrying to Russia such weapons and supplies as Britain and America could spare. He was undeterred by the prospect of battle. In 1941–42, one of his foremost objectives was to exploit opportunities to engage German forces; he thus demanded the establishment of a continuous cycle of Arctic convoys. The few merchantmen which Britain dispatched to Russia in late 1941 arrived unscathed, carrying small quantities of tanks, aircraft and rubber. The Germans barely noticed their passage.

In 1942, however, as the British began to transport substantial shipments eastwards, Hitler's forces intervened with mounting vigour. The experiences of the "PQ" convoys, as they were designated, and of the return "QP" series, became one of the war's naval epics. Even before the Germans entered the story, Arctic weather was a terrible foe. Ships often found themselves ploughing through mountainous seas, forty feet from trough to wave crest, while laden with a topweight of hundreds of tons of ice. More than a few men were lost overboard, and a monstrous wave once stripped the armoured roof from the cruiser *Sheffield*'s forward turret; the merchantman *J.L.M. Curry* sprang its plates and foundered in a storm. On the Murmansk passage, almost every ship suffered weather damage, to which even the greatest ships were vulnerable. Midshipman Charles Friend served aboard a carrier: "I remember looking out from a furiously rolling and pitching *Victorious* to see *King George V*, nearly eight hundred feet long, climbing up the slope of a wave . . . These waves were moving mountains . . . the billows a thousand feet from crest to trough . . . even *Victorious*'s high freeboard did not always prevent her from taking it green, the bow driving through the crest of a wave which crashed down on her flight deck . . . One banged down so hard the forward aircraft lift was put out of action . . . The sea had bent the four-inch armour."

British dockworkers, especially in Glasgow, gained a deplorable reputation for carelessness in cargo stowage which contrasted with painstaking American practice. Not only did much matériel arrive damaged at Murmansk, but ships' very survival was threatened by loads breaking loose. On 10 December 1941, for instance, crewmen on the 5,395-ton tramp steamer *Harmatis* opened a hatch after noticing smoke rising, to discover a flaming lorry careering about the hold, smashing crates and igniting bales. A mate wearing the ship's only smoke hood descended into the fiery shambles, playing a hose until he was overcome. The captain relieved him, and eventually suppressed the flames so that the ship could limp back to the Clyde.

Crews were obliged to labour relentlessly, hacking dangerous weights of ice from upperworks and guns, testing weapons on which lubricants froze. Men moved sluggishly in heavy layers of clothing which never sufficed to exclude the cold. Alec Dennis, the first lieutenant of a destroyer, tried to nap on deck because he knew that if he took to his bunk he would be pitched out: "While one could keep one's body reasonably warm, I found it impossible to keep my feet warm in spite of fur-lined boots." He spent the first hour of every four off watch thawing his frozen feet sufficiently to be able to sleep. Crews subsisted on a diet of "kye"—cocoa—and corned-beef sandwiches served at action stations, snatching sleep during brief intervals between German attacks. They hated the darkness of Arctic winter, but unbroken summer daylight was worse. The beauty of the Northern Lights mocked the terrible vulnerability of ships beneath their glow. The unlucky *Harmatis* experienced another drama on 17 January 1942: she was struck by two U-boat torpedoes, one of which blasted open a hatch, strewing the rigging with clothing blown loose from the cargo. As seawater flooded into her gashed hull, the captain stopped the ship to prevent her from driving under. Somehow the damage was contained. The *Harmatis* was towed into Murmansk by tugs, amid further attacks by Luftwaffe Heinkels.

Others were less fortunate: when a torpedo detonated in the magazine of the destroyer *Matabele*, only two survivors were rescued. The sea was dotted with corpses in life jackets, men who froze to death before help could reach them, for the cold killed within minutes. George Charlton, serving in a destroyer sunk by gunfire when the heavy cruiser *Hipper* attacked a convoy in the last days of December 1942, described the horror of attempting to climb the scrambling net of a rescuing trawler: "I waited for the swell to take me up to the net and then I just [pushed] my arms and legs through the mesh and I was left hanging there until two ratings came down over the side and pulled me aboard, with a third helping me up by the hair. I flopped on the deck . . . and then the numbness started wearing off and the cold hit me. I have never before or since felt anything like the pain that wracked my body."

PQ11, in February 1942, was the last convoy to enjoy a relatively easy passage. Its successor encountered severe early difficulties in pack ice. Thereafter, PQ12 played blindman's buff with the *Tirpitz*, which intelligence reported was at sea. Ships' masters vented their rage when a BBC news bulletin announced that "a valuable cargo is on its way to Russia." As so often in the war, the demands of propaganda clashed with those of operational secrecy. In March, the Royal Navy had its best chance of the year to sink the German battleship, when Albacore torpedo bombers intercepted and attacked it at sea; two planes were lost, but no hits scored. Churchill angrily contrasted the Fleet Air Arm's failure with the achievement of Japanese aircraft three months earlier in sinking two British capital ships. The most plausible explanation was that the Japanese off Malaya were highly trained and experienced fliers, while most of the Albacore crews were relative novices.

A quarter of PQ13's twenty-one merchantmen, 30,000 tons of shipping, were lost to U-boats and bomber attacks after the convoy became badly scattered in a storm. A torpedo malfunction caused the cruiser *Trinidad* to inflict crippling damage on itself while attempting to sink a damaged German destroyer. As for merchant-ship survivors, the experience of those from the *Induna*, sunk by a U-boat on 30 March, was not untypical. Two lifeboats got away in the darkness, carrying many badly burned or scalded men. Hypothermia quickly killed the injured—seven died on the first night. The boats' fresh water froze solid. A lifeboat was eventually found occupied by nine men of whom only one, a Canadian fireman, remained alive. Of *Induna*'s crew of sixty-four, twenty-four were rescued, among whom all but six lost limbs to frostbite.

Because of the *Tirpitz* threat, each convoy required the protection of almost as many warships as there were merchantmen. Destroyers provided close protection against U-boats. Merchantmen were fitted with AA guns, and the assembled ships could mount a formidable barrage against attacking bombers. Cruisers offered cover against German destroyers as far east as Bear Island, to the north of Norway—*Edinburgh* fought off such an assault on PQ14. Over the horizon lurked big ships of the Home Fleet, hoping to intervene if German capital units sortied.

Two days east of the Icelandic assembly point, a German long-range aircraft—usually a Focke-Wulfe Condor—approached the convoy and thereafter circled just out of gun range, transmitting position signals to the Luftwaffe in Norway. Sailors hated the taunting menace of "Snoopy Joe," harbinger of almost continuous air and U-boat attacks for days thereafter. The slow stammer of ships' automatic weapons, the black puffs of exploding shells filling the sky, pillars of water from near misses and detonating torpedoes, the roar of low-flying aircraft and dull explosions of bombs bursting belowdecks imposed themselves on a seascape sculpted by waves, ice and "Arctic smoke"—a layer of mist that often overlay the freezing water.

Primitive air cover was introduced in April 1942 with the first CAM ship—a merchantman fitted with a catapult-launched Hurricane, whose pilot was expected to parachute into the sea after completing his only sortie. The CAM ships' planes seldom achieved success—they were usually launched too late—and demanded almost suicidal courage from their fliers, who had at best an even chance of being snatched from the sea before they froze. Each convoy experienced its own variation of tragedy. Six homeward-bound ships of QP13 were lost after straying into a British minefield off Iceland. When PQ14's commodore's ship was torpedoed, the engine-room staff were immediately blown to fragments as its cargo of ammunition exploded. Forty others survived to jump into the sea, where all but nine died from blast injuries inflicted when a trawler attempted to depth-charge the attacking U-boat. Far to the west, a destroyer was cut in half when it crossed the bows of the battleship *King George V,* which itself became a dockyard case as a result of damage inflicted by detonation of the stricken destroyer's depth charges. The cruisers *Trinidad* and *Edinburgh* were sunk after bitter engagements and noble damage-control efforts. An engineer officer of the mortally injured *Trinidad* refused to abandon his stokers, almost invariably doomed men when ships sank. Though concussed by bomb blast, he was last seen crawling to try to free them from beneath jammed hatches, even as the cruiser foundered. His name should be known to posterity: Lt. John Boddy.

Not all those engaged in the Arctic battles displayed such heroism. On the Allied side, while some merchant navy personnel showed remarkable spirit, others too readily fled damaged vessels, like the American crew of the *Christopher Newport,* who boarded a rescue ship jauntily dressed in their best suits and carrying baggage, abandoning 10,000 tons of munitions. Panic-stricken British sailors on several occasions lowered lifeboats so clumsily that their occupants were tipped into the sea. As for the Germans, convoy crews were surprised by the irresolution of some Luftwaffe pilots, who failed to press attacks through heavy barrages. The German navy, meanwhile, was hamstrung by Berlin's insistence on making all decisions about when and whether to deploy capital ships. Again and again, disgusted Kriegsmarine officers were ordered to break off action and scuttle for the safety of Norwegian fjords.

As the convoy battles of 1942 became progressively harder and more costly, merchant service officers voiced dismay about their treatment by the navy. They resented the fact that its big cruisers turned back at Bear Island because the air threat farther east was deemed unacceptable. They complained that escorts often abandoned their charges to hunt U-boats. They found it incomprehensible that, when cargoes were thought so precious, little air cover was provided. Above all, they protested about the fact that they were expected to sail day after day through the most perilous waters in the world, knowing nothing of what was happening save what they could see from their ice-encrusted upper decks. "One of the things about being in the Merchant Navy was that you were treated like children," said one ship's master later. "We were kept in the dark. It was most unsettling."

Merchantmen crawled across the chill sea more slowly than a running man, exposed to bomb and torpedo assaults more deadly than those of the Atlantic campaign. A cruiser senior officer warned the Admiralty in

May: "We in the navy are paid to do this sort of job. But it is beginning to ask too much of the men of the Merchant Navy. We may be able to avoid bombs and torpedoes with our speed—a six- or eight-knot ship has not this advantage." Some Americans recoiled from the hazards of the Russian voyage: there was a mutiny aboard the aged tramp steamer *Troubadour* when twenty men refused to sail, suppressed by the ship's Norwegian captain with the aid of a U.S. Navy armed guard. Those responsible, "an unhappy, polyglot mixture of sea-going drifters and extravagantly paid American seamen earning danger money on top of their wages," were committed to a Russian jail on arrival at Murmansk.

Yet Churchill angrily rejected the Royal Navy's urgings to suspend convoy operations during the perpetual daylight of Arctic summer. "The Russians are in heavy action and will expect us to run the risk and pay the price entailed by our contribution," he wrote. "The operation is justified if half gets through. Failure on our part to make the attempt would weaken our influence with both our major allies." The experience of PQ16 seemed to vindicate his determination. Thirty-six ships sailed from Iceland on 21 May; Luftwaffe attacks were frequent but often halfhearted. Despite many U-boat alarms, on the twenty-sixth only one ship was sunk. A destroyer dropped its doctor in a small boat to board a damaged Russian ship and take off three badly wounded men, on whom he later operated. The *Ocean Voice* was hit by a bomb which blew a huge hole in her side. Yet in calm seas, she was able to keep station and at last reached Russia "with God's help," in the words of a sailor.

Some ships ran out of antiaircraft gun ammunition, but many attacks were beaten off. Men on the upper decks of the Polish destroyer *Garland* suffered shocking casualties from bomb near misses. At Murmansk, the words "LONG LIVE POLAND" were found scrawled on the ship's upperworks in its crew's blood; "They were hard men," a merchant navy officer said respectfully. All but seven ships of the convoy got through, and some 371 crewmen and gunners from lost vessels were rescued by extraordinary feats of courage and skill. Adm. Sir John Tovey, C-in-C of the Home Fleet, whose caution Churchill deplored, asserted that "the strategical situation was wholly favourable to the enemy," but acknowledged that PQ16's success was "beyond expectations."

Yet the following month witnessed the most discreditable episode of the Royal Navy's war. PQ17, comprising thirty-six ships, most of which were American, sailed from Iceland on 27 June, carrying 594 tanks, 4,246 vehicles, 297 aircraft and over 150,000 tons of military and general stores. The British knew from Ultra that the Germans planned a major effort against the convoy, including a sortie by capital ships code-named

Rosselsprung—"Knight's Move." Hitler had declared that "Anglo-American intentions . . . depend on sustaining Russia's ability to hold out by maximum deliveries of war materials." At last, he recognised the importance of the Arctic convoys. The Admiralty assumed operational direction of PQ17 and its supporting units, because it had access to the latest Ultra intelligence, and experience showed that Tovey, at sea in his flagship, could not effectively control a large and widely dispersed force maintaining wireless silence.

Early skirmishes were of a familiar character. A Luftwaffe Condor took up station off Jan Mayen Island on 1 July. He-115 torpedo-carrying seaplanes made an unconvincing and unsuccessful attack, during which the U.S. destroyer *Wainwright* charged headlong towards the attacking aircraft, firing everything it had. Yet on 3 July, the Admiralty ordered the convoy's cruiser screen to turn away west, towards the German capital ships which it now believed were at sea. Next day three merchantmen were sunk. That evening, a disbelieving Captain "Jackie" Broome, commanding the escort, received a signal from London: "Secret and immediate. Owing to threat from surface ships convoy is to disperse and proceed to Russian ports." Thirteen minutes later, a further brief signal confirmed: "Convoy is to scatter." After reluctantly passing the order to his charges, Broome closed on a merchantman and addressed its master through a loudhailer: "Sorry to leave you like this, goodbye and good luck. It looks like a bloody business."

The *Tirpitz* indeed sortied briefly on 6 July, only to be ordered to return to Norway, to the disgust of its crew and escorts. A German destroyer captain wrote that day: "The mood is bitter enough. Soon one will feel ashamed to be on the active list . . . watching other parts of the armed forces fighting while we, 'the core of the fleet' just sit in harbour." But the Germans had no need to risk their big ships: the Luftwaffe and U-boats sank twenty-four of PQ17's merchantmen, struggling unprotected on lonely courses to Russia. Among their civilian crews, 153 men perished while British warships lost none; the shame of the Royal Navy was plain to behold, as were the disgust of the Americans and contempt of the Russians. It is indeed possible that PQ17 would have been destroyed by the *Tirpitz*. But the navy's response of "every man for himself," the abandonment of the convoy by its escort, breached the tradition of centuries and inspired lasting mistrust within the merchant service, at a time when its morale was anyway precarious.

The decision resulted from a personal intervention by the First Sea Lord, Adm. Sir Dudley Pound. Pound already commanded scant confidence among his peers, and was in failing health. It is extraordinary that he was not sacked, but Churchill found him sympathetic, and thus he retained his post until shortly before his death in October 1943. A government minister, Philip Noel-Baker, was sent to Glasgow to address returning PQ17 survivors at St. Andrew's Hall. "We know what the convoy cost us," he told them. "But I want to tell you that whatever the cost, it was well worth it." He was howled down by embittered men. The government threw a censorship blanket over the entire episode, suppressing an eyewitness account by correspondent Godfrey Winn, who had sailed with the convoy. Only after the war was the magnitude of the Admiralty's blunder revealed to the public.

PQ18 did not sail until September 1942, when it lost thirteen ships out of forty, ten of them to air attack. Among naval ratings and merchant seamen alike, it was now agreed that the Arctic passage represented the worst ordeal of the war at sea. Winn questioned Cmdr. Robert Sherbrooke, recovering from severe wounds received when he won a VC for his part in one of the battles, about the loss of the *Bramble*, in which the correspondent had sailed with PQ17. Sherbrooke said: "There was just a sudden flash of light on the horizon and that was all." Thus did nemesis strike many ships. A seaman described meeting survivors of the cruiser *Edinburgh* and finding them "rather sad and twitchy chaps." Some men who served on the convoys remained afterwards traumatised by their experiences.

In the winter of 1942 another reckless Admiralty decision was made: to run some single merchantmen to Russia unescorted, manned by volunteer crews lured by cash bonuses of £100 an officer, £50 a man. Five out of thirteen such ships arrived. Of the remainder, one ran aground on Spitzbergen, where its survivors suffered weeks of appalling privation—most died of gangrene following frostbite, before a handful were rescued by a passing Norwegian ski patrol. On another ship, the *Empire Archer*, there was a riot among firemen—the sweepings of Scotland's notorious Barlinnie jail—who gained access to rum intended for Archangel. Two sailors were stabbed before discipline was restored.

Even when ships reached Russia, they found little to cheer them. "The arrival in Kola Inlet was eerie," wrote one sailor. "It was December and pretty dark. There were great swirls of fog, black water and white snow-covered ice. The bare rocks on either side of the inlet were menacing and silence was broken only by constant sounding of mournful fog-horns of various pitches . . . I felt that if Hell were to be cold, this would be a foretaste of it." At Murmansk they remained subject to almost daily Luftwaffe attack. A bomb fell into the bunker of the freighter *Dover Hill*, where it lodged unexploded beneath twenty feet of coal. Her captain and crew laboured for two days and nights, removing coal in buckets, before with infinite caution they were able to hoist the bomb to the deck for defusing. Ashore, Russian hospitality was frigid, facilities negligible. Some British seamen arrived proclaiming an enthusiasm for their Soviet comrades-in-arms, which vanished amid the bleak reception. American sailors, denied every comfort to which they were accustomed, recoiled in disgust. The Allies were permitted to harbour no delusions that Western assistance merited Soviet gratitude. In the words of a Russian after the war, "God knows we paid them back in full—in Russian lives." Which was true.

The turn of the year proved the critical landmark of the campaign. Weather and the enemy—especially U-boats armed with acoustic homing torpedoes—ensured that service on Arctic convoys never became less than a miserable and alarming experience, but losses fell dramatically. In 1943 the Royal Navy was at last able to deploy escort carriers and powerful antisubmarine and antiaircraft defences. The Germans, hard-pressed in Russia and the Mediterranean, were obliged to divert much of their air and U-boat strength from Norway. Hitler refused to sanction major warship attacks on convoys until an ill-judged sortie was attempted by *Scharnhorst* in December 1943, which resulted in its sinking off the North Cape by a British fleet led by the battleship *Duke of York*.

The United States began to move massive supplies by other routes: half of all wartime American shipments reached Russia through its Pacific ports, a quarter through Iran, and only a quarter—4.43 million tons—via Archangel and Murmansk. The human cost of the Arctic convoys was astonishingly small by the standards of other battlefields: though 18 warships and 87 merchantmen were lost, only 1,944 naval personnel and 829 merchant seamen died serving on Arctic convoys between 1941 and 1945. The Germans lost 1 battleship, 3 destroyers, 32 U-boats and a substantial number of aircraft. Given their extraordinary opportunities for strategic dominance of the Arctic in 1942, what is remarkable is not how many Allied ships they sunk, but how few.

The Royal Navy counted the Russian convoys among its most formidable wartime challenges. It was the service's misfortune that the professionalism and courage which characterised its performance were tarnished by the memory of PQ17. The Fleet Air Arm never distinguished itself in the north, partly for lack of good aircraft. Some of the navy's most senior officers failed to display imagination to match the courage and seamanship of their subordinates. They refused to acknowledge, as Churchill and Roosevelt always did, that aid must be seen to be sent to Russia, no matter the cost. If the supplies shipped in 1941–42 were of greater symbolic than material importance to the outcome of the war on the Eastern Front, they were a vital earnest of Western Allied support for the decisive campaign to destroy Hitler.

3. The Ordeal of Pedestal

BETWEEN 1940 AND 1943, the Mediterranean witnessed some of the bloodiest fighting of the Royal Navy's war. British submarines, based on Malta when conditions there allowed, attacked Axis supply lines to North Africa with some success. Battle squadrons sought to assert themselves in the face of the Italian navy, U-boats and the Luftwaffe. Adm. Sir Andrew Cunningham inflicted severe damage on the Italian fleet in his November 1940 carrier air strike against Taranto, and in the surface action off Cape Matapan on 28–29 March 1941. But every capital ship sortie into open waters within range of the enemy was a perilous venture, which took a harrowing toll. The carrier *Illustrious* was badly damaged by German bombing in January 1941. On 25 November that year, the battleship *Barham* blew up, with the loss of most of its crew, after being torpedoed by a German submarine. The battleships *Queen Elizabeth* and *Valiant* rested for seven months on the floor of Alexandria harbour after falling victim to an attack by courageous Italian human-torpedo crews on 19 December 1941. The Royal Navy, having lost five capital ships in a month, was for a time obliged to cede the central Mediterranean to the Axis. There was a steady drain of British cruiser and destroyer losses to mines, bombs and torpedoes. For some months in 1941, the navy suffered severely while holding open a sea link to besieged Tobruk, which was deemed symbolically if not militarily important.

The pervasive strategic reality was that the Royal Navy remained vulnerable in the Mediterranean until the British Army could gain control of the North African littoral, providing the RAF with bases; in 1942, the hazards were increased by German deployment of U-boat reinforcements. But Winston Churchill conducted the war effort on the basis that Britain must be seen to challenge the enemy at every opportunity, especially when the army accomplished so little for so long. Malta, within easy range of Axis Sicilian air bases, suffered almost three years of intermittent bombardment. In March and April 1942 the little island received twice the bomb tonnage dropped on London during the entire blitz; its people almost starved, and its resident submarine flotilla had to be withdrawn. The requirement to sustain Malta became a priority for the Royal Navy, and every supply ship had to be fought through in the face of air, U-boat and surface attack. Each convoy demanded a supporting fleet operation: there had to be battleships in case Italian heavy units sortied, carriers to provide air cover, and cruiser and destroyer escorts. Each venture precipitated an epic battle. The most famous, or notorious, took place in August 1942, when Malta's shortages of oil, aircraft and food attained desperate proportions: Operation Pedestal was launched to bring succour.

Vice Adm. Neville Syfret took command of the battle fleet that sailed from the Clyde on 3 August, escorting fourteen merchantmen. Several of these were chartered American ships, notably the tanker *Ohio*, manned by British crews. All had been fitted with antiaircraft armament manned by soldiers, and on the passage to Gibraltar the convoy intensively exercised both gunnery and manoeuvre. The ships that set forth on 10 August to make the Malta passage formed a mighty array: the battleships *Nelson* and *Rodney*; the fleet carriers *Victorious*, *Indomitable* and *Eagle*; the old carrier *Furious*, ferrying Spitfires to reinforce the island as soon as the range narrowed sufficiently to fly them off; six cruisers; twenty-four destroyers and a flotilla of smaller craft. To one cadet aboard a merchantman it was "a fantastically wonderful sight."

Only weeks had elapsed since the Royal Navy's Arctic humiliation, and the service felt on its mettle: a destroyer captain, Lt. Cmdr. David Hill, said: "There was a strong touch of desperation and bloody-mindedness following PQ17." One of the Pedestal destroyer flotillas, led by Jackie Broome, had endured that ghastly experience. A host of German and Italian eyes, watching Gibraltar from Spain and North Africa, saw the fleet sail. Axis commanders were undeceived by a feint convoy which sailed simultaneously from Alexandria, trailing its coat in the eastern Mediterranean. "I felt indeed that some of our party were entering the narrow seas on a desperate venture," wrote George Blundell of the battleship *Nelson*, "and prayed to the Ruler of Destiny for his favour."

On 11 August, amid a still, azure sea, the *Furious* began flying off its Spitfires, which set course for Malta, 550 miles distant, where most arrived safely. But now the first disaster struck. In the western Mediterranean, Asdic was confused by freak underwater conditions created by the confluence of warm seas with colder Atlantic currents: ships were thus acutely vulnerable to submarine attack. Even as the fighters were being launched, a salvo of torpedoes fired by U-73 struck the *Eagle*, which sank in eight minutes with the loss of 260 of her complement of 1,160 men. "She presented a terrible sight as she heeled over, turned bottom up and sank with horrible speed," wrote an awestruck witness. "Men and aircraft could be seen falling off her flight deck as she capsized . . . It makes one tremble. If anyone took a good film of it, it should be shown throughout the country . . . I remember thinking of the trapped men." That evening the *Furious*, its flight deck now empty, turned for home and safety. One of her escorts, the destroyer *Wolverine*, spotted an Italian submarine and raced in to ram; the Axis boat sank, but *Wolverine* suffered severe damage.

At 8:45 p.m. the first enemy air attack was launched against Pedestal, by thirty-six He-111s and Ju-88s flying from Sicily. These achieved no hits, and four German aircraft fell to the intense AA barrage. The next day at noon, a much more serious strike took place, by seventy bombers and torpedo carriers with fighter escort. The ensuing battle lasted two hours. The freighter *Deucalion* was damaged and later sunk off the Tunisian coast by a torpedo bomber, despite gallant efforts to save the ship by her master, Capt. Ramsay Brown. During the afternoon, the convoy survived a submarine ambush unscathed. The destroyer *Ithuriel* rammed and sank another Italian boat, at the cost of crippling herself.

That evening of the twelfth, the Luftwaffe and Italian air force came again. A hundred bombers and torpedo carriers sustained attacks from every direction and altitude, designed to swamp the defence. Ships' AA crews fired almost continuously; empty cases massed in heaps beside gun mountings; the brilliant sky became pockmarked with thousands of black puffs; and the noise of screaming aircraft engines competed with the stammer and thud of every calibre of armament. The destroyer *Foresight* was sunk, the carrier *Indomitable* badly damaged by three armour-piercing bombs. Still short of the Sicilian Narrows, Syfret withdrew his capital ships westwards, leaving a close escort headed by six cruisers, commanded by Rear Adm. Harold Burrough, to fight the convoy through to Malta.

Pedestal's agony now began in earnest. Within an hour of Syfret parting company, the Italian submarine *Axum* achieved a brilliant triple success: in a single attack, it sank Burrough's flagship, *Nigeria*, and the antiaircraft cruiser *Cairo*, also hitting the tanker *Ohio*. These losses wiped out the convoy's fighter direction capability, for the two cruisers carried the only radio sets capable of voice communication with Malta-based planes. Then, as the light began to fade, with British ships losing formation and huddling into a scrum, the Luftwaffe came again. Ju-88s sank the merchant ships *Empire Hope* and *Clan Ferguson* and crippled the *Brisbane Star*. Soon afterwards, a submarine torpedo damaged the cruiser *Kenya*. In darkness in the early hours of 13 August, German and Italian motor torpedo boats launched a series of attacks which persisted for hours. The defence was feeble, because Burrough decided that to illuminate the battlefield with starshells would help the enemy more than his own gunners. The cruiser *Manchester* was fatally damaged, four more merchantmen sunk and a fifth hit. The only compensation for suffering such losses in the Mediterranean's warm summer waters was that far more survivors could be rescued than in the Arctic or even the Atlantic.

At daybreak the Luftwaffe returned, sinking another merchantman. The *Ohio* suffered further damage, but limped onwards until renewed attacks later in the morning stopped her engines. Two more merchantmen were crippled, and had to be left behind with a destroyer escort. At 4:00 p.m., in accordance with orders, Burrough's three surviving cruisers turned back for Gibraltar. Three merchantmen—the *Port Chalmers*, *Melbourne Star* and *Rochester Castle*, the last with its deck almost awash— struggled to cover the final miles into Malta shepherded by small craft from the island. At 6:00 in the evening on 13 August, as cheering crowds lined the old fortifications, they steamed into Grand Harbour. The Germans set about demolishing the stragglers, sinking the damaged *Dorset* and hitting *Ohio* yet again. By a miracle attributable partly to its rugged American construction, the tanker maintained way, towed by a destroyer and two minesweepers. On the morning of 15 August, the Catholic Feast of the Assumption of Our Lady, the *Ohio* reached safety and began to offload. Her master, Capt. Dudley Mason, was awarded the George Cross; the *Brisbane Star* also completed the passage.

The Pedestal convoy delivered 32,000 tons of stores, 12,000 tons of coal and two months' supply of oil; five merchantmen survived out of fourteen. The navy's aggressive posturing dissuaded the Italian fleet from joining the battle. Mussolini's battleships were immobilised anyway by lack of fuel, and RAF aircraft dropped flares over five cruisers which put to sea, convincing them that they faced unacceptable risk if they persevered. Lt. Alastair Mars, commanding the submarine *Unbroken*, extracted some revenge for British warship losses by torpedoing the cruisers *Bolzano* and *Muzio Attendolo*. But after the Pedestal battle was over, Cmdr. George Blundell of the battleship *Nelson* looked back in deep gloom: "Most of us felt depressed by the party. Operation 'M' for Murder we call it. 'The navy thrives on impossibilities,' said the BBC. Yes, but how long can it go on doing so?"

The three-day drama of Pedestal was almost matched by the experiences and sufferings of other Malta convoys and their escorts. Not all those who sailed distinguished themselves: there were shameful cases of merchant-ship crews abandoning their ships unnecessarily, of seamen scuttling for lifeboats while their vessels were still steaming. A disgusted Captain Brown of the *Deucalion*, some of whose men quit their posts prematurely, said later, "I could never have imagined that any Britishers could have shown up in such poor colours." But the overall story is one of a fine endeavour. By the winter of 1942, the worst of Britain's Mediterranean travails were over. Ultra decrypts enabled Allied warships and aircraft to wreak increasing havoc with Rommel's supply line: Axis shipping losses in the Mediterranean rose from 15,386 tons in July to 33,791 in September, 56,303 in October and 170,000 in the two months that followed. In November, Montgomery was victorious at El Alamein and the Americans landed in North Africa. The siege of Malta was relieved soon afterwards.

Holding the island since 1940 had cost the Royal Navy 1 battleship, 2 carriers, 4 cruisers, 1 minelayer, 20 destroyers and minesweepers and 40 submarines. The RAF lost 547 aircraft in the air and another 160 destroyed on the ground. Ashore, Malta's defence forfeited the lives of 1,600 civilians, 700 soldiers and 900 RAF personnel. Afloat, 2,200 warship crewmen, 1,700 submariners and 200 merchant seamen perished. Thereafter, in 1943 and 1944, Allied dominance of the Mediterranean remained contested and imposed continuing losses, but the strategic advantage tilted relentlessly away from the Axis. The Royal Navy's critical responsibilities in the last two years of the war became those of escorting Allied armies to new battlefields, and organising and protecting a succession of massive amphibious landings. If the threat from Germany's submarines and aircraft persisted to the end—British warships suffered severely in the ill-fated autumn 1943 Dodecanese campaign—the Royal Navy had won the decisive battles of the European war at sea; not in actions between fleets, but by sustaining Britain's global rights of passage in the face of air power and U-boats. In fulfilment of this responsibility, most of its captains and crews upheld the service's highest traditions.

CHAPTER TWELVE

THE FURNACE: RUSSIA IN 1942

A PHENOMENON created by the strong emotions and fantastical experiences war brought upon Russia was a resurgence of religious worship, which Stalin did not seek to suppress. At Easter 1942, Moscow's overnight curfew was lifted, and Dr. Sof'ya Skopina attended the great Orthodox cathedral in Moscow's Elokhovskaya Square. "We arrived at 8 p.m. There was a small queue to bless the *kulich* [Easter bread] and eggs. An hour later there was such a crowd that one couldn't turn and no air to breathe. Amid the throng, women screamed, 'They've crushed me! I'm going to faint!' The atmosphere grew so humid that moisture ran down the columns. Candles passed from one person to another sent smoke curling into spirals. There were many young people (I don't know why they had come there). Some mums came with their kids, and a lot of military men. There were people even sitting on the cross with the picture of Christ. It was like a football crowd. At 11 p.m. a priest appeared and announced that 'Our friends the British are about to arrive.' We could no longer breathe and went outside, where we saw several cars drive up. It was the British [embassy delegation]."

Army nurse Evdokiya Kalinichenko wrote in May: "We're having a little break, for the first time this month. We've made the wounded men comfortable, dried ourselves out, had a wash in a real *banya* [bath house]. We've been on so many roads. All kinds of roads . . . Mostly country roads, often mud-bound, rutted and degraded by rain, holes, bumps. One's heart breaks when the vehicle jolts: most of the passengers are gravely wounded, and for some such jolting can be fatal. Now, however, it is so quiet around us that it is hard to believe there is war anywhere on the planet. We wander about in the woods and gather bunches of flowers. The sun shines, the sky is blue. We keep peering upwards by force of habit, but see only passing clouds. We think the Germans have at last been stopped and won't try to go any further—they've learnt their lesson on the approaches to Moscow."

Kalinichenko hoped too much, too soon. Though the Russians had mass, and could replace their horrific 1941 losses, they still lacked the combat power and logistical support to sustain deep penetrations. The New Year offensive by five *fronts* (the equivalent of Western army groups), personally directed by Stalin, petered out even before the spring thaw arrested movement. The Germans held their line south of Leningrad, sustaining the threat to the city; they moved to cut off the Volkhov Front and destroy the Second Shock Army. Its commander, Lt. Gen. Andrey Vlasov, was captured, and subsequently raised a Cossack "Russian Libera-tion Army" for the Nazis.

In the Crimea, the Germans blocked the western exit from the Kerch Peninsula, trapping a vast Russian army, then counterattacked. Between 8 and 19 May, Manstein achieved another triumph, shattering the Crimean Front and taking 170,000 prisoners. Seven thousand survivors took refuge in limestone caves until the Germans blasted the entrances with explosives and pumped in gas. Lt. Gen. Gunther Blumentritt, who became a Wehr-macht army commander, wrote of the Russians rather as he might have described wild beasts he could not respect, but grudgingly feared:

> Eastern man is very different from his Western counterpart. He has a much greater capacity for enduring hardship, and this passivity induces a high degree of equanimity towards life and death . . . Eastern man does not possess much initiative; he is accustomed to taking orders, to being led. [The Russians] attach little importance to what they eat or wear. It is surprising how long they can survive on what to a Western man would be a starvation diet . . . Close contact with nature enables these people to move freely by night or in fog, through woods and across swamps. They are not afraid of the dark, nor of their endless forests, nor of the cold . . . The Siberian, who is partially or completely Asiatic, is even tougher . . . The psychological effect of the country on the ordinary German soldier was considerable. He felt small and lost in that endless space . . . A man who has survived the Russian enemy and the Russian climate has little more to learn about war.

Manstein favoured bypassing the fortress of Sevastopol, but Hitler insisted on its capture. The giant 1,350-ton 800mm siege gun "Big Dora" was brought forward, utilising enormous labour because it could move only on twin railway tracks. Franz Halder dismissed Dora, an example of wasteful Nazi industrial effort on prestige weapons, as "an extremely impressive piece of engineering, but quite useless." Its seven-ton shells and 4,000-strong crew contributed much less to the capture of the city than the dogged efforts of Manstein's infantry. The defenders were also pounded from the air. A Luftwaffe dive-bomber pilot, Capt. Herbert

Paber, wrote: "One explosion next to another, like poisonous mushrooms, shot up between the rocky hideouts. The whole peninsula was fire and smoke—yet in the end thousands of prisoners were taken even there. One can only stand amazed at such resilience . . . That is how they defended Sevastopol all along the line . . . The whole country had to be literally ploughed over with bombs before they yielded a short distance."

When the city finally fell on 4 July after a siege of 250 days, the NKVD's units were among those which escaped, after massacring all their prisoners. The dreadful losses in the Crimea were attributed to the incompetence of the Soviet commander, Stalin's favourite Lev Mekhlis, who rejected pleas for units to be allowed to dig in as a symptom of defeatism. The only redeeming feature of the disaster was that Mekhlis was sacked. Sevastopol cost the Germans 25,000 dead and 50,000 tons of artillery ammunition. The attackers were again impressed by the stubbornness of the resistance.

Meanwhile, farther north, as the ground dried out after the thaw, on 12 May Gen. Semyon Timoshenko launched a thrust by the Southwestern Front towards Kharkov, which failed disastrously. Yet again, a German counterattack encircled the Russians, and yet again Stalin refused to permit a retreat, causing the loss of more than a quarter of a million men. The army commander and some of his officers shot themselves rather than accept captivity. The survivors were driven eastwards in rout. One man said, "We wept as we retreated. We were running anywhere to get away from Kharkov; some to Stalingrad, others to Vladikavkaz. Where else would we end up—Turkey?"

Hitler's confidence revived: he dismissed Germany's losses in the previous year's fighting, and accepted the view of Col. Reinhard Gehlen, the Eastern Front intelligence chief, that Stalin's reserves were exhausted. By August, German weapons output would regain full momentum, following a disastrous July 1941 decision, rescinded only in January 1942, to cut arms and ammunition production in anticipation of victory. It was extraordinary that Hitler retained the loyalty and obedience of his officers after the strategic madnesses of the previous campaign and the privations of winter. In the Crimea in January 1942, an embittered German soldier itemised his diet: one hot meal a day—cabbage soup with potatoes in it—half a loaf of bread every second day, some fat, a little cheese and hard honey.

Yet even on such fare, the Wehrmacht remained a formidable fighting force. Most of Germany's generals, in the dark recesses of their souls, knew that they had made their nation and its entire army—it was a myth that only the SS committed atrocities—complicit in crimes against humanity, and especially Russian humanity, such as their enemies would never forgive, even before the Holocaust began. They saw nothing to lose by fighting on, except more millions of lives: it deserves emphasis that a large majority of the war's victims perished from 1942 onwards. Only victories might induce the Allies to make terms. Hitler's April directive for the summer operations called for a concentration of effort in the south; the objectives of Operation Blue were to destroy the Red Army's residual reserves, seize Stalingrad and capture the Caucasian oilfields.

Stalin misjudged German intentions: anticipating a new thrust against Moscow, he concentrated his forces accordingly. Even when the entire Blue plan was laid before him, after being found on the body of a Wehrmacht staff officer killed in an air crash, he dismissed it as disinformation. But Russia's armies remained much stronger than Hitler realised, with 5.5 million men under arms and rapidly increasing tank and aircraft production. Criminals and some political prisoners were released from the gulag's labour camps for service—975,000 of them by the war's end. Berlin estimated Russia's 1942 steel output at 8 million tons; in reality, it would attain 13.5 million tons.

The first phase of Blue, expected to take three weeks, began on 28 June with an assault towards the Don. Against Stalin's armies, Hitler deployed 3.5 million Germans and a further million Axis troops—Italians, Romanians, and the Spanish "Blue" Division dispatched by Franco as a goodwill gesture—with spectacular initial success. When *Pravda* correspondent Lazar Brontman arrived in Voronezh, 300 miles northwest of Stalingrad, at first he found the city relaxed and secure in its remoteness from the enemy. He was amused one evening by the droll spectacle of scores of women in the park dancing with one another in the absence of male partners. Women also policed the city: Brontman observed that they directed traffic more efficiently than men, but used their whistles too much.

Within days, however, the mood darkened dramatically. Farther west the Russian line broke, precipitating yet another headlong retreat. German bombers began to pound Voronezh's streets, "ironing the city without meeting resistance," and prompting a great exodus of fugitives. Profiteers who owned vehicles charged desperate people three, four, five thousand roubles for the privilege of a ride eastwards. One by one, the city's factories and government offices shut down. When its inhabitants learned that the Germans were only thirty miles away, Brontman wrote that Voronezh was "psychologically prepared for surrender," and indeed the city was overrun a few days later.

The advancing panzers were delayed by rain and mud more than by the Red Army, and in early July reached their initial objectives. Stalin mandated the only authorised Russian strategic retreat of the war: when the Germans continued their advance east beyond Voronezh, they found themselves attacking empty space. Russian forces escaped from an intended envelopment at Millerovo, prompting Hitler to sack Field Marshal Fedor von Bock for the second time, then splitting his Army Group South into two new commands, A and B, commanded respectively by Field Marshal Wilhelm List and Gen. Maximilian von Weichs. But the Führer exulted in the progress of the campaign, which thus far had been a mere armoured victory ride; his infantry were scarcely called upon to fight, and losses were negligible. New swathes of Soviet territory fell into German hands. Through July the panzers swept on southwards towards Rostov, savagely mauling the Russian South *front* as its formations sought escape across the Don. Hitler commissioned Gen. Friedrich Paulus, a staff officer eager to prove himself as a field commander, to lead the Sixth Army in a dash for Stalingrad.

Most of Germany's generals immediately recognised the folly of this move. The strategic significance of Stalin's name city was small, irrelevant to the main objective of clearing the Caucasus and securing its oil. Moreover, Hitler's eagerness for a symbolic triumph was matched by the determination of Stalin to deny this to him. If Stalingrad fell, the Soviet leader feared a renewed German thrust in the north, against Moscow. He thus determined that the Volga city must be held at all costs, and committed to its defence three armies from his strategic reserve. The stage was set for one of the decisive battles of the war, a collision between the personal wills of the two dictators.

THE SPIRIT of many Russians was unbroken, but the catastrophes of spring and summer ate deep into morale. Some people nursed hopes that the Western Allies would relieve their plight. Pavel Kalitov, the commissar of a partisan group in Ukraine, wrote on 8 July: "We are very happy because England is bombing Romania with such success, and the Americans are going to send a landing force to France." Such expectations were precious but spurious. British bombing received much more propaganda attention than its achievements justified, and the Second Front was still almost two years away. Until 1943, arms and food deliveries from the West made only a small contribution to matching enormous Soviet needs and commitments. Whatever Stalin's people achieved in 1942, they must achieve it almost unaided.

It is hard to exaggerate the sufferings of Russian soldiers in the face of the elements and their own leaders' bungling, as well as the enemy.

"The night was terribly dark," wrote Capt. Nikolai Belov, describing his unit's detrainment behind the front. "The whole battalion set off in the wrong direction. We walked in circles all night, 30 km in terrible mud." Two weeks on, he recorded: "We have only a couple of old rifles for the whole battalion." On 10 May, his unit took up positions near a village named Bolshoi Sinkovets: "We have had no food for two days. Everyone is starving." Two days later, the battalion was issued with forty-one rifles for 500 men. On 17 May, they "speed-marched" thirty miles, losing forty stragglers who could not keep up. This was unsurprising, since the men had not eaten for two days. Belov wrote: "Everyone is frustrated with the commanders—and not without reason." Day after day, their ordeal continued. "Arrived in Zelyonaya Dubrava, having marched 35 km during the day. It is unbearably hot, we are terribly tired. Again there is nothing to eat. Lots of men are unable to keep up. Sedov is crying. He is quite unable to walk." Belov's men were reduced to grubbing in the fields for rotting potatoes left from the previous year's harvest. Their first actions against the Germans resulted in murderous losses: on 15 July, he reported his company's strength reduced to five men.

At midsummer 1942, the Western Allies' view of Russia's predicament remained bleak. A British intelligence officer wrote on 15 July: "I have the inescapable feeling that much as the Germans may have lost, the Red Army has lost more . . . Sevastopol was . . . a fair feat of Soviet arms and demonstrated the enormous power of the Red Army on the defensive—given the right conditions of terrain . . . [But it] is still not capable of dealing with the Germans in the open terrain of South Russia . . . On the whole the Germans have most things in their favour . . . They possess a better fighting machine . . . How far the Germans will be able to exploit their success will depend on the ability of the Red Army to retain some form of cohesion in retreat until they have gone back behind great natural obstacles or into country more suitable for the defence."

It is important to view the events of the year in context. In 1941, Russia suffered 27.8 percent of its total war losses. But in 1942 Kharkov, the Crimea and the Kerch Peninsula disasters accounted for even larger casualties. When Stalingrad was added, the year as a whole cost Russia 28.9 percent of its overall casualties in the conflict, 133 percent of the Red Army's frontline strength. Posterity knows that Stalin learned vital lessons: he started to delegate military decisions to competent generals and the worst blunderers were dismissed. The weapons created by Russia's industrial mobilisation and production beyond the Urals began to reach her armies, increasing their strength while that of the Axis shrank. But none of this was apparent to the world in the summer of 1942. Germany still seemed irresistible on the battlefield, Russia at its last gasp.

Almost all British, and also later American, attempts to collaborate operationally with Stalin's people foundered on the rocks of their ally's secretiveness, incompetence, ill-will and paucity of means. The Royal Navy's requests for the aid of Soviet warships and aircraft to cover British convoys approaching Murmansk and Archangel yielded meagre responses. In August 1942, an RAF Catalina delivered to northwest Russia two SIS agents, whom the Soviets had agreed to parachute into northern Norway. Their hosts instead detained the two men incommunicado for two months before dropping them, still in summer clothing, inside Finland rather than Norway, where they were swiftly arrested, tortured and shot. Thereafter, the British recognised that cooperation with the Russians was an exclusively one-way proposition; that the consequences of placing Allied personnel at the mercy of Soviet goodwill were often fatal.

Nonetheless, the Western governments went to extravagant lengths to preserve a semblance of unity. When Gen. Władysław Anders, who had suffered in Stalin's prisons between 1939 and 1941, met Churchill in Cairo in August 1942, the Pole vehemently denounced the Soviet Union: "There was, I said, no justice or honour in Russia, and not a single man there whose word could be trusted. Churchill pointed out to me how dangerous such language as I was using would be if spoken in public. No good, he said, could come of antagonising the Russians . . . Churchill closed the talk by saying that he believed Poland would emerge from the war a strong and happy country." Anders allowed himself to be persuaded that "we Poles were now going home (so we thought) by a different route, a longer one, indeed, but one with fewer hardships." The Western Allies exerted themselves to sustain this delusion.

THE GERMANS encountered the first units of the Stalingrad *front* on 23 July, some eighty-seven miles west of the city. That night, Hitler made what proved the decisive blunder of the war in the east. He issued a new directive, declaring the objectives of Blue completed. Army Group A was ordered to overrun the Caucasus oilfields, 745 miles beyond its existing positions—a longer advance than the German drive from the Siegfried Line to the Channel coast in May 1940. Its formations soon found themselves attempting to sustain a front 500 miles wide with hopelessly inadequate forces, against stubborn Russian resistance. Meanwhile Army Group B commenced operations designed to close up to a line along the

Volga and secure Stalingrad. Manstein was transferred northwards with five infantry divisions and the siege artillery he had used at Sevastopol, to end the tiresome resistance at Leningrad: following a change of policy, Berlin was now impatient to occupy the city. The next news from the Sixth Army showed that its progress towards Stalingrad had become sluggish. Hitler, irked, ordered that the Fourth Panzer Army should be diverted from the Caucasus to support Paulus. He thus divided his strength in a fashion which rendered each element of his forces too weak to attain its objectives.

But August 1942 was another season of Russian catastrophes. One of Stalin's favourites, the old Bolshevik warhorse Marshal Semyon Budenny, presided over a series of shambolic defeats in the northern Caucasus. The Sixth Army wrecked Russian forces on the Don east of Kalach, taking 50,000 prisoners; an entire Soviet tank army collapsed, with crews abandoning their vehicles in panic. On 21 August, Paulus launched a dash from the Don to the Volga, blasting a path through the defenders with waves of dive-bombers. In two days, his forces reached the river nine miles north of Stalingrad. The city's capture seemed imminent, and he dispatched to Hitler a draft of his plans for Sixth Army's move into winter quarters. Farther south, on 9 August mountain troops took Maikop, the most accessible of the Caucasian oilfields, where Russian demolitions proved so thorough that it was deemed necessary to bring equipment from Germany to drill new wells. Army Group A's spearheads began pushing east for the Caspian; the Seventeenth Army was directed southwards through the mountains towards the Black Sea.

The entire Caucasian advance was hamstrung by Hitler's orders to divert available fuel and ammunition supplies to Paulus. Among the Nazi hierarchy in Berlin, however, there was another surge of optimism: Rommel was at the gates of Cairo, armaments production was rising, Germany's Japanese allies had achieved extraordinary triumphs and the implications of American naval successes at the Coral Sea and Midway were barely comprehended. Dönitz's U-boats were devastating Atlantic convoys; an Italian submarine commander reported that he had sunk an American battleship, and was decorated by Mussolini for his flight of fantasy. German civilian morale revived.

Only the technocrats who knew the economic and industrial secrets of the Reich were undeluded. The manpower situation remained desperate, and Germany was increasing aircraft output by sustaining production of obsolescent types. General Halder wrote in his diary on 23 July: "The chronic tendency to underrate enemy capabilities is gradually assuming grotesque proportions." In September, German difficulties mounted swiftly. Troops in the southern mountains encountered snowstorms, and repeated changes of objective wreaked havoc with operations. Again and again, German advances were delayed or halted by lack of fuel—the First Panzer Army found itself immobilised for three weeks, conceding a precious breathing space to Stalin's commanders. Almost all available Luftwaffe support was diverted to Stalingrad, heedless of the cost to operations elsewhere. On 12 September, the first German troops entered the city.

Along the length of the front, Russian soldiers and civilians alike understood little of the Germans' huge difficulties, seeing only the miseries imposed upon their own people by battlefield failure, slaughter and starvation. On 23 October Commissar Pavel Kalitov wrote in dismay from Logovo, on receiving the order for yet another retreat: "The civilians are howling. Everything is to be evacuated. Everywhere there is weeping, tears, grief. Just think of it: winter is about to begin, they must go out into the cold with their little ones . . . Where are they to go? Our units are falling back. The Germans are exploiting a weak point in our line. Our newspapers often use such phrases as: 'under pressure of superior enemy forces.' But what about us? Why are we unable to mass such 'superior forces'? What is wrong? The past sixteen months have taught us many lessons. It is so hard to abandon settlements . . . More victims, more bloody torture, more curses levelled at us. [The peasants say]: 'That's what they are like, our protectors.'"

An old woman spoke scathingly to Vasily Grossman about her country's rulers: "These fools have allowed [the enemy] to reach the heart of the country, the Volga. They've given them half of Russia." From the Kremlin came new slogans: "Not a step back . . . The only extenuating circumstance is death." Stalin, facing disaster with half the European Soviet Union in German hands, made an appointment with reality which proved critical. In September he named Zhukov as the nation's deputy supreme commander, then dispatched him to oversee the defence of Stalingrad and to prepare a major counteroffensive. He recognised the need to subordinate ideology to military necessity: the prohibited word "officer" was restored to the Red Army, and unit commanders were liberated from their subordination to commissars; henceforward, promotions would be determined by competence. The value of medals as incentives was acknowledged: by 1945 the Red Army had issued 11 million, against the U.S. Army's 1.4 million.

Stalin, profiting from experience as Hitler would not, delegated operational control of the battlefield, though his supreme authority was never in doubt. Such drastic steps were indispensable to remedy the Red Army's lamentable summer performance. "We have to learn and learn," wrote Commissar Kalitov on 4 September 1942. "For a start, we must stop being so careless." Nikolai Belov gloomily described an inspection by a senior officer of the army battle training staff: "Results deplorable. The Youssefs"—the Red Army's derisive term for men from Kazakhstan—"cannot turn left or right. What a terrible lot—complete mutton-heads. If we are given more Kazakhs we can consider ourselves doomed." But the Red Army was indeed learning, however painfully, and was receiving formidable reinforcements of men, tanks and aircraft.

In the autumn and winter of 1942, the grey, charmless industrial city of Stalingrad became the scene of some of the most terrible fighting of the war. On Sunday, 23 August, the Germans heralded their assault with an air raid by 600 aircraft: 40,000 civilians are said to have died in the first fourteen hours, almost as many as perished in the entire 1940–41 blitz on Britain. Thereafter, the Luftwaffe struck relentlessly. "We ploughed over the blazing fields of the Stalingrad battlefield all day long," wrote Stuka pilot Herbert Pabst. "It is incomprehensible to me how people can continue to live in that hell, but the Russians are firmly established in the wreckage, in ravines, cellars, and in a chaos of twisted steel skeletons of the factories." Paulus launched his first major ground attack on 13 September, and thereafter the struggle was waged amid a landscape of ruins. Gen. Vasily Chiukov, commanding the Sixty-second Army, wrote: "The streets of the city are dead. There is not a single green twig on the trees; everything has perished in the flames."

The concrete masses of the city's transport hubs and industrial plants were swiftly reduced to rubble. Each became a scene of slaughter, their unlovely names etched into the legend of Russia's Great Patriotic War: the grain elevator beside the Number Two station, the freight station, the Number One station, the Lazur chemical plant, the Red October metal works, the Dzerzhinsky tractor factory and the Barricades gun foundry. In the first phase of the battle, the Russians held a perimeter thirty miles by eighteen, which shrank rapidly. At Stalin's insistence three infantry armies were thrown into a counterattack against the northern flank—and beaten back. The Germans, in their turn, launched repeated efforts to capture two landmarks: Point 102, a Tatar mound that rose some 350 feet above the city, and the Volga crossing point just beyond Red Square, through which reinforcements and supplies reached the city and casualties were evacuated. On some nights, as many as two or three thousand Russian wounded were ferried in darkness across the mile of ice-floed water to the eastern bank.

Each boat that took out casualties brought in men and ammunition. Reinforcements were herded aboard ferries to run the gauntlet of the crossing under Luftwaffe attack—sometimes in daylight, such were the exigencies of the siege. Aleksandr Gordeev, a naval machine gunner, watching pityingly as soldiers clung to the deck rails rather than obey orders to descend into the hold: "The officers made them move down by kicking them, NCOs were swearing and shouting. Baida [his petty officer] and two big sailors were grabbing men who resisted and pushing them down the ladder. Crates of shells, bullets and rations were brought aboard. Looking at the stack of ammunition boxes five steps from our Maxim gun, I could imagine what would happen if they were hit." Soon afterwards, he watched another ferry carrying casualties sunk by Stukas. "The wounded, more than a hundred of them, were sitting or lying in the cabins while fugitives clambered up from the hold. There was a general, continuous howling sound that swelled above the bomb explosions."

New units were rushed into the battle as fast as they arrived. Sixty-second Army's commander Gen. Vasily Chuikov said, "Time is blood." Detonations of bombs and shells, the crackle of small arms and the thud of mortars seldom ceased, day or night. Chuikov remarked later of Stalingrad, "Approaching this place, soldiers used to say: 'We are entering hell.' And after spending one or two days here, they said: 'No, this isn't hell, this is ten times worse than hell.' A young woman soldier said: 'I had been imagining what war was like—everything on fire, children crying, cats running about, and when we got to Stalingrad it turned out to be really like that, only more terrible.' " She had joined the service with a group of friends from her home town of Tobolsk, in Siberia. Most were posted to the embattled city, and few left it alive.

The battle was fought in conditions that enabled Russian soldiers to display their foremost skill, as close-quarter fighters. There was no scope for sweeping panzer advances or imaginative flanking manoeuvres. Each day, German soldiers, guns and tanks merely sought to batter a path to the Volga yard by yard, through mounds of fallen masonry in which Russians huddled, cursed, starved, froze, fought and died. A letter was taken from the body of a dead defender, written by his small son: "I miss you very much. Please come and visit, I so want to see you, if only for one hour. My tears pour as I write this. Daddy, please come and see us."

Chuikov expressed to Vasily Grossman his sense of oppression: "There's firing and thunder all around. You send off a liaison officer to find out what's happening, and he gets killed. That's when you shake all over with tension . . . The most terrible times were when you sat there like an idiot, and the battle boiled around you, but there was nothing you could do." On 2 October, Chuikov's headquarters were engulfed by a torrent of blazing oil from nearby storage tanks which burst after being hit by German bombs. Forty of his staff died as a pillar of smoke and flame rose hundreds of feet into the sky. The tractor plant was the scene of nightmare clashes as filthy, exhausted and half-starved defenders strove to repulse German tanks crashing through the rubble. At one moment the Soviet bridgehead on the west bank of the Volga shrank to a depth of a mere hundred yards.

The Russians fought with a desperation reinforced, as always, by compulsion. The price of unauthorised retreat was death. Vasily Grossman wrote: "On those anxiety-filled days, when the thunder of fighting could be heard in the suburbs of Stalingrad, when at night one could see rockets launched high above, and pale blue rays of searchlights roamed the sky, when the first trucks disfigured by shrapnel, carrying the casualties and baggage of retreating headquarters, appeared in the streets of the city, when front-page articles announced the mortal danger for the country, fear found its way into a lot of hearts, and many eyes looked across the Volga." Grossman meant, of course, that men yearned for escape eastwards from the cauldron. Those who made such attempts paid the price: some 13,500 soldiers were executed at Stalingrad for alleged cowardice or desertion, and many more were killed out of hand. In a typical report of 23 September, Beria reported that during the preceding twenty-four hours his NKVD "blocking detachments" had detained 659 people: 7 "cowards" and 1 "enemy of the people" were shot in front of their units. A further 24 were still held, including 1 "spy," 3 "betrayers of the motherland," 8 "cowards" and 8 "enemies of the people."

Paulus launched repeated attacks, but again and again his forces proved just too weak to break through. There was no scope for subtlety, merely a hundred daily death grapples between Germans and Russians who shared identical privations. Chuikov deployed his forces as close as possible to the enemy line, to frustrate Luftwaffe strafing. Bombardment had wrecked the city, but as the Western Allies would later discover, ruins create formidable tank obstacles, and are more easily defended than open streets and intact buildings. Almost every soldier was always hungry, always cold. Snipers and mortars rendered careless movement fatal; many men died collecting ammunition or queuing at field kitchens. So did women. Chuikov later paid unstinting tribute to their contribution as signallers, nurses, clerks, and air defence spotters.

The icy wind burnt faces deep red. Each day brought its own local crisis, while by night the Russians shifted across the river just sufficient reinforcements to sustain their precarious perimeter. Moscow sentimentalised many episodes for propaganda purposes, such as the story of a marine named Panaiko whose Molotov cocktail ignited, transforming him into a human pillar of flame. The doomed man stumbled towards a German tank, where he dashed a second Molotov against the engine grille, engulfing both tank and hero in fire. If some such tales were apocryphal, many were not. "Courage is infectious here, just as cowardice is infectious in other places," wrote Vasily Grossman, and he was right. Stalin's orders were simple and readily understood: the city must be held to the last man and woman.

It was Hitler's ill-fortune that the battle perfectly suited the elemental spirit of the Red Army. A panzergrenadier officer wrote: "We have fought for fifteen days for a single house, with mortars, machine-guns, grenades and bayonets. The front is a corridor between burnt-out rooms . . . The street is no longer measured in metres, but in corpses. Stalingrad is no longer a town. By day it is an enormous cloud of burning, blinding smoke; it is a vast furnace lit by the reflection of the flames. And when night arrives— one of those scorching, howling, bleeding nights—the dogs plunge into the Volga and swim desperately for the other bank. The nights of Stalingrad are a terror for them. Animals flee this hell; the hardest stones cannot bear it for long; only men endure."

IT IS IMPORTANT to recognise that, while Chuikov's battle was critical, elsewhere along hundreds of miles of front fighting continued unabated through the autumn and winter, killing more people than perished at Stalingrad. "Hello, my dear Marusya and daughter Tanya!" the partisan commissar Pavel Kalitov wrote home from Ukraine. "This is to tell you that so far I am alive and in good health. We are still in the same place, i.e., the upper reaches of the river Shelon. We are experiencing hard fighting right now. The Germans have sent against us tanks, aircraft, artillery and mortars. Our partisans are fighting like lions. Vasya Bukov killed fifteen Germans with a rifle on 7 June. It is very hard to deal with them because they have the firepower. We are entirely dependent on local people for supplies, and they are really very good here. The Germans are many and we are few, that's why we don't sleep more than 2–3 hours a day. Yesterday I went to the *banya* [bath house] after the battle, and remembered how in peacetime one could sip a little glass of vodka after the *banya* and have a proper rest, and go fishing at weekends. How is your sister Shura feeling now? Has she put on a little weight now that you are feeding her after her experience of starvation in Leningrad?" He concluded optimistically, "The fascists aren't fighting as well this year as they did last."

Conditions in Leningrad progressively eased, though Russia's second city remained under bombardment. Its inhabitants were still desperately hungry, but most received just sufficient food to sustain life. In March

1942, the authorities launched a campaign to clear the streets of snow, debris and rubble, in which hundreds of thousands of citizens participated. In April, a new commander was appointed, Lt. Gen. Leonid Govorov. Though a taciturn man, the forty-five-year-old gunner was intelligent, cultured and humane. The NKVD reported from Leningrad during the summer: "In connection with the improvement in the food situation in June, the death rate went down by a third . . . The number of incidents of use of human flesh in food supply decreased. Whereas 236 people were arrested for this crime in May, in June it was just 56."

Yet for soldiers on the line in the north, horror remained a constant. Nikolai Nikulin noted in his diary on 18 August that all that was left of his own division was some cooks and NCOs. He complained that the morning issue of porridge was often laced with shrapnel, and he was tormented by thirst: "During the night I crawled twice to a shell crater for water. It was as thick and brown as coffee, and smelt of explosives and something else. In the morning, I saw a black crooked hand protruding from that crater. My tunic and trousers are as stiff as cardboard with mud and blood, the knees and elbows holed by crawling on them. I have thrown away my helmet—not many people wear them here; one normally shits into a helmet, then throws it out of the trench. The corpse near me stinks unbearably; there are so many of them around, old and new. Some turn black as they dry, and lie in all sorts of postures. Here and there in the trench one sees body parts trampled into the mud—a flattened face, a hand, all as brown as the soil. We walk on them."

At the end of August, the Germans suddenly abandoned their strategy of containment, and launched a major offensive to take Leningrad. When this failed, the Russians countered with their own attack, which achieved dramatic gains. Some cultural life revived in the city: there were art exhibitions, concerts, and a performance of Shostakovich's Seventh Symphony in the Philharmonic Hall. The people of Leningrad now had sufficient faith in their own survival to turn their minds to the plight of their fellow sufferers in Stalingrad. Vera Inber wrote: "It shows in the expression on people's faces, in the trams, on the streets: all the time we feel for Stalingrad . . . Now everything will be decided at Stalingrad—the whole fate of the war."

Through the winter of 1942, Leningrad continued to be bombed and shelled. One barrage began during a theatre performance: partway through the second act of the premiere of a comedy about the Baltic Fleet, *The Wide Wide Sea*, an actor appeared in front of the curtain and demanded of the audience, "What shall we do, comrades? Take shelter or continue?" There was thunderous applause and cries of "Continue!" On 12 January

1943, Govorov was ready to launch a new offensive to break the blockade. Zhukov revisited the city, and set his own stamp on operations. As usual indifferent to casualties, he demanded caustically, "Who are these cowards of yours who don't want to fight?" On 16 January, the key position of Shilisselburg was recaptured, and two days later it was formally announced that the blockade was broken. In the city, its famous poet Olga Berggolts wrote, "This happiness, the happiness of liberated Leningrad, we will never forget. The cursed circle is broken." On 3 March another citizen, Igor Chaiko, wrote, "A thought is forming in fiery letters in my mind: I can overcome anything . . . Spring is a symbol of life. The Germans are shelling us again, but the menace is shrinking in the sunlight."

Cats, almost of all which had been eaten, suddenly became useful again, to dispel a plague of rats: an entire trainload of feline warriors was dispatched to the city. German shelling, now inspired by mere malice rather than military purpose, continued throughout 1943—July witnessed the worst bombardment of the siege. Only in January 1944 did the Red Army launch the assault that finally pushed back the Germans beyond artillery range of the city. But Leningrad's fate was decided in the spring of 1942, when it became plain that its surviving inhabitants could be fed. It was officially stated that 632,253 people died in the course of the siege, but the true figure is assumed to be at least a million. Soviet propaganda suppressed reporting of much that happened during the city's agony. When Olga Berggolts visited Moscow to broadcast at the end of 1942, she was warned to say nothing about the siege's horrors: "They said that the Leningraders are heroes, but they don't know what that heroism consists of. They didn't know that we starved, they didn't know that people were dying of hunger."

Strategically, the northern struggle was much less important than the battle for Stalingrad. Nonetheless, Leningrad's experience was at least as significant in showing why the Soviet Union prevailed in the Second World War. It is unthinkable that British people would have eaten one another rather than surrender London or Birmingham—or would have been obliged by their generals and politicians to hold out at such a cost. Compulsion was a key element in Leningrad's survival, as in that of Stalin's nation. If the city's inhabitants had been offered an exchange of surrender for food in February 1942, they assuredly would have given up. But in the Soviet Union no such choice was available, and those who attempted to make it were shot. Both Hitler and Stalin displayed obsessive stubbornness about Leningrad. That of Stalin was finally rewarded, amid a mountain of corpses. A people who could endure such things displayed qualities the Western Allies lacked, which were indispensable to the destruction of

Nazism. In the auction of cruelty and sacrifice, the Soviet dictator proved the higher bidder.

EVEN AS THE DEFENDERS of Leningrad were experiencing a fragile revival of life and hope, farther east and south the Stavka launched its strategic counterstrokes. Operation Mars, which began on 25 November 1942, is almost forgotten, because it failed. Some 667,000 men and 1,900 tanks attempted an envelopment of the German Ninth Army which cost 100,000 Russian lives, and was repulsed. A battle that elsewhere in the world would have been deemed immense was scarcely noticed amid the eastern slaughter. Some men found any alternative preferable to fighting on. "Just as I lay down to rest before breakfast," wrote Capt. Nikolai Belov, "a runner came from the Commissar, summoning me to HQ. It turned out that soldier Sharonov had shot himself. What a scoundrel! He left the drill parade pleading sickness and ran into me on the way to his quarters, all doubled up. I ordered him to stay in my dugout under guard, but finding it momentarily empty he took the opportunity to shoot himself."

Fortunately for Stalin, Zhukov and the Allied cause in the Second World War, the other great Soviet operation of the winter, Uranus, was vastly more successful than Mars. The Germans lacked strength adequately to man their enormous front. There was a 300-mile gap between the Second Army at Voronezh on the upper Don and the Fourth and Sixth Panzer Armies southeastwards at Stalingrad. Short of manpower, von Weichs, the army group commander, deployed Hungarian, Italian and Romanian formations to cover the flanks of the Sixth Army: German intelligence then failed to identify powerful Soviet forces massing against the Romanians. On 19 November Zhukov opened his offensive, hurling six armies against the northern Axis perimeter, followed by a thrust westward the next day by the Stalingrad *front* south of the city.

A German antitank gunner, Henry Metelmann, was supporting the Romanians when the Russian offensive struck. "The whole place trembled, bits of earth fell on us and the noise was deafening. We were sleep-drunk, and kept bumping into each other, mixing up our boots, uniforms and other equipment, and shouting out loudly to relieve our tension. We went out from one bedlam into another, an inferno of noise and explosions . . . Everything was in utter turmoil and I heard much shouting and crying from the Romanian forward line . . . Then we heard the heavy clanging of tracks. Someone further along quite unnecessarily shouted: 'They are coming!' And then we saw the first of them, crawling out of the greyness." The Russian armour rolled over Metelmann's gun, all of its crew save himself, and two Romanian armies, whose soldiers surrendered in tens of thousands. Many were shot down, while survivors in their distinctive white hats were transported downriver by barge to prison camps. A Russian sailor, gazing upon a crowd of POWs staring listlessly at the ice floes, observed that the captives had been eager to glimpse the Volga: "Well, they've seen the Volga now." Romania paid dearly for its adherence to the Axis, suffering 600,000 casualties in the course of the eastern campaigns.

On 16 December the river froze, and the ice quickly became thick enough to bear trucks and guns. In the ruins of Stalingrad, fighting ebbed. The critical battles were now taking place south and westwards. Five days later, Soviet tanks completed a perfect double envelopment behind Paulus's Sixth Army: Zhukov's spearheads met east of the Don crossing at Kalach. Many times in the course of the war the Russians achieved such encirclements; many times also, the Germans broke out of them. What was different here was that Hitler rejected the pleas of Sixth Army's commander for such a retreat. Paulus was ordered to continue his assault on Stalingrad, while Manstein began an attack from the west to restore contact with the Sixth Army. By 23 December, his spearheads had battered a passage to within thirty miles of Stalingrad. Then they stuck. Manstein urged Paulus to defy Hitler and break out to join him, as was still feasible. The Sixth Army's commander refused, condemning 200,000 men to death or captivity. Manstein's forces were spent, and he ordered a general retreat.

ALONG THE ENTIRE GERMAN FRONT in the east, the approach of Christmas prompted a surge of sentimentality. Every Sunday afternoon, most men within reach of a radio listened to the request programme *Wunschkonzert für die Wehrmacht*, broadcast from Berlin to provide a link between soldiers and families at home. Relentlessly patriotic, it highlighted such numbers as "*Glocken der Heimat*" ("Bells of the Homeland") and "*Panzer rollen in Afrika vor*" ("Panzers Roll in Africa"). Soldiers loved to hear Zarah Leander sing "*Ich weiss es wird einmal ein Wunder gescheh'n*," a special favourite of German civilians: "I know, one day a miracle will happen / And then a thousand fairy tales will come true / I know that a love cannot die / That is so great and wonderful."

Many Germans, especially the young, were gripped by a paranoia no less real for being rooted in Nazi fantasies. Luftwaffe pilot Heinz Knoke succumbed to emotion on Christmas Eve, listening to "*Stille Nacht, Heilige Nacht*"—"Silent Night": "This is the most beautiful of all German carols. Even the British, the French and the Americans are singing it tonight. Do they know that it is a German song? And do they fully appreciate its true significance? Why do people all over the world hate us Germans, and yet still sing German songs, play music by such German composers as Beethoven and Bach, and recite the works of the great German poets? Why?" Paratrooper Martin Poppel wrote in the same spirit from Russia:

> Our thoughts and conversations turn towards home, to our loved ones, our Führer and our Fatherland. We're not afraid to cry as we stand to remember our Führer and our fallen comrades. It's like an oath binding us together, making us grit our teeth and carry on until victory . . . At home, they'll be sitting under the Christmas tree as well. I can see my brave old Daddy, see him stand and drink with reddened eyes to the soldiers. And my courageous mother, she'll certainly be crying a bit, and my little sister too. But one day there'll be another New Year when we can all be together, happily reunited after a victorious end to the mass slaughter of the nations. That superior spirit which moves the young people must lead us to victory: there is no alternative.

The sentiments of these young men, cogs in a war machine that had wreaked untold misery, reflected the triumph of Goebbels's educational and propaganda machine as well as the tragedy of Europe to which it contributed so much. That Christmas of 1942 in Russia, millions of German soldiers approached a rendezvous with the collapse of their leader's insane ambitions that would hasten many to their graves.

Göring professed the Luftwaffe's ability to supply the German forces isolated in the Stalingrad pocket—though the most rudimentary calculation showed that such airlift capacity was lacking. Through December, as ammunition and rations dwindled, Paulus's men lost ground, men, tanks, and soon hope. On 16 January 1943, a Wehrmacht officer at Stalingrad wrote in a valedictory letter to his wife: "The implacable struggle continues. God helps the brave! Whatever Providence may ordain, we ask for one thing, for strength to hold on! Let it be said of us one day that the German army fought at Stalingrad as soldiers never before in the world have fought. To pass this spirit on to our children is the task of mothers." To most of those trapped in Paulus's pocket, however, such heroic sentiments represented flatulence.

On 12 January, four Russian *fronts* struck at Army Group Don, north of Stalingrad, driving back the Axis forces in disarray. The Pasubio Division, part of the Italian Eighth Army in the Don pocket, found itself struggling westwards. Without fuel, the hapless troops were obliged to ditch heavy weapons and take to their feet. "Vehicles complete with loads were being abandoned along the road," wrote artillery lieutenant Eugenio Corti. "It broke my heart to see them. How much effort and expense that equipment must have cost Italy!" If exhausted men sought to snatch rides on German vehicles, they were thrown off with yells and curses.

Corti made ineffectual efforts to preserve discipline in his unit. "But how can you expect people who are unused to being well-ordered in normal civilian life to become orderly . . . simply because they find themselves in uniform? As enemy fire rained down, the rabble quickened its stumbling pace. I now witnessed one of the most wretched scenes of the whole retreat: Italians killing Italians . . . We had ceased to be an army; I was no longer with soldiers but with creatures incapable of controlling themselves, obedient to a single animal instinct: self-preservation." He cursed his own softness, in failing to shoot a man who defied orders that only the wounded should ride on the few sledges. "Countless instances of weakness like mine accounted for the confusion in which we found ourselves . . . A German soldier in our midst was beside himself with contempt. I had to admit he was right . . . we were dealing with undisciplined, bewildered men."

At a dressing station, "the wounded were lying atop one another. When one of the few orderlies tending them appeared with a little water, to the groaning was added the cries of those he inadvertently trod upon. Outside, straw had been laid on the snow, on which several hundred men were lying . . . it must have been –15 or –20 degrees. The dead lay mingled with the wounded. One doctor did the rounds: he himself had been twice wounded by shell splinters while performing amputations with a cut-throat razor."

Whichever of the warring armies held the ascendant, Russian sufferings persisted. In a peasant hut, Corti came upon a stricken family. "I was greeted by the corpse of a gigantic old man with a long whiteish beard lying in a pool of blood . . . Cowering against a wall, terror-stricken, were three or four women and five or six children—Russians, thin, delicate, waxen-faced. A soldier was calmly eating cooked potatoes . . . How warm it was in that house! I urged the women and children to do their eating before more soldiers arrived and gobbled the lot." Axis troops were often bemused and impressed by the stoicism of the Russians, who seemed to them victims of communism rather than enemies. Even after the alien invaders had brought untold misery upon their country, simple country-folk sometimes displayed a human sympathy for afflicted and suffering

Axis soldiers which moved them. Corti wrote: "During halts on those marches many of our compatriots were rescued from frostbite by the self-less, maternal care of poor women."

Throughout that terrible retreat, Hitler's allies cursed the Luftwaffe, which dropped supplies only to German units. Corti wrote: "We watched those aircraft avidly: we found their form and colour repugnant and alien, like the uniforms of German soldiers . . . If only the familiar outline of some Italian plane had come into sight! If only the slightest thing had been dropped for us, but nothing came!" The Italians' misery was compounded by censorship at home which kept their families in ignorance of those perishing in the snow: "Back in the distant *patria* nobody knew of their sacrifice. We of the army in Russia lived out our tragedy while the radio and newspapers went on about other things altogether. It was as if the entire nation had forgotten us."

Corti recoiled from the spectacle of Germans massacring Russian prisoners, though he knew that the Red Army often did likewise to its own captives. "It was extremely painful—for we were civilised men—to be caught up in that savage clash between barbarians." He was torn between disgust at the Germans' ruthlessness, "which at times disqualified them in my eyes from membership of the human family," and grudging respect for their strength of will. He deplored their contempt for other races. He heard of their officers shooting men too badly wounded to move, of rapes and murders, of sledges loaded with Italian wounded hijacked by the Wehrmacht. But he was also awed by the manner in which German soldiers instinctively performed their duties, even without an officer or NCO to give orders. "I . . . asked myself . . . what would have become of us without the Germans. I was reluctantly forced to admit that alone, we Italians would have ended up in enemy hands . . . I . . . thanked heaven that they were with us there in the column . . . Without a shadow of a doubt, as soldiers they have no equal."

Again and again, German tanks and Stukas drove back pursuing Russian armour, enabling the retreating columns to struggle on amid murderous Soviet mortaring. One Italian soldier's testicles were sliced away by a shell splinter. Thrusting them in his pocket, the man bound the wound with string and trudged onwards. Next day at a dressing station, he lowered his trousers; fumbling in his pocket, according to Eugenio Corti's account, he proffered to a doctor "in the palm of his hand the blackish testicles mixed with biscuit crumbs, asking whether they could be sewn back on." Corti survived to reach the railhead at Yasinovataya, and thence travelled through Poland to Germany. A hospital train at last bore him home to his beloved Italy. At the end of 1942 an Italian general asserted that 99 percent of his fellow countrymen not merely expected to lose the war, but now fervently hoped to do so as swiftly as possible.

IN JANUARY 1943, the German line in the east suffered a succession of crippling blows. On the twelfth, in the far north, the Russians launched an attack which, at the end of five days' fighting, opened a corridor along the shore of Lake Ladoga that broke the siege of Leningrad. A simultaneous assault farther south recaptured Voronezh and wrecked the Hungarian formations of Hitler's armies. In late January, Soviet forces closed on Rostov, threatening German forces in the Caucasus, which were soon confined to a bridgehead at Taman, just east of the Crimea. On 31 January, Paulus surrendered the remains of the Sixth Army at Stalingrad. Zhukov became the first wartime Soviet commander to receive a marshal's baton, soon joined by Alexander Vasilievsky, the chief of the General Staff, and Stalin himself. On 8 February the Russians entered Kursk, and a week later Rostov; they took Kharkov on the sixteenth.

Stalingrad transformed the morale of the Red Army. A soldier named Ageev wrote home: "I'm in an exceptional mood. If you only knew, then you'd be just as happy as I am. Imagine it—the Fritzes are running away from us!" Vasily Grossman was disgusted by what he perceived as the gross egoism of Chuikov and other commanders, vying with one another to claim credit for the Red Army's victories: "There's no modesty. 'I did it, I, I, I, I, I . . .' They speak about other commanders without any respect, recounting some ridiculous gossip." But, after the horrors and failures of the previous year, who could grudge Stalin's generals their outburst of triumphalism? The struggle for Stalingrad had cost 240,000 Russian dead, many of them consigned to unmarked graves because superstition made *frontoviks*, as Russians termed fighting soldiers, reluctant to wear identity capsules, the Red Army's equivalent of dog tags. A further 320,000 sick or wounded men were evacuated. A grand total of some 600,000 military and civilian dead perished around Stalingrad and in related battles. But this butcher's bill seemed acceptable as the price of a victory that changed the course of the war.

The Allied world rejoiced alongside Stalin's people. "The killing of thousands of Germans in Russia makes pleasant reading now," wrote British civilian Herbert Brush on 26 November 1942, "and I hope it will be kept up for a long time yet. It is the only way to convert young Germans. I wonder how the Russians will treat the prisoners they capture . . . it will show whether the Russians are really converted to civilised life." The answer to Brush's speculation was that many German prisoners were killed or allowed to starve or freeze, because the contest in barbarism had become unstoppable.

The Red Army achieved stunning advances in the first months of 1943, gaining up to 150 miles in the north, before coming to a halt beyond Kursk. Soviet generalship sometimes displayed brilliance, but mass remained the key element in the Red Army's successes. Discipline was erratic, and units were vulnerable to mass panics and desertions. Command incompetence was often compounded by drunkenness. Capt. Nikolai Belov recorded scenes during an attack that were not untypical:

> The day of battle. I slept through the artillery bombardment. After about 1½ hours, I woke and ran to the telephone to check the situation. Then I ran up the communication trench to 1st Rifle Battalion, where I found its commander Captain Novikov and chief of staff Grudin dashing about with pistols in their hands. When I asked them to report, they said they were leading their men to attack. Both were drunk, and I ordered them to holster their weapons.
>
> There were piles of corpses in the trenches and on the parapets, among them that of Captain Sovkov, whom Novikov had killed—I was told that he had shot a lot of [our own] soldiers. I told Novikov, Grudin and Aikazyan that unless they joined the forward company, I would kill them myself. But instead of advancing towards the river, they headed for the rear. I gave them a burst of sub-machine-gun fire, but Novikov somehow found his way back into the trench. I pushed him forward with my own hands. He was soon wounded, and Grudin brought him in on his back. Both of them, notorious cowards, were of course delighted. Assuming command of the battalion myself, in the evening I crossed the Oka river to join the leading company of Lieutenant Util'taev. When night fell, I advanced with three companies, but the assault failed.

The fundamental cause of the disasters which befell the German armies in Russia in the winter of 1942–43 was that they had undertaken a task beyond their nation's powers. The Wehrmacht was saved from immediate disaster only by the generalship of Field Marshal Erich von Manstein. Hitler had said grudgingly back in 1940, "The man is not to my liking, but he is capable." Manstein was almost certainly the ablest German general of the war. In March he stabilised his line, launched a counterattack which retook Kharkov, and checked the momentum that had borne forward the Soviet spearheads from the Volga to the Donets, thus securing Hitler another breathing space.

But for what? The balance of advantage on the Eastern Front had shifted decisively and irrevocably against Germany. The power of the Soviet Union and its armies was growing fast, while that of the invaders shrank. In 1942, Germany produced just 4,800 armoured vehicles, while Russia built 24,000. The new T-34 tank, better than anything the Germans then deployed save the Tiger, began to appear in quantity—Chelyabinsk, one of Stalin's massive manufacturing centres in the Urals, became known as Tankograd. That year also, Russia built 21,700 aircraft to Germany's 14,700. The Red Army deployed 6 million men, supported by a further 516,000 NKVD troops. In the winter fighting of 1942–43, Germany lost a million dead, along with vast quantities of matériel.

The Wehrmacht's combat performance remained superior to that of the Red Army: until the end of the war, in almost every local action the Germans inflicted more casualties than they received. But their tactical skills no longer sufficed to stem the Russian tide. Stalin was identifying good generals, building vast armies with formidable tank and artillery strength, and at last receiving large deliveries from the Western Allies, including food, vehicles and communications equipment. The 5 million tons of American meat that eventually reached Russia amounted to half a pound of rations a day for every Soviet soldier. Allied food shipments probably averted a starvation catastrophe in the winter of 1942–43.

Of the Red Army's 665,000 vehicles in 1945, 427,000 were American-built, including 51,000 jeeps. The United States provided half the Red Army's boots—loss of livestock made leather scarce—almost 2,000 railway locomotives, 15,000 aircraft, 247,000 telephones and nearly 4 million tyres. "Our army suddenly found itself on wheels—and what wheels!" said Anastas Mikoyan with a generosity uncharacteristic of Stalin's ministers. "When we started to receive American canned beef, fat, powdered eggs and other foodstuffs, this was worth a lot of extra calories." Mikoyan believed that Lend-Lease supplies shortened the war by a year to eighteen months.

It was plain to Hitler's commanders that victory in the east was no longer attainable. The only issue for Germany was how long its armies could withstand Russia's relentlessly growing strength. When spring prompted the melting of the Volga's ice, among a host of horrors revealed by the thaw were the bodies of a Russian and a German, victims of Stalingrad, clasped in a death embrace. Yet already that German's living compatriots were more than 300 miles westward, embarked upon a retreat that would never be reversed.

CHAPTER THIRTEEN

LIVING WITH WAR

1. Warriors

THE EXPERIENCE OF WAR was extraordinarily diverse. The Eastern Front, where 90 percent of all Germans killed in combat met their fate, overwhelmingly dominated the struggle against Hitler. Between 1941 and 1944, British and American sailors and airmen fought at sea and in the sky, but relatively small numbers of Western Allied ground troops engaged the Axis in North Africa, Italy, Asia and the Pacific. Much larger Anglo-American forces spent those years training and exercising: when the 1st Norfolks went into action at Kohima in June 1944, for instance, it was the battalion's first battle since leaving France through Dunkirk in May 1940. Many other British and American units experienced equally protracted delays before joining the fray. The conflict was a pervasive circumstance for the peoples of Britain and its white dominions, and to a lesser extent the United States, but it imposed serious peril and hardship on only a relatively small minority of men "at the sharp end" of ground combat. At sea, fatalities in most naval battles were counted in hundreds. In the sky, airmen suffered high proportionate losses, but these were dwarfed by those of the eastern land campaign.

The Soviet Union suffered 65 percent of all Allied military deaths, China 23 percent, Yugoslavia 3 percent, the United States and Britain 2 percent each, France and Poland 1 percent each. About 8 percent of all Germans died, compared with 2 percent of Chinese, 3.44 percent of Dutch people, 6.67 percent of Yugoslavs, 4 percent of Greeks, 1.35 percent of French, 3.78 percent of Japanese, 0.94 percent of British and 0.32 percent of Americans. Within the armed forces, 30.9 percent of Germans conscripted into the Wehrmacht died, 17.35 percent of the Luftwaffe (including paratroopers and ground personnel), 34.9 percent of the Waffen SS. Some 24.2 percent of Japanese soldiers were killed, and 19.7 percent of naval personnel. Japanese formations committed against the Americans and British in 1944–45 lost far more heavily—the overall statistics are distorted by the fact that throughout the war a million of Hirohito's soldiers remained in China, where they suffered relatively modest losses. One Russian soldier in four died, against one in twenty British

Commonwealth combatants and one in thirty-four American servicemen. Some 3.66 percent of U.S. Marines died, compared with 2.5 percent of the U.S. Army and 1.5 percent of the U.S. Navy.

The war promoted an almost contradictory blend of callousness and intense sentimentality. A modest number of those fighting contrived to enjoy themselves, usually when their own side was winning—Germans and Japanese in the early years, Americans and British thereafter. Young people who relished adventure found this readily available. Lt. Robert Hichens of the Royal Navy wrote in July 1940: "I suppose our position is about as dangerous as is possible in view of the threatened invasion, but I couldn't help being full of joy . . . Being on the bridge of one of HM ships, being talked to by the captain as an equal, and knowing that she was to be in my sole care for the next few hours. Who would not rather die like that than live as so many poor people have to, in crowded cities at some sweating indoor job?" Hichens was killed in 1942, but he was a happy warrior.

Special forces—the "private armies" regarded with mixed feelings by more conventional warriors—attracted bold spirits careless about risking their lives in piratical enterprises by land and sea. Between 1940 and 1944, partly because Churchill's soldiers were unable to confront the Wehrmacht in Europe, British raiding units conducted many small operations of a kind the U.S. chiefs of staff mistrusted, though American airborne units and Rangers later played conspicuous roles in the northwest Europe campaign. The prime minister promoted raids on German outposts to show aggression, test tactics and equipment, and sustain a façade of momentum in the British war effort. Probably the most cost-effective of these took place on the night of 27 February 1942, when a small contingent of the newly formed Parachute Regiment assaulted a German radar station on a clifftop at Bruneval, near Le Havre on the French coast.

The objective was reconnoitred by local French Resistance workers before 120 paratroopers led by Maj. John Frost dropped into thick snow, secured the position against slight resistance from the surprised Luftwaffe radar crew, and held it while an RAF technician, Flight Sergeant Charles Cox, coolly dismantled key components of its Wurzburg scanner. The force then fought its way down to the beach for evacuation by landing craft, having lost only two men killed and six taken prisoner. The captured technology proved invaluable to British scientific intelligence. Churchill and the chiefs of staff were impressed by this first test of their paratroops, and endorsed a big expansion of such units. The Bruneval raid, trumpeted by Allied propaganda, was indeed a fine example of daring and initiative, aided by luck and an unusually feeble German response.

Such operations worked best when carried out by small forces pursuing limited objectives; more ambitious raids achieved more equivocal outcomes. A month after Bruneval, 268 commandos landed at Saint-Nazaire, while an old destroyer rammed the gate of the port's big floating dock. Next day, five tons of explosive detonated as planned aboard the destroyer, destroying the lock gates and killing many German sightseers as well as two captured commando officers who had concealed their knowledge of the impending explosion. But 144 of the attackers were killed and more than 200 army and naval personnel were taken prisoner. During the big assault on Dieppe in August 1942, the Germans suffered 591 ground casualties, but two-thirds of the 6,000 raiders, mostly Canadian, were killed, wounded or captured. By 1944, when Allied armies were deployed in major campaigns, British commando and airborne forces had been allowed to outgrow their usefulness, absorbing a larger share of elite personnel than their battlefield achievements justified. In the earlier war years, however, they made a useful morale contribution and delighted their participants.

Many professional soldiers welcomed the career opportunities Hitler provided. Those who survived and displayed competence gained promotions in months that in peacetime would have taken years; commanders unknown outside their regiments one summer could achieve fame and fortune by the next. In five years Dwight Eisenhower—admittedly an exceptional example—rose from colonel to full general. "One of the fascinations of [the] war," in the words of British lieutenant general Sir Frederick Morgan, "was to see how Americans developed their great men so quickly . . . Ike grew almost as one watched him."

Britain's Sir Bernard Montgomery advanced from being a lieutenant general in August 1942, unknown outside his service, to become an army group commander and national hero just two years later. At lower levels, many regular officers who entered the war as lieutenants became colonels or brigadiers by their mid-twenties. Horatius Murray, for instance, in 1939 after sixteen years' service had only attained the rank of major, but finished the war as a lieutenant general. On the other side, the Wehrmacht's Capt. Rolf-Helmut Schröder remembered his campaign experience "with gratitude," despite being wounded three times. Likewise Maj. Karl-Gunther von Haase, who survived captivity in Russian hands: "In the early war years we were proud to belong to the German army. I look back on my military career not without satisfaction."

Some people found that bearing their share of their nation's struggle for conquest or freedom rendered sorrows tolerable and ennobled loneliness and danger. But the humbler their personal circumstances, the slighter seemed the compensations for sacrifice. William Crawford, a seventeen-year-old boy 2nd class serving aboard the battle cruiser *Hood*, wrote home miserably: "Dearest Mum . . . I know it's wrong to say but I sure am fed up. I feel kind of sick, I can'nae eat and my heart's in my mouth. We struck bad weather today. Talk about waves as big as houses, they're crashing over our bows . . . I wonder if it would do any good Mum if you wrote to the Admiralty and asked them if there was no chance of me getting a shore job at Rosyth. You know, tell them you have got two sons away and that. Be sure to tell them my age. If only I could get off this ship it would not be so bad." Crawford, however, was still aboard *Hood* when she was sunk with almost all hands in May 1941.

As his letter illustrates, stoicism was no more universal among sailors at sea than soldiers on the battlefield. "I am absolutely fed up with everything," a naval paymaster, Cmdr. Jackie Jackson, wrote to his wife from the Mediterranean in May 1941. "The dirt and filth, the flies and heat and more than anything the fact that I am not hearing from you." He complained that he had received only one letter in six weeks, "the most depressing I have ever received in my life. Add to that a cable which more or less implied that the house has been wrecked and you can get a fair idea of how much I want to hear from you occasionally, and at the same time how I dread it, as I am probably going to have even worse news and more complaints . . . I've had a hideous time and I wonder why I'm alive." It is easy to see why such people as Winston Churchill, George Patton or pilots flying Mustangs or Spitfires—a small and privileged minority—enjoyed the war. It is equally apparent why many others—especially a Russian infantryman or Chinese peasant, a Polish Jew or Greek farmer—could not.

Most of those who fought clung stubbornly to their own amateur status, performing a wholly unwelcome duty before returning to their "real" lives. As a twenty-four-year-old lieutenant in action against the Germans with the King's Own Scottish Borderers, Peter White reflected: "It must take about seven years . . . to make a being feel really like a soldier and not just a civilian dressed up. The situation seemed so ludicrously unreal and yet grimly real at the same time. We could at least comfort ourselves with the knowledge that the poor blighters opposite us were in the same boat even though it was a boat of their seeking." John Hersey wrote of the marines on Guadalcanal: "The uniforms, the bravado . . . were just camouflage. They were just American boys. They did not want that valley or any part of its jungle. They were ex-grocery boys, ex–highway laborers, ex–bank clerks, ex-schoolboys, boys with a clean record . . . not killers."

RAF corporal Peter Baxter lamented: "My whole generation . . . are wasting some of the finest years of their lives in the dreary business of war. Our manhood has come to full fruition, but it is stifling and decaying in these wasted years . . . The deadening, paralysing influence of service life has blighted my middle twenties." Many young men had never before lived away from home, and they hated the indignities and discomforts of barracks existence. Frank Novy, a twenty-one-year-old, spent his first night in the army at a depot in Leeds. "After a few minutes on the palliasse I heard complaints from all sides. My own was terribly hard, and I had no pillow, my teeth were aching and soon I had a headache. I felt depressed and tired out. I tried to sleep, but I kept thinking of home, and all I had left went round and round in my head, ceaselessly, persistently . . . At times I felt so depressed that I wanted to cry, but couldn't."

Recruits found themselves growing new skins. Len England described how a fellow soldier delivered a stream of wisecracks to a girl behind the counter in the YMCA, then turned to England and said in surprise, "I've never flirted before in my life. I've only been in the army five days, and now look at what I'm doing." England observed that he and his new comrades felt like different people, "more authoritative and self-assertive in uniform." Educated men recoiled from the crude banality of barracks vocabulary: among Americans, everything seemed to be "tough shit"; an alleged coward "was shaking like a pup shitting carpet tacks"; and civilians who escaped military service were "4-F bastards."

No sentence was complete without its obscene expletives: the fucking officers made them dig fucking foxholes before they received fucking rations or stood fucking guard. Even the most delicately reared recruits acquired this universal military habit of speech, though officers' messes aspired to more gentility. Cultured men were pained by translation into a world in which art, music, and literature had no place. Capt. Pavel Kovalenko of the Red Army wrote one night in the line: "After dinner I sat down to read Nekrasov. My God, when will I be able to spend as much time as I want enjoying Pushkin, Lermontov, Nekrasov. I saw a photograph of Tolstoy as a young man in officer's uniform . . . Tears choked in my throat, almost overwhelming me."

Capt. David Elliott of the Welsh Guards found himself "terribly depressed" on returning to his barracks in Britain after a weekend leave: "There is nothing so utterly boring, so utterly narrow and so utterly petty as regimental soldiering which lacks the accompaniment of a state of battle . . . Certainly in this battalion there is no charity, no loving kindness, no loyalty . . . Among the officers, if not among the men, there are many problem children." While embryo airmen revelled in the thrills of flight training, few recruits found comparable compensations in discovering how to become infantrymen. Pfc. "Red" Thompson, from Staten Island, New York, felt that he acquired limited skills: "I learned to take care of myself; to be wary, to look and listen; and to dig holes." Every soldier became reflexively familiar with the order "Get your gear on and stand by to move out," usually with scant notion of where he was going. Ignorance of anything beyond a man's field of vision was the norm. As a 1942 recruit training in North Carolina, nineteen-year-old Missourian Tony Moody decided that he and his comrades cherished no lust for glory: "We somehow hoped we wouldn't be in harm's way."

Pressures on manpower caused the conscription of more than a few recruits who should never have been obliged to serve. "My comrades were mostly from Yorkshire and Lancashire," wrote the eighteen-year-old Pvt. Ron Davidson.

> The 1930s had been a bad time for many and physically some found things very difficult and others were barely literate. I remember one who did not make the grade, aneuretic and also sub-normal—needless to say he had been passed A1 by the army doctors! He could just about dress himself, but the intricacies of army gear were beyond him and we used to get him into it. We used to lay out his kit in the prescribed manner, but this was done at night so [he] slept on the wooden floor which he regularly wet. The army in its wisdom decided [he] was "idle" and a malingerer and set about "waking him up a bit." This took the form of huge P[hysical] T[raining] I[nstructor]s chasing him all over the barrack square, yelling in his ear the most frightful obscenities.

This misfit was eventually discharged, but most rifle platoons included one or two subnormal men, whose conduct in battle was unsurprisingly erratic. British soldier William Chappell avowed his own submission to military service, but never ceased to ache for the civilian world from which he had been torn: "I accept this life. I accept the loss of my home, the collapse of my career, the bomb that injured my mother, the wide scattering and disintegration of the web of friendship I had woven so painstakingly for myself . . . I still want the same things. More chocolate; longer hours in bed; easily acquired hot baths, delicious, varied and delicate food; all my own possessions around me . . . I am bothered by my feet, sick of khaki, bored and annoyed by my companions, all the monotonous, slow, fiddle-de-dee of army life. I long for it all to be finished with, and sometimes vaguely envy those who have gone."

An American officer wrote from the Pacific: "When the tents are down, I think every man feels a loneliness because he sees that this wasn't home after all. As long as there were four canvas walls about him, he could kid himself a little . . . Standing on barren ground surrounded by scrap lumber piles and barracks bags with nothing familiar on his horizon he feels uprooted and insecure, a wanderer on the face of the earth. That which is always in the back of his mind now stands starkly in the front: 'Will it ever end, and will I be here to see it?' " Staff Sgt. Harold Fennema wrote to his wife, Jeannette, in Wisconsin: "So much of this war and army life amounts to the insignificant job of passing time, and that really is a pity. Life is so short and time so precious to those who live and love life that I can hardly believe myself, seeking entertainment to pass time away . . . I wonder sometimes where this is going to lead." Yet if camp life was monotonous, at least it was closer to home than the theatres of war. Pfc. Eugene Gagliardi, a nineteen-year-old newspaper pressman from Brooklyn, regarded his entire later experience of service in Europe as "a nightmare. All my good memories of the army were before we went to France."

Active service, when it came, changed everything. The American correspondent E. J. Kahn wrote from New Guinea: "As an urban selectee's military career progresses, he changes gradually from a preponderantly indoor being into a wholly outdoor one." The marine Eugene Sledge recoiled from the brutish state to which the battlefield reduced him: "The personal bodily filth imposed upon the combat infantryman by living conditions on the battlefield was difficult for me to tolerate. It bothered almost everyone I knew . . . I stunk! My mouth felt . . . like I had gremlins walking around in it with muddy boots on . . . Short as it was, my hair was matted with dust and rifle oil. My scalp itched, and my stubble beard was becoming an increasing source of irritation in the heat. Drinking water was far too precious . . . to use in brushing one's teeth or in shaving, even if the opportunity had arisen."

Combat opened a chasm between those who experienced its horrors and those at home who did not. In December 1943, the Canadian Farley Mowat wrote to his family from the Sangro front in Italy: "The damnable truth is we are in really different worlds, on totally different planes, and I don't really know you any more, I only know the you that was. I wish I could explain the desperate sense of isolation, of not belonging to my own past, of being adrift in some kind of alien space. It is one of the toughest things we have to bear—that and the primal, gut-rotting worm of fear."

The great Duke of Wellington justly remarked, "Believe me, not every man who wears a military uniform is a hero." In all armies, soldiers serving with forward combat units shared a contempt for the much larger number of men in the rear areas who fulfilled roles in which they faced negligible risk: the infantry bore 90 percent of global army casualties. An American or British rifleman who entered France in June 1944 faced a 60 percent prospect of being killed or wounded before the end of the campaign, rising to 70 percent for officers. Armoured and artillery units suffered much smaller proportionate losses, and those in the huge logistics "tail" were exposed to no greater statistical risk of death or mishap than industrial workers at home.

Bombardment imposed an intense trauma. "There was nothing subtle or intimate about the approach and explosion of an artillery shell," wrote Eugene Sledge, remembering Peleliu:

> When I heard the whistle of an approaching one in the distance, every muscle in my body contracted. I braced myself in a puny effort to keep from being swept away. I felt utterly helpless. As the fiendish whistle grew louder, my teeth ground against each other, my heart pounded, my mouth dried, my eyes narrowed, sweat poured over me, my breath came in short irregular gasps, and I was afraid to swallow lest I choke. I always prayed, sometimes out loud. I felt utterly helpless . . . To me, artillery was an invention of hell. The onrushing whistle and scream of the big steel package of destruction was the pinnacle of violent fury and the embodiment of pent-up evil. It was the essence of violence and of man's inhumanity to man. I developed a passionate hatred for shells. To be killed by a bullet seemed so clean and surgical. But shells would not only tear and rip the body, they tortured one's mind almost beyond the brink of sanity. After each shell I was wrung out, limp and exhausted.

Enforced passivity in the face of bombardment was among the most dismal predicaments of every soldier. "Give a Jock a rifle or a bren gun and allow him to use it, and however frightened he may be he will face up to most things," wrote Capt. Alastair Borthwick of the 5th Seaforth Highlanders. "Put him, inactive, in a trench and danger becomes progressively more difficult to bear. Fear is insidious, and it grows in inactivity." Most soldiers discovered a special horror in enduring a mortar barrage—one fancifully likened the sudden, repetitive dull crumps to the sound of a woman beating a carpet. Bombs which detonated in overhead trees broadcast deadly wood splinters and steel shards across the area below. Peter White was overcome by pity for one of his soldiers amid such an assault:

> Young Cutter, who was really quite unsuitable for such a pastime, gave way completely each time we listened with fascination to the plopping of the bombs' ascent from the enemy hill and lay quivering during the tantalisingly long wait for the whisper of their descent which sounded

for a moment before our surroundings erupted to shattering crashes painful to the ear. As each climax came, the whimpering misery of Pte. Cutter broke out in an uncontrollable stream of verbal pleading. He recovered enough in between to murmur "I'm sorry, Sir" . . . I felt a wealth of sympathy for Cutter, but dared not show it for I felt he would just collapse the more. He had so lost control of himself by the time a pause arrived long enough for us to scamper out and continue digging that I told him to stop where he was until he had collected his wits. He was in such a state his condition might have put ideas into the heads of others. He grovelled in the sand moaning "Oh God! Oh God, when will it stop . . . Sir . . . I, sorry. God! Oh stop it." No one mocked him or made fun. We had all tasted too vividly of the ordeal ourselves to feel anything but great compassion.

With experience, men overcame their initial delusion that all those who found themselves beneath a storm of high explosive must be doomed to die: they discovered that most soldiers survive most battles. Thereafter, it became a matter of personal taste whether an individual decided that he himself was bound to be among the fortunate or condemned to join the dead. "We had learned our first lesson, that fate, not the Germans or Italians, was our undiscriminating enemy," wrote a Royal Engineers corporal in Sicily. "With the same callousness as Army orders; without fairness or judgement. 'You and you dead, the rest of you, on the truck.' " Farley Mowat wrote in August 1943 with the gaucherie of his twenty-two years: "It's hard for guys my age to grasp that nobody lives forever. Dying is just a word until you find out differently. That's trite but horribly true. The first few times you almost get nicked you take it for granted you are almost immortal. The next few times you begin to wonder. After that you start looking over your shoulder to make sure old Lady Luck is still around."

Many men fantasised about earning the privilege of a light wound, what the British called "a Blighty one," which would enable them honourably to escape the battlefield. Chance, however, was often ungenerous: a young officer of the Burma Rifles was flown fresh from India to join an embattled Chindit column in 1944. On the very night of his arrival, he had been in action for less than two hours when a bullet lodged in his right thigh, severing his penis and right testicle. Corp. James Jones wrote of Guadalcanal: "It's funny, the things that get to you. One day a man near me was hit in the throat, as he stood up, by a bullet from a burst of MG fire. He cried out, 'Oh My God!' in an awful, grimly comic, burbling kind of voice that made me think of the signature of the old Shep Fields' Rippling Rhythm band. There was awareness in it, and a tone of having expected it, then he fell down, to all intents and purposes dead. I say 'to all intents and purposes' because his vital functions may have continued for a while."

Jones suggested that some men found consolation in resigning themselves to the apparent inevitability of their own deaths: "Strangely, for everyone, the acceptance and the giving-up of hope create and reinstil hope in a kind of reverse-process mental photonegative function. Little things become significant. The next meal, the next bottle of booze, the next kiss, the next sunrise, the next full moon. The next bath. Or as the Bible might have said, but didn't quite, Sufficient unto the day is the existence thereof."

The grotesque became normal. "One learned to accept things one would not have thought possible," said Dr. Karl-Ludwig Mahlo, a German army medical officer. Hans Moser, a sixteen-year-old gunlayer with an 88mm flak battery in Silesia, was surprised to find himself unmoved when an explosion killed the neighbouring crew, leaving their gunpit strewn with body parts: "I was so young I didn't think a lot about anything." A U.S. infantryman, Roscoe Blunt, watched the impact of a shell on a fellow soldier: "The man disintegrated, leaving only patches and puddles of flesh and bone spattered in the mud. Graves registration would never find this one, not even his dog tags. Another unknown soldier. I sat and ate my food. I had not known him."

Most men under fire focused upon immediacies and loyalties towards one another. Their hopes and fears became elemental, as described by a British lieutenant, Norman Craig, in the desert: "Life was so free of all its complexities. What a clarity and a simplicity it really had! To stay alive, to lead once more a normal existence, to know again warmth, comfort and safety—what else could one conceivably demand? I would never chide circumstance again, never question fate, never feel bored, unhappy or dissatisfied. To be allowed to continue to live—nothing else mattered." Comradeship was fundamental: "Nobody has the courage to act in accordance with his natural cowardice with the whole company looking on," said a Luftwaffe NCO named Walter Schneider, pleased with his own paradox.

The intimacy forged by even a few weeks of shared battle experience caused some units to behave with cynical ruthlessness towards newcomers—outsiders. A veteran American staff sergeant said about Anzio, where his unit had eight replacements killed within twenty-four hours of their arrival: "We weren't going to send our own guys out on point in a damnfool situation like that. We had been together since Africa, and Sicily, and Salerno. We sent the replacements out ahead." It was the same in every army: "The company was the *heimat*," said SS lieutenant Helmut Gunther, "the people you wanted to be with. What mattered about being wounded was separation from your unit. You had a completely different feeling towards those who had been with you a long time as distinct from those who hadn't. A few months are an eternity for a soldier in war." Some Scottish soldiers of the 51st Highland Division mutinied at Salerno in September 1943, rather than accept posting to another formation.

Only a small number of warriors articulated hopes more ambitious than those for personal survival. One of these was a British officer who wrote to his parents before being killed in his first North African battle: "I should like you to know what it is I died for . . . There is, I feel, both in England and America a tremendous surge of feeling, a feeling which, for want of a better word, I shall call 'goodness.' It is not expressed by the politicians or the newspapers, for it is far too deep for them. It is the heartfelt longing of all the 'middling folk' for something better—a world more worthy of their children, a world more simple in its beliefs, nearer to earth and to God. I have heard it so often among soldiers in England and America, in trains, in factories in Chicago and in clubs in London, sometimes so poorly expressed that one can hardly recognize it, but underlying it all there is that craving for a new life."

All this was true. While Winston Churchill saw himself conducting a struggle to preserve the greatness of the British Empire, most of his fellow countrymen yearned instead for domestic change, most vividly anticipated in the Beveridge Report, published in November 1942, which laid the foundations of Britain's postwar welfare state. The *Spectator* editorialised: "The report has almost eclipsed the war itself as a subject of discussion in the country; it has been keenly debated by British troops overseas." Capt. David Elliott wrote to his sister, after hearing a discussion among his guardsmen about Beveridge: "If it is not accepted *in toto* I feel there will be a revolution." Independent Labour MP Aneurin Bevan told the House of Commons with unwonted accuracy: "The British Army is not fighting for the old world. If hon. Members opposite think we are going through this in order to keep their Malayan swamps, they are making a mistake."

There was a striking contrast between the attitudes of European and Asian peoples, who sought social and constitutional change as a reward for victory, and that of Franklin Roosevelt's fellow countrymen, who were largely content with the society they had got. A *New York Times* writer observed sardonically about the American overseas: "Tea from the British and *vin rouge* from the French have only confirmed his original convictions: that America is home, that home is better than Europe." Ernie Pyle recorded the aspirations of soldiers whom he met before the invasion of Sicily, overwhelmingly dominated by the hunger to go home: "These gravely yearned-for futures of men going into battle include so many things—things such as seeing the 'old lady' again, of going to college, of holding on your knee just once your own kid, of again becoming champion salesman of your territory, of driving a coal truck around the streets of Kansas City once more and yes, of just sitting in the sun once more on the south side of a house in New Mexico . . . It was these little hopes that made up the sum total of our worry rather than any visualization of physical agony to come."

Men's obsessive ambition to return to where they belonged became more emphatic when such "physical agony" came. U.S. Army nurse Dorothy Beavers wrote a letter for "a beautiful young man, a captain, who had lost both arms and legs. Yet he still seemed thrilled that he could say: 'I'm going home.' " When the American machine gunner Donald Schoo's driver had a hand blown off, the man ran in circles yelling hysterically, "I'm going home! Thank you, God! I'm going home!" A soldier who received a "Dear John" letter from his spouse told a reporter: "Any guy overseas who says he's in love with his wife tells a damn lie . . . He's in love with a memory—the memory of a moonlit night, a lovely gown, the scent of a perfume or the lilt of a song."

Isolation was a towering sensation, even for men serving amid legions of their compatriots. "I see all these thousands of lonely soldiers here," John Steinbeck wrote from the British capital in 1943 about the GIs on its streets. "There's a kind of walk they have in London, an apathetic shuffle. They're looking for something. They'll say it's a girl—any girl, but it isn't that at all." Although soldiers often talk about women, under the stress and unyielding discomfort of a battlefield most crave simple pleasures, among which sex scarcely features. A U.S. Marine Corps lieutenant colonel in the South Pacific fantasised about his ambitions on returning home: "I'm going to start wearing pyjamas again . . . I'm going to polish off a few eggs and several quarts of milk . . . A few hot baths are also in order . . . But I'm saving the best for last—I'm going to spend a whole day flushing a toilet, just to hear the water run."

It is striking to contrast such modest ambitions, common to most soldiers of the democracies, with the martial enthusiasm of some of Hitler's men, especially those of the Waffen SS, which persisted in surprising degree until the last months of the war. An American-born Italian woman wrote with mingled bewilderment, repugnance and fascination about two German officers she met in 1943: "They are the most highly specialized human beings that I have ever encountered: the 'fighting man.' Both of them are under twenty-five; both have taken part in the campaigns of

Poland, France, Russia—and now Italy. One of them, risen from ranks, commanded for six months a company of Russian deserters . . . It is impossible to convey the depth of conviction in his voice, while he expounded to us the familiar doctrines which had been taught him: the needs of *Gross Deutschland*, Nordic racial superiority, the inevitability of Germany's entry into the war (in spite of all Hitler's efforts to make peace with England), his pride in his country and his men, and above all his unshakeable certainty, even now, of victory."

It is an enduring enigma how a German army overwhelmingly composed of conscripts, as much citizen soldiers as were their Allied counterparts, should have shown itself consistently their superior. Part of the answer must lie in the supreme professionalism of the officer corps and its combat doctrine; through the ages Germany had produced formidable soldiers, and under Hitler their performance attained its zenith, albeit in an unspeakable cause. Beyond this, the role of compulsion became almost as important as it was in Stalin's armies. German soldiers who fled a battlefield or deserted knew they were subject to execution, a sanction imposed with increasing frequency as the Nazi empire crumbled. The Wehrmacht shot nothing like as many of its own men as did the Russians, but by 1945 penal executions ran into tens of thousands. Allied commanders, desperate to persuade their own men to try harder, often lamented their inability to impose deterrent capital sentences on deserters.

But more important to residual German resistance was the contribution of a core of fanatics, notably Waffen SS formations. A decade of Nazi indoctrination moulded excellent junior leaders. Even when it was plain that the tide of war had turned irreversibly against Hitler, many Germans made extraordinary sacrifices to preserve their homeland from Russian retribution. Not every member of the Wehrmacht was a hero: in 1944–45, a growing number showed themselves willing and even eager to surrender. But the ethos of Hitler's army—like those of Russia and Japan—differed importantly from that of the British and American forces. The price of allowing men to retain some civil liberties and freedom of choice, and of forgoing brutal sanctions upon the weak, was that the Western armies were obliged to compensate by firepower and patience for their soldiers' lesser willingness to accept sacrifice.

2. Home Fronts

NIKOLAI BELOV of the Red Army wrote in his diary at the end of 1942: "Yesterday I received a whole bunch of letters from Lidochka. I sense that she isn't having an easy time back there with the little ones." Captain

Belov understated his wife's predicament. In many societies, civilians suffered more than soldiers. The Romanian Mihail Sebastian never saw a battlefield, but wrote in December 1943: "Any personal balance sheet gets lost in the shadow of war. Its terrible presence is the first reality. Then somewhere, far away, forgotten by us, are we ourselves, with our faded, diminished, lethargic life, as we wait to emerge from sleep and start living again." Although statistics are drastically distorted by the mortality in Russia and China, it is notable that globally more noncombatants perished between 1939 and 1945 than uniformed participants. It is hard to use the phrase "home front" without irony in the context of Russia's war, in which tens of millions found themselves in the condition described by the Ukraine partisan commissar Pavel Kalitov in September 1942, at the hamlet of Klimovo: "A pale, thin woman sits on a bench with a baby in her arms and a girl of about seven. She is weeping, poor wretch. What are her tears about? I would do anything to be able to help these miserable human beings, to ease their pain."

Three weeks later, he described a similar scene in Budnitsa: "What is left of it? Heaps of ruins, chimneys sticking out, scorched chairs. Where there were roads and paths, there are thorns and weeds. No sign of life. The village is under constant artillery fire." Shortly afterwards, Kalitov's unit received an army order to clear all civilians from a fifteen-mile zone behind the front; they were to be permitted to take their belongings, but no forage or potatoes. Kalitov wrote unhappily: "We've got to work with the civilians, to prepare them so that they do this without resisting. It's a tough business: many people are living almost entirely off potatoes. To demand that they leave these for the troops means sentencing them to terrible hardships, even death. A family of refugees stands in front of me now. They are so thin and gaunt, one can see through them. It is especially hard to look at the little ones—three of them, one a baby, the others a little older. There is no milk. These people have suffered as much as us, the soldiers, or even more. Bombs, shells and mines no longer scare them." He marvelled at what human beings showed themselves able to endure.

Even those Russians who did not suffer siege or bombardment spent the war labouring in conditions of extreme privation: they received 500 calories a day less nourishment than their British or German counterparts, a thousand fewer than Americans. Some 2 million perished of hunger in territories under Soviet control, while a further 13 million died under bombardment or in German-occupied regions; prisoners in the gulag's labour camps occupied the lowest place in the hierarchy of priority for rations, and one in four of them died in each of the war years. Russians suffered widespread scurvy as a consequence of vitamin deficiency, together with many other conditions associated with hunger and overwork. "We had no life of our own outside the factory," said Moscow woman Klavdia Leonova, who worked in a textile plant making army tunics and camouflage netting.

Throughout the war, her production line operated around the clock, its workers organised in two twelve-hour shifts. They were fed badly baked bread and kasha—a porridge made with burned wheat—distributed at the work benches. "We did not starve, but we were always very hungry and often ate potato peelings . . . Sunday was in theory a day off, but the factory Party Committee often called on us for outside work, such as digging trenches or bringing in timber from the forests around Moscow. We had to load lorries with pitprops which were so heavy they would have been a burden even for a professional weightlifter . . . We lived with the peasants . . . the women regularly abused the regime. They abused us too, because we collected berries and mushrooms in the woods which they had hoped to sell to us."

In the unoccupied Western nations, some people prospered: criminals exploited demand for prostitution, black-market goods and stolen military fuel and supplies; industrialists made enormous profits, many of which somehow evaded windfall taxes; farmers, especially in the United States, where incomes rose by 156 percent, experienced greater prosperity than they had ever known. "Farm times became good times," said Laura Briggs, daughter of an Idaho smallholder. "Dad started having his land improved . . . We and most other farmers went from a tarpaper shack to a new frame house with indoor plumbing. Now we had an electric stove instead of a woodburning one, and running water at the sink where we could do the dishes; and a hot water heater; and nice linoleum."

But far more people hated it all. Lt. David Fraser, a Grenadier Guardsman, identified an important truth about the circumstances of millions, soldiers and civilians alike: "People were not where they belonged, so that the effect was of a dream from which one hoped one day to awake." In April 1941, Edward McCormick wrote to his son David, who had enlisted with his brother Anthony, and was now embarked with an artillery regiment for the Middle East. "To Mummy, in particular," their father said,

> the whole war centres round you and Anthony. The chief motivating force in her life, ever since you were born, has been your health, happiness and safety. These are still her instinctive thoughts, and you don't need me to tell you therefore how devastating this parting with you both has been to her. I feel it too, and it appals me to think of the hardship, danger and filth which will probably be your experience. There

is no doubt whatever, in my mind, that this war had to come. A Nazi victory can only mean the enjoyment of life by a very small number of chosen Germans, and the souls of all people under them will be engulfed. You and Anthony are helping to rid the world of this plague and, while personal feelings make me wish you were far away from it all, I am filled with pride . . . at what I know you will achieve. Mum and I send you our fondest love and blessings and pray for your well-being and safe return to us. DAD

It would be more than four years before the McCormick family was re-united, a separation common to scores of millions. And although enlistment in uniform was the commonest cause of displacement and the sundering of families, these misfortunes also took many other forms. Half the population of Britain changed residence in the course of the war, some because they were evicted to make way for servicemen, some because their houses were destroyed, most because wartime duties demanded it. A significant part of the Belgian fishing fleet adopted a new life at the port of Brixham, in Devon, while some Danish fishermen worked from Grimsby, in Lincolnshire. Elsewhere in Europe, more brutal imperatives intervened. In January 1943, for instance, a British nurse named Gladys Skillett found herself giving birth to a child not in the British Channel Islands that were her rightful home, but in the maternity ward of a small German hospital at Biberach. She was one of 834 civilians on occupied Guernsey deported to the Reich in September 1943 to spend the rest of the war in an internment camp as hostages; there should have been 836 of them, but an elderly major and his wife from Sark slashed their wrists before embarkation. Mrs. Skillett forged a lifelong friendship with the wife of a Wehrmacht soldier who shared her hospital room in Biberach, and who gave birth to a healthy son on the same day as her own arrived.

Bianca Zagari was a mother of two in a prosperous Italian family, who fled from their home city of Naples in December 1942, when American bombing began. A party of fourteen including in-laws, nephews and nieces, maid and governess, they settled in the remote and impoverished Abruzzo region, renting two houses in a village in the Sangro Valley, accessible only on foot. There, they eked out an uncomfortable existence until, to their horror, in October 1943 once again bombs began to fall around them; they were only eighteen miles from Monte Cassino, in an area bitterly contested between the German and Allied armies. Zagari and her children fled with the villagers; as they clambered into the hills, a peasant told her, in local dialect she could barely comprehend, that the bombing had claimed most of her relations: "Signora, the ten dead are yours." She wrote: "Now it is dawn and others are climbing up from Scontrone, terrified. Each one gives me a horrific detail: a hand, a little foot, two plaits with red bows, a body without a head."

Her husband, Raffaele, survived, but most of his family perished. The survivors existed for weeks in caves in the mountains, learning skills such as Zagari had never known—lighting fires and building rough shelters with scant help from the unsympathetic local people, who cared only for their own. "I have to ask for everything from everyone—it is like begging for alms." When the Germans found them, all the men were conscripted for forced labour: "They took one while he was digging under ruins for his mother." After months of misery, one day she fled across the mountains with her two children and her jewel case. Eventually a pitying German lorry driver gave them a lift to Rome. "We arrive via the Porta San Giovanni. I feel I am dreaming—I see nannies with children playing calmly. The war seems a distant rumour. Everyone asks where we have come from. No one understands the answer that we have come from Scontrone where nine members of the family have been killed. At the Corso hotel, where the concierge knows us and tries to help, we hear another guest threatening that he will refuse to patronise the establishment again if it admits such vagabonds as ourselves."

The Zagaris were able to exploit their wealth to deliver them from the worst privations, as most Italians could not. When the icy winter of 1944 came, disease and lack of fuel and food imposed a bitter toll on civilians, especially children. One mother said: "Suddenly my little girl became unwell. The doctor said it was colitis—a death which took five hours, an indescribable agony. The house was freezing and Gigeto [her husband] ran to buy lots of bottles to fill with hot water. I put her in our bed and held her close with the bottles around her. 'Gigeto,' I screamed, 'Santina must not die.' But she did." Many people who had lost their homes by bombardment or expulsion were reduced to a primitive mountain existence, as a young girl described: "The cold and damp of the caves got into our bones. My mother crouched in a corner clutching my three-month-old brother in her arms. She told me to go into the town and find a doctor. I ran like a hare, but found that he was away from home—at the house of the Podestàs whose son had a high temperature like my brother. Eventually he gave me a prescription—but he wouldn't give me any of the drugs that were on his table. He said he would come and visit, but when he arrived my little brother was already dead." Their distraught mother said, "My baby boy died because my milk was bad because I didn't eat enough." She was one among millions.

People displaced from their homes and countries spent much of the war waiting: for orders or visas, an opportunity to flee from looming peril or permission to travel. A twenty-one-year-old English girl, Rosemary Say, having escaped from German internment into the Vichy zone of France, kicked her heels for weeks in Marseilles among an unhappy community of fellow fugitives: "It was sad to see the waste of intellect and ability as the delays lengthened and the future for many continued to look bleak. Had he got his visa at last, had he been arrested or just scarpered into the countryside to try his luck? We waited and wondered. But if the person didn't come back he was soon forgotten. We were only really held together by a common wish to be off and away and to begin our lives again . . . There was a lot of suspicion and hopelessness . . . Feelings ran high and quarrels were loud and violent. We all shared the worry of our uncertainty."

The Ukrainian teenager Stefan Kurylak was shipped westwards by the German occupiers to labour for an Austrian Alpine farming family, devout Catholics named Klaunzer. On first sighting the boy, Frau Klaunzer burst into tears; without knowing why, the young Ukrainian followed suit. It was explained to him that the Klaunzers' son had been killed on the Eastern Front a few weeks before. Frau Klaunzer kept mouthing one of the few German phrases Stefan could understand: "Hitler no good! Hitler no good!" Stefan was thereafter treated with kindness and humanity. He worked on the family land, not unhappily, until the end of the war, when his hosts begged him in vain to stay on as one of themselves.

Few such experiences were so benign. A fourteen-year-old Pole, Arthur Poznanski, returned to the Piotrkow ghetto one day in October 1942 from the Hortensja glassworks, where he and his younger brother Jerzyk worked. He was handed a crumpled note by a member of the ghetto's Jewish militia. It was from his mother. There had been a deportation: "We are being taken. May God help you, Arthur. We cannot do anything more for you, and whatever may happen, look after Jerzyk. He is but a child and has got no one else, so be his brother and parent. Goodbye . . ." Arthur, passionately moved, kept repeating to himself, "I'll try! Yes, I'll try!" But he thought, "How? I felt so lonely and helpless." The boys spent the rest of the war in concentration camps, separated by hundreds of miles, but both miraculously survived; the rest of their family perished.

The British endured six years of austerity and spasmodic bombardment. The blackout promoted moral as well as physical gloom. Yet the circumstances of Churchill's islands were much preferable to those of continental societies, where hunger and violence were endemic. Like North America, Britain was shielded by expanses of sea, relative personal freedom and wealth. Privileged Britons remained privileged indeed: "The extraordinary thing about the war was that people who really didn't want to be involved in it were not," the novelist Anthony Powell wrote afterwards.

This was true, within a limited social milieu. The week before D-Day, as 250,000 young American and British soldiers made final preparations for hurling themselves at Hitler's Atlantic Wall, in London Evelyn Waugh wrote in his diary: "Woke half drunk and had a long, busy morning—getting my hair cut, trying to verify quotations in the London Library, which is still in disorder from its bomb, visiting Nancy [Mitford, at her bookshop]. At luncheon I again got drunk. Went to the Beefsteak [Club], which I have just joined . . . Back to White's [Club]—more port. Went to Waterloo in an alcoholic stupor, got the train to Exeter and slept most of the way."

Waugh was untypical; many of the friends with whom he caroused were on leave from active service, and several were dead a year later. The German V-weapon assault was about to commence, inflicting fresh death and destruction on war-weary Britons. But, just as life in New York or Chicago was much more comfortable than life in London or Liverpool, so Londoners were vastly better off than the inhabitants of Paris, Naples, Athens, or any city in the Soviet Union or China. The Lancashire housewife Nella Last reflected in October 1942 that her war had thus far inflicted little hardship or suffering, "in comparison to three-quarters of Stalingrad being demolished during the first bombardment. We have had food, shelter and warmth when millions have had none—what will be the price we will have to pay?—we cannot expect to go on 'escaping,' there *is* no escape for any of us. I saw a neighbour's baby today and I felt a sudden understanding for those who 'refuse to bring babies into the world now.' All this talk of 'new worlds' and 'after the war,' no talk of the suffering, the anguish, before all this is over."

Mrs. Last was unusually sensitive; most of her compatriots were too preoccupied by their own present troubles to concern themselves with the larger but remote miseries of others. On 22 November 1942, Phyllis Crook, another housewife, wrote to her thirty-two-year-old husband serving in North Africa: "Christmas is going to be a beastly time and I'm hating the thought of it. However it's got to be got on with 'as usual' and I have been busy trying hard to get things for all the kids of our acquaintance. It would be so easy to say 'I can't get anything' and leave it at that. It is so cold . . . How I wish I could retire for the winter instead of constantly shivering. Chris [their small son] asked God to make you a good boy tonight! Well my love news seems very scarce and I must say goodnight. Life seems too mouldy for words. I wonder when we shall see you again. It all seems horribly far away and doesn't bear too much thinking about. Look after yourself, my dear and don't go going into any danger, as Daddy would say! All my love always, dearest Phil. PS Joyce is now working in a factory 11 hours a day. John Young has had malaria."

Mrs. Crook's woes would seem trivial, her self-pity contemptible, to many people of war-ravaged nations. Her own life and those of her children were unimperilled, and they were not even hungry. But separation from her husband, the necessity to occupy lodgings far from her east London home, the drab monotony of wartime existence seemed to her, like many others, sufficient causes for unhappiness. And ten days after writing that letter she became a widow when her husband was killed in action.

News of the violent and premature deaths of distant loved ones was a pervasive feature of the wartime experience. Often, little was known of their fate, as J. R. Ackerley noted in a poem published in the *Spectator:*

> We never knew what became of him, that was so curious;
> He embarked, it was in December, and never returned;
> No chance to say Good-bye, and Christmas confronting us;
> A few letters arrived, long after, and came to an end.
>
> The weeks dragged into months, and then it was December.
> We troubled the officials, of course, and they cabled about;
> They were patient but busy, importunities without number;
> Some told us one thing, some another; they never found out.
>
> There's a lot go like that, without explanation;
> And death is death, after all; small comfort to know how and when;
> But I keep thinking now that we've dropped the investigation;
> It was more like the death of an insect than of a man.

Countless families struggled to come to terms with loss. Diana Hopkinson, the wife of a British Army officer, described a reunion with her husband on a station platform in Berkshire, after a long separation during which they received news that his brother had been killed in action. "His strange uniform, his strangely thin face glimpsed in the dimmest light, gave me a feeling of artificiality. Even in our kisses there was something unreal. In bed there was a terrible sadness to overcome—Pat's death—before we could make love. When at last he turned towards me, we made love as if we were partners in a solemn rite, strange, speechless, but familiar."

The Sheffield housewife Edie Rutherford was just preparing tea when her young neighbour, the wife of an RAF pilot, knocked on the door. "Her face was wooden and she jerked out: 'Mrs. Rutherford, Henry is missing,' thrust the telegram into my hand. Of course I just opened my arms and took her in and let her have a good weep the while I cursed audibly this blasted war. 'He isn't dead. I'm sure he isn't dead. He was home only last Wednesday. He's alive somewhere and worrying because he knows I'll get this telegram to upset me' . . . It is difficult to know what to say to a wife in such trouble. I did my best, poor lass. Felt myself as if my inside had fallen out. I wish to goodness this war would end."

Another housewife, Jean Wood, recorded: "I had a very nice lady and her husband, neighbours. She was having her son on leave and she didn't have any meat for him. But that particular day the butcher let me have some rabbit . . . a taste treat. I didn't want the rabbit, 'cause I'd rather give my small children an egg, if I could get eggs. So I took the rabbit round to her. She was so thrilled. On that particular day, her son was killed. We could have flung the rabbit anywhere, for all we cared. He was such a nice boy, a young officer, nineteen years old." They were all "nice boys," to those obliged to mourn them.

Muriel Green, one of Britain's 80,000 "land girls" providing agricultural labour, burst into tears on the last night of a home leave in Norfolk in June 1942. "I cried because of the war. It has altered our life which can never be the same. To see the desolate emptiness of the seaside upsets me. When you are away and Mother writes to say the latest desecration, the latest boy missing, the latest family to sacrifice, it is just words. But in the home it is mortifying. Life will never be so sweet as before the war, and the last two summers and early '39 were the most perfect years of my life when all seemed young and gay. I could have cried for hours had I not known it was upsetting Mother."

The American Dellie Hahne was one of many women who married the wrong man amid the stress and emotional extravagance of the time, and repented at leisure during the years that followed. "He was a soldier. He could not be anything but a marvelous, magnificent human being," she said, with the ruefulness of one who learned better. She came to pity others who experienced domestic miseries: "Pregnant women who could barely balance in a rocking train, going to see their husbands for the last time before the guys were sent overseas. Women coming back from seeing their husbands, traveling with small children. Trying to feed their kids, diaper their kids. I felt sorriest for them. It suddenly occurred to me that this wasn't half as much fun as I'd been told it was going to be. I just thanked God I had no kids."

Many children clung to parting memories of fathers from whom they became separated for years—in some cases forever. The little Californian

Bernice Schmidt was nine when her parents got divorced. As a newly single man, her thirty-two-year-old father, Arthur, thus became eligible to be drafted. He was given leave from training camp before embarkation and took his three children to a Los Angeles amusement park. He told them how homesick he was, and gave each a little parting present: Bernice's was a pin in the shape of two hearts held together with an arrow, inscribed "Bernice, love daddy." Private Schmidt was killed in action with the 317th Infantry on 15 November 1944. His daughter never forgot the day that news came, because it was her twelfth birthday. One day in October 1942, Nella Last was gazing at a neighbour's children. Their mother touched her arm and asked, "What are you thinking about?" Mrs. Last said, "Oh, I don't know. Always be glad that your Ian is only seven." The woman said simply, "I *am*."

Until 1943, when Stalingrad and bombing began to change everything, most German civilians save those who lost loved ones found the conflict a numbing presence rather than a trauma. "Is it possible that one can get used to war?" mused Mathilde Wolff-Monckeburg, the elderly wife of an academic living in Hamburg, in 1941. "This question tantalises me and I am afraid of a positive reply. All that was unbearable at first, all that was impossible to fathom, has by now become somehow 'settled,' and one lives from day to day in frightening apathy . . . We still have our comforts and warmth, we have enough to eat, we occasionally have hot water, we do not exert ourselves apart from daily shopping expeditions and small household duties." Like all Germans save National Socialist functionaries, who enjoyed privileges in food as everything else, she complained chiefly about the dreariness of rations: "One grows ever more sensitive to the emptiness inside and greed for the unobtainable becomes ever more intense," Wolff-Monckeburg wrote in June 1942. "Glowing fantasies multiply in tantalising colours when one thinks of large juicy beefsteaks, new potatoes and long asparagus with lumps of golden butter. It is all so degrading and miserable—and there are people who call this a 'heroic' period." But if Germans complained of privation, this was slight by global standards: whereas British output of consumer goods fell by 45 percent between 1939 and 1944, Germany's declined only by 15 percent. If its people disliked what they were obliged to eat— their annual consumption of potatoes rose from 12 to 32 million tons— they experienced severe hunger only when the war ended in May 1945; the Nazis starved the conquered nations to keep their own citizens fed.

More than any other aspect of the war, food or lack of it emphasised the relativity of suffering. Globally, far more people suffered serious hunger, or indeed died of starvation, than in any previous conflict, including

World War I, because an unprecedented range of countries became battlefields, with consequent loss of agricultural production. Even the citizens of those countries which escaped famine found their diets severely
restricted. Britain's rationing system ensured that no one starved and the
poor were better nourished than in peacetime, but few found anything to
enjoy about their fare. A land girl, Joan Ibbertson, wrote: "Food was our
obsession . . . In my first digs the landlady never cooked a second vegetable, except on a Sunday; we had cold meat on Monday, and sausage for
the rest of the week. Sometimes she cooked potatoes with the sausage, but
often she left us a slice of bread each. The two sausages on a large, cold,
green glass plate greeted us on our return from a day on leeks or sprouts,
and a three-mile cycle ride each way . . . A neighbour once brought round
a sack of carrots, which he said were for the rabbits, but we benefited from
this act of kindness . . . We had dried eggs once a week for breakfast, but
the good lady in charge liked to cook it overnight, so it resembled, and
tasted like, sawdust on toast. We had fishpaste on toast, too, some mornings . . . One Christmas we were allowed to buy a chicken. My bird was so
old and tough that we could hardly chew through it."

Each week a British adult was entitled to four ounces of lard or butter, twelve ounces of sugar, four ounces of bacon, two eggs, six ounces of
meat, two ounces of tea and unlimited vegetables or home-grown fruit
"off-ration," if available. Most households resorted to improvisation to
supplement authorised issues. Derek Lambert, then a small boy, recorded
a scene at his family's table: "One morning a jar was put on the breakfast
table with supreme nonchalance . . . My father, an undemonstrative man,
spread the nectar on his bread and bit into it. He frowned and said: 'What
was that?' 'Carrot marmalade,' said my mother. With unusual delibera-
tion, he picked up the jar, took it into the garden and poured it onto the
compost heap."

Yet any Russian or Asian peasant, or Axis captive, would have deemed
carrot marmalade a luxury. Kenneth Stevens was a prisoner in Singapore's Changi jail. He wrote: "In this place one's mind returns continually
and dwells longingly on Food . . . I think of Duck and Cherry Casse-
role, Scrambled Eggs, Fish Scallops, Chicken Stanley, Kedgeree, Trifle,
Summer Pudding, Fruit Fool, Bread & Butter Pudding—all those lovely
things were made just perfectly 'right' in my own home." Stevens died in
August 1943 without ever again tasting such delicacies. Only in 1945 did
his wife receive his diary from the hands of a fellow prisoner and share his
anguished fantasising from the brink of the grave. Meanwhile, the average
height of French girls shrank by four inches and of boys by just under three
inches between 1935 and 1944. Tuberculosis stimulated by malnutrition

increased dramatically in occupied Europe, and by 1943 four-fifths of Belgian children were displaying symptoms of rickets. In most countries city dwellers suffered more from hunger than country people, because they had fewer opportunities for supplementing their diet by growing their own produce. The poor lacked cash to use the black market, which, in all countries, continued to feed those with means to pay.

In the matter of diet, Canada, Australia and New Zealand escaped lightly, and Americans scarcely suffered at all. Rationing was introduced to Roosevelt's people only in 1943, and then on a generous scale. *Gourmet* magazine gushed tastelessly: "Imports of European delicacies may dwindle, but America has battalions of good food to rush to appetite's defence." Meat was almost the only commodity in short supply, though Americans complained bitterly about that. A housewife named Catherine Renee Young wrote to her husband in May 1943: "I'm sick of the same thing . . . We hardly ever see good steak any more. And steak is the main meat that gives us strength. My Dad just came back from the store and all he could get was blood pudding and how I hate that." But whatever the shortcomings of wartime quality, American domestic meat consumption fell very little in quantity, even when huge shipments were exported to Britain and Russia.

Every nation with power to do so put its own people first, heedless of the consequences for others at their mercy. The Axis behaved most brutally, and with the direst consequences: Nazi policy in the east was explicitly directed towards starving subject races in order to feed Germans. Such was the regime's administrative incompetence that food imports to the Reich, and consequent Soviet deaths, fell far short of the hopes of Agriculture Minister Herbert Backe and his "Hunger Plan." People in occupied regions displayed extraordinary ingenuity in hiding crops from the occupiers, and clung tenaciously to life in defiance of the predictions of Nazi nutritionists, who anticipated 30 to 40 million fatalities. But many people indeed perished. Prewar Soviet agriculture was grossly inefficient, and much farmland had been overrun by the Wehrmacht. Even when it was reclaimed, machinery had been seized or destroyed, the countryside laid waste. In pursuit of the Wehrmacht's policy of seeking to live off the land, German soldiers in the east consumed an estimated 7 million tons of Russian grain, 17 million cattle, 20 million pigs, 27 million sheep and goats and over 100 million domestic fowls.

The Japanese throughout their empire adopted draconian policies to provide food for their own people, which caused millions to starve in Southeast Asia. China also suffered appallingly, its peasants despoiled by both the Japanese and Nationalist armies. In Henan Province in 1942, when unseasonable frost and hail were followed by a plague of locusts, millions left their land and many perished, to the horror of Western eye-witnesses: "As they died the government continued to wring from them the last possible ounce of tax . . . Peasants who were eating elm bark and dried leaves had to haul their last sack of grain to the tax collector's office."

Though the Allies were not responsible for anything like the human toll exacted by the Axis, their policies displayed a harsh nationalistic self-ishness. The United States insisted that both its people at home and its armed forces abroad should receive fantastically generous allocations of food, even when shipping space was at a premium. For every pound of supplies the Japanese transported to their island garrisons, many of whom—at Rabaul, for instance—spent the second half of the war engaged in subsistence vegetable gardening rather than combat operations, the United States shipped two tons to its own forces. American reluctance to feed their men on local supplies was increased by the shortcomings of some nations' canning processes: eight U.S. airmen died in an outbreak of botulism after eating Australian tinned beetroot. American specialists were thereupon dispatched to raise local standards. Maj. Belford Sea-brook, of the famous New Jersey agribusiness, introduced its principles to Australia. Coca-Cola established forty-four bottling plants in theatres of war, which produced 95 percent of all soft drinks sold in camp PXs. The United States reduced agreed allocations of meat to Britain to maintain supplies to its own civilians and soldiers; Gen. Brehon Somervell, a noto-rious anglophobe, supported his transportation chief's 1943 assertion that the British people "were still living 'soft' and could easily stand further reductions."

For Italians, hunger was a persistent reality from the moment the country became a battlefield in 1943. "My father had no steady income," recalled the daughter of a once-rich Rome publisher. "Our savings were spent, we were many in the house, including two brothers in hiding. I went with my father to the [public] soup kitchen because my mother was ashamed to do so. We made our own soup from broad-bean skins. We had no olive oil . . . A flask of oil cost 2,000 lire when our entire house had cost only 70,000. We bought whatever was available on the black market, bartering with silver, sheets, embroidered linen. Silver was worth less than flour; even our daughters' dowries were exchanged for meat or eggs. Then in November with the cold weather we had to exchange goods for coal: the longest queues formed at the coal merchants. We carried the sacks back on our own, because it was better that no man showed his face [lest he should be conscripted for forced labour]."

"Hunger governed all," the Australian correspondent Alan Moorehead wrote from Italy. "We were witnessing the moral collapse of a people. They had no pride any more, or dignity. The animal struggle for existence governed everything. Food. That was the only thing that mattered. Food for the children. Food for yourself. Food at the cost of any debasement or depravity." Prostitution alone enabled some mothers to feed their families, as British sergeant Norman Lewis witnessed in 1944. At a municipal building in the outskirts of Naples, he encountered a crowd of soldiers surrounding a group of women who were dressed in their street clothes,

> and had the ordinary well-washed, respectable shopping and gossiping faces of working-class housewives. By the side of each woman stood a small pile of tins, and it soon became clear that it was possible to make love to any one of them in this very public place by adding another tin to the pile. The women kept absolutely still, they said nothing and their faces were as empty of expression as graven images. They might have been selling fish, except that this place lacked the excitement of a fish market. There was no solicitation, no suggestion, no enticement, not even the discreetest and most accidental display of flesh . . . One soldier, a little tipsy, and egged on constantly by his friends, finally put down his tin of rations at a woman's side, unbuttoned and lowered himself onto her. A perfunctory jogging of the haunches began and came quickly to an end. A moment later he was on his feet and buttoning up again. It had been something to get over as soon as possible. He might have been submitting to field punishment rather than the act of love.

In December 1944, when there was hunger verging upon starvation in Italy and indeed all Europe, a British embassy official in Washington visited Assistant Secretary of War John J. McCloy to protest against the policy of shipping extravagant quantities of supplies to U.S. forces overseas, while liberated civilians were in desperate straits: "'In order to win the war,' he demanded of McCloy, 'were we not imperilling the political and social fabric of European civilization on which the future peace of the world depended?'" This drew from Mr. McCloy the immediate rejoinder "that it was a British interest to remember that, as a result of the complete change in the economic and financial position of the British Commonwealth which the war had brought about, we, in the U.K., depended at least as much upon the U.S. as we did upon Europe. Was it wise to risk losing the support of the U.S. in seeking the support of Western Europe? This was what was involved." The shocked British official persisted in pressing the case for feeding Europe's civilians. McCloy stuck to his guns, asserting that it would be fatal for Britain "to argue that the war in the Pacific should be retarded in order that the civilian population of Europe should be fed."

The Foreign Office in London professed acute dismay on receiving the minute of this meeting, but British impotence in the face of U.S. dominance remained a towering reality. That only a relatively small number of Italians died of starvation between 1943 and 1945 was due first to the illicit diversion of vast quantities of American rations to the black market, and thereafter to the people—much to the private enrichment of some U.S. service personnel; and to the political influence of Italian-Americans, which belatedly persuaded Washington of the case for averting mass starvation.

The British government, in its turn, imposed extreme privation on some of the peoples of its empire, to maintain the much higher standard of nourishment it deemed appropriate at home. In 1943, allocations of shipping to Indian Ocean destinations were slashed, for good strategic reasons but at deplorable humanitarian cost. Mauritius suffered shocking hardships, as did some East African countries where white settlers made fortunes from wartime agricultural production, exploiting conscripted native labour paid derisory wages.

The 1943–44 Bengal famine, of which more will be said below, prompted a brutally callous response from Britain's prime minister. When Wavell, then viceroy, heard of the massive British 1945 airlift to Holland, where people had been reduced to eating tulip bulbs, he noted bitterly: "A very different attitude [exists] towards feeding a starving population when the starvation is in Europe." Greeks also suffered from the British blockade of Hitler's empire—at least half a million died of hunger. Churchill was assuredly right that concessions to allow food imports into Greece and other occupied nations would have served the Wehrmacht. But a fundamental reality persists: the Allied powers provided for their own peoples levels of nourishment which they denied to others, including societies notionally under their protection.

3. A Woman's Place

THE MOBILISATION of women was a critical social phenomenon of the war, most comprehensive in the Soviet Union and Britain, though Adam Tooze has shown that Germany also used female workers more widely than formerly supposed. The Japanese social ethos precluded the elevation of women to positions of responsibility, but they played a critical role in factories, and by 1944 provided half of Japan's agricultural labour force.

Prewar Britain used women workers much less than the Soviet Union, but quickly conscripted them under the pressures of siege. Some thus found a fulfilment they had not known in peacetime: Peter Baxter's fifty-five-year-old mother worked as a clerk in the British Ministry of Supply, "and is, I suspect, enjoying herself more than she has done for years," her son wrote. "She has a quick brain, and it is stimulating for her to be using her wits instead of toiling through a load of housework . . . I can't help thinking that, much as my mother has loved her children, she might perhaps have been happier all these years if she could have kept on with a business career as women do in Russia."

Many girls suffered, however, when thrust into a male-dominated, shamelessly chauvinistic factory world, as was Rosemary Moonen: "My initiation into factory life was shattering. Being a hairdresser in a high-class salon situated in a select area of the town, I was a somewhat genteel, reserved type of girl. To be plunged abruptly into a world of coarse, ill-bred men and women, where language was foul and bluer than the bluest sky, was an experience . . . harsh and unreal." The foreman to whom Moonen was first introduced tossed her a broom contemptuously, saying: "Here! Take this! And sod around!"

> I was stung to humiliation before the rest of the girls . . . He returned thirty minutes later to find me sitting on a box doing nothing. Furiously he demanded "What the blankety blank I thought I was doing?" Summoning all my courage I retorted that until he had the decency to show me the job I had to do, presuming it was to help the war effort, I intended staying where I was. Somewhat taken aback he treated me to a stream of foul language, calling me some of the filthiest names imaginable. I was so angry and disgusted by this time, that I brought up my hand and slapped him hard across the cheek . . . He apologised grudgingly, and took me to a machine, and demonstrated the pedals, handbrakes and rollers for me to operate . . . At the end of that shift I went home and wept bitterly. How was I ever going to stand the atmosphere?

Sarah Baring was a peer's daughter whose sole prewar occupation had been that of a dancing debutante. Now she found herself drilling alloy sheets in an aircraft parts factory, which she hated: "The airless workplace, the indescribable food, the damp floors which even soaked through the wooden clogs we wore on our feet, the twit of a shop steward who hadn't the courage of a flea . . . the bullying and oppressive attitude of the manager . . . I had to take the odd day off and lie in bed fighting constant fatigue." Baring was fortunate enough to be able to exploit her fluency in German to eventually gain a transfer to Bletchley Park.

Every nation sought to elevate and glamorise the role of women war workers as a stimulus to recruitment. In America in 1942, Redd Evans and John Jacob Loeb composed a popular ditty:

> All the day long,
> Whether rain or shine
> She's a part of the assembly line.
> She's making history.
> Working for victory,
> Rosie the Riveter.

The original of Rosie the Riveter, who became an American feminist icon, was twenty-two-year-old Rose Will Monroe from Pulaski County, Kentucky. Like millions of Americans, she relocated to war work—in her case on the Willow Run B-24 and B-29 assembly lines at Ypsilanti, Michigan. She was made the star of a propaganda movie, and in May 1943 Norman Rockwell produced a famous painting of Rosie the Riveter, published as a *Saturday Evening Post* cover, though his physical model was an Arlington, Vermont, telephonist. By 1944, 20 million American women were working, a 57 percent increase on the 1940 figure. The progress of black civil rights in the United States, though extremely sluggish, was importantly enhanced by the recruitment into factories of African-American women, often working alongside whites. All female workers, however, remained severely disadvantaged by lower pay, earning on average $31.50 a week against the male average of $54.65. Many were employed in shipyards, which briefly spawned a "Wendy the Welder" propaganda character, based on Janet Doyle of the Kaiser Richmond Liberty yard in California. Canada followed suit by promoting "Ronnie the Bren Gun Girl."

It would be mistaken to romanticise the role of Rosie: the U.S. industrial workforce remained overwhelmingly male-dominated, and the lifestyle of that early generation of working women was often wretched. A vast, squalid trailer park grew up beside Ford's Willow Run plant. Some workers commuted as much as sixty miles daily rather than endure life there. Wages were high, but there was social concern about "eight-hour orphans"—the children of working wives simply abandoned at home through the day. A few such hapless offspring, it was discovered, were left in cars at factory parking lots. Moreover, many of the new workers took time to acquire appropriate skills. Some "Rosies," like their male counterparts, were less than competent, a reality reflected in the structural limitations of some of the ships they built. Likewise, the intense agricultural effort on both sides of the Atlantic was sometimes blighted by ill-judged production decisions and inadequate skills. In April 1942 Muriel Green, working in a market garden in southern England, reflected glumly on the waste of much of her effort growing vegetables: "I suppose in everything there is waste: that is what is the matter with this country. There seems so little full effort and so little result—so far."

In Russia, the plight of both women military conscripts and civilians was vastly worse. *Pravda* correspondent Lazar Brontman recorded in his diary the desperate efforts of Moscow housewives to escape factory service. Those with children under eight were exempted until the summer of 1942, but thereafter this age limit was lowered to four. Women begged for office jobs of any kind to avoid labour in the ZIS vehicle works. Brontman recorded the droll assignment of some privileged women who became "hooves"—avoiding more demanding duties by working in a Moscow theatre imitating the sound of galloping horses during a play about Soviet cavalry. More than 800,000 Russian women served with Stalin's armies. For some, including ninety-two who became Heroes of the Soviet Union, the experience may have been uplifting. The female "rabbit units" of the Red Air Force, named in self-mockery for an incident early in the war when desperately hungry female flight trainees ate "like rabbits" raw cabbages which they found on a station, became famous. A handful of women served as snipers at Sevastopol and Leningrad, and in 1943 large numbers of female graduates began to emerge from sniping schools. Their superior breathing control was found to promote marksmanship, and they played a useful role in the latter war years—though not, contrary to myth, at Stalingrad.

Some women, however, recoiled from the experience of battle. Nikolai Nikulin witnessed an incident on the Leningrad front, during shelling which left a sentry writhing in agony on the ground. A girl nurse sat sobbing beside him, "tears running down her filthy face that has not seen water for many days, her hands shaking in panic." The wounded man himself eventually pulled down his trousers and bandaged a shocking thigh wound, while seeking to calm the girl. "Daughter, please don't be scared! Don't cry." Nikutin observed dryly, "War is not a place for girls."

Many women in uniform were ruthlessly sexually exploited. Capt. Pavel Kovalenko wrote one day: "I went to visit the tank regiment. The unit commander had got drunk celebrating his new rank of lieutenant-colonel and was snoring away. I was struck by the spectacle of the prostrate figure curled up beside him—his 'campaign wife,' as it turned out." "Campaign wives" became a phenomenon of Russia's war, and only a fortunate minority gained wedding rings from the experience. "The PPZh is our great sin," sighed Vasily Grossman, using the Red Army's slang phase for commanders' sexual abuse of its women. Thousands were evacuated when they became pregnant, deliberately or otherwise. Almost the only concession to their sex was that they were eventually granted a tiny extra ration of soap.

Meanwhile, women labouring in fields and factories in the absence of their menfolk suffered chronic hunger and were often required to perform tasks beyond their physical strength. Hernias became commonplace among those who struggled daily with heavy loads or were harnessed to the plough in lieu of dead oxen. Grossman reflected in the dark days of August 1942: "Villages have become the kingdoms of women. They drive tractors, guard warehouses, queue for vodka. Tipsy girls are out singing— they are seeing a girlfriend off to the army. Women are carrying on their shoulders the great burden of work. Women dominate. They feed and arm us now. We do the fighting. And we don't fight well. Women look and say nothing. There's no reproach [in their eyes], not a bitter word. Are they nursing a grievance? Or do they understand what a terrible burden a war is, even an unsuccessful one?"

Housewife Valentina Bekbulatov wrote to her son at the front, describing the family's desperate circumstances: "Dear Vova! I received the money that you sent, but you didn't need to bother, it's not enough anyway to help us in our poverty, and you deprive yourself even of this meagre support. I earned only twenty-six roubles this month, so you can imagine what our situation is like—there is no chance to buy anything at the market. We are waiting for milk. Uncle Pazyuk came over recently, he brought some household stuff to exchange for flour. Aunt saw her three sons off to the army—Aleksey, Egor and Aleksandr. Aleksey has already been in a battle, Egor is in the Far East, and from Aleksandr there aren't any letters . . ."

Evdokiya Kalinichenko was wounded in the leg as an army nurse, discharged and sent back to the university she had previously attended, which was evacuated to Kazakhstan. From there, she wrote to her family, painting a picture which captures a fragment of the vast collective tragedy of her people:

It sometimes seems to me that our university is a refuge for all the miserable refugeless and homeless (oh, I won't be able to post this letter!). [She feared the wrath of the censors, but posted it anyway.] Shura was at the front. Whether or not she was married there, she returned with a child. Ah, Mayusha, you can't imagine how people look at such girls, and what a hard time they have. She is a little older than I, completing her second year when the war began. She has neither friends nor acquaintances, only the university. She was allowed to start in the third year and given a place in the hostel. The baby is four months old, a girl who cries day and night. She needs dry nappies, yet Shura possesses only the clothes on her back. She needs to be washed, but the water freezes in her room. We drag home every piece of wood we can find. Yesterday, I spotted a huge board by the wall on my way home. It was a theatre advertisement, in red letters on black background: "Othello." [They used it for firewood.] This means that for a couple of days Shura will be able to unwrap the little girl's blankets, dry her nappies . . . Dusya, my namesake, helps Shura in everything. She is also a student, although she must be nearing forty . . . If it wasn't for her, the little girl would have been long dead from cold and hunger. Aunt Dusya works as a loader at the bakery, and secretly brings some flour in her pockets. Shura makes soup from it, eats herself and feeds the little girl. People say that Dusya's own children were killed by bombs. She talks to no one, is very thin, dark, dresses like a man and smokes *makhorka* [shag tobacco].

Only a quarter of us are men, and even they are cripples. For some reason legs are the limbs most often hit—and they are cut off. Every second man here is without a leg. Most amputations are made very high. Petya (who sits next to me in lectures) has no legs at all, [only] artificial ones. He has trouble moving about. He can't get used to them, and anyway he is weak. He has a very sweet, shy face, and his eyes are very blue. His voice is soft. How could he have commanded a platoon? It becomes especially hard for Petya to move about when our bread ration arrives two or three days late. His face turns grey, cheekbones sharper, eyes bleaker . . . When we get very tired cutting and collecting firewood Petya jokes a lot, trying to amuse me and the girl next to me. His stories are not particularly funny, but we laugh and laugh at them.

Damn this war . . . One sees only cripples . . . To my mind the most wretched is a captain, a sapper. He has no face, but instead just a terrible blue, purple and green mask. It is fortunate that he is blind, and so cannot see himself. People say that, before the war, he was a handsome man. Even now he is tall, slender, and neat. We think that if he had a child he would be born again in it, and everyone would see what he once was like. If only this damn war would end. They are killing and maiming the best. We need to be very strong, to survive it.

One of Evdokiya's fellow students was a young man named Vitya, once very handsome, now deeply embittered by the loss of a leg. She wrote that he had become hardened, "turned to stone." He refused to see his family, even his mother, though he wrote to them. In one such letter, Vitya described the life of their town, where he had learned to ride a bicycle: "I push the pedals with one foot, and manage fine. The streets are empty, there are wrecked houses everywhere, empty shells. Evenings in the town park are unimaginably peaceful, there is even music. There are lots of girls, all blonde, and our officers are having a good time with them . . . as if there was no war now. These young ladies are nicknamed 'German shepherds' because they are indifferent to whether their men are Russian or German. I said as much to one, and she replied: 'You are jealous? Someone'll turn up for you too, my poor cripple, but not as good.' I threw my crutch at her."

All the combatant nations deployed women as nurses, a role many found rewarding. Dorothy Beavers was twenty-two in 1942, the daughter of an Ohio small farmer whose mother still drove a horse and buggy, with no phone at home. She worked in a little local hospital, and suggested to her father that she should join the army medical branch. Her two brothers had already gone into the service, and after some thought he said, "Maybe you should go and take care of them." She married an army doctor in Winchester, England, the night before sailing for France in June 1944, and landed on Utah Beach still clutching her bridal bouquet. "The job came naturally to me," she said. But it was a revelation to find herself treating eighteen- and nineteen-year-olds who had lost not only limbs, but sometimes their buttocks or "whole chunks of their hips." No one could call Lieutenant Beavers and her kind publicity seekers, but they all appreciated recognition back home. She was thrilled when a little paragraph about herself and a photograph appeared in the *Ohio State Journal*.

The Russians and Yugoslav partisans were the only fighting peoples to deploy women for combat functions. The British dispatched a small number of female agents to occupied territories under the orders of the Special Operations Executive (SOE), and women fulfilled vital administrative and support functions for both the Allied and Axis armed forces. They were treated with condescension by most senior officers, most of which had been born in the nineteenth century. Western Allied commanders, if not their Soviet counterparts, deplored the intrusion into service relationships of sexual temptations and tensions, actual or potential. Nimitz, at Pearl Harbor, declined to accept any females on his staff. Sir Arthur Harris of Bomber Command said, "I always believed that women in uniform should either be so beautiful that they felt no possible threat to themselves from any other woman, or so old and ugly that they were past it."

The RAF employed some German-speaking women to monitor enemy voice-radio transmissions. Most enthusiastically embraced the role, though a few displayed genteel scruples. Air Vice-Marshal Edward Addison, commanding the RAF's electronic countermeasures group, received a protest visit from a member of the Women's Auxiliary Air Force (WAAF), the daughter of a prewar bank manager in Hamburg, who recoiled from the demands of eavesdropping on Luftwaffe night-fighter conversation. She said she was embarrassed by the obscenities, common to airmen of all nationalities, that echoed across the airwaves. Most women were more robust. Working alongside combat personnel, or in the various branches of civil defence, they adapted to both the disciplines and the horrors. RAF pilot Ken Owen dismissed sentimental stereotypes about the relationship between crews and female ground staff at bomber stations: "It's bloody rubbish all that stuff about the WAAFs waving us off and so on. They became as callous and phlegmatic as we were."

For some girls, war proved as much of an adventure as it was for eager young male warriors: daily life acquired an exciting urgency. The German aristocrat Eleonore von Joest said, "I was young, I found it really interesting. I thought, 'All this is life.' " After von Joest, then aged nineteen, took part in the horrific 1945 mass exodus from East Prussia, her mother declared sardonically, "My daughter even managed to have fun on the trek." The barriers of sexual licence were dramatically extended. Many women of all nationalities felt a sentimentality, even a duty, towards fighting men on the brink of the grave. British land girl Muriel Green wrote one day in 1941 about her newly discovered passion for a French-Canadian soldier: "I am . . . almost in love! Or is it in love with love? What it is to be young and foolish! It certainly is good for morale in wartime to be made love to! . . . He is lonely and so am I. We are both away from home and friends . . . I am not quite sure whether I promised to go back to Canada with him or not! I will be his friend anyway! I blame the war for this." A few weeks later she described how she unwillingly allowed a Scottish soldier embarking for overseas to kiss her on their last date: "I did not want to really . . . but they were going away . . . and I may be the last girl he will kiss before he goes, maybe the last girl he will ever kiss. Bless him. He is too nice to be killed."

Green, who was twenty-two, expressed deep unhappiness early in the war, as quoted above, but exulted in pleasures she later discovered, romance notable among them. She looked back on 1944 as "one of the happiest [years] of my life. I have had good health, good friends, good working conditions with money to spend (if there had been anything to buy) and a jolly time. The war has progressed and left many scars. I am one of the lucky devils who have no scars." She later added: "Hostel life has changed nearly all the girls here to wife-pinchers . . . Eligible bachelors are so short . . . We all blame the war and go on enjoying life as it comes which in this place is life with other women's husbands."

The reverse of the coin, of course, was that men serving overseas were troubled by fears about the fidelity of their loved ones at home. Staff Sgt. Harold Fennema wrote from Europe to his wife in Wisconsin, "Honey, it's pitiful the number of times you hear fellows say that their last letter mentioned someone back home who is having a baby, and her husband has been overseas for a year or more. Unfaithfulness is probably the soldier's biggest cause for worry." Capt. Pavel Kovalenko of the Red Army wrote in a similar vein in July 1943: "The war has shaken all family values. Everything has gone to the dogs. Everyone lives for today. One needs a lot of strength and endurance to resist human temptations, to remain unstained. I have to resist, the honour of one's marriage is sacred."

Few husbands were as strong-minded as Kovalenko amid the sexual opportunities of war and the strains of long absences from home. As for wives and daughters, those in occupied countries who succumbed sexually to their invaders, whether voluntarily or under duress, almost invariably experienced social ostracism in their communities if they survived until the liberation. If some women enjoyed new freedoms, responsibilities and rewards, many more suffered grievously and were exploited mercilessly. The pregnant wife of an Italian in hiding described the misery of her daily existence in 1943: "I would sometimes queue from seven in the morning to three in the afternoon . . . I had to take my two small children with me. I found a place selling 'sanguinaccio' [blood sausage], which I found disgusting but my little girl ate. I had boils on my legs which I was told were caused by lack of vitamins. My husband was desperate for cigarettes and I found a tobacconist who supplied me. When I got home exhausted, all my husband wanted to do was make love. He would jump on me while I still held the shopping bag. When I refused, he accused me of having a lover." Some young warriors discovered compensations in conflict—adventure and a test of manhood—denied to most women, who recognised only its miseries and horrors. If the war dramatically expanded women's opportunities and responsibilities in some societies, it also intensified their exploitation, above all sexual, in a world arbitrated by force.

CHAPTER FOURTEEN

OUT OF AFRICA

EVEN WHEN THE United States dispatched troops to the Mediterranean theatre, by the end of 1942 the Western Allies deployed only sixteen divisions for ground operations against the Germans and Italians. The critical factors in the struggle against Hitler that year were Russia's survival and resurgence, matched by soaring American weapons production. On land, at sea and in the air, Allied forces began to receive the fruits of the United States' prodigious industrial efforts, with tanks and aircraft reaching the theatres of war in unparalleled numbers. America built almost 48,000 aircraft and 25,000 tanks in 1942, against Germany's 15,400 planes and 9,200 tanks. In 1939, just 29 shipyards were building for the U.S. Navy; by 1942 there were 322, which would deliver over 100,000 new ships and small craft to the U.S. Navy and Maritime Commission before VJ-Day came.

For the rest of the war, Western Allied operations were powerfully influenced by the need to concentrate appropriate shipping to land armies on hostile shores under fire in both the Pacific and European theatres. To achieve this, huge numbers of specialised, shallow-draught vessels were designed and built. The British led the way with the creation of LSTs—Landing Ships, Tank—capable of making an ocean passage, then offloading twenty tanks and up to a hundred other vehicles through their bow doors. The United States adopted the 2,286-ton model, larger than most destroyers, and built 1,573 by the end of the war. The construction of smaller vessels was dominated by the flamboyant, tough-talking, hard-drinking New Orleans boatbuilder Andrew Higgins, who styled himself "Mr. Landing Craft." Born in Nebraska in 1886, he offered his first design, the Eureka, to the U.S. Marine Corps in 1938. Its key features, conceived a decade earlier for Higgins's inshore craft used by rumrunners, revenue agents, oil drillers and trappers, were a propeller recessed in a semitunnel and a "spoonbill" bow. Its limitation was that troops disembarked over the sides. Higgins was then shown a photograph of a Japanese vessel with a bow ramp being used in China. He immediately telephoned his chief engineer and gave instructions for a prototype to be built, which was successfully tested on Lake Pontchartrain a month later. The Hig-

gins boats—designated as LCVPs, Landing Craft, Vehicle, Personnel—
were ordered in large numbers. The population of New Orleans grew
by 20 percent in 1942, largely because of the influx of workers needed to
build his boats, for which his company received orders worth $700 mil-
lion. Higgins became a legendary figure in wartime industry, turning out
some 20,000 craft. But he was financially reckless, and his company went
broke soon after the conflict ended.

Experience under fire in North Africa showed that wooden vessels were
highly vulnerable. Steel variants were introduced, many of them assembled
by a Florida farm-machinery contractor, which between 1943 and 1945
carried millions of Allied troops and tens of thousands of vehicles into battle. The Americans built a total of 42,000 such small craft and the British
3,000, nearly half of them in 1944; the United States also made 22,000
DUKW ("duck") amphibious trucks and amtracs, the latter used almost
exclusively in the Pacific. Yet even this vast inventory—what Americans
christened the "'gator navy"—never sufficed to satisfy demand: 2,470 small
craft were required merely for the initial phase of D-Day in Normandy.

Shortage of assault shipping was a chronic constraint on Allied strategy,
and Churchill frequently lamented British dependence on U.S. bottoms.
No amphibious operation could be mounted unless Washington willed it.
Britain's forces also called upon Lend-Lease for a growing proportion of
their weapons requirements. Britain's production of tanks fell from 8,600
in 1942 to 4,600 in 1944, of artillery pieces from 43,000 to 16,000. The
United States eventually provided 47 percent of the British Empire's
armour, 21 percent of small arms, 38 percent of landing ships and landing
craft, 18 percent of combat planes and 60 percent of transport aircraft. So
great became American capacity that deliveries to Britain amounted to only
11.5 percent of U.S. 1943–44 production: 13.5 percent of aircraft, 5 percent of food, and 8.8 percent of guns and ammunition. British industry
meanwhile focused on heavy bombers—the strategic air offensive engaged
around one-third of national output, which does much to explain why Britain attached such importance to its achievements and shortcomings.

AFTER PEARL HARBOR, there was an interval of thirty months—a long time in
the context of a seventy-one-month war—before America's military and
industrial mobilisation translated into large armies deployed on European
battlefields, though U.S. air and maritime power impacted sooner. Most
of the soldiers who later fought in northwest Europe enjoyed the luxury—
and endured the boredom—of more than two years' training before being
committed to action: the majority of U.S. formations did not see their first

battlefield until 1944. In 1942 the United States sent most of its marine corps and a few army divisions to the Pacific, and tens of thousands more soldiers to Iceland and Northern Ireland.

Americans began to descend on Britain in large numbers. Some warmed to the quaintness of Churchill's battered islands, but many questioned their inhabitants' commitment both to the mid-twentieth century and to waging war effectively. "The English were kind to us, especially when they got to know us," wrote an armoured officer, Haynes Dugan. "There were some wonderful parties, although supplies were low." Dugan never forgot one such gathering, at which a young Welsh paratroop officer sang in his own language. The American was bemused to discover that, amid the national clothing shortage, a woman guest was wearing a dress made from her own curtains. He recorded, "The shopkeepers had a favorite saying: 'It isn't rationed, old boy, we simply can't get it!' "

Bob Raymond, an airman from Kansas City, came to Britain to serve first with the RAF and later with the USAAF. He wrote home in May 1942: "The force of tradition and precedent is so strong that thinking in politics, business, religion, etc. seems to have congealed. They are the most economically backward people I've ever encountered. Labor-saving devices and short-cut, direct business methods are heartily resisted . . . Too much tea-drinking, Friday-to-Monday weekends, holidays etc." A U.S. government survey of domestic opinion on 25 March 1942 reported: "Americans have a greater confidence in the intensity of the Russian war effort than in the intensity of the British war effort; they feel that Russians are putting our Lend-Lease supplies to better use . . . Lack of confidence in British war effort has become more strongly marked since the fall of Singapore." The British were under no illusions about their low standing: "The Americans . . . knows us chiefly as a nation suffering from a slow decay," asserted a January 1943 War Office report, "a nation of superior, unfriendly, discourteous people, set in the old ways of inefficiency, clinging to old dreams of a greatness which we cannot perpetuate . . . We deceive ourselves if we think the soil is clean. The seeds of distrust and dislike lie dormant in it."

Throughout 1942 Britain continued the relentless naval struggle to hold open its global supply lines. The RAF's offensive against Germany slowly gathered momentum, joined by some USAAF bomb groups. A weak, predominantly Indian army confronted the Japanese on the Burmese frontier. The U.S. chiefs of staff were impatient to land in France, offering a token troop contribution to what would have been an overwhelmingly British forlorn hope. Churchill dismissed this idea out of hand, and convinced Roosevelt that the Allies should instead pursue the attainable objective of securing victory in the Mediterranean. North Africa thus persisted as the only theatre in which substantial British ground forces fought the Axis. In the desert, the men of the Eighth Army girded themselves for new efforts in a wilderness where neither side had the smallest emotional stake. The British officer Keith Douglas wrote:

> The great and rich men who cause and conduct wars . . . have so many reasons of their own that they can afford to lend us some of them. There is nothing odd about their attitude. They are out for something they want, or their Governments want, and they are using us to get it for them . . . It is exciting and amazing to see thousands of men, very few of whom have much idea why they are fighting, all enduring hardships, living in an unnatural, dangerous, but not wholly terrible world, having to kill and to be killed, and yet at intervals moved by a feeling of comradeship with the men who kill them and whom they kill, because they are enduring and experiencing the same things.

Neither Churchill nor his people doubted the dominant importance of the struggle in Russia, but North African operations mattered much to British self-respect. In the winter of 1942–43, these also offered an important, probably indispensable opportunity for some U.S. formations to gain combat experience and for curbing the hubris of their generals. During much of the preceding year, however, it seemed doubtful that the British could even hold Egypt. MP Harold Nicolson wrote: "A whisper is going round that our troops do not fight well . . . Our men cannot stand up to punishment. And yet they are the same men as man the merchant ships and who won the Battle of Britain. There is something deeply wrong with the whole morale of our Army." Churchill told a secret session of the Commons debating the desert campaign: "The conduct of our large army . . . does not seem to have been in harmony with the past or present spirit of our forces." Following the ignominious surrender of Tobruk on 21 June, Auchinleck dismissed Ritchie, his field commander, and took personal charge of the Eighth Army. But at the end of the month, beaten at Mersa Matruh, his battered formations retreated yet again, to the El Alamein line inside Egypt.

British fortunes were at their lowest ebb. It was widely agreed that desert generalship and tactics in the first six months of 1942 had been deplorable, the Gazala battles scandalously mishandled. Morale was wretched. It seemed plausible to both sides that Rommel might reach Cairo, and Egypt be lost to the Allies. The strategic impact of such a blow would have been limited, because the Axis lacked resources for exploitation. But the cost to

British prestige, already badly tarnished, would have been appalling. Panic swept Egypt, and the Royal Navy's Mediterranean Fleet quit Alexandria. Lt. Pietro Ostellino wrote exultantly to his wife on 2 July 1942, in a letter that emphasised residual fascist enthusiasm among some Italians who clung to hopes of military success: "Things here get better and better. As you will have heard from the radio and newspapers, the English and their allies are taking such a beating that they will find it difficult to raise their heads again. They deserve it! Our soldiers are simply marvellous. We cannot fail to be victorious now."

Washington agreed. The leaders of the U.S. Army believed, and continued to assume until late autumn, that the British campaign was lost; that the Eighth Army had shown itself fatally inferior to the Afrika Korps, which was destined to sweep onwards and seize the Nile Delta. During July, gloom suffused the British in Cairo, matched by visible exultation among Egyptians. On the notorious "Ash Wednesday," Middle East headquarters conducted bonfires of secret documents and many families fled to Palestine. To the shame of the Mandate authorities there, several hundred Jews fleeing Egypt who applied for sanctuary, including some working for the British, were refused entry visas. Officials asserted blandly that they were unable to breach immigration quotas.

Yet the British predicament was not as bad as they themselves supposed. Some civilians, even in occupied Europe, made shrewder deductions from meagre and deceitful Nazi bulletins than did Allied soldiers on the battlefield. Victor Klemperer, the great Dresden Jewish diarist, wrote on 8 July 1942: "I assume that England and Russia exaggerate by 100 per cent, Goebbels and Co by 200 per cent . . . In Russia Hitler's victories are killing him; in Egypt he really could win. But . . . Rommel appears to have been brought up short before Alexandria." Klemperer was right: Rommel's condition was unenviable. The outnumbered Axis army stood at the end of a tenuous 1,500-mile supply line. Allocations of fuel and weapons from Germany were always inadequate. Empowered by Ultra decrypts, the Royal Navy and the RAF began to inflict heavy attrition on fuel, tank and ammunition shipments across the Mediterranean.

The RAF in North Africa gained strength, while the Luftwaffe weakened; the first American Grant tanks, almost a match for Rommel's panzers, reached the Eighth Army. Strategically, it would have profited the Germans to withdraw to a line inside Libya, easing their own supply difficulties and increasing those of the British. Whatever delusions Rommel's soldiers cherished, his army lacked enough strength to make a final push for Alexandria with a realistic prospect of success. But vanity and ambition often caused "the Desert Fox" to overreach himself, and Hitler urged ill-judged aggression upon the Afrika Korps even more insistently than Churchill pressed his own commanders.

Auchinleck was well placed to frustrate Axis purposes, merely by holding his ground. American and British forces were to land at the opposite end of North Africa in November—Operation Torch—and this made it unnecessary for the Eighth Army to take risks. Once the Allies established themselves in Morocco, Algeria and Tunisia, Rommel's position in Egypt would become untenable. But as autumn approached, the success of Torch seemed ill-assured, especially in Washington. For the British, there was also the imperative of national prestige. Since 1939 Churchill's armies had suffered repeated defeats—indeed humiliations—often by smaller enemy forces. Spirits at home were low. Churchill's people had grown morbidly sensitive about the contrast between the heroic struggle waged by the Russians and their own nation's feeble battlefield showing. A British victory was desperately needed, and only in the desert was this attainable. The defeat of the Afrika Korps in Egypt was scarcely relevant to the war's outcome, but had become an issue of immense importance to morale, and was perceived as such by the prime minister.

On 1 July, when the Germans attacked again, they were repulsed in what became known as the first battle of El Alamein. In the encounters which followed neither side gained a decisive advantage. But what mattered was that Rommel was denied a breakthrough—although, given the opposing forces' respective strengths and detailed Allied foreknowledge of German intentions, it would have been disgraceful had he achieved one. In the first days of August Churchill arrived in Cairo with Gen. Alan Brooke, to see for himself how things stood. He sacked Auchinleck, who was replaced as Eighth Army commander by Brooke's nominee, Lt. Gen. Sir Bernard Montgomery, and as Middle East C-in-C by Gen. Sir Harold Alexander. A month later, on 30 August, Rommel attacked at Alam Halfa. Montgomery, provided by Ultra with full details of German plans, drove him back. The general then addressed himself to training Britain's troops for his own offensive. He had two critical advantages: large U.S. tank reinforcements were arriving and the Desert Air Force had gained dominance of the sky.

THE VOLUME of Ultra intelligence was now increasing dramatically, with critical influence in every theatre. In earlier years, decrypts were priceless, especially to the naval war, but their flow was erratic. From mid-1942 onwards, with a few important breaks, the Allies became privy to much of their enemies' signal traffic; the penetration of German and Japanese ciphers made a massive contribution to victory. Beyond the achievements of British and American decrypters, it was a secondary miracle that the Axis powers never seriously suspected that their most secret communications were being accessed by the enemy. Not all important traffic was read all the time: Axis telephone landlines, always the link of choice where available, remained secure. The quality of Allied analysis and exploitation varied in accordance with the prejudices of field commanders and their intelligence chiefs. For instance, Ultra would later reveal the December 1944 German armoured buildup in the Ardennes, but staffs failed to draw appropriate conclusions about an impending offensive. Knowing the enemy's hand did not of itself diminish the strength of his cards, and provided no guarantee of success in clashes between armies and fleets. But Ultra revealed to the Allies more about what the other side was doing and planning than had been vouchsafed to any previous combatants in history.

The Ultra achievement owed much to three Polish mathematicians, led by Marian Rejewski, who conducted critical early work on the German Enigma code machine between 1932 and 1939, after acquiring a commercial example of the ciphering device. The French assisted, providing the Poles with a list of 1931 Wehrmacht keys, acquired from a German source. Ironically, through Rejewski served with the Polish army in Britain between 1943 and 1945, he was never told of the rich fruits of his own pioneering achievements. In 1939 the Poles presented both the British and the French with reconstructed Enigma machines. The following year, these enabled the British Code and Cypher School at Bletchley Park to begin to break some German and Italian messages. At intervals thereafter, captures at sea of further Enigmas and monthly settings lists reinforced Bletchley's armoury of knowledge.

Ultra was a collective Allied designation for a large variety of Axis keys, more than 200 by 1945, some of which proved slow to surrender their secrets. Luftwaffe signals were broken first, towards the end of May 1940, followed by army and navy traffic. In 1941, a substantial volume of Wehrmacht messages were being read and their contents passed to Allied field commanders with an average delay of six hours. This proved too slow to influence tactical decisions in ground fighting. It became progressively understood that Ultra could be used most effectively to guide strategy, as it was during the summer 1942 Alamein battles.

Allied handling of Ultra intelligence became superbly sophisticated, with information passed to commanders by locally deployed Special Liaison Units whose role was not merely to protect secrecy, but also to ensure that no initiative or preemption of German action revealed Allied foreknowledge. If a prospective naval target was located at sea through cryptanalysis, whenever possible reconnaissance aircraft overflew the enemy before an attack to mask Ultra's role. From 1942 onwards, Bletchley Park became an industrial centre, with 6,000 staff working in a hutted township, processing a flood of messages in shifts around the clock. The heart of its operation was Colossus, the electromechanical bombe which dramatically speeded exploration of multiple mathematical possibilities. The codebreaking teams were dominated by some hundreds of brilliant academics, most of them mathematicians and German-speakers. The most influential personalities, both in their early thirties, were Alan Turing, sometimes described as the father of the computer, and Gordon Welchman. Some young men performing vital, and perforce absolutely secret, roles at Bletchley were chided by outsiders for their absence from the front. One received a letter from his former headmaster, asserting that his doggedly civilian status disgraced his old school.

The picture of enemy operations provided by Ultra was always incomplete, but it offered a reliability no intelligence provided by spies could match. For instance, the Allies could launch D-Day on 6 June 1944 confident that the enemy was still oblivious of their objective and timing. Churchill permitted some Ultra information about the Eastern Front to be passed to Moscow. Stalin was never officially informed of the Bletchley Park operation, but Moscow was well briefed by British traitors, who supplied their NKVD handlers in London with a steady flow of decrypts.

Full Anglo-American intelligence-sharing began only in 1943. The United States had broken the Japanese diplomatic cipher before the war, but their handling of Ultra never matched the interservice integration achieved by the British, partly because of army-navy rivalry. The U.S. Army ran its own decryption operation at Arlington Hall, Virginia, eventually employing some 7,000 staff. The navy team, based in bleak subterranean quarters at the Fourteenth Naval District, Pearl Harbor, was led by Cmdr. Joseph Rochefort, the awesomely brilliant Japanese-speaker, cryptanalyst and intuitive thinker who contributed so much to victory at Midway. Rochefort's men read some messages in the Japanese navy's JN-25 operational cipher soon after the outbreak of war and achieved fragmentary breaks at vital moments in 1942, which proved the most important Ultra achievements of the Pacific war. Thereafter, however, for some months JN-25 defied Rochefort's team, leaving naval intelligence dependent upon coast watchers and traffic analysis. In 1943 the operational code was again broken, and thereafter provided a stream of data for the rest of the war.

Bletchley Park and Arlington Hall played key roles in breaking Japanese army codes in 1943, the first being that of military attachés overseas. Captures of Japanese codebooks laid open bulk military signal traffic in

1944. Whereas in January that year Arlington Hall read fewer than 2,000 of the enemy's army messages, in March this increased to 36,000, decisively influencing MacArthur's New Guinea strategy. Interception of Japanese communications faltered during the 1944–45 Philippines campaign, when the army's main codes changed, causing a further interruption of decryption. In general, U.S. naval operations were more importantly influenced by Ultra than were those of the armies in the Pacific campaigns. No codebreaking achievement could eliminate the difficulties of assaulting strongly defended enemy positions. But the collective contribution of U.S. and British cryptanalysts to the war effort was greater than that of any other such small body of men in history. Their operations provided the supreme example of the Western Allies' imaginative integration into the war effort of their cleverest civilian intellects.

IN THE AUTUMN of 1942, Churchill was passionately impatient for the Eighth Army to attack. Once the Torch landings took place, the glory of every subsequent British success would have to be shared with the Americans. Alexander and Montgomery were relentlessly chivvied from London, though the foxy little field commander stuck to his own timetable. A cold, incisive, self-consciously professional soldier, "Monty" was determined to impose on British operations an order and discipline which had hitherto been absent. He has sometimes and not unjustly been described as "a good World War I general," most comfortable with limited set-piece operations. His most conspicuous attribute was "grip"; between August and October 1942, in a remarkable fashion he revived the confidence of the desert army. Reinforcements now gave the British a decisive advantage: the Eighth Army deployed 195,000 men against 104,000 Germans and Italians, 1,029 tanks against 489, 750 aircraft against 675, and enjoyed a massive superiority of artillery.

Keith Douglas, traversing the rear areas of the Eighth Army to join an armoured regiment, was fascinated by the spectacle of men and machines massing in the sands for battle: "Lorries appeared like ships, plunging their bows into drifts of dust and rearing up suddenly over crests like waves. Their wheels were continually hidden in dust-clouds: the ordinary sand being pulverized by so much traffic into a substance almost liquid, sticky to the touch, into which the feet of men sank almost to the knees. Every man had a white mask of dust in which, if he wore no goggles, his eyes showed like a clown's eyes."

On the other side of the hill, Rommel's army inhabited the same environment, but was prey to increasing gloom about its predicament. It bears emphasis that its most numerous component was Italian, not German, and like most of his countrymen, Vittorio Vallicella was dejected: "We are stuck in this desolate plain of El Alamein, tired, hungry, with little water, filthy and full of lice. We know that our Great Leader [Mussolini] is 660 kms from the front, furious because we have been unable to open the gates of Alexandria for him." He added: "For sixteen months we have led this life: kept going with a canteen of water (if lucky); at the mercy of fleas and lice. Maybe at this point we can only hope that a bomb takes us out and puts an end to our suffering." He recorded a comrade's suicide as the seventeenth in his unit since March 1941. The RAF strafed constantly: during one attack, Vallicella's companions were rash enough to seek cover under a vehicle which suffered a direct hit, killing them all. The "bomb-happy" Vallicella gained a respite of a few hours' sleep in a German field hospital before being sent back into the line.

The Italian army's supply system had collapsed, leaving its men dependent on German largesse. The Afrika Korps was irked by Italian scrounging, to which Vallicella and his comrades responded by resort to *"arrangiarsi,"* loosely translated as "every man for himself." "What will become of us?" mused the soldier. "How can we keep fighting so far from our supply bases and at the mercy of air attack? Not a week goes by when our supply columns are not machine-gunned and destroyed. Lack of water, food, arms, drives our morale to rock bottom." Many Italian soldiers were subsisting entirely on canned and dried food. After the first week, Vallicella wrote: "We are at the end of our tether; if our logistics have always been inadequate, now they scarcely exist." He and his comrades roamed the battlefield, scavenging food and water, draining fuel from the tanks of wrecked vehicles. The Folgore Division suffered shocking casualties: "Those young men supported only by mortars and the odd machine-gun wrote a page of history. Hundreds were wiped out for a regime that didn't even know how to provide them with the equipment they needed to fight."

Lt. Norman Craig, describing his own sensations as Alamein began, reflected on the challenge of junior leadership: "Before an attack fear is universal. The popular belief that in battle there are two kinds of person— the sensitive, who suffer torment, and the unimaginative few who know no fear and go blithely on—is a fallacy. Everyone was as scared as the next man, for no imagination was needed to foresee the possibility of death or mutilation. It was just that some managed to conceal their fear better than others. Officers could not afford to show their feelings as openly as the men; they had more need to dissemble. In a big battle a subaltern had little or no influence over the fate of his platoon—it was the plaything of the gods. His role was essentially histrionic. He had to feign a casual and cheerful optimism to create an illusion of normality and make it seem as if there was nothing in the least strange about the outrageous things one was asked to do. Only in this way could he ease the tension, quell any panic and convince his men that everything would come out right in the end. Inwardly I marvelled that they did not take to their heels. They grumbled and looked apprehensive, but nothing more . . . [The NCOs were thinking,] 'If an officer can do it, we damn well can.' The men looked to the NCOs and said, 'We'll go wherever the bloody corporals go.' Thus an army stands firm."

On 23 October, Montgomery launched Operation Lightfoot, the opening phase of the twelve-day second Alamein battle, which began with a devastating bombardment. Vittorio Vallicella was chatting with some Germans, drinking captured tea, when British shells began to fall upon them. "I have seen many enemy barrages, but the intensity of this one is beyond our experience." Men choking amid the acrid fumes of explosions watched tongues of flame leaping up across the desert. Vallicella took refuge in a dugout, seeking comfort in the companionship of others: "Together we feel less fear." He described one scene hard to imagine in any army save that of Mussolini. Ordered by a lieutenant to load the dead onto a truck and drive them to a temporary cemetery beside a field hospital, he refused. The officer threatened him with a pistol. At that moment their colonel arrived, remonstrated fiercely with the lieutenant and snatched the weapon from his hand; the crestfallen officer collapsed into tears. Vallicella and his comrades took the bodies to a field hospital, where nurses helped with the grisly task of unloading. They told the soldiers that their main task for days past had been to lay the dead in mass graves; even the necessary bulldozers had to be borrowed from their German allies.

For almost a week, Axis forces beat back repeated British attacks. In London, Churchill fumed. Lt. Vincenzo Formica recorded a surge of exultation in his unit on 1 November: the Italians briefly supposed that the British had abandoned their efforts to break through. They were heartened by the news of heavy tank losses which panzers had imposed on Montgomery's armoured units: "Officers and men, who had lived through the fighting and suffered for months amid the Egyptian desert through the hottest part of the year, saw that all their suffering and sacrifices were to be rewarded with the prize every warrior craves: Victory. We assumed we would be launching a counterattack. The word was 'Christmas in Alessandria!' "

Within twenty-four hours, however, the picture changed dramatically. Montgomery afterwards claimed that Alamein was fought to his original plan. In truth, he was obliged to shift his focus of attack northwards, but the Eighth Army's dominance of the battlefield was not in doubt. Attrition imposed intolerable losses on the Axis forces, whose fuel shortage had become acute. "All our illusions were shattered on the night of 2 November," wrote Lieutenant Formica. They set off behind a tank column, only to discover that its leader was lost. At last their colonel appeared, and personally guided them to the Ariete Division's concentration area. There "it became very plain to me that the whole military situation had changed—to our disadvantage. Long columns of vehicles from different units and even different formations were moving so chaotically as to make it obvious these were not organised bodies pursuing objectives. Conditions were appalling: poor visibility, vehicles bogged in sand, collisions. I looked down from our vehicle on silent and exhausted infantrymen. Occasionally I glimpsed the plumes of the Bersaglieri, upon whom so much glory and sand had been heaped."

Rommel, returning from sick leave to the battlefield, signalled Berlin that he was embarking upon a full-scale retreat, revealed by Ultra to the triumphant British. By 4 November, the Eighth Army was advancing in pursuit across open desert, while Axis units sought escape. Formica wrote that day: "As we drove, vehicles of every sort crossed my path, carrying pale and battered men. When I questioned officers and soldiers I realised that our whole line had cracked. It seemed impossible! . . . 'Look,' said my battalion commander. 'There are the English tanks.' I saw the enemy . . . silent and still like some treacherous wild beasts, half hidden in the early-morning mist."

Lt. Pietro Ostellino wrote that night: "We could see flares all around us in the starry sky: red for English and green for German. We had been moving slowly, at the best speed possible given the terrain and the darkness, when I was forced to abandon my tank in the desert because it couldn't keep up with the others." He and a handful of fellow Italians drove trucks westwards through the darkness, occasionally pausing so the officer could dismount and check his compass, until a German vehicle chanced upon them. Ostellino asked for news of the British, and though they had no language in common the Germans made plain that the enemy were all around them, that their only hope was to cover distance before dawn.

They paused briefly around midnight to eat and doze. Ostellino was woken by a shout, walked to investigate, and came upon the remains of an infantry battalion, heading for El Daba. "The men were at the end of their tether and desperately thirsty. Only the officers, who all had southern accents, sustained some spirit and energy and urged their men to keep going . . . It was a pitiful scene when those men driven to desperation by thirst and exhaustion went down on their knees around me so that I could

Victors celebrate at Bataan

Indian refugees on the flight from Burma that killed uncounted thousands

American prisoners in the Philippines

War in the Pacific: *Lexington*'s crew abandon ship during the Battle of the Coral Sea; and (below) Japanese dead on Guadalcanal

Australians evacuate a casualty during the struggle on Papua New Guinea's Kokoda Trail

Chipping ice on an Arctic convoy; and (below) survivors of a sunken U-boat huddle aboard an American warship during the Battle of the Atlantic

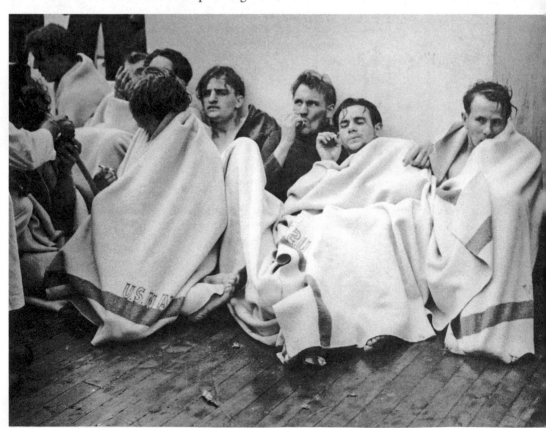

Women of the WRNS—Women's Royal Navy Service—push out a submarine torpedo for loading. Britain mobilised a larger proportion of its female population for war service than any other nation save the Soviet Union.

Some of Chiang Kai-shek's unhappy soldiers, of whom more than a million died in their 1937–45 struggle against the Japanese

A retreating German on the Eastern Front

Collateral damage: the Soviet Union in 1943

Women riveters in an American dockyard

A twelve-year-old Russian worker at the Perm aero-engine factory

The Red Army advances

One of Zainul Abedin's sketches from life—and death—
of victims of the 1943–44 Bengal famine

give them a drink." He found their colonel, an little veteran of the First World War with one eye covered by a black patch, following his men in a field car. The old man said pityingly, "We officers have other spiritual resources but my soldiers, poor fellows, can think only of their thirst." In truth, throughout the desert campaign Italian leadership was deplorable.

The Eighth Army's armoured units sped westward, their tracks churning sand, their crews thrilled that months of deadlock were broken. "The view from a moving tank is like that in a camera obscura or a silent film," wrote Keith Douglas, "in that since the engine drowns all other noises except explosions, the whole world moves silently. Men shout, vehicles move, aeroplanes fly over, and all soundlessly: the noise of the tanks being continuous, perhaps for hours on end, the effect is of silence." On and on they drove, though heavy rain and Montgomery's caution prevented them from converting success into destruction of Rommel's army. Vicenzo Formica noted in some embarrassment the contrast between the chaotic Italian rout and the ordered withdrawal of the Afrika Korps. "I met Captain Bondi, the Ariete's German liaison officer, cordially disliked by our men. He pointed to parties of German soldiers who were retreating on foot, very tired but still in perfect order, even as enemy shells fell between their files."

Vittorio Vallicella found the experience of retreat considerably less disagreeable than much else that had happened to him since 1941. He drove fast westwards with only six companions, successfully avoiding the roadblocks established to halt stragglers and reassemble broken units. For some days they were troubled by no news and no officers, and outpaced RAF strafing. They found dumps of petrol and oil to sustain their flight, and even managed to shoot a gazelle for fresh meat: "In the tragedy of the war these are some of our best days." Such good things came to an end, however: one of the group became sick, and on arrival at a field hospital they found themselves once more under military discipline. Each man was presented with a copy of an order of the day which ended with the words: "Every effort, every sacrifice will reap a happy and precious reward for the greatness of our country—*nostra patria*." Vallicella wrote: "Reading this order makes us want to throw up. Some generals always have the word *Patria* on their lips while they themselves are merely busy organising their messing arrangements."

Panzer officer Tassilo von Bogenhardt said: "All the fight seemed to have gone out of the men . . . We were carpet-bombed, dive-bombed and machine-gunned . . . The last thing I remember [before being wounded and evacuated] is blowing up my panzer when the petrol had run out, and watching the flames slowly envelop it. It was then that I knew this was the end of our Afrika Korps . . . I remember wondering why the British advanced so cautiously . . . if they only knew. I almost wished they did know."

Rommel was able to extricate a substantial part of his forces, but the Eighth Army had taken 30,000 Axis prisoners and destroyed large quantities of weapons and equipment. This time, for Rommel's retreating army there would be no further tilt of the seesaw eastwards. The British had achieved the only substantial land victory of the western war for which they would share laurels with no ally. In the course of December, the Germans turned and fought several fierce rearguard actions, but on each occasion the Eighth Army prised them from their positions and pushed on. Tripoli fell on 23 January 1943. Three days later, Montgomery's forces found themselves in Tunisia, where the last protracted phase of the North African war was fought out.

THE TORCH LANDINGS in Vichy French Algeria and Morocco on 8 November 1942 represented the first big combined operation against the Germans by the U.S. and British armies. Churchill and Roosevelt decreed it in the face of strong opposition from the U.S. chiefs of staff, who saw the Mediterranean merely as the focus of British imperialistic ambitions. Once it was acknowledged that there could be no continental D-Day in 1942, the president accepted the prime minister's view that some significant military gesture must be made to sustain a sense of Allied momentum; North Africa was the only plausible objective. Torch involved an initial Anglo-American force of 63,000 men and 430 tanks. It was hoped that Vichy French forces would offer no resistance to the two American assault divisions. Instead, however, these incurred 1,500 casualties in early actions ashore and were obliged to hit back hard.

A Foreign Legionnaire manning a Vichy battery above Casablanca described the gunners' horror when American planes fell upon their uncamouflaged positions: "In five minutes it was all over. I crept out of the ditch where I had flung myself when the first bomb fell . . . Out of thirty men and one officer, fifteen men and the officer were dead; ten more were wounded. The two guns were out of commission and two trucks were on fire. For a moment I felt great bitterness in my soul as I saw my comrades scattered all around. Ever since the fall of France, we had dreamed of deliverance, but we did not want it that way." On 10 November, the Allied supreme commander, Gen. Dwight Eisenhower, brokered a cease-fire. Thereafter, French forces progressively joined the Allied front against the Germans, though hampered by lack of weapons and—in the case of some officers—of enthusiasm for their new cause.

The North African advances thrilled the people of the Allied nations, once they dared to believe that these were more than mere swings of the pendulum. The land girl Muriel Green scribbled on 11 November: "Suddenly realized the news has become exciting. I had grown so tired of advances and withdrawals in Egypt for the past few years I did not realize this one was anything to jump about over. It is marvellous the Americans striking the other side, I really think things are beginning to happen and that victory is on the way." Some Germans were of the same opinion. "It is enormously impressive to see how sea power prevails," wrote Helmuth von Moltke, who yearned for Hitler's downfall, on 10 November after the Torch landings. "It advances like a colossus." To the Russians, the war in Africa usually seemed of scant relevance to the immensity of their own struggle. But tidings of Torch and Alamein reached the Red Army and gave its soldiers a small new infusion of hope. Even as Muriel Green was composing her diary in western England, on the Eastern Front Capt. Nikolai Belov wrote, "Good news came today: the Americans and English are giving the Germans a real thrashing. Though Africa is very far, now it feels so close."

In the town of Derna, 400 miles west of Alamein, one November day a party of Italian soldiers hungry for information met some Germans, one of whom who spoke good Italian. This man was a proud Nazi who insisted that the Axis would achieve victory in 1943. He had just been listening to the radio, he said, which announced Germany's capture of Stalingrad. That obviously meant the end of the Russians. The Italians were in no mood to be so credulous. "We hope he is right," wrote one, "but find his optimism unconvincing." Their scepticism was soon vindicated.

During the early stages of the North African campaign, U.S. commanders feared a possible German intervention through Spain. Once this failed to materialise, the invaders were securely ashore and the Vichy French abandoned resistance, the Allies anticipated swift clearance of the entire littoral. In this they were confounded. Hitler made an unexpected decision to send more men to North Africa. After twenty months in which he had denied Rommel support that might have yielded victory, the Führer now chose to reinforce failure. By air and sea, 17,000 German troops and supporting armour moved from Italy into Tunisia, with the acquiescence of its Vichy French resident-general. The Allies still had numerical superiority, but all the American troops and many of the British were green. The Luftwaffe provided effective air support to the German ground forces, led locally by Gen. Jürgen von Arnim.

Vittorio Vallicella and his comrades of Italy's dwindling desert contingent spent Christmas 1942 on the Tunisian shore, nursing homesickness and sheltering from British bombs: "At midnight mass, I gaze upon sad faces. The English upset us by launching an air raid, and everyone rushes to their posts. It is thus that we spend Christmas Eve rather than eating the feast Doliman"—their hugely admired cook—"had promised." Next day, however, matters improved: the master chef prepared for them pasta with ragù, boiled potatoes, a slice of meat, and—to their astonishment—panettone, "never seen in these parts." Doliman proudly showed them its box: "Panettone Motta." Their Christmas lunch was washed down with half a litre of wine and half a mess tin of brandy. "Never has a meal been so good. We end the day swimming naked in the Mediterranean while our loved ones are almost certainly immersed in fog." Vallicella had the good fortune to be taken prisoner by the French soon afterwards, and spent the next three years as an agricultural labourer in their hands; he did not return to his beloved homeland until 1947.

Amid winter rain and mud, the Germans were able to frustrate Allied efforts to rush Tunis: in a series of January offensives, von Arnim's formations drove back ill-equipped French forces and held open the supply line to the Afrika Korps farther east. In February, they achieved a series of smashing successes against the Americans, destroying two tank, two infantry and two artillery battalions of Lt. Gen. Lloyd Fredendall's corps in a single forty-eight-hour operation. Rommel then launched an attack through the Kasserine Pass, which drove back Eisenhower's forces in humiliating disarray. The Americans learned lessons, often forced upon the British before them, about the quality of enemy armour, the speed of the Germans' actions and reactions and the ruthlessness with which they pressed every advantage. Some U.S. units panicked in a fashion which inspired contempt among senior British officers, including Alexander, who should have known better. The performance of the British First Army in Tunisia revealed many shortcomings, both in the skills of its soldiers and in the abilities of its commander, Gen. Kenneth Anderson. Sensible English people understood the folly of patronising their allies. RAF corporal Peter Baxter wrote in his diary: "I think the Americans merely lack training in battle conditions, and maybe aren't too sure what they're supposed to be fighting the Germans for." Both these suppositions were true.

Whatever setbacks Eisenhower's army suffered, the tide of war in North Africa was running overwhelmingly in the Allies' favour. The caution of the Italian high command denied Rommel a chance to exploit a brief opportunity to outflank and destroy Allied forces in northern Tunisia. The Americans were reinforcing rapidly, while German strength was shrinking. On 22 February 1943 Rommel was obliged to break off his offensive. Next day, he was promoted to become C-in-C Army Group

Africa. A week later, Ultra revealed his intention to use all three of his weak panzer divisions to strike Montgomery's Eighth Army, which was approaching the Axis Mareth line in southern Tunisia. The German push at Medenine on 6 March was easily thrown back; Rommel, a sick man, left Africa for the last time.

Soon Montgomery was attacking Mareth with a large superiority of tanks and aircraft. After the failure of his first assault on 19 March, he conducted a successful outflanking operation deeper inland, but the Germans were able to withdraw intact to new positions at Wadi Akarit. Meanwhile, the Americans regained the ground lost in the small disaster at Kasserine. At the urging of Alexander, now Eisenhower's deputy, chaotic Allied command arrangements were reorganised; the most visibly incompetent American officers were replaced with a ruthlessness the British might profitably have emulated. Through April, the Allies steadily pushed back the Axis line. By early May, von Arnim's forces were confined to a pocket seldom more than 60 miles from the Mediterranean coast, along a 150-mile front where the British confronted them in the east and the Americans farther west.

The Allies tightened their grip on the Axis Mediterranean supply route, achieving record sinkings of ships. Von Arnim's shortage of armour, ammunition, fuel and food worsened. It became plain that his resistance could not be much prolonged; indeed, it was remarkable that he sustained the struggle for so long against much superior Allied forces—at no time in North Africa did Eisenhower's and Alexander's soldiers find their task easy. In April, the U.S. II Corps was frustrated in an attempted breakthrough, but Montgomery finally achieved success at Wadi Akarit, driving back his opponents to a new line. On 22 April, Alexander launched an all-out offensive: the First Army attacked towards Tunis, Gen. Omar Bradley's corps at Bizerta and the French towards Pont du Fahs. The British Eighth Army failed to smash the new German line at Enfidaville. On Montgomery's advice, Alexander transferred two of his divisions to the First Army, to deliver a final assault along the Medjez–Tunis road, with massive air and artillery support. The combined pressure on von Arnim's front proved irresistible: Tunis, Bizerta and Pont du Fahs fell on the same day, and two wrecked German panzer armies disintegrated. The last Axis pocket surrendered on 13 May, and 238,000 prisoners fell into Allied hands.

Victory had required almost five months' more fighting than the Anglo-American high command had anticipated in November, after El Alamein and Torch. But Hitler's reinforcement of failure rendered success, when it came, correspondingly greater. Initial American hubris was punished by Wehrmacht skill, but Eisenhower and his colleagues displayed sense and humility in learning the lessons. Weaknesses of command, tactics, equipment and junior leadership were addressed to some effect before the Allied armies began to cross the Mediterranean.

The British Army was vastly cheered by the sense of redemption that accompanied its arrival in Tunis. After almost three years of hard campaigning, it had achieved a victory which won enthusiastic applause at home. Despite the overblown acclaim lavished on Montgomery, the Eighth Army's commander had shown himself a steady professional. His record was tarnished by failure to destroy Rommel's army after Alamein, the sluggishness of his subsequent pursuit and some important failures against German defensive positions. British lieutenant general Sir Frederick Morgan, a bitter critic, asserted that "the pursuit of Rommel across Africa was in the nature rather of a stately procession than of a rout of a defeated army." But Montgomery had proved himself the ablest British general of the war thus far, with a shrewd awareness of the limitations of his citizen army.

The North African campaign established the reputations of the Allied commanders who would dominate the big western battles in Europe— "Monty," Alexander, Eisenhower, Patton, Bradley. It was their good fortune to face the Germans when the Allies had substantial material superiority and the Wehrmacht had suffered debilitating losses in Russia. There is no reason to suppose that any of the battlefield stars of 1942–45 would have fared better than their French and British predecessors, had they borne responsibility for the earlier campaigns of the war. The first requirement of a general eager to forge a great reputation is to lead an army with sufficient strength to overcome its opponents.

By May 1943, after the Germans' epic defeat at Stalingrad and expulsion from North Africa, there was no doubt among the Allied nations, and little among the Axis peoples, about the outcome of the war. Lt. Vicenzo Formica, whose hopes of desert victory were so high on 1 November 1942, reflected wretchedly on the disillusionment that had followed: "I think back with pride to those far-off days, and my heart bleeds on contemplating the reality of life around us today. I am a prisoner in a concentration camp [his description of his POW camp] in the middle of North America." Yet, if the tide was now running strongly for the Allies, great uncertainties persisted about the course and duration of the war. It seemed plausible that the Nazi empire might survive until 1947 or 1948. While Churchill ordered the church bells of Britain rung for victory in North Africa, much more pain and hardship lay ahead before the Allies would enjoy real cause for celebration.

CHAPTER FIFTEEN

THE BEAR TURNS: RUSSIA IN 1943

IN 1943, while the Western Allies were still conducting modest operations in the Mediterranean, the Soviet Union inflicted on Germany a series of massive defeats, causing irreparable losses of men, tanks, guns and aircraft. The superiority of Stalin's armies grew alongside the confidence of his generals. Soaring weapons output increased the Red Army's advantage: the Russians were building more than 1,200 T-34s a month, while the Germans produced only 5,976 Panthers and 1,354 Tigers, their best tanks, during the whole war. After the triumphs of the winter, Stalin's people had no doubt of final victory. Nonetheless, until the end they were obliged to fight hard and to accept massive casualties.

The plight of Russia's civilians remained dire, with millions nudging starvation even when the tide of war ebbed from their immediate vicinity. In January 1943, some people who had sent their families out of Moscow when the city seemed doomed now brought them back, but Lazar Brontman was deterred by continuing shortages of fuel, electricity and rations. "Everyone talks incessantly of food," the journalist wrote. "We recall the menus of dinners gone by, and if somebody dines in richer and more fortunate company, he afterwards torments others with details of the dishes served." In the printworks of *Pravda*, it was necessary to remove lightbulbs as soon as the daily edition was dispatched to prevent them from being stolen. Amid the fuel famine, wooden fences vanished from Moscow's streets and suburbs. Subzero temperatures obliged office staff to work in overcoats and gloves.

Battlefield successes provided satisfaction but scant cause for exuberance, because so many people continued to die. Again and again in 1943, the Russians accomplished dramatic encirclements, only to find the Germans smashing their way free, conducting fighting withdrawals with their customary skill. "The Russians weren't very good," asserted a Waffen SS gunner, Capt. Karl Godau. "They just had the masses. They attacked in masses, so they lost in masses. They had good generals and good artillery, but the soldiers were poor stuff." Such condescension was overstated, but it remained true that Soviet middle-ranking leadership was weak, organisation often collapsed on the battlefield, and men paid in blood for repeated tactical blunders.

The machine gunner Aleksandr Gordeev deplored the crudity of his own army's tactics: "The frontal attacks puzzled me. Why advance straight into German machine-gun fire? Why not make flank attacks?" He briefly deluded himself that his own company, reduced to one-third strength, would be spared from making further assaults, but instead early one morning it was reinforced by rear-area personnel, some of them clerks. They were issued double rations of vodka, "and those who wanted it drank more." Gordeev's assistant gunner was reassigned as a rifleman, and "walked off as though assured he was facing death." He was replaced by a soldier sweating with terror and limping from the consequences of a self-inflicted wound. Gordeev wrote, "The situation was pretty shitty; this wasn't a company, but a drunken mob"; it was nonetheless plunged back into battle.

In Nikolai Belov's sector of the front, on the morning of 20 February 1943, a Russian bombardment designed to pound the Germans fell instead on his own men, who suffered heavily even before meeting the enemy. After a day of bloody fighting, at 4:00 p.m. he himself was wounded. He lay between the trenches for four hours before darkness fell and submachine gunners were able to drag him back into the trenches, and thence to the rear for treatment. Belov returned to his battalion three weeks later to find almost all its officers gone, most of them dead: "Major Anoprienko left for the [Military] Academy. Division commander Colonel Ivanov is killed. Captain Novikov shot [presumably for dereliction of duty], Grudin killed. Dubovik killed. Alekseev died of wounds. Stepashin stripped of rank and sentenced to ten years [imprisonment]."

But Russia could endure such losses, and even such clumsy, brutal warmaking. Stalin's forces were now much larger than those of Hitler, and their superiority was growing steadily: some Soviet weapons systems were better than those of the Wehrmacht. Russian air power was increasingly formidable, as ever more of the Luftwaffe's declining strength was diverted to defend the Reich from Allied bombers. For a time in the spring of 1943, the Germans looked incapable of holding any line east of the Dnieper, 400 miles from Stalingrad. Indeed, it seemed plausible that Hitler's Army Groups A and Don could be prevented even from getting back to the river. As thousands of prisoners were herded into cages, Russian soldiers savoured booty, notably including clothing: many men in Ivan Melnikov's unit seized the opportunity to replace the cloths wrapped around their feet with German boots. "It was hard to take off our foot bandages, for they had stuck to the skin and one had to tear them off rag by rag," Melnikov wrote with clinical dispassion. "Using water unsparingly, we washed our blistered, bleeding feet. Some of us put on socks that we found . . . Then we marched onwards full of cheer."

At the end of January, a fast tank force directed by Southwest Front commander Nikolai Vatutin crossed the Donets east of Izyum and raced south towards Mariupol, on the Sea of Azov, to get behind the Germans. On 2 February, Zhukov and Vasilevsky launched an ambitious two-pronged attack, one spearhead driving southwestwards, past Kharkov towards the Dnieper, the other heading northwest for Smolensk by way of Kursk, which fell on 8 February. Kharkov was captured a week later, and within days Soviet forces approached the Dnieper crossings at Dnepropetrovsk and Zaporozhye.

Thereafter, however, Russian difficulties increased. Panzers wrecked Vatutin's mobile force by superior tactics and gunnery. Manstein took command of Army Group South and launched a series of punishing offensives. Before the spring thaw reduced the battlefield to mud, which as usual immobilised armour, on 11 March the Germans retook Kharkov, where many Russians experienced extraordinary odysseys. On 8 March, the medical orderly Aleksei Tolstukhin found himself trapped by the German advance on the city. He wrote later to his parents: "For ten days I wandered around the steppe, trying to get back to the Red Army. I was frozen, starving and very tired. On the eleventh day I found a straw stack and fell asleep in it. I was woken by a heavy blow on the back from a rifle butt. I opened my eyes to find Hitler's men standing over me. After that, a new icy and hungry life began for me, with endless beatings. I cannot describe to you all that I have suffered. I can't bear to talk about it. Only on 17 September did I find an opportunity to escape. At ten in the morning of 21 September I walked through the front line 20 km from Poltava . . . I still cannot believe that I am back with my own people." Corporal Tolstukhin escaped the draconian sanctions often imposed on escaped prisoners by their own commissars and was merely returned to duty. He was soon wounded by shrapnel, though not badly enough to escape the battlefield; on 16 November, he was killed on the bank of the Dnieper.

The Germans, meanwhile, endured ample miseries of their own. "We never heard a frank admission of defeat," wrote Guy Sajer. When his unit began to pull back from the west bank of the Don, "as most soldiers had never studied Russian geography, we had very little idea of what was happening." But after Stalingrad, fear of encirclement gnawed at every German. Sajer and a handful of fellow infantrymen made their escape in

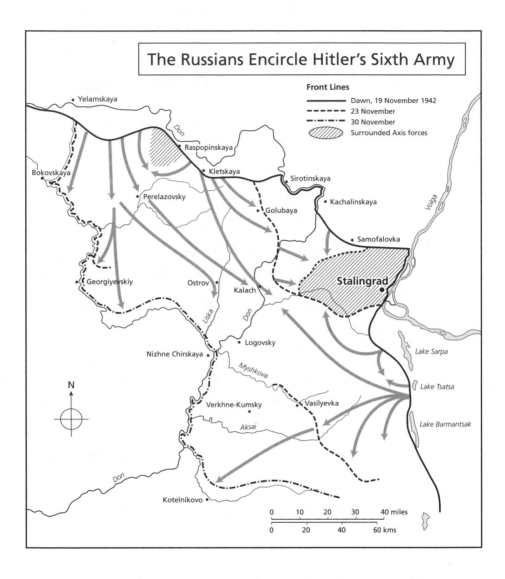

The Russians Encircle Hitler's Sixth Army

Front Lines
——————— Dawn, 19 November 1942
- - - - - - - 23 November
—·—·—·— 30 November
▨ Surrounded Axis forces

darkness, in a Russian truck towed by a tank. "The windshield became caked with mud, and Ernst waded through the liquid ground to scrape it away with his hand ... Behind us the wounded had stopped moaning. Maybe they were all dead—what difference did it make? Daylight dawned on faces haggard with exhaustion." The party halted and an engineer NCO shouted, "One hour's rest! Make the most of it!" The towing tank's commander shouted back, "Fuck you! We'll leave when I've had enough sleep!" There was a fierce altercation between the two men, the engineer seeking to pull rank. The tankman said, "Shoot me if you like, and drive the tank yourself. I haven't slept in two days, and you're to leave me the hell alone." They got away two hours later, but the experience emphasised that German soldiers, like their foes, could flag in the face of acute adversity.

On 18 March two panzer divisions took advantage of a railway embankment to race their tanks in column to Belgorod and retake the city. In the north, Hitler reluctantly authorised a withdrawal from the Rzhev salient, which no longer presented a credible threat to Moscow. This enabled Army Group Centre to shorten its line by 250 miles, and created a sufficient concentration of strength to stem an offensive by Rokossovsky. As the Germans fell back, millions of Russians beheld the devastation and carnage left behind them. Many who remained unmoved by the familiar plight of adults gave way to emotion on witnessing the tragedies of the very young. Capt. Pavel Kovalenko wrote on 26 April: "We understand the horrors of war, its relentless laws written in blood. But children, these blossoms of life, the blossoms of blossoms, these innocent holy souls, the beauty of our lives . . . they, who have done no harm to anyone . . . are suffering for the sins of their parents . . . We've failed to protect them from the beast. One's heart bleeds, one's thoughts freeze with horror at the sight of small bloodsoaked bodies, with gnarled fingers and distorted little faces . . . They bear mute testimony to indescribable human suffering. These small, frozen, dead eyes . . . reproach us, the living."

In the village of Tarasevichi, by the Dnieper, Vasily Grossman met a teenage boy. "They are so frightening, these old, tired, lifeless eyes of children. 'Where is your father?' 'Killed,' he answered. 'And mother?' 'She died.' 'Have you got brothers or sisters?' 'A sister. They took her to Germany.' 'Have you got any relatives?' 'No, they were all burned in a partisan village.' And he walked into a potato field, his feet bare and black from the mud, straightening the rags of his torn shirt." A million such encounters forged the mood of Russia's soldiers as the time approached when they would enter the territories of Hitler's people. The Soviet propagandist Ilya Ehrenburg wrote: "Not only divisions and armies . . . [but] all the trenches, graves and ravines with the corpses of the innocents are advancing on Berlin." A Soviet propaganda slogan said: "The soldier's rage in battle must be terrible. He does not merely seek to fight; he must also be the embodiment of the court of his people's justice."

Grigory Telegin wrote to his wife on 28 June 1943: "I received the letter telling me that your brother Aleksandr was killed on 4 May . . . My heart has become like stone, my thoughts and feelings reject pity; hatred towards the enemy burns in my heart. When I look through my sights, firing point-blank at these beasts on two legs, and see their split skulls and mutilated bodies, I feel a great joy and laugh like a child in the knowledge they will not come back to life. I will describe a typical day in action. 5 June. The rising sun's rays are reflected in flashes from our tank turrets. Droplets of fog hang like crystals on the leaves of the trees. Three green rockets signalled the attack. At 0700 our tanks advanced in column, then extended into line in a clearing. We could clearly see the wooden houses of the village."

Russian shells were exploding in the German positions. The attackers glimpsed figures running towards the rear, prone bodies crushed beneath their own tank tracks. But mines and antitank guns caught first one Soviet tank, then a second, then a third, which burst into flames. Telegin continued: "My heart sickens at the thought of my friends, still firing from the burning vehicles. Anger and hatred drive us on, overtaking the stricken tanks. We crush enemy machine-gun pits and anti-tank guns with their crews." Reaching the far side of the village, he saw German trenches ahead, between woods and ditches impassable by tanks. Identifying nearby the tank of his friend Misha Sotnik, he ran his own T-34 alongside. They switched off their engines and held a brief shouted exchange. Agreeing to advance one on each side of the German trenches, they started up again and lurched onwards.

During the ensuing struggle, a direct shell hit wrecked Telegin's machine gun and optics. As the hours dragged on amid smoke and dust, the crew became so thirsty that some men at times drifted into unconsciousness. Then the engine overheated and died. Stranded under fire, they took another direct hit which concussed the driver and caused Telegin briefly to pass out. "We gasped like fish, our lips cracked, mouths dry. We opened the driver's hatch and saw ten metres away a crater filled with water. Bullets buzzed around us, but I rolled out of the hatch, crawled towards the water and drank. I brought water for my comrades in messtins, and we revived." For the next ten hours they remained prisoners of their stinking, sun-baked steel box. Then, at last, the driver's experiments with the choke were rewarded, and the engine roared. "We pulled back. An ambulance drove up, and I saw a familiar silhouette on a stretcher. It was Misha Sotnik, a sub-machine gun bullet in his head. Unable to hold back my tears, I kissed Misha's blue lips and said farewell."

Even when the tide of war had turned, and indeed until the last months, Stalin's armies suffered a relentless haemorrhage of deserters, many of them "Eldash" or "Youssefs"—Asians. Nikolai Belov recorded his own battalion's losses on 13 June 1943: "Two more men have deserted to the enemy, making a total of eleven, most of them Eldash." Red Army statistics showed 1,964 of its soldiers deserting to the enemy in April 1943, 2,424 in May, 2,555 in June. The usual penalties were imposed on those caught making such an attempt. Belov wrote of one execution: "Today a Youssef was shot in front of the unit for trying to desert to the Germans. Creepy feeling." On 2 June he recorded laconically: "Two more men tried to desert today. Luckily they got blown up on mines and were dragged back." Like many Red officers, he felt able to rely only on his own racial group, writing after reinforcements reached the unit: "They are green-horns, born 1926. Such youngsters. But what is good about them is that they are well-trained and all of them Russian. These men won't desert."

The enemy had his own morale problems. Belov was astonished to learn from a neighbouring unit that two Wehrmacht soldiers, one of them a sergeant, had surrendered. "This is the first time I've heard of Germans coming over to us. Their lives are not so good, then." Capt. Pavel Kovalenko had the same experience on 31 March: "A German deserter appeared completely out of the blue. There was a knock at the door. 'Who is there? Come in!' The door opened and a Fritz appeared. Everyone grabbed their guns. He took out a gold watch and gave it to one soldier, handed a gold ring to another, his rifle to a third. Then he raised his hands. He is from Westphalia, a coal miner, aged twenty-two. His father had told him to desert."

But some Germans did not despair, even when they fell into Russian hands. Nikolai Belov cited the example of a prisoner brought in by his reconnaissance platoon, "a big fellow of twenty-two. Where do these scoundrels get such youths from? He said that they will launch an offensive in a month, and want to finish the war this year. Germany will of course win." Hitler scraped together reinforcements which enabled him by June 1943 to deploy in Russia just over 3 million German troops. He acknowledged that a general offensive remained impracticable, but insisted on a single massive thrust. His attention focused upon the bulge in the Soviet front west of a monosyllabic place-name that would enter the legend of warfare: Kursk. The scale of the eastern conflict is emphasised by the fact that the salient was almost as large as the state of West Virginia, nearly half the size of England. It featured some low hills and contained many ravines and streams, but most of the region was open steppe—dangerous ground for a tank advance against effective antitank fire. Underground iron-ore deposits caused wild compass variations, but this scarcely mattered when neither side had cause for uncertainty concerning the whereabouts of the enemy.

For the Kursk attack, Hitler concentrated much of the combat power of the Wehrmacht, together with three fresh SS panzer divisions, 200 of his new Tiger tanks and 280 Panthers. Yet the limited scope of Citadel, as his operation was code-named, contrasted with the sweeping offensives of 1941 and 1942 and emphasised Hitler's diminished means. The Russians readily identified the threat, aided by detailed intelligence provided by their Swiss-based "Lucy" spy ring. At a key Kremlin meeting on 12 April, Stalin's generals persuaded him to allow the Germans to take the initiative. They were content for the panzers to impale themselves on a defence in depth, before the Red Army counterattacked. Through spring and early summer, Soviet engineers laboured feverishly to create five successive lines studded with minefields, bunkers and trenches, supported by massive deployments of armour and guns. They massed 3,600 tanks against the attackers' 2,700; 2,400 aircraft against the Luftwaffe's 2,000; and 20,000 artillery pieces—twice the German complement. Some 1.3 million Russians faced 900,000 Germans.

Manstein, commanding Army Group South, spent three months assembling his forces, but few Germans other than the Waffen SS formations deluded themselves about Citadel's prospects of success. Lt. Karl-Friederich Brandt wrote wretchedly from Kursk: "How fortunate were the men who died in France and Poland. They could still believe in victory." Manstein no longer aspired to achieve the Soviet Union's defeat; he sought only a success which might oblige Stalin to acknowledge stalemate, a strategic outcome that would persuade Moscow to accept a negotiated peace rather than fight to a finish.

Russian soldiers advanced to the defence of Kursk through lands laid waste by their enemies. Eighteen-year-old Yuri Ishpaikin wrote to his parents: "So many families have lost their fathers, brothers, the very roofs over their heads. I have only been here a few days, but we have marched far through a devastated country. Everywhere lie unploughed and unsown fields. Only chimneys and stone ruins survive in villages. We saw not a single man or beast. These villages are real deserts now. At night the whole western side of the sky is lit up, copper-red. It makes the soul rejoice to pass an undamaged village. Most houses are empty, but chimney smoke curls from a few, and a woman or boy comes out onto the porch to watch the Red Army pass." Ishpaikin, like many others, would never leave the Kursk battlefield.

"It grew hot as early as 0800 and clouds of dust billowed up," wrote Pavel Rotmistrov, commanding a guards tank army as its long columns moved into the salient. "By midday the dust rose in thick clouds, settling in a solid layer on roadside bushes, grainfields, tanks and trucks. The dark red disc of the sun was hardly visible through the grey shroud of dust. Tanks, self-propelled guns and tractors, armoured personnel carriers and trucks were advancing in an unending glow . . . Soldiers were tortured by thirst and their shirts, wet with sweat, stuck to their bodies. Drivers found

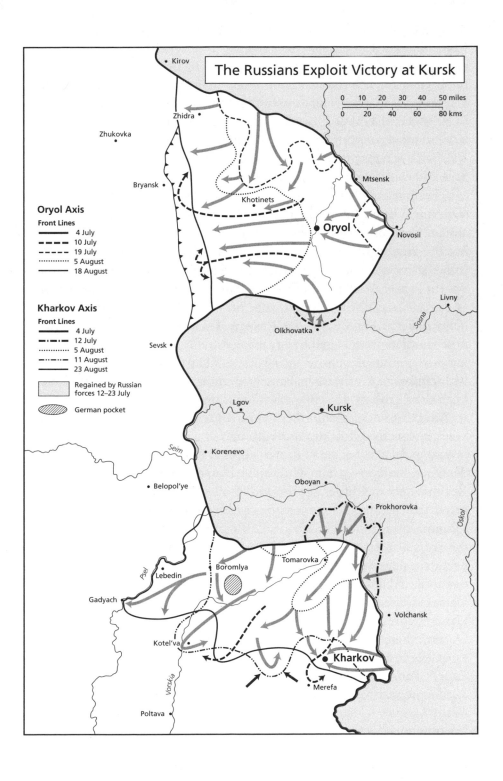

The Russians Exploit Victory at Kursk

0	10	20	30	40		50 miles
0	20		40		60	80 kms

Kirov

Zhidra

Zhukovka

Bryansk

Khotinets

Mtsensk

Oryol

Novosil

Oryol Axis

Front Lines

———— 4 July
━━━━ 10 July
- - - - 19 July
·········· 5 August
———— 18 August

Livny

Sosna

Olkhovatka

Sevsk

Kharkov Axis

Front Lines

———— 4 July
—·—·— 12 July
·········· 5 August
—··—··— 11 August
———— 23 August

Regained by Russian
forces 12–23 July

German pocket

Lgov

Kursk

Seim

Korenevo

Oskol

Belopol'ye

Oboyan

Prokhorovka

Psel

Lebedin

Boromlya

Tomarovka

Gadyach

Volchansk

Kotel'va

Kharkov

Voriskla

Merefa

Poltava

the going particularly hard." Those who could write penned last letters, while illiterate men dictated to comrades. Twenty-year-old Ivan Panikhidin had survived a serious wound in the 1942 fighting. Now, approaching the front again, he professed pride about taking part in a struggle vital to his country: "In a few hours we shall join the fighting," he told his father. "The concert has already begun, we just need to keep the music going: I write to the accompaniment of the German barrage. Soon we shall attack. The battle is raging in the air and on the ground . . . Soviet warriors stand firm in their positions." Panikhidin was killed a few hours later.

The Luftwaffe battered the Russian lines for days before the assault, achieving a direct hit on the billet of Rokossovsky, who was fortunately absent. German artillery fire was met by a Russian counterbarrage, blasting the ground where formations were massing to advance. On 5 July Model's forces lunged forward from the north, while in the south the Fourth Panzer Army struck. From the outset, each side recognised Kursk as a titanic clash of forces and wills. Stuka dive-bombers and SS Tiger tanks inflicted heavy losses on Russian T-34s. Many of the new German Panthers were halted by breakdowns, but others forged on, crushing Soviet antitank guns in their path, while panzergrenadiers grappled with Zhukov's infantry, using flamethrowers against trenches and bunkers. Both sides' artillery fired almost without interruption.

After three days, the northern German armies had advanced eighteen miles, and seemed close to a breakthrough. Rokossovsky's army withstood savage assaults, but some of its units broke. A SMERSH (morale) report denounced officers whom it deemed blameworthy: "The 676th Rifle Regiment showed little appetite for combat—its second battalion commanded by Rakitsky left its positions without orders; other battalions also succumbed to panic. The 47th Rifle Regiment's Lt. Col. Kartashev and the 321st's Lt. Col. Vokoshenko panicked, lost control, and failed to take necessary steps to restore order. Some senior officers showed themselves cowardly and deserted the battlefield: the 203rd Artillery Regiment's CO Gatsuk showed no interest in his unit's operations and with telephonist Galieva retired to the rear areas, where he resorted to drink."

But others held fast, and Model's armour suffered massive attrition, especially from Russian minefields. In the south, by 9 July almost half of Fourth Panzer Army's 916 fighting vehicles were disabled or wrecked. Across the vast battlefield, a jumble of armour and men milled, surged, clashed, recoiled. Flame and smoke filled the horizon. Commanders heard a confusion of German and Russian voices competing in urgency on their radio nets: "Forward!," "Orlov, take them from the flank!," "*Schneller!*," "Tkachenko, break through into the rear!," "*Vorwärts!*" The correspondent Vasily Grossman noted that everything on the battlefield including food became black with dust. At night, exhausted men were unnerved by the sudden descent of silence: the cacophony of the day seemed more acceptable because it was more familiar.

On 12 July Zhukov launched his counterthrust, Operation Kutuzov, against the northern Orel salient. A German tank officer wrote: "We had been warned to expect resistance from PaK [antitank guns] and some tanks in static positions . . . In fact we found ourselves taking on a seemingly inexhaustible mass of enemy armour—never have I had such an overwhelming impression of Russian power and mass as on that day. The clouds of dust made it difficult to get support from the Luftwaffe and soon many of the T-34s had broken through our screen and were scurrying like rats across the battlefield." In the mêlée of armour, some tanks of the rival armies collided, halting in a tangle of tortured steel; there were many exchanges of fire at point-blank range. Across hundreds of miles of dusty plain and blackened wreckage, the largest armoured forces the world had ever seen lunged at each other, twisting and swerving. Turret traverse was often a lethal race, in which survival was determined by whether a Russian or German tank gun fired the first round. By nightfall on 12 July, rain was falling; the two armies embarked on the usual struggle against the clock, exploiting darkness to recover disabled tanks, evacuate wounded and bring forward fuel and ammunition.

The important reality was that German losses were unsustainable: Manstein's assault had exhausted its momentum. Even where the Russians were not advancing, they held their ground. That same day 2,000 miles away, the six U.S. and British divisions that had landed in Sicily began to sweep across the island. Hitler's nerve broke. On 13 July, he told his generals he must divert two SS panzer divisions, his most powerful formations, to strengthen the defence of Italy. He aborted Citadel. Zhukov surveyed the battlefield with Rotmistrov. The tank general wrote: "It was an awesome scene, with battered and burned-out tanks, wrecked guns, armoured personnel carriers and trucks, heaps of artillery rounds and pieces of track lying everywhere. Not a single blade of grass was left standing on the darkened soil." The Germans kept attacking for a few days more, in hopes of salvaging something that Berlin might claim as a victory, but they were soon obliged to desist. Manstein's reputation for invincibility was among the casualties of Kursk, though he never accepted responsibility for failure.

Behind the front, partisans staged fierce attacks on German communications, executing 430 rail demolitions on 20–21 July alone. Hapless train crews, Russians conscripted by the occupiers, were summarily shot when they fell into guerrilla hands. By mid-1943 the Russians claimed to deploy 250,000 partisans in Ukrainian and other eastern wildernesses beyond German control. Their guerrilla activity made far more impact than that of any western European resistance movement, aided by Moscow's indifference to Wehrmacht reprisals against the civilian population. "The Germans sent tanks, aviation and artillery against this partisan region," wrote a Russian correspondent when he visited a liberated area, "and they crushed it. Every village has been reduced to ashes. Their inhabitants fled into the forest . . . Partisan detachments dispersed, because it was impossible for big groups to survive. They are unable either to hide (the Germans keep combing the woods) or to support themselves. Food is very scarce. Sivolobov's detachment has lived exclusively off the meat of slaughtered cows and horses for two months. They couldn't stand the sight of meat any more. There was no bread, no potatoes, nothing . . . Civilians are better off. They have managed to tuck some food away, for instance burying stuff in fake graves. The enemy realised that something was going on, but when they started digging one up, they found only a dead German! The terror is awful. In some places they are shooting boys no older than ten as 'Bolshevik spies.' "

Model's army sustained a tigerish defence in the Kursk salient until 25 July, then started to fall back. On 5 August, the Germans lost Orel and Belgorod. On the twenty-fifth the Russians regained Kharkov—and this time kept it. Soldier Alexander Slesarev wrote to his father: "We're crossing liberated territory, land that has been occupied by the Germans for two years. People emerge joyfully to greet us, bringing apples, pears, tomatoes, cucumbers and so on. In the past, I knew Ukraine only from books, now I can see with my own eyes its natural beauties and many gardens." The resumption of Soviet rule was not an unmixed blessing for Stalin's people. "It is a shame, when you travel around liberated villages, to see the cold attitude of the population," wrote another soldier. The Germans had permitted peasants to sow and harvest their own plots; the returning Soviets reimposed rigorous collectivisation, which provoked some protest riots recorded by Lazar Brontman. Every tractor and almost every horse was gone, so that land could be tilled only with spades and rakes, sometimes by women pulling ploughs. Even sickles were seldom available.

Local communities struggling for subsistence displayed bitter, sometimes savage hostility to refugees who passed by—in their eyes, such people were locusts. A peasant woman wrote from Kursk Province: "It's hard now that we don't have cows. They took them from us two months ago . . . We're ready to eat each other . . . There isn't a single young man

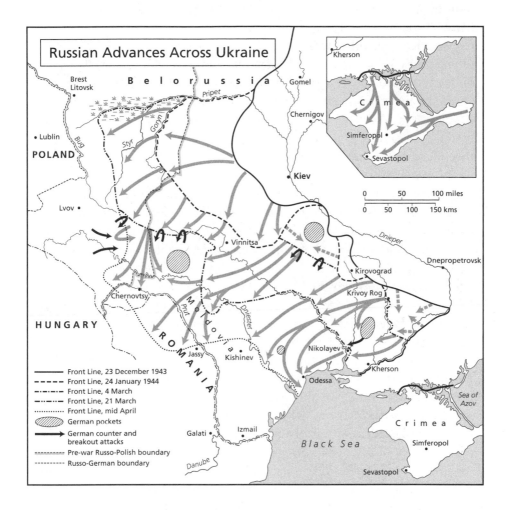

Russian Advances Across Ukraine

———	Front Line, 23 December 1943
- - - -	Front Line, 24 January 1944
·-·-·-·	Front Line, 4 March
··-··-··	Front Line, 21 March
············	Front Line, mid April
▨	German pockets
➤	German counter and breakout attacks
....	Pre-war Russo-Polish boundary
- - - - - -	Russo-German boundary

at home now that they're fighting at the front." Another woman wrote to her soldier son, lamenting that she was reduced to living in the corridor outside her sister's one-room flat. Yet another told her soldier husband: "We have not had bread for two months now. Its already time for Lidiya to go to school, but we don't have a coat for her, or anything to put on her feet. I think Lidiya and I will die of hunger in the end. We haven't got anything . . . Misha, even if you stay alive, we won't be here." In the village of Baranovka, which had been occupied by the Germans for seven months, Lazar Brontman found only a few farm buildings still standing. The former manager of the local collective farm was living in a cowshed with his wife and three small daughters. Their stomachs were distended by starvation.

The man told the correspondent, "We've seen no bread for three months. We eat grass." Then he asked fearfully, "Will the Germans come back?" Brontman gave them a kilo of bread, which they gazed on as a precious delicacy. Another family, whom Brontman invited to share a brew of tea, refused the offer; they had lost the habit of such luxuries, they said dully. Yet these people lived in what was once one of Russia's greatest agricultural regions. Censors intercepted a letter from a mother named Marukova in liberated Oryol to her son in the Red Army: "There is no bread, to say nothing of potatoes. We are eating grass and my legs refuse to walk." Another mother, this one named Galitsina, in the same district wrote likewise: "When I get up in the morning I don't know what to do, what to cook. There is no milk, bread or salt, and no help from anyone."

The Germans staged their initial withdrawal from Kursk in good order, but no one on either side doubted that they had suffered a calamitous defeat, sustaining half a million casualties in fifty days of fighting. Stalin, triumphant, displayed his revived self-confidence by issuing new orders to rein in Zhukov and Vasilevsky. After the triumph of Stalingrad, five subsequent attempts to achieve matching envelopments of German armies had failed. In the future, he decreed, the Red Army would launch frontal assaults rather than encirclements. By the end of August, eight Soviet *fronts* were conducting nineteen parallel offensives towards the Dnieper along a line of 660 miles from Nevel to Taganrog. On 8 September, Hitler authorised a withdrawal behind the river, where the Russians were improvising crossings with any means to hand. They staged one of their few massed air drops of the war on the west bank, landing 4,575 paratroopers, of whom half survived.

The Russian armies drove forward in the same desperate fashion in which they had retreated in the previous year, numbed by daily horrors. Victory at Kursk meant little to a soldier such as Private Ivanov of the 70th Army, who wrote despairingly to his family in Irkutsk: "Death, and only death awaits me. Death is everywhere here. I shall never see you again because death, terrible, ruthless and merciless is going to cut short my young life. Where shall I find strength and courage to live through all this? We are all terribly dirty, with long hair and beards, in rags. Farewell for ever." Private Samokhvalov was in equally wretched condition: "Papa and Mama, I will describe to you my situation, which is bad. I am concussed. Very many of my unit have been killed—the senior lieutenant, the regimental commander, most of my comrades; now it must be my turn. Mama, I have not known such fear in all my eighteen years. Mama, please pray to God that I live. Mama, I read your prayer . . . I must admit frankly that at home I did not believe in God, but now I think of him forty times a day. I don't know where to hide my head as I write this. Papa and Mama, farewell, I will never see you again, farewell, farewell, farewell."

Pavel Kovalenko wrote on 9 October: "We passed through the area where the 15th Regiment had been trapped. There are corpses everywhere and smashed carts. Many bodies have their eyes poked out . . . Are the Germans human? I cannot come to terms with such things. People come—and they go. Senior Lieutenant Puchkov got killed. I am sorry about the lad. Last night a cavalryman trod on a mine. Both soldier and horse were blown to pieces. When night fell I sat shivering by the fire, my teeth chattering with wet and cold."

Next day, his unit trudged into a Belorussian settlement named Yanovichl. "What's left of it? Just ruins, ashes and charred remains. The only living souls are two cats, their fur scorched. I stroked one of them and gave it some potatoes. It purred at me . . . Everywhere there are lots of unharvested potatoes, beetroot and cabbage. Before driving away the population, the Germans suggested that they bury their belongings. Now, these pitiful relics of domestic felicity lie scattered in gardens. The Germans have taken everything useful. One house has survived out of three hundred, the rest succumbed to flame. An old woman sits grieving. Her eyes are lifeless, gazing frozen into the far distance. She has nothing left, and icy winter is almost upon us."

Day after day as the Red Army advanced, such scenes were repeated. "I was shaken by the ferocity of the tank battles," said Ivan Melnikov. "What did people feel in those steel boxes under fire? I once saw ten or eleven burned-out T-34s in one place, a ghastly sight. Almost all the bodies lying nearby were badly burnt, while those who had stayed in their tanks had turned into firebrands, lumps of charcoal." One night a reconnaissance section from his unit was caught in the open under German flares; four of its six men were killed, and the next day the Germans amused themselves by using the bodies for target practice. "[They] were a terrible sight by evening: shapeless, torn by bullets, their faces blown off, arms severed."

Commanders drove units so far and fast that horses pulling baggage carts became too weary to eat their hay. Many animals lay dead by the roadside amid rows of hastily dug German graves, skulls, half-decayed corpses, abandoned sledges and burnt-out vehicles. "We march in the footsteps of war," mused Kovalenko. "Chaos is majestic in its way. I contemplate this vista of destruction and death with pain and helplessness in my soul."

As snow once more closed down the battlefield in the last months of 1943, the Russians held a large bridgehead beyond the Dnieper around

Kiev, and another at Cherkassy. The Germans lost Smolensk on 25 September, and retained only an isolated foothold in the Crimea. On 6 November, the Russians took Kiev. Vasily Grossman described an encounter with infantrymen near the shattered city that day:

> The deputy battalion commander, Lieutenant Surkov, has come to the command post. He hasn't slept for six nights. His face is heavily bearded. One can see no tiredness in him, because he is still seized by the terrible excitement of fighting. In half an hour, perhaps, he will sink into sleep with a field bag under his head, and then it would be useless to try to wake him. But now his eyes are shining, and his voice sounds harsh and excited. This man, a history teacher before the war, seems to be carrying with him the glow of the Dnieper battle. He tells me about German counterattacks, about our attacks, about the runner whom he had to dig out of a trench three times, and who comes from the same area as he, and was once his pupil—Surkov had taught him history. Now, they are both participating in events about which history teachers will be telling their pupils a hundred years from now.

Over half the Soviet territory lost to Hitler since 1941 had been regained. By the end of 1943, the Soviet Union had suffered 77 percent of its total casualties in the entire conflict—something approaching 20 million dead. "The enemy's front is broken!" wrote Kovalenko triumphantly on 20 September. "We are advancing. We are moving slowly, groping our way. Everywhere are traps, minefields. We've advanced 14 km during the day. There was a 'little misunderstanding' at 14.10. A group of our aircraft got confused and strafed our column. It was dismaying to see them firing at their own people. Men were wounded and killed. It is so bad." He added on 3 October:

> Our organisation both on the march and in action leaves much to be desired. In particular, infantry-artillery coordination is poor: the gunners fire at random. [We have suffered] colossal casualties. There are only sixty men left in each of our regiment's battalions. What are we supposed to attack with? The Germans are resisting ferociously. Vlasov soldiers [Cossack renegades] are fighting alongside them. Dogmeat. Two have been captured, teenagers, born 1925. [We should] not mess about, but shoot the sons-of-bitches.

Three days later, he wrote: "We are advancing again, but with scant success—just a little progress here and there. We have few infantry, and are desperately short of shells. The Germans burn every village. Our reconnaissance units operating in their rear areas have led a lot of civilians out of the forest where they had been hiding. We seem stuck in the swamps. When shall we get out of here? Rain, mud."

Capt. Nikolai Belov's unit was in the same plight: "The weather and mud are dreadful. We face a winter amid forests and swamps. Today, we set off at 1000 and advanced about six kilometres in twenty-four hours. There is no ammunition. Rations are short because supplies have fallen behind. Many men are without boots."

Few Russian soldiers saw much cause for rejoicing, because they knew how long the road to Berlin still was. An elderly officer named Ignatov wrote to his wife, complaining of the poor organisation of the army: "The soldiers with whom I fought in 1917–18 were much better disciplined. We receive completely untrained replacements. As a veteran of the old army, I know what a Russian soldier should be like; whenever I try to bring these men up to the mark they moan and complain of my harshness. We were sent into battle without spades, though they had promised them to us. We are sick of promises we no longer believe." An NCO in Vladimir Pershanin's unit was sent with his lieutenant to recover the identity capsules of eight of his men killed when the officer lost his way, and led them into the path of a German machine gun: " 'You shit!' said the Sergeant, not addressing the Lieutenant directly, but spitting towards him. 'Eight lives for fuck-all!' "

The German predicament, however, was vastly worse. "This morning the combat strength of 39th Infantry Division was down to six officers and roughly three hundred men," wrote one commander in a 2 September morale report. "Apart from their dwindling strength, the men's state of fatigue gives rise to great anxiety . . . Such a state of apathy has arisen among the troops that draconian measures do not produce the desired results, but only the good example of officers and 'kindly persuasion.' " Ghastly scenes took place during the flight to the Dnieper, as discipline broke down in a fashion unprecedented for the Wehrmacht. "Frantic men were abandoning everything on the bank and plunging into the water to try to swim to the opposite shore," wrote a soldier. "Thousands of voices were shouting towards the grey water and the opposite bank . . . The officers, who had managed to keep some self-control, organised a few more or less conscious men, like shepherds trying to control a herd of crazed sheep . . . We heard the sounds of gunfire and explosions punctuated by bloodcurdling screams." Many men eventually crossed on improvised rafts.

Once more, the German army regrouped; once more it prepared to hold a line with dogged determination. Many more battles lay ahead. Panzer officer Tassilo von Bogenhardt mused on the paradox that almost all his men were by now resigned to death, yet their morale remained high: "Each German soldier considered himself superior to any single Russian, even though their numbers were so overpowering. The slow, orderly retreat did not depress us too much. We felt we were holding our own." But soon afterwards he was badly wounded and captured; he somehow survived the ensuing three years as a prisoner. The year 1943 on the Eastern Front had brought upon the invaders of Russia irredeemable catastrophe, and to Stalin's armies the assurance of looming triumph.

CHAPTER SIXTEEN

DIVIDED EMPIRES

1. Whose Liberty?

WINSTON CHURCHILL stretched an important point by telling the House of Commons on 8 December 1941: "We have at least four-fifths of the population of the globe on our side." It would have been more accurate to assert that the Allies had four-fifths of the world's inhabitants under their control, or recoiling from Axis occupation. Propaganda promoted an assumption of common purpose in the "free" nations—among which it was necessary to grant nominal inclusion to Stalin's people—in defeating the totalitarian powers. Yet in almost every country there were nuances of attitude, and in some places stark divergences of loyalty.

South America was the continent least affected by the struggle, though Brazil joined the Allied cause in August 1942 and sent 25,000 of its soldiers to participate—albeit almost invisibly—in the Italian campaign. Most of the nations that escaped involvement were protected by geographical remoteness. Turkey was the most significant state to sustain neutrality, having learned its lesson from rash involvement in World War I on the side of the Central Powers. In Europe, only Ireland, Spain, Portugal, Sweden and Switzerland were fortunate enough to have their sovereignty respected by the belligerents, most for pragmatic reasons. Ireland had gained self-governing dominion status in 1922, although until 1938 Britain retained control of four strategically important "treaty ports" on its coastline. In 1939–40, as the former mother nation began its struggle for survival against the U-boats, Winston Churchill was tempted by the notion of reasserting by force his country's claims upon these naval and air bases. He was dissuaded only by fear of the impact on opinion in the United States, where there was a strong Irish lobby.

The Atlantic "air gap" was significantly widened, and many lives and much tonnage lost, in consequence of the fanatical loathing of Irish prime minister Éamon de Valera for his British neighbours. Almost every warship and merchantman that sailed past the Irish coastline in the war years felt a surge of bitterness towards the country which relied on Britain for most of its vital commodities and all its fuel, but would not lift a finger to help in its hour of need. "The cost in men and ships . . . ran up a score which Irish eyes a-smiling on the day of Allied victory were not going to cancel," wrote corvette officer Nicholas Monsarrat. "In the list of people you were prepared to like when the war was over, the man who stood by and watched while you were getting your throat cut could not figure very high." Yet because of Ireland's divided sovereignty and loyalties, even Northern Ireland, still a part of the United Kingdom, never dared to introduce conscription for military service. The perverse outcome was that more Catholic southern Irishmen than Protestant northerners—who loudly asserted their commitment to the crown—served in Britain's wartime armed forces, though the services of most southerners were purchased by economic necessity rather than seduced by ideological enthusiasm for the Allied cause.

The Swedes asserted their status with a rigour promoted by proximity to Germany and thus vulnerability to its ill-will: they arrested and imprisoned scores of Allied intelligence agents and informants. Only in 1944–45, when the outcome of the war was no longer in doubt, did the Stockholm government become more responsive to diplomatic pressure from London and Washington, and less zealous in locking up Allied sympathisers.

Switzerland was a hub of Allied intelligence operations, though the Swiss authorities foreclosed all covert activities they discovered. They also denied sanctuary to Jews fleeing the Nazis, and profited enormously from pocketing funds deposited in Swiss banks by both prominent Nazis and their Jewish victims, which later went unclaimed because the owners perished. The daughter of a rich French Holocaust victim, Estelle Sapir, said later: "My father was able to protect his money from the Nazis, but not from the Swiss." Switzerland provided important technological and industrial support to the Axis war effort, in 1941 increasing its exports to Germany of chemicals by 250 percent, metals by 500 percent. The country became a major receiver of stolen goods from the Nazi pillage of Europe, and banked what the OSS, Washington's covert operations organisation, categorised as "gigantic sums" of fugitive funds. The Swiss unblinkingly paid to the Nazis the proceeds of life insurance policies held by German Jews, and the Bern government dismissed postwar recriminations about such action as "irrelevant under Swiss law." Only a fraction of Switzerland's enormous profits from wartime misappropriations were ever acknowledged, and an even smaller portion paid out to Jewish victims and their families. The war proved good for business in the ice-hearted cantons.

Among the belligerents, unsurprisingly, the more distant was a given Allied country from the consequences of Axis aggression, the less ill-will its people displayed towards the enemy. For instance, an Office of

War Information poll in mid-1942 found that one-third of Americans expressed willingness to make a separate peace with Germany. A January 1944 opinion survey showed that while 45 percent of British people professed to "hate" the Germans, only 27 percent of Canadians did so.

For most people in Europe and Asia, the conflict was a pervasive reality. Families in the Asian republics of the Soviet Union found their menfolk conscripted for the Red Army, prison camps established within sight of their villages and food chronically short. A Japanese air raid on the northern Australian port of Darwin on 19 February 1942 killed 297 people, most of them service personnel on ships in the harbour. Though the attack was never repeated on anything like such a scale, and Australia was thereafter troubled only by sporadic small-scale Japanese naval intrusions, the country's sense of invulnerability was shattered. Tribesmen on Pacific islands and in Asian jungles were enlisted to serve one army or another, though often oblivious of what their sponsors were fighting about. Even in parts of Russia, the same ignorance obtained: beside the Pechora River, inside the Arctic Circle, a gulag camp boss described how local villagers "had a very vague understanding about what was going on in the world. They did not even know very much about the Soviet war with Germany."

Large majorities in the belligerent nations—with the notable exception of Italy—supported the causes championed by their respective governments, at least unless or until they started losing. But minorities dissented, and thousands were imprisoned in consequence, some of them by the democracies. So too were people whose allegiance was deemed suspect, sometimes grossly unjustly: Britain in 1939 detained all its German residents, including Jewish fugitives from Hitler. The historian G. M. Trevelyan was among the prominent figures who denounced indiscriminate internment, saying that the government failed to recognise "the great harm that is being done to our cause—essentially a moral cause . . . by the continued imprisonment of political refugees." America made the same mistake in the hysteria following Pearl Harbor when it interned its Nisei Japanese. The governor of Idaho, supporting drastic measures, said: "The Japs live like rats, breed like rats and act like rats. We don't want them."

At the outbreak of war, the United States was by no means a homogeneous society. American Jews, for instance, suffered suspicion, if not hostility, from their own countrymen, exemplified by their exclusion from country clubs and other elite social institutions. A wartime survey showed that Jews were mistrusted more than any other identified ethnic group except Italians; a poll in December 1944 showed that while most Americans accepted that Hitler had killed some Jews, they disbelieved reports that he was slaughtering them in millions.

Black Americans had cause to regard the "crusade for freedom" with scepticism, for much of their country was racially segregated, as were the armed forces. At army recruit John Capano's training camp in South Carolina, there was a sign outside a local restaurant: "Niggers and Yanks not welcome." He said, "It was a very white troop, which fought running battles with the blacks in the motor pool." 1940 witnessed six recorded lynchings of black Americans in the South, four of them in Georgia, and many more floggings, three of them fatal. Virginia matrons delivered a formal protest about Eleanor Roosevelt's presence at a mixed dance in Washington: "The danger," they wrote to the president, "lies not in the degeneration of the girls who participated in this dance, for they were . . . already of the lowest type of female, but in the fact that Mrs. Roosevelt lent her presence and dignity to this humiliating affair; that the wife of the President of the United States sanctioned a dance including . . . both races and that her lead might be followed by unthinking whites."

The 1942 influx of large numbers of black workers to join the labour force in Detroit provoked vociferous white anger, which in June erupted into serious rioting. The following year witnessed further racial disturbances, in Detroit against blacks and in Los Angeles against Mexicans. The president adopted a notably muted attitude towards the Detroit clash, and indeed until his death remained circumspect about racial issues. The proportion of black workers in war industries rose from 2 percent in 1942 to 8 percent in 1945, but they remained underrepresented. America's armed forces enlisted substantial numbers of African-Americans, but entrusted only a small minority with combat roles, and sustained a large measure of segregation; the American Red Cross distinguished between "colored" and "white" blood supplies. Cynics demanded to be told the difference between park benches marked *"Juden"* in Nazi Germany and those labelled "Colored" in Tallahassee, Florida.

At the outbreak of war even many white Americans, immigrants or children of immigrants, defined themselves in terms of the old-world national group to which they belonged, notably including almost 5 million Italian-Americans: until December 1941, their community newspapers hailed Mussolini as a giant. One published letter writer applauded the German invasion of Poland, and predicted that, "as the Roman legions did under Caesar, the New Italy will go forth and conquer." Even when their country declared war on Mussolini, many Italian-Americans hoped for a U.S. victory that somehow avoided imposing an Italian defeat.

By 1945, however, an immense change had taken place. The shared experience of conflict, and especially of military service, accelerated a remarkable integration of America's national groupings. Anthony Carullo, for instance, had emigrated to the United States from southern Italy with his family in 1938. When he joined the army and served in Europe, he had to address letters home to his sisters, because his mother understood no English. But when he was asked, "If we send you to Italy, are you willing to fight Italians?" the twenty-one-year-old replied doughtily, "I'm an American citizen. I'll fight anybody." The German-born sergeant Henry Kissinger afterwards asserted that it was the war that made him a real American. Between 1942 and 1945, millions of his compatriots of recent immigrant stock discovered for the first time a shared nationalism.

Much more complex and brutal issues of loyalty confronted societies occupied by the Axis, or subject to colonial rule by the European powers. In some countries, to this day it remains a matter of dispute whether those who chose to serve the Germans or Japanese, or to resist the Allies, were guilty of betrayal or merely adopted a different view of patriotism. Many Europeans served in national security forces which opposed Allied interests and promoted those of the Germans: French gendarmes consigned Jews to death camps. Despite the legend of Dutch sympathy promoted by Anne Frank's diary, Holland's policemen proved more ruthless than their French counterparts, dispatching a higher proportion of their country's Jews to deportation and death.

France was riven by internal dissensions. Especially in the early years of occupation, there was widespread support for the Vichy government, and thus for collaboration with Germany. A German officer working with the Armistice Commission in 1940–41, Tassilo von Bogenhardt, asserted that he found his French counterparts "very interesting to talk to . . . I suspected that the fortitude of the British in the face of our bombing rather annoyed them . . . [They] admired and respected Marshal Pétain as much as they detested the communists and Front Populaire." Some 25,000 Frenchmen served as volunteers in the SS Westland Division. Though the colonial authorities in a handful of France's African possessions "rallied" to de Gaulle in London, most did not. Even after the United States entered the war, French soldiers, sailors and airmen continued to resist the Allies. In May 1942, when the British invaded Vichy Madagascar to preempt a possible Japanese descent on the strategic island, there was protracted fighting. Madagascar is larger than France—1,000 miles long. Its governor-general signalled to Vichy: "Our available troops are preparing to resist every enemy advance with the same spirit which inspired our soldiers at Diego Suarez, at Jajunga, at Tananarive [the sites of earlier encounters between Vichy forces and the Allies] . . . where each time the defence became a page of heroism written by '*La France.*' "

Clashes at sea made it necessary for the Royal Navy to sink a French frigate and three submarines; in the Madagascar shore campaign, 171 of the defenders were killed and 343 wounded, while the British lost 105 killed and 283 wounded. When the governor ordered the submarine *Glorieux* to escape to Vichy Dakar, its captain expressed frustration at being denied an opportunity to strike a blow at the British fleet: "All on board felt the keen disappointment I did myself at sighting the best target a submarine could ever be given without also having a chance of attacking it." The defenders of Madagascar finally surrendered only on 5 November 1942. Once again, few prisoners chose to join de Gaulle. Everywhere Vichy held sway, the French treated captured Allied servicemen and civilian internees with callousness, and sometimes brutality. "The French were rotten," said Mrs. Ena Stoneman, a survivor from the sunken liner *Laconia* held in French Morocco. "We ended up thinking of them as our enemies and not the Germans. They treated us like animals most of the time." Even in November 1942, when it was becoming plain that the Allies would win the war, the opposition mounted by French troops shocked Americans landing in North Africa.

In mainland France, the Resistance enjoyed support from only a small minority of people until the Germans' 1943 introduction of forced labour persuaded many young men to flee to join maquis groups, for which they afterwards fought with varying degrees of enthusiasm. To challenge the occupiers was difficult and highly dangerous. Given the strong French tradition of anti-Semitism, there was little appetite for assisting Jews to escape the death camps. Much of France's aristocracy collaborated with the Germans, as well as with the Vichy regime which governed central and southern France until the Germans took them over in November 1942.

There were honourable exceptions, however, notable among them Countess Lily de Pastré. She was born in 1891, her mother a Russian and her father a rich French member of the Noilly Prat vermouth dynasty. In 1916 she married Count Pastré, who had his own fortune derived from a nineteenth-century family shipping business. One of their three children, Nadia, assisted wartime Allied escape lines. In 1940 the countess was divorced, but continued to live in style at her family's Château de Montredon, south of Marseilles. She began to lavish her fortune on making Montredon a haven for artists, many of them Jewish, who had escaped from the German-occupied zone. She created an organisation, Pour que l'Esprit Vive—"So that the spirit may survive"—to finance and shelter people at risk. Up to forty fugitives at any one time—writers, musicians, painters—became long-stay guests at the château, including such artists as André Masson and the Czech Rudolf Kundera, together with the Jewish pianist Clara Haskil and harpist Lily Laskine. Pastré arranged for Haskil's treatment for a brain tumour and her subsequent escape to Switzerland.

There were regular recitals and afternoon concerts by residents. To stimulate her guests' creativity, the countess offered a 5,000-franc prize for the best interpretation of a Brahms piano work. The highlight of her wartime career was a moonlight performance of *A Midsummer Night's Dream* staged on 25 July 1942, with a cast of fifty-two and incidental music played by an orchestra with a Jewish conductor. Costumes were created by the young Christian Dior, mostly from Montredon's curtains. Lily de Pastré's activities were brutally curtailed in the latter part of the war, after the Wehrmacht took over her château. Some of her former guests, such as German Jewish composer Alfred Tokayer, were arrested and shipped to death camps. But the countess's efforts to succour some of the most vulnerable victims of Nazi persecution stand in distinguished contrast to the passivity of most of France's rich, who declined to risk loss of their property as well as their lives. She died broke in 1974, having exhausted her huge fortune in the service of philanthropy, much of this during the war years.

Elsewhere, some small countries showed bolder defiance than did the French. The Danes, alone among European societies, refused to participate in the deportation of their Jews, almost all of whom survived. Few of the 293,000 people of the tiny Grand Duchy of Luxembourg welcomed its incorporation into Hitler's empire. During the 1940 German invasion, seven of Luxembourg's eighty-seven defenders were wounded; the ruling family and ministers escaped to London to form a government in exile. When a plebiscite on the German occupation was held in October 1941, 97 percent of the population declared their opposition. Berlin shrugged off this vote, declared all Luxemburgers German citizens, and began conscripting them into the Wehrmacht. They responded by calling a general strike, which was broken by the execution of twenty-one trades unionists and the deportation of hundreds more to concentration camps. It would be mistaken to idealise Luxembourg's resistance to the Nazis: its postwar government convicted 10,000 citizens of collaboration, and 2,848 Luxemburgers died in German uniform. But most of the duchy's people made plain their rejection of Nazi hegemony.

Farther east, large numbers of Ukrainians and citizens of the Baltic states enlisted in the Wehrmacht, disliking Stalin's Soviet Union more than the Nazis. Ukrainians provided many of the guards for Hitler's death camps, and in February 1944 Nikolai Vatutin, one of Stalin's best generals, was killed by anti-Soviet Ukrainian partisans who attacked his vehicle. In occupied Yugoslavia, the Germans exploited ethnic animosities, deploying Croat Ustaše militia against the Serbs. The Ustaše, together with Cossacks in German uniforms, committed ghastly atrocities against their fellow countrymen. In the later war years, the Germans recruited soldiers of any subject power willing to serve in their uniform—Cossacks, Latvians, even a few Scandinavians, French, Belgian and Dutch troops.

Perhaps the most exotic formations in Hitler's armies were the 13th and 23rd SS Divisions, largely composed of Bosnian Muslims and led by German officers; for parade appearances, these men wore the tasselled fez. Heinrich Himmler described the Muslim Waffen-SS as "among the most honourable and true followers of the Führer Adolf Hitler due to their hatred of the common Jewish-English-Bolshevik enemy." This was an exaggeration, since 15 percent of the formations' men were Catholic Croats, but Himmler promoted Muslim support by establishing a special mullah military school in Dresden, and the mufti of Jerusalem created an "Imam School" in Berlin, to educate SS officers about shared Nazi and Muslim ideals. One of the Muslim formations' commanders, a bizarre figure named Karl-Gustav Sauberzweig who liked to address his soldiers as "children, children," asserted that "the Muslims in our SS divisions . . . are beginning to see in our Führer the appearance of a Second Prophet." But Sauberzweig was removed from command of the 13th SS Division after it performed poorly in Yugoslavia in 1944, and Muslim recruits contributed scant combat power to Hitler's forces.

Guerrilla war against the Axis occupiers, promoted by Allied secret organisations, has been romanticised in postwar literature, but its strategic impact was small. Resistance groups were seldom homogeneous in motives, makeup or effectiveness, as the Italian Emanuele Artom—later executed by the Germans—noted in his diary in September 1943: "I must record reality in case decades hence psuedo-liberal rhetoric applauds the partisans as purist heroes. We are what we are: a mixture of individuals— some acting in good faith, some political *arrivistes*, some deserters who fear deportation to Germany, some driven by a yearning for adventure, some by a taste for banditry. In the ranks are those who perpetrate violence, get drunk, make girls pregnant."

So it was among resistance movements all over occupied Europe. Both sides acted with considerable brutality: there was embarrassment in the SOE's French Section when a courier, Anne-Marie Walters, denounced her British chief in southwest France, Lt. Col. George Starr, for implication in the systematic torture of collaborators and prisoners. During subsequent investigations in Britain, a senior SOE officer, Col. Stanley Woolrych, wrote that, despite his admiration for Starr's achievements in the field, "I feel that his record has been somewhat marred by a streak of sadism which it is going to be extremely hard to ignore . . . There is no doubt . . . that they tortured prisoners in a fairly big way." Walters's allegations were hushed up, but they highlighted the passions and cruelties that characterise irregular warfare.

It is unsurprising that only small minorities supported resistance, because the price was so high. Peter Kemp, an SOE officer in Albania, described a 1943 episode when he and his British party sought refuge in a village after ambushing a German staff car. Stiljan, their interpreter, conducted a long argument with an indignant figure at a half-open door, which was finally slammed in his face. "He will not have us," explained Stiljan. "They have heard the shooting on the road and they are very much afraid, and very enraged with us for causing the trouble." Who could blame such people? They knew they would face appalling reprisals, while the young foreign adventurers moved on to make mischief for the Axis elsewhere. Kemp acknowledged: "As time went on it became more and more obvious that we could offer the Albanians little inducement to take up arms compared with the advantages they could enjoy by remaining passive. I must confess that we British liaison officers were slow to understand their point of view; as a nation, we have always tended to assume that those who do not wholeheartedly support us in our wars have some sinister motive for not wishing to see the world a better place."

THE EUROPEAN OVERSEAS EMPIRES were riven by divisions which became more acute where colonies were subject to occupation. In Indochina, through a variety of complex anomalies the French flag continued to fly until March 1945; a Vichy regime led by Adm. Jean Decoux administered the country in accordance with the orders of a Japanese military mission. In September 1940, Japanese troops emphasised their absolute dominance by attacking two Tonkinese towns and killing 800 French troops before withdrawing into southern China. The confusion of local loyalties intensified when Vichy warships fought a brisk series of actions against the neighbouring Siamese, who attempted to secure disputed border territory in Laos and Cambodia. The Japanese thereupon intervened to enforce a French retreat, to secure the interests of their Siamese clients. From July 1941 onwards, 35,000 Japanese troops acted as they chose in Indochina, which was incorporated in Japan's so-called Greater East Asia Co-Prosperity Sphere. The Vichy *colons* preserved shreds of personal freedom as long as they, like European acolytes of the Nazis, implemented the policies of their Axis masters. In March 1945, on orders from liberated Paris, French troops launched a disastrous uprising, quickly and brutally suppressed by the Japanese, who then assumed full control of the country.

The Vietnamese, Laotians and Cambodians suffered appallingly from 1942 onwards, as the Japanese pillaged their countries: elderly Vietnamese later said that their experiences were worse than those of their later wars of independence. Rice, corn, coal and rubber were shipped to Japan; many rice fields were compulsorily planted with jute and cotton to meet the occupiers' textile requirements. Denied their own produce, local people began to starve on a staggering scale. In Tonkin, by 1945 at least 1.5 million Vietnamese, and perhaps many more, had died of hunger in an area which before the war was the world's third-largest grower of rice. The French colonial authorities suppressed local protests and insurrections with a brutality the Japanese could not have surpassed.

The communist Vietminh movement was the chief political beneficiary of Vietnamese misery, gaining substantial support in northern areas where Tokyo's economic policies caused the most distress. There was no significant armed resistance to the Japanese until the summer of 1945, because the passionately anti-imperialist Americans refused to fly Free French officers into Vietnam from China. Only in the summer of that year did the OSS ship arms to the Vietminh, in a belated attempt to foment anti-Japanese activity. The weapons were warmly welcomed by their leader, Nguyen That Thanh, better known as Ho Chi Minh; OSS officers on the ground displayed unreserved enthusiasm for his guerrillas, epic naïveté about their politics and bitter animosity towards local French colonialists.

The Vietminh—by that time numbering about 5,000 active supporters—were happy to fight the French, but showed no interest in engaging the Japanese. They either stored their weapons in readiness for the postwar independence struggle or brandished them to impose their will on the rural population. Under pressure from Washington, the OSS persuaded the guerrillas to make some show of engaging the occupiers; one group staged a noisy demonstration against a small Japanese supply column, which turned and fled without suffering much harm. On another occasion, on 17 July 1945, a Vietminh battalion led by Vo Nguyen Giap attacked a Japanese outpost at Tâm Doa, killing eight of its forty defenders and capturing the remainder. But this appears to have been the sum of the Vietminh contribution to the Allied cause, in return for U.S. deliveries of several tons of weapons and equipment, which were later used against the returning French colonialists.

BY FAR THE MOST IMPORTANT overseas element in the Allied war effort was, of course, the British Empire. London's relations with the white self-governing dominions were conducted with considerable clumsiness and indeed ruthlessness under the exigencies of global conflict, and policy towards the black and brown nations of the empire was uncompromising. The prime minister asserted his determination to sustain hegemony over India, and outraged American opinion by declaring in November 1942 that he had not become the king's first minister in order to preside over the liquidation of the British Empire. Most of his people were warmly sentimental about the contribution of Indian and colonial troops to the war effort, heedless of the fact that their services were purchased for cash and only rarely inspired by loyalty to, or even understanding of, the Allied cause. James Mpagi from Kampala, Uganda, said: "We thought perhaps war was something very simple . . . perhaps the same thing as if people were quarrelling for a cow or [between] neighbouring villages."

Britain took for granted the loyalty of its black and brown peoples, and in 1939 this was promptly expressed in the form of messages of support from colonial governors and prominent citizens. There was no significant dissent: black Africa and the Caribbean eventually contributed some 500,000 recruits to the war effort; three African divisions carried arms in Burma, while most other black soldiers performed labour service. Britain never introduced military conscription in its African possessions, but strong local pressure and sometimes compulsion were exercised to mobilise tribesmen who served in British uniform under the command of white officers. Batison Geresomo of Nyasaland recalled later: "When we heard about the conflict, we were not sure . . . whether they will be taking everybody by force . . . the white man came in all the districts to recruit soldiers. Some were taken by the chiefs' force and some went on their own wish." In addition, conscription for agricultural labour service was widely introduced in East Africa, much to the profit of white settler farmers. Local chiefs in the Gold Coast colony bowed to the wishes of the authorities by urging their young men to enlist. Recruiting bands sang songs to attract men, one punning the Akan word *barima*—"brave man"—with Burma.

> Barima ehh *yen* ko ooh!
> Barima *yen* ko ooh!
> Yen *ko* East Africa, Barima
> Besin, na yen *ko*!
>
> Brave men and warriors let us go [enlist]
> Brave men and warriors let us go [enlist]
> Let us go to East Africa and Burma
> Come let us go [enlist]

Kofi Genfi described the recruiting process in Ashanti, where the local district commissioner, Captain Sinclair, was charged with fulfilling manpower quotas. Sinclair, in turn, allotted each local chief a share: "Sinclair . . . had the list, he knew how many men from each village there would be. He would take the truck . . . and bring the men." In Bathurst, Gambia, in 1943 more drastic measures were employed: 400 "corner boys"—street urchins—were rounded up and enlisted on the orders of the British governor; a quarter deserted during training. In Accra, one man described how he was snatched off the street by soldiers while visiting his brother. In Sierra Leone, those arrested for illicit diamond mining were sent to the army, an option extended to some of those convicted by the courts as an alternative to imprisonment.

Many Africans became genuine volunteers for military service, however, because they wanted work and pay. Though all claimed to be eighteen, some were significantly younger. Few had any comprehension of what war might entail, and there were widespread desertions when units were ordered overseas. Nyasaland soldiers of the King's African Rifles, destined for Burma, sang a song called *"Sole,"* an adaptation of the English word "sorry" which can also mean "trouble."

> *Sole, sole, sole,*
> We don't know where we are going,
> But we are going away,
> *Sole, sole, sole,*
> Perhaps we are going to Kenya,
> We are sorry we are leaving home,
> But it is the war. Time of trouble,
> *Sole, sole, sole.*

Some Africans articulated a simple kind of patriotism: "Our boss was involved . . . the colonial power," said a Sierra Leonean who served in Burma. "And when the boss is involved—or when the head of the household was in trouble—everybody had to go to his support . . . If we had not gone to . . . fight against the Japanese we would all be speaking Japanese today." Only a handful of black recruits were granted commissions, of whom the most notable was twenty-one-year-old Seth Anthony from the Gold Coast, a teacher and prewar Territorial soldier. He was sent to Britain for officer training at Sandhurst, served in Burma, and finished the war as a major. One of his men said later that they liked to fight under him because he had "powerful juju." But Anthony was an extreme rarity in the British Army, though the RAF eventually commissioned some of its fifty West African recruits. Assumptions and assertions of racial superiority were implicit, if not explicit, in every aspect of policy. When, for instance, two companies of the King's African Rifles reached the outskirts of Addis Ababa in April 1941, they were halted by an order from army headquarters: it was considered more appropriate for the imperial entry into the Abyssinian capital to be led by a white South African unit, which duly leapfrogged past the disgruntled KAR.

Britain's imperial forces suffered significant disciplinary difficulties and embarrassments. In December 1943 the Mauritius Regiment, provoked by poor leadership and wretchedly insensitive handling by its white officers, staged a sit-down strike at its camp on Madagascar; 500 men were eventually court-martialled, of whom two were sentenced to death, though the penalty was later commuted. A further 24 men received sentences of seven to fourteen years' imprisonment, and the regiment was disbanded. Desertion rates were notably high in the Gold Coast Regiment, with 15 percent of its 1943 strength posted as absent, 42 percent of these from Ashanti.

There was much discontent among black Africans serving overseas about their rates of pay and conditions, much inferior to those of white soldiers. The South African forces set the pay of their "coloured"—mixed-race—recruits at half the white rate, and that of black soldiers at two-thirds of the coloured rate, on the grounds that the latter could more cheaply support their families in the style to which they were accustomed. Like the United States until 1944, South Africa refused to deploy black soldiers in combat roles, though it recruited them for labour service; it was thus disingenuous that early recruiting posters depicted black soldiers in uniform carrying knobkerries and assegais. Volunteers were slow to come forward, knowing that the country's institutionalised racial discrimination would persist in the armed forces: even in besieged Tobruk, white South African army canteens would not serve black soldiers.

In India, segregated brothels were established for the British Army's black Africans, though one Catholic commanding officer's scruples caused him to insist that his unit's establishment should be closed down. In 1942, there was a mutiny in the 25th East African Brigade in East Africa: Gen. Sir William Platt reported "numerous incidents in almost all Somali units . . . refusals to obey orders, sit-down strikes, desertion with weapons, untrustworthiness as guards, collusive thefts, occasional stone-throwing and drawing of knives." In India during 1944 there were clashes between black soldiers and civilians near the Ranchi rest camp in which six Indians were killed and several women raped.

The British drew comfort from the fact that these disturbances were less serious than a major mutiny by black French *tirailleurs* which took place at Thiaroye, near Dakar, that year, and uprisings by battalions of the Belgian Force Publique in the Congo. Commanders were dismayed, however, by the conduct of some colonial units on the battlefield, such as the King's African Rifles battalion which broke and ran when first exposed to fire in Burma, and two battalions of the 11th East African Division which refused to cross the Chindwin River into Burma, saying, "We will do whatever we're told to do, but we are not going any further." Brig. G. H. Cree reported that, given the widespread grievances of the African formations, "We were lucky to have escaped with a few flare-ups instead of a more general revolt."

It is important to view such remarks and incidents in the wider context: hundreds of thousands of African troops performed their duty as labourers or riflemen under fire with considerable courage and some effectiveness. But it seems foolish to romanticise their contribution. They had no stake in Allied victory, and most served as mercenaries, drawn from societies schooled to obey white masters. A Rhodesian officer recorded the burial of African battlefield dead in the unyielding stony soil of Somaliland:

> Poor Corporal Atang, self-abnegation and retiring modesty were part of you in life . . . How it would distress you to know that your grave is giving such trouble and keeping weary men from rest . . . They lower him gently. The bloodstained blanket is thrust aside . . . Lastly there is Amadu, the Musselman [sic] who died clutching his beloved Bren gun. The sergeant major of D company and a group of co-religionists are there. Two descend into the grave, the body being passed to them from the stretcher, they lower it slowly to the bottom . . . In a high, resonant voice the chief mourner intones an old Arabic phrase, a prayer for the dead.

Here was a sentimental view of the contribution of colonial subjects, to be contrasted with that of the black South African Frank Sexwale, who called the conflict "a white man's war, a British war. South Africa belonged to Britain; everything that the Afrikaaner did, he got the notion from the master, Britain." Sexwale's perception accurately reflected the indifference of almost all his black and coloured compatriots to the struggle, but he overlooked the complexities of white South African sentiment. Among Afrikaaners there was a long-standing pro-German tradition. Field Marshal Lord Smuts, South Africa's prime minister and a close friend of Churchill's, only narrowly defeated a 1939 parliamentary motion demanding his country's neutrality. Having dragged South Africa into the war,

Smuts ensured that it made a substantial contribution to the Allied cause. From beginning to end, however, he faced domestic opposition, and never dared to introduce conscription. White volunteers remained in limited supply, and towards the end of 1940, antiwar demonstrations took place in Johannesburg. Some avowed pro-Nazis were interned for the duration, including future Nationalist prime minister John Vorster.

In Australia, support for Britain was much stronger. In 1939, tens of thousands of volunteers responded like Rod Wells, who thought, "There's a war going on! The Old Country needs help . . . Let's go and show them what we can do." Three divisions of such men fought with distinction in the Mediterranean, and a further two later joined them in New Guinea and other Pacific campaigns. But the war also revealed political stresses and divisions "down under." Most of the half million Americans who passed through Australia between 1942 and 1945 warmed to the country socially, but their commanders deplored Australian parochialism, vicious trades union practices especially in the docks, and supposed lack of energy in pursuing the war. MacArthur suggested sourly that the Australian spirit had been corroded by twenty years of socialist government. On 26 October 1942, the *New York Times* military correspondent Hanson Baldwin published a lacerating critique of the Australian war effort:

> The normal difficulties of waging a coalition war have been increased in Australia by one factor about which Australians themselves complain—the labor problem. There is no question in the opinion of many Australians that Australian labor's insistence upon its "rights," its determination to work no longer than a stated number of hours and to knock off Saturday afternoons and holidays, and its general attitude toward and approach to the war, have hampered the full development of the United Nations' war effort in Australia. The labor attitude in the "land down under" can perhaps best be described as "complacency"; many of the workers seem primarily interested in retaining peacetime privileges.

Baldwin observed that the consequence of Australian labour unions' obstructionism was that many logistical tasks had to be performed by American soldiers. He concluded: "Many of us in the democracies of all countries, loving personal liberty and our casual, easy, carefree ways of life of peacetime, have forgotten that war is a hard taskmaster and that the ways of peace are not the ways of war." Baldwin's remarks caused a storm in Australia, where they were deeply resented, but they were founded in harsh reality, and the British government shared the correspondent's sentiments. Many Australians earned admiration as warriors, but a substantial number exercised their democratic privileges to stay away from the battlefield.

In Canada likewise, overseas military service remained voluntary, causing the army to suffer a chronic shortage of infantrymen. Though Canadians played important roles in the northwest Europe and Italian campaigns, the Battle of the Atlantic and the bomber offensive, most of French Canada wanted no part in the struggle. "A nasty evening in Montreal, where the French Canadians booed and spat at us and several of us were thrown out of bars," recorded an RAF flight trainee among a party in transit through the region. In August 1942, a sullen 59 percent of French-Canadians told pollsters they did not believe they would have had to participate in the war but for Canada's membership in the British Empire.

In the Middle East and Asia, some subject peoples displayed fiercer opposition to the conflict. They paid little heed to the nature of the German, Italian and Japanese regimes, merely choosing to view their colonial oppressors' enemies as their own prospective allies. The British exercised de facto rule over Egypt not as an acknowledged colonial possession but through a draconian interpretation of the bilateral defence treaty. Many, indeed most Egyptians, gave passive support to the Axis; King Farouk took impending British defeat for granted. One of his army officers, Capt. Anwar Sadat, the twenty-two-year-old son of a government clerk who later became Egypt's president, wrote: "Our enemy was primarily, if not solely, Great Britain." In 1940, Sadat approached Gen. Aziz el-Masri, the inspector-general of the army and a well-known Axis sympathiser, and said, "We are a group of officers working to set up an organisation for the purpose of driving the British out of Egypt."

In January 1942 demonstrators thronged the streets of Cairo, crying out, "Forward Rommel! Long live Rommel!" British troops and armoured cars surrounded the royal palace until Farouk acceded to British demands. That summer, Egyptian army officers eagerly anticipated their liberation by Rommel's Afrika Korps. They were thrilled by the arrival in Cairo of two German spies, Hans Eppler and another man known only as "Sandy." Captain Sadat was crestfallen, however, to witness the frivolous behaviour of the two agents, whom he found living on the Nile houseboat of the famous belly dancer Hikmet Fahmy. He wrote: "The surprise must have shown on my face, because Eppler laughingly asked: 'Where do you expect us to stay? In a British army camp?' " The German said Hikmet Fahmy was "perfectly reliable." He and his colleague spent drunken evenings at the Kitkat nightclub, and changed large sums of forged British banknotes through a Jew who allegedly charged 30 percent commission.

Sadat wrote long afterwards, with the unembarrassed anti-Semitism of his people: "I was not surprised at a Jew performing this service for the Nazis because I knew that a Jew would do anything if the price was right." The British arrested the entire spy ring and suppressed internal dissent with little difficulty. But they could not credibly idealise Egypt's role in the Allied camp.

Britain's Asian empire manifested the most conspicuously divided allegiances. In 1939, nationalists in Malaya staged antiwar demonstrations, harshly suppressed by the local colonial authorities. An Indian member of the Malay civil service said that, "although his reason utterly rebelled against it, his sympathies instinctively ranged themselves with the Japanese in their fight against the Anglo-Saxons." Indian nationalist leader Jawaharlal Nehru wrote: "It [is] obvious that the average man in India is so full of bitterness against the British that he would welcome any attack on them." Some of his compatriots rejoiced in the spectacle of fellow Asians routing white armies and navies. "We couldn't help gloating at the beating the British were getting at the hands of the Germans," said Dr. Kashmi Swaminadhan. "This, in spite of our being anti-Hitler." Lady Diana Cooper wrote before the deluge in 1942: "I could see no particular reason why the 85 per cent Chinese and 15 per cent Indian and Malayan citizens of Singapore should fight, as Cockneys do, *against* people of their own shade, and *for* the dear good English." Indeed, few did so.

In Malaya and Burma, the new rulers were able to enlist the services of many local people and some Indians who felt no loyalty to the expelled British. But against these should be cited the example of such a man as the Indian P. G. Mahindasa, teacher of the English school in Malacca settlement. He wrote before his execution by the Japanese for listening to the BBC on his radio: "I have always cherished British sportsmanship, justice and the civil service as the finest things in an imperfect world. I die gladly for freedom. My enemies fail to conquer my soul. I forgive them for what they did to my frail body. To my dear boys, tell them that their teacher died with a smile on his lips." In Malaya, the Chinese communist Chin Peng, who later became leader of the violent anti-British independence movement, remarked on the irony that he received an OBE from a grateful British government for promoting terrorism and murdering Malays who collaborated with the Japanese.

Many people in Burma, Malaya and the Dutch East Indies, together with more than a few in the Philippines, at first welcomed the invading Japanese as liberators. Even ardent foes of European imperialism were soon disillusioned, however, by the arrogance and institutionalised brutality of their new masters. Examples are legion: far more local people died as slaves on the notorious Burma Railway than did Allied prisoners. Of almost 80,000 Malays sent to work there, nearly 30,000 perished, alongside 14,000 whites; the rail link also cost the lives of 100,000 Burmese, Indians and Chinese. When cholera broke out at Nieke on the Burma-Thailand border, infecting large numbers of Tamils performing forced labour on the railway, the Japanese set fire to a barracks housing 150 stricken patients. Elsewhere, any man or woman who displeased the occupiers was treated with systemic sadistic cruelty. Sybil Kathigasu, the Catholic wife of a Perak planter, was tortured in Taiping jail, while her daughter was hung from a tree over a fire. She shamed them into freeing the child, but herself emerged from the ordeal crippled for life.

A minimum of 5 million people in Southeast Asia died in the course of the war, many of them in the Dutch East Indies, either at Japanese hands or as a result of starvation imposed by Tokyo's diversion of food and crops to feed its own people. The price of rice soared, while harvests fell by one-third; tapioca was exploited as a substitute. The writer Samad Ismail wrote wearily in 1944: "Everyone feels affection for tapioca; embraces, exalts and extols tapioca; there is nothing else they discuss other than tapioca, in the kitchen, on the tram, in a wedding gathering—always tapioca, tapioca and tapioca." But while a tapioca diet provided some bulk, it did nothing to reverse the chronic vitamin deficiency that became endemic in Japanese-occupied societies. Hunger did more than anything else to alienate the subject peoples of Tokyo's Greater East Asia Co-Prosperity Sphere, however strong their dislike of their former European overlords.

2. The Raj: Unfinest Hour

BRITISH-OCCUPIED INDIA, as nationalists regarded the subcontinent, experienced bitter wartime upheavals and distress. The jewel in the crown of Britain's empire, second only to China as the largest and most populous landmass in Asia, became a huge supplier of textiles and equipment to the Allies. It manufactured 1 million blankets for the British Army—the wool clip of 60 million sheep—together with 41 million items of military uniform, 2 million parachutes and 16 million pairs of boots. It was a source of fury to Churchill that India's sterling balances—the debt owed by Britain to the subcontinent in payment for goods supplied—soared on the strength of this output. "Winston burbled away endlessly," wrote India Secretary Leo Amery on 16 September 1942, "that it was monstrous to expect that we should not only defend India and then have to clear out, but be left to pay hundreds of millions for the privilege."

But could Indians refuse to be defended? Before the conflict began, nationalist demands for self-government and independence had become clamorous, enjoying overwhelming enthusiasm from the Hindu majority except in the so-called princely states. The maharajahs' territories survived as feudal fiefdoms, whose rulers knew that once Indians ruled their own country, their privileges would be swept away. They provided islands of support for British hegemony, because they thus preserved their own. Elsewhere, however, almost every educated Hindu wanted the British to go. The question was when: the onset of war caused some influential figures to argue that the independence struggle should be postponed until the greater evil of fascism was defeated. Veer Damodar Savarkar, though a nationalist, suggested pragmatically that his people should exploit the opportunity to acquire military and industrial skills which would be priceless to a free India.

The League of Radical Congressmen urged that active participation in the war would "not be thereby helping British imperialism, but on the contrary weakening it, by developing and strengthening the anti-fascist forces in England and Europe." Likewise M. N. Roy: "The present is not England's war. It is a war for the future of the world. If the British government happens to be a party to the war, why should the fighters for human liberty be ashamed of congratulating it for this meritorious deed? The old saying that adversity brings strange bedfellows is not altogether meaningless. If it was justifiable for the Soviet government to make the non-aggression pact with Nazi Germany, why should it not be equally permissible for the fighters for Indian freedom to support the British government so long as it is engaged in war against fascism?" Some of his compatriots adopted the view of Lt. A. M. Bose, the nephew of India's most famous scientist and himself a cosmopolitan who had travelled widely in Europe. Bose wrote to a British friend: "I am now in the army since three years as I wanted to do my bit to fight the Nazis."

Several hundred Indians, boasting such exotic names as "Tiger" Jaswal Singh, Piloo Reporter, "Jumbo" Majundan and Miroo Engineer, flew for the Indian Air Force; Engineer, one of four flying brothers, once took a girlfriend into the air in his Hurricane. But though Indian fliers wore the same uniforms and adopted the same slang as their RAF brethren, they sometimes suffered the casual racism of British officers, who called them "blackies." A fighter pilot, Mahender Singh Pujji, was dismayed when his ship stopped in South Africa en route to Britain: "I was shocked to see the treatment of Indians and Africans there. I and my colleagues were very angry." In England and later the Western Desert, he never adapted to British food, and subsisted largely on eggs, biscuits and chocolate. Indian personnel knew that they remained second-class airmen in their commanders' eyes, denied the best aircraft and glamorous assignments; but they made a significant contribution to the 1944–45 Burma campaign, flying thousands of reconnaissance and ground-attack sorties in support of the Fourteenth Army.

Other Indians, however, adopted a more nuanced and cautious attitude to the conflict. Chakravarti Rajagopalachari, a Congress leader and premier of the Madras presidency, said in June 1940 that it might seem small-minded to raise domestic issues when Britain was in the midst of a life-and-death struggle against a merciless enemy. "Yet every nation has its own life to look after . . . We do not serve civilisation by forgetting our rights. We cannot help the Allies by agreeing to be a subject people. On the contrary, such surrender would help the Germans."

Nehru, in a letter from the prison cell he frequently occupied, pointed out to the viceroy of India, Lord Linlithgow, that his supporters had often held back from injuring the Raj: "In the summer of 1940, when France fell and England was facing dire peril, Congress . . . deliberately avoided [direct action], in spite of a strong demand for it . . . because it did not want to take advantage of a critical international situation or to encourage Nazi aggression in any way." He wrote likewise on the day after Pearl Harbor: "If I were asked with whom my sympathies lay in this war, I would unhesitatingly say with Russia, China, America and England." But for the Congress president, there remained an essential qualification. Churchill refused to grant independence to India; in consequence, Nehru asserted, "there is no question of my giving help to Britain. How can I fight for a thing, freedom, which is denied to me? British policy in India appears to be to terrify the people, so that in anxiety we may seek British protection."

Following Japan's entry into the war, Mahatma Gandhi demanded that the British should leave forthwith, to make India a less desirable invasion objective. In 1942, the nationalists' "Quit India" movement gained widespread support and stirred rising popular unrest. Congress moved from a policy of noncooperation towards one of outright rejection of British rule. On 21 January Lord Linlithgow reported to London: "There is a large and dangerous potential fifth column in Bengal, Assam, Bihar and Orissa, and . . . indeed, potentiality of pro-enemy sympathy and activity in eastern India is enormous." To the nationalists' surprise, even in this darkest hour of Britain's eastern fortunes, the imperial power declined to negotiate. Most of Congress's leaders were imprisoned, some for long periods; Gandhi himself was released only in 1944, on grounds of ill-health. Widespread violence erupted, most seriously in Bombay, the Eastern United Provinces and Bihar, with attacks on symbols of the Raj—government buildings, railways, post offices—and some sabotage.

In August 1942 spontaneous riots broke out, following the failure of Sir Stafford Cripps's mission to persuade Congress to shelve its political demands until peace came. The British restored order with considerable ruthlessness: the viceroy came close to authorising aerial strafing of the dissidents, an option he described only half ironically as "an exhilarating departure from precedent." There were mass punitive whippings of convicted rioters, and tens of thousands of troops and *lathi*-wielding police were deployed against demonstrators. There are credible reports of policemen in disaffected areas engaging in rapes and indeed gang rapes of arrested women; several hundred demonstrators were shot down, many homes were burned.

In parts of northwest India, for some months a reign of terror prevailed. On 29 September in Midnapore, for instance, a procession led by a seventy-three-year-old woman named Matongini Hazra converged on Tamluk's courthouse. An ardent follower of Gandhi, she had already served six months' imprisonment for demonstrating in front of the viceroy. Now, accompanied by several women blowing conches, she advanced on the police and army cordon securing the courthouse, carrying a flag. When the security forces opened fire, a bullet struck her left hand, causing her to transfer the flag to her right. She was hit again before a third bullet struck her full in the temple. Three teenage boys were among others killed before the demonstrators fled.

In the short term, repression was successful in restoring order. The Indian Army remained almost entirely staunch. But all save the most myopic British imperialists recognised that their rule had lost the consent of the governed. It was a source of embarrassment to thoughtful politicians that in 1942, in the midst of a war against tyranny, some fifty battalions of troops—more than were then committed against the Japanese—had to be deployed to maintain internal control of India. It may be argued that there were overwhelming practical objections against surrendering power to Congress when the Japanese army stood at the gates. But it was among the ugliest aspects of British conduct of the war that in order to hold India, it was necessary not merely to repulse external invaders but also to administer the country under emergency powers, as an occupied nation rather than a willing cobelligerent. Some of the repressive measures adopted in India were similar in kind, if not in scale, to those used by the Axis in occupied countries. Reports of excesses by the security forces were suppressed by military censorship.

The British in India displayed a casual racism, and sometimes brutality, which caused sensitive witnesses to recoil. Troop-Sergeant Clive Branson was a peacetime artist born in the subcontinent, a former member of the communist International Brigade in Spain. He wrote of his compatriots' behaviour: "Those bloody idiots in the regular army . . . treat the Indians in such a way which not only makes one tremble for the future, but which makes one ashamed of being one of them . . . Never will any of us . . . forget the unbelievable, indescribable poverty in which we have found people living wherever we went." If those at home knew the truth, said Branson, "there would be a hell of a row—because these conditions are maintained in the name of the British."

There were grievances in the ranks of the Indian Army, mostly about soldiers' inferior conditions of service compared to those of their British counterparts. One group of men wrote jointly to their commanding officer: "In the eyes of Mahatma Gandhi all are equal but you pay a British soldier Rs75/- and to an Indian soldier you pay Rs18/- only." Another man complained: "An Indian subadar salutes a British soldier, but the British soldier does not salute an Indian subadar. Why is this so?" Nor were Indians the only victims of the Raj's harsh governance: in December 1942, 2,115 Japanese civilian internees were held by the British at the Purama Quila camp outside Delhi in scandalous conditions of squalor and privation; by the year's end 106 of them had died, some of beriberi and dysentery. The Japanese empire presided over many worse things, on a vastly greater scale; but the deaths at Purama Quila reflected deplorably on British competence as well as humanity.

Americans, from their president downwards, never entirely forgave Churchill and his nation for the manner in which the peoples of the subcontinent were excluded from the ringing promises of freedom enshrined in the Atlantic Charter. Americans serving in India—performing liaison and logistical tasks, training Chinese soldiers and flying bomber operations against the Japanese—recoiled from British treatment of its inhabitants and believed their own behaviour more sympathetic. Indians were less convinced: a letter writer to the *Statesman* newspaper denounced the conduct of the Americans as vigorously as that of the British, describing them uncharitably as "venereal disease–ridden and seducers of young women." The British saw hypocrisy as well as moral conceit in criticism of their imperial governance by an ally which sustained racial segregation at home.

Most of Churchill's political colleagues recognised the inevitability of granting early independence to India, and hesitated only about the timing. But the old Victorian imperialist remained implacable: he clung to a delusion that British greatness derived in substantial measure from the Raj, and was disgusted by the perceived treachery of Indian politicians who sought to exploit Britain's vulnerability and sometimes rejoiced in its misfortunes. Throughout the war, the prime minister spoke and wrote about Indians with a contempt that reflected his only acquaintance with them, as a nineteenth-century cavalry subaltern; his policies lacked the compassion which generally characterised his leadership.

By the autumn of 1942 more than 30,000 Congressmen were imprisoned, including Gandhi and Nehru. But British treatment of dissenters throughout their empire was incomparably more humane than that accorded by the Axis to domestic foes and occupied nations. For instance, Anwar Sadat was jailed after being implicated in his conspiracy with the German spies in Cairo, but so casually guarded that he was able to make two easy escapes; after the second, in 1944, he remained free, though in hiding, for the rest of the war. In India, Nehru could write letters freely, enjoy such favourite books as Plato's *Republic* and play badminton during a relatively privileged fortress incarceration. But his weight fell dramatically, and confinement weighed as heavily upon the fifty-two-year-old Indian leader as on any other prisoner. In one letter, he told his wife, Betty, to abandon the notion of sending him Bradley's *Shakespearean Tragedy* "when there is tragedy enough at present."

Some nationalists believed that drastic methods should be employed to get the British out. In 1940 Subhas Chandra Bose, the Congress president, demanded a campaign of civil disobedience. When Gandhi rejected this, Bose resigned his post and made his way to Berlin via Kabul. Once in Germany, he recruited a small "Indian Legion" from prisoners captured in the Western Desert, which served the Third Reich without notable distinction. In the summer of 1943 Bose returned to Southeast Asia. The Japanese granted his "provisional Indian government" a nominal seat in the occupied Andaman and Nicobar Islands, and he was soon attracting big crowds for public meetings under Japanese auspices. Wearing uniform and top boots, he spoke in terms that mirrored Churchill's call for blood, toil, tears and sweat. Indian National Army recruits, he told his audiences, must face "hunger, thirst, privation, forced marches and death. Only when you pass this test will freedom be yours." INA soldiers called Bose *Netaji*—"Esteemed Leader." One of them, Lt. Shiv Singh, said: "After being captured in Hong Kong, Gen. Mohan Singh and Bose said . . . 'You are fighting for a very small sum of money indeed, now come and fight for your country.' We volunteered without any force being used . . . I thought *Netaji* . . . was number-one leader, above Gandhi."

Bose formed a women's brigade, the Rani of Jhansi Regiment, in honour of a heroine of the 1857 rising against the British, and marched with it from Rangoon to Bangkok. One recruit asserted in a radio broadcast: "I am not a doll soldier, or a soldier in mere words, but a real soldier in the true sense of the word." A contingent of 500 reached Burma from Malaya late in 1943, but the women were disappointed to find themselves relegated to nursing duties. Men's units were deployed against Slim's army in Assam and Burma. One soldier, P. K. Basu, said later: "I did not believe that the INA would actually succeed, but I believed in the INA"; two INA regiments were named for Gandhi and Nehru. There was a yawning gulf between Bose's rhetoric and the INA's contribution to the Axis war effort. When its poorly armed units were deployed in battle, their Japanese sponsors treated them with disdain, and few showed stomach for serious fighting. Some imperial Indian troops shot INA prisoners out of hand, but the British were embarrassed by the renegade force's very existence and dismayed to find that a substantial number of Indians regarded Bose as a hero—as they do today.

THE MOST SERIOUS BLOT upon the wartime Raj, and arguably upon Britain's entire war effort, was the 1943–44 Bengal famine. The loss of Burma deprived India of 15 percent of its food supplies. When a series of floods and cyclones—natural catastrophes to which low-lying East Bengal is chronically vulnerable—struck the region, wrecking its 1942 harvest, the population fell prey to desperate hunger. Much transport was destroyed, further impeding movement of food supplies. A Bengali fisherman named Abani was among millions who lost their livelihoods. "We could not afford to buy a net . . . The moneylender would not give me a loan. The moneylender himself had no money. Our family possessions had been destroyed in the flood: of eight cows we only saved one." By December, people were dying. In the following year, their plight became catastrophic. In October 1943 a relief worker named Arangamohan Das reported from Terapekhia bazaar on the Haldi River. "There I saw nearly 500 destitutes of both sexes, almost naked and reduced to bare skeletons. Some of them were begging for food . . . from the passers by, some longing for food with piteous look, some lying by the wayside approaching death hardly with any more energy to breathe and actually I had the misfortune of seeing eight peoples breathe their last before my eyes."

Censors intercepted a letter from an Indian soldier embittered by his experience during leave: "We come home to our own villages to find the food is scarce and high-priced. Our wives have been led astray and our land has been misappropriated. Why does the Sarkar [government] not do something about it *now* rather than talking about post-war reconstruction?" Why not, indeed? The British government refused to divert scarce shipping to famine relief; India Secretary Leo Amery at first adopted a cavalier attitude. Even when he began to exert his influence in favour of intervention, the prime minister and cabinet remained unsympathetic. In 1943, sailings to Indian Ocean destinations were cut by 60 percent, as shipping was diverted to sustain Allied amphibious operations, aid to Russia and Atlantic convoys; the British cabinet met only 25 percent of Delhi's requested food deliveries. Churchill wrote in March 1943, applauding the minister of war transport's refusal to release ships to move relief supplies: "A concession to one country . . . encourages demands from all the others. [The Indians] must learn to look after themselves as we have done . . . We cannot afford to send ships merely as a gesture of goodwill." A few months later, he said: "There is no reason why all parts of the British Empire should not feel the pinch in the same way as the Mother Country has done."

But the British diet remained incomparably more lavish than that of the Indian people. Bengalis use the phrase *payter jala*—burning of the belly—to describe hunger, and many bellies burned in 1943 and 1944. Gourhori Majhi of Kalikakundu said long afterwards: "Everyone was crazed with hunger. Whatever you found, you'd tear it off and eat it right there. My family had ten people; my own stomach was wailing. Who is your brother, who is your sister—no one thought of such things then. Everyone is wondering, how will I live? . . . There was not a blade of grass in the fields." Many women resorted to prostitution, and some families sold their daughters to pimps.

Even at this extremity there were no reports of cannibalism such as took place in Russia, but there were many child murders. The newspaper *Biplabi* reported on 5 August 1943: "In Sapurapota village . . . a Muslim weaver was unable to support his family and, crazed with hunger, wandered away. His wife believed that he had drowned himself . . . Being unable to feed her two young sons for several days, she could no longer endure their suffering. On [23 July] she dropped the smaller boy torn from her womb, the sparkle of her eye, into the Kasai's frothing waters. She tried in the same way to send her elder son to his father, but he screamed and grabbed onto her . . . She discovered a new way to silence her child's searing hunger. With feeble arms she dug a small grave and threw her son into it. As she was trying to cover him with earth a passer-by heard his screams and snatched the spade from his mother's hand. A [low-caste Hindu] promised to bring up the boy and the mother then went away, who knows where. Probably she found peace by joining her husband in the Kasai's cold torrent."

There were widespread cholera outbreaks, with people dying in the streets and parks of major cities: by mid-October 1943, the death rate in

Calcutta alone had risen from its usual 600 a month to 2,000. Jawaharlal Nehru's sister-in-law wrote from a relief centre describing "rickety babies with arms and legs like sticks; nursing mothers with wrinkled faces; children with swollen faces and hollow-eyed through lack of food and sleep; men exhausted and weary, walking skeletons all of them." She was appalled by "the look of weary resignation in their eyes. It wounded my spirit in a manner that the sight of their suffering bodies had not done." In October Wavell, by now India's viceroy, belatedly deployed troops to move relief supplies. Thereafter, government efforts to assist the population steadily increased, but at least 1 million and perhaps as many as 3 million people were dead, and immense political damage had been done. There was no doubt of the logistical difficulties the British faced in assuaging the consequences of natural disaster while fighting a great war. But Churchill responded to Wavell's increasingly urgent and forceful pleas for aid with a brutal insensitivity which left an irreparable scar on Anglo-Indian relations.

Nehru wrote from prison on 18 September 1943: "Reports from Bengal are staggering. We grow accustomed to anything, any depth of human misery and sorrow . . . More and more I feel that behind all the terrible mismanagement and bungling there is something deeper . . . the collapse of the economic structure of Bengal." He added on 11 November: "The Bengal famine has been the final epitaph of British rule and achievement in India." Churchill stubbornly refused concessions to nationalist sentiment, dismissing objections from the Americans and their Chinese clients. Leo Amery recoiled in dismay from Churchill's ravings: "Cabinet . . . [Winston] talked unmitigated nonsense, first of all treating Wavell as a contemptible self-seeking advertiser, and then talking about the handicap India is to defence, and how glad he would be to hand it over to President Roosevelt."

Yet few British people, fighting for their lives, were much troubled by displays of Indian alienation or imperial repression. They cheered themselves with knowledge that the vast Indian Army, 4 million strong, remained loyal to the Raj. Indian divisions made a notable contribution to the East Africa, Iraq, North Africa and Italian campaigns, and played the principal role in the 1944–45 struggles for Assam and Burma. British wartime policy could be deemed a success, in that by 1944–45 disorder was almost entirely suppressed; strikes and acts of sabotage dwindled. But posterity can see the irony that while Britain fought the Axis in the name of freedom, to retain control of India it practised governance without popular consent, and adopted some of the methods of totalitarianism.

Britain's wartime treatment of its subject races remained humane by

German or Japanese standards; there were no arbitrary executions or wholesale massacres. But India was not the only imperial possession in which the exigencies of emergency were used to justify neglect, cruelty and injustice. In 1943, famines afflicted Kenya, Tanganyika and British Somaliland; at various moments there were food riots in Tehran, Beirut, Cairo and Damascus. While these were caused by circumstances of war, the imperial power was parsimonious in apportioning resources to alleviate their consequences. While British rule reflected moderate rather than absolute authoritarianism, it scarcely sufficed to promote support—and especially Indian support—for retention of imperial hegemony. The only narrowly plausible defence of British wartime rule of India is that the country was so vast, with such potential for turbulence, that indulgence of domestic dissent would have threatened an irretrievable loss of control, to the advantage of the Axis. The common experience of battle forged some sense of battlefield comradeship between British and imperial soldiers, white, brown and black alike. But the stress of war, rather than strengthening the bonds of empire as Britain's jingos liked to pretend, dramatically loosened them.

The leaders of the Grand Alliance depicted the war as a struggle for freedom against oppression, good against evil. In the twenty-first century, few informed people even in former colonial possessions doubt the merit of the Allied cause, the advantage that accrued to mankind from defeat of the Axis. But it seems essential to recognise that in many societies contemporary loyalties were confused and equivocal. Millions of people around the world who had no love for the regimes of Hitler, Mussolini or Hirohito felt little greater enthusiasm for Allied powers whose vision of liberty vanished, it seemed to their colonial subjects, at their own front doors.

CHAPTER SEVENTEEN

ASIAN FRONTS

1. China

AS EARLY AS 1936, the American correspondent Edgar Snow, a passionate admirer and friend of Mao Tse-tung's, wrote: "In her great effort to master the markets and inland wealth of China, Japan is destined to break her imperial neck. This catastrophe will occur not because of automatic economic collapse in Japan. It will come because the conditions of suzerainty which Japan must impose on China will prove humanly intolerable and will shortly provoke an effort of resistance that will astound the world." Snow was right about the outcome of Japanese imperialism, though not about the military effectiveness of Chinese resistance. Wartime Allied strategy in the Far East was powerfully influenced by America's desire to make China not only a major belligerent, but a great power. Enormous resources were lavished upon flying supplies from India to Americans, notably airmen, supporting the Nationalist regime of Chiang Kai-shek "over the Hump" of the Himalayas, after Japan's conquest of Burma severed the land link in 1942, and the United States built airfields in China from which to deploy its bombers.

All these efforts proved vain. China remained a chaotic, impoverished, deeply divided society. Chiang boasted an enormous paper army, but his regime and commanders were too corrupt and incompetent, his soldiers too scantily equipped and motivated, to make significant headway against the Japanese. Logistical and operational difficulties crippled USAAF missions out of China. In the north, in Yennan Province, Mao's communists held sway, and professed antagonism to the Japanese. But Mao's strategy was dominated by the desire to build his strength for a postwar showdown with Chiang. Between 1937 and 1942, both the Nationalists and the communists inflicted substantial casualties on the invaders—181,647 dead. But thereafter they acknowledged their inability to challenge them in headlong confrontations which drained their threadbare resources to little purpose. Chinese historian Zhijia Shen has written in a study of Shandong Province: "Local people were much more influenced by pragmatic calculation than by the idea of nationalism . . . When national and local interests clashed, they did not hesitate to compromise national interests."

Though Mao deluded some Americans into supposing that his guerrillas were making war effectively, for much of the conflict he maintained a tacit truce with the Japanese, and indeed became secret partners with them in the opium trade. While the Nationalists recorded 3.2 million military casualties during the Japanese occupation, the communists acknowledged only 580,000. Latterly, Chiang devoted as much military energy to holding his ground against Mao as to fighting the Japanese. He was unembarrassed by his own equivocations. He said: "The Japanese are a disease of the skin; the communists are a disease of the heart."

Nonetheless, the occupation of half of China constituted a massive drain upon Tokyo's resources, and cost Japan 202,958 dead between 1941 and 1945, compared with 208,000 men killed fighting the British, and 485,717 army and 414,879 naval personnel lost in combat with the United States. The country was vast: even if organised opposition was weak, large forces were indispensable to make good Tokyo's claims on territory and to control a hostile and often starving population. In the north, Japan's Kwantung Army held Manchuria (they called the puppet state they create there Manchukuo); its North China Area Army was based in Beijing; and the headquarters of the Central China Expeditionary Forces was in Shanghai. All estimates are unreliable, but it seems reasonable to accept the figure of 15 million Chinese wartime dead as a direct consequence of Japanese military action, starvation or plagues, some of these deliberately fostered by biological warfare specialists of the Japanese army's Unit 731.

The Japanese were the only large-scale wartime users of biological weapons. Unit 731 in Manchuria operated under the supremely cynical cover name of the Kwantung Army Epidemic Protection and Water Supply Unit. Thousands of captive Chinese were murdered in the course of tests at 731's base near Harbin, many being subjected to vivisection without benefit of anaesthetics. Some victims were tied to stakes before anthrax bombs were detonated around them. Women were laboratory-infected with syphilis; local civilians were abducted and injected with fatal viruses. In the course of Japan's war in China, cholera, dysentery, plague and typhus germs were broadcast, most often from the air, sometimes using porcelain bombs to deliver plague fleas. An unsuccessful attempt was made to employ such means against American forces on Saipan, but the ship carrying the putative insect warriors was sunk en route.

That the Japanese attempted to kill millions of people with biological weapons is undisputed; it is less certain, however, how successful were their efforts. Vast numbers of Chinese died in epidemics between 1936 and 1945, and modern China attributes most of these losses to Japanese action. In a broad sense this is just, since privation and starvation were consequences of Japanese aggression. But it remains unproven that Unit 731's operations were directly responsible. For instance, over 200,000 people died during the 1942 cholera epidemic in Yunnan. The Japanese released cholera bacteria in the province, but many such epidemics took place even where they did not do so. It was difficult, with available technology, to spread disease on demand with air-dropped biological weapons. Yet even if Japan's genocidal accomplishments fell sort of their sponsors' hopes, the nation's moral responsibility is manifest.

Between 1942 and 1944 big battlefield encounters in China were rare, but Japanese forces conducted frequent punitive expeditions to suppress dissent or gather food. One of the most ferocious of these took place in May 1942, designated by the Japanese high command as an act of vengeance for America's Doolittle raid on Tokyo. More than 100,000 troops were dispatched into Chekiang and Kiangsi Provinces, with support from the biological warfare unit. By September, when their mission was deemed fulfilled and the columns withdrew, a quarter of a million people had been killed. Throughout the war, Chiang's capital of Chungking was routinely bombed by Japanese aircraft, and raids inflicted heavy civilian casualties in several other cities.

The files of the medical branch of the Tokyo War Ministry show that in September 1942, enslaved "comfort women" were servicing Japanese soldiers at 100 stations in northern China, 140 in central China, 40 in the south, 100 in Southeast Asia, 10 in the southwest Pacific and 10 on southern Sakhalin. Women were deployed in proportions of one to every forty soldiers. Around 100,000 were centrally conscripted, in addition to many others recruited locally. Hirohito's warriors were issued with condoms branded "Assault No. 1," though many disdained to use them. Chinese peasants called their Japanese occupiers "the *YaKe*," meaning dumb, because scarcely any Japanese condescended to learn or speak Chinese. "The *YaKe* treatment" described the piercing of a man's or woman's legs with a sharpened bamboo, the customary punishment for supposed Chinese disobedience.

One of its victims was a nineteen-year-old girl, Lin Yajin, who like many of her contemporaries bore *YaKe* scars for the rest of her life. She was a peasant's daughter in Hainan Province, one of six children, when she was seized by Japanese soldiers in October 1943. They took her to their base camp and questioned her perfunctorily about local guerrilla activity. She sobbed in terror through her first night of captivity; during the second, four men filed into the hut where she was held.

One of them was an interpreter who told me the others were officers and then left. All three raped me. As I was a virgin, it felt very painful so I screamed very loudly. When they heard me cry they said nothing, just continued to fuck me like animals. For ten days, every evening three, four or five men did the same. Usually, while one of them raped me the others watched and laughed.

I tried to escape but it was very difficult. Even when you went to the lavatory, you were guarded by a soldier—a Bengali who didn't rape us. Then I was moved to another village, called Qingxun, only one and a half kilometres from my home. Here also several soldiers came every day. Even when I had my period they still wanted to fuck me. After one month I was sick. My face was yellow and my whole body was dropsical. When the Japanese soldiers realised what had happened—I had caught a venereal disease—in the end they let me go home. I found my father was also seriously ill, and a month later he died—my family was so poor we had no money for a doctor. My mother treated me with herbs from the fields. It took quite a long time for my sickness to be cured. By then it was the summer of 1944. Four other girls were taken to the Japanese camp with me, and in 1946 I learned that all of them had died of venereal disease. Later, when the villagers learned that I'd been raped by Japanese, they too mocked and beat me. I have been alone ever since.

Deng Yumin, from Xiangshui in Baoting County, suffered a similar fate. Like many of her people, members of the Miao ethnic minority, she was conscripted for forced labour in 1940, living in a work camp and first planting tobacco, then road building. One day, the overseer told her she had been chosen for special work. She was taken to meet a Japanese officer, who she thought was about forty years old. Through an interpreter,

he told me I was a pretty girl, and he wanted me to be his friend. I didn't have a choice, so I nodded to tell him I agreed. A few days after, late in the evening the interpreter took me to meet that officer again, and left me alone with him. His name was Songmu. He immediately took me in his arms, then groped my body. I struggled instinctively, but there was nothing I could do. He did what he liked. When I went back where I worked, I was very ashamed to tell the other girls what had happened. After that he raped me every day. I was a virgin, fourteen years old. I hadn't started my periods. I didn't feel very much. It just felt very painful.

It was like that for more than two months. One day the interpreter took me to Songmu's place. He was not there. I saw another two officers whom I had never met. I wanted to leave and call Mr. Songmu but one of the officers stopped me and closed the door. They said they wanted to marry me. When I resisted, they slapped my face—one was about twenty years old, the other about fifty. Both of them raped me that day. I told Mr. Songmu what happened. He just grinned and said it was a little thing. I was so angry. I had a good feeling about him until then, but from that day I started to hate him very much. A week later the interpreter asked me again to see Mr. Songmu, but I said I didn't want to see him any more. He said that if I refused, the soldiers would kill me and my family and all the villagers. So I had to see Mr. Songmu again, and after that not only he but also other officers raped me very often. Once three officers came, and one held my arms and another my legs while the third raped me, and they all laughed wildly. It was like that until the end of the war.

If Japanese conduct in victory had been barbaric, amid defeats it became progressively more murderous. The principal victims of their Asian rampages were not the British, Australians or Americans, whose pride and prestige were more vulnerable than their citizens, but the native inhabitants of the societies over which Tokyo assumed hegemony, China foremost among them. "Terrible things were done by Japan in China," says the modern Japanese writer Kazutoshi Hando, but many of his compatriots still decline to acknowledge this.

Not only Japanese nationalists, but also some modern Western historians, argue that the United States provoked Japan into war in 1941. They suggest that conflict between the two nations was avoidable, and propound a theory of moral equivalence, whereby Japanese wartime conduct was no worse than that of the Allies. But the Japanese waged an expansionist war in China, massacring countless civilians, for years before President Roosevelt imposed economic sanctions. A contemporary Japanese nationalist later sought to justify his nation's policies by asserting: "America and Britain had been colonising China for many years. China was a backward nation . . . we felt Japan should go there and use Japanese technology and leadership to make China a better country." The record shows that Japanese conduct in China was both wholly self-interested and shamelessly barbaric. But sufficient numbers of Japanese remained convinced of their nation's "civilising mission" and of the legitimacy of their claims upon an overseas empire to render their government implacably opposed to withdrawal from China, even when Japan began to lose the war and to ponder negotiating positions. While European imperialism was indisputably exploitative, the Japanese claimed rights to pillage Asian societies on a scale and in a fashion no colonial regime had matched.

American enthusiasm for the Nationalist regime, and for China's potential as an ally, persisted until 1944, when the Japanese launched their last major conventional offensive of the war, Operation Ichigo. This was designed to eliminate American bomber airfields in China and open an overland route to Indochina. It conclusively exposed the impotence of Chiang Kai-shek's army, whose formations melted away in its path. Vast new areas of central and southern China were overrun—almost bloodlessly for the Japanese, though emphatically not for the Chinese. Once more, they died in their thousands and hundreds of thousands, as the warring armies swept over them. It is remarkable that Japan embarked on Ichigo at a moment in the war when such an ambitious operation had become strategically futile; its only significant achievement, beyond slaughter, was to disabuse Washington of its illusions about China. By 1945 the U.S. chiefs of staff had abandoned notions of seizing Taiwan and using it as a stepping-stone to create a perimeter on the mainland. They recognised that the country was incapable of participating effectively in the war. China was merely a great victim, second only to Russia in the scale of its sufferings and losses, and was denied the consolation of any redemptive military achievement.

2. Jungle Bashing and Island Hopping

AT THE JANUARY 1943 Casablanca summit conference, the Western Allied leadership reasserted the priority of defeating Germany, but agreed to devote sufficient resources to the war against Japan to maintain the initiative—the Americans committed themselves to a target figure of 30 percent of their war effort. This compromised the doctrine of Germany First more than the chiefs of staff cared to admit, but reflected the imperative created by American domestic opinion, so much more strongly committed to Japan's defeat than to that of Germany. U.S. commanders thereafter decided that resource limitations ruled out an early assault on Rabaul. The USAAF was unwilling even to allocate long-range bombers to conduct a major air offensive against this, Japan's key base in the southwest Pacific, before 1944. The chiefs of staff thus agreed that in 1943 Allied forces would pursue modest objectives: advancing up the Solomons to Bougainville, while MacArthur's forces addressed the north coast of New Guinea. The latter was an exclusively U.S. Army and Australian operation, though dependent on naval support.

The U.S. Navy and Marine Corps were unfailingly sceptical about southwest Pacific operations, which was directed towards ultimate recapture of the Philippines. They saw them as a sop to MacArthur's ego rather than a path to victory. The admirals preferred instead to exploit naval and air power to thrust across the central Pacific through the Marshall, Caroline and Mariana Islands, the shortest route to Japan. It was a measure of the United States' vast wealth that, instead of making a choice between these strategies, a decision was taken to undertake both simultaneously. Thereafter, Nimitz and MacArthur conducted parallel but separate and implicitly competitive campaigns.

The British, meanwhile, addressed themselves once more to Burma. Their retreat had ended in May 1942. In December that year, after the usual seasonal paralysis imposed by the monsoon, Wavell made a first tentative attempt to strike back, committing an Indian division against the port of Akyab, in the Arakan region of Burma facing the Bay of Bengal. Two attempted assaults failed, as did another thrust towards Donbaik in March 1943. The British field commander, Lt. Gen. Noel Irwin, held a reckless press conference at which he sought to explain Allied setbacks by asserting that "in Japan the infantryman is the *corps d'élite*," while the British "put our worst men into the infantry." It would take years, he said, to train Indian troops to the necessary standard to beat the Japanese. Allied censors smothered publication of his remarks, but they reflected the defeatism, incompetence and incoherence prevailing among British commanders in the East. Churchill minuted the chiefs of staff: "I am far from satisfied with the way the Indian campaign is being conducted. The fatal lassitude of the Orient steals over all these Commanders."

Although 4 million Indian soldiers eventually bore arms for the Allies and substantial British resources were deployed in the subcontinent, the generals were slow to renew effective operations. Churchill fumed about the large forces deployed in northeast India, who were achieving wretchedly little; he once described the Indian Army as "a gigantic system of outdoor relief" because of the small number of fighting divisions it provided. Some 450,000 mainly Indian troops, along with some British units, confronted 300,000 Japanese holding Burma, but little useful was done to prepare this army for battle. Lt. Dominic Neill of the Gurkhas—Britain's beloved Nepalese mercenaries—who arrived in India in 1943, said: "Neither I nor my Gurkha soldiers received any tactical training whatsoever until we came face to face with the Japanese."

The only good news from Burma that year was generated by an operation far behind the enemy front, engaging 3,000 British troops led by the eccentric, indeed mentally unstable, Brig. Orde Wingate. His "Chindits" accomplished little of military value at a cost of 30 percent losses, but they created a highly serviceable propaganda legend. Their survival behind enemy lines, despite appalling sufferings, was held to demonstrate that British soldiers could sustain jungle warfare, a proposition many people had come to doubt. Before the Chindit columns left India, Wingate made it plain that no casualties could be carried, and thus badly wounded men must be put out of their misery. This policy might have been merciful, given their inevitable fate in Japanese hands, but it proved hard for Allied soldiers to fulfil. After one Chindit action, Gurkha lieutenant Harold James found himself obliged to follow Wingate's orders: "I had a wounded Gurkha, shot to bits in great pain, and dying. After agonizing for a bit, I gave him a lethal dose of morphia . . . The Gurkhas were amazing, they just accepted it . . . To my horror I found another very seriously wounded Gurkha. I said, 'I've just had to do it.' George looked at me as if to say 'You do it again.' I protested, 'There's no way I'm going to do it twice.' He gave the chap a lethal dose."

Another survivor of the 1943 Chindit foray, Dominic Neill, was among those who realised how little the columns accomplished, beyond creating a legend of suffering and sacrifice. "The newspapers back in India had banner headlines about Wingate's expedition. We couldn't believe our eyes. We had achieved absolutely nothing, we had been kicked out by the Japs again. The publicity was the work of the authorities in GHQ Delhi grasping at any straws after the defeat in 1942, closely followed by the disastrous Arakan campaign of 1942/43." But Churchill thrilled to the exploits of the Chindits, which seemed to provide an honourable contrast to the inertia that suffused the main army in India.

In August 1943, the Japanese achieved a useful propaganda coup of their own by declaring Burma an independent state. Many Burmese were briefly seduced, their enthusiasm increased by Japanese success in repulsing Britain's Aykab offensives. But in Burma as elsewhere, the occupiers' arrogance, cruelty and economic exploitation progressively alienated their subjects. However eager were the Burmese to throw off British rule, evicting the Japanese became a more pressing concern. In the first half of the Asian war, only hill dwellers assisted British arms. By 1944, however, the Japanese faced the hatred of Burma's townspeople as well as guerrilla activity by the tribes.

The autumn monsoon put an end to each year's campaigning season on the India-Burma frontier as effectively as did the spring thaw in Russia. Thus, after the failure of British and Indian forces to break through in the Arakan, 1943 passed without significant progress on the Burma front. Churchill was obliged to content himself with using Indian formations to assist the Allied campaigns in North Africa and Italy. Critics of the Indian Army argued then, and have maintained since, that its romantic reputation was significantly higher than its performance justified. Some units, Gurkhas notable among them, displayed skill, courage and tenacity. Others did not. The British imperial endeavour against the Japanese persistently lagged behind that of the United States.

Yet even in the Pacific, until massive resources reached the theatre during 1944, there were long pauses between successive American initiatives. In June 1943, MacArthur and the Southwest Pacific Area (SWPA) commander, Adm. William Halsey, began their new campaigns in New Guinea and the Solomons. The seizure of New Georgia took a month of tough fighting. Thereafter, Halsey leapfrogged several Japanese-defended islands to land 4,600 men on Vella Lavella. By December, the Americans had secured positions on Bougainville and captured Cape Gloucester at the western end of New Britain. By January 1944 a major air offensive against Rabaul had rendered the base almost useless to Japanese ships and aircraft. Its 100,000-strong garrison became strategically irrelevant; since the troops could move nowhere, they could safely be left to rot.

The expansion of the U.S. Navy made possible a growing Pacific buildup in the course of 1943. Four huge *Essex*-class fleet carriers and five light carriers provided the core of fast task forces which included battleships and cruisers for shore bombardment and destroyers for radar picket and antisubmarine escort duties. A vast fleet train of oilers and supply vessels enabled the fighting ships to sustain up to seventy days of continuous operations, far beyond the Royal Navy's capabilities. There were also escort carriers to provide close support for the amphibious armadas, hundreds of PT boats for inshore work, together with repair and hospital vessels. Though these ships were overwhelmingly manned by landsmen without previous seagoing experience, officers and crews displayed skills of navigation, gunnery and seamanship which entirely outclassed those of their enemies. The steep decline in the Japanese Combined Fleet's operational performance, from high professionalism in December 1941 to faltering ineptitude a year or two later, was one of the strangest and most notable phenomena of the war.

Those Japanese pilots who got close enough to see an American task force below them were awed by its size, often covering hundreds of square miles of ocean. The U.S. Navy in the last two years of the war projected long-range power such as the world had never seen, and grew larger than all the other combatant navies put together. Substantial elements of this fleet were deployed in support of each of the island assault operations that dominated the latter phase of the eastern war. Nimitz's central Pacific offensive opened in November 1943, with landings on the tiny atoll of Tarawa in the Gilbert Islands. There was no scope for strategic deception, because the only credible objectives for American assault were a handful of island air bases. The U.S. Navy and Marine Corps advanced from one foothold to the next, knowing that the Japanese had fortified them all in anticipation of their coming.

Adm. Raymond Spruance's Gilberts' armada included nineteen carriers, twelve battleships and their support vessels, together with an invasion force of 35,000 Marines and 6,000 vehicles. The Americans at sea that day, contemplating the display of their nation's power around them, felt invincible. U.S. carrier aircraft wrecked every local Japanese airfield with bombs and gunfire; before the landings, Spruance's heavy guns bombarded the island for three hours, delivering 3,000 tons of shells. Yet the experience that followed proved one of the most bitter of the U.S. Marine Corps' war. On Betio, the main islet, less than two miles long and 700 yards wide, the Japanese had created bunkers of concrete, steel and felled palm trees which were almost impervious to bombs and shells. Marine Karl Albrecht was shocked by his first sight of the beach as his craft approached: "It was lined with amphtracs, all of which appeared to be burning and smoking . . . The attack appeared to have dissolved in confusion. I was terror-stricken and amazed at the same time. We were Americans and invincible. We had a huge armada of warships and a division of Marines. How could this be happening? I discovered the rows of Marines along the beach weren't lying there waiting for orders to move. They were dead."

A wide offshore reef checked the assault boats, so that thousands of marines were obliged to wade the last few hundred yards to the shoreline with agonising sluggishness, under Japanese fire. A navy pilot gazing down on the scene said later: "The water never seemed clear of tiny men, their rifles over their heads, slowly wading beachwards. I wanted to cry." Four days of fighting followed, among blasted palm trees and skilfully camouflaged defences. When the shooting stopped, the marines had suffered 3,407 casualties and almost all the 4,500 Japanese defenders were dead—just 17 prisoners were taken. Every participant in the battle was shocked by its intensity. It was a painful experience for the American people, as well as for the marines, to discover how hard they had to fight to overcome a sacrificial defence. National hubris, the doctrine of American exceptionalism, was affronted by the revelation that a primitive enemy could resist overwhelming firepower, that the path to victory made close-quarter combat and its sacrifices mandatory. Though significant tactical lessons were learned from Tarawa, the same infantry experience would be repeated in later island battles. From a global and especially Russian perspective, U.S. losses were small for important strategic gains, but they seemed very terrible when the prizes were mere atolls of coral and palm trees.

Nothing could alter the campaign's fundamentals: to defeat Japan, U.S. forces must seize strongly defended Pacific air and naval bases. No application of superior technology and firepower could avert the need for American soldiers and marines to expose their bodies to a skilful and stubborn foe. Even now that it was plain the Allies would win the war, Japan's commitment remained unshaken. Japanese strategy, such as it was, required extraction of the highest possible blood price from the Americans for every small gain, to erode their will and persuade them to negotiate. It is often claimed that Japan's militarists alone insisted on continuing the war, but the generals enjoyed powerful support from conservative politicians, many fervent Japanese nationalists, and from the emperor. In November 1943, at the first conference of the Greater East Asia Co-Prosperity Sphere in Tokyo, Hirohito was warned that the Solomons were about to fall. His response was to goad his generals: "Isn't there some place where we can strike the United States? When and where are you people ever going to put up a good fight? And when are you ever going to fight a decisive battle?"

Cultural revulsion underpinned the hatred which characterised Allied conduct of the Asian war. Japan's savagery towards its prisoners and subjects was now well-known, and often repaid in kind. Japanese willingness to fight to the death rather than surrender, even in tactically and indeed strategically hopeless circumstances, disgusted Allied troops. American and British soldiers were imbued with the European historical tradition, whereby the honourable and civilised response to impending defeat was to abandon the struggle, averting gratuitous bloodshed. Americans in the Pacific, like British soldiers in Burma, felt rage towards an enemy who rejected such civilised logic. The Japanese, who had been merciless in victory, now showed themselves determined to cull every possible human life from their inexorable descent towards defeat.

If the Allies had confronted their foe on a major landmass where there was scope for motorised manoeuvre, they would have achieved victory much more quickly: overwhelming U.S. superiority in tanks, artillery and air power would have smashed the relatively primitive Japanese army, as did the Russians in Manchuria in August 1945. As it was, however, the long series of Pacific battles, miniature in scale by European standards, enabled the Japanese to exploit their defensive skills and sacrificial courage without suffering much disadvantage from lack of artillery and air support. They excelled in camouflage and harassment—"jitter tactics." Even in Japan's years of defeat, its soldiers retained a remarkable psychological dominance of the battlefield. The U.S. Marine Corps was probably America's finest fighting ground force, excepting the army's airborne divisions, and achieved some remarkable things in the Pacific campaigns, but Americans never matched the skills of their opponents, or indeed of the Russians, as night fighters. The more urban and "civilized" a society, the harder it becomes to train its soldiers to adapt to the lifestyle imposed by infantry fighting amid raw nature. The higher the input of technology to a given branch of war, the more emphatic was American excellence: their carrier pilots, for instance, had no superiors. Peasants, however, often make the most stoical riflemen.

ONCE U.S. PLANES could operate from Tarawa, they swiftly destroyed Japanese air capability throughout the Marshall Islands. In early February 1944, the marines were pleasantly surprised by the ease with which they captured the Majuro, Kwajalein and Roi-Namur Atolls—a personal triumph for Nimitz, who overruled all his subordinates to insist upon assaulting the central Marshalls rather than the heavily defended easternmost islands. They then took Eniwetok, at the extreme northwestern end of the Marshall chain, while Spruance's carrier aircraft devastated the key Japanese base at Truk, in the Carolines. The speed of these successes enabled Nimitz to advance the timetable for the next phase of his campaign, scheduling an attack on the Marianas for June rather than September 1944.

A powerful competitive element entered U.S. conduct of the struggle. MacArthur, fearful that the New Guinea campaign would seem a backwater, accelerated his own operations. His troops seized the Admiralty Islands three months ahead of schedule, thus encircling Rabaul and forcing the Japanese to withdraw up the northern coast of New Guinea. In April 1944, he staged his most daring and dramatic coup of the war, capturing Hollandia in Dutch New Guinea, bypassing 40,000 Japanese troops, and in June repulsing a strong Japanese counterattack along the Driniumor River. His forces also captured the Vogelkop Peninsula, at the western end of New Guinea, together with the nearby island of Biak, which became an important air base.

There is a persuasive argument, advanced by the U.S. Navy at the time and by many historians since, that MacArthur's campaign became redundant at the end of 1943; that the only purpose of his subsequent bitter and bloody campaign in the Philippines was to fulfil the personal ambitions of its commander at the expense of many Filipino lives, along with those of several thousand Americans. U.S. dominance of air and sea had become so great that Japanese forces in the southwest Pacific were incapable of transporting troops to threaten Allied strategic purposes. In late 1943 U.S. submarines, decisive contributors to victory, began to wreak havoc upon Japan's supply links to its overextended empire. Many Japanese island garrisons were starved of weapons and ammunition as well as food.

Yet it is characteristic of all wars, and especially of the greatest in human history, that events and personalities acquire a momentum of their own. MacArthur existed. He held a grand title, and had been exalted by propaganda into the most famous of American warlords. His public-relations machine was the most effective branch of his headquarters. Though Roosevelt and his associates, together with most of the nation's military leaders, thought him a charlatan, when a 1945 poll asked Americans whom they considered their greatest general, 43 percent replied MacArthur against 31 percent for Eisenhower, 17 percent for Gen. George Patton and 1 percent for Gen. George Marshall. SWPA's supreme commander had a physical presence, strength of will and personal authority greater than those of the U.S. chiefs of staff. Although MacArthur was never given the massive resources he demanded, he exercised a political and moral influence which sufficed to sustain his campaign and enable him to pursue his chosen personal objectives. Rationally, the United States might have halted its ground operations against Japan in 1944 once the Marianas had been secured. From its air bases, the USAAF's Superfortress bombers could reduce the enemy's homeland to ashes. Together with naval blockade, which crippled Japanese industry and above all oil supplies, irresistible air bombardment made eventual Japanese capitulation inevitable. America's last bloody island campaigns of 1944–45, like the belated British advance into Burma, did little to advance the outcome of the war.

But this is a perspective accessible only to posterity. At the time, it would have seemed unthinkable—save to the airmen fiercely ambitious to show that they could defeat Japan on their own—to halt ground operations. The U.S. Marine Corps and Army divisions deployed in the Pacific expected to keep fighting, and so did their commanders and the nation at home. Once great peoples are committed to the business of killing, there is a bleak inevitability about the manner in which they continue to do so until their enemies are prostrate. In the spring of 1944, the Japanese were still far from acknowledging defeat.

CHAPTER EIGHTEEN

ITALY: HIGH HOPES, SOUR FRUITS

1. Sicily

IN SEPTEMBER 1939, wiseacres in Britain said, "The generals learned their lesson in the last war. There are going to be no wholesale slaughters." To this Evelyn Waugh responded with characteristic waspishness, "How is victory possible except by wholesale slaughters?" His question, while mischievous, was entirely to the point. To defeat Nazi Germany, it was indispensable for its enemies to destroy the Wehrmacht. It was the Western Allies' extreme good fortune that the Russians, and not themselves, paid almost the entire "butcher's bill" for doing this, accepting 95 percent of the military casualties of the three major powers of the Grand Alliance. In 1940–41, the British Empire defied Hitler alone. Thereafter, the United States made a dominant material contribution to Germany's defeat, by supplying aid to Russia and Britain which assumed massive proportions from 1943 onwards, and by creating great air and naval armadas. The Anglo-American bomber offensive made an increasingly heavy impact on Germany. The Western Allied armies, however, by deferring a major landing on the Continent until 1944, restricted themselves to a marginal role. The Russians eventually killed more than 4.5 million German soldiers, while American and British ground and air forces accounted for only about 500,000. These figures emphasise the disparity between respective battlefield contributions.

For Churchill's and Roosevelt's soldiers to have played a decisive role in the ground war against Germany, they would have needed to land on the European continent at least forty divisions, and probably more, in 1943 before the Russians achieved their great victories. These armies did not exist, with the length of training and scale of equipment that American and British military leaders deemed essential. Equally important, shipping was lacking to transport such a force to the Continent and keep it supplied thereafter. The Luftwaffe remained relatively potent: its nemesis came in the following year, at the hands of the USAAF's Mustang fighters over Germany. Allied dominance of French airspace, which proved absolute in 1944, would have been contested had the Allies landed earlier.

The Americans were willing to risk landing a small army in France in

1943, or even in 1942. The British, who would have had to provide most of the men, were not. They judged, almost certainly rightly, that unless they deployed overwhelming strength they would suffer another disaster, as painful as those of the early war years. Even if a continental campaign in 1943 had proved sustainable, it would have cost hundreds of thousands more casualties than the Anglo-American armies suffered in 1944–45, since they would have faced German forces much stronger than those deployed in Normandy on and after D-Day, following a further year of attrition on the Eastern Front.

The expanses of sea separating the Western Allies from occupied Europe posed a challenge for invasion forces that had to cross them, but they also quarantined the Anglo-Americans from German interference. Roosevelt and Churchill were able to exercise the luxury of choice denied to the Red Army, which continuously confronted Hitler's armies. Capt. Pavel Kovalenko was among many Russians embittered by the Western Allies' supposed pusillanimity, which conveniently ignored the Soviet Union's ignominious role between 1939 and June 1941. Kovalenko wrote from the front on 26 March 1943: "Winston Churchill made a speech on the radio, [saying]: 'I can imagine that some time in the next year or possibly the one after, we shall be able to accomplish the defeat of Hitler.' What can one expect from these bastards of 'allies'? Cheats, scoundrels. They want to join the fighting when the outcome is decided."

Churchill, strongly aware of such sentiments, minuted his chiefs of staff in March 1943: "Everywhere the British and Americans are over-loading their operational plans with so many factors of safety that they are ceasing to be capable of making any form of aggressive war. For six or eight months to come, Great Britain and the United States will be playing about with half a dozen German divisions [in North Africa and Sicily]. That is the position to which we are reduced, and which you should labour sedulously to correct." But the British and Americans found it impossible to launch a grand ground commitment in Europe in 1943; instead, they opted for limited operations against the Axis southern flank. At Casablanca Churchill's delegation had secured American agreement to a landing in Sicily, which it was then hoped might take place in early summer. Much emphasis was also placed on Pointblank, the Combined Bomber Offensive designed to pave the way for the invasion of France. By the time of the subsequent Washington summit in May, the protracted endgame in North Africa had pushed back the Sicilian target date to July. The U.S. chiefs of staff remained unhappy about diverting strength from the prospective French campaign, but in Washington they acknowledged that no landing in northwest Europe could take place that year. They believed that the British were exploiting the shipping shortage to escape a French invasion commitment which they disliked. British caution was real enough, but so was the transport issue. It would be intolerable for Allied armies to linger idle in England until the following summer; Italy was meanwhile their only credible objective.

The Allies knew how desperately many Italians yearned to escape from the war. Iris Origo, the American-born writer who occupied a castle in southern Tuscany, wrote in April: "A marked change has come over public opinion. The active resentment and dismay which followed upon the Allies' landing in North Africa and the bombing of Italian cities has given place to a despairing apathy . . . everyone says quite openly: 'It is Fascism that has brought us to this.' " It was plain that Italy would soon quit. The British assumed that once this happened, most of the country would fall into Allied hands: Ultra indicated that the Germans did not intend to mount a major campaign in the lower peninsula, but merely to hold a mountain line in the north. Here was an example of the dangers posed by enjoying a privileged view of the enemy's hand. The Allies thought they knew Hitler's mind; but he frequently changed it, and redealt the cards.

Churchill and his generals were thus far right, that it was essential to attack the Italian mainland, the only battlefield where Anglo-American ground forces could engage the Germans in 1943. But they were inexplicably and culpably ill-informed about the geographical, tactical, political and economic problems they would meet there. They underestimated the difficulties of advancing through mountainous territory against a skilful and stubborn defence. They expected that Italy would provide a springboard for an early offensive against Germany's southern flank. "The Mediterranean," the British chiefs of staff asserted in Washington, "offers us opportunities for action in the coming autumn which may be decisive . . . We shall have every chance of breaking the Axis and of bringing the war to a successful conclusion in May 1944."

The Americans agreed to the Italian commitment, subject to an understanding that come autumn, several divisions would be withdrawn, for redeployment to Britain to prepare for D-Day. As late as 27 July 1943, the British Joint Intelligence Committee correctly forecast an imminent Italian surrender, but mistakenly assumed that Hitler's forces would thereafter withdraw to the Maritime Alps and positions covering Venice and the Tyrol. Churchill's chiefs of staff were more cautious, anticipating some German reinforcement of Italy. But Allied operations against Mussolini's country were launched amid British assurances of easy pickings, which prompted enduring American bitterness when confounded by events.

On 10 July an armada of 2,590 warships and transports began to disembark 180,000 troops on the coast of Sicily, under the command of Gen. Sir Harold Alexander. The British landed in the east, the Americans in the southwest. Strong winds wreaked havoc with the airborne plan, causing many gliders to fall into the sea—69 out of 147 which took off from Tunisia were thus lost, drowning 252 British paratroopers, and just 12 landed safely on their assigned zones. Reckless antiaircraft fire from the Allied fleet cost more casualties among the transport planes. Four Italian divisions offered little resistance on the beaches, which was fortunate, since many invaders were put ashore in the wrong places. Even some Germans showed little fight: an American paratrooper who landed helpless and alone amid one of their units was amazed when three enemy soldiers approached him. Their leader said in perfect English, "We surrender. For three years and eight months we've been fighting all over Europe, Russia and North Africa. That's long enough in any army. We're sick of it all."

The defence was hampered by the fact that, while Gen. Albert Kesselring commanded in Italy, Mussolini had insisted that an Italian, Gen. Alfredo Guzzoni, should control Axis forces in Sicily, a responsibility he was woefully unfit to fulfil. But most men of the two German formations on the island, soon reinforced by elements of a third, threw themselves into the battle with their usual determination. The Luftwaffe paratrooper Martin Poppel wrote on 14 July, after his unit took their first prisoners, British airborne soldiers: "In my opinion their spirit is none too good. They tend to surrender as soon as they face the slightest resistance, in a way that none of our men would have done." He added after an action a week later: "The Tommies obviously thought that their artillery fire yesterday had made us withdraw, and arrived early this morning with three lorries packed full of infantrymen. Hitched up behind 3.7cm and 5.7cm anti-tank guns. Clearly they didn't understand our paratroopers and had learned nothing from their experiences yesterday. Everything was quiet. My boys let the motorcycle escort past and only let them have it when the lorries were right next to them. Within a matter of seconds the first truck was in flames, with Tommies jumping off as best they could. At the end of it we counted fifteen dead and brought back eleven prisoners. In the evening we fetch the anti-tank guns back—they'll strengthen our positions considerably." Poppel spoke well only of British artillery, which commanded German respect throughout the war: "You have to hand it to Tommy, he gets his Forward Observation Officer in position bloody quickly and his artillery fires itself in very fast."

The Germans suffered not only from Allied guns, but also from air attacks. They discovered that their enormous sixty-ton Tiger tanks, while formidable weapons, were quite unsuited to the rough terrain of Sicily: Axis counterattacks, notably against the American beachheads, were easily repulsed. Martin Poppel's braggadocio about his own unit's performance should not mask the fact that another Luftwaffe division, the Hermann Göring, proved the most inept German formation on the island. Its commander, Gen. Paul Conrath, wrote furiously on 12 July: "I had the bitter experience of watching scenes during these last few days which are unworthy of a German soldier . . . Personnel came running to the rear, crying hysterically, because they had heard a single shot fired somewhere in the landscape . . . 'Tank panic' and the spreading of rumours are to be punished by the most severe measures. Withdrawal without orders and cowardice are to be dealt with on the spot, if necessary by shootings." Germans were infuriated by widespread reports of Italian officers abandoning their men.

Italian soldiers streamed into the Allied lines to surrender "in a mood of fiesta," as an American put it, "their personal possessions slung about them, filling the air with laughter and song." A lieutenant wrote home: "A queer race these Italians. You'd think we were their deliverers instead of their captors." Some Americans responded brutally to such docility: in two separate incidents on 14 July, an officer and an NCO of the U.S. 45th Division murdered large groups of Italians in cold blood. One, Sgt. Horace West, who killed thirty-seven with a Thompson submachine gun, was convicted by a court-martial, but later granted clemency. The other, Capt. John Compton, assembled a firing squad which massacred thirty-six Italian prisoners. Compton was court-martialled but acquitted, and was later killed in action. Patton, whose military ethic mirrored that of many Nazi commanders, wrote that "in my opinion these killings have been thoroughly justified." He agreed to the courts-martial only under pressure. Disclosure of both incidents was suppressed, because Eisenhower feared enemy reprisals against Allied prisoners. If Germans had been responsible, they would have been indicted for war crimes in 1945, and probably executed.

On the Allied right, Montgomery's two corps took Syracuse as planned on the first day, but thereafter made slow progress, hampered by lack of transport. "This is *not* tank country," a British officer complained, while one of Montgomery's soldiers grumbled that Sicily was "worse than the fuckin' desert in every fuckin' way." A British officer, David Cole, described the experience of "plodding along mile after dusty mile in a temperature of 95 degrees in the shade" until he looked down on the plain of Catania with his commanding officer.

The panorama before us was magnificent. Thirty miles to the north, dominating the horizon was the huge, misty, snow-capped conical mass, 10,000 feet high, of Mount Etna . . . Along the coast, the city of Catania was dimly visibly, shimmering in the heat. All this would have constituted a picture of great beauty and tranquillity, had it not been for the thud of shells, with their tell-tale puffs of black smoke, exploding near the river. The reality was that down in front of us, concealed in slit-trenches and ditches and sheltered behind buildings and whatever cover they could find, two armies were facing each other in mortal conflict.

A British airborne unit took the Primosole bridge intact, only to be forced back by counterattacks when it ran out of ammunition. Luftwaffe paratroopers thereafter conducted a staunch defence of the bridge against assaults characterised by sluggishness, lack of imagination and failures of communication. A shortcoming of the British Army throughout the war was the poor quality of its wireless sets, manifest in the Primosole operations. The Germans had better radios than their enemies, a significant battlefield advantage. The differential was most marked on the Eastern Front, where in 1941–42 most Russian planes and tanks lacked wirelesses altogether; even in 1943 only company commanders' tanks were fitted with them. Poor British communications contributed to disaster in the 1940 French and 1941 Cretan campaigns. As late as September 1944, the failure of radio links throughout the 1st Airborne Division contributed significantly to its defeat at Arnhem, and represented a professional disgrace to the British Army. The RAF between 1942 and 1945 deployed some of the most advanced electronic technology in the world, but British military wirelesses remained unreliable, and this weakness sometimes significantly influenced the course of battles, as it did in Sicily.

At Primosole, two battalions of the Durham Light Infantry suffered 500 casualties. Tank-infantry coordination was poor, and two German 88mm guns destroyed a succession of Shermans advancing across open ground. Some of the attackers afterwards described the fighting as among the bloodiest of their war. Yet the Germans held the ground with an improvised battle group, chiefly composed of engineers and signallers rather than infantrymen. It remains a mystery why Montgomery, confronted with strong resistance, did not outflank the defenders by sending troops by sea to Catania. The Primosole bridge was eventually overrun, but the advance had been seriously delayed.

Alexander tasked the Americans merely to protect the British flank. In consequence, they were denied an opportunity to push north across the island, with the possibility of trapping a panzer division which was withdrawing eastward. Patton, losing patience with his restricted role, sent a corps racing for Palermo in the northwest. He reached the city on 22 July, taking many Italian prisoners, but his thrust baffled Kesselring, because it was strategically futile. Alexander's acquiescence in this American dash in the opposite direction from the German main forces reflected his usual lack of grip. It was obvious to every thoughtful officer that the campaign would be decided in eastern, not western Sicily. But as Allied soldiers picked their wandering paths across the island, only their opponents displayed clarity of purpose.

The Germans were hampered, however, by shortages of ammunition and supplies, and by the abject performance of their allies. General Conrath wrote bitterly: "The Italians virtually never gave battle and presumably will not fight on the mainland either. Many units in Sicily, either led by their officers or on their own, marched off without firing a single shot . . . 90 per cent of the Italian army are cowards and do not want to fight." The readiness of Italian soldiers to abandon the struggle availed their nation little: in Sicily its long agony began. As town after town became a battlefield, battered by bombs and shells, Mussolini's war-weary subjects suffered terribly. Troina, west of Mount Etna, became the focus of days of fierce fighting. A correspondent described the scene in the town after its eventual capture by the Americans: "A ghostly old woman lying amid crumbling plaster and shattered timber . . . stretched out her hands to us, stared out of sightless eyes, and moaned like the wind whining through pine trees. We went on to the church. Light was shining through a hole in the roof. Below it an unexploded 500lb bomb lay on the floor. Some American soldier breathed heavily in my ear: 'God, that was a miracle' . . . In the mayor's office we found a few of the living wounded that our soldiers had pulled out of the wreckage. On a wooden bench lay the thin form of a girl about ten years old. Her black hair was streaked with gray powder plaster. One of her legs was completely wrapped in bandages . . . In her two hands she clutched a cracker which a soldier had given her. She didn't move but only stared at the ceiling."

ON 25 JULY in Rome, King Victor Emmanuel and Marshal Pietro Badoglio contrived the arrest of Mussolini. Europe's first fascist leader scarcely protested at his own downfall. His spirit was broken, he was resigned to defeat and seemed chiefly concerned to save his skin. The ex-Duce spent the ensuing weeks of captivity, first on offshore islands then at a ski resort in the Apennines, eating prodigious quantities of grapes, reading a life of

Christ and attending mass for the first time since childhood. It is doubtful that he much relished "rescue" by Otto Skorzeny's Nazi commandos on 12 September. Though restored to puppet power in northern Italy, he knew that his game was played out. So did Hitler, who for months had been casting about for an alternative leader of Italy's fascists; he restored Mussolini only because he could identify no substitute.

The Duce's fall precipitated a moment of exhilaration among the Allies and their sympathisers around the world. Many people found wartime life endurable only because they were sustained by spasmodic injections of hope. Amid local victories or reports of regime change, they experienced pathetic surges of excitement or relief. Victor Klemperer, the Dresden Jewish diarist who clung to a precarious liberty, noted many landmark occasions when he supposed Germany's defeat imminent. On 27 July 1943, he exulted at Mussolini's fate: "The end is now in sight—perhaps another six to eight weeks! We put our money on a military dictatorship [in Germany]." A fellow Jew shared his euphoria, saying of his workplace, "We don't really need to turn up in the morning now," and speculating about whether Hitler would survive another month. Such moments of fevered and misplaced optimism sufficed to carry people on both sides of the conflict just a little further through their sorrows and privations, staving off despair.

The political upheaval in Rome persuaded Hitler that Sicily must be evacuated. The Germans retreated eastwards in good order, fighting a succession of delaying actions. The tank gunner Erich Dressler, appalled by the wreck of his own unit and the inferiority of the defenders' resources, was baffled by Allied sluggishness: "With more grit the tommies could have finished the whole lot of us . . . I thought, it is all over. But for some reason or other they suddenly stopped." On the night of 11 August, the Germans began to ferry their forces across the Strait of Messina, more than two miles wide, to the Italian mainland. Although Ultra flagged the enemy's intention, neither the Allied air forces nor the Royal Navy intervened effectively to prevent the Axis from withdrawing 40,000 German and 62,000 Italian soldiers together with most of their tanks, vehicles and supplies. This was a shocking failure. A German naval officer, Baron Gustav von Liebenstein, masterminded an evacuation which some described as a miniature Dunkirk: arguably, indeed, it was more successful, because all three German divisions reached the mainland in full fighting order. The Americans entered the port of Messina late on 16 August, just ahead of the British. The German commander, Gen. Hans Hube, completed his withdrawal from the island the following morning.

The Sicilian campaign taught the Anglo-Americans painful lessons. Amphibious and related air operations were poorly planned and clumsily managed. Coordination between air and ground forces was lacking. If Italian troops had fought with the same determination as the Germans, the invaders would have been pushed back into the sea. The Americans were dismayed by Alexander's lack of grip, contemptuous of Montgomery's sluggishness and irked by their ally's apparent desire to relegate them to a subordinate role. The British, in their turn, were exasperated by the reluctance of American commanders, especially Patton, to conform to agreed plans. Each partner criticised the combat performance of the other's troops. Both found it hard to overcome defenders holding high ground dominating the island's few roads. The Germans executed masterly ambushes and demolitions, a foretaste of their tactics up the length of Italy during the next two years. The invaders failed to exploit sea power to outflank resistance, and merely conducted a succession of slogging matches.

Fifty thousand Germans had held half a million Allied soldiers at bay for five weeks. The invaders made much of the perils posed by Tiger tanks, Nebelwerfer mortars, and "spandau" machine-gun and artillery fire; the difficulties of attacking in steep terrain; the heat; and malaria and combat-fatigue losses. But it was plain that, though overwhelming Allied superiority eventually prevailed, the Wehrmacht's soldiers had fought more convincingly than their Anglo-American counterparts. Again and again Allied forces failed—as they would again fail in northwest Europe—to translate captures of ground into destruction of enemy forces. The Germans were so baffled by their own escape, and by Allied failure to launch an amphibious operation into Calabria to cut them off, that some cherished a fantastic theory that Alexander had acquiesced in their withdrawal for political reasons.

The Sicilian campaign represented the only significant summer 1943 land operation against the Germans by the United States and Britain, engaging eight Allied divisions and costing 6,000 dead. During the same season, 4 million men were locked in combat around Kursk and Orel, where half a million Russians perished. Some German civilians, desperate for an end of the war, lamented the sluggishness of Western Allied progress. Mathilde Wolff-Monckeburg wrote on 14 August: "We hoped and hoped that things would move even faster." There are explanations for the modest Western Allied ground commitment in 1943, but it is easy to see why the Russians regarded it with such contempt. So too did some participants. Lt. Col. Lionel Wigram, one of the British Army's

most energetic and imaginative officers, submitted a report analysing failures he had observed at first hand. He criticised set-piece frontal attacks,
overdependence on artillery and refusal to exploit infiltration to work
behind defenders in close country. He urged that every battalion should
be relieved of some twenty-odd of its soldiers who invariably ran away
in action. He concluded: "The Germans have undoubtedly in one way
scored a decided success in SICILY. They have been able to evacuate their
forces almost intact having suffered very few casualties . . . They have
inflicted heavy casualties on us. We all feel rather irritated as a result."
This recklessly frank assessment reached Montgomery's ears: his vanity
pricked, he sacked Wigram from command of his battalion. No heed was
taken of the colonel's just strictures.

Apologists for the British and American armies assert that respect for
the German defence of Sicily, like many other Axis battlefield achievements, cannot mask its ultimate failure. Kesselring's forces were evicted
from the island. They lost. This is true, and important. It is among the
themes of this book that the Wehrmacht fought many battles brilliantly
well, but that Germany made war very badly. Nonetheless, repeated Anglo-
American failures to destroy Hitler's armies, despite successes in displacing
them from occupied territory, meant that the Red Army remained until
1945, as it had been since 1941, the main engine of Nazism's destruction.

2. The Road to Rome

THE ALLIED ASSAULT on the Italian mainland began on 3 September, when
Canadians of the Eighth Army landed in Calabria without meeting resistance; Kesselring, commanding the German defence, had decided to fight
his first battle farther north. Five days later, on 8 September, as Allied leaders assembled for a summit in Quebec, Marshal Badoglio's government in
Rome announced Italy's surrender, prompting renewed optimism about
a swift advance up the peninsula. On the ninth, Lt. Gen. Mark Clark's
Fifth Army landed at Salerno. This proved one of the critical actions of
the western war, but not in the fashion the invaders anticipated. Col. Bill
Darby's U.S. Rangers achieved initial success on the extreme left of the
Allied line, clearing the Amalfi coast resort villages and securing the Chi-
unzi Pass, with its distant view of Naples. But elsewhere the Germans
deployed rapidly to meet the invaders and launched a series of smashing
counterattacks. Clark's one American and one British corps found themselves penned in four small beachheads under intense fire.

On 13 September, Kesselring's forces drove a wedge between U.S.
and British elements which brought his panzers within a mile of the sea.

The amphibious armada offshore suffered heavy attacks by the Luft-waffe, employing new radio-controlled glider bombs. Clark panicked and proposed reembarking the army. Though Eisenhower and Alexander overruled him, for hours chaos dominated the beachhead, especially after darkness fell. "In the belief that our position had been infiltrated by German infantry, [American troops] began to shoot each other," wrote a British eyewitness, "and there were blood-chilling screams from men hit by the bullets. We crouched in our slit trench under the pink, fluttering leaves of the olives, and watched the fires come closer, and the night slowly passed . . . Official history will in due course set to work to dress up this part of the action at Salerno with what dignity it can. What we saw was ineptitude and cowardice spreading down from the command, and this resulted in chaos."

Lt. Michael Howard of the Coldstream Guards wrote: "Shells whined swiftly over us like lost souls. Moan, moan, moan they wept." Some British as well as American units behaved deplorably: the Scots Guards official history acknowledged "a general feeling in the air of another Dunkirk." Only an intense naval bombardment, pounding the German front, averted disaster. "For God's sake, Mike," said Eisenhower to the U.S. VI Corps commander, Maj. Gen. Mike Dawley, a few hours before Dawley was relieved and sent home as a colonel, "how did you manage to get your troops so fucked up?" Lt. Peter Moore of the Leicestershire Regiment wrote:

> During the night the Germans had positioned mortars and spandaus to cover the whole perimeter. The first sign of the impending bombardment was the familiar tung, tung, tung, tung, tung, tung of mortar bombs being dropped down the barrel and fired. We waited tensely and in seconds came the screaming whoosh-bang, whoosh-bang, whoosh-bang as the bombs exploded among us. At the same time the spandaus opened up with long bursts of rapid fire over our heads, tearing through the vines. The mortaring was very accurate and soon we had many wounded and a few killed. It was very difficult to go to the help of the wounded because of the intense machine-gunning. We fired our Bren guns and rifles to give cover as they crawled or were manhandled to a cave which we had found. The exchanges of fire continued all day. I had persuaded myself into a state of resignation. I did not see how we could sustain a prolonged attack and just hoped that whatever fate awaited me would be quick. I always carried the Army Prayer Book, and I gained enormous comfort and solace from reading through the order of Matins and Evening Prayer, the familiar canticles, psalms and prayers.

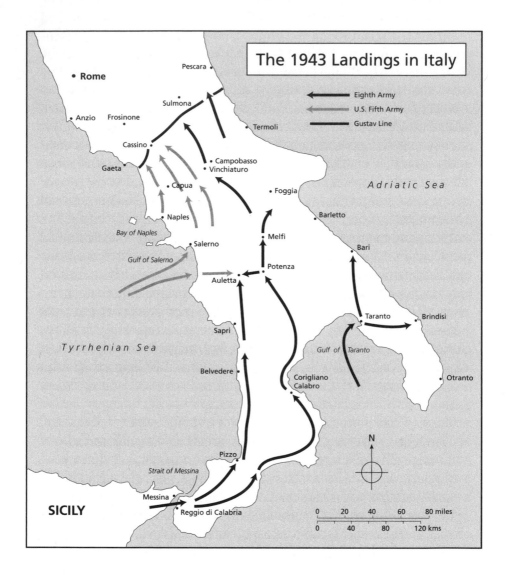

The 1943 Landings in Italy

Eighth Army
U.S. Fifth Army
Gustav Line

Rome
Pescara
Sulmona
Anzio Frosinone
Termoli
Cassino
Gaeta
Campobasso
Vinchiaturo
Capua
Foggia
Naples
Barletto
Bay of Naples
Melfi
Salerno
Bari
Gulf of Salerno
Potenza
Auletta
Sapri
Gulf of Taranto
Tyrrhenian Sea
Taranto
Brindisi
Belvedere
Corigliano
Calabro
Otranto
N
Pizzo
Strait of Messina
Messina
SICILY
Reggio di Calabria

| 0 | 20 | 40 | 60 | 80 miles |
| 0 | 40 | 80 | 120 kms |

After days of heavy fighting, Kesselring's counterattack was beaten off. "In the first grey hints of light, we buried the German dead," wrote Michael Howard. "These were the first corpses I had handled: shrunken pathetic dolls lying stiff and twisted, with glazed blue eyes. Not one could have been over 20, and some were little more than children. With horrible carelessness we shovelled them into their own trenches and piled on the earth. The scene remains etched in my mind: the hunched, urgent diggers, the sprawling corpses with their dead eyes in a cold dawn light that drained all colour from the scene, leaving only mournful blacks and greys.

When we had finished, we stuck their rifles and bayonets above the graves and scuttled quickly back under cover. It was a scene worthy of Goya."

Once again, Allied firepower had turned the scale. "The heavy naval barrages were especially unpleasant," noted a German officer. Every movement of Kesselring's forces was met by a storm of shelling and air attacks. If Allied soldiers were appalled by Salerno, the Wehrmacht scarcely enjoyed the experience. "Here we got our first taste of what superior material force really meant," said the panzer gunner Erich Dressler ruefully. "First came low-flying bombers in such close formation that one could not distinguish the individual squadrons, whilst artillery and mortars plastered us for hours." Again and again the panzers thrust forward, and again and again they were halted. Kesselring's casualties in the battle totalled only 3,500, including 630 killed, against 5,500 British and 3,500 American, but the Germans lacked sufficient combat power to reach the sea. They mauled the invaders, as they would do later at Anzio and in Normandy. But they could not expel them in the face of immensely potent artillery and air support.

The unimpressive Allied showing, against smaller Axis forces, nonetheless exercised a decisive influence on the subsequent campaign. Kesselring began to withdraw northwards, but Salerno convinced him that the Wehrmacht's skills could sustain a long delaying action in the Italian Peninsula, terrain ideally suited to defence. Hitler agreed, and scrapped his earlier plan for a strategic withdrawal to the northern mountains. The Allies' Mediterranean assault was thus far successful, in that it persuaded him to withdraw sixteen divisions from the Eastern Front to reinforce Kesselring. But the stage was set for eighteen months of slow and costly fighting in some of the most unyielding country in Europe. "The Tommies will have to chew their way through us inch by inch," a German paratrooper wrote in an unfinished letter found on his corpse at Salerno, "and we will surely make hard chewing for them."

Kesselring settled himself to conduct a series of defensive battles, which the Allies found painfully repetitive. At each stage they bombed and shelled the German positions for days before their own infantry advanced into machine-gun, artillery and mortar fire. After days or weeks of attrition, the Germans made a measured withdrawal to a new mountain or river line, protected by demolition of bridges, rail links and access roads. Everything of value to the civilian population as well as to the Allies was pillaged or destroyed. It was estimated that 92 percent of all sheep and cattle in southern Italy together with 86 percent of poultry were taken or killed by the retreating army. With the malice that so often characterised German behaviour, Kesselring's men destroyed much of Naples's cultural heritage before abandoning the city, burning whole medieval libraries, including the university's 50,000 volumes. Delayed-action bombs were laid in prominent buildings, where they inflicted severe casualties after the city's liberation. Some Allied soldiers behaved no better than their enemies, vandalising priceless artifacts.

Churchill remained wedded to a belief, indeed an obsession, that a big campaign in Italy could open a path into Germany. The Americans, however, decided that further Mediterranean operations offered only bitter fruits; once some good bomber airfields had been secured, they sought to divert forces as swiftly as possible to the invasion of France, and they were surely correct. British enthusiasm for a southern strategy was justified in 1942–43, but forfeited credibility as the cross-Channel attack loomed, and as the difficulties of achieving a breakthrough in Italy became apparent. Allied forces must stay there, to tie down Germans who would otherwise fight in France or Russia. But no important victory was achievable, certainly not by field commanders of such meagre abilities as Alexander and Clark.

By the end of September, thirteen Allied divisions confronted seven German, while a further eleven of Kesselring's formations secured the country behind the front, employing the most brutal methods everywhere that partisans attempted to challenge their mastery. Through the autumn months the Allies battered their way slowly up southern Italy, checked at every turn by demolitions, ambushes, stubbornly defended river crossings and hill features. "If the 'liberation' of Italy goes on at this rate," Countess Iris Origo wrote bitterly from occupied territory in October, "there will be little enough left to free; district by district, the Germans are leaving a wasteland." The Gustav Line along the Garigliano and Sangro Rivers was contested for weeks, during which torrential storms reduced the battlefield to a quagmire. "I don't think we can get any spectacular results so long as it goes on raining," Montgomery reported to Brooke shortly before relinquishing command of the Eighth Army to return to England to direct the Normandy invasion. "The whole country becomes a sea of mud and nothing on wheels can move off the roads."

Morale slumped. "Italy would break their backs, their bones, and nearly their spirits," the American historian Rick Atkinson has written. "All roads lead to Rome," said Alexander ruefully, "but all the roads are mined." Booby traps and antipersonnel devices inflicted a steady toll of casualties. "A man's foot is usually blown loose at the ankle," a U.S. Army doctor noted, "leaving the mangled foot dangling on shredded tendons. Additional puncture wounds of both legs and groin make the agony worse." Evacuating casualties from the mountains was a nightmare task, four men being required to carry each stretcher. The Germans created imaginative obstacles: north of the Sangro, they felled a half-mile-long line of roadside poplars. Before Allied armour could pass, these had to be cleared by bulldozers at the rate of one tree an hour.

Most men's memories of the campaign were dominated not by the sun and natural beauty with which popular imagination endowed Italy, but by the horror of winter conditions. "The ground for fifty yards outside is MUD—six inches deep, glistening, sticky, holding pools of water," gunner officer John Guest wrote home. "Great excavations in the mud, leaving miniature alps of mud, show where other tents have been pitched in the mud, and moved on account of the mud to other places in the mud. The cumulative psychological experience of mud . . . cannot be described. Vehicles grind along the road beneath in low gear. Either side . . . is a bank of mud, thigh-deep. The sides collapse frequently and the huge trucks, like weary prehistoric animals, slide helplessly down into the ditches . . . My men stand in the gun-pits stamping their feet in the wet, their heads sunk in the collars of greatcoats. When they speak to you they roll their eyes up because it makes their necks cold to raise their heads. Everyone walks with their arms out to help them keep their balance." In November, the Canadian soldier Farley Mowat wrote from Italy to a friend in Britain: "I hate to disillusion you about the climate, but it must be the worst in the whole bloody world. It either burns the balls off you in summer, or freezes them off in winter. In between, it rots them off with endless rain. The only time I'm comfortable is in my sleeping bag, wearing woollen battledress and burrowed under half a dozen extra blankets."

The U.S. battalion commander Lt. Col. Jack Toffey, a hero of the Italian campaign, mused aloud about how to develop his men's killing instincts, to instil in them the tigerish lust to close with the enemy which alone could win battles: "Our boys aren't professionals, and you have to condition them to enjoy killing." By November, more than half the soldiers whom Toffey led ashore had become casualties. Another American likened fighting in Italy to "climbing a ladder with an opponent stamping on his hands at every rung." The combat artist George Biddle wrote: "I wish the people at home, instead of thinking of their boys in terms of football stars, would think of them in terms of miners trapped underground or suffocating to death in a tenth-story fire . . . cold, wet, hungry, homesick and frightened."

By 1 December, seventeen Allied divisions were deployed against thirteen German ones. The invaders enjoyed overwhelming air support, but this was of limited assistance in winter weather against defenders deeply dug into the mountains. In the four battles of Monte Cassino, fifty miles south of Rome, between January and May 1944, bombing destroyed one of the great medieval monasteries of Europe without significantly furthering the ground advance. The Allied armies, which now comprised a remarkable conglomeration of British, American, French, New Zealand, Polish, Canadian and Indian troops, displayed courage and fortitude in conditions resembling those of the Eastern Front, or of Flanders in World War I, but their sacrifices achieved little. Poor generalship and ill-coordinated attacks, together with German skill and intractable terrain, caused the failure of assault after assault. France's Gen. Alphonse Juin was the only Allied commander to emerge from the mountain campaigns with an enhanced reputation: a marshal who had voluntarily dropped a rank to fight in Italy, Juin was far better fitted to direct operations than either Alexander or Clark.

The American field ambulance service won warm praise, retrieving casualties hour after hour and day after day under continuous fire. One driver's vehicle was blasted into a ditch by a near miss, after which he went forward on foot and brought in four Indian casualties one by one "under a hail of fire . . . Day and night, and non-stop if necessary, those American boys would carry on. They could always be trusted to get through, no matter how sticky the situation." The 1/2 Gurkha Rifles spearheaded one of many attacks on Cassino. "The leading companies walked into a death trap. This scrub proved to be thorn thicket seeded with anti-personnel mines, its outskirts threaded with trip-wires linked to booby traps. Behind this deadly barrier stormtroopers lay in wait, in machine-gun posts less than fifty yards apart. Between these nests foxholes sheltered enemy tommy-gunners and bomb-throwers. A shower of grenades arched out of the night . . . The leading platoons dashed into the undergrowth and blew up almost to a man. Colonel Showers fell shot in the stomach. Two-thirds of the leading company was struck down within five minutes, yet the survivors continued to force their way forward. Riflemen were found afterwards with as many as four trip-wires around their legs. Naik Birbahadur Thapa, although wounded in many places, managed to burst through the scrub and seize a position . . . Stretcher-bearer Sherbadur Thapa made sixteen trips across this deadly ground before he was killed. An unscathed handful battled on until ordered to withdraw. Seven British officers, four Gurkha officers and 138 other ranks had fallen." In six weeks, the 4th Indian Division suffered more than 4,000 casualties. Its own officers conceded that as a fighting formation it was never the same again.

Spirits were no higher on the other side of the hill. "I feel that much will be written in the future about these battles," wrote Sgt. Franco

Busatti, a member of a fascist pioneer unit still serving alongside the Germans, "and I am curious to know the answers of tomorrow to the 'why' of today." Swept along in the retreat of Kesselring's army, he was struck by the contrast between Italian soldiers, chronically disordered, and the Germans, disciplined even in defeat. "The war will be won by either the Germans or the English and Americans," he wrote fatalistically. "The Italians are irrelevant." Like many of his countrymen, Busatti eventually decided that he owed allegiance to neither side: deserting the battlefield, he took refuge with his family at their home in Citta di Castello until the end of the war.

For the Allies, however, there was an iron imperative to renew the assault. Capt. Henry Waskow, a twenty-five-year-old Texan, led his diminished company on an attack against one of innumerable German mountain positions, known only as Hill 730, on the moonlit night of 14 December 1943. "Wouldn't this be an awful spot to get killed and freeze on the mountain?" he murmured wryly to his runner. He felt a sudden yearning for toast. "When we get back to the States, I'm going to get me one of those smart-aleck toasters where you put the bread in and it pops up." A few seconds later, he was mortally wounded by a shell fragment when the Germans spotted the advancing Americans. Waskow left behind a letter for his family, of a kind which many young men wrote: "I would like to have lived. But, since God has willed otherwise, do not grieve too much, dear ones, for life in the other world must be beautiful, and I have lived a life with that in mind all along . . . I will have done my share to make the world a better place . . . Maybe when the lights go on again all over the world, free people can be happy and gay again . . . If I failed as a leader, and I pray God I didn't, it was not because I did not try." It was only because many young men of many nations shared Waskow's dogged commitment to do "the right thing," as each belligerent society defined it, that the war could be carried on.

THE PRINCIPAL VICTIMS of the campaign were the people of Italy. If Benito Mussolini had preserved Italian neutrality in 1940, it is possible that he might have sustained his dictatorship for many years in the same fashion as General Franco of Spain, who presided over more mass murders than the Duce, yet was eventually welcomed into membership of NATO. It is unlikely that Hitler would have invaded Italy merely because Mussolini clung to nonbelligerent status; the country had nothing Nazi Germany valued except views. As it was, however, between 1943 and 1945 the catastrophic consequences of adherence to the Axis were visited upon Italy. For many months even before Badoglio's surrender, his fellow countrymen saw themselves not as belligerents, but instead as helpless victims of Hitler. Iris Origo wrote in her diary: "It is . . . necessary to . . . realise how widespread is the conviction among Italians that the war was a calamity imposed upon them by German forces—in no sense the will of the Italian people, and therefore something for which they cannot be held responsible." If this sentiment reflected naïveté, it was nonetheless widely held.

The overthrow of Mussolini, far from bringing a cessation of bloodshed and freeing Italy to embrace the Allies, exposed the land to devastation at the hands of both warring armies. On 13 October, the new government declared war on Germany. The view of many Italians about their nation's change of allegiance, and about the Germans, was expressed in a letter one man wrote two days later: "I won't fight on their side—nor, since we have been guilty of *betrayal*, against them, although I think them disgusting." Iris Origo noted, "The great mass of Italians *'tira a campare'*—just rub along." Emanuele Artom, a member of a Turinese Jewish intellectual resistance group, wrote: "Half Italy is German, half is English and there is no longer an Italian Italy. There are those who have taken off their uniforms to flee the Germans; there are those who are worried about how they will support themselves; and finally there are those who announce that now is the moment of choice, to go to war against a new enemy." Artom himself was captured, tortured and executed in the following year.

Nazi repression and fear of being deported to Germany for forced labour provoked a dramatic growth of partisan activity, especially in the north of Italy. Young men took to the mountains and pursued lives of semibanditry: by the war's end, almost 150,000 Italians were under arms as guerrillas. Political divisions caused additional factional warfare in many areas, notably between royalists and communists. Some fascists continued to fight alongside the Germans, while the Allies raised their own Italian units to reinforce the overstretched Anglo-American armies. Few such recruits proved enthusiastic: when an Italian artillery battery fighting with the Allies was inspected by the king's son, Crown Prince Umberto, the gunner Eugenio Corti found himself pitying the royal visitor, "leader of a people skilled in discovering scapegoats for their own cowardice," united only in a desperate desire for all the belligerents to quit their shores.

In June 1944, amid the euphoria of the advance on Rome, Alexander made a gravely ill-judged broadcast appeal to Italy's partisans, calling on them to rise against the Germans. Many communities consequently suffered savage repression when the Allied breakthrough proved inconclusive. After the war, Italians compared Anglo-American incitement to a partisan revolt, followed by their subsequent abandonment of the population to retribution, with the Russians' failure to succour Warsaw during its equally disastrous rising in the autumn of 1944. The lesson was indeed the same: Allied commanders who promoted guerrilla warfare behind the Axis lines bore a heavy moral responsibility for the horrors that followed, in exchange for marginal military advantage.

The Germans, having previously regarded their Italian allies as mere poltroons, now viewed them as traitors. "We are poor wretches, poor beings left to the mercy of events, without homeland, without law or sense of honour," wrote Lt. Pedro Ferreira of the Italian forces in Yugoslavia, where many of his comrades were shot by the Germans after the armistice. "Italians, after this shame, can never again lift up their heads and speak of honour. Are we betrayed or betrayers? What fate will be in store for us when we have changed our flag three times in two days?" Kesselring ruled Italy with a ruthlessness vividly documented in his order of 17 June 1944: "*The fight against the partisans must be conducted with all means at our disposal and with utmost severity.* I will protect any commander who exceeds our usual restraint in the choice and severity of the methods he adopts against partisans. In this connection the principle holds good that a mistake in the choice of methods in executing one's orders is better than failure or neglect to act." He added on 1 July: "Wherever there is evidence of considerable numbers of partisan groups a proportion of the male population will be shot."

The most notorious massacre of innocents was carried out at Hitler's behest, with Kesselring's endorsement, under the direction of Rome's Gestapo chief, Lt. Col. Herbert Kappler. On 23 March 1944, partisans attacked a marching column of the Bozen Police Regiment in the Via Rasella. Gunfire and explosives killed 33 Germans and wounded 68, while 10 civilians were also killed. In reprisal, Hitler demanded the deaths of 10 Italians for each German. Next afternoon, 335 prisoners were taken from the Regina Coeli prison to the Ardeatine Caves. They were a random miscellany of actors, lawyers, doctors, shopkeepers, cabinetmakers, an opera singer and a priest. Some were communists, and 75 were Jews. Two hundred of them had been seized in the streets near the Via Rasella following the partisan attack, though none was involved in it. In batches of five they were led into the caves and executed, the bodies left where they fell. Though the Germans used explosives to close the shaft in a half-hearted attempt to conceal the massacre, this was rendered ineffectual by the stench that soon seeped forth. The caves became a place of pilgrimage and tears.

Elide Ruggeri was one of a handful of survivors of another massacre, in the churchyard at Marzabotto, a picturesque little town at the foot of the Apennines, where in September 1944 Waffen SS troops exacted a terrible revenge on the civilian population for local partisan activities. "All the children were killed in their mothers' arms," she later recounted. Though herself badly hit, she lay motionless under the dead. "Above and beside me were the bodies of my cousins and of my mother, whose stomach had been ripped open. I lay motionless all that night, through the next day and the night following, in rain and a sea of blood. I almost stopped breathing." At dawn on the second day, Ruggeri and four other wounded women crawled out from beneath the heaped corpses. Of her own family, 5 had been killed. In all, 147 people died at the church, including the priests who had been officiating when the SS arrived; 28 families were wiped out. At nearby Casolari a further 282 victims perished, including 38 children and 2 nuns. The final local civilian toll was 1,830, and moved Mussolini to make a vain protest to Hitler. It is bizarre that Kesselring, under whose orders the SS acted, was reprieved from execution at Nuremberg.

If the Allied invaders never matched such horrors, they were parties to lesser crimes against humanity: French colonial troops, especially, committed large-scale atrocities. "Whenever they take a town or a village, a wholesale rape of the population takes place," wrote a British NCO, Norman Lewis:

Recently all females in the villages of Patricia, Pofi, Supino and Morolo were violated. In Lenola . . . fifty women were raped, but—as these were not enough to go round—children and even old men were violated. It is reported to be normal for two Moroccans to assault a woman simultaneously, one having normal intercourse while the other commits sodomy. In many cases severe damage to the genitals, rectum and uterus has been caused. In Castro di Volsci a doctor treated 300 victims of rape . . . Many Moors have deserted, and are attacking villages far behind the lines. Today I went to Santa Maria a Vico to see a girl said to have been driven insane as the result of an attack by a large party of Moors . . . She was unable to walk . . . At last one had faced the flesh-and-blood reality of the kind of horror that drove the whole female population of Macedonian villages to throw themselves from the cliffs rather than fall into the hands of the advancing Turks.

Such Allied excesses, matched by the effects of air and artillery bombardment through the long struggle up the peninsula, ensured that few Italians gained much joy from their "deliverance." Two soldiers of the 4th

Indian Division were chasing a chicken around a farmyard when a window of the adjoining house was thrown open: "A woman's head appeared, and a totally unexpected English voice called out '—— off, and leave my ——ing 'ens alone. We don't need no liberation 'ere.'"

Italy's surrender precipitated a mass migration of British prisoners of war, set free from camps in the north of the country to undertake treks through the Apennines towards the Allied lines. A defining characteristic of these odysseys, many of which lasted months, was the succour such men received from local people. Peasant kindness was prompted by an instinctive human sympathy, rather than enthusiasm for the Allied cause, and deeply moved its beneficiaries. The Germans punished civilians who assisted escapers by the destruction of their homes, and often by death, yet sanctions proved ineffectual: thousands of British soldiers were sheltered by tens of thousands of Italian country folk whose courage and charity represented one of the noblest aspects of Italy's unhappy part in the war. Farley Mowat arrived in the country with a contempt for its people, but changed his mind after living among them. "Now it turns out they're the ones who are really the salt of the earth. The ordinary folk, that is. They have to work so hard to stay alive it's a wonder they aren't as sour as green lemons, but instead they're full of fun and laughter. They're also tough as hell . . . They ought to hate our guts as much as Jerry's but the only ones I wouldn't trust are the priests, lawyers, and the big shopkeepers, landowners and such."

The wild Italian countryside and the hospitable customs of its inhabitants prompted desertions from the Allied armies on a scale greater than in any other theatre. The rear areas teemed with military fugitives, men "on the trot"—overwhelmingly infantry, because they recognised their poor prospects of survival at the front. Thirty thousand British deserters were estimated by some informed senior officers to be at liberty in Italy in 1944–45—the equivalent of two divisions—and around half that number of Americans. These are quite extraordinary figures, which deserve more notice in narratives of the campaign, though it should be noted that official histories set the desertion numbers much lower, partly because they omit those who, by a technically important distinction, were deemed merely to be "absent without leave." In a rest area behind the front, Lt. Alex Bowlby chanced on a man who had quit his own platoon dining with an Italian family. The errant soldier finished his meal, left the house and stole the bewildered young officer's jeep before anyone thought to stop him. Amid the chronic discomforts and terrors of the campaign, Bowlby noted that most of his men performed their duties at the edge of mutiny. One would-be deserter removed by the military police shouted back defiantly at his comrades, "I'll be alive when you're all fucking dead." Alexander itched to reintroduce the death penalty as a deterrent, and a British divisional commander, Bill Penney, agreed: "Shooting in the early days would probably have been an effective prophylactic." But capital punishment was deemed politically unacceptable.

Both the Germans and the Allies distributed broadsheets to the population, making competing demands for their aid. Iris Origo wrote: "The peasants read these leaflets with bewildered anxiety as to their own fate, and complete indifference (in most cases) to the main issue: *Che sara di noi?*—What will become of us? All that they want is peace—to get back to their land—and to save their sons. They live in a state of chronic uncertainty about what to expect from the arrival of soldiers of any nationality. They might bring food or massacre, liberation or pillage." On 12 June 1944, Origo was in the garden of her castello rehearsing *Sleeping Beauty* with her resident complement of refugee children, when a party of heavily armed German troops descended from a truck.

Full of fear, she asked what they wanted, to receive an unexpected answer: " 'Please—wouldn't the children sing for us?' The children sing *O Tannenbaum* and *Stille Nacht* (which they learned last Christmas)— and tears come into the men's eyes. '*Die Heimat*—it takes us back to *die Heimat*!' So they climb into their lorry and drive away." Less than two weeks later, the area was occupied by French colonial troops. Origo wrote bitterly: "The Goums have completed what the Germans begun. They regard loot and rape as the just reward for battle, and have indulged freely in both. Not only girls and young women, but even an old woman of eighty has been raped. Such has been Val d'Orcia's first introduction to Allied rule—so long and so eagerly awaited!"

Allied forces sustained a sluggish advance up the peninsula, but from the summer of 1944 onwards, it was a source of some dismay to Alexander's soldiers that Mediterranean operations and sacrifices commanded diminishing attention at home. "We are the D-Day dodgers in sunny Italee," they sang, "always on the vino, always on the spree." The world saw that the outcome of the war hinged upon events much farther north, in France and Germany. But the Italian front occupied the attention of one-tenth of Hitler's ground forces, which would otherwise have been deployed on the Eastern Front or in France. Allied air bases in Italy made possible a heavy and effective bomber assault on Germany's Romanian oilfields. It is hard to imagine how the campaign might have been accelerated, avoided or broken off. But it yielded neither glory nor satisfaction to those who fought, or to the hapless inhabitants of the battlefield.

3. Yugoslavia

THE ITALIAN CAMPAIGN prompted a surge of British enthusiasm, with tepid American acquiescence, for raising the tempo of anti-Axis operations in neighbouring Yugoslavia. Throughout the war, Churchill embraced every nation which displayed a willingness to join the struggle against Hitler: this was a fundamental tenet of his foreign policy, lent urgency in 1940–41 by Britain's desperate circumstances. The consequence was to make bedfellows of some societies with which the democracies had little or nothing in common, of which Yugoslavia was a striking example. From 1943 onwards, its accessibility from Italy, together with the wider strategic significance of the Balkans, made it the focus of many British hopes.

Granted statehood in 1918 amid the collapse of the Hapsburg empire, the country was an ill-assorted ragbag of mutually hostile ethnic groups and conflicting ideologies, ruled as a dictatorship until 1941 by Prince Paul on behalf of the teenage King Peter. Most of the country was extraordinarily primitive. A communist partisan described a typical peasant community: "Many had never been even in the nearby towns. [The women] wore hand-woven dresses open down to the navel, so that their breasts flopped out. They greased their hair with butterfat, parted it in the middle, then tucked it up over their foreheads. Their vocabulary was meagre, except concerning livestock and the like . . . The men were on a markedly higher level than the women, for they had seen something of the world in the army, on jobs and through trade."

"The country was very, very wild indeed," wrote Capt. Charles Hargreaves, who served among the Serbs as an SOE officer, "and there was nothing much in the way of roads. The houses were rather like English Tudor cottages, made of beam and brick, to the extent that when one went through a doorway the ground had been hollowed out and there were rushes or bracken on the floor. The people lived a way of life which vanished in England five hundred years ago . . . They were very kind, very good—they'd give you anything. Going into one house, we'd been walking for a very long time and we were sat down and two of the daughters came in and removed our boots, washed our feet and dried them with their hair. It was really quite biblical."

What took place in Yugoslavia during the war years was overwhelmingly an internecine ethnic and political conflict. Neither the Axis cause nor that of the Western Allies commanded much emotional enthusiasm. German atrocities bred hatred, but also achieved their purpose of instilling fear. Many Yugoslavs, desperate to avoid exposing themselves to the occupiers' wrath, opposed violent acts of resistance. Some 1.2 million perished—approximately matching the war's combined British, American and French fatalities; but a majority were killed by hostile ethnic or political groups of their fellow countrymen, rather than by the major belligerents.

In the spring of 1941, Hitler bludgeoned Prince Paul into signing the Tripartite Pact, to secure Yugoslavia's mineral resources and acquiescence in his invasion of Greece. This provoked a violent reaction from Serb nationalists. On 27 March they staged a coup to overthrow the regency and install an anti-Axis government in the name of young King Peter. Hitler, enraged by this supposed betrayal, responded by invading the country on 6 April. The king and government fled, and the Germans achieved an almost bloodless occupation. Hitler set about dismembering the country. Northern Slovenia was incorporated into the Reich. Croatia was granted independence and its fascist Ustaše militia assumed a powerful and bloody role in sustaining Axis control of the country. In May 1941, the Ustaše unleashed a reign of terror designed to cleanse Croatia of its 2 million Serbs. Meanwhile, Dalmatia and southern Slovenia were ceded to Italy. Macedonia, which was given to Bulgaria, experienced brutalities which turned its people decisively against rule from Sofia. As a result of wholesale ethnic cleansing, only 2,000 of Skopje's prewar population of 25,000 Serbs, for instance, remained in the city by the spring of 1942. The whole country was thrown into turmoil, a cycle of repression, sporadic resistance and a struggle for survival by millions of hapless people.

In London, the British welcomed the exiled Yugoslav rulers as heroes, and began to give what little assistance was in their power to the Chetnik resistance movement in Serbia led by royalist colonel Draža Mihailović. Yet in 1943 it became increasingly clear that the Chetniks were more interested in gaining political control of Yugoslavia than in challenging the Axis occupiers. Mihailović was persuaded by the ferocity of reprisals— one hundred Yugoslavs shot for each German killed—that it was futile to challenge the Axis at such a cost.

Communists led by the Croatian Josip Broz—"Tito"—appeared to be fighting more actively. Their propaganda was skilfully conducted, to persuade both the Yugoslav people and the Western Allies that they would resist the occupiers as the Chetniks would not; Tito also won support across ethnic divides. "The army of Mihailović was completely peasant-based and hadn't got much discipline," said a British liaison officer, Robert Wade, "whereas Tito's lot, ruthless though he was, behaved like the Brigade of Guards by comparison. No drilling, but when they were told to keep their distance they kept their distance—they were properly led and you could see the difference." Charles Hargreaves agreed: "Sometimes [the Chetniks] would be quite prepared to do small things, perhaps to ambush a train or convoy, but nothing very big, nothing that would have involved too much German loss of life . . . Their main intention was to secure control of the country after the war." Maj. Basil Davidson of the SOE, an impassioned supporter of Tito, said cynically: "Unfortunately the Cetniks took the view that it was up to us to win the war against the Germans and up to them to win the war inside Yugoslavia against the communists, who had meanwhile formed a much stronger and more effective resistance."

In December 1943, Churchill shifted his support decisively towards the communist leader, who claimed to have 200,000 men under arms. In this, the prime minister was influenced by some illusions: that Tito's partisans "were not real communists"; that they could be persuaded to forge an accord with King Peter; and that they were single-mindedly committed to the struggle against the Axis. Communist sympathisers in the SOE's Cairo headquarters contributed to this roseate perception; London was ignorant of the fact that for some months in 1943 Tito negotiated with the Germans for a truce which would enable him to crush Mihailović and committed most of his forces to kill Chetniks. Milovan Djilas was with a group of partisan negotiators who spent some days at German headquarters, where officers professed revulsion at the Yugoslavs' manner of making war. "Look what you have done to your own country!" they exclaimed. "A wasteland, cinders! Women are begging in the streets, typhus is raging, children are dying of hunger. And we wish to bring you roads, electricity, hospitals."

Only when Hitler rejected any deal with the communists did conflict resume between partisans and occupiers. The subsequent bloodbath radicalised much of the population, and enabled Tito to create a mass movement. His followers eventually gained control of large rural areas. But they lacked the strength required to take important towns or cities until the Red Army arrived in 1944, and they were as committed as the Chetniks were to achieving postwar domination. Thirty-five Axis divisions were deployed in Yugoslavia, but few were first-line troops, and this concentration reflected Hitler's obsessive fear of an Allied landing in the Balkans as much as the need to secure the country against Tito. The partisans' military achievements were less significant than London allowed itself to believe. From late 1943 onwards, the Allies began to send Tito weapons in quantities far larger than those supplied to any other European resistance movement. But most were used to suppress the Chetniks and secure the country for Tito in 1944–45, rather than to kill Germans.

The struggle in Yugoslavia, where so many enmities overlapped, assumed a murderous character and complexity, of which Tito's deputy Milovan Djilas cited an example. "Covered with orchards and rising from the confluence of two mountain streams, the still undamaged town of Foca seemed to offer charming and peaceful prospects. But the human devastation inside it was immeasurable and inconceivable," he wrote. "In the spring of 1941 the Ustaše—among them a good number of Moslem toughs—had killed many Serbs. Then the Chetniks . . . proceeded to slaughter the Moslems. The Ustaše had selected twelve only sons from prominent Serbian families and killed them. While in the village of Miljevina they had slit the throats of Serbs over a vat, apparently so as to fill it with blood instead of fruit pulp. The Chetniks had slaughtered groups of Moslems whom they tied together on the bridge over the Drina and threw into the river. Many of our people saw groups of corpses floating, caught on some rock or log. Some even recognised their own families. Four hundred Serbs and 3,000 Moslems were reported killed in the region of Foca."

Hapless townspeople and villagers were obliged to endure the presence of partisans living off the land—which meant off their own meagre produce. They saw their valleys turned into battlefields and witnessed the execution of thousands of real and alleged collaborators by one faction or another, together with wholesale slaughters carried out by the Axis occupiers in reprisal for partisan actions. Hatreds were implacable. Almost every community and family suffered loss. Djilas acknowledged the horror of many local people when the communists avenged themselves—for instance, burning the Chetnik village of Ozrinici: "Though quite a few of them took joy in the misfortunes of Ozrinici, and understood the military reasons for our action, the peasants simply couldn't get it into their heads that the communists could act like the invaders and the Chetniks . . . Harsh communist counter-measures . . . made the peasants reticent and double-faced: they sided with whoever came along and tried to wriggle out of any risky commitment." Even Djilas's own aunt Mika reproached him: "You are fighting for a just cause, but you are harsh and bloody."

At every halt on the partisans' interminable marches, they encountered wretchedness: "All the villages in the Sutjeska valley had been destroyed. First the Ustaše burned down the Orthodox villages and then the Chetniks burned the Moslem villages. The only houses and people left were in the neighbouring hills. The devastation was all the more horrifying in that here and there a shaky doorframe, a blackened wall or a charred plum tree stuck out of the tall weeds and undergrowth. Though lush greenery swayed in the cool breeze on either side of the swift river, my memories of those days are weighed down with bitterness, hurt and horror."

In a society in which rival nationalisms, feuds and the cult of vengeance were endemic, by 1944 brutality was institutionalised. All the warring parties shared responsibility for dreadful bloodshed, much of it inflicted upon people whose only crime was to belong to another race or creed. The partisans often accepted into their own ranks captured Chetniks willing to change sides. Djilas was dismayed by the fate of a tall, dark girl who rejected her captors' advances, saying defiantly, "It would be immoral to change one's views!" He was impressed by her courage, and saddened to hear that she diminished herself in his eyes by collapsing into trembling sobs at her execution. He consoled himself with the reflection that, while all her group were shot, none was tortured in accordance with the usual custom: "The executions were carried out by Montenegrins, who volunteered so as to avenge their comrades killed . . . The condemned were led away at night, in groups of twenty." Both executioners and their victims appeared equally uncomfortable with their role: "They couldn't be told apart, except that some had rifles and stars while others had wire around their wrists . . . As usual no effort was made to bury them properly; their legs and arms stuck out of the mound. Civil war has little regard for graves, funerals, requiems." The partisans were embarrassed only when their accompanying British military mission stumbled upon the "spilled brains, smashed faces, contorted bodies." Tito demanded tetchily, "Couldn't they have done it somewhere else?"

Meanwhile, Axis forces contributed their own share of slaughter. A squeamish soldier of the Italian Alpini wrote: "After we had been at Podgorica for a couple of days, we all set off together to a nearby pass where the partisans have come off best in an attack on one of our columns. Thirty-eight vehicles have been destroyed, the drivers and escorts massacred—all of them! The bodies are mutilated. An order goes out: two days of carte blanche. We destroy or rather are present at the destruction of anything we meet. Our veterans are the chief perpetrators. We are shocked and terrified by the yells of soldiers and the terror of the hapless inhabitants . . . This is the first, unforgettable confrontation with a reality that shames us as men."

The partisans were amazed that Italy's surrender in September 1943, which removed the principal prop of Croat domination, prompted no lessening of the Ustaše's appetite for slaughter. When Tito's men taunted captured fascists that they had lost the war, the doomed prisoners shouted back, "We know, but there's still time to rub out a lot of you!" Condemned Croats sang, "Oh Russia, all will belong to you / But of Serbs there will be few." Djilas wrote: "This was war with no quarter, no surrender, no letting bygones be bygones." He reflected in Tolstoyan terms on the fates that drove the struggle: "Why were doctors from Berlin and professors from Heidelberg killing off Balkan peasants and students? Hatred for Communism was not sufficient. Some other terrible and implacable force was driving them to insane death and shame. And driving us, too, to resist and pay them back. Perhaps Russia and communism could account for this to some extent. Yet this passion, this endurance which lost sight of suffering and death, this struggle for one's manhood and nationality in the face of one's own death—this had nothing to do with ideology or with Marx and Lenin." The partisans often found themselves obliged to abandon their own casualties, or to dispatch the most gravely wounded. Djilas described how one husband acceded to the pleas of his desperately injured wife to finish her off, choosing a moment when she was dozing. A father did the same for his daughter: "He survived the war, withered and sombre, and his friends regarded him as a living saint."

The Western Allies were bitterly disappointed when, in 1945, the support of the Red Army enabled Tito to secure control of Yugoslavia. The German invasion had unleashed domestic forces that the Anglo-Americans proved powerless to control. Even if they had denied arms to Tito, the Red Army's arrival in 1944 would have ensured that a communist regime was installed in Belgrade. Tito was one of the major figures of the war: he exploited Allied support with notable diplomatic skill and secured lifelong mastery of his country. But his claims to have played an important part in overthrowing Nazi tyranny are more questionable. Yugoslavia's partisans were the most numerous and pestilent of the insects buzzing about the open wounds of the Axis in its decay, but their role was slight alongside that of the Allied armies.

CHAPTER NINETEEN

WAR IN THE SKY

1. Bombers

YOUNG MEN OF ALL NATIONS perceived romance in playing their parts in the war as knights of the air. "I saw myself as something like a gladiator of old," wrote Ted Bone, who in 1941 became a nineteen-year-old volunteer for RAF aircrew service. "Not for me the horrors of hand-to-hand combat with a rifle and bayonet—I would be firing at another fighter plane." Young men of "the Lindbergh generation" exulted in the notion of flying fast and nimble single-engined, single-seat aircraft, which granted pilots a power over their own destinies unusual among twentieth-century warriors. It was ironic, therefore, that many such dreamers found themselves instead committed to aerial bombardment of cities, one of the more barbarous features of the conflict; Bone himself became a Lancaster gunner. Bombing killed well over a million people in Europe and Asia, including many women and children. Some of the bravest, best-educated and most highly trained scions of their societies became rivals in a struggle to devastate their enemies' centres of civilisation.

Neither they nor their commanders saw the mission in such terms, of course. Airmen thought not of victims on the ground, unconsidered because rarely visible, but instead about their own destinies above. In exchange for a passage to the sky, they accepted an enhanced risk of death, as well as a responsibility to shoot, bomb and strafe. Geoff Wellum, who flew a Spitfire for the first time as an eighteen-year-old on the eve of the Battle of Britain, described the sensation: "I experience an exhilaration that I cannot recall ever having felt before. It's like one of those wonderful dreams, a Peter Pan sort of dream. The whole thing feels unreal . . . What a pity . . . that an aeroplane that can impart such a glorious feeling of sheer joy and beauty has got to be used to fight somebody."

The New Yorker Harold Dorfman, who survived a tour as a B-24 navigator over Germany, said later: "I would not trade the experience for anything in the world." At a USAAF base in England, Corp. Ira Wells, a B-24 gunner, read accounts of ground fighting and thought with pity of Allied soldiers: "We had all the glory. I realised how fortunate we were to be in the air. I was more frightened in London during the V2 rocket attacks than in the air on missions." Dorfman and Wells were relatively unusual, because few bomber airmen enjoyed their work in the way that many fighter pilots did. This was not because they agonised much, or at all, about the fate of those who died beneath their bomb doors; it was because flying for eight or ten hours either in daylight formation amid flak and fighters like the men of the USAAF, or through lonely darkness, as did those of the RAF, imposed relentless strain and frequent terror. They were denied the thrill of throwing a high-performance fighter across the sky. The monotony of bombing missions was shattered only when crews encountered the hellish sights and sounds of combat and bomb runs over the cities of Germany or Japan.

Although Laurie Stockwell was a sensitive young Englishman, it never occurred to him to question the ethics of his own part, as a pilot, in bombing Germany. Like almost all his kind, he simply saw himself performing, without fervour, an exceptionally hazardous role in a struggle to remove the dark threat bearing down upon Western civilisation. He wrote to his mother in 1942:

> I have never spoken to you of my feelings and thoughts about this war, and I hope I will never speak of them again. Do you remember a small boy saying he would be a conscientious objector if war came? Things happened to change that small boy's view, talk of brutality, human suffering, atrocities, but that did not have any great effect on changing my mind, for I realise that we all are capable of doing these deeds of which we read so much nowadays. It is the fact that a few people wish to take freedom from the peoples of the earth that changed my views. News of atrocities only breeds hate, and hate is contemptible in my eyes. Why should I then fight in the war which only brings disgust into my thoughts? It is so that I might live in happiness and peace all my days with you . . . I am also fighting so that one day happiness will again rule the world, and with happiness that love of beauty, of life, contentment, fellowship among all men may return. You may have noticed that I have not mentioned fighting for one's country, for the empire; that to me is just foolishness.

Stockwell died over Berlin in January 1943. Randall Jarrell, an airfield control-tower operator who became a poet of the USAAF crews' experience, wrote:

> In bombers named for girls, we burned
> The cities we had learned about in school—

Till our lives wore out; our bodies lay among
The people we had killed and never seen.

Most young men conscripted for war service wanted to fly, but few achieved their aspirations. Air forces picked only the brightest and fittest adolescents for probable death. The RAF navigator Ken Owen, a Welshman, said, "Perhaps a quarter of our sixth form at Pontypridd grammar school became aircrew; more than half of them were killed." Yet those accepted for flying duties exulted in their status as an elite; they received a popular adulation unmatched by any other breed of warrior.

In the first year of Britain's war, circumstances forced the RAF to rush new pilots into the line, sometimes with no more than twenty or thirty hours' experience in the planes they flew in combat. Thereafter, however, the British and Americans trained airmen requiring the highest skills—pilots and navigators—for up to two years before committing them to action. Instructors "washed out" many candidates, but despite intensive tuition, wartime pilots often killed themselves because their skills were inadequate to handle high-performance aircraft, even before engaging the enemy. Youth and the mood of the times encouraged recklessness. In the course of the war, the RAF lost in nonoperational accidents 787 officers and 4,540 other ranks killed, 396 officers and 2,717 other ranks injured. Among U.S. airmen of all services, 13,000 died accidentally. Taking off and landing a fighter, designed to be inherently unstable, required meticulous care. Misjudgement was often punished by death—in the first two years of the war 1,500 Luftwaffe trainees were killed learning to fly the Bf-109. Managing a bomber was little easier, especially if it suffered a technical mishap.

An aspect of the conflict common to warriors in all three dimensions was that navigation was a life-and-death science. A British Army training report noted that soldiers would forgive almost any fault in their officers except incompetent map reading, which at best wasted energy and at worst got them killed. Ships were sunk by straying carelessly into minefields. Airmen who lost their way, especially over the sea, often died when their fuel ran out. Antisubmarine patrol duty, roaming far out over empty oceans, was a wearisome task, demanding special navigational care: errors killed as many crews as enemy action or mechanical failure. Even when electronic aids and beacons were introduced, a dismaying number of planes fell into the sea because inexpert airmen flew reciprocal courses or were unable to fix their positions in poor weather.

The Germans, Italians and Japanese entered the conflict with highly trained pilots, and until 1942 most of the Luftwaffe's aircraft were superior to those of the RAF or USAAF; the Japanese and Italians also had some good types. "With the start the Germans had, it was a miracle we ever caught up," said British bomber group commander Edward Addison. The Luftwaffe's close support for the Wehrmacht was a key factor in German victories between 1939 and 1942. Göring's squadrons failed, however, as a strategic bomber force. Before the blitz on Britain, senior airmen of most nations were imbued with a mystical faith. They deluded themselves that societies would succumb to panic in the face of the mere fact of assault from the air; the collapse of morale would provoke industrial disintegration and, thus, defeat. The destruction of Guernica by the Condor Legion during the Spanish Civil War, along with the bombing of Nanjing, Warsaw and Rotterdam, promoted delusions about the vulnerability of civilian populations. More protracted experience disproved these, however. "[A] vital lesson—one that has taken even air specialists by surprise," wrote Maj. Alexander Seversky, a leading American air strategist, in 1942,

> relates to the behaviour of civilian populations under air punishment. It had been generally assumed that aerial bombardment would quite quickly shatter popular morale . . . The progress of this war has tended to indicate that this expectation was unfounded. On the contrary, it now seems clear that despite large casualties and impressive physical destruction, civilians can "take it." On the whole, indeed, armed forces have been more quickly demoralised by air power than unarmed city dwellers. These facts are significant beyond their psychological interest. They mean that haphazard destruction of cities . . . is costly and wasteful in relation to the tactical results obtained. Attacks will increasingly be concentrated on military rather than on random human targets. Unplanned vandalism from the air must give way, more and more, to planned, predetermined destruction.

Bombers achieved results only in proportion to the weight of explosives they could drop accurately on designated targets; mass was critical. The Luftwaffe and the Japanese air forces had formidable capabilities for supporting their respective ground forces and navies, as well as for killing refugees and promoting terror, but their aircraft carried small bombloads. The Luftwaffe inflicted pain and destruction during the 1940–41 blitz on Britain, but nowhere near sufficient to make a decisive impact on the ability of Churchill's nation to continue the war. Thereafter, Germany's air force suffered a steady decline: when the first generation of Axis airmen was killed off, training of their successors languished. Both the Germans and the Japanese made a critical strategic mistake, to which fuel famine contributed, by failing to allocate resources to sustain a flow of proficient pilots. By 1944–45, Axis flying skills were wholly outclassed by those of their American and British counterparts. The Russians displayed the same ruthlessness in training and expending airmen as in everything else. By 1943 they had some good aircraft and able pilots, but their technology was less advanced, and they suffered savage losses.

In the second half of the war, the Western Allies produced superb planes in vast numbers, but the Germans introduced only two good new types—the FW-190 and the revolutionary Me-262 jet fighter. Numbers of the latter were too small and pilot skills inadequate to avert the Luftwaffe's eclipse in the sky. The Japanese Zero, which so daunted the Allies in 1941–42, became wholly outclassed. It has been described as "an *origami* aircraft"—light, graceful, superbly manoeuvrable, but frail and offering negligible concessions to pilot safety; for instance, it lacked cockpit armour. Cmdr. David McCampbell, the U.S. Navy's top-scoring air ace of the war, said: "We learned very early that if you hit them near the wing roots, where the fuel was, they would explode right in your face." The Japanese army and naval air forces posed no significant challenge to the Allies in 1944–45 except through kamikaze attacks, an expedient of desperation.

Allied airmen, once deployed to operational fighter or bomber squadrons, until the last eighteen months of the war confronted a statistical probability of their own extinction. Romantic delusions faded as they learned to anticipate a destiny as a bloody jam of crushed flesh and bones, or surmounting a petrol-fuelled funeral pyre. To be sure, their daily lives on the ground were privileged; they were spared the mud and discomfort to which foot soldiers were subjected. But they were less likely to survive; Ernie Pyle wrote: "A man approached death rather decently in the air force. He died well-fed and clean-shaven."

More than half the RAF's heavy-bomber crews perished, 56,000 men in all. The USAAF's overall losses were lower, but among 100,000 of its men who participated in the strategic offensive against Germany some 26,000 died, and a further 20,000 were taken prisoner. "You were resigned to dying every night," said a British Whitley bomber pilot, Sid Bufton. "Before setting out you looked around your room: golf clubs, books, nice little radio—and the letter to your parents propped up on the table." Unsurprisingly, Allied casualties were proportionately heaviest when the Axis dominated the war, and fell steadily once the tide turned. From 1943 onwards, it was the turn of German and Japanese airmen to do most of the dying: less than 10 percent survived until the end.

The Allied air chiefs' principal preoccupation was strategic assault on Germany—the offensive against Japan began in earnest only in March

1945—by which they aspired to win the war on their own. The RAF was obliged to abandon daylight bombing after a bloody initiation in 1939–40. Thereafter, its squadrons mounted a night offensive, which made little material impact on Germany until 1943: they lacked mass as well as navigational and bomb-aiming skills. The first British bombs which fell on Berlin at the end of August 1940 inflicted only random damage, though they shocked the capital's inhabitants and killed a few civilians. One young mother retired to a shelter when the warning sirens sounded, but was reluctant to disturb her two sleeping children, whom she left in bed: they perished when the house received a direct hit. After that story was published, Berliners took more heed of sirens.

An RAF squadron commander described Bomber Command's early operations over Germany as "groping." This was exemplified by the experience of Sgt. Bill Uprichard, who flew a Whitley of 51 Squadron on a mission against oil refineries at Politz on the Baltic in poor weather on the night of 29 November 1940. Outbound, after spending two and a half hours in thick cloud over the North Sea, suddenly the sky opened to reveal a brilliantly lit city below. Uprichard and his crew realised they must be passing neutral Sweden, and hastily reset their course. They blind-bombed Politz by dead-reckoning—estimating their own time over target—then turned for home in impenetrable cloud. Without warning they found themselves facing heavy antiaircraft fire. Uprichard wrote:

> I woke up! The wind had been stronger than I thought and we were flying a course taking us straight over the heavily defended Friesian Islands. We crossed the North Sea still in cloud and it was difficult to get a pinpoint on anything. I spent a lot of time—probably too much— flying up and along the Yorkshire coast hoping to see a break. It was raining heavily . . . By this time our fuel was very low—only about 20 mins. left—so for the first time I put out an emergency signal PAN-PAN-PAN and in two ticks Linton-on-Ouse came up with a magnetic course. We were then on the verge of abandoning the aircraft. It was a matter of a long time-glide home. We made it, but the refuelling party told me we had virtually nothing left in the tanks.

Throughout 1940–41, naïveté persisted within the RAF about the effectiveness of Bomber Command's operations. "The briefings were very, very good," said Ken Owen, a nineteen-year-old navigator. "They made us feel we were going to hit an important target, doing important damage to the Germans. And of course we all listened to the BBC bulletins next morning, which trumpeted our success; there was a tremendous amount of self-delusion. We thought we were knocking hell out of them. Maybe twelve times [out of thirty 'trips'] I think we bombed the right place; otherwise it was either the wrong place or ploughed fields."

Despite the limited impact of the strategic air offensive in its early years, most of the RAF's leaders retained a visionary faith not only in what bombing might do, but also in what it had already accomplished. In September 1942, Air Marshal Sir Wilfred Freeman wrote to Britain's air chief Sir Charles Portal complaining of the extravagant claims made by some commanders: "In their efforts to attract the limelight they sometimes exaggerate and even falsify facts. The worst offender is C-in-C Bomber Command." Freeman cited claims published in the media about the achievements of some recent raids on Germany: "The damage at [Karlsruhe and Düsseldorf] is described as fantastic. I believe this to be untrue . . . I suggest that you might . . . send a circular letter to commanders-in-chief . . . impressing on them the need to adhere strictly to the unvarnished truth in accounts of operations . . . I am alarmed about the effect which the present tendencies must shortly have on the good name of the R.A.F."

But, during the long years before Western Allied armies engaged the Germans in strength, it suited not only the air chiefs, but also Britain's prime minister and America's president, to collude in proclaiming the triumphs of bombing. Sir Arthur Harris, who became Bomber Command's C-in-C in February 1942, said: "Winston's attitude to bombing was 'Anything to put up a show.' If we hadn't [used Bomber Command] we would only have had the U-boat war, and as he said, defence of our trade routes was not an instrument of war." Churchill regarded the bomber offensive as a vital weapon in Western relations with Stalin, in some small degree assuaging the Soviet warlord's bitterness about alleged Anglo-American sluggishness in launching a second front.

Ken Owen flew his first 1942 trip, to Kassel, in a mood of euphoria. "I was in a daze. It was sheer excitement—the briefing, sitting in the aircraft preparing for take-off. There was bright moonlight. We found the target—and plenty of flak. I was far more scared on the second 'op.' My feet were cold, I was sweating under my arms. It didn't take long for two kinds of reputations to be established: first, there were the 'gen crews'— the real 'press-on types'; then there were the ones who didn't like it at all. Two or three were voted most likely to get the chop, some because they were so frightened they were likely to do something stupid . . . One or two pilots were shit-scared; one or two gunners froze in their turrets. Sometimes people got the chop because of a terrible lack of discipline in their crews."

Airmen became intimately familiar with the stench of hot rubber and petrol in the planes, sometimes also of cordite from their hammering guns and vomit from frightened men. Several times, Owen's wireless operator threw up as the aircraft took violent evasive action. "If you were coned [by searchlights], you'd fly towards somebody else in the hope they'd pick them up instead of you. There was a tremendous element of cynicism and callousness—'Thank Christ it's someone else.' I honestly can't remember the names of many of the men who got the chop. They were only there about a fortnight. We were quite slow to realise that flying was becoming a dangerous occupation; that element of excitement kept us going, and morale was high. There were problems, of course, but I never blamed higher authority because I felt that we were all learning together."

The intimacy of the relationships between members of bomber crews is a cliché, but it was by no means universally valid. B-24 navigator Harold Dorfman respected his pilot's skill, but "we hated each other . . . After a row on a training flight, we never talked to each other except about the mission." Jack Brennan, from Staten Island, was twenty-one when he joined the air force, to his family's fury. " 'We could have kept you out,' they said. But I was one of the kids who wanted to be a hero." The experience of flying twenty-four missions against Germany with an incompetent and cowardly pilot cured him of such delusions. "All the time, I wished I had gone into something else. We got hit almost every trip. The only good thing was that we had decent living conditions compared with the guys on the ground." His crew's combat experience ended ingloriously, when the pilot persuaded them to parachute over Sweden while on a mission to Berlin. Brennan was one of three survivors, and he revelled in the comfort and safety of his subsequent experience as an internee: "It was like a summer camp."

The nature of life and death on bomber stations discouraged relationships outside a man's own crew. "If you had losses to the degree we had losses, you didn't get terribly attached to people," said Etienne Maze, who flew RAF Halifaxes. "They came and they went. By the time you had done ten 'ops,' you were a very old boy." On the day Ted Bone saw some acquaintances on a "missing" list, he merely recorded in his diary: "Good bods Pyatt, Donner etc. Cleaned bike, wrote home, had crumpets and cocoa for supper in the billet." An American B-17 crewman wrote: "We learned to live as perhaps once we were long ago, as simply as animals without hope for ourselves or pity for another."

Bomber operations imposed unique stresses upon participants, who knew the odds against surviving a "tour." They boarded their planes at calm, well-regulated bases; flew out into the whitest heat of war over

Europe; landed back amid the fields of Norfolk or Lincolnshire; visited the pub among local yokels the following evening; then did it all again two or three days later. Pilots, especially on night operations, enjoyed considerable personal latitude which they could exercise for good or ill. Most displayed remarkable determination and devotion to duty, but some faltered. Air Vice-Marshal Sir Ralph Cochrane, 5 Group's commander, personally interviewed one pilot who turned for home when approaching Hamburg: the man offered as his only excuse that he found his aircraft drifting away from the main "stream." This man told the group commander that the crew had discussed their choices over the intercom and agreed to abandon the mission. "When I asked him why he, as captain, didn't take the decision, he replied that they were all members of the sergeants' mess, and it was their lives as well as his, so obviously he had to consult them."

Ron Crafter, an electronic countermeasures operator aboard a Halifax, was hit in the face by shell splinters during an attack on V1 launching sites in June 1944. "The wounds were superficial, but I panicked. I have since found it rather difficult to live with—the most important moment of my life and I was found wanting. I have tried to convince myself that as I was only nineteen it was excusable." So it was, of course. A significant minority of expensively trained airmen, after suffering such experiences, failed to complete their tours. The spirits of many reached their lowest ebb in the winter of 1943, during the RAF's so-called Battle of Berlin. "Thirty sorties in an operational tour, with a loss rate of 4 per cent, was near the limit of human endurance . . . It was clear that morale was bad," Ralph Cochrane acknowledged.

Many men who flinched were treated with considerable harshness, because their superiors feared that indulgence would promote emulation. Reg Raynes was a wireless operator, the sole survivor of a Hampden that crashed on a Norfolk beach in 1941 after returning badly shot-up from Berlin: "I clearly remember the complete silence as we went down. Both engines were gone and the rest of the crew never spoke." His next memory was of finding himself at a psychiatric hospital at Matlock in Derbyshire, from whence he was posted back to a bomber station, automatically demoted in rank. "I was unfit for flying duties, and no one seemed to know what to do with me. All they could see was a Wop/air gunner walking about in a rather aimless manner, and I don't think they ever realised I was mentally ill."

One morning he reported sick with acute head pains, and was sent to another hospital near Newcastle. "They took away my uniform and gave me an ill-fitting blue suit, white shirt and red tie. Apart from a sergeant brought back from Tobruk, all the rest of the patients were army privates, misfits who had slipped through the call-up by mistake. None of them had ever seen a gun, they discussed getting their 'ticket' [out of the service] all day, and they nearly all did." Raynes was discharged from the air force in 1943; he suffered severe psychiatric difficulties for the rest of his life, but received only a 30 percent disability pension.

Some men whom the RAF branded "LMF"—"lacking moral fibre"— were given menial ground jobs; others were dispatched to "Aircrew Refresher Centres"—punishment barracks—of which the most notorious was located outside Sheffield. Ken Owen said: "You joked about getting the chop, about flying reciprocal courses, but never about Sheffield." Yet Owen was among a small minority of airmen who not only survived a tour of thirty operations, but undertook another, with a new crew in a Lancaster. "For the second tour," he said, "we were far more cynical and suspicious. [We asked ourselves]: 'What sort of rear-gunner is this Macpherson? Let's hope the little bastard can stay awake.' We were far more efficient, far more determined to be efficient, far more determined to survive; there was more talk about collisions over the target; we knew the German night-fighter system had improved enormously." One night Owen and his crew came back from a raid on the German rocket-development site at Peenemünde with two engines knocked out and the plane riddled with shrapnel holes inflicted by flak. They abandoned it over Norfolk, and were lucky enough to parachute safely to the ground, where they all met in the Hunstanton police station. "I hated the whole business, then."

American airmen flying daylight missions found it especially harrowing to witness at close quarters horrors invisible to the RAF's night fliers. A B-17 pilot wrote of one mission: "When a plane blew up, we saw [its crew's body] parts all over the sky. We smashed into some of the pieces. One plane hit a body which tumbled out of a plane ahead. A crewman went out of the front hatch of a plane and hit the tail assembly . . . No chute. His body turned over and over like a bean bag tossed into the air . . . A German pilot came out of his plane, drew his legs into a ball, his head down. Papers flew out of his pockets. He did a triple somersault through our formation. No chute." If wartime airmen were indeed an elite, they paid a heavy price for their privileges, facing greater risks than any other combatants save infantry riflemen and submariners.

2. Targets

UNTIL 1943, the most important achievement of the Allies' strategic air offensive was that it obliged the Germans to divert growing numbers of their fighters and dual-purpose 88mm guns from the Eastern Front to defence of the Reich. Berlin alone was defended by a hundred batteries of sixteen to twenty-four guns, each manned by crews of eleven. Though many gunners were teenagers ineligible for the front, the diversion of firepower and technology was important. Historian Richard Overy argues convincingly that the German war effort suffered severely from the need to commit resources to home defence. Bomber Command and the USAAF made an important contribution by obliging the Luftwaffe to divert almost its entire 1943–45 fighter strength to Germany, conceding near-total air superiority over both eastern and western battlefields to the Allies. It is also plain that, while Albert Speer, the minister of armaments and war production, contrived to increase output even amid the massive air attacks of 1944, vastly more weapons would have been built—with serious consequences for the Allied armies—if factory operations had been unimpeded.

Between 1940 and 1942, only 11,228 Germans were killed by Allied bombing. From January 1943 to May 1945, however, a further 350,000 perished, along with unnumbered tens of thousands of foreign POWs and slave labourers. This toll compares with 60,595 British people killed by all forms of German air bombardment including V-weapons between 1939 and 1945. During 1943, Bomber Command's night offensive grew dramatically in strength, and the USAAF began to deploy formidable forces. Its chief, Gen. Henry "Hap" Arnold, brilliantly promoted his service's expansion, "supported as he was by a thoroughly able and quite unscrupulous staff," in the words of an admiring British colleague. The USAAF's wartime manpower rose from 20,000 to 2 million, from 17 air bases to 345, and from 2,470 aircraft to 80,000, while the U.S. Navy acquired 7,500 planes of its own. A steadily growing proportion of American bomber strength was deployed against Germany from British bases.

THE OUTSTANDING precision-bombing feat of the war was the RAF's May 1943 attack on the Ruhr dams, an epic of ingenuity, skill and courage, though its economic significance was modest. As early as 1937, the Air Ministry identified Germany's water supply as a key factor in steel production, and in 1940 the chief of Air Staff, Sir Charles Portal, urged an attack on reservoirs. The difficulty was to find appropriate means. Scientist and aircraft designer Barnes Wallis was independently pursuing the same purpose, and conceived the notion of bouncing depth charges against dam walls. In February 1943 his project won official backing, despite the scepticism of Sir Arthur Harris. Wallis was asked to produce the weapons in time for an attack in May, when the Ruhr reservoirs would be full. A senior staff officer wrote, with conspicuous naïveté: "The operation against the dams will not, it is thought, prove particularly dangerous," because the targets were defended lightly, or not at all. Initial tests were carried out with a spherical charge, but in April Wallis determined upon a cylindrical alternative, backspun before release by an electrically driven pulley so that it would "crawl" down a dam wall to detonate thirty-three feet below the water's surface. Astonishingly, in barely a month the four-ton weapons were built, and Lancasters specially modified to carry them.

The specially formed 617 Squadron trained throughout April and early May to carry out the attack. Contrary to popular myth, not every man was a volunteer, nor were all crews highly experienced. Some had flown fewer than ten previous operations against Germany, and several flight engineers had never been in action at all. This makes all the more remarkable the achievement of twenty-four-year-old Wing Commander Guy Gibson, a fierce disciplinarian and obsessively dedicated airman, in preparing his unit to launch the attack on the night of Sunday, 16 May. Nineteen crews took off. The Möhne and Eder dams were identified as priority targets; it was recognised that the third objective, the earth-banked Sorpe, though industrially vital, was less vulnerable to Wallis's depth charges.

The Möhne was breached by the fourth weapon dropped, the Eder by the third and last available to the attacking Lancasters. Most of the aircraft directed to the Sorpe were shot down en route, and two crews returned home without attacking. The two charges dropped failed to breach the dam, as did another aimed at the Bever, mistakenly identified as the Ennepe. Eight crews failed to return, a punitive casualty rate: six of them fell victims to antiaircraft fire during the low-level flights to and from the Ruhr in bright moonlight, indispensable to bombing accuracy.

The destruction of the Möhne and Eder created a sensation and won the admiration of the world. The moral impact of the attack was enormous, not least on Germany's leaders, and much enhanced the prestige of Bomber Command. Gibson received a VC. Some of the popular enthusiasm for "the Dambusters" derived from the fact that destroying precision industrial targets seemed a much less morally uncomfortable activity than burning cities and civilians. But the flooding of the Möhne valley killed 545 Germans and 749 foreigners, the latter Ukrainian women slave labourers and French and Belgian POWs. The loss of water imposed only temporary inconvenience upon Ruhr steel production, partly because Harris failed to launch follow-up attacks with conventional bombs to prevent the dams from being repaired. But thereafter the Germans felt obliged to divert substantial resources to reservoir defence. If the economic impact of "the Dambusters' raid" was limited, the propaganda achievement was great. All those involved richly merited their laurels.

IN 1943, the German economy staggered in the face of the combined pressures of shortages of coal, steel and manpower, compounded by massive destruction in the Ruhr achieved by Bomber Command and the USAAF. This was the first year in which the air offensive inflicted massive damage on the Nazi war machine. The July firestorm in Hamburg, created by the heaviest air raids in history, killed 40,000 people and destroyed 250,000 dwellings. "We were told the British [bombers] would avoid Hamburg because they would need the town and its harbour later on," one of its traumatised citizens, Mathilde Wolff-Monckeburg, wrote amid the rubble. "We lived in a fool's paradise." By extraordinary exertions and the skills of Gen. Erhard Milch, the Luftwaffe managed to double its 1942 aircraft output, producing 2,200 combat aircraft a month by the summer of 1943. But its new models, the He-177 and Me-210, proved failures which wasted vital resources. The later versions of the Bf-109, which with the FW-190 remained the mainstays of Germany's daylight air defence until the war's end, were outclassed by Allied fighters. The August 1943 suicide of Luftwaffe chief of staff Hans Jeschonnek represented an admission of his service's defeat.

Adam Tooze has made an important and persuasive case against Albert Speer's claims to have created a German armaments production "miracle" between 1942 and 1945. Many of Speer's crisis expedients failed: for instance, the revolutionary Type XXI U-boat was rushed into production in 1944 so hastily that technical shortcomings rendered it incapable of useful service. A coal and steel famine persisted until the war's end—the civilian allocation of fuel was cut to a level 15 percent below that of the meagre British domestic ration. Germany lost access to Ukrainian metal ores in 1943. Merely fulfilling ammunition requirements absorbed more than half the army's steel allocation, together with the services of 450,000 workers; a further 160,000 were building tanks, and 210,000 manufacturing other weapons.

Germany's 1943 production of 18,300 armoured vehicles was far outstripped by the Allies' 54,100—29,000 of these Russian—though Reich factories doubled deliveries between autumn 1942 and spring 1943. German ammunition output peaked in September 1944. From 1943 onwards, the Allies outgunned the Axis in every category of weapon, save tank armament, by ever-growing margins.

This makes it all more remarkable that, in the face of so many handicaps and misjudgements, German forces were able to sustain a ferocious resistance until May 1945. In assessing the Third Reich's industrial experience and the work of Speer and Milch—Jeschonnek's successor as Luftwaffe chief of staff—historical revisionism can be overdone. By 1943, and indeed earlier, the Reich was set upon a course that could lead only to economic collapse. But Allied soldiers fighting the Germans would have derived little comfort from this knowledge as they faced devastating artillery and mortar barrages, and strove to challenge Tigers and Panthers with their own inferior tanks.

The critical weakness of the Allied bomber offensive was poor intelligence, which caused it to become, in Churchill's rueful words, a bludgeon rather than a rapier. Ultra offered little help in divining what was happening inside Germany, because most industrial data was transmitted on paper or by landline rather than radio. Even as the destructive power of the RAF and USAAF grew, the "bomber barons" remained ill-informed about the choke points of Nazi industry, which Sir Arthur Harris was anyway little interested in identifying. Having embarked on a campaign to wreck Germany's cities, he sustained this with obsessive dedication until 1945. The USAAF, doctrinally committed to precision bombing, devoted much more energy to pinpointing key target systems: in August and October 1943, for instance, the Eighth Air Force suffered shocking casualties attacking ball-bearing plants at Schweinfurt, with indifferent success. On the first raid 147 of 376 aircraft were lost, and on the second 60 out of 291, with a further 142 damaged.

These disasters increased Harris's contempt for precision bombing of what he called "panacea targets." It has been justly observed that, although the British and American leaderships at the Casablanca conference in January 1943 mandated a combined bomber offensive, what actually took place was a competition between the RAF and USAAF, each independently pursuing its own doctrine. Adam Tooze believes that Harris's "Battle of the Ruhr," which began with an attack on Essen on 5 March 1943, came close to achieving a decisive victory by wrecking German coal and steel production. Göring expressed astonishment that the Allies did not continue their attacks on the Ruhr, "because there we are in some places having to deal with production bottlenecks that present enormous dangers," as Goebbels recorded. But Bomber Command underrated the importance of maintaining pressure on industrial cities already attacked, which Harris too readily erased from his target list on the evidence of aerial photographs showing roofless buildings.

In July 1943 Harris, supposing the Ruhr sufficiently devastated, shifted Bomber Command's focus of attack first to Hamburg, then to Berlin. Over

Hitler's capital his squadrons, operating at extreme range in winter weather against a huge and widely dispersed target area, suffered severely—losses on every mission rose to an unacceptable average of more than 5 percent. At the end of 1943, Bomber Command headquarters dispatched a report to all its groups and stations, proclaiming in the most fanciful terms the results of its attacks: "These raids on the German capital do indeed mark the beginning of the end . . . The Nazis' military and industrial organization, and above all their morale, have by these attacks suffered a deadly wound from which they cannot recover."

On 7 December, Harris wrote to the prime minister, asserting that if he could deliver a further 15,000 Lancaster sorties against Germany's major cities, the Nazi regime would collapse by 1 April 1944. Bomber Command almost fulfilled his appointed mission quota, but Germany's resistance remained unbroken. The C-in-C's extravagant predictions damaged his credibility with the prime minister and the service chiefs, including Sir Charles Portal. By the early spring of 1944, when Bomber Command was diverted to join the USAAF in attacking preinvasion targets in France, its casualties in the "Battle of Berlin" had become prohibitive. But Harris's iron will enabled him later that summer to renew his assault on Germany's cities, which continued until April 1945.

Bombing did not make the decisive impact upon civilian morale that the British aspired to achieve: factories continued to produce and orders to be obeyed, just as in Britain in 1940–41. It was always an irony, rooted in arrogantly chauvinistic assumptions, that the RAF set out to do to Germany just what the Luftwaffe had failed to do to Churchill's people. But the misery of urban Germans became very great; the Nazi regime was driven to increasingly desperate expedients to explain to its own people their vulnerability to air assault. Newspaper headlines after the May 1943 dams raid asserted that it was "the work of Jews." The public was unconvinced: security police reported that many citizens merely asked why the Luftwaffe was incapable of such achievements. In June a municipal foreman in Hagen watched a British night raid on nearby Wuppertal:

> Hundreds of flak guns are roaring away . . . The air is humming with many aircraft engines. There are innumerable searchlights wandering around the sky. It's raining shrapnel . . . There are five enemy aircraft caught in a searchlight cone; they fly towards us, are furiously shot at, and fly past above us. Later we see an aircraft going down in flames. The whole thing goes on for an hour and a half . . . In the west the sky is red . . . Long convoys of trucks come through the town, laden with all kinds of household goods. Distraught people sit beside their

few belongings. Refugees are arriving at the main station. They stand there with their fire-blackened faces, owning nothing more than they stand up in. It's total misery. The mood in the town is dire. Everywhere there's the question being asked: when will it be our turn?

In June 1943, a citizen of Mülheim wrote: "Our Führer ought now to give the order to destroy the big cities in England, too." Hitler would certainly have done this if he could, but the Luftwaffe was incapable of returning to finish what it had left off in May 1941. A few thoughtful Germans feared that the growing havoc visited on their land represented a judgement on the Nazis' crimes: on 20 December 1943, the Protestant bishop of Wurttemberg roused Berlin's ire by writing to the head of the Reich Chancellery to suggest that his flock were "often feeling that the suffering they were having to endure from the enemy bombing raids was in retribution for what was being done to the Jews." He was sternly enjoined to show "greater reticence in such matters."

As bombing intensified and civilian morale slumped, oppression and compulsion were employed ever more ruthlessly to sustain Nazi hegemony. In 1943, the courts passed a hundred death sentences a week on citizens deemed guilty of defeatism or sabotage: two branch managers of Deutsche Bank and a senior executive of an electricity combine were among those executed for expressing gloom about the war's outcome. To maintain output, the aircraft industry adopted a seventy-two-hour working week. As slave labour became increasingly important, Milch urged ever more draconian measures to increase its productivity; he wrote of foreign and POW workers: "These elements cannot be made more efficient by *small means. They are just not handled strictly enough.* If a decent foreman would sock one of those unruly guys because the fellow won't work, then the situation would soon change. *International law cannot be observed here.* I have asserted myself very strongly . . . I have very strongly represented the point of view that prisoners, with the exception of the English and the Americans, *should be taken away from the military authorities.* Soldiers are not in a position . . . to cope with these fellows . . . If [a prisoner of war] has committed sabotage or refused to work, I will have him hanged, right in his own factory." Hitler's "wonder weapons," the V-1 flying bomb and V-2 rocket, were produced by slaves in conditions of appalling hardship and brutality. Industrial output was sustained only by ruthless exploitation of captive manpower. The commitment to high-technology "revenge weapons," estimated to have cost the Reich around one-third of the resources expended by the Allies on the Manhattan atomic-bomb project, represented a massive and futile burden on a shrinking war economy.

Though the RAF inflicted huge damage on Germany, it was left to the USAAF to achieve the most important victory of the air war, in the early months of 1944, by means which surprised its own commanders. The Mustang long-range fighter, capable of escorting Flying Fortresses and Liberators all the way to Germany and outfighting any opponent when it got there, became available in large numbers. The USAAF embarked on a major campaign against aircraft factories, pounding them for six consecutive days during "Big Week" in February, and forcing the Luftwaffe to commit every available fighter to their defence. It quickly became plain that the ground destruction achieved by the bombers was less significant than the startling success of American pilots in air combat. In a single month, the Luftwaffe lost one-third of its fighters and one-fifth of its aircrew. In March, half the Germans' remaining air strength was destroyed; in April 43 percent of residual capability, in May and June 50 percent.

German production remained remarkably high: as late as September 3,538 aircraft of all types were built, of which 2,900 were fighters. But the Luftwaffe's total 1944 output of 34,100 combat aircraft was dwarfed by the Allies' 127,300, of which 71,400 were American, and the Germans' loss of pilots was calamitous. The USAAF thereafter began to address synthetic oil plants, the Reich's principal source of fuel once the Russians overran the Romanian oilfields in April 1944, with an immediate impact on fuel supplies: the Luftwaffe found many of its planes grounded, aircrew training crippled. When D-Day came in June, Göring's shrunken squadrons were unable to offer significant support to the Wehrmacht. Thereafter the air bombardment of Germany attained massive proportions, while RAF and USAAF losses fell. Whereas in a typical March 1943 attack, around 1,000 aircraft delivered 4,000 tons of bombs, by February 1944, average force size had tripled; by July, the Allies deployed 5,250 planes of all types against Germany, with a bomb capacity of 20,000 tons. In the course of that year and the first months of 1945, they reduced the Reich's conurbations to rubble. By November 1944, attacks on the rail network had made it almost impossible to ship steel produced in the Ruhr to manufacturing plants elsewhere.

The moral effect of the USAAF's daylight raids was immense: the German people were appalled to witness huge formations of enemy planes, their condensation trails searing the high air, parading with impunity over their homeland. "The white stripes moved slowly along the edge of the sky," wrote an onlooker as bomb groups of the Eighth Air Force flew overhead, "calmly, on a straight course, unhurried. They came closer. When our eyes had got used to the bright lights we saw, bathed in the sunlight, the bright dots at the tips of the stripes; in neat squadrons they swept past—one, after a couple of minutes another, then a third, a fourth, a fifth . . . People alongside us started counting the tiny silver dots. They had already got to four hundred. But there was still no end to be seen."

Varied weights of Allied attack fell upon 158 German cities. Braunschweig, a typical example, was the target of twelve raids which destroyed one-third of its buildings and killed 2,905 people. The steel centre of Essen experienced 635 "enemy aircraft approaching" warnings between September 1939 and December 1943, followed by a further 198 warnings in the ensuing nine months. Each one obliged Essen's weary citizens to take refuge in their shelters and bunkers for hours. Germany's rural population was subjected to deliberate air attacks only in 1945, but nowhere was wholly safe: on the night of 17 January 1943 a single stray bomb fell on the little rural community of Neuplotzen in Brandenburg, west of Berlin, killing eight people. A cross was erected near their graves, engraved with the words: "They were torn from the midst of daily life by a spiteful death. Faith in victory conquers distress."

As destruction mounted, so too did Nazi malevolence towards the Allied fliers responsible: Martin Bormann, Hitler's secretary and most trusted aide, sent a notice to local authorities on 30 May 1944 ordering that no citizen should be punished for assaulting or killing downed enemy airmen. There were around 400 recorded incidents of British and American airmen being killed out of hand after parachuting or crashing. Fighter-bomber pilots, who strafed at low level in the last phase of the war, incurred special hatred. Among recorded examples, on 24 March 1944 four airmen were killed in Bochum, on 26 August seven American airmen were killed in Russelheim and on 13 December three RAF men were beaten to death by an enraged crowd in Essen. In February 1945, a member of a factory fire brigade who voiced strong protests about the maltreatment of captured Allied airmen was shot by the Gestapo.

Germany's city dwellers were obliged to spend up to half of each twenty-four hours in cellars and shelters. Nazi officials' exploitation of privileged access to the best-protected refuges caused widespread resentment. In a public shelter in Bochum, party members were reported to have "made themselves comfortable with a few crates of beer" while less fortunate citizens were exposed to the fury of bombardment. Hitler devoted vast resources to his personal safety: 28,000 workers and a million cubic metres of concrete—more than the weight of materials employed throughout 1943–44 on all Germany's public shelters—were used to construct his East Prussian headquarters and Berlin bunker. A twenty-two-year-old Luftwaffe auxiliary described her disgust about the experience of a night in a Krefeld public bunker in November 1944:

At the front of the room men and women of all ages were knocking back schnapps . . . Thick clouds of tobacco smoke make sleep impossible. From one corner there came a jumble of noise of women shrieking and men mumbling drunkenly . . . Children and old people lay asleep among the adults, wrapped in woollen blankets and tattered rags, on wooden plank beds or in chairs. Everywhere there were slumped, exhausted bodies and haggard faces . . . a terrible fug of the smell of dirty underclothes, sweat and stale air almost took your breath away. A long way away a child was quietly weeping, while from the other side there came the sound of snoring and groaning.

Savage penalties were imposed on air-raid looters: on 5 March 1943 Kasimir Petrolinas, a sixty-nine-year-old Lithuanian, was caught by a policeman taking three damaged metal bowls, value one reichsmark, from rubble in Essen. After a special court convicted him, within hours he was shot by a firing squad. In March 1944 an eighteen-year-old named Ilse Mitze was charged with stealing eight vests, five pairs of knickers and thirteen pairs of stockings following an October 1943 raid on Hagen. In her defence, it was said that she had earlier helped to dig out victims. Her employer admitted that she was "difficult" and "had a sweet tooth," but added that she was "industrious and respectable." Hagen's medical officer, giving evidence, dismissed her as "a stupid, impudent and mendacious psychopath." She was condemned to death, a sentence which caused even the local security authorities to protest. Mitze was nonetheless guillotined in Dortmund in May and her fate proclaimed on wall posters to deter others.

The inhabitants of Germany's cities experienced a scale of terror and devastation far beyond anything the Luftwaffe inflicted on Britain in 1940–41: a successful bomber attack unleashed a vision of hell. Mathilde Wolff-Monckeburg wrote from Hamburg during its July 1943 firestorm: "For two whole hours this ear-splitting terror goes on and all you can see is fire. No one speaks. Tense faces wait for the worst at every gargantuan explosion. Heads go down automatically whenever there is a crash, and features are trapped in horror."

The grotesqueries of destruction were boundless. Ursula Gebel wrote of a November 1943 attack on Berlin, during which many bombs fell on the city zoo. "That afternoon . . . I had been at the elephant enclosure and had seen the six females and one juvenile doing tricks with their keeper. That same night, all seven were burnt alive . . . The hippopotamus bull survived in his basin, [but] all the bears, polar bears, camels, ostriches, birds of prey and other birds were burnt. The tanks in the aquarium all ran dry; the crocodiles escaped, but like the snakes they froze in the cold November air. All that survived in the zoo was the bull elephant named Siam, the bull hippo and a few apes."

Martha Gros lived in Darmstadt, near Frankfurt. On the night of 12 September 1944, this large industrial town suffered an attack by Bomber Command's 5 Group which killed at least 9,000 people. "We stood in the fartherest corner of the shelter," she recounted:

> There was Hauptmann R. in full uniform, me, Fräulein H and G, holding each other's hands and listening to [the planes] zooming over us. One of the first explosions was close. My heart fluttered, there was a fearful crash, the walls shook. We heard cracking noises, then a collapse and hissing flames. Plaster began to fall on us, and we expected the ceiling to collapse. The lights had failed. About thirty seconds later there was a second terrible explosion, the door blew open and I saw, bathed in bright light, the staircase above collapsing and a river of fire pouring downwards. The safety curtains were burning.
>
> I shouted "Let's get out," but Hauptmann R. grabbed me: "Stay here, they're still over us." At that moment the house opposite was hit. A tongue of flame, about five metres long, whipped towards us, cupboards and other furniture burst open and fell on us. A terrible pressure forced us against the wall. Now R. shouted: "Get out and hold hands." By using all his strength he dragged me out from under the wooden wreckage. I dropped my cash box and pulled Miss H with me, and she grabbed Mr. G. We climbed through the hole leading to the back. Our house was burning. I heard the ceilings collapse, watched my beds go up in flames. In the midst of the garden it was incredibly hot and there was so much smoke that we all knelt on the ground, holding our heads as low as possible, and occasionally scooping up earth and holding it against our hot faces.

In cellars and shelters beneath a nearby hospital, under battery emergency lighting, sheets were soaked in salad oil to ease the pain of hideously burned casualties, most of whom died. Water was cut off. A stench of roasted flesh filled the air. Doctors operated hour after hour, far beyond exhaustion. The corpses of some of the dead appeared unmarked—they had succumbed to asphyxiation or internal injuries inflicted by blast. Many people suffered eye damage from acrid fumes or blazing fragments whirling through the air. Ottilie Bell described a near miss: "There was a crash, the lights went out, the radio went dead. We all fell on our knees, mouths wide open. My sister-in-law was praying loudly for our lives. Our puppy, barely six weeks old, started barking with terror."

Housewife Grete Siegel said: "We were all petrified . . . Old women leaned against their garden walls in nightgowns and caps, shivering with terror and cold. Those who had been burned had blisters the size of fists on their faces, necks, everywhere. One woman had strips of skin hanging from her face . . . I glimpsed a charred corpse, about sixty centimetres long, lying on its face. That's how all of them were . . . In the *Palaisgarten* we saw countless bodies, nearly all of them naked: one had only a sock on, others just suspender belts or a strip of shirt; there was a young blonde girl, who looked as if she was smiling." In cellars, dead victims of suffocation sat like ghosts, wrapped in blankets and with cloths tied in front of their faces: "The stench was horrific." When morning came on 13 September, in Martha Gros's words, "there was a deathly silence in the town, ghostly and chilling. It was even more unreal than the previous night. Not a bird, not a green tree, no people, nothing but corpses." Ottilie Bell said, "All one could see were smouldering ruins. Not a single house left standing in our thousand-metre-long street."

Between 1943 and 1945, such scenes were repeated day after day, night after night, in Germany's cities. Beyond the sufferings of the civilians, the morale of their menfolk on distant battlefields suffered grievously from hearing the tidings from home—and eventually from seeing the destruction for themselves. "What a homecoming it was!" wrote a German soldier who returned from the Russian front in 1944. "We had heard, of course, about the Allied air attacks on the German cities. But what we saw from our [train] windows was far beyond what we had expected. It shocked us to the very core of our being. Was this what we had been fighting for in the east? . . . The faces of the civilians were grey and tired, and in some of them we could even see resentment, as if it was our fault that their homes had been destroyed and so many of their dear ones burnt to cinders." Italy was not spared. Lt. Pietro Ostellino wrote home from North Africa: "I heard today that enemy aircraft have once more bombed our great and beautiful Turin . . . The bombing of an open city is horrible. When aircraft vent their fury on us in the front line, so be it. We are soldiers and must bear the consequences of war. But for the defenceless civilians it is an act of subhuman cruelty and savagery."

IN 1944-45, the Anglo-American bomber offensive became the supreme expression of the two nations' industrial might and technological prowess.

Much of eastern and southern England was transformed into a chequer-board of air bases overlaid on farmland, ringed by concertina wire, and variously designated for training, transport, fighters or bombers. There were 110 USAAF and RAF airfields in Norfolk alone, each occupying 600 acres of flatland; a Bomber Command station was manned by some 2,500 ground personnel, around 400 of them women, and a revolving cast of 250 airmen. This was war conducted by timetable, in accordance with a deadly daily routine sustained for years.

In the last months of the war, USAAF and RAF losses over Europe fell steeply, but operational flying never became a safe activity. Alan Gamble's crew, a characteristic national mix of the period—Australian pilot, American tail gunner, Scots navigator and mid-upper gunner, the rest English—began operations in February 1945 eager to be "in at the finish . . . We hoped to make a name for ourselves." All had completed earlier tours with Bomber Command. On 7 February, they took off with a force of a hundred Lancasters for a daylight attack on an oil refinery at Wanne-Eickel. Crossing the French coast, they saw ahead of them an angry black cloud, and climbed to maximum altitude in an attempt to avoid it. Instead, the plane began to ice up dramatically. It was soon "waffling about like a drunken duck," in Gamble's words.

They pressed on, but after a debate on the intercom decided to make for nearby Krefeld, in the Ruhr. The plane was at 8,500 feet and they had just released their bombs when there was a violent lurch as the starboard wing began to buckle "as if it was going to wrap itself around us." The Lancaster rolled over and began to spin. "Prepare to abandon aircraft!" called Geoff, the pilot, as he struggled to regain stability. Gamble, convinced of imminent death, thought, "Dear God, this is it—I hope it doesn't hurt too much." Suddenly, the plane momentarily righted itself. The crew seized parachutes and one by one leapt from the forward hatch. Gamble was alarmed to find himself descending towards a turbulent river, but managed to steer away onto land. His crew was unusually lucky: all landed alive and survived the ensuing three months as prisoners.

Until the end, cities were pounded mercilessly. A woman in Braunschweig wrote on 9 March 1945: "The planes are over Berlin every day, sometimes twice a day. The poor, poor people. How do they stand such suffering? Everyone is totally worn out." A Berliner, Karl Deutmann, wrote of one USAAF attack: "We heard, behind the metre-thick walls of our bunker and for more than an hour, nothing but the awful rumbling and thunder of the carpet of falling bombs, with the lights flickering and sometimes almost going out . . . When we left the bunker the sun had disappeared, the sky darkened with clouds. Fed by numberless small and big fires, a vast sea of smoke hung over the whole of the inner city . . . In the Neuburgerstrasse . . . the girls' trades school had been hit; hundreds of girls had been sheltering in the cellar. Later the parents were standing in front of the shattered bodies, mangled and stripped naked by blast, no longer able to recognise their own daughters." In Hagen a diarist wrote on 15 March 1945: "Fear and panic rule among the public. There is no public building left in the town, no business, and hardly any street. Only mountains of rubble and debris. I am churned up to the depths of my being and cannot describe all the horror. The air is filled with an eerie hissing and roaring. I stand around with others, baffled and not knowing what to do."

Only a limited number of British and American people gave much thought to the fate of Germany beneath air bombardment, partly because their governments persistently deceived them about the nature of the campaign: the reality of area bombing, the targeting of cities, was concealed beneath verbiage about industrial installations. The USAAF, doctrinally and morally committed to precision attack, never publicly admitted that its operations, and especially radar-guided blind bombing, inflicted almost as much injury upon civilian life and property as did the area attacks of the RAF. Moreover, it was asking much to invite the Allied peoples, who had themselves suffered so much from German aggression, to be overly troubled about German civilian casualties.

Some informed British people were more dismayed by the cost to architecture than to human beings: the aesthete and National Labour MP Harold Nicolson expressed shock at public indifference to the destruction of Europe's cultural heritage. "It is a reproach to democratic education," he wrote in the *Spectator* in February 1944, just a year before Dresden was bombed, "that the peoples of Britain and America should be either indifferent or actually hostile to these supreme expressions of human intelligence. It is a reflection upon our leaders that they have shown but a perfunctory awareness of their responsibilities. And it will be a source of distress to our grandchildren that we, who might have stood firm as the trustees of Europe's heritage, should have turned our faces aside."

Nicolson was correct in anticipating that future generations would recoil in dismay from the strategic bomber offensive, but he misjudged the nature of their revulsion: in the twenty-first century, it is the indiscriminate bombardment of civilians, more than the devastation of baroque palaces, that rouses strong emotions. More than a few Germans, and even some Anglo-American critics, see a moral equivalence between Nazi wickedness in massacring innocents, especially Jews, and Allied wickedness in burning cities. This seems mistaken. The bomber offensive was designed to achieve the defeat of the Axis and the liberation of Europe. The Nazis' mass murders not only killed far more people, but lacked the justification of pursuing a strategic purpose. Instead, they were conducted solely to fulfil Nazi Germany's ideological and racial objectives. Techno-logical determinism was the decisive factor in the worst excesses of bomb-ing, which took place in 1945 when the war was obviously approaching its conclusion: vast air forces existed, and thus they were employed. Years of conflict against a barbaric enemy had coarsened Allied sensibilities, shrunk humanitarian instincts. This is unremarkable.

When it was all over, the American and British airmen who had partic-ipated in the strategic offensive against Germany, at such risk and sacrifice to themselves, were dismayed to find their campaign the object of criti-cism and indeed opprobrium. They had bombed the Nazi war economy into a state of collapse; unfortunately, however, their achievement came too late to secure the credit which the air chiefs thought their due, because the Allied armies stood on the brink of completing the Reich's defeat by their own exertions. The bomber offensive made a significant contribu-tion to the outcome, but reached its terrible maturity too late to claim success on its own terms.

Critics concluded that the Allies had paid an unacceptable moral price for a marginal strategic achievement. Sir Arthur Harris said: "It all boils down to the fact that everybody dislikes bombers because they drop things on them, and everybody loves the fighter because it shoots down the bomber." He once wrote bitterly: "I have no intention . . . of going down to History as the author, or sole executant, of the Strategical plans to destroy the cities of Germany." He himself, he asserted, "never had strategical control of the Bomber Offensive . . . only tactical control with which to implement the strategical directives . . . received."

He quoted the remark of Gen. John Burgoyne after accepting defeat in the American War of Independence: "I expect ministerial ingratitude will be displayed, as in all countries and at all times has been usual, to remove the blame from the order to its execution." Harris added, "In my experi-ence, I doubt he ever spoke a truer word." He had a point. Harris was a formidable commander, if an unlovable human being, who developed a personal obsession with destroying Germany's cities, and displayed the spirit of an ancient Roman in fulfilling this end: *Delenda est Carthago*. But if his superiors dissented from his conduct of Britain's bomber forces, it was their duty to sack him. As it was, Churchill and the chiefs of staff permitted Harris to pursue to the blazing end the policy they themselves had man-dated back in 1942; he was the enforcer of area bombing, not its architect.

It is unjust that fighter pilots of all nations today retain a popular adulation often denied to bomber aircrews. Moral strictures upon strategic air attack should properly be deployed against those who instigated it. The killing of civilians must always be deplored, but Nazi Germany represented a historic evil. Until the last day of the war, Hitler's people inflicted appalling sufferings upon the innocent. The destruction of their cities and the deaths of significant numbers of their inhabitants seems a price they had to pay for the horrors they unleashed upon Western civilisation, and represents a far lighter toll than Germany imposed upon the rest of Europe.

CHAPTER TWENTY

VICTIMS

1. Masters and Slaves

ALMOST EVERY CITIZEN of the nations that participated in the war suffered consequences, but in widely varying degree. Historians describe events chiefly in terms of clashes of arms, which of course determined outcomes. But the conflict should also be understood as a human experience which changed the lives of hundreds of millions of people, many of whom never saw a battlefield. Fear of injury or death created the most obvious apprehension, especially in the new age of air bombardment. But beyond this, there were many other causes of distress: about food and health; the absence of loved ones; the dissolution of communities. There were simple sorrows, such as being unable to give presents to loved ones. "Eva's birthday," Victor Klemperer, a Jew rendered destitute by Nazi confiscation of all that he owned, wrote of his wife in Dresden on 12 July 1944. "My hands quite empty again, not even a flower." Nor was it necessary to be subject to Axis hegemony to suffer grievously: Stalin deported eastwards vast numbers of Soviet citizens from minorities whose loyalties he deemed suspect, notably Chechens and Crimean Tatars, some 3.5 million in all. An unquantified but large proportion of these people died in consequence, some from typhus which broke out during their transportation. Their sufferings, unlike those of Hitler's victims, are scarcely recorded, but it is known that four Heroes of the Soviet Union were among the deportees; Beria's purges spurned discrimination.

Among other victims of the Soviets were 1.5 million Poles deported to Siberian exile or the gulag in 1940–41, in furtherance of Stalinist ethnic-cleansing policies; at least 350,000 perished of starvation or disease, and a further 30,000 were executed. Edward Matyka, a twenty-one-year-old soldier, naïvely supposed that the Russians would not impede his escape to Romania from the German-occupied region of Poland. But he was arrested by a Soviet patrol in January 1940, imprisoned, and awarded a sentence of five years' hard labour for "illegal crossing of the border and attempts to carry out spying on behalf of the enemies of the Soviet Union." In October, after weeks of travelling on prison barges, he and his comrades were required to march forty miles in bitter cold to reach their labour camp: "Four hundred shadows of men moved after one another slowly, with difficulty, making their way through deep snow . . . We went through forest and the column began to stretch and thin out as the weak and owners of baggage dropped out."

At their camp, they spent the next eighteen months in conditions of ghastly privation. Some mornings, even in the prison hospital, Matyka awoke to find his hair covered with white hoarfrost. Each day, an average of twelve men perished. The Pole wrote of his desolation: "I was so far from my dear ones and I lay ill among unknown dying people. I knew that if I died, I would be forgotten like those whose lifeless bodies were carried out each day and that my family would never know what had happened to me. I cried like a helpless child that has been wronged, and prayed for a miracle." He was sent to work inside the Arctic Circle at a camp named Ust-Usa, canning meat for prison consumption. By the time he and his comrades were finally freed, they had completed a 600-mile railway, laid with their bare hands. Matyka wrote bitterly, "The bones of Poles and other prisoners probably lie under every sleeper."

Felicks Lachman, another Polish prisoner in the gulag, afterwards wrote a bitter little poem:

> Lice bugs bugs lice
> More bugs more lice
> Rats fleas gnats flies
> And bread-devouring mice
>
> Dirt mud no soap
> Stench filth to cope
> No faith no hope
> In darkness we grope
>
> Our beds bare planks
> Our mates sheer cranks
> Our dreams long ranks
> Of American tanks.

In the Soviet Union's desperate circumstances of July 1941, Stalin amnestied 50,295 Poles who were released from prisons and camps, together with a further 26,297 from POW cages and 265,248 from special settlements and exile. A substantial number of soldiers subsequently joined the Polish communist army raised inside the Soviet Union. In the following year 115,000 others, 73,000 of them military personnel and the remainder women and children, were astonished to receive permission to leave Russia for Iran, where they became a British responsibility. Though Foreign Secretary Anthony Eden recognised the Poles' ghastly plight, "living in harrowing conditions, diseased and threatened with death by starvation," this was not a burden welcomed by their new hosts. The British colonial authorities in Cairo wrote to the Foreign Office in June 1942 expressing acute alarm about the scale of the Polish migration: "To put matters brutally if these Poles die in Russia the war effort will not be affected. If they [are allowed] to pass into Persia, we, unlike the Russians, will not be able to allow them to die and our war effort will be gravely impaired. Action must be taken to stop these people from leaving the USSR before we are ready to receive them . . . however many die in consequence."

This shamelessly callous analysis illustrates the brutalisation of some of those directing the Allied war effort in the face of so many competing tragedies. The Polish migration went ahead anyway: a British medical officer in Iran responsible for the care of the arriving refugees reported that 40 percent were suffering from malaria, and almost all from dysentery, diarrhoea, malnutrition or typhoid. Nearly two years elapsed before these Polish soldiers were medically fit to join the Allied armies fighting in Italy, where they served with distinction until the war's end. Their dependents were shuffled from camp to camp, in humane but nonetheless unhappy British captivity. Many were shipped to India, and thence in 1945 to Britain, where most chose to spend the balance of their lives. Whatever the shortcomings of British behaviour towards these Poles, the fundamental reality was that they were victims of a murderous persecution by the Soviet Union, a power joined with the democracies in a supposed "crusade for freedom."

In Europe, meanwhile, an estimated 20 million people were displaced from their prewar homes, often in circumstances of terrible hardship. One evening in 1940, Szmulek Goldberg, a Jew from Łódź, took his girlfriend, Rose, to the nearby sports club where they had spent many happy hours. It was now bomb damaged and shuttered. They wandered into the derelict gymnasium where Szmulek once won a dance contest, partnering his mother. "I had dressed in my flashy clothes and brown felt hat for the last time. We stopped and I turned to Rose. 'My name is Szmulek Goldberg,' I said in a formal, introductory tone. 'My name is Rose,' she replied, her eyes glistening with moisture. I bowed to her and she curtsied in return. We waltzed through the stillness to music we heard only in our hearts." That night, amid Rose's sobs and a long embrace, Szmulek said his farewells. He fled Łódź and survived—but spent the last years of the war in Auschwitz-Birkenau. He never saw his girl again.

A powerful sensation among hundreds of millions of people was that of injustice: they did not believe they merited the plagues of peril, privation, loneliness and horror that had swept them away from their familiar lives into alien and mortally dangerous environments. "I don't believe I am wicked," wrote the British gunner Lt. John Guest, "and I don't believe the majority of people, Germans included, are either—certainly not wicked enough to have been deservedly overtaken by this war."

The peoples of countries ruled by the Axis were in worse condition, of course: almost all found themselves at the mercy of both the enemy's soldiers and new collaborationist administrations. A Chinese in Malaya, Chin Kee On, wrote: "The former social order was reversed. The 'nobodies' of yesterday became the 'big shots' of today. The former scum and dregs of society, such as ex-convicts, notorious gentleman-crooks, swindlers and well-known failures became the new elite, riding high in official favour and power." On Java, two young Dutch girls travelling with their mother aboard a hopelessly overcrowded train were startled to be denied the seats to which they were accustomed. An elderly Indonesian noted their confusion. *"Ya Njonja, daly Iain sekarang,"* he said sardonically to the mother—"Yes madam, things are changed."

That Dutch family soon fell victim to far worse misfortunes. Elizabeth van Kampen, the daughter of a planter, spent the years between her fifteenth and eighteenth birthdays in a Japanese internment camp with her mother and two sisters, clinging precariously to life as they suffered malnutrition, lice, beriberi, dysentery and repeated attacks of malaria. Most of Mrs. van Kampen's teeth fell out; her husband perished at the hands of the Kempeitai police. Elizabeth tried to preserve her sanity by dreaming of her past idyllic colonial childhood, and of a world beyond walls, but "how can you dream while you are locked up in a dirty, overcrowded prison, when you are lying on a filthy mattress full of bugs? How can you dream while your stomach cries for food? How can you dream without a sound of music? I was seventeen years old, but I became scared to dream at all."

In the occupied countries, law was no longer an absolute, but became whatever the conquerors chose that it should be. Few Germans were as squeamish as the Abwehr official Helmuth von Moltke, who during a visit to Oslo found himself occupying a requisitioned Norwegian home. "The . . . disgusting thing was the feeling of having entered a stranger's house, to sit there like thieves, while the owner, as I knew, sat in a concentration camp." In Łódź in April 1940, the Slazak family was evicted from their small flat and shop, which were given to their neighbours, who were ethnic Germans; George's mother wept bitterly. "My dear father was a gentle giant. I had never known him to lose his temper. Seeing the Bucholts take our home and shop, he shook with anger, but could say nothing with two Gestapo men present."

German and Japanese carpetbaggers who had achieved little status or respect in their own societies became proconsuls in their nations' new possessions; Takase Toru, from 1942 to 1945 a powerful figure in Japanese-ruled Singapore, taunted Chinese business leaders: "I have been to Malaya three times before, and seen many of you at dinner table . . . but you had not paid any notice to me then." The Japanese extorted a "gift" of 50 million straits dollars from the Chinese community, renamed many streets and advanced clocks two hours to Tokyo time. During the brief 1942 honeymoon between the Burmese and their "liberators," a Japanese classical theatre troupe performed in Rangoon, singing:

> Let us dance happily,
> And if we dance happily,
> It will be in the heart of Tokyo,
> Joy! Joy!
> In the midst of Tokyo flowers.

But Japanese arrogance and brutality soon destroyed the goodwill of the Burmese people. Malays likewise recoiled from their new masters' conduct, exemplified by their ubiquitous habit of urinating in public. The local population was outraged by the Japanese custom of administering a rebuke by a slap in the face. The occupiers grudgingly modified this practice in 1943, decreeing that only senior officers, colonels and above, could physically abuse natives; but scant heed was paid to the restriction. Christopher Bayly and Tim Harper, vivid chroniclers of the Asian experience, have written: "The Japanese seemed hardly more culturally sensitive than the British and were certainly more brutal."

Hans Frank, the Nazi ruler of Poland, wrote in his 1942 diary: "Humanity is a word that one dares not use . . . The power and the certainty of being able to use force without any resistance are the sweetest and most noxious poison that can be introduced into any government." This is an important statement, for it captures the exhilaration experienced by many Germans and Japanese on finding themselves, together with their local acolytes, occupying posts which conferred absolute powers of life and death. In ordinary peacetime life, men's and women's actions are constrained not only by law but by social convention; even those who might feel no moral inhibitions about pillaging, injuring or killing others are subject to machinery which prevents them from doing so. But the men who exercised authority under the totalitarian regimes, emphatically including that of the Soviet Union, knew themselves to be liberated from all constraints and safeguards upon the sanctity of human life, provided only that killings advanced the purposes of the system they served. This huge, terrible freedom thrilled its beneficiaries: the few Nazi officeholders who afterwards gave honest testimony described their exercise of power in lyrical terms.

It was hard for victims, accustomed to lives in ordered communities, to grasp the implications of their absolute impotence. The chasm between a bourgeois society going about its lawful business and the *Arbeit Macht Frei* entrance arch to Auschwitz was initially too wide for comprehension. Occupation and subjection seemed bad enough; only progressively did it become apparent that there could be higher gradations of suffering. Ruth Maier, a young Austrian Jewish refugee living in Oslo, wrote on 25 April 1941 about her quest for a U.S. visa: "I've been to the American Consulate about it. I'm sure to get a visa after the war. But not before then . . . So we need to be patient." The hapless girl did not yet understand that her inability to secure a visa was no mere inconvenience, but a matter of life and death—her own: five months afterwards, she was deported and murdered. As late as 1944 Edith Gabor, the eighteen-year-old daughter of a Budapest diamond merchant, heard reports of the fate of Europe's Jewish communities. "But we thought: 'Oh, this is something that happens to other people, in other countries.' " She herself was frightened, but not frightened enough. Later that year she was transported to the first of a succession of concentration camps where she narrowly survived unspeakable horrors. All the rest of her family save one brother were gassed.

Many people met death far from any battlefield. The Jews of Europe suffered the most dramatic fate, but millions of other civilians—Russians, Poles, Yugoslavs, Greeks, Chinese, Malays, Vietnamese, Indians—were extinguished by wilful murder, chance explosion, disease or starvation. Their deaths were no less terrible because they took place in circumstances of obscurity, in some ruined village rather than at Auschwitz or Majdanek, and unaccompanied by any redemptive opportunity to offer resistance or win medals. Helmuth von Moltke of the Abwehr was appalled to learn of mass hostage shootings in occupied territories, writing to his wife on 21 October 1941:

In one area in Serbia two villages have been reduced to ashes, 1,700 men and 240 women have been executed. This is the "punishment" for an attack on three German soldiers. In Greece 220 men of one village have been shot. The village was burnt down, women and children were left there to weep for their husbands and fathers and homes. In France there are extensive shootings while I write. Certainly more than a thousand people are murdered in this way every day and another thousand German men are habituated to murder. All this is child's play compared with what is happening in Poland and Russia. May I know this and yet sit at my table in my heated flat and have tea? Don't I thereby become guilty too? What shall I say when I am asked: "And what did you do during that time?" Since Saturday, the Berlin Jews are being rounded up.

The Holocaust is today often discussed in isolation. In one sense, this is logical, because the Jews were singled out for genocide, but the records of Auschwitz-Birkenau, the most notorious of the death camp complexes, emphasise the numbers from other racial groups who shared the fate of Jewish deportees. The best available statistics show that a total of 1.1 million Jews arrived at the camp, of whom 100,000 survived; among 140,000 non-Jewish Poles, half survived; of 23,000 gypsies, all but 2,000 perished; all of the 15,000 Soviet POWs died; about half of 25,000 others—mostly political prisoners—were killed. In addition to almost 6 million Jews murdered by the Nazis, over 3 million Russians died in German captivity, while huge numbers of non-Jewish civilians were massacred in Russia, Poland, Yugoslavia, Greece and other occupied countries.

It thus seems important to assess the Holocaust against the background of Hitler's governance of his empire. One of the most moving and enlightened advocates of pursuing such context was Ruth Maier. As a twenty-two-year-old refugee in Oslo, barely a month before her own deportation and murder in Auschwitz, she wrote in her diary: "If you shut yourself away and look at this persecution and torture of Jews only from the viewpoint of a Jew, then you'll develop some sort of complex which is bound to lead to a slow but certain psychological collapse. The only solution is to see the Jewish question from a broader perspective . . . within the framework of the oppressed Czechs and Norwegians, the oppressed workers . . . We'll only be rich when we understand that it's not just we who are a race of martyrs. That beside us there are countless others suffering, who will suffer like us until the end of time . . . if we don't . . . if we don't fight for a better . . ." She broke off to express exasperation about the persistence of her own instinct to see the Jewish tragedy as unique, but her mental confusion does not diminish the nobility and unselfishness of this very young woman's words from the threshold of the grave.

One of Hitler's greatest mistakes, from the viewpoint of his own interests, was that he attempted to reshape the eastern lands that fell under his suzerainty in accordance with Nazi ideology while still fighting the war. Almost all comparisons between Hitler and Churchill are otiose, but one seems significant: Britain's leader provoked the exasperation of his ministers, as well as that of humbler fellow countrymen, by his refusal to seriously address domestic social reform until victory was achieved. Germany's leader, in contrast, launched a drastic reordering of conquered societies in the east within weeks of their occupation. He conducted wholesale expulsions of indigenous populations to make way for German colonists, and slaughtered large numbers of people, notably Jews and social and political activists, heedless of whether they offered resistance to his hegemony. Ignoring the human horror—as of course did the Nazis—these policies imposed enormous economic and agricultural disruption on Hitler's war machine. Some members of designated lesser races enlisted in Nazi service to secure food or pay, or because they hated Jews, or because they merely relished opportunities for exercising dominion and indulging cruelty; but oppression embittered millions of Stalin's former subjects who might have become willing German acolytes.

In occupied western Europe in 1940–41, the Nazis encountered many active or potential collaborators. The leaders of Vichy France were eager to pursue a partnership with the Reich, which could have gained the support of many people in France, and conceivably led to French belligerence against Britain. But Hitler's economic exploitation of Pétain's nation, notably by imposing an artificially high exchange rate for the mark against the franc, progressively alienated the French, even before the 1943 introduction of forced labour in Germany, the detested Service de Travail Obligatoire.

The Nazis' mass deportations from Poland, Czechoslovakia and Ukraine gravely damaged agricultural production. Many of the ethnic German colonists intended to replace the native inhabitants proved reluctant, as well as technically unqualified, to fulfil their appointed destinies. All history's successful empires have rested partly on force majeure, but partly also upon offering conquered peoples compensations for subjection: stability, prosperity and the rule of law. The Nazis, by contrast, offered only brutality, corruption and administrative incompetence. They themselves would have argued that their cruelties were successful in suppressing strategically significant resistance to occupation everywhere save in Yugoslavia and Russia. This was true, but it is only part of the story.

Many of the occupied countries, and especially France, made useful contributions to the German war economy under compulsion: in all, they

supplied some 9.3 percent of the Reich's armaments, and Danish agriculture provided 10 percent of Germany's food needs. But Hitler might have
fared better had he offered conquered peoples incentives as well as threats,
rewards as well as draconian confiscations of property and commodities.
The Nazis' view of economics was grotesquely primitive: they regarded
wealth creation as a zero-sum game, in which for Germany to gain, someone else must lose. The consequence was that, from 1940 onwards, Hitler's empire was progressively pillaged to fund his war, a process that could
end only in its bankruptcy.

The Nazi hierarchy was slow to comprehend the folly of slaughtering
prospective slaves amid the national manpower crisis created by mobilisation of most of Germany's population of military age. Adam Tooze has
calculated that, in all, 7 million men of working age—notably Jews, Poles
and Russian POWs—were killed or allowed to die by the Germans, most
between 1941 and 1943. He describes the Holocaust as "a catastrophic
destruction of labour power." The Nazis in 1941–42 reasoned that their
difficulties in feeding the German people were best assuaged by eliminating every unwanted mouth within their reach. At a Berlin meeting
attended by Göring on 16 September 1941, food shortages were highlighted. The *Reichsmarschall* declared it to be unthinkable to reduce rations
for Germany's civilian population, "given the mood at home." Hitler's
people required material as well as moral reassurance that the war was
worth fighting.

The only answer, the Nazis concluded, was to reduce provision for
native inhabitants of the occupied territories and Russian POWs. On
13 November, Quartermaster-General Eduard Wagner told his heads
of department that "prisoners of war who are not working will have to
starve." Thus Russian prisoners began to die in vast numbers, some of
hunger and others at the hands of guards granted unlimited licence to kill
to control the herds of desperate humanity for which they were responsible. By 1 February 1942, almost 60 percent of 3.35 million Soviet prisoners in German hands had perished; by 1945, 3.3 million were dead out
of 5.7 million taken captive.

Only in 1943 did the Nazis acknowledge that hungry mouths also had
useful hands: they belatedly accepted the value, indeed indispensabil-
ity, of keeping prisoners alive to bolster Germany's shrinking industrial
labour force. When this new policy was implemented, Göring observed
with complacency that Russians performed 80 percent of the construction
work on his Ju-87 Stukas. By the autumn of 1944, almost 8 million foreign
labourers and POWs were engaged in the German economy, 20 percent
of its workforce. BMW employed 16,600 prisoners at its Munich plant

alone; though still treated with institutionalised cruelty, their rations were increased just sufficiently to sustain life. Industrial employers asked that punishments should be administered behind the wire of workers' quarters, rather than in open view on factory premises, to avoid distressing German staff. A vast complex of guarded quarters was established in and around every major German city to house foreigners of all kinds. The Munich area harboured 120 POW facilities, 286 barracks and hostels for civilians and a brothel to service them, together with 7 concentration camp outstations including a branch of Dachau, a total of 80,000 bedspaces.

It was impossible for most German civilians to credibly deny knowledge of the concentration camps or the slave-labour system: little girls living near Ravensbrück were seen playing a game of "camp guards"; prisoners were widely used for firefighting, rescue work and clearing rubble in the wake of air raids. They were also dispatched to deal with unexploded bombs, a task so often fatal that SS men convicted of crimes were preferred as guards for such squads. To ensure that slaves were readily available, local satellite camps were established in urban areas. Prisoners from Sachsenhausen, for instance, were drafted into nearby Berlin, where their striped clothing caused civilians to refer to them as "zebras." In Osnabrück, mothers complained to the SS that children in the schoolyard were obliged to witness slaves being beaten by their guards. The SS responded that "if the children aren't tough enough yet, they have to be hardened."

Local authorities were generally appreciative of such cheap labour, which the mayor of Duisburg described as "highly satisfactory." But some civilians deplored alleged coddling: a road contractor wrote in March 1944, "We are still much too soft on POWs and other labour squads in our streets. I say, better throw one man overboard than let us drown." The SS frequently used prisoners to collect loot from wrecked buildings for their own profit—in Düsseldorf two men were shot lest they reveal their jailers' racketeering. Civilian doctors frequently signed false death certificates for prisoners shot or beaten to death; in this as in much else, the German medical profession displayed its readiness to oblige the Nazi regime. Slave labourers continued to die even after being enlisted in the service of Reich industries, partly because a tension persisted between the need for their services and Nazi reluctance to feed them. By one calculation, 170,000 of 2.77 million Russian civilian workers perished, along with 130,000 Poles and 32,000 Italian POWs.

From 1943 onwards, however, prisoner mortality declined sharply. Even some Jews were kept alive, notably as workers at the huge IG Farben complex beside Auschwitz-Birkenau. The major Holocaust killings, save those of Hungary's Jews, were already completed. Foreign workers and slaves never provided a wholly satisfactory substitute labour force—they were thought to underperform their German counterparts by at least 15 percent, perhaps as much as 30 percent. It was a folly, as well as a barbarity, to suppose that starved and brutalised slave labourers could achieve as much useful productivity as those treated with minimal humanity. The concentration camp system, which the SS sought to make a profit centre, was inefficient even on its own terms, but slave labour alone made it possible for Germany to continue the war until 1945.

2. Killing Jews

THE EDIFICE OF HOLOCAUST literature is vast, yet does not satisfactorily explain why the Nazis accepted the economic cost of embarking upon the destruction of the Jewish people, diverting scarce manpower and transport to a programme of mass murder while the outcome of the war still hung in the balance. The answer must lie in the deranged centrality of Jewish persecution not merely to National Socialist ideology but to Germany's policies throughout the global conflict. The Nazis were always determined to exploit the licence granted to a government waging total war to fulfil objectives that otherwise posed difficulties even for a totalitarian regime. Göring asserted at a key party meeting on 12 November 1938, following *Kristallnacht*: "If, in the near future, the German Reich should come into conflict with foreign powers, it goes without saying that we in Germany should first of all let it come to a showdown with the Jews."

At that time, Nazi policy still promoted the emigration of German Jews, but a November 1939 article in the SS journal *Schwartze Korps* asserted the commitment to "the actual and definitive end of Jewry in Germany, its total extermination." Many such remarks were made openly and publicly by leading Nazis: Hitler made his notorious "prophecy" in a speech to the Reichstag on 30 January 1939, asserting that war would result in "the annihilation of European Jewry." He sought to make it plain that every Jew within his reach was a hostage for the "good behaviour" of the Western powers. If the British and French declined to acquiesce in his ambitions—above all if they chose to oppose these with force—the consequences would be their responsibility.

The Western powers treated such remarks as hyperbolic. Even when Hitler embarked on his rampage of hemispheric conquest, the democracies found it difficult to conceive that the people of a highly educated and long-civilised European society could fulfil their leaders' extravagant rhetoric and implement genocide. Despite mounting evidence of Nazi crimes, this delusion persisted in some degree until 1945, and even for a time afterwards.

The Nazi T4 euthanasia programme, which began in July 1939, killed German and Polish inmates of psychiatric units, categorised as "unfit for further existence," at a rate of some 5,000 a month in 1940. Most were gassed, though some were shot, under Gestapo and SS supervision with assistance from doctors; between 4,000 and 5,000 of the 70,000 victims were Jewish. The T4 programme was historically important, because at an early stage it demonstrated the German government's willingness to undertake an annihilatory process, minutely bureaucratised from Berlin, to eliminate a subgroup surplus to the Third Reich's requirements. Once one minority had been slaughtered wholesale, no further moral barrier stood in the path of the Holocaust: the dilemmas facing the Nazi leadership related only to timing and logistical feasibility.

For more than two years after war came, the priority of securing victory was held to require postponement of an absolute elimination of European Jewry. Between August 1939 and the summer of 1942, when the death camp programme achieved full capacity, the Nazis contented themselves with killing large numbers of people in many countries on an arbitrary and opportunistic basis. During the first months after German troops entered Poland, some 10,000 Poles were murdered—a mixture of Jews and non-Jews deemed inimical to German interests. Designated SS Einsatzgruppen—death squads—followed the armoured spearheads. Their commanders were granted generous discretion about selecting victims, which some exploited to eliminate prostitutes, gypsies and the mentally ill. Around 60,000 Polish Jewish soldiers were segregated from their fellow POWs and earmarked for later disposal; all of Poland's 1.7 million Jews were designated for resettlement in ghettos. Early in 1940, the Nazis embarked on the enforced removal of 600,000 Jews from areas of the country now incorporated in the Greater Reich; the deportees were transferred to the "General Government" rump, which was administered separately. Large numbers, displaced without provision for their shelter or feeding, perished within months.

At this stage, Nazi policy was still incoherent. There was much discussion about deportation: in May 1940 Himmler presented a memorandum to Hitler about the possibility of shipping Europe's Jews to Africa or Madagascar. The Reichsführer SS mentioned the radical alternative of the "Bolshevist method of the physical extermination of a people," but rejected this as "un-Germanic and impossible." It was agreed that as many

Jews as possible should perish in the course of the normal business of administering occupation, but there was no commitment to their systematic slaughter.

During the next two years, and especially after the invasion of Russia, Germans killed Jews at whim, on a scale largely determined by availability of manpower and resources. A German ordnance sergeant from a bakery company recalled: "I saw these people being rounded up and then just had to look away, as they were clubbed to death right before our eyes . . . A great many German soldiers, as well as Lithuanians, stood there watching. They did not express either assent or disapproval—they just stood, totally indifferent." A handful of German officers displayed the courage to protest: Col. Walter Bruns, an engineer who chanced upon a massacre of Jews while out riding near the Rumbuli forest in Latvia on 30 November 1941, submitted a formal report to Army Group North. He also made a personal visit to army headquarters at Angerburg to deliver a further copy. No formal response was forthcoming, save that the chief of staff urged that in future such killing "must be done with greater caution."

The Einsatzgruppen were relatively few and small; they achieved some impressive massacres, notably in Ukraine, but their victims were still numbered only in tens of thousands. Energetic efforts by the SS Mounted Brigade in the Pripet Marshes during early August 1941 accounted for 6,504 Jewish victims. The unit's final report for the month cited 15,878 killings, though the real total was probably over 25,000. The logistical difficulties of wholesale murder proved immense, even when labour-saving expedients were adopted, such as herding victims into mass graves before shooting them. At such a sluggish pace, the process of "solving Europe's Jewish problem" would require decades, and in the late summer of 1941 SS commanders began to demand a much more radical and comprehensive approach. In September, Einsatzgruppe C proposed working the Jews to death: "If we entirely dispense with the Jewish labour force, then the economic rebuilding of Ukrainian industry . . . is virtually impossible. There is only one possibility . . . the solution of the Jewish problem via the full-scale deployment of the Jewish labour force. That would bring with it the gradual liquidation of Jewry."

Late in July 1941, a new policy was adopted: confinement of eastern European Jews to ghettos, where they became easier to control and deploy for labour service, while freeing up outside accommodation. The Wehrmacht strongly supported this measure, because it resolved administrative difficulties in its rear areas. The SS extended the range of Jewish murder victims to include many more women and children, but after experiencing the practical difficulties of industrial killing, few SS officers yet felt able to accept a challenge as ambitious as exterminating the entire race. Through the winter of 1941–42 they focused upon packing the ghettos, then completing regional cleansing processes by killing all those Jews found outside them, most in rural areas. Ghetto living conditions were unspeakable: from August 1941 onwards, 5,500 Jews died each month from starvation and disease out of Warsaw's total ghetto population of 338,000, and mortality was comparable elsewhere.

Final victory in Russia was still assumed to be imminent. Until this came, with a consequent liberation of resources, most of the Nazi leadership favoured deferring a "Final Solution." Heinrich Himmler, however, was less patient: he saw swift eradication of Jews in the occupied territories both as a national priority and a means of extending his personal authority. He flaunted his mandate as Reichskommissar "for the strengthening of the German nation," even though at that stage Hitler had made no decision about "Germanisation" of occupied Soviet territory. It may sound trite to emphasise the centrality of the influence of the SS upon the Holocaust, but it is nonetheless necessary. The most powerful fiefdom in Nazi Germany pursued the extinction of the Jews almost heedless of its impact on the country's war making. As John Lukacs has observed, Himmler focused far more single-mindedly on this objective than did Hitler.

In September 1941, the Führer confirmed Himmler's victory in his contest with Alfred Rosenberg for authority over eastern Europe: the Reichsführer SS was given explicit licence to conduct ethnic cleansing in the east. This decision marked the onset of the Third Reich's systematic campaign of genocide. Amid expectations of looming victory, commitments were made that became significant impediments to Germany's war effort when faced with the rising spectre of defeat, yet they were never reversed. Himmler pursued the extermination of Jews with a concentration of purpose conspicuously absent from every other aspect of Nazi policy making. Any rational assessment of Germany's predicament in late 1941 demanded dedication to winning the war, above all against the Soviet Union. If this was achieved, the Third Reich could thereafter order its polity as it wished; if not, then National Socialism was doomed. But Himmler committed the SS to a task which could contribute nothing to German victory, and indeed diverted resources from its achievement.

Through the autumn and into the winter of 1941, the pace of slaughter accelerated: scores of towns and villages were systematically purged of Jews. In October, when a Soviet "stay-behind" commando unit blew up the Romanian army's newly established headquarters in Odessa, Romanian troops assisted by German SS men killed some 40,000 of its Jews. On 18 and 19 October, the SS murdered all 8,000 Jewish inhabitants of Mariupol, and a week later another 1,800 in Taganrog. Week after week the process continued, in towns the world had never heard of—Skadovsk and Feodosiya, Kertsh and Dzhankoy, Nikolayev and Kherson. Mental-asylum patients were killed as a matter of course, whatever their religious affiliation. The SS also shot large numbers of prisoners whom they identified as "of Asiatic appearance," and began the work of murdering gypsies, which became systematic in 1942. POW camps were combed for Russian Jews and commissars; those identified, at least 140,000 in all, were removed and shot. It seems important to emphasise that by the time the Final Solution was agreed, at least 2 million Soviet POWs had already been killed or allowed to die. All moral barriers to mass murder had been broken down, and ample precedent for wholesale killing established, before the major massacres of Jews were ordained.

In the winter of 1941, administrative confusion persisted about whether Jews capable of forced labour service should be kept alive. Local commanders adopted diverse policies: in Kaunas 1,608 men, women and children "ill or suspected of being infectious" were murdered on 26 September, followed by a further 1,845 in a "punishment operation" on 4 October, and 9,200 more after a new screening on 29 October. On 30 October, the head of the German civil administration in Slutsk in western Russia made a formal protest to the general commissioner in Minsk about the massacre of the city's Jews. "One simply could not do without the Jewish craftsmen," he said, "because they were indispensable for the maintenance of the economy . . . All vital enterprises would be paralysed with a single blow if all Jews were liquidated."

His complaints, he said, had been brushed aside by the commander of the police battalion carrying out the killings, who expressed astonishment "and explained that he had received instructions . . . to make the city free of Jews without exception, as they had also done in other cities. The cleansing had to take place on political grounds, and nowhere had economic factors so far played a role . . . During the action the city itself offered a horrible picture . . . The Jews, among them also craftsmen, were brutally mistreated in a frightfully barbarous way. One can no longer speak of a Jewish action, it appeared much more like a revolution." None of this, of course, deflected Himmler or his officers: on 29–30 November more than 10,000 inhabitants of the Riga ghetto were shot outside the city, and another 20,000 a week later. By December, most Jews in the Baltic states were dead; thousands of collaborators recruited by the Germans as "local voluntary troops" participated enthusiastically in the killings. For the rest of the war, Latvians, Lithuanians, Estonians and Ukrainians played an important part in implementing Himmler's Jewish extermination programme—over 300,000 were eventually enlisted as auxiliaries to the SS, men who might otherwise have credibly served in Hitler's armies.

The Wehrmacht was wholly complicit in Himmler's operations, even though the SS did most of the killing. On 10 August 1941, the Sixth Army commander, Walter von Reichenau, cited in an order the "necessary execution of criminal, Bolshevist and mainly Jewish elements" which the SS must carry out. Manstein described Jews on 20 November as "the middleman between the enemy at our backs and the remains of the Red Army." Karl-Heinrich von Stülpnagel of the Seventeenth Army cautioned his units on 30 July not to shoot civilians indiscriminately, but instead to concentrate upon "Jewish and communist inhabitants." The Wehrmacht routinely provided logistical support for SS massacres, together with troops to cordon killing fields. On many documented occasions, army units participated in shootings, despite orders from higher commanders against such sullying of soldierly honour. Soviet partisan activity provided a pretext for "security operations," such as that for which the orders issued by the Wehrmacht's 707th Division's commander in Belarus are preserved. "Jews," he wrote on 16 October 1941, "are the only support the partisans have for surviving now and over the winter. Their annihilation must therefore be carried out uncompromisingly." Without the Wehrmacht's active assistance, mass murder on the scale that took place in 1941–42 would have been impossible. By the end of 1941, at least half a million eastern European Jews were dead.

The elimination of European Jewry assumed an ever-higher priority on the Nazis' agenda: Hitler convinced himself that the August 1941 Atlantic Charter, together with America's looming entry into the war, were driven by Jewish influence on the United States government. This lent a new urgency to his determination to kill their coreligionists in Europe. During the months and years that followed, Germany's leader came to view this as an objective as important as military victory, and even as a precondition for achieving it. Attempts to discern rationality in Nazi strategy, especially from 1941 onwards, founder in the face of such a mind-set.

Peter Longerich, one of the more authoritative historians of the Holocaust, has convincingly argued that the Nazi leadership's commitment to executing the Final Solution through designated death camps was not made until the end of 1941: "The leadership at the centre and the executive organizations on the periphery radicalized one another through a reciprocal process." Construction of the first purpose-built extermination camp at Bełżec, near Lublin, began only on 1 November 1941. Longerich cites evidence that, until very late that year, key SS officers were still talking of mass deportations rather than extermination, and were chiefly preoccupied with how best to organise and mobilise Jews for slave labour. That autumn, anti-Jewish propaganda within the Reich was sharply increased, to prepare public opinion for the deportation of German Jews to the east. If the distinction sounds arcane between shipping the condemned to a wilderness where they were expected to starve and gassing them wholesale, it was significant in the evolution of the Holocaust.

When the U.S. commitment to the Allied cause became explicit, Hitler could no longer discern advantage in sparing Jews within his reach. "In autumn 1941," writes Longerich, "the Nazi leadership began to fight the war on all levels as a war 'against the Jews.' " The construction of gas chambers commenced at Chelmno, Bełżec, Auschwitz and elsewhere. Gas trucks had already been employed for the murder of mental patients in Germany and parts of the Nazi empire. Himmler welcomed wider use of such technology, not least to ease the psychological strain which mass shootings imposed on his SS. By autumn 1941, Zyklon B was killing selected prisoners at Auschwitz and elsewhere—though at that stage, most victims were non-Jews. Local initiatives by SS officers, rather than a coherent central directive, determined who died.

In mid-October 1941, mass deportations of Jews from the Reich began, with thousands being dispatched variously to Łódź, Riga, Kaunas and Minsk. Among the designated victims there were more than a few suicides, and in the light of events it is hard to suggest that those who took this course were ill-advised. Hans Michaelis was a retired lawyer in Charlottenburg. Just before being transported, he sent for his niece. "Maria," he said, "I don't have much time. What should I do? What is easiest, what's the most dignified? To live or to die? To suffer a terrible fate or to end one's own life?" His niece wrote: "We speak. We examine both possibilities. We ask ourselves what his late wife . . . would have advised. Again he grabs the clock." Then he said, "I have 50 hours left here, at most! . . . Thank God that my Gertrud died a normal death, before Hitler. What would I give for that! . . . Maria, see how time flies!" As at last they parted, she said, "Uncle Hans, you will know the right thing to do. Farewell." Hans Michaelis took poison.

A Berliner named Hilde Meikley watched the removal of local Jews: "Sadly I have to say that many people stood in the doorways voicing their pleasure as the wretched column went by. 'Just look at those cheeky Jews!' someone shouted. 'They're laughing now, but their last hour has come.' " The victims were permitted to carry 110 pounds of baggage apiece. All their valuables were seized at the departure stations, where body searches were conducted and passengers were required to pay fares. Luggage was loaded onto freight wagons, never to be seen again by its owners. Local authorities took possession of vacated housing, which was reallocated to eager new tenants. The rhetoric of Alfred Rosenberg, the minister for the occupied eastern territories, and Goebbels, acknowledging the fact of the deportations to the world, was uncompromising. Rosenberg told a November 1941 press conference: "Some six million Jews still live in the east, and this question can only be solved by a biological extermination of the whole of Jewry in Europe. The Jewish question will only be solved for Germany when the last Jew has left German territory, and for Europe when not a single Jew stands on the European continent as far as the Urals."

If the Nazis bore responsibility for the Holocaust, they were assisted in their crimes by some, if not most, of the regimes of occupied Europe. Anti-Semitism, albeit less homicidal than in Germany, was a commonplace phenomenon. Mihail Sebastian, a Jewish writer briefly conscripted into the Romanian army, noted the attitude of many of his fellow soldiers, which contributed to their acquiescence in Nazi dominance of Romania's polity: "Voichita Aurel, my comrade in the Twenty-First Infantry, said something yesterday about Captain Capsuneanu, something that sums up a whole Romanian style of politics: 'He's a real mean bastard who'll beat you and swear at you. But there's one good thing about him: he can't stand yids and lets us have a go at them too.'" Sebastian wrote: "That is precisely the consolation that the Germans offer the Czechs and Poles, and which they are prepared to offer the Romanians." The German occupation of France institutionalised a French anti-Semitism that was already widespread, and which the Vichy government was happy to make explicit.

SO MANY PROMINENT NAZIS spoke explicitly and publicly about their intentions towards the Jews that it remains remarkable that the Allied national leaderships were reluctant to accept their words at face value. Informed citizens in both Britain and America drew appropriate conclusions about what was happening, reinforced by eyewitness testimony from eastern Europe. Mrs. Blanche Dugdale, a passionate British crusader for Jewish interests, wrote a letter published in the *Spectator* that December: "In March 1942, Himmler visited Poland, and decreed that by the end of the year 50 per cent of the Jewish population should be 'exterminated' ... and the pace seems to have been hastened since. Now the German programme demands the disappearance of all Jews ... Mass-murders on a scale unheard-of since the dawn of civilization began immediately after the order was issued." Mrs. Dugdale gave an account of the deportations, identifying Bełżec, Sobibór and Treblinka as death camps. "Certain it seems that Polish Jewry will be beyond help if the murder-campaign cannot be stopped before the war ends." Helmuth von Moltke of the Abwehr informed the British by secret letter via Stockholm in March 1943: "At least nine-tenths of the [German] population do not know that we have killed hundreds of thousands of Jews. They go on believing they have just been segregated . . . farther to the east . . . If you told these people what has really happened they would answer, 'You are just a victim of British propaganda.'"

Within some Allied nations there was equivalence, or worse, in defining attitudes to the greatest of all Nazi persecutions. Anti-Semitism was etched deep into Russian history and attitudes: in Moscow at Easter 1942, for instance, one of countless rumours sweeping the city asserted that Jews had been committing ritual murders of Orthodox children—the ghastly old eastern European "blood libel" against the Jewish people. In 1944, the NKVD reported hearing people assert that "Hitler did a good job, beating up the Jews." The revelation of the death camps posed a dilemma for Moscow, which the Soviet authorities never entirely resolved. They could not applaud the Nazis' slaughter of the Jews, but one historian has called the Holocaust "an indigestible lump in the belly of the Soviet triumph." To acknowledge its enormity was to require a sharing of the Russian people's overpowering sense of victimhood, which they were most unwilling to concede. In Soviet correspondents' wartime dispatches, all references to explicitly Jewish suffering were excised by the censor. In 1945, when Russians heaped abuse on their defeated enemies, observant Germans noticed that almost the only charge not laid at their door was that of persecuting the Jews.

In Poland, where anti-Semitism was widespread, some people cited reports that Jews had welcomed the Red Army in September 1939 as evidence of their perfidy. When Jews in the Warsaw ghetto staged a brief and doomed revolt in 1943, a Polish nationalist underground paper wrote on 5 May: "During the Soviet occupation . . . Jews regularly stripped our soldiers of their arms, killed them, betrayed our community leaders, and openly crossed to the side of the occupier. [In one small town] which in 1939 was momentarily in the hands of the Soviets . . . Jews erected a triumphal arch for the Soviet troops to pass through and all wore red armbands and cockades. That was, and is, their attitude to Poland. Everyone in Poland should remember this." In the spring of 1944 some Jewish soldiers deserted from the Polish corps based in Scotland, citing disgust at anti-Semitism, which they said was no less apparent in the exile army than in their homeland.

Anglo-Saxons were not immune from such sentiments. The British soldier Len England expressed shock at the attitudes of many of his barrack-room comrades, of a kind later vividly portrayed in Irwin Shaw's description of U.S. Army service in his novel *The Young Lions*. England wrote: "Two of the most intelligent people I have yet met are confirmed Jew-baiters. The argument usually runs like this: where are the Jews in the army? There are none because they all have managed to get the soft jobs and have wangled out of conscription. In just the same way, the Jews were always the first to leave danger areas. The Jews hold the purse-strings, the country has been taken over by them. Individual Jews may be pleasant enough, but as a race they are the root of all evil."

Murray Mendelsohn, a U.S. Army engineer whose father had emigrated from Warsaw in 1914, was conscious of latent, if not active, anti-Semitism in his barrack room. His education and intelligence incurred the suspicion of his comrades, many of them former miners and construction workers. They nicknamed him "brain" without admiration, "Not because I was that smart, but by comparison. I learned to be very inconspicuous." When the men of Easy Company of the 506th Airborne cursed their hated first commander, Lieutenant Sobel, they did so as the "fucking Jew." As late as June 1945, when the concentration camps had been exposed to the world, an increasingly deranged Gen. George Patton denounced liberals who "believe that the displaced person is a human being, which he is not, and this applied particularly to the Jews, who are lower than animals."

Though Churchill denounced in the most passionate terms reports of the Nazi extermination programme, his government—like that of Franklin Roosevelt—was unwilling to accept large numbers of Jewish refugees, even if the Germans could be persuaded to release or trade them. When Americans were polled in November 1938 about whether they believed Jewish fugitives from Hitler should be granted special immigration rights to enter the United States, 23 percent said yes, 77 percent no. In August 1944 some 44 percent of Australians who were asked if they would accept a settlement of Jewish refugees in the empty north of their country rejected the notion, against 37 percent in favour. As late as December 1944, another survey of American opinion on the admission of Jews to the United States showed that 61 percent thought they should be given no greater priority than other applicants. A British Colonial Office official commented cynically on a December 1942 report about the death camps: "Familiar stuff. The Jews have spoilt their case by laying it on too thick for years past." A Foreign Office official likewise deplored special pleading by "these wailing Jews."

The Polish underground worker Jan Karski made his way to London in the autumn of 1942 after a fantastic odyssey across Europe, to provide an eyewitness account not only of his country's sufferings, but explicitly of conditions in the Jewish ghettos, and of the extraordinary achievement he claimed of having penetrated the Nazi death camp at Bełżec. While he was received courteously enough by the Polish exile prime minister, Gen. Władysław Sikorski, by Foreign Secretary Anthony Eden and later in Washington by President Roosevelt, he was afflicted by a dismal sense of awareness that the horrors he described somehow lost their force and magnitude in safe, unoccupied Allied capitals. "In London these things bulked small," he wrote. "London was the hub of a vast military wheel, the spokes of which were made up of billions of dollars, armadas of bombers and ships and staggering armies that had suffered great loss. Then, too, people asked where did Polish sacrifice rank next to the immeasurable heroism, sacrifice and sufferings of the Russian people? What was the share of Poland in this titanic undertaking? Who were the Poles? . . . We Poles had no luck in this war." Karski was discouraged by his own leaders from over-emphasising the Jewish persecution, lest it should detract from the force of his account of the plight of Poland as a whole.

Arthur Schlesinger, relatively highly informed by his work for the Office of Strategic Services, wrote of his own state of knowledge about the fate of Europe's Jews in 1944: "Most of us were still thinking of an increase in persecution rather than a new and barbaric policy of genocide . . . I cannot find colleagues who recall a moment of blazing revelation about the Final Solution." Likewise the British intelligence officer Noel Annan: "It took some time . . . for the enormity of Germany's crimes against the Jews to sink in. In intelligence we knew of the gas ovens, but not of the scale, the thoroughness, the bureaucratic efficiency with which Jews had been hunted down and slaughtered. No one at the end of the war, as I recollect, realised that the figure of Jewish dead ran into millions." In the entire archive of Britain's wartime secret service, no mention occurs—or none at least which survives—about persecution of the Jews or the Holocaust, probably because the SIS was never invited to investigate these issues. Contrary to much popular modern mythology, the operational difficulties of bombing transport links to the death camps would have been very great, especially in 1942 when most of the Holocaust killings took place. Allied leaders considered reports of Jewish suffering in the context of atrocities being committed against occupied populations all over Europe.

The American diplomat George Ball wrote later: "Perhaps we were so preoccupied with the squalid menace of the war we did not focus on this unspeakable ghastliness. It may also be that the idea of mass extermination was so far beyond the traditional comprehension of most Americans that we instinctively refused to believe in its existence." Many Europeans and Americans who had been appalled by reported German atrocities in Belgium in 1914 concluded angrily after the First World War that they had allowed themselves to be fooled by Allied propaganda, for it emerged that the killings of civilians had been exaggerated. A world war later, the Western powers were determined not to be similarly deluded again. It was to the perverse credit of British and American decency that many people were reluctant to suppose their enemies as barbaric as later evidence showed them to have been. George Orwell wrote in 1944: "'Atrocities' had come to be looked on as synonymous with 'lies.' But the stories about German concentration camps were atrocity stories: therefore they were lies—so reasoned the average man." Surveys found that most of Roosevelt's nation continued to regard the Germans as fundamentally decent and peaceful folk, led astray by their leaders. As late as May 1945, when newsreels of the concentration camps had been shown around the world, 53.7 percent of American respondents told pollsters they thought only a small part of the German people were "naturally cruel and brutal."

None of the above diminishes in the smallest degree the responsibility of the Nazis, and of the German people, for the Holocaust. But it should be acknowledged that, even when overwhelming evidence became available, the Allied nations were slow to respond to the death camps. Though little could have been done to save their inmates, any more than for the millions of Russian prisoners who died in German hands, an insouciance pervades Allied documentation of the period which does scant credit to Britain or the United States. Even if Jews were not persecuted in the Anglo-Saxon societies, they were not widely loved. There remained until 1945 a resolute official unwillingness to assess their tragedy in a separate dimension from the sufferings of Hitler's other captives, and of the occupied societies of Europe. Such insensitivity merits understanding, but rightly troubles posterity.

IN THE WINTER OF 1941-42, a large number of Jewish deportees from Germany were shot immediately on their arrival at eastern destinations, but these killings were carried out at the discretion of local SS commanders; no general order was issued, decreeing either their preservation or their extinction. Late in November there was an eccentric intervention by Himmler himself, ordering a temporary halt to the killing of Reich Jews as distinct from easterners, though this check was soon reversed. To a remarkable degree, regional autonomy and logistical convenience— shortage of accommodation and food or, contrarily, of labour—still decided who lived and who died; but large-scale killings of eastern Jews, especially those unfit for work, continued through the winter. In Serbia, thousands of Jews and gypsies were executed in retaliation for partisan activity; local German commanders knew that prioritising such people as victims ensured Berlin's approval.

Only one further step remained to be taken by the Nazi leadership: to order a transition from inflicting death arbitrarily and regionally towards imposing it by direct order from the top, in pursuit of an agreed policy of total extermination. In a speech on 12 December 1941, following his declaration of war on the United States, Hitler made plain his commitment to the destruction of the Jews, in supposed retaliation for their responsibility for the conflict. The implementation of the genocide programme was entrusted to the SS's deputy chief, Reinhard Heydrich, to whom Himmler later paid unstinting posthumous tribute: "He was a character of rare purity with an intelligence of penetrating greatness and clarity. He was filled with an incorruptible sense of justice. Truthful and decent people could always rely on his chivalrous sentiment and humane understanding." These virtues were skilfully concealed on 20 January 1942, when at the Wannsee conference Heydrich mapped the road to the death camps. There is no record that he articulated an explicit commitment to murder all of Europe's Jews, not least because the logistical obstacles remained formidable. Starvation still had a useful part to play; where convenient, victims could be worked to death. But the intended outcome was no longer in doubt: the "Final Solution" of the Jewish problem would be accomplished in stages, only the last of which must await the war's end.

There was considerable detailed discussion about the construction of extermination camps and the virtues of gas. The principal outcome of the conference was agreement that the SS would in future exercise absolute authority over the fate of Europe's Jews; that no other Reich agency could appeal against its decisions; and that henceforward, policy would be directed towards the overarching aim of cleansing the entire Nazi empire. This was implemented with remarkable speed: in mid-March 1942, almost three-quarters of all those who perished in the Holocaust were still alive; eleven months later, the same proportion were dead.

A ministerial adviser enquired of SS-Brigadeführer Odilo Globocnik whether it might not be prudent to burn the bodies of the Nazis' Jewish victims, rather than bury them: "After us there might come a generation that doesn't understand the whole business!" Globocnik replied, "Gentlemen, if there is ever a generation after us so feeble and weak-kneed that it doesn't understand our great achievement, the whole of National Socialism will have been in vain . . . Bronze tablets should be buried stating that it was we who had the courage to carry out this momentous and so necessary task." Yet it is striking that, while Nazi leaders repeatedly and publicly averred their commitment to eliminating Europe's Jews, detailed implementation of the Final Solution remained a closely guarded secret: even Hitler and his associates feared the global response, and especially the impact upon their own people, of public revelation of the death camps.

In the spring of 1942 Himmler refined a scheme to exploit concentration camp labour for both armaments production and the private profit of the SS. However, systemic incompetence and corruption ensured that little of value to the Reich was produced under SS auspices; on the contrary, the camp programme was a drain on Germany's transport, manpower and general economic resources. Though millions of prisoners were put to work, mostly of a primitive kind, the SS never seriously attempted to reconcile its desire to extract useful services from its slaves with a consequent need to treat them with minimal humanity. Because its foremost aspiration was to produce mass death, it failed to produce much else save a ghastly harvest of human hair, gold teeth and discarded clothing.

At the beginning of June 1942, amid further mass deportations from the districts of Lublin and Galicia, the SS extended the policy of dispatching victims immediately on their arrival in camp reception areas. The concept of resettling Jews in the east had been abandoned, although a figleaf of pretence was sustained. Germany's leaders now anticipated that their summer offensive in Russia would end the war, and thus the usefulness of Jewish slave labour. The Slovakian government acquiesced in the shipment of 50,000 of its citizens to Auschwitz. A programme of deportations of western European Jews was introduced, conducted in collaboration with local security forces—the Nazi empire lacked resources to cleanse the occupied territories without the assistance of indigenous bureaucracies and law-enforcement agencies. Among the explicit purposes of the German government was to ensure that as many foreign regimes as possible were complicit in the massacre of Jews. In this, it achieved considerable success.

Posterity is fascinated by the ease with which the Nazis found so many ordinary men—to borrow the title of Christopher Browning's classic study—willing to murder in cold blood vast numbers of innocents, of all ages and both sexes. Yet there is ample evidence in modern experience that many people are ready to kill others to order, once satisfied that this fulfils the wishes of those whose authority they accept. Hundreds of thousands of Russians were complicit in the deaths of millions of their fellow countrymen at the behest of Stalin and Beria, before the Holocaust was thought of. Germany's generals may not themselves have killed civilians, but they were happy to acquiesce in and even enthuse about others doing so.

Postwar testimony shows that implementation of the Final Solution required only a modicum of patience and practice to overcome the scruples of some novice mass murderers. On 13 July 1942, Reserve Police Battalion 101 arrived in a convoy of trucks at the Polish village of Josefów, whose inhabitants included 1,800 Jews. Mostly middle-aged reservists from Hamburg, on their arrival they were ordered to gather around their commander, fifty-three-year-old Maj. Wilhelm Trapp, a career policeman affectionately known to the unit as "Papa Trapp." In a choking voice and with tears in his eyes, he told them they had a most unwelcome assignment, ordered at the highest level: to arrest all Jews in the village, remove to a camp men of working age, and kill the remainder. He said this was justified by Jewish involvement with partisans, and the Jews' instigation of the American boycott that had injured Germany. He then invited any man who felt unable to perform this unpleasant duty to step aside. Several policemen indeed declined to participate, and after the killings began their number increased. At least twenty were permitted to return to barracks.

Yet a sufficiency of others stayed to do the business: one man later recalled that his first victim vainly begged for mercy, on the grounds that he was a decorated World War I veteran. Georg Kageler, a thirty-seven-year-old tailor, killed his initial batch easily enough, but then fell into conversation with a mother and daughter from Kassel, who were destined to die next. He appealed to his platoon leader to be excused, and was sent to guard the marketplace while others did his share of shooting. Another man who quit during the slaughter explained that he became distressed by the poor marksmanship of a comrade: "He always aimed his gun too high, producing terrible wounds in his victims. In many cases the entire backs of victims' heads were torn off, so that the brains sprayed all over. I simply couldn't watch it any longer." One member of the battalion, Walter Zimmerman, later gave evidence: "In no case can I remember that anyone was forced to continue participating in the executions when he declared that he was no longer able to . . . There were always some comrades who found it easier to shoot Jews than did others, so that the respective commando leaders never had difficulty finding suitable shooters."

Christopher Browning shows that during the weeks and months that followed, most of Reserve Police Battalion 101's members overcame initial revulsion and became hardened killers. To be sure, they resorted to alcohol to render their duties tolerable, but they performed them with a growing accession of brutality. Lt. Hartwig Gnade, for instance, degenerated from a mere murderer into a sadist: at a mass killing at Łomazy on 16 August, while he waited for 1,700 Jews to finish digging their own mass grave, he selected twenty elderly, heavily bearded Jews and made them crawl naked before him. As they did so, he screamed at his squad, " 'Where are my non-commissioned officers? Don't you have any clubs yet?' The NCOs went to the edge of the forest, fetched themselves clubs, and vigorously beat the Jews with them." By the time Battalion 101 completed its contribution to the Holocaust in November 1943, its 500 men had shot at least 38,000 Jews, and herded a further 45,000 aboard trains for Treblinka. Browning found no evidence that any sanction was imposed upon those who refused to kill; in one of the most highly educated societies in Europe, it was easy to find men willing to murder those whom their rulers defined as state enemies, without employing duress.

Many Jews in their last moments invoked the Almighty as their refuge and sought His help as killers descended upon their communities. Nineteen-year-old Ephrahim Bleichman's uncle Moshe was shot by Polish gendarmes after fresh meat was found in his house, and his cousin Brucha was killed by scavengers who wanted her fresh bread. Young Bleichman thought: "If this tragedy was God's will, nothing could be done. Yet my family . . . depended on God, not man to rectify the situation. I could neither abide by their philosophy, nor dispute it. The propaganda machine combined with systematic harassment cowed many of us into apathy. [They] felt powerless." Ephrahim took to the forest when he heard that a German deportation was imminent, and survived in hiding for many months. "We shared the forest with owls, snakes, wild hogs and deer. On windy nights, the tree branches made strange noises. The shadows of bushes resembled intruders ready to pounce on us. The natural movements of animals made us always worry that enemies were afoot. It took us a long time to accustom ourselves to the nights." By the summer of 1942, all Soviet Jews in areas under Nazi control had been killed. Thereafter, even as Germany's military predicament worsened, the pace of slaughter quickened. There were wholesale deportations from Greece and Bulgaria in 1943. The Warsaw ghetto rising in April that year provoked intensified persecution in Poland, Holland, Belgium, France, Croatia and Slovakia.

MANY GREAT TESTIMONIES by victims of the Holocaust have been preserved, but one of the most astonishing was revealed to the world only sixty years after its author's death. Irène Némirovsky was born in Kiev in 1903, the daughter of a rich banker who had translated himself from the Ukrainian ghettos and pogroms to a large mansion in St. Petersburg. She grew up in lonely luxury, travelling regularly with her family to France. They fled the revolution in 1917, enduring considerable hardships before reaching Paris two years later, where her father rebuilt his fortune. Irène had been writing since she was fourteen. In 1927, she published her first novella; by the outbreak of war she was an established French literary figure, author of nine novels, one of which had been filmed, and married with two daughters. In 1940, when the Germans occupied Paris, she retreated to a rented house in the village of Issy-l'Evêque, in Saône-et-Loire. There, in the following year, she embarked upon what she intended to become a trilogy about the war, on the epic scale of *War and Peace*. She had few illusions about her own likely fate, and wrote despairingly in 1942: "Just let it be over—one way or the other!" Though she had converted to Catholicism, there was no escape from the Nazi blight upon her race: on 13 July she was arrested by French police and deported to Auschwitz, to be murdered at Birkenau on 17 August. Her husband was killed shortly afterwards.

Némirovsky had completed the first two volumes of her remarkable work. Her daughters, who survived the war in hiding, miraculously preserved her manuscripts, written in a tiny script reflecting the author's shortage of ink and paper. The girls could not bring themselves to read this sole memorial of their mother until more than half a century had passed. Then one of them, Denise, painstakingly transcribed the manuscript with the aid of a magnifying glass, and hesitantly passed it to a publisher. *Suite française* was published in France in 2004 and became a worldwide sensation. Its first volume describes the French experience of June 1940, the plight of millions of refugees. The second focuses upon the relationship between a German soldier of the occupying army and a Frenchwoman. The pathos is extraordinary, of a Jew doomed to die portraying with acute sympathy the sentiments and behaviour of those who would become her murderers. Her account of French society under occupation, its sufferings, manifestations of quiet courage and also of moral betrayal, forms one of the most remarkable literary legacies of the war. Cool, wry analysis was matched by a warm compassion, displayed as she herself awaited a death in which she knew that the French people were complicit with the Germans. Némirovsky is now recognised as one of the most remarkable witnesses of her time and of her race's tragedy.

WHILE A VAST NUMBER of Germans were directly or indirectly complicit in the massacre of the Jews, a small minority displayed high courage in succouring the persecuted, at mortal risk to themselves. A young Berlin shoemaker named August Kossman, a communist, hid Irma Simon, her husband and son in his little apartment for two years. The teenager Erich Neumann's mother, a café owner, sheltered a young Jewish family friend in Charlottenburg for five months. A Jewish fugitive named Max Krakauer compiled a list at the end of the war of all those Berliners who had assisted his long struggle to escape death, and recalled sixty-six names. Rita Knirsch's mother sheltered a young man named Solomon Striem, a family friend, saying to her daughter, "Rita, you must tell nobody about this! . . . I cannot just turn this poor hunted man away." Such extraordinarily courageous people sustained a shred of the honour of German civilisation.

In 1944, when the Nazis occupied Hungary and Slovakia, it was the turn of most of their surviving 750,000 Jews to climb aboard transports, to perish in the last massive killings of the Holocaust. Thereafter, as Allied victory loomed, Jews who had survived thus far found their prospects improved: more people were willing to risk hiding them. But most of those whom Hitler had chosen as his preeminent victims were already dead.

CHAPTER TWENTY-ONE

EUROPE BECOMES A BATTLEFIELD

ON 3 NOVEMBER 1943, Hitler announced to his generals a strategic decision that no further reinforcements would be dispatched to the Eastern Front. He reasoned that German forces still held a wide buffer zone protecting the Reich from the Russians; he must reinforce Italy, where Anglo-American armies were established, and France, where they were certain soon to land. Yet even as he sought to address the western threats, on 14 January 1944 the Russians renewed their assaults in the north. Strategic retreat was the obvious response, because the German threat to Leningrad was no longer credible; but the Führer, after some vacillation, once more insisted that his forces should hold their positions. "Hitler could think only in lines, not in movements," sighed a German officer, Rolf-Helmut Schröder, long afterwards. "If he had allowed his generals to do their job, so much could have been different." The Russians broke through, fragmenting the German line; on 27 January, Stalin declared Leningrad officially liberated. Hitler sent Model, his favourite general, to retrieve the situation, but within a month the new commander pulled back more than a hundred miles, to prepared positions along the river Neva, Lake Peipus and Lake Pskov. Then the spring thaw imposed its usual check on operations.

Between January and March repeated Soviet thrusts made little progress. The weather imposed difficulties on all the combatants, but afflicted the Russians most, because they were attempting to advance. On 11 February, Zhukov persuaded Stalin to approve a new attempt at encirclement. This time he sought to cut off six German divisions on the west bank of the Dnieper between two Soviet bridgeheads. The manoeuvre was eventually successful, and earned Ivan Konev a marshal's star, but on 17 February, 30,000 German troops broke out; yet again, the Wehrmacht demonstrated the ferocity with which it could respond to desperate circumstances.

Farther south, through March three Ukrainian *fronts* battered their way westwards. The German commanders in their path, Kleist and Manstein, defied Berlin's explicit injunctions by conducting major withdrawals to save threatened formations from destruction. Hitler responded by sacking both field marshals, replacing them with Model and the brutish Ferdinand Schörner, whom he deemed to have the ruthlessness indispensable to the times. Schörner mounted a stubborn defence of the Crimea against his own judgement, but was eventually obliged to accept the inevitable: on 12 May 27,000 survivors of the garrison's 150,000 men were evacuated by sea. The Russians had held Sevastopol for 250 days, but the Germans abandoned the fortress after defending it for only 7.

Capt. Nikolai Belov wrote from the front in mid-April: "Everything is melting. There will be a terrible amount of mud here, and it won't clear up till June." That spring, the condition of the Russian people improved a little. The Luftwaffe could spare few aircraft to bomb cities and civilians and in many places German prisoners were put to work, clearing debris. Across thousands of square miles of contested territory, soldiers and civilians picked a path between wrecked vehicles, abandoned trenches, uncleared mines and burnt-out villages. In communities clinging to the precipice of survival on a daily ration of ten ounces of bread, local people grudged food to German POWs, but admitted that they were good workers. The NKVD and SMERSH—"the Soviet bacillus of mistrust," in Catherine Merridale's phrase—conducted a ruthless hunt for alleged traitors, collaborators and spies in areas that had been occupied by the Wehrmacht. In Chernigov, for instance, during February the bodies of four hanged traitors, one of them a woman, swung for days from a gallows in the central square.

Kiev's inhabitants warned visitors to beware of some local girls: "They slept with Germans for a piece of sausage." A steady stream of refugees returned to the city, pushing their pathetic property on carts and wheelbarrows. Trams began to run again, some shops and cinemas reopened; water could be drawn at street hydrants, and even electricity became sporadically available. But long queues waited hours for a chance to purchase any commodity, and the streets remained uncleaned. Nazi propaganda posters, images of "Hitler the Liberator," still clung to some walls. Destitution was the common condition of tens of millions of Russians: when three little street urchins approached the *Pravda* correspondent Lazar Brontman on a street in Yelsk, he expected them to plead for money or food. Instead, they asked, "Uncle, have you got a little pencil, by any chance? At school we have nothing to write with." Brontman gave them a pencil. "They forgot even to thank me and disappeared hurriedly down the street, staring at their new acquisition, and apparently arguing about who should be its owner."

In May 1944, 2.2 million German troops confronted the Russians; Hitler derived comfort from the fact that the enemy was still 560 miles from Berlin at the westernmost point of the front. He believed the main Soviet summer effort would come in northern Ukraine, and apportioned his strength accordingly. But he was wrong: the objectives of Zhukov's impending Operation Bagration, the most spectacular Soviet offensive of the war, lay in the zone defended by Army Group Centre. Scheduled to commence in June, its scale reflected the enormous resources now available to the Red Army. Some 2.4 million men, 5,200 tanks and 5,300 aircraft would make an initial thrust towards Minsk; in the second phase, the 2nd Baltic and 1st Ukrainian *fronts* would punch forward on both flanks, exploiting the breakthrough. Bagration was hugely ambitious, but at last the Red Army's capabilities and the Wehrmacht's vulnerability rendered such strokes possible.

Just praise has been lavished upon the ingenuity and success of British and American deception operations in World War II, but less attention has been paid to the matching achievement of Soviet *maskirovka*, literally "camouflage." This became progressively more sophisticated in 1943, and attained its zenith in deluding the enemy about the objectives of Bagration. Large resources were committed to building dummy tanks, guns and installations, to persuade the Germans that the main Russian thrust would come in northern Ukraine, where fake roads and crossings were also created. Meanwhile, Soviet formations facing Army Group Centre maintained static defensive deployments; reinforcements moved up only by night under rigorous blackout, and until the last moment were held thirty to sixty miles behind the front. Zhukov's intentions were revealed on a strict need-to-know basis to only a handful of senior officers. The Germans identified 60 percent of the Soviet forces facing Army Group Centre, but missed a vital guards tank army, and supposed they would meet only 1,800 tanks and self-propelled guns, instead of the real 5,200. The Wehrmacht's eastern intelligence chief, the highly regarded Reinhard Gehlen, was entirely misled by the Russian *maskirovka*, as skilful and significant as similar Anglo-American operations before D-Day. The collapse of Hitler's residual illusions in the east waited only upon Russian readiness to strike.

Around the world that spring, cynicism persisted about the modest Anglo-American contribution to the struggle, compared with that of the Soviets. The Polish corps commander in Italy, Gen. Władysław Anders, wrote gloomily in mid-April: "The course of the war is still the same; the Red Army continues to gain victories and the British are either being defeated, as in Burma, or, together with the Americans, have stuck fast in Italy." The Western Allied invasion of Normandy is customarily described as the Second Front; yet in southern Europe around one-tenth of Hitler's army, including some of its best formations, was already embattled on a mountain line south of Rome and on the coast farther north. Successive Allied attacks on German positions around Monte Cassino were characterised by lack of coordination, imagination, and indeed competence. The sixth-century Benedictine monastery was battered into rubble, thousands of tons of bombs and shells were expended, and many British, Indian, New Zealand and Polish lives were lost, but still the Germans held on.

The Anglo-American corps that landed on the coast farther north at Anzio in January, in fulfilment of Churchill's personal vision, was confined to a narrow perimeter which the Germans attacked fiercely and repeatedly. "So back we go to World War I," wrote a young officer of a Scottish regiment holding the line there. "Oozing thick mud. Tank hulks. The cold, God, the cold. Graves marked by a helmet, gashed with shrapnel. Shreds of barbed wire. Trees like broken fishbones . . ." The routines of trench life and incessant bombardment dulled men's senses. "Efficiency in general and combat efficiency in particular suffer when individuals remain too long and too constantly under the gun," wrote Lt. Col. Jack Toffey of the U.S. Army. Behind the front, existence under siege became bizarrely domesticated: "This beachhead is the craziest place I have ever seen," a U.S. signals officer wrote to his brother in New Jersey. "The boys have their own private horses, chickens, livestock, bicycles and everything else that the civilians left." Some men planted vegetable gardens.

In February, the Germans launched a massive counterattack on the perimeter. "I never saw so many people killed around me before in all my life," said an Irish Guards corporal. An NCO, watching as swine snuffled around the bodies of the dead in no-man's-land, mused bitterly, "Is this what we are fighting for, to be eaten by pigs?" The Germans found the experience of Anzio as tough as the Allies did. "Spirits are not particularly high since 4½ years of war start to get on your nerves," wrote one of Kesselring's soldiers with some understatement. Another man observed on 28 January that he had been unable to get his boots off for a week: "The air roars and whistles. Shells explode all around us." The February assault cost the Germans 5,400 casualties, and their army log reported: "It has become very difficult to evacuate the wounded. All ambulances, even the armoured ones, have been lost, making it necessary to use assault guns and Tiger tanks." Some Allied units broke, streaming in flight towards the rear—and so too did several German ones, in the face of annihilatory U.S. and British artillery fire. The Allies expended 158,000 rounds during the February battles, ten for each one fired by the Wehrmacht.

Meanwhile farther south, though the Allies were still pinned in the mountains, their foes found nothing to celebrate. The German corps commander at Cassino, Gen. Fridolin von Senger und Etterlin, told an aide: "The rotten thing is to keep fighting and fighting and to know all along that we have lost this war . . . Optimism is the elixir of life for the weak." Von Senger, a rare and indisputable "good German," soldiered on like the fine professional he was. But his men endured hell under Allied bombing and shelling, which levelled the town below as well as the monastery on the mountain. Explosions flung men about like "scraps of paper." A German lieutenant described the March air attacks: "We could no longer see each other. All we could do was to touch and feel the next man. The blackness of night enveloped us and on our tongues was the taste of burnt earth." Yet as clouds of dust subsided and the Allied infantry and tanks began to advance, still the Germans fought back. Craters and rubble created by the bombing obstructed the attackers, not the defenders. "Unfortunately we are fighting the best soldiers in the world—what men!" Alexander wrote ruefully to Brooke on 22 March.

The breakthrough in Italy, when it came, was too late and too incomplete to promote triumphalism: on 12 May Alexander launched his first intelligently planned attack, with Allied forces making two simultaneous thrusts. Deception persuaded Kesselring to fear a new amphibious landing behind his front and thus to hold back his reserves. Gen. Alphonse Juin's men of the French Expeditionary Corps played a prominent role in overrunning the Hitler Line southwest of Cassino, while Polish forces overcame the defences north of the monastery. The Americans attacked on the left, just inland from the sea. The Germans, their front broken, began a general retreat northwards. On 23 May Alexander ordered a breakout from the Anzio beachhead, besieged for four months. Many German units were reduced to one-third strength or less. "My heart bleeds when I look at my beautiful battalion," one CO wrote to his wife. "See you soon, I hope, in better days."

Operation Diadem, as the May offensive was code-named, offered the Allies their only opportunity between 1943 and 1945 to achieve the comprehensive defeat of Kesselring's armies in Italy, by cutting off their retreat. The consequences of Gen. Mark Clark's disdain for this objective, because of his obsession with gaining the personal glory of taking Rome, has passed into the legend of the war; his disobedience of orders emphasised his unfitness as an army commander. Alexander, a weak commander-in-chief, was not the man to control the anglophobic Clark, and himself bore significant responsibility for Allied sluggishness in exploiting Diadem. When the Italian capital fell on 4 June, Kesselring made good his withdrawal to a strong new defensive position, the Gothic Line, on a northwesterly axis anchored in the Apennines between Spezia, on the west coast, and Pesaro, on the east.

But it seems just to measure the disappointments the Allies experienced in Italy during June 1944 alongside those suffered by their armies elsewhere: the Wehrmacht displayed consistent skill and determination in escaping from encirclements on both the Eastern and Western Fronts. Again and again the Russians trapped German armies, only to see them break out. If Clark had closed the Italian roads leading north, Kesselring's retreating forces would probably have smashed through anyway. The failure of Diadem to translate tactical into strategic success was matched a few weeks later by the escape of substantial German forces through the Falaise Gap in Normandy, and by American unwillingness to cut off von Rundstedt's withdrawal from the Bulge in January 1945.

In Italy, the Allies had to content themselves with escaping from the miseries of the winter stalemate and advancing 250 miles. Once it became clear that decisive victory in the theatre remained unattainable, to Churchill's fury the Americans insisted upon winding down the campaign: they withdrew six U.S. and French divisions to join the battle for France. For the last eight months of the war, in Washington's eyes the only merit of residual Italian operations was that they engaged twenty German divisions which would otherwise have been defending the Reich against Eisenhower or Zhukov.

HITLER RECEIVED NEWS of the Italian retreat with uncharacteristic fatalism. In the late spring of 1944 he knew that within weeks his armies must face a major Russian offensive. It was vital first to repulse the Anglo-American invasion of France, which was plainly imminent. If this could be achieved, it was unlikely that the Western Allies could mount a new assault on the Channel coast before 1945; most of the German forces in the west could be shifted to the Russian front, dramatically improving the prospects of repelling Stalin's offensive. If this was an implausible scenario, as Germany's generals thought, it was by nurturing such hopes that Hitler rationalised his strategy. Everything hinged upon the outcome of Eisenhower's invasion attempt.

On the Allied side, there was a matching awareness of the stakes. A comparison of paper strengths suggested that the Anglo-Americans must prevail, above all because of their overwhelming air power. But amphibious operations in the Mediterranean had done nothing to promote complacency: in Sicily, and again at Salerno and Anzio, forces had landed in chaos, and come within a hair's breadth of disaster. The British had always been apprehensive about fighting a big battle in France: when Lt. Gen. Sir Frederick Morgan began his task as chief Allied planner for D-Day in 1943, he found it "evident that the project was not highly regarded by the War Office save as a high-grade training exploit . . . The British entered upon this expedition from the start with the utmost reluctance and that is to put the matter very mildly." In May 1944, Churchill and Brooke were still scarred by the shambles of Anzio.

The American and British air chiefs were also hostile. Believing themselves close to achieving Germany's defeat by strategic bombing, they bitterly resented the diversion of their aircraft to invasion support. Churchill had his own objections to bombing French rail links because of the inevitable civilian casualties, displaying a sensitivity that disgusted Bomber Command's C-in-C Sir Arthur Harris: "Personally I couldn't have given a damn if I killed Frenchmen. They should have been fighting the war for themselves. But I was being bullied all the time by Winston." Roosevelt, Marshall and Eisenhower overruled the prime minister. In the course of the war, some 70,000 French people were killed by Allied bombs: "collateral damage" in France thus included almost one-third more civilians accidentally killed than the British suffered from the Luftwaffe's deliberate assault on their island. Bombing played a critical role in slowing the German buildup after D-Day, but the price was high.

If the peoples of the Allied nations were impatient for the invasion of France, some of those who had to carry it out displayed less eagerness: British soldiers who had served for years in North Africa and Italy resented the call to risk their lives again in Normandy. They felt that it was somebody else's turn. "Who else is fighting this war?" demanded bitter soldiers of the 51st Highland Division, which was "softened, rather than hardened" by six months' training in England after its return from the Mediterranean, in the opinion of one of its senior officers. Among other Mediterranean veterans, "3rd Royal Tanks were virtually mutinous before D-Day," their brigade major, Anthony Kershaw, wrote later. "They painted the walls of their barracks in Aldershot with slogans such as 'No Second Front,' and had it not been for their new commanding officer—the best CO of an armoured regiment that I met during the war—I really think they might have mutinied in fact."

Few British units that had fought in the Mediterranean performed impressively during the northwest Europe campaign, and this seems unsurprising; they looked askance at millions of other British and American soldiers who had thus far escaped combat. On D-Day, thirty months after Pearl Harbor, half the U.S. Army's 8 million men had yet to deploy overseas, and many more had still to see action. The 24th Infantry Division, for instance, spent nineteen months performing garrison duties in Hawaii, then a further seven months in Australia training for jungle warfare; some of its men were prewar regular soldiers who became eligible for return to the United States before the formation had seen a single day of battle. While the Russians had been fighting continuously for three years, less than a dozen formations of the U.S. Army had fought the Germans. Many British soldiers had likewise been training in England since 1940: statistically, in May 1944, less than half of Churchill's army had fired a shot in anger, when account is taken of troops fulfilling support and garrison functions which did not involve combat. If the campaign Montgomery's forces afterwards fought proved arduous and bloody, it was brief in comparison with the struggle on other fronts.

Only relentless American pressure on Britain's leadership enforced the D-Day commitment. This rendered it ironic that the British secured for themselves the initial invasion commands: Montgomery directed British and U.S. ground forces, Adm. Sir Bertram Ramsay the fleet and Air Chief Marshal Trafford Leigh-Mallory the air armada. Although Dwight Eisenhower was supreme commander, Montgomery deluded himself that he might retain operational control of the Allied armies all the way to Berlin, with his American boss as a figurehead; the little general's unfailing insensitivity caused him to cling to this ambition until the last months of the war.

Meticulous planning and immense armaments promised Operation Overlord's success, but the hazards of weather and the skill of the German army fed apprehension in many British and American breasts. The consequences of failure must be appalling: civilian morale would plummet on both sides of the Atlantic; senior commanders would have to be sacked and replaced; the prestige of the Western Allies, so long derided by Stalin for feebleness, would be grievously injured, likewise the authority of Roosevelt and Churchill. Even after three years' attrition in the east, the German army remained a formidable fighting force. It was vital that Eisenhower should confront von Rundstedt's sixty divisions in the west with superior combat power. Yet the invaders were supported by such a vast logistical and support "tail" that, even when they reached their maximum strength in 1945, they would deploy only sixty American and twenty British and Canadian combat divisions. Air power, together with massive armoured and artillery strength, were called upon to compensate for inadequate infantry numbers.

Churchill and Roosevelt deserved their nations' gratitude for delaying D-Day until 1944, when their own resources had become so large, and those of Hitler were so shrunken. Allied losses in the ensuing continental campaign were a fraction of what they must have been had an invasion taken place earlier. For the young men who made the assault on 6 June 1944, however, such grand truths meant nothing: they recognised only the mortal peril each one must face to breach Hitler's Atlantic Wall. The invasion began with drops by one British and two American airborne divisions on the night of 5 June. The landings were chaotic but achieved their objectives, confusing the Germans and securing the flanks of the assault zone; paratroopers engaged enemy forces wherever they encountered them with an energy worthy of such elite formations.

Sgt. Mickey McCallum never forgot his first firefight, a few hours after landing. A German machine gunner mortally wounded the man next to him, Pvt. Bill Attlee. McCallum asked Attlee "if he was hit bad." The soldier replied, "I'm dying Sergeant Mickey, but we are going to win this damn war, aren't we?" "You damn well A we are." McCallum did not know where Attlee hailed from, but thought his choice of words suggested an East Coast man. He was passionately moved that this soldier, in his last moments, thought of the cause rather than of himself. In the hours and days that followed, many other such young men displayed similar spirit and were obliged to make a matching sacrifice. At dawn on 6 June, six infantry divisions with supporting armour struck the beaches of Normandy across a thirty-mile front; one Canadian and two British formations landed on the left, three American divisions on the right.

Operation Overlord was the greatest combined-arms operation in history. Some 5,300 ships carried 150,000 men and 1,500 tanks scheduled to land in the first wave, supported by 12,000 aircraft. On the French coast that morning, a drama unfolded in three dimensions such as the world would never behold again. British and Canadian troops poured ashore at Sword, Juno and Gold beaches, exploiting innovative armoured technology to overwhelm the defences, many of them manned by *Ostruppen* of Hitler's empire. "I was the first tank coming ashore and the Germans started opening up with machine-gun bullets," said a Canadian, Sgt. Leo Gariepy. "But when we came to a halt on the beach, it was only then that they realized we were a tank when we pulled down our canvas skirt, the flotation gear. Then they saw that we were Shermans." Pvt. Jim Cartwright of the South Lancashires said, "As soon as I hit the beach I wanted to get away from the water. I think I went across the beach like a hare."

The Americans seized Utah, at the elbow of the Cherbourg Peninsula, with only small loss. "You know, it sounds kind of dumb, but it was just like an exercise," said a private soldier wonderingly. "We waded ashore like kids in a crocodile and up the beach. A couple of shells came over but nowhere near us. I think I even felt somehow disappointed, a little let down." Farther east at Omaha Beach, however, Americans suffered the heaviest casualties of the day—more than 800 killed. The German defending unit, while not elite, was composed of better troops than those manning most of the Channel front, and sustained vigorous fire against the invaders. "No one was moving forward," wrote the AP correspondent Don Whitehead. "Wounded men, drenched by cold water, lay in the gravel . . . 'Oh God, lemme aboard the boat,' whimpered a youth in semi-delirium. Near him a shivering boy dug with bare fingers into the sand. Shells were bursting on all sides of us, some so close that they threw black water and dirt over us in showers."

A private soldier wrote: "There were men crying with fear, men defecating themselves. I lay there with some others, too petrified to move. No one was doing anything except lay there. It was like a mass paralysis. I couldn't see an officer. At one point something hit me on the arm. I thought I'd taken a bullet. It was somebody's hand, taken clean off by something. It was too much." For half the morning, the Omaha Beach assault hung on the edge of failure; only after several hours of apparent stalemate on the sands did small groups of determined men, Rangers notable among them, work their way up the bluffs above the sea, gradually overwhelming the defenders.

When news of the invasion was broadcast, across the Allied nations churches filled with unaccustomed worshippers, joining prayers for the men of the armies. On U.S. radio channels commercial breaks were cancelled, as millions of anxious listeners hung on bulletins and live reports from the beachhead. Industrial strikes were abandoned and civilian blood donations soared. In Europe, millions of oppressed and threatened people experienced a thrill of emotion. As a Dresden Jew, Victor Klemperer had more cause than most to rejoice, but he had been rendered cautious by past disappointments. He compared his wife's reaction with his own: "Eva was very excited, her knees were trembling. I myself remained quite cold, I am no longer or not yet able to hope . . . I can hardly imagine living to see the end of this torture, of these years of slavery."

As for Hitler's soldiers in France, "On the morning of 6 June, we saw the full might of the English and Americans," one man wrote in a letter to his wife which was later found on his corpse. "At sea close inshore the fleet was drawn up, limitless ships small and great assembled as if for a parade, a grandiose spectacle. No one who did not see it could have believed it. The whistling of the shells and shattering explosions around us created the worst kind of music. Our unit has suffered terribly—you and the children will be glad I survived. Only a tiny, tiny handful of our company remains." The Luftwaffe paratrooper lieutenant Martin Poppel, for so long an ardent Nazi and confident of victory, wrote on 6 June: "It turns out that this really is the Allies' big day—which unfortunately means that it's ours too." Geyr von Schweppenburg, commanding Panzergroup West, was convinced that Rommel, who directed the deployments behind Hitler's Atlantic Wall, was wrong to stake everything on a "forward defence." Von Schweppenburg had urged that the armoured divisions should be held back and massed for a counterattack. Nonetheless, like most thoughtful German officers, he believed the outcome inevitable whatever deployments the defenders had made: "No landing or lodgement attempted by the Allies could ever have been defeated by us without an air force, and this we utterly lacked."

Late in the afternoon of 6 June—much too late to have any realistic prospect of success—the 21st Panzer Division staged a counterattack on the British front, which was easily halted by antitank guns and 17-pounder Sherman "Fireflies." At nightfall, Eisenhower's forces were securely established, holding perimeters between half a mile and three miles inland which achieved linkage during the days that followed. In the German lines, Martin Poppel wrote: "We all reckon that [our] battalion has been thrown into battle alone and with few prospects of success . . . The men are damned jittery . . . Everybody is frankly shit-scared in this eerie night, and I have to curse and swear at them to get them to move."

On the beaches, reinforcements poured ashore from shuttling landing craft, so that by the end of D plus 1 Montgomery deployed 300,000 men. The first Allied fighters began to fly from improvised local airstrips. The Luftwaffe was so shrunken by months of attrition over Germany that its planes scarcely troubled the invaders. Allied pilots marvelled at the contrast between their daylight view of the beachhead, where long columns of vehicles could be seen advancing with impunity, and the stillness in the enemy's lines: the Germans knew that any visible movement they made would bring down fighter-bombers. Only during the brief hours of summer darkness were Rommel's forces able to redeploy and bring up supplies; their commander was himself later wounded by a strafing fighter.

The D-Day battle cost only 3,000 British, American and Canadian dead, a negligible price for a decisive strategic achievement. The people of Normandy, however, suffered terribly for their liberation, losing as many dead on 6 June as the invaders. Allied soldiers shocked local people by their contempt for civilian property; a Civil Affairs unit noted in Ouistreham: "Looting by troops pretty general. British prestige has fallen here today." Similarly, a Frenchwoman described the ransacking of her home in Colombières by Canadians: "It was an onslaught throughout the village. With wheelbarrows and trucks, the men stole, pillaged, sacked everything . . . There were disputes about who got what. They snatched clothing, boots, provision, even money from our strongbox. My father was unable to stop them. The furniture disappeared; they even stole my sewing machine." Looting remained a universal practice among Eisenhower's armies throughout the campaign, almost unchecked by commanders. Meanwhile, Allied bombs and shells killed some 20,000 people in northwest France during the bitter attritional fighting that now began.

Eisenhower and his generals had always recognised that the "battle of the buildup" in the weeks following D-Day would be as critical as the landings: if the Germans could concentrate forces in Normandy more swiftly than the Allies, the invaders might still be evicted—as Hitler hoped and demanded. Deception planners made a vital contribution, by their brilliantly sophisticated Operation Fortitude, which convinced the Germans of a continuing threat to the Pas de Calais, where important forces lingered for weeks. But, though Allied air force destruction of rail links and road bridges slowed the arrival of reinforcements, throughout June and July new formations rolled into Normandy, to be hurled piecemeal into the cauldron. The eleven-week campaign became by far the most costly of the western war, and Normandy the only battlefield where casualty rates at times briefly matched those of the Eastern Front. Though D-Day had huge symbolic significance and commands the fascination of posterity, the fighting that followed was much bloodier: for instance, while D Company of the British Ox & Bucks Regiment triumphantly seized "Pegasus bridge" across the Caen Canal early on 6 June for the loss of only two killed and fourteen wounded, next day it suffered sixty casualties in an inconclusive little action at Escoville.

Montgomery had declared ambitious initial objectives for the British on the eastern flank, including seizure of the city of Caen. Unsurprisingly, however, momentum was lost on 6 June, as troops advancing inland from the beaches were delayed by a maze of German strongpoints and hastily deployed blocking forces. During the succeeding days, dogged fighting consolidated the beachhead and gained some ground, but German formations, notably including the 12th SS Panzer Division, prevented a decisive breakthrough. Again and again British troops pushed forward, only to be checked by enemy tanks and infantry fighting with their accustomed energy.

"The attack entailed crossing about one thousand yards of open cornfield which fell away from Cambes Wood," wrote an officer of the King's Own Scottish Borderers. "We had barely crossed the start-line when the enemy reacted fiercely, with well-sited machine-guns and intense mortar fire which enfiladed the companies as they moved forward. It was a situation almost reminiscent of some First World War battlefield . . . We could see the tracer bullets flicking off the corn." Pvt. Robert Macduff of the Wiltshires said: "One of the scenes which will live forever in mind is the arms and legs on the roadside covered in maggots. The smell was vile. Someone had been killed, someone had gone forever . . . There but for the grace of God go I." Brig. Frank Richardson, one of Montgomery's ablest staff officers, wrote afterwards of the Germans, whom he admired boundlessly: "I have often wondered how we ever beat them."

But the Wehrmacht was also capable of extraordinary blunders, and made many in Normandy, especially before its commanders grasped the significance of the Allies' power to punish daylight movement. "Here we encountered one of the most terrible images of the war," wrote a German NCO near Brouay on 8 June. "The enemy had virtually cut to pieces units of the Panzer Lehr Division with heavy weapons. [Half-tracks] and equipment had been ripped apart; next to them on the ground, and even hanging in the trees, were body parts of dead comrades. A terrible silence covered all." On 9 June a dozen Panthers of the 12th SS Panzer Division launched a reckless headlong charge against Canadians emplaced at Bretteville. Sergeant Morawetz of the SS described what followed:

> The whole company drove as a body, at high speed and without any stops, in a broad front . . . After a muffled bang and a swaying, as if a track had been ripped off, the vehicle came to a stop. When I looked to the left, I happened to see the turret being torn off the panzer driving on the left flank. At the same moment, after another minor explosion, my vehicle began to burn . . . Paul Veith, the gunner sitting in front of me, did not move. I jumped out, then I saw flames coming out of the open hatch as if from a blowtorch . . . To my left, other burning panzers . . . The crews burned without exception on their faces and hands . . . The whole area was under infantry fire.

Within minutes seven Panthers were destroyed by antitank guns; their commander returned from receiving treatment for wounds inflicted in an earlier action to find his regiment sorely depleted. He was exasperated by the attack's futility: "I could have cried with rage and sorrow."

The Americans fought a series of hard battles to secure the Cherbourg Peninsula, where the small fields, steep banks and dense hedges of the *bocage* country enabled the defenders to inflict heavy losses for every small gain. "We had to dig them out," said a U.S. infantry officer. "It was a slow and cautious business, and there was nothing dashing about it. Our men didn't go across the open fields in dramatic charges . . . They did at first, but they learned better. They went in tiny groups, a squad or less, moving yards apart and sticking close to the hedgerows on either end of the field. They crept a few yards, squatted, waited, then crept again." Soldiers of the U.S. airborne divisions, who had expected to be withdrawn from combat after D-Day to prepare for another assault, instead fought on in Normandy for five weeks; they displayed an energy and commitment lacking in some infantry formations, and made a vital contribution. An operational report from the U.S. First Army highlighted "the urgent need for the development of an aggressive spirit in the infantry soldier . . . Many units do not acquire this attitude until long after their entry into combat and some never acquire it. On the other hand units containing specially selected personnel such as airborne and Rangers exhibited an aggressive spirit from the start."

Whenever the Germans attempted to attack, they were devastated by artillery, fighter-bombers and antitank guns; but the strategic imperative to advance rested upon the Allies. The British lost vast numbers of tanks in a series of unsuccessful attempts to break through to Caen and beyond. Local successes were often undone by enemy counterattacks. "We were essentially defensive and the Germans essentially both attacking by nature and also fighting for their existence," wrote Maj. Anthony Kershaw. "We are not very dashing soldiers and the English cavalry has never been very good." Allied infantry assaults were unimaginative, coordination with armour poor.

MASS, GENERALSHIP and the institutional effectiveness of armies chiefly influence battlefield outcomes, and so they did in Normandy. But the quality of rival weapons systems, especially tanks, also played an important role. The British and U.S. armies had excellent artillery. The Americans equipped their infantry with a good semi-automatic rifle, the M-1 Garand, but a poor support weapon, the BAR. Their 2.36-inch handheld "bazooka" antitank rocket—named for a weird wind instrument invented by American comic Bob Burns—lacked adequate penetration. The British Army boasted a reliable rifle, the .303 Mk IV Lee-Enfield, and the much-loved Bren light machine gun.

The Germans had better weapons; in particular, they could generate extraordinary violence with their belt-fed MG-42 machine gun, known to the Allies as the "spandau," of which some 750,000 were produced. On the battlefield, the MG-42's rasping 1,200-rounds-per-minute (rpm) rate of fire sounded far more lethal than the slow hammer of the Bren's or

BAR's 500 rpm. The British and Americans also had Vickers and Browning heavy machine guns, but the MG-42, easily manufactured from metal stampings and capable of changing barrels in five seconds, was a key factor in the German army's tactical performance. So too was the Panzerfaust handheld antitank projector: deadly at close range—much more so than the U.S. bazooka or British PIAT—and produced at the rate of 200,000 a month, the Faust played an important part in checking Allied armour in 1944–45, when the Wehrmacht was short of antitank guns. The 88mm dual-purpose gun and Nebelwerfer multibarrelled mortar were also used to formidable effect.

All the European armies had submachine guns for close-quarter fighting. The British 9mm Sten was an adequate weapon produced in millions at a cost which fell to under £3. The U.S. Army's .45-calibre Thompson was valued for its reliability, but cost £50 apiece to manufacture. Most American units in 1944–45 used the cheaper and simpler M-3 "grease gun." Allied soldiers were envious of the German MP-38 and MP-40 machine pistols. They called these Schmeissers, though that designer had nothing to do with their creation—they were made at the works of Berthold Giepel. Towards the end of the war, the Germans also acquired small numbers of an excellent assault rifle, the MP-43, forerunner of a generation of European infantry weapons thereafter.

BUT THE ALLIES' most serious problem was the inferiority of their tanks: numerical advantage counted for little when British and American shells often bounced off well-armoured German Panthers and Tigers, while a hit on a Sherman, Churchill or Cromwell was almost invariably fatal. "A sheet of flame licked over the turret and my mouth was full of grit and burnt paint," wrote a shocked British tank officer after his Cromwell was hit by an 88mm shell from a Tiger. " 'Bale out,' I yelled and leaped clear . . . There were my crew, hiding under a currant bush, miraculously all safe. Joe, the driver, white and shaking, crouched with drawn revolver. He looked like a cornered rat . . . The Tiger drove off undamaged, its commander waving his hat and laughing . . . Our hands shook so much that we could hardly light our cigarettes." Though Allied tanks were infinitely replaceable, it is hard to overstate the impact of German tank superiority on the morale of Allied units. Capt. Charles Farrell wrote: "There was, I think, no British tank commander who would not happily have surrendered his 'fringe benefits' for a tank in the same class as the German Panther or Tiger."

"We were all rather frightened," wrote a British tank officer about a night spent on the Bourgebus ridge during one of the most bitter armoured clashes, "and two men from my troop corporal's tank came up and said they would rather face a court-martial than go on. I explained that we all felt much the same but were not given the option." Two days later, when one of this officer's tanks was hit, the crew baled out. "I never saw the gunner and wireless operator again. They were cases for the psychiatrist and the M.O. sent them away. Those fellows had been in nearly every battle the regiment fought, and each had baled out at least twelve times before."

Peter Hennessy was ordered to investigate the fate of another tank of his Sherman squadron which had halted immobile a few yards ahead. His driver dismounted, clambered up the hull, glanced into the turret and ran hastily back. "Christ!" he said, "they're all dead in there. What a bloody mess." An 88mm round had ricocheted around the interior, killing the entire turret crew and terminating in the codriver's back. A few moments later a shocked and emotional figure lifted the driver's hatch of the stricken tank and emerged, the sole survivor.

Formations which had previously served in the Mediterranean were not the only ones to find the conflict in France a ghastly experience: some men who had never before seen action recoiled from this ferocious initiation. "There were a lot of problems in Normandy and some of the units of the British Army, bluntly, were not in very good shape," wrote Lt. Michael Kerr. "[They] had had many years in Britain before going into battle." Some green units seemed slow to treat their task with the absolute commitment necessary: a Waffen SS officer was baffled to observe British infantry advancing behind their tanks on 18 June, "strolling, hands in pockets, rifles slung on their shoulders, cigarettes between their lips."

Lt. Tony Finucane felt that the doctrine of reliance upon artillery and air support corroded proper infantry spirit. His own unit advanced, he said, "knowing that with the first burst of spandau everyone would go to ground and that would be it for the day. So much for dash, verve and pursuit—those who tried such antics were usually caught by our own 25-pdrs." Finucane believed responsibility for many of the problems properly rested with senior officers at brigade and divisional level, some of whom had no more experience of battle than did their men. "It was not necessarily the training of the army in U.K. which was wrong. Rather was it that many senior officers were inexperienced and may have viewed themselves as 'above' training."

It is hard to exaggerate the strain imposed upon every man by responsibility to join the spearhead of an attack. Ken Tout described the agonisingly slow progress of a typical armoured advance: "The front tanks are venturing slowly and agonisingly towards the first blank, savage corners. Their caution filters slowly back along the column, dictating a snail's pace . . . The morning drags slowly by, the sluggish progress of the clock accentuated by our jolting, ten-yards-at-a-time advance as we wriggle about in our tight coops, like battery hens, trying to restore circulation in legs, buttocks and shoulders." A Lancers officer edged his Sherman forwards into a wood, ordering his squadron to follow him. The commander of the next tank forgot to switch off his set before speaking into the intercom, and thus the entire unit heard him order, "Driver left, driver left." The reply came, "But he's gone right, sergeant." The tank commander said, "I know bloody well he's gone right, but I'm not following that f—ing c—t, it's too f—ing dangerous."

"It was a hell of a day," wrote a British company commander describing his unit's experiences on 25 June with a frankness unusual among Allied soldiers:

> The first shock was that this advance was supposed to be protected by smoke, but we were utterly exposed . . . Two members of the company couldn't stand it and shot themselves in the foot in quick succession . . . Off we go, the blast from a shell knocks me over, but only one little flesh wound . . . Where are the boys? Not here. I go back—"Come on." Through the hedge again, still no boys. Back again—"COME ON." They came, through more hedges . . . Bloody murder; people dropping dead. Hitlerjugend prisoners . . . During the attack one of my platoons ran away and was brought back at pistol-point by Tug Wilson, my second-in-command . . . We were being counterattacked by infantry and two tanks. The same platoon ran away again . . . Eventually it all died down. The enemy retired, leaving two knocked-out tanks and quite a lot of dead.

Soldiers who fought on foot and those who rode on tracks were almost unfailingly sceptical of each other's tactics. "We discussed the forthcoming advance with the delicate, genteel bargaining that always took place between tank and infantry," wrote a British infantryman, Lt. Norman Craig, of an exchange with an armoured officer. "Myself, hoping to persuade the tanks to go in front; he politely determined that they should not. The infantryman considered the tank an overpowering leviathan, which should be hurled indiscriminately into the assault; the tank man looked on the infantry as a convenient expendable mass, useful for neutralising anti-tank guns."

Throughout the northwest Europe campaign, Allied senior officers vented frustration at infantrymen's insistent thraldom to artillery. Forrest Pogue recorded some American commanders' comments: "They kept saying that the infantry failed to take cover, failed to take advantage of artillery preparation, failed to advance boldly, failed to dig in properly. [Under heavy fire] it was digging in which saved them, yet in basic [training] we dug only one foxhole. Artillery is used very extensively. I have been in many [command posts] when somebody would say they saw two or three Germans several hundred yards away. 5–30 rounds were frequently dropped on them."

Much depended on local junior leadership, and too many brave junior leaders died. "The spirit of human aggression has a magical tendency to evaporate as soon as the shooting starts," wrote Norman Craig, "and a man then responds to two influences only—the external discipline that binds him and the self-respect within him that drives him on . . . Courage is essentially competitive and imitative." The commanding officer of a British infantry battalion said: "On an average, in a platoon of twenty-five, five will do their best to fight . . . and fifteen will follow a lead. The rest will be useless. This applies to the whole infantry corps, and if the junior officers and NCOs will not go, the situation is pretty bad."

A tank officer, Michael Rathbone, wrote: "I have drawn my revolver to halt fleeing infantrymen; they came running by my tank when we were repairing a track damaged by a mine. I prayed we should never have to fight again with the 59th Division." Likewise Peter Selerie, another armoured officer: "We were often critical of the infantry . . . I remember that an infantry battalion melted away after incredibly heavy mortaring together with 'air burst' salvos. They had unfortunately neglected to dig in properly and had lost their officers and the bulk of their NCOs. The Kensingtons machine-gun battalion held the line supported by our tanks." Riflemen always suffered far heavier casualties than did tank crews, and well the riflemen knew this.

Most soldiers going into battle for the first time were less frightened than they became once they had experienced its reality. When the American infantryman Royce Lapp landed in France, "None of us were too scared then, because we didn't know what we were getting into." Likewise men of a U.S. cavalry unit clustered curiously around the first corpse they saw, that of a German officer. Their commander, Lt. Lyman Diercks, a twenty-eight-year-old postal worker from Bryant, Illinois, harangued his soldiers. "I told them it was very likely some of us wouldn't survive the war. We had to be like a family. I didn't expect them to be heroes, but if they became cowards they'd have to live with it all their lives. And while I was talking to them, I was really talking to myself."

When a shell landed close to a Canadian sergeant in Normandy, he exclaimed, "Shit and shit some more!" A newly arrived replacement asked if he was hit. The NCO said no, "he had just pissed his pants. He always pissed them, he said, when things started and then he was okay . . . Then I realized something wasn't quite right with me, either. There was something warm down there and it seemed to be running down my leg. I felt, and it wasn't blood. It was piss . . . I said, 'Sarge, I've pissed too' . . . He grinned and said, 'Welcome to the war.' " Fear afflicted other men in other ways. A Canadian prisoner was led into a Waffen SS regimental headquarters, under intense Allied bombardment. To his amazement, the staff were sheltering under map tables while singing a rousing chorus of "O Beautiful German Rhine" to the accompaniment of a mouth organ. The Canadian shook his head and mumbled in confusion, "War is a merry thing!" Some unglamorous tasks imposed disproportionate risks: "The first men to die in most battles were the phone linesmen," said a Waffen SS gunner, Capt. Karl Godau. Field telephone communications were vital when few units had tactical radios: linesmen were constantly obliged to expose themselves under fire to repair breaks caused by shelling or passing vehicles, and many were killed doing so.

A panzer staff sergeant, captured by the Americans, offered his interrogators a comparison between the Eastern and Western Fronts: "The Russian won't let you forget for one moment . . . that you are fighting on his soil, that you represent something he loathes. He will endure the greatest hardships . . . True, the average soldier lacks the resourcefulness of the American, but he makes up for it with a steadfastness I have never seen matched. If nine men get killed in an attempt to cut through wire, the tenth will still try—and succeed. You Americans are masters of your equipment, and your equipment is very good. But you lack the Russians' tenacity."

Yet if both sides suffered terribly in Normandy, German losses were worse, and irreplaceable. As early as 16 June Kurt Meyer's 12th SS Panzer Division was weakened by 1,149 casualties and its tank strength was halved; during a briefing at his command post, Meyer wrote: "I see worried faces . . . Without talking about it openly we know we are approaching a catastrophe . . . Faced with the enemy's enormous naval and air superiority, we can predict the breakdown of the defensive front . . . We are already surviving on subsistence level. Up to now we have received neither a single replacement for comrades wounded or killed, nor one tank or gun."

The SS Panzergrenadier Fritz Zimmer recorded in his diary at the end of June that his company was reduced to eighteen men; a week later, on 8 July, he fought the last action of his own war:

From 6:30 to 8 a.m. again heavy drum fire. After this Tommy attacks with great masses of infantry and many tanks. We fight as long as possible, but realise we are in a hopeless position. When the survivors try to pull back, we find ourselves already surrounded . . . I crawled back under continuing fire as fast as possible. Some comrades tried to do the same, unsuccessfully. I still cannot understand how nothing happened to me, with shells falling two or three metres in front, behind and beside me. Splinters whizzed about my ears. I worked my way to within about two hundred metres of our lines. It was hard work, always on my stomach, only occasionally on hands and knees, for three or four kilometres. Attacking Tommies passed me five or six paces away without noticing me in the high corn. I was nearly at the end of my tether, my feet and elbows incredibly painful and my throat parched with thirst, but I rolled on. Suddenly the vegetation thinned and I had to cross an open field. I was only ten metres from the next cornfield when three Tommies suddenly appeared and took me prisoner. I was immediately given a drink and a cigarette. At the collection point I met my Unterscharführer and other comrades from my company.

By 22 July the Luftwaffe paratrooper Martin Poppel lay in hospital, recovering from wounds inflicted in Normandy and increasingly fearful for the future of his nation's cause. "How did the poor buggers at the front and the exhausted civilian population at home deserve to be so badly led? We have many anxious questions about the future and our prospects in this long war. Even the most confident among us have doubts." Another soldier wrote to his wife on 12 August: "My darling Irmi, it doesn't look too good—that would be saying too much—but you know the cheerfulness with which I go about life . . . Man is a creature of habit. The roar of gunfire and explosion of bombs, which at first are hard on the nerves, lose their terrors after two or three days . . . The last three days we have had the most wonderful summer weather—sun, warmth and blue skies—so utterly at odds with everything else we see around us. Oh well, it will turn out all right in the end. Just have as much faith in my luck as I do and everything will look brighter, a thousand kisses to you, my darling Irmi and the children, your Ferd."

A comrade wrote likewise to his family on 10 August: "My darling wife and darling children . . . the rumble of gunfire comes ever closer. When I hear it my thoughts wander back to you, my dearest, and the question of whether I shall ever see you again rises before me. The battle could reach me any time now. What will be my fate? . . . Last night I was with you in my dreams. Ah, how beautiful it was! Can you imagine, my darling, how it feels to wake from such an idyll to the thunder of guns? I carry your image in my heart. It is such a heavy feeling. I should like to fly home to you my dearest! What will be my fate? How good it was to be allowed a few wonderful days with you in Fallingbostel, my dear loyal wife!" Both the letters quoted above were found by an American soldier on their authors' corpses.

THROUGH THOSE SUMMER MONTHS, the British and American peoples thought of little else save their armies' struggle in Normandy. But in Berlin, Hitler confronted an even graver threat: less than three weeks after the landings in France, in the east the Soviets launched Operation Bagration, which became the greatest offensive of the war and the last to be launched from Russian soil. Hitler's refusal to allow a strategic retreat during the spring left his forces defending a 1,400-mile front, with few reserves. Two-thirds of the entire German army was still deployed against the Russians, but this was not enough to meet an assault by 2.4 million men and more than 5,000 tanks, deploying twice the firepower committed to the Soviets' 1943 assaults.

Stalin said in a speech to his people on May Day 1944: "If we are to deliver our country and those of our allies from the danger of enslavement, we must pursue the wounded German beast and deliver the final blow to him in his own lair." The Russian word for "lair" is *berloga*. Thus, armoured crews painted on their tanks not "On to Berlin!" but "On to *berloga!*" On 22 June three Soviet *fronts* under Zhukov's command struck at the 700,000 men of Army Group Centre. Simultaneously, a partisan offensive in the German rear almost severed Field Marshal Ernest Busch's lines of communication. The Russians concentrated 400 guns a mile for their preliminary bombardment, along a front of 350 miles. They had total air superiority, thanks in large measure to the Western Allies' destruction of the Luftwaffe over Germany.

When Zhukov's infantry and tanks stormed forward into the palls of smoke and dust shrouding the defenders' positions, German phone lines were dead, command links broken. Busch's formations were shattered where they stood, vainly attempting to execute Hitler's demand for a rigid, no-retreat defence. Designated "fortresses" at Vitebsk, Orsha, Mogilev and Bobruysk were ordered to hold out to the last man. The consequences were catastrophic. The Russians swept forward in an irresistible tide, bypassing the "fortresses" and driving headlong westwards. On 28 June Model was hastily transferred to replace Busch, but the situation was irretrievable. Minsk fell on 4 July, while in the north the attackers thrust towards Riga, on the Baltic, which was soon encircled.

The Red Army never displayed much tactical subtlety, save perhaps in harassing the enemy through the hours of darkness, a skill in which its men surpassed the Western Allies. A British analyst has written: "In Soviet thinking the concept of economy of force has little place. Whereas to an Englishman the taking of a sledgehammer to crack a nut is a wrong decision and a sign of mental immaturity . . . in Russian eyes the cracking of nuts is clearly what sledgehammers are for." Russian attacks emphasised massed artillery bombardment and sacrificial tank and infantry advances, often led by "staff battalions"—penal units of political and military prisoners offered the possibility of reprieve in return for accepting the likelihood of extinction. Some 442,700 men served in them, and most died. The Russians continued to suffer higher casualties than did the Germans. If all soldiers find it hard to describe to civilians afterwards what they have endured, for Russians it was uniquely difficult. Even in the years of victory, 1943 to 1945, the Red Army's assault units accepted losses of around 25 percent in each action, a casualty rate the Anglo-American forces would never have accepted as a constant. Of 403,272 Russian soldiers who completed tank training in the course of the war, 310,000 died.

The poet David Samoilov noted, "This was the last Russian war in which most of the soldiers were peasants." Partly in consequence, Stalin's soldiers were even more superstitious than most warriors. Some, for instance, thought it unlucky to curse while loading a weapon; many wore good-luck charms and crosses. If relatively few admitted a formal allegiance to banished Christianity, many crossed themselves before going into action. Song played a big part in the army's culture. Men sang as they marched, and in the evenings around their fires—mostly ballads heavy with sentiment, lacking the cynicism of British soldiers' favoured numbers. With so many *frontoviks* quickly wounded or killed, it was estimated that Russian soldiers spent an average of only three months together. But men said that inside a week they learned more about one another than in a year of civilian life. The Red Army offered its men neither sex education nor condoms. Those who developed venereal diseases were sometimes punished by the denial of medical treatment. Children sometimes marched with the regiments, because they had lost everything and only the army offered them some hope of subsistence.

A Soviet report on 25 August 1944 described the Germans still resisting effectively: "The enemy's use of self-propelled guns and tanks to cover their retreats makes it difficult for us to engage their infantry. In these circumstances, our infantry often behave indecisively. The nature of our units has changed significantly during the last few months. Many consist overwhelmingly of green replacements. There are few men who have served since 1941. Many who have fought since 1943 complain about the inexperience of replacements." Soviet operations were punctuated with displays of stunning incompetence, often influenced by drunkenness. The cruelties inflicted on ordinary soldiers by their superiors explain the fact that even in 1944–45 some Russian soldiers continued to desert to the Germans. It can be said of Stalin's men, as of the Japanese, that their barbarous conduct towards other races merely mirrored their own rulers' treatment of themselves. But Russian higher commanders now displayed an impressive confidence in the handling of large forces and the coordination of all arms, aided by American-supplied communications equipment.

The Red Army advanced more swiftly than Eisenhower's forces in 1944–45, partly because its soldiers lived off the land and required much lower scales of supply; they were the least cosseted of the war. Among the long list of comforts and facilities routinely provided to Western Allied troops but denied their Russian counterparts were razors, delousing chambers, pencils, ink, paper, knives, torches, candles, games. Vodka was the only Red Army–issue stimulant to morale, and some sections pooled their rations, so that men could take turns to drink themselves into stupefaction. To the end, many men advanced to attack while suffering hunger, lice, piles, toothache, bleeding gums caused by scurvy, and sometimes tuberculosis.

The foremost Russian advantages in waging war were a willingness to accept almost unlimited casualties, together with men's knowledge of the draconian penalties awaiting those who flinched or failed. Russian units confronted with German resistance were never permitted to adopt the familiar Anglo-American expedient of taking cover and calling for artillery and air support. They were expected to drive on, heedless of obstacles or minefields, and to pay the price: there were always more men. On 5 July, the first phase of Bagration ended with the German Ninth Army destroyed. The First Panzer Army and the Fourth Army had each lost around 130,000 of the 165,000 men with which they started the battle. Vast columns of bedraggled German prisoners shuffled to the Russian rear, flotsam of the once-invincible Wehrmacht. The 1st Belorussian *front* now swung west towards Warsaw, while two other army groups headed for East Prussia and into Lithuania. On 13 July, the 1st Ukrainian *front* began an advance towards the Vistula. By the month's end, Vilnyus and Brest-Litovsk were in Russian hands.

Poles had a dark joke in 1944, about a bird which falls out of the sky into a cowpat, to be rescued by a cat; its moral, they said, was that "Not everyone who gets you out of the shit is necessarily your friend." The Soviet "liberation" of Poland, which began with Bagration, obliged its people to exchange the rule of one tyranny for another. On 14 July the Stavka issued an order to all Russian commanders: "Soviet troops . . . have encountered Polish military detachments run by the Polish émigré government. These detachments have behaved suspiciously and have everywhere acted against the interests of the Red Army. Contact with them [is] therefore forbidden. When these formations are found, they must be immediately disarmed and sent to specially organised collection points for investigation." The Russians murdered thousands of Poles whose only crime was a commitment to democratic freedom. Most notoriously, they declined to succour the August Warsaw Uprising. Russians nursed a historic hatred for the Polish people, and indulged this in 1944–45 with indiscriminate savagery towards both sexes.

Even as the Red Army approached the Vistula, its Karelian *front* drove deep into Finland, breaching the Mannerheim Line, which the Finns had defended so staunchly in 1940. The Finnish people paid dearly for their second challenge to Stalin: on 2 September the Helsinki government signed an armistice which rendered its eastern territories forever forfeit. Hitler refused to evacuate the Baltic Courland Peninsula in Latvia, though his generals pleaded that the forces holding the perimeter there might contribute importantly to the defence of Germany. Twenty-one divisions—149,000 men and 42 generals—remained beleaguered in Courland until May 1945.

When Bagration reached its triumphant conclusion, the Russians claimed to have killed 400,000 Germans, destroyed 2,000 tanks and taken 158,000 prisoners. The victors were struck by the poor physique of many captured Germans; one soldier wrote, "They all looked pitiful. They are like bank clerks. Many of them wear glasses." By the end of August 1944 the Russians stood on the Vistula, almost within reach of Warsaw and at the border of East Prussia. They were besieging Riga, and in the south had reached the Danube. In two months they had advanced 450 miles. A Russian officer marvelled at the endless wrecked tanks he and his men passed on their lines of march westwards, which he fancifully likened to "camels on their knees." As the Red Army savoured its dominance of the battlefield, for the first time men found opportunities to enjoy the pleasures of living and fighting in the territories of other nations. "One night you sleep under the open sky, the following night you are sunk into a feather bed like a nobleman," Gennady Petrov wrote to his parents from Ukraine. "I am living so well I have no complaints about anything save lack of music records and camera film."

On the far left of the Soviet line, on 20 August two Ukrainian *fronts* began a drive into southeast Europe of which the objectives were politi-

The 1944 Thrust into Poland

Front lines: 1944

Belorussia	Ukraine
23 June	13 July
4 July	18 July
28 July	28 July
29 August	29 August

German counterattacks
German pockets
Prewar Russo-Polish boundary
Russo-German boundary: 1940

cal rather than military. Stalin, bent upon securing most of the Balkans ahead of the Western Allies, committed his forces first against Romania, which surrendered on the twenty-third. The Romanians' change of allegiance cost them dear: by 25 October their army had suffered a further 25,000 casualties, after being conscripted to assist the Red Army to evict the Germans from their country. On 5 September Russia declared war on Bulgaria, which was officially fighting only the Anglo-Americans. Facing overwhelming Soviet might, the Bulgarians surrendered four days later. A communist government was installed in Sofia, enabling the Red Army to shift forces to Transylvania and Yugoslavia—Belgrade fell on 19 October.

Only a Nazi-engineered coup in Budapest on 15 October prevented the Hungarian government from also yielding to the Soviets: by 30 December, Budapest was under siege. The Soviet summer advances obliged Hitler to recognise that most of the Balkans had become indefensible. In late October, the Germans began to evacuate Greece. Gen. Maximilian von Weichs, the theatre commander, was thereafter chiefly concerned to use his 600,000 men—mostly drawn from low medical categories and service personnel—in Albania and Yugoslavia, to protect the right flank of Army Group South. Along the entire Eastern Front, the German predicament was dire. The Soviets' looming triumph was delayed only by the logistical difficulties of fuelling and supplying huge forces in regions of few roads and wrecked railways; their armies halted to rearm and regroup. Hitler's generals knew that when the Russians chose to advance again, the Wehrmacht could merely delay the inevitable.

If great wars were ever fought rationally, the moment had come for Germany to surrender, as it had surrendered in 1918 before the Fatherland became a battlefield. In 1944, by contrast, many of its greatest cities had been devastated by an Allied bombing offensive which was now approaching its peak. The Luftwaffe was shattered, the armed forces starved of fuel, men, tanks, vehicles and artillery. It is unsurprising that the leading Nazis were committed to fight on, because they could expect only death at the hands of the victors. It is debatable whether Hitler himself, in his innermost consciousness, preserved real hopes of retrieving his fortunes. But he had committed himself to a policy of total, indeed perpetual, war. If he was to be denied victory, in the last months of his rule he seemed content instead to preside over a titanic cataclysm, matching in scale the collapse of his titanic ambitions.

Posterity is more puzzled by the failure of other Germans to accept the logic of their predicament, to depose the Nazis and save hundreds of thousands of lives by abandoning the struggle. Such an initiative could only credibly have come from the generals. The 20 July 1944 bomb plot, the only concerted military attempt to decapitate the Nazi regime, was conducted with stunning incompetence and lack of conviction, and engaged a relatively small number of officers. A legend of anti-Nazi resistance was created, and is today sustained, chiefly to bolster the revival of postwar German self-esteem. Col. Claus von Stauffenburg would almost certainly have been successful in killing Hitler had he remained in the Führer's headquarters to detonate his bomb instead of hastening back to Berlin. Many other officers had opportunities to achieve the same end, had they been willing to sacrifice their own lives.

As it was, a perverted sense of duty caused most of the Wehrmacht's leadership to follow the Nazi regime to the end, to their perpetual dishonour. Among themselves, Germany's generals often mocked the character and conduct of the gangsters and grotesques by whom their country was led; yet their own slavishness towards Hitler seldom flagged. At a meeting on 27 January 1944, when he called on every officer to display loyal and fanatical support for National Socialism, Manstein called out, "And so it will be, my Führer!" He later claimed that his interjection was intended ironically, but few believed him. He and his kind placed their reputations as members of the soldierly caste, committed to fulfil to the last their military responsibilities and oath to Hitler, ahead of the interests of the society they professed to serve. They made an explicit or implicit choice to fight and die as servants of the Third Reich, rather than as protectors of the nation, whose interests could only credibly be served by securing peace on any terms, or indeed none. The Waffen SS panzer officer Hubert Meyer wrote in outrage about the 20 July plot: "It was incomprehensible that soldiers would attempt a coup against the supreme military leadership while they were themselves involved in bitter defensive fighting against the enemy who demanded 'unconditional surrender,' not willing to negotiate a ceasefire or even peace." Many Wehrmacht officers, even those hostile to the Nazis, shared his sentiments.

Helmuth von Moltke of the Abwehr explained the continuing support of a sufficiency of Germans for Hitler in a secret letter written in English to his former Oxford tutor, and dispatched from Stockholm in March 1943: "There are a great many people who have profited from the Third [Reich] and who know that their time will be up with the Third [Reich]'s end. This category does not only compromise some few hundred people, no it runs into hundreds of thousands. Further there are those who supported the Nazis as a counterbalance against foreign pressure and who cannot now easily find their way out of the tangle; even where they believe the Nazis to be in the wrong they say that this wrong is counterbalanced by a wrong done to us before . . . There are those who . . . say: if we lose this war we will be eaten up by our enemies and therefore we have to stand this through with Hitler." Moltke observed that Germany's soldiers were "continuously led into positions where there is no choice but to fight. Their mind is occupied with the enemy as fully as the housewife's with her requirements." He repeated a remark made by Hitler to Manstein: "The German general and soldier must never feel secure, otherwise he wants to rest; he must always know there are enemies in front and at his back, and that there is only one thing to be done and that is to fight." Von Moltke's analysis remained valid until 1945.

The soldiers abandoned the civilians to their despair. In Hamburg, old Mathilde Wolff-Monckeburg wrote on 25 June 1944: "No one ever laughs any more, no one is light-hearted or happy . . . We are waiting for the final act." She added a few weeks later: "For days we have had no water; everything is chipped and broken and frayed; travelling is out of the question; nothing can be bought; one simply vegetates. Life would have no purpose at all if there weren't books and human beings one loves, whose fate one worries about day and night."

Germany's military leaders earned the contempt of posterity for indulging the mass murderers who led their country, while claiming to absolve themselves of complicity in the Nazis' crimes. To contemplate revolt in the last phase of a struggle for national survival demanded a moral courage such as few German officers had. They knew the carnage they had wreaked in Russia; they could expect no mercy from Stalin's people, and fear of impending Soviet vengeance became a dominant motivation for millions of German soldiers. It provided a perverse and spurious justification for the generals' refusal to turn on Hitler. Their reasoning was vacuous, because sustained resistance merely delayed the inevitable. Yet even the more intelligent clung to fantastic hopes that the Western Allies would deliver them from the Russians. A career officer, Capt. Rolf-Helmut Schröder, believed that once the Americans had defeated Germany, they would confront the Soviet Union: "We thought it impossible the Americans would accept that the Russians should overrun Germany."

The war retained its stubborn, murderous, futile momentum. In the last months of the European struggle, while some German soldiers were visibly grateful to be taken prisoner, many sustained a stubborn defence. They showed a much greater will for sacrifice than had the French in similar circumstances in 1940, or most British troops thereafter. The Wehrmacht's performance can partly be explained by compulsion—the fact that deserters and alleged cowards were ruthlessly shot, in their thousands during the last months. Between 1914 and 1918, 150 death sentences were passed on members of the kaiser's army, of which just 48 were carried out. By contrast, between 1939 and 1945 more than 15,000 military executions were officially listed, and the real total was substantially higher. Beyond mortal sanctions, the immediate realities of the battlefield—the presence of the enemy in the next field or street—imposed its own logic. Even in its death throes, the Third Reich proved able to persuade many Germans to display extremes of futile stubbornness.

AFTER A MONTH of fighting in Normandy, the Anglo-American armies held a secure perimeter twenty miles inland. But bad weather impeded air operations and the landing of supplies. Every small advance demanded huge effort and cost casualties on a scale that thoroughly alarmed the Allies, especially the British. When Operation Epsom at the end of June failed to envelop Caen—originally planned as a D-Day objective—Montgomery summoned heavy bomber support: Lancasters duly devastated the city on the evening of 7 July, enabling British and Canadian troops to move into the northern ruins. On 18 July, a formidable armoured force was committed to Operation Goodwood, designed to take Falaise. Montgomery broke off this attack at the end of its second day, after losing 4,000 casualties and 500 tanks, one-third of all British armour in Normandy. The Shermans were replaced readily enough, but the attackers were chastened by their failure. "Our nerves were shot," wrote tank commander John Cropper of the mood in his crew at the end of July. "Ritchie and Keith started an argument, on music I think. Within seconds they were literally screaming at each other. I had to be very firm with them to break it up . . . It was a long time before either of them uttered another word."

Meanwhile on the Allied right, Gen. Omar Bradley's First Army progressed painfully through the *bocage*, where difficult conditions were worsened by German flooding of low ground. The Americans lost 40,000 casualties in two weeks, before reaching dry ground around Saint-Lô from which a major armoured assault could be launched. Operation Cobra was preceded by a massive heavy bomber attack, which crippled the German Panzer Lehr Division in its path. On 25 July, the Americans began an advance on Coutances which met little effective resistance: the German army in Normandy was crumbling. Bradley's forces were soon racing south, with the Germans falling back ahead of them. Avranches fell on 30 July, and seizure of an intact bridge at Pontaubault opened the way west into Brittany, south to the Loire and east to the Seine and the so-called Paris-Orleans gap. Patton, commanding the newly activated U.S. Third Army, dispatched a corps on a dash southeastward to Mayenne and Le Mans, reaching the latter after advancing seventy-four miles in a week.

Yet although senior German officers now recognised strategic retreat as essential, most of their line held. Hitler insisted on a new counterattack, disclosed to the Allies by Ultra: in darkness in the early hours of 7 August, Rommel's successor, Field Marshal Gunther von Kluge, launched a major counteroffensive designed to separate the U.S. First and Third Armies. During the night the panzers retook Mortain and pushed forward seven miles. With the coming of daylight, however, disaster fell on them. Allied fighter-bombers quickly destroyed forty out of seventy attacking tanks. For four more days the Germans strove to regain momentum, but U.S. infantry held their positions supported by massive artillery fire.

On Montgomery's front, progress remained slow. Late on 7 August Gen. Henry Crerar's Second Canadian Army attacked south of Caen.

In darkness, his tanks made some headway, before the assault ran out of steam soon after daybreak. Other Canadian and Polish armoured units took over, but their inexperience, and a bungled bomber strike which devastated several spearhead units, halted operations once more; inconclusive fighting continued on the road to Falaise until 10 August. Montgomery's formations faced the bulk of the surviving German armour. It was nonetheless painful for them to progress so sluggishly, when the Americans in the west were sweeping forward in triumph.

With Patton's forces moving so fast, Bradley saw an opportunity to trap an estimated twenty-one German formations—or, more accurately, their remains. If the Third Army swung north to Alençon and the Canadians could reach Falaise, only fourteen miles would separate them. Montgomery accepted the plan. One of Patton's corps dashed for Alençon against negligible opposition and pushed through the town to reach the outskirts of Argentan on the evening of 12 August. At this point, Bradley made one of the most controversial decisions of the campaign, halting the advance. His professed reason—to avoid the risk of a collision with the advancing Canadians—does not merit serious examination. More plausibly, and probably prudently, he flinched from placing relatively weak forces in the path of the retreating Germans, wounded tigers.

The Canadians were still fighting hard. Again and again they faced fierce actions with enemy rearguards who sometimes fought to the last man. The rate of attrition in some armoured encounters was extraordinary: on the morning of 8 August, for instance, one 17-pounder "Firefly" of the Northamptonshire Yeomanry knocked out three Tigers and a panzer Mk IV; but an hour later a single German Mk IV, posted hull down in a gully, knocked out seven tanks of the same regiment before itself being destroyed. The Canadians finally reached Falaise on 16 August, twenty hours after American and French troops launched the Anvil landings in southern France against slight opposition. That day, as Patton's army hastened eastwards, meeting few Germans and hysterically rejoicing French crowds, Hitler authorised a strategic withdrawal from Normandy.

In the so-called Falaise pocket, 150,000 Germans suffered relentless Allied air and artillery bombardment. "The floor of the valley was seen to be alive," wrote an Allied officer near Trun, ". . . men marching, cycling and running, columns of horse-drawn transport, motor transport, and as the sun got up, so more targets came to light . . . It was a gunners' paradise and everybody took advantage of it . . . Away on our left was the famous killing ground, and all day the roar of Typhoons went on and fresh columns of smoke obscured the horizon . . . the whole miniature picture of an army in rout. First a squad of men running, being overtaken by men on bicycles, followed by a limber at a gallop, and the whole being overtaken by a Panther tank crowded with men and doing well up to 30mph."

On the evening of 19 August Polish and American troops met at Chambois, allegedly closing the Falaise gap. Allied fighter-bombers destroyed thousands of vehicles in the pocket. But for two more days German fugitives trickled through. The Germans lost 10,000 killed at Falaise, and five times that number taken prisoner. "My driver was burning," wrote the SS Panzergrenadier Herbert Walther. "I had a bullet through the arm. I jumped onto a railway track and ran." Hit again in the leg, he managed a further hundred yards before "I was hit in the back of the neck with a big hammer—a bullet had gone in beneath the ear and come out through the cheek. I was choking on blood. There were two Americans looking down at me and two French soldiers who wanted to finish me off." But a remarkable number of fugitives got away; it became a cliché of the historiography of the war to assert that the German armies in France were destroyed, but this was not entirely true. They suffered some 240,000 casualties during the campaign, and forty divisions were wrecked. It was nonetheless an extraordinary achievement that a further 240,000 men and 25,000 vehicles crossed the Seine eastwards between 19 and 31 August.

On the river below Rouen, a five-mile-long queue of German armour and vehicles stood immobile but almost unscathed through an entire day and night, while German engineers laboured to repair a damaged railway bridge, the only feasible crossing; heavy rain kept the Allied air forces away until the passage was opened. Sporadic artillery fire inflicted some losses, but thousands of men and vehicles were soon on their way towards Germany. More got across the river on a ferry improvised from two barges by a naval unit at Elbeuf. If these were only fragments of an army, they proved invaluable to Hitler in the weeks that followed, forming the skeleton on which a western defence of the Reich was improvised. SS panzer officer Herbert Rink wrote: "We were shell-shocked and exhausted. Once behind the West Wall, we could join all the defeated, decimated German units, all those who had made it through 600km of horrifying, crushing battle . . . We, who had come depleted and exhausted from the inferno of Caen, through the breakout from the pocket at Falaise, through the nerve-racking retreat across France and partisan-plagued Belgium—we had gathered our strength and rebuilt our confidence." If Rink's last assertion was an exaggeration, it was indisputable that von Rundstedt, who succeeded as C-in-C in the west after the suicide of von Kluge, was able to establish and defend a new line.

The Germans abandoned Paris without a fight. Gen. Philippe Leclerc's

Free French armoured division entered the capital on 25 August to find the Resistance claiming possession, a legend that launched the resurrection of France's national self-respect. The Allied armies embarked on a dramatic pursuit which carried them into eastern Belgium and the liberation of Brussels. On 1 September, Eisenhower assumed operational command of the Anglo-American forces, relegating Montgomery to leadership of the Anglo-Canadian 21st Army Group with the sop of promotion to field marshal. The Western Allies were convinced that by achieving victory in Normandy they had brought Germany to the verge of defeat. Most of France was free, at a cost of only 40,000 dead. At the beginning of September 1944, they anticipated final victory before the year's end. In the event, their hopes took significantly longer to fulfil, but "the remainder of the war," wrote Geyr von Schweppenburg, commanding Panzergroup West, "was only a prolonged epilogue."

CHAPTER TWENTY-TWO

JAPAN: DEFYING FATE

WAR IS PRODIGIOUSLY WASTEFUL, because much of the effort made by rival combatants proves futile, and the price is paid in lives. It is easy for historians to identify not merely battles but entire campaigns which need not have been fought, because outcomes were already ordained in consequence of events elsewhere. Much effort and human sacrifice contribute little to final victory. But when great forces have been created and deployed, it is almost inevitable that they will be used. As long as the enemy refuses to acknowledge defeat, it is deemed intolerable for armies to stand idle, bombs to remain in their dumps. During 1944, the U.S. Navy gained overwhelming dominance of the Pacific. Blockade rendered inevitable the collapse of an enemy wholly dependent on imported fuel and raw materials; American submarines achieved the strangulation of Japanese commerce which Germany's U-boats had failed to impose on Britain. Seldom in history has such a small force—16,000 men, 1.6 percent of the sea service's strength, with never more than 50 boats deployed—gained such decisive results. American submarines were responsible for 55 percent of all Japan's wartime shipping losses, 1,300 vessels totalling over 6 million tons; their destructive achievement climaxed in October 1944, when they sank 322,265 tons of shipping. Thereafter, Japanese losses diminished only because they had little cargo tonnage left to sink; Japan's bulk imports fell by 40 percent.

It is extraordinary that Hirohito's nation went to war knowing the importance and vulnerability of its merchant shipping, yet without seriously addressing convoy protection; the Tokyo regime built huge warships for the Combined Fleet, but grossly inadequate numbers of escorts. Japanese antisubmarine techniques lagged far behind those of other belligerents. Their radar and airborne antisubmarine capabilities were so feeble that American boats could often operate on the surface in daylight. While the Germans lost 781 U-boats and Japan 128, the Imperial Japanese Navy sank only 41 U.S. submarines; 6 more foundered in accidents. American submariners suffered a loss rate comparable with airmen—almost one man in four—but the results they achieved were so important that this sacrifice was cheap at the price. The U.S. investment of industrial resources in submarines was a fraction of that lavished on the B-29 Superfortress bombers which belatedly joined the assault, and the undersea arm contributed far more to victory.

Japanese island garrisons found themselves isolated, immobilised and starving. A soldier on Bougainville wrote on 14 September 1944: "Old friendships dissolve when men are starving. Each man is always trying to satisfy his own hunger. It's much more frightening than meeting the enemy's assaults. There is a vicious war going on within our ranks. Can spiritual power degenerate to this?" American air and naval dominance denied Japan any chance of launching an effective strategic counterstroke. Its soldiers, sailors and airmen still enjoyed many opportunities to die bravely, to inflict suffering and death on their foes and the oppressed subjects of their empire. But the nation's fate was sealed.

It was rationally unnecessary for the Allies to launch major ground operations in Southeast Asia—or, for that matter, the Philippines. If they merely maintained naval blockade and air bombardment, the Japanese people must eventually starve, their oil-deprived war machine would be reduced to impotence. Given the nature of war, democracies and global geopolitics, however, "eventually" was not soon enough. In the spring of 1944, it was taken for granted that Allied forces must attack the Japanese wherever possible. The British had confronted them for two years on the northeast frontier of India without making significant advances, but now at last resources, including large numbers of U.S. transport aircraft, became available to mount an offensive with overwhelming superiority.

Churchill opposed an overland operation to reconquer Burma; Gen. "Vinegar Joe" Stilwell complained bitterly to Marshall in July 1944 that "[The British] simply do not want to fight in Burma or reopen communications with China." This was true. "India is not at present a suitable base from which to launch large-scale operations," asserted a joint Anglo-American report in the spring of 1944. "Her transport system is already overtaxed, her political situation unsatisfactory, and her economic position precarious." Australia, said this document, offered far more convenient basing facilities. The British Empire's soldiers had been repeatedly worsted in jungle warfare; Churchill preferred an amphibious landing in southern Burma, below Rangoon, or better still on the tip of Sumatra, to secure a base from which to retake Malaya. Washington, however, refused to provide assault shipping merely to enable the British—as Roosevelt and his chiefs of staff saw it—to reconquer their eastern empire. Americans no longer took much trouble to salve Churchill's sensibilities, and made explicit their determination to direct the future course of the eastern war.

A U.S. official visiting London said bluntly, "It is now our turn to bat in Asia." The Americans demanded an overland assault on northern Burma, to reopen the road from India to Chiang Kai-shek's China.

Chiang declined to commit his own troops to further this objective unless or until the British advanced from Assam. Britain sulkily acceded to American wishes, though both Churchill and his local field commander, Lt. Gen. William Slim, recognised that, win or lose, the Fourteenth Army's operations could contribute little to Japan's defeat by comparison with America's Pacific campaign. The initial Allied plan for 1944 called for two of Slim's divisions to launch a new offensive in the coastal Arakan; two Indian divisions would probe from Assam into northern Burma, while Stilwell directed a thrust south from China to take Myitkyina and reopen the Burma Road. The latter operation would be supported by the deployment of an expanded Chindit force, six brigades strong, airlifted into northern Burma behind the Japanese front, then supplied by American aircraft.

Yet even as the Allies began to concentrate their forces, the enemy preempted them: two Japanese divisions attacked in the Arakan, to pin down British forces before launching a major offensive into Assam, with Imphal as its principal objective. The operation was recklessly ambitious now that Indian and British troops were deployed in such strength. Lacking air superiority, with few tanks and guns, it was folly for the Japanese to dispatch infantry hundreds of miles across terrible country against Slim's positions. The Japanese offensive provided the British with an opportunity such as they had never previously enjoyed: to fight on their own ground, with powerful artillery, armoured and air support.

The Arakan thrust was smashed so swiftly and comprehensively that Slim was able to airlift some of his units northeastwards to strengthen the defence of Imphal and Kohima, key road junctions separated by a hundred miles. The battles there in the spring of 1944 produced the heaviest fighting of the war on Britain's eastern front. Climatic conditions in Assam and Burma were as wretched as those of the Pacific, with the added hazard of mountain terrain; even before men began to fight, mere movement on precipitous hill faces strained their powers to the limit. "The physical hammering one takes is difficult to understand," said Lt. Sam Hornor, a signals officer in the 1st Norfolks.

> The heat, the humidity, the altitude and the slope of almost every foot of ground, combine to knock hell out of the stoutest constitution. You gasp for air which doesn't seem to come, you drag your legs upwards till they seem reduced to the strength of matchsticks, you wipe the salt

sweat out of your eyes. Then you feel your heart pounding so violently that you think it must burst its cage . . . Eventually, long after everything tells you you should have died of heart failure, you reach what you imagine is the top of the hill only to find it is a false crest . . . You forget the Japs, you forget time, you forget hunger and thirst. All you can think of is the next halt.

Bert May, a bugler, said of Kohima: "It was a stinking hell of a hole. All the vegetation on the ground was dead . . . Leeches, they used to get through on to any part of your body that was open. You used to get a lighted cigarette, stick it on his tail and 'bonk,' he'd pop off." For weeks after the Japanese attack began on 7 March, the issue seemed to hang in the balance. The Japanese encircled Slim's positions. There was panic at Dimapur, the big supply dump beyond Kohima. Lt. Trevor Highett of the Dorsets said later, "There are few things more unpleasant than a base in a flap. It was full of people who never expected to fight, and who couldn't wait to get out. 'Take what you like,' they said. 'Just give us a signature if you've got time.' " Then the infantrymen trudged forward to join the battle. Each day witnessed fierce small-arms and grenade battles at close quarters, as the Japanese charged again and again.

The former district commissioner's tennis court became the focus of the struggle for Kohima, with only a few yards separating the Royal West Kents' positions from those of their foes. "We shot them on the tennis court, we grenaded them on the tennis court," said company commander John Winstanley. "We held because I had constant contact by radio with the guns and the Japs never seemed to learn how to surprise us. They used to shout in English as they formed up, 'Give up' . . . One could judge just the right moment to call down gun and mortar fire . . . They were not acting intelligently and did the same old stupid thing again and again. We had experienced fighting the Japs in the Arakan, [with them] bayoneting the wounded and prisoners . . . They had renounced any right to be regarded as human, and we thought of them as vermin to be exterminated. That was important—we are pacific in our nature, but when aroused we fight quite well."

The battlefield was soon reduced to a barren, blackened wilderness, stripped of vegetation by blast, pockmarked with craters and foxholes, festooned with the coloured parachutes with which supplies were dropped to the garrison. The stench of death and putrid flesh hung over everything. "We were attacked every single night," said Maj. Frankie Boshell, a company commander in the Berkshires, who relieved the West Kents. "On the second night they started at 1900 and the last attack came at 0400 next morning. They came in waves, like a pigeon shoot. Most nights they over-ran part of the battalion position, so we had to mount counterattacks." His company lost half of its 120 men at Kohima, and other units suffered in like proportion. Sgt. Ben McCrae wrote: "Your nerves got to you. You could have sat down and cried your eyes out. Which a lot of blokes did—they got so low-spirited with it all. You were hungry, cold and wet, you thought, 'When am I going to get out of here?' You didn't, you couldn't." Sgt. Bert Fitt took out three bunkers with grenades, then found his Bren gun empty when he met a Japanese. "When you get to hand-to-hand fighting like that, you realise that you or he's going to get killed . . . You close in and hope for the best . . . I crashed the light machine-gun into his face . . . Before he hit the ground I had my hand on his windpipe . . . I managed to get his bayonet from his rifle and I finished him with that."

In action, there was a fine line between courage which heartened others and bluster which incurred their contempt. The 1st Norfolks were uncertain on which side to place their bombastic colonel, Robert Scott. Amid the carnage, Scott said ebulliently to his riflemen, "Come on you chaps, there's no need to be afraid, you are better than those little yellow bastards." When struck on the scalp by a glancing shrapnel splinter, he shook his fist at the Japanese lines and said, "The biggest bloke on the damn position and you couldn't get him! If you were in my bloody battalion I'd take your proficiency pay away!" Capt. Michael Fulton said to a fellow officer, "Well, Sam, I'd better get off and earn my MC." Fulton ran forward, and within seconds was shot through the head. At Kohima, the 1st Norfolks lost 11 officers and 79 other ranks killed, 13 officers and 150 other ranks wounded.

"Almost to a man the Japs had died without trying to escape," wrote a British company commander of the Border Regiment after a night clash farther south, on the Imphal plain. "But one was burning in the open, and his yellow limbs were black and shining like those of some fantastic Negro; another who had come out to fight was dead and sprawling, a bayonet like an outsize arrow still sticking in his chest; three more, already wounded, were running for the cover of a tall bamboo clump some thirty yards wide." Some men found the struggle too much for them: "For the first time, that day, I saw two men crack," wrote the same officer after another savage encounter at Imphal. "One, a six-foot corporal, who spent the afternoon cowering in a ditch, the other, a reinforcement who when nothing was happening in the middle of the night suddenly broke and ran—until somebody stopped him with a bayonet."

Devastating artillery, armour and air power gradually reduced the attackers. A British tank lurched down steep terraces blackened by days of bombardment to retake the tennis court at Kohima, firing at point-blank range into Japanese foxholes. Gen. Renya Mutaguchi, the Japanese commander, had launched his offensive with little logistic support, and the RAF daily battered his lines of communication. Soon the besiegers began to starve. On 31 May, without authorisation the local Japanese commander at Kohima ordered a withdrawal which collapsed into rout. On 18 July, Mutaguchi likewise bowed to the inevitable: the remnants of the Japanese forces around Imphal embarked upon a ragged, stumbling march towards the Chindwin River, racked by hunger, tormented at every twist of the mountain trails by Allied aircraft and pursuing troops.

A despairing Japanese soldier wrote: "In the rain, with no place to sit, we took short spells of sleep standing on our feet. The bodies of our comrades who had struggled along the track before us lay all around, rain-sodden and giving off a stench of decomposition. Even with the support of our sticks we fell among the corpses again and again as we stumbled on rocks and tree roots laid bare by the rain and attempted one more step, then one more step, in our exhaustion." The outcome of the twin battles of Imphal and Kohima was the heaviest defeat ever suffered by a Japanese army: out of 85,000 men committed, 53,000 became casualties. Among their 30,000 dead, as many perished from disease and malnutrition as from Allied action. Mutaguchi's forces lost all their tanks, guns and animal transport, which were irreplaceable. On no single battlefield of the Pacific campaign did Hirohito's forces suffer as severely.

After almost three years of defeat in the east, the victors' morale soared. Although a difficult campaign lay ahead in 1945, to reoccupy Burma at the end of a long, long supply line, Slim knew he had cracked the spine of the Japanese army in Southeast Asia, staking his claim to be recognised as the ablest, as well as best-loved, British field commander of the war. As for the Japanese, Mutaguchi had never anticipated that he could conquer India, but cherished hopes that the spectacle of the "Indian National Army" attacking the British might stimulate a general revolt against the Raj. Instead, the INA's performance discredited it as a fighting force. Victory in Assam and Slim's subsequent advance into Burma temporarily reasserted British authority in India. While Indian popular enthusiasm for independence remained undiminished, strikes and street violence receded.

THE CRITICAL BATTLES of 1944 took place much farther east, however. That summer, a huge accession of resources to the Pacific theatre, notably warships and planes, enabled the United States to close the ring on Japan. While men continued to die and ships to sink, the U.S. Navy's dominance changed the character of the struggle. Petty Officer Roger Bond of the carrier *Saratoga* said, "If you went out to the Pacific after . . . January of 1944, you had a completely different experience and viewpoint than those before . . . I wasn't part of the one where we truly were losing, getting chased out of the place." The Japanese were still fighting hard, but everywhere they were being forced back.

On Bougainville as on many other islands, Hirohito's soldiers paid the price for staging foolish, futile infantry attacks against well-armed defenders. An American wrote in March 1944: "Enemy dead were strewn in piles of mutilated bodies, so badly dismembered in most cases that a physical count was impossible. Here and there was a leg or an arm or a blown-off hand . . . At one point, Japanese bodies formed a human stairway over the barbed wire. Five enemy dead were piled one on top of the other, as each had successively approached the location to use a predecessor as a barricade and then fall on top of him as he in turn was killed. Farther out from the perimeter, where a little stream wound its way parallel to it, Japs killed by the concussion of thousands of mortar shells lay with their heads, ostrich-fashion, stuck under the least protection they could find."

By 1944, the United States was producing so many ships and planes that it felt able to commit large forces to the Pacific. Fulfilment of the doctrine of Germany First had always been compromised by the fact that American popular sentiment was much more strongly roused against the Japanese than against the Germans, and by the U.S. Navy's determination to be seen to win the war in the east. While Russia's struggle still hung in the balance, this had been risky. But now it was plain that Stalin's armies were triumphant, the Wehrmacht in eclipse. Eisenhower's forces in Europe were relatively large, but nothing like as numerous as would have been necessary had they confronted Hitler's legions alone. Although lavishly provided with tanks, guns, vehicles and aircraft, the Anglo-American armies were always short of infantry. Moreover, the Pacific campaigns imposed an enormous drain on Allied global shipping resources, out of all proportion to the relatively small combat forces deployed, because of the distances involved.

Service in the Pacific was an experience light-years from that of Europe, first because of its geographical isolation. The U.S. Marine pilot Samuel Hynes wrote: "Out here the war life was all there was; no history was visible, no monuments of the past, no cities remembered from books. There was nothing here to remind a soldier of his other life; no towns, no bars, nowhere to go, nowhere even to desert to." Men obliged to exist for months under open skies in tropical conditions suffered relentlessly from disease and skin disorders, even before enemy action took a bloodier toll. A marine, Frazer West, described a characteristic problem on Bougainville: "It wasn't dysentery . . . It was bad rain diarrhea—bad water . . . you can develop diarrhea real quick . . . Undoubtedly stress played a real part. We didn't even know the meaning of the word stress then, but now we do."

Amphibious operations became a Pacific routine, albeit a hazardous and challenging one. An American soldier wrote: "Even under the best conditions, the unloading phase of a landing operation is a hot, rugged chore. With a high surf pounding against a narrow strip of jungle under-growth, with a set deadline of daylight hours, and under the scorching heat of a South Sea November sun, the job was an exhausting night-mare. Working parties were punching with every last ounce of blood to get ammunition, oil, supplies, vehicles, rations and water out of the boats and above the high-water line. Shore party commanders were frantically trying to find a few square feet of dump space and discovering nothing but swamp all along the beach. Seabees and engineers were racking their brains and bodies in a desperate effort to construct any kind of road to high ground where vehicles could be parked, oil stored and ammunition stacked. But there wasn't any high ground for thousands of yards—only a few scattered small islands of semi-inundated land surrounded by a stink-ing, sticky mire. And hour after hour boats roared in to the beach jammed with supplies."

The most important Pacific operation of 1944 was the seizure of the Marianas, key to the inner ring of Japan's defences. When the U.S. Marine Corps began its assaults on Saipan, Tinian and Guam, the Japanese Com-bined Fleet sailed to meet the invaders, precipitating the largest carrier encounter of the war. "The fate of the Empire rests on this one battle," declared Adm. Soemu Toyoda on 13 June, as his ships, commanded by Adm. Jizaburo Ozawa, sailed against Spruance. But Ultra had once more revealed his plan to the Americans. The Japanese had hoped to use sub-marines and land-based aircraft severely to weaken the Americans before the main engagement. Instead, seventeen of Toyoda's twenty-five subma-rines were sunk, while his airfields on Guam and Tinian were devastated by U.S. bombing.

Both sides deployed formidable forces, but the Americans outnum-bered the Japanese by around two to one at sea and in the air, with 956 aircraft to 473, 15 carriers to 9—five times the U.S. strength at Midway. Ozawa believed he had gained the advantage when he pinpointed Spru-ance's ships, and was first to launch air strikes at 8:30 a.m. on 19 June. But these were swiftly detected by American radar, and the report was flashed to Adm. Marc Mitscher: "Large bogeys bearing 265 degrees, 125 miles at 24,000." His chief of staff, Capt. Arleigh Burke, said later, "Well that was just we were waiting for, so we launched all our fighters, the whole blooming works."

What followed became known as the "Great Marianas Turkey Shoot": of Ozawa's 373 planes dispatched, only 130 survived, having failed to inflict significant damage on the U.S. fleet. A further 50 Japanese aircraft were shot down over Guam. "[The Japanese] were just devastated," said Burke. "You could tell that from the radio conversation." In the carrier operations room, eavesdroppers were monitoring enemy radio transmissions. When at last the disconsolate Japanese airborne controller asked his commander's permission to return to the fleet, a listening American officer said, "Let's shoot him down." Burke replied with pitying condescension, "No, you can't shoot that man down. He's done more good for the United States today than any of us. So let him go home." U.S. submarines torpedoed Ozawa's flagship, the new carrier *Taiho*, and the veteran *Shokaku*. These successes cost the Americans just 29 planes; Toyoda's surviving ships turned away.

Through the night, Task Force 58, Mitscher's Fast Carriers, steamed hard in pursuit of the retreating Japanese, and the following afternoon U.S. reconnaissance planes pinpointed Ozawa's squadron. Mitscher took the daring gamble of launching strikes at extreme range, knowing that his 216 aircraft would have to be recovered in darkness. So great were American resources and so high the stakes that the carriers' air component could be deemed expendable. Exultant pilots found the Japanese, among them Don Lewis, a dive-bomber pilot.

> The carrier below looked big, tremendous, almost make-believe. I had a moment of real joy. I had often dreamed of something like this. Then I was horrified with myself. What a spot to be in. I must be crazy . . . From each side of the carrier below seemed to be a mass of flashing red dots . . . It had been turning slowly to port. It stopped. Who could ask for more? I pulled my bomb release, felt the bomb go away, started my pull-out. My eyes watered, my ears hurt, and my altimeter indicated 1,500 feet. The sky was just a mass of black and white puffs, and in the midst of it planes already hit, burning and crashing into the water below. It is strange how a person can be fascinated even in the midst of horror.

This sortie sank another carrier, *Hiyu*, and damaged two others; the Japanese were left with 35 planes, having destroyed only 20 American aircraft. A further 80 of Mitscher's force ditched from lack of fuel or were lost attempting to land in darkness, but most of the crews were recovered.

U.S. factories could readily replace the lost aircraft, while those of Japan were quite unable to rearm Ozawa. Spruance incurred criticism for breaking off the battle at this point, allegedly forfeiting a chance to complete the destruction of the fleeing Japanese. But he had inflicted a massive and irretrievable defeat on Toyoda's fleet. He had no need to hazard his own ships, and perhaps the entire Marianas operation, in dangerous waters. Spruance in the Battle of the Philippine Sea displayed a wisdom and discretion that his counterpart and rival, "Bull" Halsey, seldom matched. The action confirmed that American combat skills, as well as naval power, now wholly outclassed those of their enemies. For the rest of the war Japan's pilots displayed diminishing proficiency, and sometimes even a want of courage. U.S. carrier aircraft, notably the Hellcat fighter, dominated the sky, even when the Japanese deployed some new aircraft supposedly capable of matching them.

But victory at sea off the Marianas could not avert bloody fighting ashore. The marines' first objective was Saipan; its fourteen-mile length, and some high ground, enabled the Japanese to deploy 32,000 defenders in depth. When 77,000 U.S. Marines waded ashore on 15 June, they met machine-gun and artillery fire which inflicted 4,000 casualties in the first forty-eight hours. The planners had anticipated a three-day battle, but the island's capture took three weeks: the defenders had to be blasted from their bunkers yard by yard. An army division was committed in support of the marines; after failing to take the densely forested position ruefully dubbed Purple Heart Ridge, its commander was sacked. But day by day, even while hundreds of thousands of their compatriots were fighting a similarly brutal battle in Normandy, the invaders slowly battered a path inland.

On the night of 6–7 July 3,000 Japanese, sensing that the end was close, launched a futile, sacrificial banzai charge in which they were mown down by U.S. firepower after desperate close-quarter fighting. "We had hardly any arms," said one of the few survivors, naval paymaster Noda Mitsuharu. "Some had only shovels, others had sticks." An American officer said: "It reminded me of one of those old cattle stampede scenes of the movies. The camera is in a hole in the ground and you see the herd coming and then they leap up and over you and are gone. Only the Japs kept coming and coming. I didn't think they'd ever stop."

Mitsuharu, lying in front of the American positions with two bullets in his stomach, saw a group of his comrades crawling towards him. One raised a grenade and said invitingly, "Hey, sailor there! Won't you come with us?" Then the wounded Japanese heard a voice cry, "Long Live the Emperor!" and there was an explosion. "Several men were blown away, dismembered at once into bits of flesh . . . their heads were all cracked open and smoke was coming out." Mitsuharu himself lived to be taken prisoner. For weeks after organised resistance on the island ended on 9 July, small parties of survivors continued to attack Americans. Substantial numbers of soldiers and civilians, some of the latter under duress, killed themselves by leaping from the cliffs at Marpi Point.

On 21 July, Americans began landing on Guam, a larger island, thirty-four miles long, and a vital objective because it had the only good water supply in the Marianas chain, as well as the best harbour. The protracted resistance on Saipan had given the 19,000-strong Japanese garrison time to construct strong beach defences, but the Americans preceded the assault with one of the longest and most effective air and naval bombardments of the campaign. This wreaked havoc: organised resistance soon collapsed, though three weeks' fighting was needed to suppress isolated strongpoints and secure the island for the Americans' vast programme of airfield construction. Indeed, infantrymen were obliged to maintain patrols and to skirmish with small groups of Japanese on Guam until the end of the war.

The marines attacked their third Marianas objective, the smaller island of Tinian, on 24 July. Lt. Gen. Holland Smith, commanding the assault, considered this the best-executed amphibious landing of the campaign. Organised opposition was eliminated in twelve days, though once again Japanese survivors refused to surrender. "Nowhere have I seen the nature of the Jap better illustrated than it was near the airstrip at dusk," wrote the *Time* correspondent Robert Sherrod.

> I had been digging a foxhole for the night when one man shouted "There is a Jap under those logs!" The command post security officer was dubious, but he handed concussion grenades to a man and told him to blast the Jap out. Then a sharp ping of a Jap bullet whistled out of the hole and from under the logs a skinny little fellow—not much over 5 ft tall—jumped out waving a bayonet. An American tossed a grenade and it knocked the Jap down. He struggled up, pointed his bayonet into his stomach and tried to cut himself open in approved hara-kiri fashion. The disembowelling never came off. Someone shot the Jap with a carbine. But, like all Japs, he took a lot of killing. Even after four bullets had thudded into his body he rose to one knee. Then the American shot him through the head.

A thousand such incidents make it easy to understand why U.S. Marines and soldiers fighting in the Pacific treated their enemies as mortally dangerous wild beasts.

Informed Japanese knew that their home islands, on which millions of houses were constructed of wood and paper, now faced an ordeal by air bombardment; the Marianas airfields brought Japan's cities within range of U.S. bombers. The shore battles showed that Japanese soldiers' willingness for sacrifice could extract a high price for each American victory, but the invaders' firepower was irresistible. Nimitz's submarines were inflicting a scale of attrition on Japan's merchant fleet unsustainable by a nation dependent on imports. The combination of naval blockade and air bombardment ensured Japan's defeat, even if U.S. ground forces advanced no farther. But the Japanese government remained committed to fight on: the supremely stubborn military men who dominated Tokyo's polity believed they could still achieve a negotiated settlement, preserving at least their holdings in China, by convincing the Americans that the cost of assaulting the Japanese homeland would be unacceptably high.

Even as the marines were fighting for the Marianas, in the Southwest Pacific the United States was conducting a much more controversial campaign. Gen. Douglas MacArthur, the regional supreme commander, was bent upon personally achieving the liberation of the 17 million people of the Philippines, where he had spent much of his service life. A former chief of staff of the army with powerful right-wing friends at home, in 1944 MacArthur flirted with a presidential election run against Roosevelt, abandoning this notion only when it became plain that he could not secure the Republican nomination, far less beat the White House incumbent. He remained an immensely formidable figure, hard for the chiefs of staff to resist, his prestige raised so high by domestic propaganda that he was effectively unsackable.

Navy planners argued that, with the Marianas air bases in U.S. hands, the large Japanese army in the Philippines could be left to contemplate its own impotence while American forces addressed Iwo Jima, Okinawa and thereafter the Japanese home islands. There was a case for the United States to undertake limited operations to secure some Philippines airfields and harbours, but none for what actually followed. MacArthur was bent upon fighting his way through the entire archipelago, and so he did. Although he never gained the formal endorsement of the chiefs of staff for his purposes, no one in Washington was powerful or clear-sighted enough to stop him. Marshall once wrote memorably to MacArthur, "Remember, the Navy is on our side"; the Southwest Pacific supremo never acknowledged this.

In September 1944, carriers of Halsey's Third Fleet off the southern Philippines inflicted punitive losses on Japan's surviving air capability. On the twelfth alone, 2,400 American sorties destroyed 200 enemy planes in the sky and on the ground. Nimitz and MacArthur agreed that the island base of Peleliu should be seized before the army addressed the Philippines. On 15 September, men of the 1st Marine Division made an assault landing with massive air and naval support: 10,000 Japanese defenders, supported by deeply emplaced artillery, resisted fiercely. The ensuing campaign, which also engaged a U.S. Army division, proved a nightmare. Vast quantities of ammunition and effort had to be expended to overcome the enemy's positions bunker by bunker. It was later calculated that 1,500 artillery rounds were fired for each defender killed. The Japanese, as usual, fought almost to the last man, and 1,950 Americans perished before Peleliu's commander, Col. Kunio Nakagawa, committed suicide on 24 November. The battle, a violently intense miniature, was of doubtful value to American grand strategy. It merely reinforced the message that there was no shortcut to success in seizing Japan's Pacific outposts.

On 20 October 1944, four army divisions began to land on Leyte Island, in the midst of the Philippines. They met light opposition, and by afternoon the beachhead was sufficiently secure for MacArthur to stride ashore and deliver a grandiloquent liberation broadcast. Thereafter, however, increasingly vigorous Japanese resistance turned the campaign into an ordeal by rain, mud and blood for tens of thousands of U.S. soldiers. MacArthur's staff had ignored engineers' warnings that Leyte was unsuitable for airfield building, and American troops found themselves overwhelmingly dependent on carrier planes for air support. MacArthur's chief of public relations, Col. Bonner Fellers, had made his reputation in 1942 by dispatching daily signals from Cairo reporting British operations and intentions, which were intercepted by Rommel. Now, Fellers sustained his sorry record by repeatedly announcing victory on Leyte while MacArthur's soldiers were fighting for their lives.

Week after week and then month after month, weather and mountains, insects and enemy fire, exhaustion and swamps imposed their toll of misery upon every infantryman on the island. "They lost all account of the distance they had covered," wrote Norman Mailer, who served in the Philippines, in his fictional account of a patrol which marched in painful step with his own experience. "Everything beneath them had blurred, and the individual torments of each kind of terrain were forgotten . . . They wavered like a file of drunks, plodding along with their heads bent down, their arms slapping spasmodically at their sides . . . Their shoulders were blistered from their packbands, their waists were bruised from the bouncing of their cartridge belts, and their rifles clanked abrasively against their sides, raising blisters on their hips . . . Like litter-bearers, they had forgotten everything; they did not think of themselves as individual men any longer. They were merely envelopes of suffering."

Even as the Americans hacked a painful path across Leyte Island, at sea their foes launched an ambitious and desperate attempt to wreck the campaign. The Imperial Japanese Navy dispatched four carriers scantily provided with aircraft to make a feint from the north, designed to lure away Halsey's Third Fleet at the almost inevitable cost of their own destruction. Meanwhile, Japanese heavy units set forth to converge on Leyte Gulf, where they planned to attack the American amphibious armada and its relatively weak naval support force—Adm. Thomas Kinkaid's Seventh Fleet. Operation Sho-Go was never likely to succeed: whatever havoc the attackers contrived, American strategic superiority was overwhelming. But a change of Japanese codes and wireless silence imposed on their fleet at sea denied Halsey and Kinkaid foreknowledge of what was afoot. Only on 24 October was a powerful Japanese battle squadron, commanded by Vice Adm. Takeo Kurita, spotted entering the Sibuyan Sea between Leyte, Panay and Luzon. American submarines promptly dispatched two of its cruisers, and the Third Fleet launched carrier aircraft which sank the huge battleship *Musashi* and damaged other vessels. Kurita turned away, apparently conceding defeat. The impulsive Halsey, convinced he had seen off the Japanese, then disappeared north with his entire force of sixty-five ships in pursuit of Ozawa's carrier decoy force, which had been located by reconnaissance aircraft.

That night of 24 October, as Halsey raced away towards a far horizon, the Seventh Fleet fought a notable battle of its own. A second Japanese battle squadron was sighted closing on Leyte Gulf from the south, up the Surigao Strait. To meet this, Kinkaid deployed his old bombardment battleships, together with cruisers, destroyers and PT boats. A remarkable action followed. In darkness soon illuminated by eruptions of flame, the American mosquito craft inflicted little damage on the column of Japanese warships. But just before 4:00 a.m. destroyer torpedoes and radar-guided fire from the 14-inch and 16-inch main armament of Kinkaid's big ships sank the Japanese battleships *Yamashiro* and *Fuso*, together with three of their escorts. The heavy cruiser *Mogami* and the light cruiser *Abukuma* were also hit, and later sunk by U.S. aircraft. The surviving elements of the Japanese task force turned for home; only two heavy cruisers and five destroyers escaped. American ships suffered only thirty-nine men killed, most of these victims of friendly fire in the confusion of darkness. It had been a slaughter: the Japanese performance reflected not only inferior technology and gunnery, but resignation to sacrifice. The battle squadron had no realistic prospect of traversing the narrow waters of the Surigao Strait and achieving useful results unless it had the benefit of surprise, and unless the Americans responded as feebly as they had done two years earlier, in similar circumstances off Savo Island. This was never likely. The Japanese sailed to meet death, and duly did so.

But the most remarkable action of the battle, and indeed one of the strangest naval encounters in history, was still to come. During the night, the Japanese battle fleet mauled by Halsey's planes once more about-turned; after steaming eastward through the San Bernardino Strait, it steered south towards Leyte Gulf, undetected even when daylight came, and meeting no opposition. Just before 7:00 a.m., the five small escort carriers and seven escorts of Rear Adm. Clifton Sprague's Task Force 77.4.3—immortalised by its radio call sign Taffy 3—had just secured from predawn general quarters when a panic-stricken voice transmission from an antisubmarine patrol aircraft reported four Japanese battleships, eight cruisers and escorting destroyers less than twenty miles away and closing fast. Sprague exclaimed with understandable intemperance, "That sonofabitch Halsey has left us bare-assed!" His ships, slow floating platforms providing air support for MacArthur's troops ashore, strove desperately to open the range, while flying off such planes as they could muster. The Japanese, however, were soon firing hard and fast into Taffy 3.

Admiral Kurita, commanding the Japanese squadron, was offered an easy opportunity to annihilate the small, pathetically weak American force. Sprague's destroyers and planes lunged repeatedly and with extraordinary courage at the enemy, but they lacked numbers and armour-piercing bombs. Kinkaid's battleships were away to the south, many hours' steaming, after fighting their night duel in the Surigao Strait. The escort carriers and airmen knew that they alone must fight off the enemy battle fleet. Many pilots displayed prodigies of valour, through a few cracked under the strain of making repeated attacks: one man who landed back on the *Manila Bay* proved reluctant to take off again, to make his third torpedo attack of the morning. Capt. Fitzhugh Lee summoned the young man to his bridge. "He was pretty shaken up because he had watched his pals get shot down . . . We had just one torpedo left . . . We didn't have any other pilot on board—ours were all flying. So we loaded him up and I gave him a fight talk on the bridge and patted him on the back and said, 'Go out and do your best.' He did make a third run, and survived."

Overwhelming Japanese fire sank three American escorts and one carrier of Taffy 3 in a succession of mêlées at point-blank range; some fifty American aircraft were lost as they pummelled the Combined Fleet. But the cruisers *Chokai*, *Suzuya* and *Chikuma* sank under air attack, and Kurita's

Italians with one of their would-be liberators

Crewmen of the U.S. carrier *Intrepid* bury comrades at sea

A Hellcat pilot quits his cockpit after a flight-deck mishap

Temporary reprieve: a British bomber crew returns from a raid on Germany during the strategic air offensive which killed more than half of the RAF aircrew who took part

The price of collaboration: a street scene in liberated France

A Japanese family on Saipan encounter their first American

One of Slim's Bren gunners in Burma

Recovering wounded in France

Jumping into Arnhem

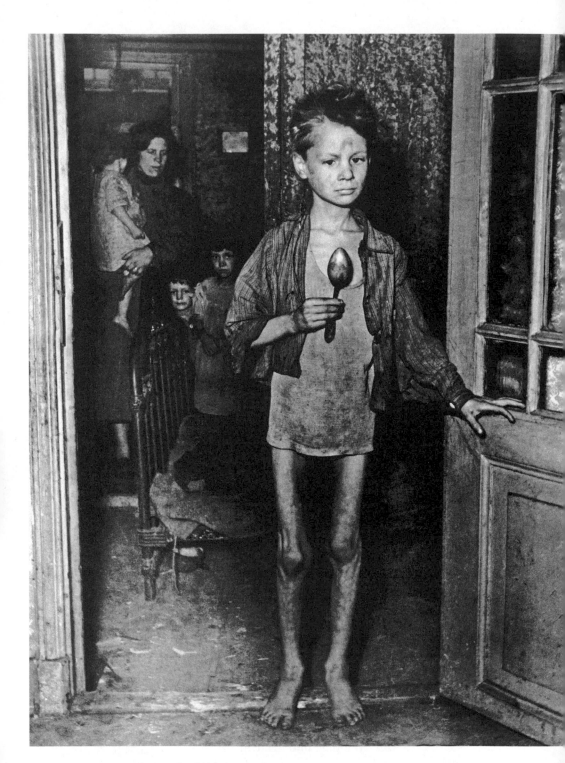

A Dutch child during his country's "Hongerwinter," 1944

Hitler's last human resorts: Wehrmacht prisoners at the Rhine, March 1945

Soviet assault guns massed for the Battle of Berlin

Ohrdruf concentration camp, April 1945

Marines on Iwo Jima

Hiroshima

nerve broke. Dismayed by the energy of American resistance, convinced that he was in the presence of elements of the Third Fleet, whose big ships would soon engage and overwhelm him, 143 minutes after the first shells were fired he broke off the action and turned for home. Taffy 3's heroics had repulsed a battle fleet in a fashion which bewildered thousands of American sailors, who earlier that morning thought themselves doomed men.

The Americans lost one further escort carrier sunk and two seriously damaged when Philippines-based Japanese planes delivered the first suicide strikes of the campaign. Halsey's aircraft duly attacked Ozawa's decoy squadron, sinking all four carriers, a light cruiser and two destroyers. The Third Fleet then turned south, to face bitter recriminations about its desertion of the Leyte squadrons. Halsey's recklessness merited his dismissal. But, given the scale of the American triumph in what became known to history as the Battle of Leyte Gulf, the largest naval clash in history, his folly was overlooked. The Japanese had committed 64 ships against 216 American and 2 Australian vessels. They lost 285,000 tons of warships, the Americans just 29,000 tons; only 2,803 Americans died, against more than 11,000 Japanese. Operation Sho-Go ended with the Imperial Navy shorn of 4 carriers, 3 battleships, 10 cruisers and 9 destroyers. The Americans lost 3 small carriers, 2 destroyers and 1 destroyer escort; several other vessels were badly hit, and would have sunk but for the energy and courage of American damage-control teams amid blazing fuel, bursting steam pipes and exploding munitions.

Leyte Gulf vividly demonstrated the collapse of Japanese naval skills: gunnery, seamanship, ship identification—and nerve. Japan's admirals conducted Sho-Go as if they expected to lose. They seemed more ready to die than to fight, a strange transition for men who, in 1941–42, showed themselves ardent and effective warriors. In many of the earlier Pacific battles, signals intelligence gave the Americans a critical edge, which they were denied in the Leyte Gulf actions. Thanks to Halsey's blunders, the power of the Third Fleet was never fully engaged. Yet at every turn, the U.S. Navy outfought its enemies. To be sure, technology and especially radar were deployed to American advantage; the destruction of Japan's naval air arm enabled Halsey's and Kinkaid's pilots to fly almost unchallenged. But the essential message of the battle was that the Imperial Navy had suffered a moral as well as a material collapse.

Leyte Island was secured at the end of December; thereafter, on 9 January 1945 U.S. forces landed on the main Philippine island of Luzon, to begin a campaign which lasted for the rest of the war against Japanese forces directed with stubborn skill by Gen. Tomoyoki Yamashita, the 1942

"Tiger of Malaya." Manila, the capital, was razed to the ground during weeks of fighting, in which forces of Japanese sailors fought almost to the last man. These men also committed massacres of civilians which lacked the smallest military purpose, but demonstrated Japan's determination to impose death upon every victim within reach, often accompanied by rape and mutilation, before meeting its own fate.

Many Filipinos who escaped Japanese savagery perished under American artillery fire; Manila was reduced to rubble, making a mockery of its liberation. Up to 100,000 of its citizens died in the ruins of their capital, alongside 1,000 Americans and 16,000 Japanese. Yamashita retreated to the mountainous, densely forested centre of the island, where he sustained a shrinking perimeter until August 1945. The U.S. Eighth Army under Eichelburger continued successive amphibious operations throughout the Philippines until the end of the war, occupying islands one by one, after battles that were sometimes fierce and costly. MacArthur could claim that he had reconquered the archipelago and inflicted defeat on its Japanese occupiers. But since those soldiers could not have been transported to any battlefield where they might influence the war's outcome, they were as much prisoners in the Philippines as was Hitler's large, futile garrison in the German-occupied British Channel Islands.

"The Philippines campaign was a mistake," says the present-day Japanese historian Kazutoshi Hando, who lived through the war. "MacArthur did it for his own reasons. Japan had lost the war once the Marianas were gone." The Filipino people whom MacArthur professed to love paid the price for his egomania in lost lives—perhaps half a million, including those who perished from famine and disease—and wrecked homes. It was as great a misfortune for them as for the Allied war effort that neither President Roosevelt nor the U.S. chiefs of staff could contain MacArthur's ambitions within a smaller compass of folly. In 1944, America's advance to victory over Japan was inexorable, but the misjudgements of the Southwest Pacific supreme commander disfigured its achievement.

CHAPTER TWENTY-THREE

GERMANY BESIEGED

IN THE FIRST DAYS of September 1944, much of the Allied leadership—with the notable exception of Winston Churchill—supposed their nations within weeks of completing the conquest of the Third Reich. Many Germans were of the same opinion, making grim preparations for the moment when invaders would sweep their country. A German NCO named Pickers wrote to his wife in Saarlouis: "You and I are both living in constant mortal danger. I have written *finis* to my life, for I doubt if I'll come out of this alive. So I'll say goodbye to you and the children." The soldier Josef Roller's father wrote to him from Trier: "I have buried all the china and silver and the big carpet in the stables. The small carpet is in Annie's cellar. I have bricked in Annie's china where the wine used to be. So if we should have gone you will find it all, but be careful in digging, so that nothing gets broken. So, Josef, all the best and keep your head down, fondest greetings and kisses from us all, your papa."

The German people understood that if the Russians broke through in the east, all was lost. "Then there'll be nothing left but to take poison," a Hamburg neighbour told Mathilde Wolff-Monckeburg, "quite calmly, as if she was suggesting pancakes for dinner tomorrow." It is more surprising that some Nazi followers still clung doggedly to hope. Konrad Moser was a child evacuee in one of many hostels for his kind, located beside a POW camp at Eichstadt on the grounds that the Allies were unlikely to bomb it. Late in 1944 when his elder brother Hans arrived to take him back home to Nuremberg, the hostel's warden said accusingly, "I know why you want him. You don't believe in final victory!" Hans Moscr shook his head and said, "I'm on leave from the Eastern Front." He took Konrad back to his parents, with whom the child survived the war.

Most of Germany's cities were already devastated by bombing. Emmy Suppanz wrote to her son on the Western Front from Marburg, describing life at home: "Café Kaefer is still open from 6:30 to 9 a.m. and from 5 to 10 or 11 p.m. Bits of plaster moulding fell off the ceilings in the last attack, though oddly enough the mirrors are still unbroken. The windows in the café and the flat above have gone, of course. Burschi had two rabbits, one fairly big white one called Hansi and a smaller grey one to which we had not yet given a name, and was eaten a fortnight ago. The cook wanted to kill Hansi also, but she didn't do it. Yesterday Burschi met me with news that Hansi had seven young ones! Sepp, the town . . . was dreadful." Such news from home ate deep into the spirit of soldiers far away, fighting for their lives.

On the other side of the hill, the Allied armies' dash across France amid rejoicing crowds infused commanders and soldiers alike with a sense of intoxication. The GI Edwin Wood wrote of the exhilaration of pursuit: "To be nineteen years old, to be nineteen and an infantryman, to be nineteen and fight for the liberation of France from the Nazis in the summer of 1944! That time of hot and cloudless blue days when the honeybees buzzed about our heads and we shouted strange phrases in words we did not understand to men and women who cheered us as if we were gods . . . For that glorious moment, the dream of freedom lived and we were ten feet tall." Sir Arthur Harris asserted that, thanks to the support of the RAF's and USAAF's bombers, the armies in France had enjoyed "a walkover." This was a gross exaggeration, characteristic of the rhetoric of both British and American air chiefs, but it was certainly true that in the autumn of 1944 the Western Allies liberated France and Belgium at much lower human cost than their leaders had anticipated. A flood of Ultra-intercepted signals revealed the despair of Hitler's generals, the ruin of their forces. This in turn induced in Eisenhower and his subordinates a brief and ill-judged carelessness. With the Germans on their knees, unprecedented rewards seemed available for risk taking: Montgomery persuaded Eisenhower that in his own northern sector of the front, there was an opportunity to launch a war-winning thrust, to seize a bridge over the Rhine at the Dutch town of Arnhem, across which Allied forces might flood into Germany.

It remains a focus of fierce controversy whether the Western Allied armies should have been able to win the war in 1944, following the Wehrmacht's collapse in France. It is just plausible that, with a greater display of command energy, Gen. Courtney Hodges's U.S. First Army could have broken through the Siegfried Line around Aachen. Patton believed that he could have done great things if his tanks had been granted the necessary fuel, but this is doubtful: the southern sector, where his army stood, was difficult ground; until April 1945 its German defenders exploited a succession of hill positions and rivers to check Patton's advance. The Allies spent the vital early September days catching their breath after the dash eastward. Gen. Alexander Patch's U.S. Seventh Army, which had landed in the south of France on 15 August and driven north up the Rhône Valley against slight opposition, met Patton's men at Châtillon-sur-Seine on 12 September. Lt. Gen. Jake Devers became commander of the new Franco-American 6th Army Group, deployed on the Allied right flank. Eisenhower's forces now held an unbroken front from the Channel to the Swiss border.

But they still lacked a usable major port. The French rail system was largely wrecked. Some planners complained that the Allied bombing prior to D-Day had been overdone, but this seems a judgement that could be made only once the Normandy battle was safely won. The movement of fuel, ammunition and supplies for 2 million men by roads alone posed enormous problems. Almost every ton of supplies had to be trucked hundreds of miles from the beaches to the armies, though Marseilles soon began to make an important contribution. "Until we get Antwerp," Eisenhower wrote to Marshall, "we are always going to be operating on a shoestring." Many tanks and vehicles needed maintenance. In much the same fashion that the Wehrmacht allowed the British to escape from the Continent amid German euphoria in 1940, an outbreak of Allied "victory disease" permitted their enemies now to regroup. By the time Montgomery launched Operation Market Garden, his ambitious dash for the Rhine, the Germans had regained their balance. Their strategic predicament remained irrecoverable, but they displayed persistent stubbornness in local defence, matched by aggressive energy in responding to Allied initiatives.

On 17 September, three Allied airborne divisions landed in Holland: the U.S. 82nd and 101st were tasked to seize river and canal crossings between the Allied front line and Arnhem; the British 1st Airborne to capture the Rhine bridge and hold a perimeter beyond it. The entire formation was dispatched to a drop zone north of the great river. The American operations were largely successful, though German demolitions at Zon enforced delay while a replacement Bailey bridge was brought forward. The British, however, farthest from Montgomery's relieving force, ran into immediate difficulties. Ultra had revealed that the remains of the 9th and 10th SS Panzer Divisions were refitting at Arnhem. Allied commanders discounted their presence, because the formations had been so ravaged in Normandy, but the Germans responded to the sudden British descent with their usual impressive violence. Scratch local forces, many of them made up of rear-area administrative and support personnel, improvised blocking positions that drastically delayed the paratroopers' march to the bridge. Model, Hitler's favourite "fireman" of the Eastern Front, was on hand to direct the German response. Some elements of the 1st Airborne Division displayed a notable lack of verve and tactical skill; they were broken up and destroyed piecemeal while attempting to advance into Arnhem. Even the small number of German armoured vehicles within reach of the town were able to maul airborne units which had few antitank weapons and no tanks.

The lone battalion that reached the bridge could only hold positions at its northern end, separated from the relieving armoured force by the Rhine and a rapidly growing number of Germans. The British decision to drop the 1st Airborne outside Arnhem imposed a four-hour delay between the opening of the first parachute canopies and Lt. Col. John Frost's arrival on foot at the bridge; this provided the Germans in their vehicles with far too generous a margin of time to respond. The British might have seized the Rhine crossing by dropping glider-borne coup de main parties directly onto the objective, as the Germans had done in Holland in 1940, and the British at the Caen Canal on D-Day. Such an initiative would have certainly cost lives, but far fewer than were lost battering a path into Arnhem. As it was, from the afternoon of the seventeenth onwards, the British in and around the town were merely struggling for survival, having already forfeited any realistic prospect of fulfilling their objectives.

There was, however, an even more fundamental flaw in Montgomery's plan, which would probably have scotched his ambitions even if British paratroopers had secured both sides of the bridge. The relieving force needed to cover the fifty-nine miles from the Meuse-Escaut Canal to Arnhem in three days, with access to only a single Dutch road; a cross-country advance was impossible, because the ground was too soft for armour. Within minutes of crossing the start line, the Guards Armoured Division was in trouble as its leading tanks were knocked out by German anti-tank weapons, and supporting British infantry became bogged down in local firefights. The American airborne formations did all that could have been expected of them in securing key crossings, but the Allied advance was soon behind schedule. The Germans were able to make their own deployments in full knowledge of Allied intentions, because they found the operational plan for Market Garden on the body of a U.S. staff officer who had recklessly carried it into battle; within hours, the document was on the desk of Model, who exploited his insight to the full.

On 20 September, when the XXX Corps belatedly reached Nijmegen, paratroopers of Gen. James Gavin's 82nd Airborne made a heroic crossing of the Waal River in assault boats under devastating fire. They secured a perimeter on the far bank which enabled the Guards Armoured's tanks to cross the bridge, which was still miraculously intact. There was then another twenty-four-hour delay, incomprehensible to the Americans, before the British felt ready to resume their advance on Arnhem.

In truth the time lag was unimportant: the battle was already lost. The Germans were committed in strength to defend the southern approaches to Arnhem. Residual resistance by the British paratroopers on the far bank was irrelevant, and Montgomery acknowledged failure. On the night of 25 September, 2,000 men of the 1st Airborne Division were ferried to safety across the Rhine downstream from Arnhem, while almost 2,000 more escaped by other means, leaving behind 6,000 who became prisoners. Some 1,485 British paratroopers were killed, around 16 percent of each unit engaged, and the 1st Airborne Division was disbanded; 474 airmen were also killed during the operation. Meanwhile the U.S. 82nd Airborne suffered 1,432 casualties and the 101st 2,118. The Germans lost 1,300 dead and 453 Dutch civilians were killed, many of them by Allied bombing.

Apologists for Market Garden, notably including Montgomery, asserted that it achieved substantial success by leaving the Allies in possession of a deep salient into Holland. This was nonsense, for it was a cul-de-sac which took the Allies nowhere until February 1945. For eight weeks after the Arnhem battle, the two U.S. airborne divisions were obliged to fight hard to hold the ground they won in September, though it had become strategically worthless. The Arnhem assault was a flawed concept for which the chances of success were negligible. The British commanders charged with executing it, notably Lt. Gen. Frederick "Boy" Browning, displayed shameful incompetence and merited dismissal with ignominy rather than the honours they received in a classic British propaganda operation intended to dignify disaster.

Montgomery's cardinal error was that he succumbed to the lust for glory which often deflected Allied commanders from their cause's best strategic interests. Gen. Jake Devers, one of the ablest though least celebrated American army group commanders of the war, wrote afterwards about the inevitability of differences between nations on ways and means, even if they were united in the goal of defeating the enemy: "This is not only true of men at the highest political level . . . it is a natural trait of professional military men . . . It is unreasonable to expect that the military representatives of nations who are serving under unified command will subordinate promptly and freely their own views to those of a commander of another nationality, unless the commander . . . has convinced them that it is to their national interests individually and collectively." Because Eisenhower lacked a coherent vision, his subordinates were often left to compete for and pursue their own. Montgomery's ambition to personally deliver a war-winning thrust, fortified by conceit, caused him to undertake the only big operation for which the Allied armies could generate logistic support that autumn across the terrain least suited to its success. He failed to recognise that the clearing of the Scheldt approaches, to enable Antwerp to operate as an Allied supply base, was a much more important and plausible objective for his army. To use a nursery analogy, in thrusting for a Rhine bridge the Allied leadership's eyes were bigger than their stomachs.

The British land worker Muriel Green revealed to her diary a surge of depression such as infected every Allied nation on hearing news of the Arnhem failure. "We all thought the war was so nearly over and now we hear of such sacrifice of lives it makes me miserable. I suppose we are taking victory so much for granted it makes such disasters seem worse." As the war entered its final phase, it became ever harder for families to endure the loss of loved ones with whom they yearned to share the fruits of peace. Ivor Rowberry, a twenty-two-year-old trainee accountant killed while serving as a signaller with the South Staffordshires, left behind words for his parents which reflected the sentiments of many fighting men of many nations:

> This . . . is a letter I hoped you would never receive . . . Tomorrow we go into action. As yet we do not know exactly what our job will be, but no doubt it will be a dangerous one in which many lives will be lost— mine may be one of those lives. Well, Mom, I am not afraid to die. I like this life, yes—for the past two years I have planned and dreamed and mapped out a perfect future for myself. I would have liked that future to materialize, but it is not what I will but what God wills, and if by sacrificing all this I leave the world slightly better than I found it I am perfectly willing to make that sacrifice. Don't get me wrong though, Mom, I am no flag-waving patriot . . . England's a great little country—the best there is—but I cannot honestly say that it is "worth fighting for." Nor can I fancy myself in the role of a gallant crusader fighting for the liberation of Europe. It would be a nice thought but I would only be kidding myself. No, Mom, my little world is centred around you and including Dad, everyone at home, and my friends at W[olverhamp]ton—*That* is worth fighting for—and if by doing so it strengthens your security and improves your lot in any way, then it is worth dying for too.

Allied hopes of breaking into Germany—or even of winning the war in 1944—did not immediately collapse at the end of September with the failure of Market Garden. Instead, they shrank progressively during the weeks that followed, as their soldiers floundered into a sea of mud and local disappointments. Too much historical attention has focused on the drama of the dash for Arnhem; even had Montgomery secured a Rhine bridge, it is implausible that he could have exploited this to break through into Germany. More promising possibilities lay in the path of Hodges's First U.S. Army, around Aachen just inside the German frontier; in early and mid-September, this nearest sector of Hitler's West Wall was scarcely defended, yet between the twelfth and the fifteenth the Americans failed in a succession of unconvincing attempts to break through. Hodges was the least impressive commander of a U.S. army, and his autumn operations were conducted with notable clumsiness. Five more weeks elapsed before the First Army occupied the ruins of Aachen. If Patton had commanded there, it is just possible that a quick breach in the West Wall might have been achieved. As it was, his Third Army battered at Metz through September, cursing the incessant rain, to no consequence except that of a mounting casualty list.

Hodges's next serious error was to launch his army into a desperate, bloody two-month struggle to clear the Huertgen forest, which was thought to threaten his right flank and rear. Four American divisions in turn suffered misery, heavy losses and soaring combat-fatigue rates in the dense woodland. The Germans doggedly held their ground, imposing a price for each small advance, and by the time the First Army emerged onto the Roer plain in early December, all hopes of an early victory had perished. Montgomery's armies, meanwhile, were obliged to spend the autumn clearing the Scheldt estuary to open Antwerp. This was a task that might have been fulfilled in days in mid-September, when the enemy was in disarray; in October and November, however, it required months of hard fighting in waterlogged terrain. Again and again, units launched attacks along narrow open causeways exposed to withering German fire.

The Scheldt estuary was defended not by SS panzers or elite infantry formations, but by the 70th "White Bread" Division, formed from medical cases, which a German naval officer described as "an apathetic, undisciplined mob." Yet it required no great skill to fire machine guns and mortars at attackers exposed in plain view: for weeks, these ailing Germans frustrated the best of the Canadian Army. The commanding officer of the Queen's Own Rifles of Canada wrote of "the utter misery of the conditions and the great courage required to do the simplest things. Attacks had to go on along dykes swept by enemy fire. To go through the *polder* meant wading, without possibility of concealment, in water that at times came up to the chest. Mortar fire, at which the Germans were masters, crashed at every rallying point . . . It was peculiarly a rifleman's fight in that there were no great decisive battles, just a steady continuous struggle." Most attacks had to be conducted by platoon-sized forces, advancing on a one-man front. So deadly was German automatic fire that the proportion of fatalities to wounded men was 50 percent higher than usual.

After a week in the Breskens pocket fighting, a single Canadian brigade had lost 533 men, including 111 killed. By the end of November, one division committed had suffered 2,077 casualties, including 544 killed or missing, and the other lost 3,650 casualties in thirty-three days, 405 men from each of its rifle battalions. This represented a rate of loss almost as heavy as that the Canadian troops suffered in the November 1917 Passchendaele battle, generally regarded as one of the worst experiences of World War I. Even low-grade German defenders could a hold a line in country where armour could not operate, bunkers provided protection against all but direct hits and the treeless landscape offered no scope for tactical subtlety.

The 1 November amphibious assault on Walcheren Island was a messy and expensive business, and a week's hard fighting was required before the Germans surrendered. The first Allied convoy to unload at Antwerp arrived only on 28 November. Given the decisive impact of supply problems on the Allied armies from late August onwards, and the miracle that Antwerp's docks had been captured intact in September, failure to seize the Scheldt approaches proved the worst single mistake of the campaign. Responsibility stretched all the way down the Allied command chain from Eisenhower. But Montgomery was the man with operational responsibility, the general who considered himself a master of war, and he must bear principal blame. "By the winter Americans had ceased to regard Monty as amusing," said Lt. Gen. Sir Frederick Morgan, "and in the cases of [Bedell] Smith and Bradley . . . contempt had grown into active hatred."

The Western Allies lost a small chance of breaking into Germany in September—small, because probability suggests that they lacked sufficient combat power to win the war in 1944—because they succumbed to the euphoria of victory in France. They lacked energy and imagination to improvise expedients to overcome their supply problems, as an advancing German army might have done. It is also arguable that the large resources committed to Pacific operations in 1944, in defiance of the "Germany First" strategy, denied Eisenhower the margin of men and shipping which might just have enabled his armies to deliver a war-winning punch. Both the U.S. and British armies were chronically short of infantry, and over-weighted with redundant antiaircraft and antitank units. In Montgomery's 21st Army Group, these absorbed 47,120 precious men, 7.1 percent of his total strength, while in Normandy only 82,000 of 662,000 British soldiers deployed were riflemen. In the course of the winter some of these units were broken up and their personnel transferred to the infantry, but until the end of the campaign too few British and American soldiers were fighting, too many performing marginal roles. Allied tactics were adversely influenced by the degree to which their armies made themselves prisoners of vehicles.

The Anglo-Americans failed to convert a big victory into a decisive one, and they paid the price in the months of fighting that followed. *Wacht*, the German Nineteenth Army's newspaper, wrote on 1 October: "The English, and even more the Americans, have throughout this war sought to avoid a very large sacrifice of lives . . . They still shrink from total commitment, the true soldierly sacrifice . . . American infantry only attack with a great armoured spearhead, and only launch an assault after a great hail of shells and bombs. If, then, they still meet German resistance, they break off the attack immediately and try again next day with their heavy firepower." If this view was self-serving, it was not wholly invalid.

The winter of 1944 proved one of the wettest for decades in western Europe. From October onwards, the weather reinforced the Germans, imposing stagnation across the front. "Dear General," Eisenhower wrote to Marshall on 11 November, "I am getting exceedingly tired of weather." If conditions were wretched for all the combatants, they hurt the Allies most, because they were trying to keep moving. Waterlogged ground rendered rapid off-road advances impossible, tanks and vehicles thrashed and flailed in mud up to their track guards and wheel hubs, air operations were drastically constricted, and the Germans exploited every water obstacle. The British had become acutely casualty-conscious as their armies shrank amid the exhaustion of national manpower reserves; they spent the winter advancing slowly through eastern Holland, sometimes making no headway for weeks. Nijmegen stands barely thirty-five miles west of Wesel, but the Reichswald forest lay in between; six months intervened between the capture of the former town on 20 September 1944 and the British crossing of the Rhine at Wesel on 23 March 1945.

For all Patton's celebrity, his army made slow progress through Alsace-Lorraine, eventually reaching the German border in mid-December. On his right, Gen. Jacob Devers's 6th Army Group met bitter resistance from Germans defending a perimeter on the west bank of the upper Rhine, the so-called Colmar pocket. Pvt. William Tsuchida, a medical aidman in the Vosges, wrote to his parents:

What a mess this whole business is. My mind is one confused conglomeration of incidents, the basic fears of night, and the waiting for daylight. The rest of it I would just as soon forget because it is so rotten.

The Allied Breakout from Normandy

ENGLAND

NETHERLANDS

GERMANY

Dover •

Dunkirk •

Calais •

Lille •

BELGIUM

⊙ Brussels

LUX.

Rhine

English Channel

6 June 1944

Somme

Cherbourg •

Dieppe •

Le Havre •

Rouen •

Oise

Reims •

Meuse

Nancy •

Paris ⊙

Seine

Marne

Epinal •

Rennes

Alençon •

Troyes •

Belfort •

Le Mans •

Orléans •

Loire

Dijon •

Saône

Pontarlier •

SWITZERLAND

Angers •

Tours •

Saumur •

Nantes •

Cher

Nevers •

Geneva •

Poitiers •

FRANCE

Vichy •

Bay of
Biscay

Limoges •

Royan •

Angoulême •

Clermont •
Ferrand

St Etienne •

Lyons •

Grenoble •

Lanslebourg •

Briançon •

ITALY

Bordeaux •

Garonne

Rhône

Toulouse •

Nice •

St Jean de Luz •

Marseilles •

Toulon •

SPAIN

Perpignan •

Mediterranean Sea

0   50   100   150 miles

0   50   100   150   200 kms

I hope everybody with the soft war jobs realises the horrible days and nights the line company men have to spend out here . . . I get in such a daze sometimes that I force myself to read something when I can, like a magazine or old letter. What it amounts to is you wonder whether you should eat now or later and hope you have a dry place to sleep tonight and hope that casualties will slow down. Everything is hope, hope.

An airborne soldier, Pfc. Bill True, was intensely moved when, one evening in the midst of the Dutch battles, a little girl approached the fox-hole occupied by himself and another man, and handed them two pillows. Here was a tiny, innocent gesture towards decencies of civilisation which otherwise seemed immeasurably remote.

ALLIED SUPPLY difficulties persisted, even when ships began to unload at Antwerp. Anglo-American soldiers required far larger quantities of food and comforts than their enemies deemed necessary, and expended prodigious quantities of ammunition to secure even modest local objectives. Eisenhower's troops advancing across Europe behaved much better than the Russians, but almost all soldiers living in fear of their lives display a cruel indifference towards the property of others. A Dutch doctor described his disgust on seeing the village of Venray, just behind the front line in Holland, after it had been occupied by British soldiers: "Words cannot describe how appalled I was when I saw how the town had been pillaged and destroyed. I spoke to an elderly English officer whose words speak for themselves: 'I'm very sorry and deeply ashamed, the Army has lost its reputation here.' "

The killing of prisoners was never institutionalised, as on the Eastern Front, but Eisenhower's men committed their share of excesses. A Canadian soldier described his experience of a patrol in Holland, in which his unit captured eight dismounted German tankers attempting to get back to their own lines. Their officer spoke good English, and the enemies chatted for some minutes about the cold, and how they would like to light a fire. They had just passed a farmhouse, he said, where there might be schnapps and a pig. Could they roast it? The Canadian said later, "The war was over for him, and I guess he was glad." Then, suddenly, the lieutenant leading the patrol turned to his Bren gunner and said, "Shoot them." The German officer who had been making jokes "sort of made a little run forward and put his arms across his chest and said something and the guy with the bren just cut loose . . . There were two, I think, still flopping like gaffed salmon, and this guy we called Whitey from Cape Breton—we called him Whitey because he was always boasting how good a coalminer he was—he shot those two with a pistol . . . It probably went into our history, I guess, as a German patrol wiped out. None of us really thought too much about it . . . But I'll tell you this, a year before, if I'd been there, I'd have been puking up my guts."

Allied forces edged towards the German border yard by painful yard. During a November attack in Alsace, within seconds of encountering devastating German machine-gun fire Pvt. Robert Kotlowitz found himself the only unwounded survivor of his platoon.

> I remember from that moment, when mass disorientation began to set in, the glob-smell of mud in my nostrils . . . the sudden drying-up of saliva in my mouth and the instant dehydration it produced; the powerful feel of my own body, as though I was carrying it as a burden; my skinny, attenuated frame, lying there on the ground, waiting; the heavy presence of limbs extending from it; my helmeted skull, quivering torso, and vulnerable crotch. The tender genitals curled dead-center at my pelvis; and my swollen bladder, burning . . . The noise of small-arms and machine-gun fire, of men's voices calling for help or screaming in pain or terror—our own men's voices, unrecognizable at first, weird in pitch and timbre. And the hum inside my own head, trying to drown out the sounds coming from all around me.

Kotlowitz lay motionless until nightfall, when he was evacuated by medics to become a combat-fatigue case. He never served in the line again. British lieutenant Tony Finucane described a battalion "advance to contact" in Holland: "We strung out across the flatland in what looked and felt like a casual stroll in the afternoon sunshine. Suddenly nearing the objective, and with men feeling for their shovels to get well dug in before nightfall, we saw a hundred yards ahead of us lots of men in grey advance in a similar formation. Imagine it! Two battalions head on in the open! Within moments a real infantry small arms battle—and pandemonium—started. We had no supporting fire, the enemy (usually referred to by ourselves as 'the wily Hun') opened up with what looked like a 20mm ack-ack gun. But in the event, with odds about evens we were better at it than they were. They backed off about half a mile."

But each such small encounter, victorious or no, imposed a loss of momentum and irreplaceable British losses. By the time Finucane found himself at Cleve in December, his platoon was reduced from thirty-five men to eleven. When his brigadier visited the forward positions and was told of the battalion's depleted rifle strength, he said with a sigh, "That's what I keep telling the General. The casualties don't look much considering the total number of men involved, but they are all fighting troops." Alan Brooke was heard to say that he wished circumstances had placed the British on the right rather than the left of Eisenhower's line. The British CIGS believed that opportunities existed in the south which Montgomery's army could have exploited more effectively than the Americans. In this, he was assuredly wrong. His view reflected only a manifestation of mutual Anglo-American mistrust, which became more pronounced as each nation's generals balefully examined the other's failures and disappointments.

Stalin, curiously enough, displayed more enthusiasm for the Western contribution to the war that winter than at any previous period, despite the Allied tensions provoked by Russian refusal to aid the embattled Poles in their ill-judged Warsaw Uprising. "A new feature of the struggle against Hitler's Germany in the past year," he told a Moscow party gathering on 6 November, "is the fact that the Red Army has not been fighting the Germans alone as was previously the case. The Tehran conference was not held in vain—its resolutions on the joint offensive against Germany from the west, east and south are being implemented with real conviction. There is no doubt that without the second front in Europe, which has engaged up to seventy-five German divisions, our forces would have been unable so quickly to break German resistance and expel Germany's armies from the Soviet Union. Equally, without the Red Army's powerful summer powerful offensive, which engaged up to two hundred German divisions, our allies would have been unable so rapidly to throw the Germans out of central Italy, France and Belgium. The challenge, the key to victory, is to keep Germany in the grip of the two fronts."

By December, when snow came, Eisenhower's armies had resigned themselves to shivering through the winter, then resuming their offensive when conditions allowed. It is hard for civilians to comprehend the miseries of an outdoor existence week after week and month after month in such conditions. "With our tent and clothing wet and half-frozen," wrote George Neill, an American soldier, "I felt numb to the point of almost not caring what happened to me." In his foxhole in darkness, "the temperature moved well below freezing. The half-frozen slush in the bottom of the hole froze solid. We just lay there in a fetal position and swore to ourselves . . . My buddies and I agreed it would be impossible to exaggerate how hopeless, miserable and depressed we felt." Such was the normal condition of millions of men on both sides of the line between October 1944 and March 1945. Trench foot became endemic, especially in formations in which morale was low and thus hygiene discipline slack. Dysentery was commonplace. The working or malfunctioning of excretory processes became an obsession for millions of men deprived of control over their bowels. In battlefield conditions, many never made it to a latrine or were unable even to lower their trousers before defecating.

If it was miserable to fight at all, it was more so in soiled clothing. Tank crews suffered special indignities. A German driver wrote: "Through my vision slit I saw many hilarious sights of brave soldiers, hanging on for dear life to the turret of a moving panzer with their trousers round their ankles and screwing up their faces in a desperate attempt to do the almost impossible." The infantryman Guy Sajer lost control of his bowels during the retreat from the Don, and grew accustomed, like all the fellow passengers in his truck, to jolting through the snow in a mess of his own excrement. Pfc. Donald Schoo suffered the same miseries during the Bulge battle. After defecating on a wooden ammunition box, "your butt hurt too much to wipe so you just pulled up your pants and went back to your hole. No one said anything about how you smelt, because everyone smelled bad."

Robert Kotlowitz was crouched in a foxhole in Alsace when his bowels suddenly exploded. He leapt forth, tore down his trousers and squatted. His buddy shouted, "Jesus Christ! Get back where you belong!" Kotlowitz, preoccupied with the demands of his body, looked on him pityingly.

> Then there was the strange assaultive sound of a rifle shot nearby, and a bullet hit the ground a few feet behind me, plowing the dirt . . . I looked ahead from my squatting position, shielding my eyes with the flat of my hand. I could see a German soldier, visible from the waist up . . . a couple of hundred yards away . . . he was laughing. All this was very clear to me: his laughter, the details of his clothing, the padded shoulders, the high collar, the bare head. I even thought that I could see his teeth . . . Then there was another shot and another clear miss. The dirt flew again. But this time I was on my feet, holding onto my pants, and in another second was in our foxhole . . . I believe the son of a bitch deliberately chose to miss me . . . he just wanted a little afternoon sport to relieve the general tedium, and I happened to be it.

Vastly worse indignities were visited on those who suffered intestinal wounds. A U.S. Army nurse, Dorothy Beavers, noted that some patients in her field hospital bore the loss of limbs with outward stoicism, while those who had undergone colostomies often "burst into tears at the sight of their own faeces in a bag." There were no limits to the miseries imposed by bullets, high explosives, sickness and vulnerability to the elements.

IN THE WINTER OF 1944, Hitler knew he faced another looming Soviet offensive. Dismissing the constraints imposed by the weather and his shrunken resources, he determined to make a crippling thrust at Eisenhower's armies before turning to meet this. Against the impassioned opposition of his generals, he launched a western offensive in the worst season of the year, at the place the Allies least expected it—the Ardennes forest, on the frontiers of Germany, Belgium and Luxembourg. The objective was to reach Antwerp, splitting the Allied front. To execute it, two new panzer armies were created, thirty divisions assembled, reserves of precious fuel stockpiled. "If you are brave, diligent and resourceful," an order of the day told shivering volksgrenadiers on 16 December, "you will ride in American vehicles and eat good American food. If, however, you are stupid, cowardly and supine, you will walk cold and hungry all the way to the Channel."

In the early hours of that morning, Operation Autumn Mist was launched against the weakest sector of Hodges's First U.S. Army. It achieved absolute tactical and strategic surprise, a breakthrough on a forty-mile-wide front as panic-stricken American troops broke and fled in disarray in the path of the SS panzers; because of thick fog, the Allied air forces were impotent to intervene. Within two days, German troops were pouring through a gaping hole—"the bulge"—in the American line. Eisenhower's British chief of intelligence, Maj. Gen. Kenneth Strong, bore a substantial share of responsibility for failing to recognise the significance of the German buildup in the Ardennes, which had been flagged by Ultra. Strong told the supreme commander that German formations identified in the area were merely resting and refitting. The fundamental failure, in which many senior American and British officers were complicit, was that they were convinced of their own mastery of the campaign and, thus, discounted the possibility of a major German thrust.

Lt. Tony Moody was one of a host of young Americans who found themselves overwhelmed by the experience of retreat. "I wasn't scared at the beginning—I got more scared: it was the uncertainty; we had no mission, we didn't know where the Germans were. We were so tired, out of rations, low on ammo. There was panic, there was chaos. If you feel you're surrounded by overwhelming forces, you get the hell out of it. I was demoralized, sick as a dog. I had frostbite. I felt pretty bad about it. I kept thinking 'oh my God, what I have got into? How much of this can I take?' I suddenly found myself quite alone, and wandered off. I stumbled into a battalion aid station and I just collapsed . . . slept twenty-four hours. The mind washes out a lot of images, but you remember the feeling of hopelessness, despair. You just want to die. We felt the Germans were much better trained, better equipped, a better fighting machine than us."

"Fear reigned," wrote Donald Burgett. His formation, the 101st Airborne, played a critical part in stabilising the front, while watching soldiers of some other units flee for their lives. "Once fear strikes, it spreads like an epidemic, faster than wildfire. Once the first man runs, others soon follow. Then, it's all over; soon there are hordes of men running, all of them wild-eyed and driven by fear." Pfc. Harold Lindstrom, from Alexandria, Minnesota, became so desperate in his misery that he found himself gazing with envy at German corpses. "They looked peaceful. The war was over for them. They weren't cold any more." He even felt pangs of envy towards comrades desperate enough to maim themselves: "No one would ever know how many accidents were genuine and how many self-made." An infantry company commander wrote of an action at Stoumont on the twenty-first: "It was so foggy that one of our men found himself ten yards from a German machine-gun before he knew it . . . Everyone had been pushed about as far as he could be. Nerves were being broken on men whom one would have thought would never weaken."

A young infantryman described his predicament one late December day when his foxhole buddy was hit: "Gordon got ripped by a machine-gun from roughly the left thigh through the right waist. He . . . told me he was hit through the stomach as well . . . We were cut off . . . We were in foxholes by ourselves, so we both knew he was going to die. We had no morphine. We couldn't ease [the pain] so I tried to knock him out. I took off his helmet, held his jaw up, and just whacked it as hard as I could, because he wanted to be put out. That didn't work, so I hit him up by the head with a helmet and that didn't work. Nothing worked. He slowly froze to death, he bled to death."

Belgian civilians suffered terribly at the hands of both sides. The Germans, during their brief reoccupation of liberated towns and villages, found time to execute scores of civilians either deemed guilty of resistance activity or, more often, murdered merely as examples to others. The savagery of some of Model's men reflected a venom characteristic of 1944–45: if they themselves were doomed to lose the war and probably to die, they were bent upon depriving as many enemies as possible of the joys of survival and liberation. Allied bombing and shelling compounded civilians' plight: in the small town of Houffalize, for instance, 192 people died, all but 8 of them from Allied bombing. Twenty-seven of the victims were younger than fifteen, and the survivors were left with ruins and destitution. Twenty inhabitants of the village of Sainlez near Bastogne were killed by bombardment that reduced every home to a shell; among them were eight members of one family named Didier: Joseph, forty-six; Marie-Angèle, sixteen; Alice, fifteen; Renée, thirteen; Lucille, eleven; Bernadette, nine; Lucien, eight; and Noël, six. Throughout the battle areas of Belgium and Luxembourg there was wholesale looting by Allied as well as German troops.

Model's panzers were exultant in the wake of their early successes, while Allied commanders were stunned and appalled. German deployment of small numbers of English-speaking commandos in American uniforms, led by Otto Skorzeny, inspired an epidemic of "fifth-column fever" that prompted the Americans to execute every such disguised enemy soldier they captured. A New Year's Day air assault on Allied airfields cost the Luftwaffe 300 aircraft to achieve the destruction of 156 American and British planes which were easily replaced. The raids further rattled Eisenhower's commanders, but in truth the strategic predicament of the Anglo-American armies was never as bad as those in the eye of the storm at first convinced themselves. They had mass, while the Germans were desperately short of tanks, aircraft, fuel and quality manpower. Behind the formidable SS panzer divisions were infantry quite incapable of matching the driving aggression that had yielded so many Wehrmacht victories in 1940–41. The logistical difficulties of supplying the German spearheads through the defiles of the Ardennes were immense; within days, Model's tanks were crippled by fuel shortages.

Sufficient American units offered stubborn resistance, especially at the vital shoulders of "the bulge," to prevent the breakthrough from becoming a rout. American reserves, notably two airborne divisions, were rushed forward. One of Bradley's soldiers watched survivors of the bitter fighting at Cheneux on 20–21 December pull back from the line. "The shattered remnants of the 1st Bn came straggling listlessly down the road, a terrible contrast to the happy battalion which had only two days before gone up the same road wisecracking and full of fight. They were bearded, red-eyed, covered with mud from head to foot, and staring blank-facedly straight to the front. No one spoke . . . They had written a page in history which few would ever know about . . . such was the confusion of places, units and deeds being churned around in the witch's brew which was the present battle."

For the Allies, powerful relief was at hand as reinforcements were fed into the line, while the German predicament worsened by the hour as American artillery delivered pulverising bombardments. "My sergeant and I jumped into a ditch," wrote a SS senior NCO, Karl Leitner, about his own experience on 21 December. "After approximately ten minutes a shell hit to the right of us, probably in a tree. My sergeant must have been badly wounded in the lung—he just gasped, and after a short time died. I had taken a piece of shrapnel in my right hip. Then a shell exploded in a tree behind. A piece of shrapnel hit me in my left ankle, other fragments slashed my right foot and ankle. I pushed myself half under my dead comrade . . . Fragments from another shell hit me in the left upper arm." It was several hours before Leitner was rescued and taken to a dressing station, during which the American barrage never let up.

Montgomery was given command of the northern sector of the front, and deployed formidable forces ready to meet the Germans if they reached the British armoured line, as most did not. On 22 December the weather cleared sufficiently to allow the Allied air forces to fly, with devastating consequences for the panzers. The German armoured spearheads advanced sixty miles at their farthest point, Foye-Nôtre-Dame, but by 3 January Hodges's and Patton's armies were counterattacking north and south, while Model's tanks had exhausted their fuel and momentum. On the sixteenth the two American pincers overcame deep snow as well as the enemy to meet at Houffalize. The Germans had suffered 100,000 casualties out of half a million men committed, and lost almost all their tanks and aircraft. The Wehrmacht infantry captain Rolf-Helmut Schröder said of his own part in the Battle of the Bulge, "We finished the battle where we had started it; then I knew—that's it." In January 1945 Schröder acknowledged the inevitability of Germany losing the war, as he had declined to do a month earlier.

The Allies lacked sufficient nerve to attempt to cut off the German retreat; Model's formations were able to withdraw in good order, with American forces following rather than crowding them. Eisenhower was content merely to restore his front after suffering the most traumatic shock of the northwest Europe campaign. The Ardennes battle left a legacy of caution among some commanders which persisted until the end of the war. "Americans are not brought up on disaster as are the British, to whom this was merely one more incident on the inevitably rough road towards final victory," in the sardonic words of Sir Frederick Morgan.

"The record of accomplishment is essentially bland and plodding," wrote that magisterial American historian Martin Blumenson. "The commanders were generally workmanlike rather than bold, prudent rather than daring, George S. Patton being of course a notable exception." Yet if Patton's reputation for energy was enhanced by his part in restoring the Ardennes front, his instinct for indiscretion remained undiminished. Visiting a field hospital, he almost committed another blunder to rival his assaults on combat-fatigue cases in Sicily. Asking one man how he had been injured, he exploded when the soldier answered, "I shot myself in the foot." Then the victim, whose ankle was shattered, added, "General, I've been in Africa, Sicily, France and now Germany. If I was going to do this to get out of the service, I'd have done it a long time ago." Patton said, "Son, I'm sorry, I made a mistake."

The worst victims of the Ardennes offensive were the German people. Most now cherished ambitions only to see the Western Allies, rather than the Russians, occupy their cities and villages. After the shocks of December 1944, however, strategic prudence became the theme of Eisenhower's operations. His armies' subsequent advance into Germany was sluggish, influenced by a morbid anxiety to avoid exposing flanks to counterattack. The Russians in the east, meanwhile, became important beneficiaries of Hitler's losses: when they launched their own great offensive on 12 January 1945, many of the German tanks which might have checked their advance lay wrecked on the Western Front. The Ardennes battle, by dissipating Hitler's armoured reserves, hastened Germany's end, and not in a fashion to its people's advantage. It ensured that the Red Army, rather than the Americans and British, led the way to Hitler's capital. Only on 28 January did Eisenhower's forces reoccupy the line they had held before Hitler launched Autumn Mist.

WHILE THE STRUGGLE in the Ardennes dominated headlines across much of the world, in Italy the Anglo-Americans continued their thankless, yard-by-yard struggle up the peninsula. Many Allied soldiers became increasingly embittered by the belief that they were suffering shocking privations for scant purpose or recognition. In some units, discipline became precarious. A platoon in Lt. Alex Bowlby's infantry battalion formed up to deliver a collective protest when they heard that a despised officer had been recommended for a Military Cross. The recommendation was cancelled, but Bowlby sensed that his men were not far from mutiny, reluctant to participate in patrols or attacks. It has been remarked that Bowlby's unit was untypically weak, that some regiments sustained higher morale and greater determination, which is undoubtedly true. But it was sometimes hard to persuade soldiers to risk and indeed sacrifice their lives when they knew that the outcome of the war was being determined elsewhere.

The last phase of the Italian campaign, in the spring of 1945, was by far the best conducted, because the Allies belatedly appointed good generals. Lucian Truscott succeeded Clark at U.S. Fifth Army in December 1944, and Richard McCreery took over the British Eighth Army from Oliver Leese. Both men displayed an imagination their predecessors conspicuously lacked, especially in avoiding frontal attacks. The push across the Po Valley, admittedly against much-depleted German forces, was a fine military achievement, albeit too late to have much influence on the war's endgame.

But there were some men fighting in Italy who had special reasons for questioning the campaign's value. The Yalta conference in early February made it plain that, following victory, a communist government would rule Poland, and that the east of the country would become Russian soil. On 13 February the Polish corps commander in Italy, Gen. Władysław Anders, sent a letter to his British commander-in-chief, reflecting on the sacrifices that his men had made since 1942: "We left along our path, which we regarded as our battle route to Poland, thousands of graves of our comrades in arms. The soldiers of II Polish Corps, therefore, feel this latest decision of the Three-Power Conference to be the gravest injustice . . . This soldier now asks me what is the object of his struggle? Today I am unable to answer this question." Anders seriously considered withdrawing his corps from the Allied line, until dissuaded by McCreery. The Poles clung to vestigial hopes that their fighting contribution to the Allied cause might yet make possible some modification of the Yalta terms in their favour. But the reality, of course, was that each of the conquering nations would arbitrate the future of the countries it occupied in the fashion that it deemed appropriate. Stalin's soldiers were already in Poland, for which Britain and France had gone to war, while the Western armies were far away.

CHAPTER TWENTY-FOUR

THE FALL OF THE THIRD REICH

1. Budapest: In the Eye of the Storm

AT THE END of October 1944, Heinrich Himmler delivered an apocalyptic speech in East Prussia, setting the stage for the final defence of the Reich: "Our enemies must know that every kilometre they seek to advance into our country will cost them rivers of blood. They will step onto a field of human mines consisting of fanatical uncompromising fighters; every block of city flats, village, farmstead, forest will be defended by men, boys and old men and, if need be, by women and girls." On the Eastern Front during the months that followed, his vision was largely fulfilled: 1.2 million German troops and around a quarter of a million civilians died during the futile struggle to check the Russian onslaught. So too did many people whose governments had rashly allied themselves with the Third Reich in its years of European dominance or who had volunteered to serve the Nazi cause. One-third of all German losses in the east took place in the last months of the war, when their sacrifice could serve no purpose save that of fulfilling the Nazi leadership's commitment to self-immolation.

Among those who found themselves in the path of the Soviet juggernaut were the 9 million people of Hungary, who found an ironic black humour in reminding one another that their nation had been defeated in every war in which it had participated for 500 years. Now they faced the consequences of espousing the losing side in the most terrible conflict of all. Early in December 1944, the Russians forced a passage of the Danube under withering fire, with their usual indifference to casualties. A Hungarian hussar gazing on corpses heaped on the riverbank turned to his officer and said in shocked wonder, "Lieutenant, sir, if this is how they treat their own men, what would they do to their enemies?" After one Soviet attack north of Budapest, the defenders dragged a writhing figure off their wire. "The young soldier, with his shaven head and Mongolian cheekbones, is lying on his back," wrote a Hungarian. "Only his mouth is moving. Both legs and lower arms are missing. The stumps are covered in a thick layer of soil, mixed with blood and leaf mould. I bend down close to him. 'Budapesst . . . Budapesst . . . ,' he whispers in the throes of death . . . He may be having a vision of a city of rich spoils and beautiful women . . . Then, surprising even myself, I pull out my pistol, press it against the dying man's temple, and fire."

Soon afterwards, the Hungarian capital became the focus of one of the most brutal struggles of the war, scarcely noticed in the West because it coincided first with Hitler's Ardennes offensive and thereafter with the massive Russian offensive farther north. During the last days of December, in deep snow Marshal Rodion Malinovsky's 2nd Ukrainian *front* closed its grip on the city. A Nazi-sponsored coup preempted an attempt by the Hungarian government to surrender to Stalin. Thereafter, the country fell into the hands of a fascist regime supported by the brutal Arrow Cross militia. The army fought on beside the Germans, though a steady stream of desertions testified to its soldiers' meagre enthusiasm.

The civilian population remained curiously oblivious of catastrophe: in Budapest, theatres and cinemas stayed open until the New Year. During a performance of *Aïda* at the opera house on 23 December, an actor dressed as a soldier appeared in front of the curtain. He offered greetings from the front to the half-empty stalls and expressed pleasure that everyone was calmer and more hopeful than a few weeks earlier, then, in the words of an opera-goer, he "promised that Budapest would remain Hungarian and our wonderful capital had nothing to fear." Families decorated Christmas trees with "Window," the silver foil strips dropped by British and American bombers to baffle German radar. Many of the city's million inhabitants, ignoring looming disaster, spurned opportunities to flee west. Some looked forward to greeting the Russians as deliverers: hearing Malinovsky's guns close at hand, the liberal politician Imre Csescy wrote, "This is the most beautiful Christmas music. Are we really about to be liberated? God help us and put an end to the rule of these gangsters."

Stalin had ordered the capture of Budapest, and at first hoped to achieve this without a battle: even when the Russians had almost completed the capital's encirclement, they left open a western passage for the garrison's withdrawal. The German front commander wanted to abandon the city; Hitler, inevitably, insisted that it should be defended to the last. Some 50,000 German and 45,000 Hungarian troops held their positions, knowing from the outset that their predicament was hopeless. One artillery battalion consisted of Ukrainians dressed in Polish uniforms with German insignia. An SS cavalry division was described as "totally demoralised," and three Hungarian SS police regiments were classified as "extremely unreliable." Gen. Karl Pfeffer-Wildenbruch, commanding the German forces, did not leave his bunker for six weeks and displayed unbridled gloom. One Hungarian general was so disgusted by his men's incessant desertions that he declared haughtily that he "would not ruin his military career" and relinquished command, reporting sick.

But, as so often, once battle was joined the combatants became locked in a struggle for survival which achieved a momentum of its own. On 30 December, a thousand Russian guns opened a barrage on Budapest that continued for ten hours daily, with air raids in between. Civilians huddled in their cellars, which failed to protect many from incineration or asphyxiation. After three days, Russian tanks and infantry began to push forward, squeezing the shrinking German perimeter on the Pest bank of the Danube, and meanwhile advancing into Buda yard by yard.

A Hungarian gunner officer, Capt. Sandor Hanak, awaited attack on 7 January behind the wooden fence of the city racecourse. "The Russkis . . . were coming across the open track, singing and arm in arm . . . presumably in an alcoholic state. Kicking the fence down, we fired fragmentation grenades and machine-gun bursts into the mass. They ran to the stands, where there was a terrible bloodbath when the assault guns fired at one row of seats after another. The Germans reported about eight hundred of them dead." When at last the Pest bridgehead was lost and the Danube bridges blown, in Buda the garrison fought street by street, house by house. In some places the Russians drove prisoners in front of them, who shouted despairingly, "We are Hungarians!" before both sides' fire tore into them. Bizarrely, a group of seventy Russians defected to the defenders, asserting that they were more afraid of retreating—to face the NKVD's machine gunners behind their own front—than of coming forward to surrender. Stalin's unwilling allies suffered heavily: on 16 January a Romanian corps reported that since October it had lost 23,000 men dead, wounded and missing—more than 60 percent of its strength.

The Russians conscripted hapless civilians to bring forward ammunition under fire. They advanced steadily through the streets, but suffered checks and slaughter wherever they were forced to cross open spaces swept by German and Hungarian guns. The plight of the defenders was worse, however: Pvt. Dénes Vass climbed over civilian and military wounded laid out along the corridors of his unit's command post. A hand reached up and tugged his coat. "It was a girl of about 18–20 with fair hair and a beautiful face. She begged me in a whisper, 'Take your pistol and shoot me.' I looked at her more closely and realised with horror both her legs were missing."

Hunger gnawed every man, woman and child. The garrison's 25,000 horses were eaten. Only 14 of 2,500 animals in the city's zoo survived—the rest were killed by Soviet fire or slaughtered for meat; for weeks, a lion roamed the underground rail tunnels until it was captured by a Soviet task force dispatched for the purpose. Following a headquarters conference on 26 January, a German officer wrote: "Leaving the room after the meeting, several commanders openly speak about Hitler's pig-headedness. Even some of the SS are beginning to doubt his leadership." The senior Hungarian general reported to the Ministry of Defence on 1 February: "Supply situation intolerable. Menu for the next five days per head and day: 5 gr. lard, 1 slice bread and horsemeat . . . Lice infestation of the troops constantly increasing, in particular among the wounded. Already six cases of typhus." The Luftwaffe sustained meagre supply drops, many of which fell into the Russian lines. Starving civilians were shot out of hand for raiding parachuted containers in search of food. In the maternity ward of a hospital, nurses clutched motherless babies to their breasts to provide at least human warmth, as the starving infants drifted towards death.

Throughout the siege, the persecution and murder of Budapest's Jews continued. On the morning of 24 December, Arrow Cross militia drove up to a Jewish children's home in Munkácsy Mihály Street in Buda and marched its inmates and their carers to the courtyard of the nearby Radetsky barracks, where they were lined up before a machine gun. This group was saved by a sudden local Russian advance which caused their intending executioners to take flight, but their parents had already been deported and killed. Many other Jews were led out to be shot on the Danube embankment, where a handful escaped by leaping into the ice-filled river.

A Hungarian army officer rebuked an Arrow Cross teenager whom he saw beating an old woman in a column being herded towards their execution place: "Haven't you got a mother, son? How can you do this?" The boy answered carelessly, "She's only a Jew, uncle . . ." An estimated 105,453 Jews died in or disappeared from Budapest between mid-October 1944 and the fall of the city. Conditions among the survivors became horrific. A witness described a ghetto scene:

> In narrow Kazinczy Street enfeebled men, drooping their heads, were pushing a wheelbarrow. On the rattling contraption naked human bodies as yellow as wax were jolted along and a stiff arm with black patches was dangling and knocking against the spokes of the wheel. They stopped in front of the Kazinczy baths . . . behind the weather-beaten façade bodies were piled up, frozen stiff like pieces of wood . . . I crossed Klauzál Square. In the middle people were squatting or kneeling around a dead horse and hacking the meat off with knives. The yellow and blue intestines, jelly-like and with a cold sheen, were bursting out of the opened and mutilated body.

The Swedish diplomat Raoul Wallenberg, who was among those trapped in Budapest, strove to check the Jewish massacres, warning German commanders that they would be held responsible. But killings continued, sometimes including the shooting of Hungarian police officers sent to protect Jews. Wallenberg was eventually murdered by the Russians.

By the beginning of February, as German casualties mounted and supplies dwindled, much of Budapest was reduced to rubble. Fires blazed in a thousand places as palaces, houses, public buildings and blocks of flats progressively succumbed. Explosions and gunfire persisted around the clock. Soviet aircraft strafed and bombed at low level, causing wounded men to scream in despair as they lay incapable of movement beneath the attacks. The grotesque became commonplace, such as an antitank gun camouflaged with Persian carpets from the opera house's props department. Terrified horses, sobbing women and children, and despairing soldiers alternately stampeded and huddled for safety.

Mastery was contested in a dozen parts of the city simultaneously. Buildings changed hands several times amid attacks and counterattacks. Hungarian soldiers who deserted in growing numbers to the Russians were offered an abrupt choice: they might join the Red Army to fight their former comrades or face transportation to Siberia. Those who chose the former were provided with identifying red cap ribbons, cut from parachute silk, and immediately thrown back into the battle. The Russians treated such renegades with surprising comradeliness: one rifle corps commander, for instance, invited Hungarian officers to dinner. After the war, it was found that the death rate had been similar among those who chose captivity and those who joined the Red Army. In a chaos of loyalties, Hungarian communist resistance groups sought to aid the Soviets, and especially to kill Arrow Cross leaders and militiamen. In late January, scores of imprisoned dissidents were shot by their fellow countrymen on the terrace of the Royal Palace, most of them after torture.

On 11 February 1945, resistance collapsed in Buda. The commander of the Hungarian antiaircraft artillery disarmed Germans in his headquarters at the Gellert Hotel, raised a white flag and had his men shoot those who defied him and sought to prolong resistance. That night, the remains of the garrison and its senior officers attempted to break out, some in small groups, others in crowds. Most were mown down by Soviet fire, so that the dead lay heaped in open spaces. The commander of an SS cavalry division and three of his officers chose suicide when it became plain they could not escape. Another twenty-six SS men likewise shot themselves in the garden of a house in Diósárok Street. A panzer division commander was killed by Soviet machine-gun fire. Old colonel János Vertessy, a Hungarian, tripped and fell on his face as he hurried along a street, breaking his last remaining tooth. "It's not my day," he said ruefully, recalling that exactly thirty years earlier he had been shot down and captured as a pilot in the First World War. Shortly afterwards, he was caught and summarily executed by the Red Army.

Two thousand wounded men lay in the cellars of the Royal Palace. In the words of a witness who came upon them, "Pus, blood, gangrene, excrement, sweat, urine, tobacco smoke and gunpowder mingle in a dense stench." Panic and factional strife overtook the doomed garrison. Two soldiers burst in on surgeons who had just opened a wounded man's stomach and began shooting at each other across the operating table. Soon afterwards fire engulfed the building, killing almost all the casualties. In the headquarters of General Pfeffer-Wildenbruch, a young NCO donned his commander's abandoned uniform—and was promptly shot dead by a crazed soldier. Stragglers roamed the city's public buildings among slashed paintings, shattered porcelain, broken furniture and abandoned personal possessions. Fires raged everywhere unchecked.

Some defenders sought to escape along the sewers by candlelight, wading through filth that sometimes rose to their waists, while the sounds of desperate fighting echoed down from the street above. They came upon the body of a handsome woman, elegantly clad in fur coat and silk stockings, still clinging to her handbag, and speculated about her identity. After advancing several hundred yards, the water level rose too high for passage. Most, including Pfeffer-Wildenbruch, were obliged to ascend through manholes into the street, where they were soon captured by the Soviets. An estimated 16,000 people, soldiers and civilians, escaped to the surrounding hills, where they roamed or lay in hiding. Some captured a Soviet bread wagon, precipitating a gunfight among themselves for its contents. Others who trudged on westwards found themselves emerging from woodland into the open ground of the Zsambek basin. Here, exposed against the snow, Soviet snipers and machine gunners shot them down in the hundreds. Throngs of desperate men were also killed in the city. A Soviet officer wrote, "The Hitlerists continued their advance towards the city exit despite their huge casualties, but soon ran into our multiple rocket-launchers firing salvos from point-blank range. It was a terrible sight." Only 700 of the 43,900 men in the Budapest garrison on 11 February reached the German front farther west; of the remainder, 17,000 had been killed and more than 22,000 taken prisoner.

A deathly silence fell upon Budapest. Fifteen-year-old Lazlo Deseo wandered back into his family's apartment after the first Russians had stormed through it. "One could howl, walking through the rooms. There are eight dead horses there. The walls are red with blood as high as a man, everything is full of muck and debris. All doors, cupboards, furniture and windows are broken. The plaster is gone. One steps over the dead horses. They are soft and springy. If you jump up and down on them, small bubbles, hissing and bloody, rise near the bullet wounds."

Survivors began to creep warily out of rubble. They were bemused by the unpredictable conduct of the victors: sometimes, on entering an apartment, Russians killed whole families; at other times they instead fell to playing with toys, then left peacefully. A Hungarian writer said of the conquerors, "They were simple and cruel like children. With millions of people destroyed by Lenin, Trotsky, Stalin or in the war, death to them had become an everyday affair. They killed without hatred and let themselves be killed without resisting." There were many executions— especially of Russians caught in German uniforms. Some postmen and tram conductors were shot, because the Russians mistook their tunics for those of Arrow Cross militiamen. Systematic looting of bank deposits and art collections was conducted under NKVD auspices, notably including those of the great Hungarian Jewish collectors; the booty was shipped to Moscow. A large proportion of Budapest's surviving women, of all ages from ten to ninety and including pregnant mothers, were raped by Red soldiers. The plight of the victims was worsened by the fact that many of the perpetrators were diseased, and in all Hungary there were no drugs to be had. Bishop Joseph Grosz wrote despairingly, "This is how things may have been in Jerusalem when the prophet Jeremiah uttered his laments."

Hungarian communists pleaded with the Soviet command to restrain its soldiers. "It is no good praising the Red Army on posters, in the Party, in the factories and everywhere," declared one such bitter appeal late in February, "if men who have survived the tyranny are now herded along the roads like cattle by Russian soldiers, constantly leaving dead bodies behind. Comrades sent to the country to promote land distribution are being asked by the peasants what use the land is to them if their horses have been taken from the meadows by Russians. They cannot plough with their noses." Such representations were vain. Stalin decreed that pillage and rape were the rightful rewards of his soldiers for their sacrifices. Poles, Yugoslavs, Czechs and Hungarians alike suffered the fate that would soon fall upon Germans.

In Budapest, even before the final collapse of the defence, the city's first cinema reopened with a showing of the Soviet propaganda film *The Battle of Orel*. Work began almost immediately on erecting statues of Soviet war heroes in public spaces. After enduring extremities of suffering, Hungarians yearned to laugh again, and cabarets were soon doing brisk business amid the rubble. The comedian Kálmán Latabár walked on stage to a standing ovation which became ecstatic when he pulled up his sleeves and trouser leg to reveal rows of watches, mocking Hungary's Soviet "liberators." A few months later, he would have been shot for less.

The capture of Budapest cost the Russians around 80,000 dead and a quarter of a million wounded. Some 38,000 civilians died in the siege; tens of thousands more were deported to the Soviet Union for forced labour, from which many never returned. The German and Hungarian forces lost about 40,000 dead and 63,000 men taken prisoner. This savage, futile battle would have been accounted an epic had it taken place on the Anglo-American front. As it was, only the Hungarians took much notice of its horrors, then or later. Within three months it was eclipsed by a matching drama, on a much larger scale, in Hitler's own capital.

2. Eisenhower's Advance to the Elbe

IN THE FIRST MONTHS of 1945, most Germans greeted the arrival of American and British forces in their country as an undeserved intrusion; if many understood that Hitler had led them to disaster, they nonetheless found it hard to accept the implications for their own domestic lives. Men of the U.S. 273rd Field Artillery occupied a house inhabited, in the words of one of its soldiers, by "a small, bird-like woman dressed in black, who tottered out from a side door. As soon as she saw us plundering her wood-pile, she started hollering in German. As we carried away armfuls, she burst into tears and wailed uncontrollably, choking on half-sentences." The Americans debated before dismissing their own scruples. " 'Hell,' said Frenchie, 'she's just as German as all the rest of the krauts.' " Like-wise a hillbilly in Pfc. Charles Felix's unit, when a voluble German woman complained bitterly that the GI intruders were scratching the furniture in her house. "I've had enough of these goddamn krauts!" expostulated the soldier. "We're over here fighting because of them and she's got the nerve to complain about her furniture! Here, lady, I'll show you some goddamn damage!" He seized a chair and threw it at the wall. Only a minority of Allied soldiers preserved lingering inhibitions towards civilians: a soldier in Aaron Larkin's engineer platoon burst into tears when ordered to evict a German family from their house to make way for his unit; Pfc. Harold Lindstrom suffered an instinctive pang of guilt when he lay down on a woman's feather bed in full infantry kit and boots.

The U.S. Army's judge advocate general recorded a steep increase in incidents of rape once Allied soldiers entered German territory: "We were members of a conquering army, and we came as conquerors," declared his postwar report. "It was only in a very exceptional case that the German victim vigorously resisted her armed attackers . . . The German victims were apparently thoroughly cowed . . . Their mortal fear was not entirely groundless, as demonstrated in a number of cases in which the Germans who sought to prevent the soldiers from carrying out their designs to commit rape were mercilessly murdered." A *Stars & Stripes* reporter who in March 1945 filed a dispatch about the high incidence of rape in the Rhineland found it suppressed by the censor, as was other "negative reporting" on Allied conduct in Germany.

There was also, of course, widespread semivoluntary copulation, which caused venereal disease rates to soar as desperate German women sold their only marketable commodity, often in order to feed their families. Many Allied soldiers recoiled from the shamelessness of German behaviour; even the educated among Hitler's people were brutalised by the privileges of oppression. Scots Guardsmen, welcomed by the aristocratic owners of a castle in northern Germany, were appalled to discover that in its adjoining park lay a small concentration camp containing 200 starving slave labourers. When a British officer remonstrated, their host replied in bewilderment, "Major, you don't understand. These people are animals—they can only be treated like animals."

The Anglo-American armies' last battles were incomparably less bloody than those in the east, because it suited both sides that it should be so. British lieutenant Peter White shouted at a fleeing German to halt: "I took aim in the middle of his back with a strong feeling of repugnance at having to fire at a man running away . . . when something seemed to tell him it was hopeless. To my intense relief he spun around, flinging his rifle into the snow and raising his hands in a swift dramatic gesture. He called out a jumbled stream of broken English in a frightened voice . . . 'Don't shoot, please sir! . . . Hitler no good . . . don't shoot . . . *Kamerad*, please!' At the same time he reached suddenly into his clothing, which nearly caused me to fire as I half-expected a pistol or grenade to be pulled out. Instead . . . he swung what turned out to be a gold pocket watch on a chain in my face as a peace offering."

The Western Allies advanced through Germany in the same measured fashion in which they had conducted their campaign since October 1944. They sought to complete the destruction of Nazism at acceptable human cost, advancing to the lines of occupation agreed with the Russians, and only temporarily and in a few areas beyond them. The Germans continued to resist, but few displayed the fanaticism that characterised the eastern battle to the end. The hard part, for the vanquished, was to identify an opportunity to quit without being shot by one side or the other. The

American aidman Leo Litwak described his experience of ministering to an elderly German shot while attempting to reach the American lines unarmed, presumably to surrender:

> He wore a gray wool uniform and cap, his eyes huge, his face pinched and unshaven, his mouth stretched as if shrieks were coming out, but it was a smothered sound, *Ohhhhh, Ohhhhh.* He saw the red crosses on my arms and helmet and reached for me and cried, *"Vater!"* Father. A spoke of femoral bone was sticking through his trousers. I slit his pants, bared the wound at mid-thigh. He'd shit small, hard, gray turds—what you might see in the spoor of an animal. The shit had worked itself down near the fracture. The stink was pungent and gagging. I put sulfa powder on the exposed bone, covered it with a compress, tied a loose tourniquet above the wound high on the thigh. He was graying fast, going into shock. He said *"Vater, ich sterbe."* Father, I'm dying. I stuck morphine into his thigh. He wasn't eased and I gave him another eighth of a grain. I watched him lapse into shock—lips blue, sweat cold, skin gray, pupils distended, pulse weak and fluttery . . . I yearned for him to be dead so we'd both be relieved from his pain.

The bulk of the Wehrmacht and the Waffen SS faced the armies of Zhukov, Konev and Rokossovsky; the Russians deployed 6.7 million men on a front extending from the Baltic to the Adriatic. The final death grapple between the forces of the two rival tyrants, Stalin and Hitler, was among the most terrible military encounters of the war, while Eisenhower's armies occupied a wing of the stage. It was entirely irrational, because the outcome was not in doubt; but the Nazis were successful in inducing a quorum of their soldiers to make a last sacrificial effort. As for those who flinched, the East Prussian schoolteacher Henner Pflug said that he ceased to gape at men hanging from trees, placards around their necks proclaiming "I am a deserter" or "I failed to defend the fatherland," because he saw so many.

Even Tito's Yugoslav partisans were grudgingly impressed by the retreat conducted by the Wehrmacht against overwhelming odds. Milovan Djilas wrote: "The German army left a trail of heroism, though the domination of Nazism has suppressed in the world's mind even the thought of such a thing . . . Hungry and half-naked, they cleared mountain landslides, stormed the rocky peaks, carved out bypasses. Allied planes used them for leisurely target practice. Their fuel ran out . . . [They] killed their own gravely wounded . . . In the end they got through, leaving a

The 1945 Western Drive into Germany

Occupied by Allied forces, 18 March 1945
British advances
U.S. advances
French advances
German pockets
Occupied by Russian forces, 16 April
Concentration camps

memory of their martial manhood. Apparently the German army could wage war . . . without massacres and gas chambers."

The paratrooper Martin Poppel's fiancée, Gerda, was one of many Germans belatedly alienated from the Nazi regime by the horrors it had brought upon her society. She wrote in January 1945 to Poppel, who was serving in Holland: "We are worn out after this terrible hail of bombs. To be hearing the howling of these things all the time, waiting for death at any moment in a dark cellar, unable to see—oh, it's truly a wonderful life. If only it would stop, they really expect too much of people. Do you still remember the lake? I think you gave me our first kiss there! Everything gone—the lovely cafés Brand and Bohning, the town hall completely burned. It's impossible even to begin to describe it. But you will be able to imagine it. You have seen Munich. Is everything going to be destroyed? Yet there is no other way out to be seen. Why do people let our soldiers go to their deaths uselessly, why do they let the rest of Germany be ruined, why all the misery, why?" She added later: "If you were still a loyal supporter of these people after the war—you know who I mean—it would inevitably separate us. What have they made of our beautiful, magnificent Germany? It's enough to make you weep. And one mustn't even think about how the others will enslave us."

Histories which depict Hitler's 1945 "armies" and "divisions" as serious fighting formations mock the reality: every unit was reduced to a fragment of its proper strength in men, tanks, artillery and transport. Between June 1944 and March 1945, the Wehrmacht lost 3.5 million rifles, so that in its last campaigns even small arms were in short supply. Many soldiers were in wretched physical condition: a medical report from a parachute artillery battery on 10 January observed that of its seventy-nine men, all but two were suffering from lice, and eighteen from eczema caused by poor diet. Efforts to sustain discipline invited derision; it must have seemed fantastic to the soldiers of 1/1120 Volksgrenadiers that in January, as the Reich collapsed, their CO Major Beiss issued an order of the day deploring personal slovenliness: "Rifles will be carried on the right shoulder, barrel up. If I should again see a 'Sunday sportsman' wandering about with his rifle pointing downwards, he will be punished by seven days' close arrest. Fresh dirt graces a soldier, but old filth exposes laziness. If I again see any man with a 'lion's mane' or any other fancy hairstyle, I shall personally cut his hair."

It is a commonplace among armies, especially those facing adversity, that men must never be left idle to brood. In the early days of 1945, when the war was going very badly indeed for Germany, a panzer company commander, Lt. Tony Saurma, sought to divert his men's leisure hours with lectures: he once addressed them for an hour about the United States, its cornbelt, industrial areas and great cities. He knew, as did his audience, that the country would soon loom large in their lives, if they were fortunate enough to survive. What was remarkable was not that hundreds of thousands of Germans abandoned the war in its last months, but that others continued to resist—a few even professing to find their predicament acceptable. An SS panzer platoon commander, posted to Hungary, wrote of a lull behind the battlefield in mid-February: "Rations were excellent. We learned from the civilian population the various uses of paprika. The people were very friendly. During the evenings we drove to see films in Nové Zámky."

The 1 February Western Allied combined chiefs of staff meeting, held on Malta before the Yalta summit, endorsed Eisenhower's plan to entrust his main effort, in this last phase of the campaign, to Montgomery's 21st Army Group in northern Germany, reinforced by Gen. William Simpson's U.S. Ninth Army. The heavy bomber forces were directed to assault Germany's transport infrastructure, including such rail centres as Dresden* and Leipzig in the path of the Russian advance. But the ground advance proved slow: Montgomery's next big attack, Operation Veritable, ran into trouble in the Reichwald forest; Simpson's formations were held back until 23 February by German flooding of large areas of their front. Only after painful fighting did Montgomery's forces close up to the Rhine between the Dutch border and Koblenz on 10 March.

In Germany's desperate circumstances, Hitler adopted a familiar panacea: changing generals. Kesselring, who had conducted the brilliant defence of Italy, succeeded von Rundstedt as commander in the west. Yet Kesselring was no more capable than his predecessor of sustaining a coherent campaign with fifty-five enfeebled divisions against Eisenhower's eighty-five full-strength formations backed by overwhelming air power. Hodges's First Army secured the Ludendorff rail bridge over the river at Remagen on 7 March, and immediately began to establish a perimeter on the eastern bank; Patton seized his own bridgehead at Oppenheim, farther south, on 22 March. The last Germans on the western bank of the Rhine were mopped up three days later. On the twenty-fourth, Montgomery's troops staged their huge set-piece Rhine crossing at Wesel, marred only by heavy casualties among airborne units which parachuted onto the far bank: the defenders proved to be lavishly equipped with antiaircraft artillery, if nothing else.

At the end of the month, Bradley's spearheads linked with Simpson's forces at Lippstadt to encircle Model's Army Group B in the so-called Ruhr pocket; Model shot himself on 17 April, and 317,000 of his men became Allied prisoners. The Americans, rather than the British, now had the best opportunities for a swift final advance. To Montgomery's fury, his formations were relegated to the secondary task of clearing northern Germany as far as Hamburg and Lübeck. It was thought urgent to push forces across the base of the Danish peninsula, to protect Denmark from any threat of Soviet occupation. Eisenhower formally abandoned

---

* The destruction of Dresden occupies such a prominent place in the popular legend of the war that it is striking to notice that the latest research suggests that 25,000 victims died there on 13–14 February, rather than the hundreds of thousands once supposed. This does not influence the controversy about whether the bombing was necessary, but it indicates that it caused far fewer deaths than the 1943 bombing of Hamburg or the 1945 Tokyo firestorm.

Berlin as an objective and informed Stalin accordingly. He diverted two armies south towards the Austrian border, to forestall any Nazi attempt to create a "National Redoubt" from which to keep the war going after the Russians and Anglo-American forces met in northern Germany. The "National Redoubt" was a figment of the imagination of Eisenhower's intelligence staff; this division of forces decisively weakened his main central thrust and left the Russians to occupy Czechoslovakia.

It is hard, however, to make a plausible case that any of this changed the postwar political map of Europe, as the supreme commander's detractors claimed. The Allied occupation zones had been agreed many months earlier, and confirmed at the Yalta summit in February. The Russians got to eastern Europe first. To have frustrated their imperialistic purposes, sparing central Europe from a Soviet tyranny in succession to that of the Nazis, it would have been necessary for the Western Allies to fight a very different and more ruthless war, at much higher cost in casualties. They would have had to acknowledge the possibility, even the probability, of being obliged to overcome the Red Army as well as the Wehrmacht. Such a course was politically and militarily unthinkable, whatever Churchill's brief delusions that eastern European freedom might be recovered by force.

Stalin's obsessive determination that the Soviet Union should accomplish the capture of Berlin accorded with the vision of his people: they saw this symbolic triumph as the only proper end of their struggle, the fulfilment of everything for which they had striven since 1941. Militarily, it might have been feasible for Eisenhower's forces to reach Hitler's capital before the Red Army, but such an advance would have precipitated a clash between the Allies. The Russians would have been outraged by any attempt to deprive them of their prize.

Soviet conduct throughout March and April was prompted by paranoia about Western intentions. Stalin lied again and again to Washington and London, professing his own indifference to Berlin as an objective; he could not credit the notion that the Americans and British would spurn a chance to beat the Red Army to the German capital. The Soviet encirclement of Berlin partly addressed the requirement of taking it from Hitler, but partly also that of ensuring its denial to Roosevelt and Churchill. There was a further consideration: the Russians were desperate to secure the Nazis' nuclear scientists and research material. Knowing from his agents in the West that the Americans were close to perfecting an atomic bomb, Stalin wanted everything that might help to kick-start the rival Soviet project: the Kaiser Wilhelm Institute for Physics in Dahlem was identified as a vital objective for the Red Army.

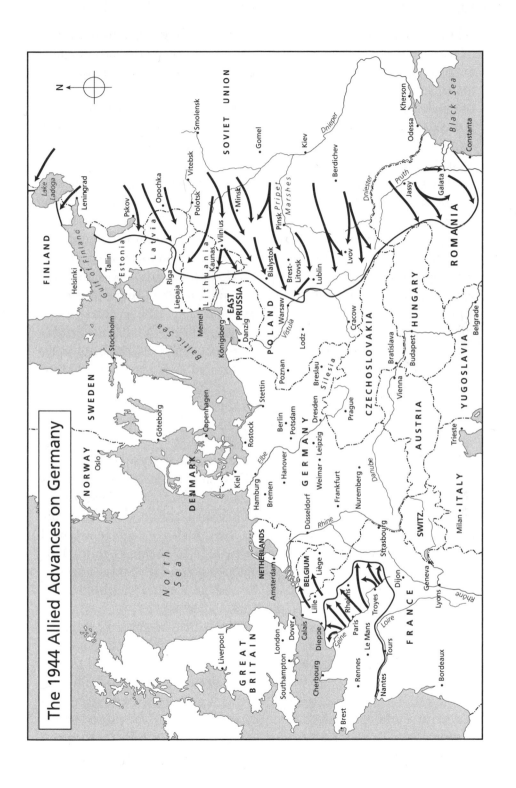

The 1944 Allied Advances on Germany

In the final stage of the western war, the Anglo-American armies advanced in the face of sporadic and ill-coordinated opposition. As always, the infantry bore most of the pain of clearing pockets of resistance. Service in a tank crew was never a sinecure, but in the last six weeks of the northwest Europe campaign, the Scots Guards tank battalion—for instance—lost only 1 officer and 7 other ranks killed, along with a handful of men wounded. Meanwhile in the same period, the infantry of the 2nd Scots Guards lost 9 officers and 76 other ranks killed, 17 officers and 248 other ranks wounded. Some Allied units encountered groups of fanatics, stubbornly defending river crossings and key junctions. One by one these were overcome, until the victors approached the Elbe. On 12 April, the First Army was ordered to stop short of Dresden and wait for the Soviets. Russian and American patrols met at the little Saxon town of Strehla on the Elbe on the morning of 24 April, followed later that day by the celebrated encounter upstream at Torgau, amid exuberant Anglo-American enthusiasm and wary and stilted Russian formality. The British reached the Baltic port of Lübeck on 2 May, allaying Allied fears that the Soviets would attempt to occupy Denmark. Fortunately for the Danish people, Russian attention was overwhelmingly focused elsewhere: upon Berlin, the capital and last bastion of Nazism.

3. Berlin: The Last Battle

STALIN ASSUMED personal responsibility for the final great operations of the war, chiefly in order to deny the personal glory to Zhukov, who was relegated to command of the 1st Belorussian *Front*. On 12 January the Soviets launched a general offensive out of their Vistula bridgeheads. Outnumbering the defenders by ten to one, their tanks and infantry streamed westward, crushing everything in their path. In an almost hysterical bulletin broadcast on 20 January, Berlin Radio described the Soviet offensive as "a mass invasion, to be compared in scale and significance with the past comings of the Mongol hordes, the Huns and Tatars."

The commentator Hans Fritsche asserted that the enemy's objective was "total destruction," and that defeat "would signal the end of civilisation." He claimed that Germans now had the advantages of short lines of communication and their "impassioned determination to defend their homeland." Germany, he said, had become "Europe's bulwark against the barbarian hordes descending from the eastern steppes." He expressed dismay at the failure of the British to align themselves with the German people against the Bolsheviks; far from dismissing the threat of defeat, as so often in the past, the Nazis called on their people for a desperate

The Russian Drive to the Oder

resistance in an admittedly desperate situation. "Germany's leadership is now faced with the most serious crisis of the war," declared Berlin Radio on 22 January. "Withdrawals and disengagements are no longer possible, because our armies are disputing territory of vital importance to German war industry . . . The utmost effort is required from every German. The German people are responding willingly to this call, because they know that our leadership has always in the past been able to restore situations in spite of all difficulties."

If Hitler's people were gripped by despair, those of Stalin were exultant: the war correspondent Vasily Grossman expressed a sense of "fierce joy" as he, who had seen so many battles since 1941, witnessed the crossing of the Vistula. He wrote a little later: "I wanted to shout, to call to all our brothers, our soldiers, who are lying in the Russian, Ukrainian, Belorussian and Polish earth, who sleep forever on our battlefields, 'Comrades, can you hear us? We've done it.' " The casualties of the Vistula offensive were staggering, even by the standards of the Eastern Front: the Russians inflicted slaughter on every formation in their path. In January alone, 450,000 Germans died; in each of the ensuing three months, more than 280,000, a figure that included victims of the Anglo-American bombings of Dresden, Leipzig and other eastern cities. During the final four months of the war, more Germans perished than in the whole of 1942–43. Such numbers emphasise the price paid by the German people for their army leadership's failure to depose the Nazis and quit the war before its last terrible act.

Early in February, the C-in-C of Army Group Vistula wrote: "In the Wehrmacht we find ourselves in a leadership crisis of the gravest magnitude. The officer corps no longer has firm control of the troops. Among soldiers there are the most serious manifestations of disintegration. Examples of soldiers removing their uniforms and exploiting every possible means to acquire civilian clothing in order to escape are far from isolated." Further humiliations were heaped upon Germany's generals: Guderian was interrogated by security chiefs Ernst Kaltenbrunner and Heinrich Müller about his role in the evacuation of Warsaw against Hitler's orders.

The chief impediment to the Soviet advance was the weather. A sudden thaw slowed to a crawl armoured movement through slush and mud. By 3 February, Zhukov's and Konev's armies held a line along the Oder from Kustrin, thirty-five miles east of Berlin, to the Czech border, with bridgeheads on the western bank. On the fifth, Hitler's commander in Hungary reported: "Amid all these stresses and strains, no improvement in morale or performance is visible. The numerical superiority of the enemy, combined with knowledge that the battle is now being fought on German soil, has proved very demoralising for the men. Their only nourishment is a slice of bread and some horsemeat. Movement of any kind is hampered by their physical weakness. In spite of all this and six weeks' unfulfilled promises of relief, they fight tenaciously and obey orders." The Russians acknowledged this with grudging respect in a 2 March intelligence report: "Most German soldiers realise the hopelessness of their country's situation after the January advances, though a few still express faith in German victory. Yet there is no sign of a collapse in enemy morale. They are still fighting with dogged persistence and unbroken discipline." Hitler rejected his generals' urgings to evacuate the beleaguered Courland Peninsula on the Baltic, where 200,000 men who might have reinforced the Reich lingered in impotence.

On the central front, the Russians temporarily halted. It is plausible that Zhukov could have continued his advance, exploiting momentum to seize Berlin, but the logistics problems were formidable. Stalin's armies had no need to take risks. Farther north, Rokossovsky pushed on through the snows of Prussia. Russian soldiers derived deep satisfaction from witnessing the destruction they had seen wreaked upon their own homeland now overtaking German territory. One man wrote from East Prussia on 28 January 1945: "Estates, villages and towns were burning. Columns of carts, with dazed German men and women who had failed to flee, crawled across the landscape. Shapeless fragments of tanks and self-propelled guns lay everywhere, as well as hundreds of corpses. I recalled such sights from the first days of the war . . ." His memories were, of course, of the struggle in Mother Russia. Landowners in East Prussia and Pomerania rash enough to remain in their homes, sometimes because of age or infirmity, suffered terrible fates: to be identified by the invaders not merely as Germans, but also as aristocrats, invited torture before death.

Millions of refugees fled westwards before the Soviets. The strong survived their journeys, but many children and old people perished. "At least we were young," said Elfride Kowitz, a twenty-year-old East Prussian. "We could cope with it better than the old." The snowclad landscape of eastern Europe was disfigured by tens of thousands of corpses. Fugitives shared dramas of fantastic intensity which made them briefly companions in adversity, who ate or starved, lived or died, trekked and slept with one another until some new shift of circumstances separated them. "In these situations," said the schoolteacher Henner Pflug, "people were thrown together in great intimacy for hours, days, weeks, then sundered again."

One among the great host of dispossessed German women wrote, "The world is a very lonely place without family, friends, or even the familiarity of a home." She learned the meaning of desperation when she saw other housewives, frantic for warm clothing in the icy weather, dash past soldiers engaging the Russians with rifles and mortars to reach a *Schloss* where they had heard there was a garment store, to seize whatever they could lay their hands on. Fleeing with two small children, she herself plumbed a depth of exhaustion wherein she could no longer push uphill the cart carrying their pathetic baggage: "I leaned on all our worldly goods and wept bitterly." Two passing French POWs took pity, and helped them over the crest. A few days later, a farmer in whose house she briefly sought refuge urged her to leave her son behind for adoption by himself. "He promised me the earth if I would leave him. What future had the child? There, he might have a good and safe home." But this mother clung to a reserve of stubborn courage which enabled her to refuse. "I had set myself a task—to take the children to safety and see them grow up. How? I did not know.

I just tackled each day as it came." This little family at last reached the sanctuary of the American lines, but many other such stories lacked happy endings.

The advancing Soviet legions resembled no other army the world had ever seen: a mingling of old and new, Europe and Asia, high intelligence and brutish ignorance, ideology and patriotism, technological sophistication and the most primitive transport and equipment. T-34s, artillery and katyusha rocket launchers were followed by jeeps and Studebaker and Dodge trucks supplied under Lend-Lease, then by shaggy ponies and columns of horsemen, farm carts and trudging peasants from the remote republics of Central Asia, clad in foot cloths and rags of uniform. Drunkenness was endemic. German harmonicas provided musical accompaniment for many units, because they could be played in rattling trucks. The only discipline rigorously enforced was that which required men—and women—to attack, to fight, and to die. Stalin and his marshals cared nothing for the preservation of civilian life or property. When one of Vasilievsky's officers asked for guidance about the proper response to wholesale vandalism being committed by his men, the commander sat silent for several seconds, then said, "I don't give a fuck. It is now time for our soldiers to issue their own justice."

Near Toruń, in Poland, one such man, Semyon Pozdnyakov, glimpsed a German soldier in no-man's-land between the armies, shuffling towards his own lines, head bent low, wounded right arm held close to his body, his left arm limply dragging a machine pistol. Pozdnyakov challenged him, shouting, "*Fritz, halt!*" The German dropped his weapon and raised his left hand in a feeble gesture of surrender. As a group of Russians approached him, they saw blood on the man's face, and empty, despairing eyes. "*Hitler kaput,*" he said mechanically. The Russians laughed at the words they now heard so often, and an officer told them to take the man to the rear. "*Nein! nein!*" said the German, thinking he was to be shot. Pozdnyakov roared at him angrily, "Why are you shouting, you half-dead fascist? You're afraid of death? Didn't you treat our people the same way? We should finish you off, and be done with you." Such was indeed the fate of many Germans, who sought mercy in vain.

Reckless abuse of weapons caused significant numbers of Russians to kill one another in rage or carelessness; they pulled triggers as readily as their Western counterparts might spit or blaspheme. For all its commanders' military sophistication, this was a barbarian army, which had achieved things such as only barbarians could. Paradoxically, its educated elements were driven by a sense of righteousness greater than any that stirred American or British soldiers. They cared nothing for Stalin's 1939 devil's bargain with Hitler, nor for Soviet aggression against Poland, Finland and Romania. They recognised only that Russia had been invaded and devastated, and now they were approaching a reckoning with the nation responsible.

Vyacheslav Eisymont, a former history teacher who served as an artillery observer, wrote from East Prussia on 19 February: "We stay in all sorts of places: sometimes in a shed, sometimes a bunker, and right now a house. It is spring weather, wet, sometimes raining. There are civilians who failed to escape, now being sent to the rear . . . We saw them as we advanced on Königsberg: old men, women and children with shouldered bundles, in long crocodiles trudging along the roadsides—the road itself was occupied by our column. That night, we saw terrible things. But our battery commander spoke for many when he said: 'Sure, you look, and you feel saddened by the sight of old people and children on foot and dying. But then you remember what they did in our land, and you feel no pity!' "

In February Konev advanced across the Oder towards Dresden, before halting at the Neisse; in the weeks that followed, his principal achievement was to secure Pomerania and Upper Silesia. Early in March a half-hearted SS panzer counteroffensive in Hungary, undertaken in pursuit of Hitler's fixation with recovering lost oilfields, was easily repulsed. On 16 March, two Soviet *fronts* began to push for Vienna. Even that dedicated Nazi field marshal Ferdinand Schörner told Hitler on 20 March: "I must report that the military worthlessness of troops in [Upper Silesia] exceeds my worst expectations. Almost without exception, they are exhausted. Formations have been broken up, mingled with alarm and Volkssturm units. Their military value is shockingly low. North of Leobschutz there is no one deserving of the name of a German soldier. My impression is that the Russians can do anything they choose, without great exertion or expenditure of strength." The Second Panzer Army in Hungary reported to the army high command without irony on 10 April, "To improve morale, an execution was carried out on the battlefield."

Corp. Helmut Fromm, facing the Russians in Saxony, wrote in his diary at Easter: "I'm sitting in my candle-lit O[bservation] P[ost] 500 metres from the Ivans. An icy wind is blowing through the tarpaulin. Shelling continues all night, interspersed with machine-gun fire and my neighbour's snoring. When I walked along the trench an hour ago, an NCO told me the Americans are in Heidelberg. Now, I'm cut off from all my loved ones, and they must be worrying about me. I wonder where my brother is. I am convinced I will see them again, because I believe in God. How long will this madness continue? May God have mercy on his people. This has been a long crusade, strewn with corpses and tears.

Please grant us an Easter followed by redemption." Corporal Fromm was sixteen years old.

Guy Sajer, serving with the Grossdeutschland Division, wrote: "We no longer fought for Hitler, or for National Socialism, or for the Third Reich or even for our fiancées or mothers or families trapped in bomb-ravaged towns. We fought from simple fear . . . We fought for ourselves, so that we shouldn't die in holes filled with mud and snow; we fought like rats." A German lieutenant protested wearily to his fiancée: "To be an officer means always having to swing back and forth like a pendulum between a Knight's Cross, a birchwood cross and a court-martial." A Berlin woman wrote: "These days I keep noticing how my feelings towards men . . . are changing. I feel sorry for them; they seem so miserable and powerless. The weaker sex. Deep down we women are experiencing a kind of collective disappointment. The Nazi world—ruled by men, glorifying the strong man—is beginning to crumble, and with it the myth of 'Man.' "

A Russian soldier wrote to his wife from East Prussia on 19 April:

Hello my darling! For the past fortnight I have been moving almost daily, sleeping in bunkers, tents, or simply under the open sky. Since yesterday, however, we have been quartered in a house and sleeping in beds . . . Our unit has earned this, for we've played our parts in the assault on Königsberg, and of course we've taken it. Our planes bombed the city for three days. The earth shook under artillery bombardment, which enveloped the city in clouds of smoke. At first the Fascists fought back fiercely, but they could not endure this hell. They seemed to be short of ammunition and had no air support either . . . There were masses of prisoners. The radio has announced: 'Allied patrols have crossed the border into Czechoslovakia!' Everything is bound to finish soon! Perhaps it still won't be over—there is also Japan, damn it . . . But one would imagine that once the European war ends, the Allies will try to finish that quickly.

As the German food distribution system collapsed, from late March onwards civilians began to suffer severe hunger even in areas still held by the Wehrmacht. And they knew worse was to come. A Berlin teenager named Dieter Borkovsky was riding the city's S-Bahn on 14 April, amid a throng of passengers loudly venting their anger and despair. Suddenly a soldier, adorned with medals which seemed absurdly incongruous on his small, dirty figure, shouted, "Silence! I've got something to tell you. Even if you don't want to listen to me, stop whingeing. We have to win this war. We must not lose our courage. If others win the war, and they do to us only a fraction of what we have done in the occupied territories, there won't be a single German left in a few weeks." Borkovsky wrote: "It became so quiet in that carriage one could have heard a pin drop."

When the Russians reached Lubbenau, sixty miles south of Berlin, Hildegard Trutz, the wife of an SS officer, hoped that clutching her two young children would spare her from rape. "My God! What a fuss I made with the first one! I can't help laughing when I think of it now. I held Elke in my arms and pushed Norfried in front of me, hoping that would soften his heart. But he simply pushed Norfried aside and threw me on the ground. I cried and clung onto Elke, but the Russian just went ahead until I had to let go of her. He was quite quick about it, and the whole thing didn't take more than five minutes . . . I soon found that it was much better not to resist at all, it was all over much quicker if you didn't."

Friedrike Grensemann came home from work to find her father preparing to obey a summons to join the Volkssturm. He handed her his pistol, saying, "It's all over, my child. Promise me that when the Russians come you will shoot yourself." Then he kissed her and went off to die. Few Germans were any more impressed than Herr Grensemann by the home guard's mobilisation. They parodied the song *"Die Wach am Rhein"*: "Dear Fatherland, set your mind at rest/The Führer has called the Grandpas up." Berliners stripped shops of such food as they could buy, then retired to the cellars that became their refuges through the days that followed. Ruth-Andreas Friedrich risked a brief sortie to the street in darkness, during a pause in Russian air raids. She saw the eastern sky reddened "as if blood had been poured over it," and listened to the now incessant gunfire, "a grumbling like distant thunder. That's no bombing, that's . . . artillery . . . Before us lies the endless city, black in the black of night, cowering as if to creep back into the earth. And we're afraid."

The Danish correspondent Jacob Kronika wrote that many Berliners now fervently desired their leader's end. "Years ago they shouted 'Heil!' Now they hate the man who calls himself their Führer. They hate him, they fear him; because of him they are suffering hardship and death. But they have neither the strength nor the nerve to free themselves from his demonic power. They wait, in passive desperation, for the final act of the drama."

Behind the front, the Nazis indulged a final orgy of killing: jails were emptied, their occupants shot; almost all surviving opponents of the regime held in concentration camps were executed, and lesser victims massacred with a dreadful carelessness. On 31 March at Kassel-Wilhelmshöhe station, 78 Italian workers suspected of looting a Wehrmacht supply train were rounded up and shot by firing squads. West of Hanover, the Gestapo

murdered 82 imprisoned slave labourers and POWs. On 6 April, 154
Soviet prisoners were killed in a prison at Lahde, and a further 200 at
Kiel. In the Nazis' last days of power over life and death, Hitler's doomed
creatures sought to ensure that the joy of liberation was denied to all those
within their reach.

Hundreds of thousands of prisoners were herded westwards, away
from the Russians, and many were literally marched to death. Hugo Gryn,
a Jew, described his experiences among a column of starving slaves on
the road to Sachsenhausen: "When we left Lieberose, we were marched
some distance away, stopped, and then heard lots of firing and then [there
was] smoke. They killed and set on fire everybody who could not move
out. This march was dreadful. Snow, mud. And when dusk came, turn left
or turn right, walk into the nearest field, get down. In the morning, get
up, except for those who could not get up, then we would move forward,
wait a while, hear the shots and move on." Almost half of the 714,211
concentration-camp prisoners held in the Reich in January 1945 were
dead by May, along with many more POWs. On 12 April, the Berlin Philharmonic Orchestra gave its last performance, organised by Albert Speer.
Beethoven's Violin Concerto was performed with Bruckner's Fourth Symphony. So too was the finale of Wagner's *Götterdämmerung*.

A LAST climactic battle remained. Since 1939, the spotlight of world attention had shifted again and again between place-names great and obscure:
from Warsaw to Dunkirk and Paris; London and Tobruk; Smolensk,
Moscow and Stalingrad; El Alamein and Kursk; Salerno and Anzio; Normandy, Bastogne and Warsaw again. Now, Hitler's capital became the
focus not only of many hopes and fears, but also of a vast concentration
of military power: the three Soviet *fronts* that massed before Berlin comprised 2.5 million men and 6,250 armoured vehicles, supported by 7,500
aircraft. In darkness in the early hours of 16 April, Zhukov launched a
frontal assault against the Seelow Heights, east of the city. The operation
was among the most brutish and unimaginative of Russia's war. Its commander was so impressed by watching his bombardment devastating the
defences that after thirty minutes he gave the order to start the attack.
A Russian engineer wrote home that night: "Along the whole length of
the horizon it was bright as daylight. On the German side, everything
was covered with smoke and thick fountains of earth in clumps flying up.
There were huge flocks of scared birds flying around in the sky, a constant
humming, thunder, explosions. We had to cover our ears to prevent our
eardrums breaking. Then tanks began roaring, searchlights were lit along

all of the front line in order to blind the Germans. Then people started shouting everywhere, '*Na Berlin!*' "

Russian infantry ran forward into the German minefields, while the first tanks clattered towards the heights. Briefly, it seemed that the artillery had silenced the defences. But then the Germans opened fire. They had pulled back from their forward positions, so that Zhukov's bombardment fell on empty trenches. As Soviet tanks thrashed in deep mud on the slopes in their path, the attackers began to suffer terrible casualties. "We moved across terrain cratered from shellfire," wrote Soviet sapper Pyotr Sebelev. "Everywhere lay smashed German guns, vehicles, burning tanks and many corpses . . . Many of the Germans surrender. They don't want to fight and give their life for Hitler." But many more continued to shoot. "Why drag out the misery?" mused one despairing member of the Wehrmacht, whose wife and three children had drowned when the *Wilhelm Gustloff* refugee ship was torpedoed in the Baltic on 15 April. "But then, there's still the other blokes. Many of them I've known for years. Am I going to leave them in the lurch?"

Gen. Gottfried Heinrici's defenders inflicted three Russian casualties for each of their own. There was no display of inspired Soviet generalship: Zhukov's hordes merely threw themselves forward again and again. The Germans poured fire into the attackers, destroying tanks in the hundreds and killing men in the thousands. For two days, six Soviet armies battered at the Seelow line without achieving a breakthrough. Konev, in the south, was ordered to push forward two tank armies, while Rokossovsky, in the north, diverted forces to support Zhukov. On 18 April, the Wehrmacht corporal Helmut Fromm wrote from Konev's sector: "Now we're in front of Forst. The Russians have got a bridgehead across the Neisse, and attacked this morning at eleven. We had to pull back. I was left with a machine-gun and two men. I'm the only one who knows how to use a *Faust*—most of the others have only done office work. Then we rode very fast on bicycles up the Breslau–Berlin autobahn . . . Ivan's guns are firing. Ten minutes ago Bohmer and Bucksbraun were wounded—Bohmer's very badly cut up. We carried him back on a plank, screaming. Whose turn is it next? Gunfire from the road. To our left a flak 88 is under fire. I'm trying to dig as deep as I can. In the sky above us a Russian tank-buster is circling . . . If I survive, I shall give thanks to God."

Hitler declined to send reinforcements to Heinrici, leaving the Ninth Army to hold the Oder positions as best it could. Mass, not manoeuvre, at last enabled Zhukov to swamp the defences and push forward to reach Hitler's outer Berlin line on 21 April; the capture of the Seelow Heights had cost the Russians 30,000 dead, the Germans 12,000. The attackers hastened on towards the city along the main road, Reichstrasse 1, as fugitives and deserters scurried and stumbled to stay ahead of them. "They all seem so miserable, so little like men any more," wrote a Berlin woman watching German soldiers shuffle past her apartment building on 22 April. "The only thing they inspire is pity, no hope or expectations. They already look defeated, captured. They stare past us blindly, impassively . . . They're obviously not too concerned about us, *Volk* or civilians or Berliners or whatever we are. Now we're nothing but a burden. And I don't sense they're the least ashamed of how bedraggled they look, how ragged. They're too tired to care, too apathetic. They're all fought out."

By 25 April, Zhukov and Konev had encircled the German capital—an attempt by Gen. Walther Wenck's Twelfth Army to break the ring and bring relief was easily frustrated. The Russians began a weeklong struggle to batter a path through the city street by street, block by block. The antitank ditches dug with such labour by tens of thousands of Berliners proved as futile as all such obstacles, but barricades of rubble heaped on old trams and rail trucks were more effective. Regular troops supported by old men and teenagers of the Hitler Youth fought the Russians with small arms, grenades and panzerfausts. The boy soldiers who died fighting for Berlin would have seemed especially tragic victims, had there not been so many others. Dorothea von Schwanenflugel described an encounter with one unhappy little figure, "a mere child in a uniform many sizes too large for him, with an anti-tank grenade lying beside him. Tears were running down his face, and he was obviously very frightened of everyone. I very softly asked him what he was doing there. He lost his distrust and told me that he had been ordered to lie in wait here, and when a Soviet tank approached he was to run under it and explode the grenade. I asked how that would work, but he didn't know. In fact this frail child didn't even look capable of carrying such a grenade." Another Berlin woman wrote likewise:

You see very young boys, baby faces peeping out beneath oversized steel helmets. It's frightening to hear their high-pitched voices. They're fifteen years old at the most, standing there looking so skinny and small in their billowing uniform tunics. Why are we so appalled at the thought of children being murdered? In three or four years the same children strike us as perfectly fit for shooting and maiming . . . Up to now being a soldier meant being a man . . . Wasting these boys before they reach maturity obviously runs against some fundamental law of nature, against our instinct, against every drive to preserve the species.

Like certain fish or insects that eat their own offspring. People aren't supposed to do that. The fact that this is exactly what we are doing is a sure sign of madness.

Neither side enjoyed scope for tactical subtlety in the battle for Berlin, there were merely a thousand savage local encounters in which the attackers measured each advance in yards. Again and again the first men to push forward were killed, the lead tanks destroyed; Soviet artillery and bombers pounded the defenders; whole streets were reduced to rubble. Siege artillery, 203mm howitzers, was brought forward to blast buildings whose occupants fired back over open sights while dust and smoke clogged the air. Stalin goaded his marshals by telephone from Moscow: tens of thousands of men paid with their lives as Zhukov and Konev conducted not a coordinated assault but a race to fulfil their rival ambitions.

"Berlin . . . presented a dreadful scene," wrote a Swedish Red Cross representative, Sven Frykman, surveying the beleaguered city by night. "A full moon shone from a cloudless sky so you could see the awful extent of the damage. A ghost town of cave dwellers was all that was left of this world metropolis . . . The imperial palace, all the splendid castles, the prince's palace, the Royal Library, Tempelhof, the buildings along the Unter den Linden—hardly anything was left. Because of the moonlight which shone through all these empty windows and doorways, the city gave an even more grotesque impression than by daylight. Here and there a flame was still burning after the most recent bombing raids, and the fire brigades were at work. Burst pipes on some of the streets made you think of Venice and its canals."

Helga Schneider wrote: "We are vegetating in a ghost town, without electric light or gas, without water, we are forced to think of personal hygiene as a luxury and hot meals as abstract concepts. We are living like ghosts in a vast field of ruins . . . a city where nothing works apart from the telephones that sometimes ring, glumly and pointlessly, beneath piles of fallen masonry." Not all calls were futile: the staff in Hitler's bunker were reduced to seeking information by calling numbers in chosen areas to discover where the enemy had reached. As one quarter after another was overrun and Russian voices were heard, in cellars terrified civilians muttered to one another: *"Der Iwan kommt!"*

With so many Germans running away or surrendering at any opportunity, it is extraordinary that resistance persisted for so long. Some 45,000 SS and Wehrmacht troops, together with 40,000 Volkssturm and a mere 60 tanks, held out for a week against the might of Zhukov's and Konev's armies. Street fighting is never easy, because it is hard to control and manoeuvre small groups of men clinging to precarious lodgements among buildings, and the struggle in that last week of April showed the power of despair. In Hitler's capital, the Red Army paid the price for its policy of unrestrained savagery towards German soldiers and civilians: whatever the views of Hitler and the SS, it is hard to suppose that Berlin's defenders would have fought so stubbornly had they entertained hopes of mercy for themselves or the population. As it was, the Soviet commitment to murder, rape and pillage was known to every German. Most of those manning the perimeter saw no prospect save that of death. Among the last-ditch defenders was a unit of the French Waffen SS Charlemagne Division. The commander of these doomed men, twenty-five-year-old Henri Fenet, was presented with the Knight's Cross at a ceremony held in a wrecked tram, by candlelight. Fenet already had another medal: the Croix de Guerre, earned fighting for France in 1940.

Amazingly, soldiers of the Charlemagne and some other Waffen SS units mustered sufficient determination to mount local counterattacks, one of which retook from the Russians the Gestapo headquarters building on Prinz Albrechtstrasse. Some men and boys who sought salvation in flight were summarily hanged in the streets by the SS men ranging the city. Russians and Germans alike were mocked by the contrast between the mountains of wreckage and the heaped and broken bodies littering the landscape and signs of spring breaking through. When gunfire paused even briefly, birds could be heard singing; trees blossomed until blast reduced them to blackened skeletons; tulips flowered in some places, and in the parks there was an overpowering scent of lilac. But mostly there were corpses. Germany's leaders had conducted a long love affair with death: in Berlin in April 1945, this achieved a final consummation.

On 28 April Benito Mussolini was captured and shot by partisans while attempting to escape from northern Italy. On the afternoon of the thirtieth, as Russian troops stormed the Reichstag building 400 yards from Hitler's bunker, the leader of the Third Reich killed himself and his wife. The banality of evil has seldom been more vividly displayed than by the couple's conduct in their last days. Eva Braun was much preoccupied with the disposal of her jewellery—"my diamond watch is unfortunately being repaired"—and by concealing her dressmakers' accounts from posterity— "On no account must Heise's bills be found." She wrote in a last letter to her friend Herta Ostermayr, "What should I say to you? I cannot understand how it should have all come to this, but it is impossible to believe any more in a God."

Most Germans received the news of Hitler's death with numbed indifference. The soldier Gerd Schmuckle was at a crowded inn far from Berlin when the radio bulletin was broadcast. "If—instead of this announcement—the innkeeper had come to the door and said that an animal of his had died in the stable, the sympathy could not have been less. Only one young soldier leapt up, extended his right arm and cried out 'Hail to the Führer!' All the others continued to eat their soup as though nothing of importance had occurred." In the capital sporadic fighting persisted for two more days, until Berlin's commandant, Lt. Gen. Karl Wiedling, surrendered on 2 May.

A terrible quiet, the quiet of the dead and damned, fell upon the city. "No sound of man or beast, no car, radio or tram . . . ," wrote a Berlin woman. "Nothing but an oppressive silence broken only by our footsteps. If there are people inside the buildings watching us, they are doing so in secret." She added a week later: "Everywhere there's filth and horse manure and children playing—if that's what it can be called. They loiter about, stare at us, whisper to one another. The only loud voices you hear belong to Russians . . . Their songs strike our ears as raw, defiant."

Everywhere the Soviet victors held sway, they embarked upon an orgy of celebration, rape and destruction on a scale such as Europe had not witnessed since the seventeenth century. "The baker comes stumbling towards me down the hall," wrote a Berlin woman about one of her neighbours, "white as his flour, holding out his hands: 'They have my wife . . .' His voice breaks. For a second I feel I'm acting in a play. A middle-class baker can't possibly move like that, can't speak with such emotion, put so much feeling into his voice, bare his soul that way, his heart so torn. I've never seen anyone but great actors do that."

A German lawyer, who had miraculously preserved his Jewish wife through the Nazi years, now sought to protect her from Russian soldiers. One shot him in the hip. As he lay dying, he saw three men rape her as she screamed out her Jewish identity. The anonymous Berlin woman diarist who recorded the episode wrote: "No one could invent a story like this: it's life at its most cruel—mad blind circumstance." An elderly Berliner moaned, "If only it were over, this poor bit of life." The diarist, who was herself repeatedly raped, wrote of experiencing a sense of detachment from her own physical being, "a means of escape—my true self simply leaving my body behind, my poor, besmirched, abused body. Breaking away and floating off, unblemished, into a white beyond. It can't be me that this is happening to, so I'm expelling it all from me."

A Soviet soldier wrote to a friend about German women. "They do not speak a word of Russian, but that makes it easier. You don't have to persuade them. You just point a Nagan [pistol] and tell them to lie down. Then you do your stuff and go away." In one place, the bodies of a group of raped and mutilated women were found, each with a bottle stuffed up her vagina. Vasily Grossman was dismayed to see that the men of the Red Army made no distinction among their victims: "Horrifying things are happening to German women . . . Soviet girls liberated from the camps are suffering a lot now." Alexander Solzenhitsyn, serving with Rokossovsky as a gunner officer, wrote an ironically indulgent poem about what he witnessed as his people sealed their victory:

> The conquerors of Europe swarm,
> Russians scurrying everywhere.
> Vacuum cleaners, wine, and candles,
> Skirts and picture frames, and pipes
> Brooches and medallions, blouses, buckles
> Typewriters (not of a Russian type)
> Rings of sausages and cheeses.
> A moment later the cry of a girl,
> Somewhere from behind a wall,
> "I'm not a German. I'm not a German.
> No! I'm—Polish. I'm a Pole."
> Grabbing what comes handy, those
> Like-minded lads get in and start—
> And lo, what heart
> Could well oppose?

When the former Jewish hospital at Wedding was overrun on 24 April, Russian soldiers found 800 Jews, most in desperate physical condition, whom the Nazi killing machine had miraculously overlooked. A disbelieving Soviet soldier said in broken German, *"Nichts Juden. Juden kaput."* The Russians raped the female inmates anyway: *"Frau ist frau."* A further 1,400 Berlin Jews emerged from hiding after the liberation, last survivors of a once-great community. There were also Jews in the Red Army. One terrified German family found themselves confronted by a Soviet commissar who said, "I am a Russian, a communist and a Jew . . . My father and mother were murdered by the SS because they were Jews. My wife and two children are missing. My home is in ruins. And what has happened to me has happened to millions in Russia. Germany has murdered, raped, plundered and destroyed . . . What do you think we want to do, now that we have defeated German armies?"

He turned on the eldest son of the family, demanding, "Stand up. How old are you?" The boy answered, "Twelve." The Russian said, "About as old as my son would be today. The SS criminals took him from me." He

The Final Russian Assaults

Front Lines
———— 15 April 1945
– – – 18 April
–·–·– 28 April
·········· 8 May
▲—▲ German defence lines
⬭ German pockets
➤ German counterattacks
∎∎∎➤ Anglo-American advances

drew his pistol and aimed it at the boy, provoking frenzied consternation and pleas for mercy from the parents. Finally the Russian said, "No, no, no, ladies and gentlemen. I will not shoot. But you must admit, I have enough reasons to do so. There is so much that screams for revenge." This encounter ended without bloodshed, because the Russian protagonist was unusually enlightened; many other such meetings climaxed in screams, horrors, sobbing women, wrecked homes, mutilated bodies.

Stalin was untroubled by the behaviour of his soldiers towards the Germans—or to their supposedly liberated slaves. The Soviets saw no shame, such as burdens Western societies, about the concept of revenge. The war had been fought chiefly on Russian soil. The Russian people had endured sufferings incomparably greater than those of the Americans and British. As conquerors, the Germans had behaved barbarously, their conduct rendered the more base because they spoke so much of honour and professed adherence to civilised values. Now the Soviet Union exacted a terrible punishment. The German nation had brought misery on the world, and in 1945 it paid. The price of having started and lost a war against a tyranny as ruthless as Stalin's was that vengeance was exacted on terms almost as merciless as those Hitler's minions had imposed on Europe since 1939.

In those days there were tens of thousands of suicides throughout eastern Germany. Liselotte Grunauer, a sixteen-year-old, recorded in her diary: "The pastor shot himself and his wife and daughter . . . Mrs. H. shot her two sons and herself and slit her daughter's throat . . . Our teacher Miss K. hanged herself; she was a Nazi. The local party leader S. shot himself and Mrs. N. took poison. It's a blessing that there is no gas at present, otherwise some more of us would have taken their own lives." Nor were Russian depredations confined to Germany: Tito's partisans were stunned by the excesses of the Red Army in Yugoslavia, even against people fighting for the same cause. Rape, pillage and murder were inflicted with indiscriminate abandon.

The British SOE officer Basil Irwin was astonished to witness the contempt the Soviets displayed towards their allies: "They treated us with no hostility or suspicion, but they treated the partisans like dirt . . . It was such a shock to [them], who thought here was the welcome they were giving to their brother Slavs and the great Russian army." When Stalin was taxed with this, he merely shrugged. Milovan Djilas wrote bitterly: "Illusions about the Red Army, and consequently about the communists themselves, were being destroyed." In Belgrade, Tito protested personally to the local Soviet commander, Korneyev, that his followers were dismayed by the contrast between the correct behaviour of British soldiers and the savagery of the Russians. Korneyev exploded: "I protest most emphatically against the insults being levelled at the Red Army by comparing it with the armies of the capitalist countries!"

In Yugoslavia, as everywhere that Stalin's soldiers went, the Soviet Union declined—as modern Russia still declines—to acknowledge the crimes committed by those wearing its uniform. *Pravda* observed sardonically on 22 April 1945: "The British press displays just indignation in reporting the atrocities committed by Germans in Buchenwald concentration camp . . . Soviet people can understand better than anyone else the anger and bitterness, pain and resentment that have now overtaken British public opinion . . . We saw the enemy for what he was a long time ago. Our allies have not seen what we have seen. Now they will understand us better, more readily appreciate our insistent demands for the indictment of the fascist butchers."

Following Hitler's death, Grand Admiral Karl Dönitz assumed the mantle of Führer. He postured in that role for a fortnight, attempting to buy time for German forces to escape westward from the Russians by staging partial capitulations and seeking to parley with the Americans. SS general Karl Wolff had already concluded a unilateral negotiation for the surrender of his army in Italy, signed at Caserta on 29 April. German forces in northwest Germany, Holland and Denmark surrendered to Montgomery at Lüneburg Heath on 4 May. Resistance on the American fronts ended two days later, while the Red Army closed up to the Elbe. The dying continued to the end: Capt. Nikolai Belov, whose diary vividly described his experiences in action, had been wounded five times since 1941. On 5 May 1945 he was killed in action.

Patton's army reached Pilsen and might have advanced to Prague, but the Russians insisted on taking the Czech capital themselves. They finally accomplished this on 11 May, after a disastrous uprising against the Germans by local partisans provoked a final spasm of bloodshed. Meanwhile, a delegation from Dönitz reached Eisenhower's headquarters at Reims on 5 May, seeking an exclusive surrender to the Americans. The supreme commander required a simultaneous and unconditional surrender on all fronts, which Gen. Alfred Jodl, Hitler's senior military adviser, signed on 7 May. The eighth was celebrated by all the Western Allies as VE-Day. Stalin, however, insisted on a further ceremony in Berlin, at which the Russians were full parties. This took place on 8 May, and the ninth thereafter became Russia's own appointed date of victory: in this, as in so much else, Stalin's nation chose to march to its own step.

Sporadic exchanges of fire persisted in the east for many weeks, with NKVD troops killing Poles and Ukrainians who refused to accept the substitution of Soviet tyranny for that of the Nazis. British lieutenant David Fraser wrote: "There was still too much vile cruelty in the world for us to be able to say with true satisfaction, 'Good is victorious.' " An American, Lt. Lyman Diercks, at Unterach near Salzburg in Austria, wrote: "Our celebration was low-key. An American in the town loaned us an American flag which we flew from a pole in the square. The elderly Austrian couple who owned the hotel cooked us a wonderful meal. She cried and said: 'Maybe now my son will be able to come home from Russia where he is a prisoner.' But he never did." In the British lines, Corp.

John Cropper described a sense of "instant relief—no wild cheering or running about. It was a case of thank God it's all over and we were safe at last. We had nothing to celebrate with anyway, just compo tea and normal rations. It was as if you'd had an exhausting day and you flop down in a chair at the end of it."

The American and British armies in Germany looted energetically and raped occasionally, but few men sought explicit revenge from the vanquished. The French, however, saw many scores to be paid. Maj. Albrecht Hamlin, CO of a U.S. civil affairs unit running Merzig (population 12,500), submitted a despairing report cataloguing wholesale acts of pillage following the arrival of a French cavalry unit: "Within an hour the city was in a state of complete confusion. The Chasseurs spread out . . . taking whatever houses they wished, ejecting civilians from their homes, impressing them on the street for forced labor, confiscating bicycles, automobiles, trucks, and general looting of houses and stores . . . The acts were manifestly committed as revenge upon the Germans. Reprimands to the officers were met with the repeated excuse that the Germans did these things to France, and now it was their turn."

Hamlin described indiscriminate shooting, rapes committed by French colonial troops and the killing of an American sergeant by a French patrol. "The hotel in Mettlach was systematically sacked and contents shipped by truck back into France . . . 5 April Luitwin-on-Boch reported that French soldiers had discovered the art objects and curios stored in the basement of the ceramic museum of Villeroy & Boch, and were destroying them." To compound the chaos, liberated Russian prisoners rampaged freely and American soldiers were reported killing fish with grenades in the Hausbacher Brook. By contrast the local inhabitants were entirely submissive, according to Hamlin. Though such scenes were widespread throughout Germany, in the Western Allied zone order was progressively restored during the weeks that followed. In the Russian zone, it was not. Institutionalised pillage, rape and murder persisted long after Germany's military defeat had been acknowledged. The ending of the war in the west signalled a deliverance for the soldiers of America and Britain, but the miseries of Europe and many millions of its inhabitants were much slower to abate.

CHAPTER TWENTY-FIVE

JAPAN PROSTRATE

IN THE SPRING OF 1945, Indian and British forces led by Gen. Bill Slim conducted a brilliantly successful campaign to recapture Burma. This was irrelevant to the outcome of the war—as both Slim and Churchill anticipated from the outset—because the U.S. Navy had already established a stranglehold on Japan in the Pacific. But it did something to restore the battered confidence and fallen prestige of the British Empire, and laid bare Japan's vulnerability. Churchill had sought to avoid a thousand-mile overland advance through some of the worst terrain in the world, preferring an amphibious assault on Rangoon from the south. But the Americans insisted on an attack through northern Burma, to fulfil the only strategic purpose they valued in the region—reopening the overland route to China.

Slim's army, dominated by Indian troops and including three divisions recruited from Britain's African colonies, was much stronger than that of the Japanese—530,000 men to 400,000—and supported by powerful armoured and air forces. Its chief problem was to supply an advance across mountainous and densely vegetated country almost bereft of roads. Air dropping, made possible by a large commitment of U.S. planes, became a critical factor in the campaign. At first, Slim planned to fight a battle on the Shwebo plain, west of the Irrawaddy, where his tanks and fighter-bombers could best be exploited. But a new Japanese commander, Lt. Gen. Hyotaro Kimura, decided against making a strong stand there, and instead opted for hitting the British as they crossed the river. When Ultra conveyed Kimura's intentions to Slim, he changed his own plan. He pushed some troops forward towards an Irrawaddy crossing point north of Mandalay, which the Japanese were expecting, but made his main effort much farther south, to cut off the enemy's retreat by striking against Meiktila, in their rear. Meanwhile, another British corps occupied the attention of the Japanese in the Arakan coastal region.

The success of these operations was made possible first by the Allies' strength, and second by absolute command of the air, which denied the Japanese opportunities for reconnaissance; from beginning to end of the

611

campaign, Kimura was befogged about British movements and intentions. Slim's forces, advancing from Assam, in India, began to cross the Chindwin River, where so many tragic scenes had taken place during the 1942 retreat from Burma, in December 1944. In the north, Stilwell commanded a force of five Chinese divisions, driving for the key airfield of Myitkyina. On 5 March, 9,000 men of Maj. Gen. Orde Wingate's Chindits began to fly in to jungle landing zones behind the Japanese front. Wingate himself died in a crash, but during the months that followed his units fought a succession of bitter battles. On 17 May, the Chindits and Chinese linked at Myitkyina, where they seized the airfield; the sufferings and casualties of Wingate's men were appalling, but they diverted significant Japanese forces from Slim's main advance.

Thereafter, some 40,000 tons of supplies and equipment were flown to Myitkyina, for onward shipment to China. These deliveries could do little to remedy the infirmity of Chiang Kai-shek's army, which remained incapable of inflicting much harm on the Japanese, and chiefly enriched the Nationalist warlords who stole most of the matériel before it reached their troops. Though the Japanese paid a heavy price for sustaining their occupation of eastern China throughout the war, committing a million soldiers to control its vastnesses, they had little difficulty in defeating barefoot, half-starved Nationalist troops wherever they fought them. Mao Tse-tung's communist forces in the north enjoyed some success in persuading Westerners that they were engaging the Japanese more effectively, but in reality Mao conserved his strength for the looming domestic struggle for control of China.

An Indian formation crossed the Irrawaddy north of Mandalay in mid-January. During the following month, three divisions staged the main crossing west of Sagaing, much farther south. The river was a mile wide, and the British wholly lacked the engineering and amphibious resources Eisenhower's armies deployed in Europe. But, with most Japanese forces committed farther north, they secured a bridgehead by dogged improvisation and some striking displays of courage. The ruins of Mandalay fell to the British on 20 March. This was an important symbolic victory, but Kimura was already falling back to fight the critical battle at Meiktila.

The nationalist leader Aung San's Japanese-sponsored Burma Defence Army (BDA) prepared to change sides. Some British officers resisted the notion of providing arms to his nine battalions, fearing these would soon be used against themselves. However, Lord Louis Mountbatten, Allied supreme commander in Southeast Asia, overruled them and ordered SOE officers to work with the BDA, saying, "We shall be doing no more than has been done in Italy, Romania, Hungary and Finland." Aung San met Slim, apologising for his inability to speak English. The general responded with characteristic courtesy that the embarrassment was on his side, for being unable to speak Burmese. They agreed to fight together, and on 27 March, when Slim's army was within a hundred miles of Rangoon, BDA units suddenly attacked Japanese positions. Many Burmese welcomed the opportunity for revenge on a people they had welcomed as liberators in 1942, but who had since become their oppressors. One of them, Maung Maung, wrote: "Partisans, young men from villages, left their homes to march with us. We ate the food that the villagers offered us, wooed their daughters, brought danger to their doors and took their sons with us." This was a romanticised view of a tardy and cynical switch of allegiance, comparable with the conduct of many French people in the summer of 1944; but it helped to create a legend which Burma's nationalists would later find serviceable.

By 29 April the British were at Pegu, fifty miles from Rangoon, amid torrential rain, a harbinger of the coming monsoon. On the south coast, an Indian division staged the amphibious assault Churchill had always wanted, and pushed forward to the capital against slight resistance. The Japanese army was shattered, and had lost almost all its guns and vehicles. It sustained isolated pockets of resistance to the end of the war, but faced slaughter as broken units sought to break through Slim's army, which was finally deployed as a cordon along the Sittang River to cut off their escape into Siam. In the last months, the British suffered only a few hundred casualties, while the 1945 Burma campaign cost their enemies 80,000 dead.

BUT THE MAIN BUSINESS of closing the ring on Japan was meanwhile being done in the Pacific. On the morning of 19 February, three U.S. Marine divisions began to land on Iwo Jima, an island pimple 3,000 miles west of Pearl Harbor and less than 700 miles south of Japan. An American watching the prelanding bombardment said: "We all figured nothing could live through that, and the carrier planes were giving it hell, too." But the defenders were well prepared and deeply dug in. Carnage was severe—proportionately worse than that on D-Day: at nightfall, 30,000 marines were ashore, but 566 were already dead or dying. The living trudged through volcanic ash up to their knees, in a moonscape devoid of cover; a rainstorm worsened their plight. A marine, Joseph Raspilair, wrote: "In all my life I do not think I have been as miserable as I was that night. All you could do was lay in the water and wait for morning so you could get out of the hole." Weeks of painful fighting followed. Corp. George Wayman, a bazooka man, was in such pain from wounds as he lay for hours in a shellhole that he felt tempted to draw his bayonet and kill himself; he was eventually evacuated only after hours exposed to the Japanese fire that pounded the marine perimeter.

Replacements trudged forward to reinforce line units, where many were hit before even learning the names of their comrades. Lt. Patrick Caruso kidded one such young man about being underage; soon afterwards the boy was killed, after just two hours on the island, without unslinging his rifle from his shoulder or glimpsing the enemy. The defenders' ingenuity seemed boundless: a marine was amazed to see a hillside suddenly open before his eyes, to reveal three Japanese pushing out a field gun. It fired three rounds, then was dragged back into the cave. Mortars eventually destroyed the gun, but a hundred such positions had to be taken out before the defences were overwhelmed. Officers learned to discourage men from seeking souvenirs, which the Japanese often booby-trapped. "The best souvenir you can take home is yourself," a laconic marine commander told his company.

By 27 March, when Iwo Jima was secured, the Americans had suffered 24,000 casualties, including 7,184 dead, to capture an island one-third the size of Manhattan. Its airfields proved useful to B-29s returning from missions damaged or short of fuel, but they were little employed for offensive operations. Geographically, Iwo Jima seemed a significant landmark on the way to Japan; but strategically, like so many hard-won objectives in every campaign, it is hard to argue that its seizure was worthwhile—the Marianas were vastly more important. The U.S. Navy's almost absolute command of the sea made it impossible for the Japanese to move forces from Iwo Jima, or indeed anywhere else, to impede American operations. Japan was bleeding from a thousand cuts. All that was now in doubt was how its rulers might be induced to acknowledge their defeat, and in the spring of 1945 they still seemed far from confronting reality. Japan's generals believed that a negotiated peace could be won by imposing on the Americans a heavy blood price for every gain, and, above all, by convincing Washington that the cost of invading the Japanese mainland would be unacceptably high. They sought to emphasise this by mounting a rising tempo of air attacks against the U.S. Navy.

Cmdr. Stephen Juricka, the navigating officer of the 27,000-ton carrier *Franklin*, was one of thousands of shocked witnesses of the devastation wreaked by air attack. "I saw . . . destroyers get hit, burst into flames, men jumping over the side to avoid flames . . . It did not take long for the crews of the picket destroyers to feel that they were being put out there as bait." Early on the morning of 19 March 1945, it was the *Franklin*'s turn to fall victim. Two bombs struck the flight deck, prompting a huge explosion below: "The planes just behind the elevator were spotted, ready for take-off, engines going, fully loaded with Tiny Tim [rockets], 500- and 1000-pound bombs. Sheets of flame came up and then we really started to smoke . . . Men were jumping off the flight deck . . . Two destroyers were picking people up out of the sea directly behind us . . . a lot of them injured, burned . . . We were exploding and on fire until the middle of the next afternoon." Father O'Callaghan, the ship's Catholic chaplain, was giving extreme unction to a dying man when a Tiny Tim rocket ignited and flew over his head. Most of the 4,800 crewmen on the *Franklin* were evacuated in the first hours after the attack, but 772 stayed aboard, waging an epic struggle to keep the ship afloat. The U.S. Navy had learned much about damage control since 1941, and all of it was put to use saving the carrier. As ever, some men behaved wonderfully well—and others less well.

Stephen Juricka said: "I was amazed [when] some of our big, good-looking officers whom you would expect to be towers of strength turned out to be little pipsqueak people who needed bucking up all the time, and some other little nondescript 135-pounders turned out to be real tigers . . . It was the little people who really came through . . . Seven officers left the *Franklin* over the highline [a breeches-buoy link to the cruiser *Santa Fe*] in spite of orders to return to the ship, and Captain Gehres reported every one of them and recommended court-martial."

AS EARLY AS 1939, the USAAF's Gen. Carl "Tooey" Spaatz had anticipated using America's B-29 Superfortress bomber, then only in the early stages of development, to attack Japan. Sporadic air raids took place in 1944, some launched from India, others from fields constructed at huge cost and in the face of painful local difficulties in China. A combination of technical difficulties with the early B-29s, the distance to Japan, together with shortcomings of leadership, navigation and bomb aiming, caused the USAAF's efforts to make little impact. Only in 1945 was the offensive dramatically transformed and intensified, first, by establishment of a huge network of bases on the Marianas; second, by large deliveries of aircraft; and finally, by the ascent of Maj. Gen. Curtis LeMay to leadership of the XXI Bomber Command.

LeMay was the architect of the first great fire-raising raid on Tokyo on 9 March 1945. He dispatched 325 aircraft to attack by night at low level—between 6,000 and 9,000 feet. Torrents of incendiaries fell and exploded with their characteristic sharp crackle. Only twelve bombers were lost, most destroyed by updrafts from the blazing city. Forty-two suffered flak damage, but the Japanese defences were feeble. A pilot wrote laconically next day: "We took off last night at 1835 and after a dull trip hit the coast of Japan at 0210. Even before we made landfall we could see the fires at Tokyo. We were at 7,800 and there was smoke towering above us. The radar run was perfect and we dropped in an open spot visually. The city was a 'Dante's inferno.' One night fighter made a run on us but we turned into him and lost him." He added in a letter home: "Fires were everywhere and the destruction wrought this night could have been nothing less than catastrophe." The airman was right: around 100,000 people were killed, and a million rendered homeless. More than 10,000 acres of the city, a quarter of its area, were reduced to ashes. Tokyo on the morning of 10 March looked to a Philippines veteran, Maj. Shoji Takahashi, "like the biggest and most devastated battlefield one could imagine—Leyte on a gigantic scale." He was stunned and disgusted when, in one of many reconciliatory gestures by the postwar Tokyo government to the United States, LeMay was given a Japanese decoration.

The USAAF chiefs displayed an admiration for the XXIst Bomber Command's forceful new supremo who was untinged by any moral scruple. Gen. Lauris Norstad said apologetically to LeMay's sacked predecessor, Gen. Haywood Hansell, "LeMay is an operator, the rest of us are planners. That's all there is to it." In the nights that followed, similar incendiary raids were launched against Nagoya, Osaka, Kobe and other cities. Even when the bombers began to strike in daylight, losses remained low, and a hundred new B-29s a month were arriving from America's factories. The airmen reluctantly acceded to navy requests to divert some effort to offshore mining operations: Operation Starvation, which began at the end of March, achieved dramatic results, for the Japanese were as short of minesweepers as of everything else. The first 900 mines to splash into the seas around Japan imposed further drastic cuts on its imports; when merchantmen were ordered to brave the subsurface menace, a spate of sinkings followed. By the war's end, B-29s had laid 12,000 sea mines, which accounted for 63 percent of all Japanese shipping losses between April and August 1945.

But the Superfortresses' main effort was directed against cities. Some daylight raids against aircraft factories provoked a strong response—one formation was met by 233 fighters. But so poor was the performance of both Japanese planes and their pilots that the bombers sustained a loss rate which never rose above 1.6 percent, negligible by European standards. After one raid the Japanese claimed twenty-eight B-29s destroyed, when the real figure was five. In their desperation, the defenders also adopted kamikaze tactics, with Japanese fighters ramming American bombers. Even this expedient was not always successful against the huge Superfortresses: one plane returned after suffering a suicide attack with the loss of only an engine. Its flight engineer, Lt. Robert Watson, said, "There was surprisingly little jolt when the Jap hit us, and our navigator didn't even know we'd been rammed." Weather and atmospheric conditions troubled crews more than did the enemy defences: thermals created freak effects— one Superfortress landed on Saipan in July with a section of tin roof flapping from a wing leading edge.

Much historical attention has focused upon the willingness of Japan's pilots to sacrifice themselves, but by this stage of the war few of those who flew conventional fighters showed much appetite for the fray: American airmen often remarked upon their lack of aggression. Tokyo was attacked again and again. On 5 June, when Kobe suffered once more, defending aircraft made their last significant appearance; the enemy had determined to husband his dwindling aircraft and crews to await American invasion, when it came. On the night of the fifteenth, a raid on Osaka destroyed 300,000 homes and killed thousands of people. The USAAF found itself struggling to identify worthwhile targets still intact: oil refineries were bombed, though these were marginal when the Japanese had little oil left to process; bomber losses fell to 0.3 percent.

Moral issues troubled the Superfortress crews no more than their commanders: with characteristic youthful facetiousness, every member of the 330th Bomb Group was presented with a certificate declaring that he, "having visited the Japanese emperor a total of . . . times to pay his respects with H.E., incendiaries and C-ration cans, having helped to clear the Tokyo slums and having aided in the spring plowing is hereby inducted into the royal and rugged order of EMPIRE BUSTERS." In the fourteen months of the USAAF bombing campaign against Japan, 170,000 tons of bombs were dropped, most of them in the last six months; 414 B-29s were lost and 3,015 crew killed; about 100 Japanese died for each American flier, and 65 Japanese cities were reduced to ashes. The 1944–45 air offensive took place chiefly because the B-29, conceived in the very different circumstances of 1940, had been created to carry it out. The Superfortress programme cost $4 billion, against $3 billion for the Manhattan Project. America's airmen were determined to demonstrate their ability to make a decisive contribution to victory. The fire-raising attacks did not match the impact on Japan's economy of the submarine blockade, because they took place when industry had already been crippled by lack of fuel and raw materials, but they convinced all but the intractable militarists in the Tokyo leadership that the war was lost. LeMay's role in punishing Japan for launching a war of aggression was more significant than his contribution to enforcing its surrender.

. . .

THE AMERICAN LANDING on Okinawa was designed to pave the way for what threatened to be the bloodiest battle of the Asian war—invasion of the Japanese mainland. The island, a sixty-mile sliver of fields and mountains, lay midway between Luzon and Kyushu. Okinawa was inhabited by 150,000 people who had Japanese nationality, though they were culturally distinct. The assault that began on 1 April, Easter Sunday, after days of intense bombardment, was under Nimitz's overall command. More than 1,200 vessels offloaded 170,000 soldiers and marines of the Tenth Army, while a vast covering fleet of aircraft carriers, battleships and lesser warships cruised offshore. To the Americans' surprise, the initial assault was unopposed. The Japanese had learned the lessons of earlier island battles and withdrawn beyond range of the naval bombardment; only after a week of skirmishing inland did advancing U.S. troops meet fierce machine-gun and artillery fire. The south of Okinawa had been transformed into a fortress, successive lines of positions deeply dug on high ground. In the first twenty-four hours thereafter, the U.S. XXIV Corps received 14,000 incoming shells.

At the point of collision between the rival armies, the island was only three miles wide. Gen. Mitsuru Ushijima had concentrated his 77,000 Japanese and 24,000 Okinawan auxiliaries where they were almost impregnable to frontal attack, as the Americans discovered during the weeks that followed. Heavy rain set in, churning the battlefield into a sea of mud. Again and again, U.S. soldiers and marines thrust forward—and were repulsed. Their generals demanded that they should try harder: on 6 May a U.S. corps commander visited a divisional command post and said he noted its units had suffered fewer casualties than any other formation. Officers interpreted this as a compliment until he added, "To me, that means just one thing—you're not pushing." In its first twenty-four days on Okinawa, the division had advanced 25,000 yards and reckoned to have killed almost 5,000 Japanese; in the succeeding sixteen days, however, it gained only 2,500 yards.

With the war in Europe coming to an end and the power of the United States everywhere triumphant, it seemed to Americans at home intolerable that their boys should die in the thousands to wrest from fanatics a remote and meaningless piece of real estate: there was intense public anger, directed less against the enemy than towards their own commanders. By May 1945, with Hitler vanquished, Americans took for granted impending victory in the Pacific and were increasingly cynical about the war. To prick public complacency, the U.S. Navy urged people to take a vacation on the west coast and visit the dockyards where lay crippled and blackened warships brought back from Okinawa. But the American Red Cross found itself struggling to muster volunteers to prepare surgical dressings, and there was a chronic shortage of manpower to work in weapons plants. War weariness was a dignified phrase to describe the American domestic mood: it might instead have been categorised as boredom, the disease of democracies, whose patience is always scarce.

The men fighting on Okinawa shared the American people's frustration. They demanded: why not stage an amphibious assault to outflank the defences? Why not use poison gas? Why fight this war, in its last phase before inevitable victory, in a fashion that suited Japanese suicidalists? None of these questions was satisfactorily answered. The officer commanding the Tenth Army was the unimaginative Gen. Simon Bolivar Buckner, Jr. For more than two months he conducted a campaign which seemed to its participants close kin to those of the First World War in Flanders. He launched repeated frontal attacks on fixed positions which slowly gained ground, but cost heavy casualties. The U.S. Marine Corps fared no better on Okinawa than the army units to which it liked to condescend. For once, MacArthur was probably right when he argued that the best course would be to seal off the Japanese garrison in the south of the island, leaving it to rot while U.S. forces addressed mainland Japan.

The Japanese never supposed that their stand on the island would achieve decisive results. They placed faith, instead, on an air assault of devastating intensity against the U.S. fleet, in which the key role was played by kamikazes. Suicide planes had been used with some success in the Philippines since October 1944. Though the Allies found this method of war making repugnant, from their enemy's standpoint it was entirely rational. A postwar Japanese historian commented impatiently: "There have been innumerable Japanese critics of the kamikaze attacks. Most of them, however, seem to have been made by uninformed people who were content to be mere spectators of the great crisis which their nation faced."

Against overwhelming U.S. air power, poorly trained Japanese pilots employing conventional tactics suffered punitive losses. By planning for their deaths as a certainty rather than a mere probability, fuel loads could be halved and destructive accuracy much increased. The resultant air campaign off Okinawa inflicted heavier losses on the U.S. Navy than had been contrived by the capital ships of the Combined Fleet at any moment of the war. In its closing months, Spruance's ships were obliged to fight some of their toughest and most sustained actions.

Cmdr. Fitzhugh Lee, executive officer of the *Essex*, described his experience of monitoring the Japanese bomb and torpedo strikes from the huge carrier's combat information centre:

> I can remember spending many unhappy hours in CIC watching these blips coming at us, knowing what they were doing, and hoping that our guns would shoot them down, seeing them turn around on the radar screen, and then knowing that the torpedoes were in the water and on their way to you. Those minutes seemed like years, when you are sitting there waiting to see whether you're going to get hit. CIC was not a happy place to be. It was interesting psychologically . . . my first experience of real fear—being in the face of what you thought might be death at any moment . . . Here you sat around these radar screens and watched these things happen with young seamen who were eighteen or nineteen years old, just off the farm or out of the shoestore . . . Their reactions were for the most part wonderful. Every once in a while you'd find one that couldn't take it . . . I found that I could spot when somebody was getting a little hysterical . . . If he got very emotional, it would spread so you had to think of something quick—get him out . . . We had a few who lost control of themselves and started weeping, crying, praying.

The image of Japan's kamikazes taking off to face death with exuberant enthusiasm is largely fallacious. Among the first wave of suicidalists in the autumn of 1944, there were many genuine volunteers. Thereafter, however, the supply of young fanatics dwindled: many subsequent recruits were driven to accept the role by moral pressure, and sometimes conscription. Their training was as harsh as that of all Japanese warriors, and attended by the same emphasis on corporal punishment. Kasuga Takeo, a mess orderly who served at Tsuchitura, a kamikaze base, testified to the melancholy and sometimes hysteria which attended the pilots' last hours. Some smashed furniture or sat in mute contemplation, others danced in frenzy. Takeo spoke of a mood of "utter desperation"; peer pressure, a dominant social force in Japan since time immemorial, achieved its apogee in the kamikaze programme.

A Japanese historian wrote later with a lyricism incomprehensible to most Westerners about the doomed fliers of this period: "Many of the new arrivals seemed at first not only to lack enthusiasm, but indeed to be disturbed by their predicament. With some this condition lasted only a few hours, with others for several days. It was a period of melancholy that passed with time and eventually gave way to a spiritual awakening. Then, like an attainment of wisdom, care vanished and tranquillity of spirit appeared as life came to terms with death, mortality with immortality." He cited the example of one Lieutenant Kuno, who arrived unhappy at his operational airfield, but before his last flight became positively jaunty and insisted on stripping his plane of all nonessential equipment. The writer expressed regret, however, that "a few of these pilots, unduly influenced by a grateful and worshipping public, came to think of themselves as living gods and grew unbearably haughty."

Most were merely distressed. One young trainee mused grimly as his country's plight became plain: "Now the wholesale attack by the enemy with enormous material superiority begins. The last *katastropische* stage described in *All Quiet on the Western Front* is soon to approach." Likewise, a twenty-year-old bomber pilot, Norimitsu Takushima, wrote in his diary: "Today the Japanese people are not allowed freedom of speech and we cannot publicly express our criticism . . . The Japanese people do not even have access to enough information to know the facts . . . This is just one example of the routines and demagoguery that have become the moving forces of our society . . . We are going to meet our fate led by the cold will of the government. I shall not lose my passion and hope until the end . . . There is one ideal—freedom." On 9 April 1945, Takushima's plane vanished on an operation.

Yet some such young men professed that they went willingly: Lt. Kanno Naoishi, regarded by his peers as one of Japan's most colourful fighter pilots, had rammed a B-24 and escaped with his life, but did not expect to survive for much longer. Airmen travelled between postings with a small bag of personal effects, containing things like chart pencils and underwear, bearing their names; his was jauntily inscribed "personal effects of the late Lt. Cmdr. Kanno Naoishi," for he assumed his own death and the consequent posthumous promotion granted to every flier who fell. In one of innumerable last letters left behind by kamikazes for their families, Hayashi Ichizo wrote in April 1945: "Mother, I am a man. All men born in Japan are destined to die fighting for the country. You have done a splendid job raising me to become an honourable man. I will do a splendid job sinking an enemy aircraft carrier. Do brag about me." Ichizo died off Okinawa on 12 April 1945, aged twenty-three. Nakao Takenonori wrote likewise to his parents on 28 April: "The other day I paid my visit to Kotohira Shrine and had a picture taken. I told them to send the finished photo to you. Just in case, I enclose the receipt . . . Please do not get discouraged, and fight to defeat America and Britain. Please say the same to Grandmother. I will leave behind my diary. Although I did not do much in my life, I am content that I fulfilled my wish to live a pure life, leaving nothing ugly behind me . . . I wish to express my thanks to my uncle and many other people . . . Wishing you the best for your future."

The U.S. Navy found the experience of combating the kamikazes among the bloodiest and most painful of its war. Japanese airmen carried out almost 1,700 sorties to Okinawa between 11 March and the end of June 1945. Day after day, ships' crews manned their guns to sustain barrages against diving, twisting attackers. Most of the pilots perished under the American fire, but a few always got through to immolate themselves on the flight decks and superstructures of the warships, with devastating effect as gasoline ignited, munitions exploded and sailors protected only by antiflash hoods and gauntlets found themselves caught in blazing infernos. On 12 April, almost all of 185 attackers were destroyed—but the Americans lost 2 ships sunk and 14 damaged, including 2 battleships. On the sixteenth, the carrier *Intrepid* was hit. On 4 May, 5 ships were sunk and 11 damaged. Between the eleventh and the fourteenth, 3 flagships were badly damaged, including the carriers *Bunker Hill* and *Enterprise*. From 6 April to 22 June, throughout the Pacific theatre, there were ten major suicide attacks by day and night involving 1,465 aircraft, plus a further 4,800 conventional sorties. Kamikazes sank 27 ships and damaged 164, while bombers sank 1 and damaged 63. About 20 percent of kamikaze assaults scored hits—ten times the success rate for conventional attacks. Only the overwhelming strength of the U.S. Navy enabled it to withstand such punishment.

By the time Okinawa was declared secure on 22 June, eighty-two days after Buckner's initial landing, the army and the marines had lost 7,503 killed and 36,613 wounded, in addition to 36,000 nonbattle casualties, most of them combat-fatigue cases. Additionally the U.S. Navy suffered 4,907 dead and more than 8,000 wounded. Almost the entire defending force ashore perished, together with many thousands of native Okinawans, some of whom were incited by the army to commit suicide. The Japanese were largely successful in achieving their purpose: America's losses persuaded the nation's leadership that an invasion of mainland Japan would prove immensely costly. The consequences, however, proved very different from those Tokyo intended.

Other minor ground operations continued through the weeks that followed: Australian forces landed on Borneo at MacArthur's behest and fought a bloody little campaign to secure its coastal regions; in the Philippines, U.S. troops pushed back Yamashita's shrunken perimeter in the mountains and conducted a series of amphibious landings to liberate islands in the vast archipelago. Dogged efforts persisted to persuade Japanese stragglers to surrender: one prisoner, twenty-nine-year-old Sgt.

Kiyoshi Ito, in civilian life a salesman from Nagoya, was persuaded to sign a leaflet for distribution by American troops:

> My comrades! You, who valiantly decided to resist to the end . . .
> PLEASE PAUSE A WHILE BEFORE DYING AND THINK!
> OFFICERS, NCOs AND MEN!
> . . . I need not tell you the plight we are in, when our isolated home-
> land is fighting against the whole world. Is it not only a matter of time?
> Please try to think reasonably. Leave it to Fate to decide the war. Come
> what may the Japanese people, with their glorious history of 3,000
> years, will never be exterminated. Comrades, why not consider your
> past and live anew to rebuild Japan? Throw away your weapons and
> come out of your positions. Take off your shirts and wave them over
> your heads and approach the U.S. positions in daylight, using the main
> roads. Then your worries will be over and you will receive humane
> treatment.
> I STRONGLY BELIEVE THAT THIS IS THE ONLY WAY
> AND THE BEST WAY LEFT TO SERVE OUR COUNTRY!
> An NCO of the Japanese Army, now a prisoner of war.

Such appeals were almost entirely ignored until August 1945 and beyond, as they were also in Burma, where Slim's Fourteenth Army was still mopping up Japanese remnants and preparing for Operation Zipper, an invasion of Malaya. There were many sour jokes among men fighting in the East on hearing news of VE-Day. A dispatch rider handed a signal bearing the news to the senior staff officer of a division in Burma. This dignitary called to his sergeant, "I've got a message here: the war in Europe is over." The NCO turned to his men and said, "The war in Europe is over. Five-minute break." Maj. John Randle, who had been fighting on the Burma front since April 1942, said of the mood in the summer of 1945, "We thought we would go on and on. We were wearing a bit thin by then. If my CO had said, 'You have earned a rest,' even before we went back [into Burma] in early '45, I would have taken it. But I would never have asked for it; you couldn't put your hand up and say 'I've had enough.' "

To the dismay of many senior Americans, MacArthur was designated supreme commander for Olympic, the invasion of Japan scheduled to commence in November with a landing on Kyushu. Meanwhile, LeMay's bombers continued to incinerate the enemy's cities, and Japanese industrial production approached collapse. On 10 July 1945, the U.S. Third Fleet under Halsey closed in on Japan and began its own intensive programme of carrier air strikes against the mainland, inflicting carnage and destruction upon areas that had escaped the attentions of the Twentieth Air Force. "In the forefront of the invader, his great carrier task force rampaged about . . . like a mighty typhoon," wrote the naval officer Yoshida Mitsuru in awed frustration.

Stalin had promised to join the eastern war and launch a great Manchurian offensive in August. Against Japan as against Germany, there seemed every prospect that American lives could be saved by allowing the Russians to do some of the bloodiest business of smashing the enemy. Washington was remarkably naïve in failing to recognise that Stalin intended to engage the Japanese not to oblige the United States, but because he was determined to secure his own territorial prizes. Far from requiring inducements to commit his soldiers, the Soviet warlord could not have been deflected from doing so. Of all the belligerents, Stalin sustained the most clear-sighted vision of his own purposes. Through June and July 1945, thousands of Soviet troop trains shuttled eastwards across Asia, carrying armies which had defeated Germany to complete the destruction of Japan.

Meanwhile at a score of massive, closely guarded installations across the United States, 125,000 scientists, engineers and support staff laboured to bring to fruition the Manhattan Project, the greatest and most terrible scientific enterprise of the war. Laura Fermi, wife of Enrico, one of the brilliant principals at the Los Alamos research site, wrote later that she pitied the army doctors charged with the welfare of the scientists: "They had prepared for the emergencies of the battlefields, and they were faced instead with a high-strung bunch of men, women and children. High-strung, because altitude affected us, because our men worked long hours under unrelenting pressure; high-strung because we were too many of a kind, too close to one another, too unavoidable even during relaxation hours, and we were all crackpots; high-strung because we felt powerless under strange circumstances."

In 1942 the British had made significant progress with research on an atomic bomb; their theoretical knowledge, indeed, was then greater than that of America's scientists. But, with their own island embattled, they recognised that they lacked resources to build a weapon quickly. An agreement was reached whereby British and European émigré scientists crossed the Atlantic to work with the Americans. Thereafter, Britain's contribution was quickly forgotten in Washington: the United States became brutally proprietorial about its ownership of the bomb.

Technological determinism is a prominent feature of modern warfare, and this was never more vividly manifested than in exploitation of the power of atomic destruction. Just as it was almost inevitable that once an armada of B-29s had been constructed to attack Japan, they would be thus employed, so the United States' commitment to the Manhattan Project precipitated the fate of Hiroshima and Nagasaki. Posterity sees the use of the atomic bombs in isolation; yet in the minds of most of the politicians and generals privy to the secret, these first nuclear weapons offered merely a dramatic increase in the efficiency of the air attacks already being carried out by LeMay's Superfortresses, and provoked negligible expressions of moral scruples back home.

Only a small number of scientists grasped the earth-shaking significance of atomic power. Churchill revealed the limitations of his own understanding back in 1941, when asked to approve the British commitment to developing a nuclear weapon. He responded that he was personally satisfied with the destructive power of existing explosives, though he had no objections to undertaking development of a new technology which promised more. The exchanges between Truman—who had become president following the death of Roosevelt on 12 April 1945—Stimson, Marshall and others avowed an understanding that the bomb could prove a weapon of devastating power, but little hint that this would inaugurate a new age for mankind. Marshall, for instance, until August 1945 ordered continued planning for Olympic; he was unconvinced that, even if the atomic bombs were dropped and worked as planned, they would terminate the war.

Maj. Gen. Leslie Groves, directing the Manhattan Project, was committed to utilisation of the new weapons at the earliest possible date. He was wholly untroubled by the agonising of such scientists as Edward Teller, who wrote almost despairingly to a colleague: "I have no hope of clearing my conscience. The things we are working on are so terrible that no amount of protesting or fiddling with politics will save our souls." The only issue that was significantly discussed was whether a demonstration of the bomb, rather than its use against an urban target, might achieve the desired effect. Following a 14–16 July weekend of intense debate among a panel of scientists led by Robert Oppenheimer, they reported: "Those who advocate a purely technical demonstration would wish to outlaw the use of atomic weapons, and have feared that if we use the weapons now our position in future negotiations will be prejudiced. Others emphasize the opportunity of saving American lives by immediate military use, and believe that such use will improve the international prospects . . . We find ourselves closer to these latter views; we can propose no technical demonstration likely to bring an end to the war; we see no acceptable alternative to direct military use."

Even Teller convinced himself—by no means foolishly—that the best hope for the future of mankind lay in a live demonstration that would show the world the unspeakable horrors unleashed by the use of such weapons. The atomic enterprise had a momentum of its own, which only two developments might have checked. First, Truman could have shown extraordinary enlightenment and decreed that the bomb was too terrible to be employed; more plausibly, the Japanese might have offered their unconditional surrender. Yet through mid-summer 1945, intercepted secret cable traffic, as well as Tokyo's public pronouncements, showed obdurate Japanese rejection of such a course.

Objectively, it was plain to the Allies that Japan's defeat was inevitable, for both military and economic reasons, and thus that the use of atomic weapons was unnecessary. But the prospect of being obliged to continue addressing pockets of fanatical resistance all over Asia for months, if not years, was appalling. A belief persisted in Tokyo that stalwart defence of the home islands could yet preserve Japan from accepting absolute defeat. Gen. Yoshijiro Umezu, chief of the Japanese general staff, fantasised in characteristically flatulent terms in a May newspaper article: "The sure path to victory in a decisive battle lies in uniting the resources of the Empire behind the war effort; and in mobilising the full strength of the nation, both physical and spiritual, to annihilate the American invaders. The establishment of a metaphysical spirit is the first essential for fighting the decisive battle. An energetic commitment to aggressive action should always be emphasised." A staff officer, Maj. Yoshitaka Horie, delivered a current-affairs talk to army cadets which precipitated a reprimand from an officer of the Army Education Directorate, who said: "Your lectures are so depressing that officers who hear them will start losing the will to fight. You must end on a high note, assuring them that the Imperial Army is still in fighting mood."

Some of those who are today most critical of the use of the bombs ignore the fact that for every day the war continued, prisoners and slaves of the Japanese empire in Asia continued to die in the thousands. Perversely, the Allies might have done more to confound Japan's militarists by publicly announcing that they did *not* intend to invade the mainland, but instead to continue starving and bombing the Japanese people until they surrendered, than by preparing for Olympic. Truman's greatest mistake, in protecting his own reputation, was failure to deliver an explicit ultimatum before attacking Hiroshima and Nagasaki. The Western Allies' Potsdam Declaration, issued on 26 July, threatened Japan with "prompt and utter destruction" if it failed to surrender forthwith. This phrase was pregnant with significance for the Allied leaders, who knew that the first atomic bomb had just been successfully tested at Alamagordo. But to the Japanese, it merely heralded more of the same: firebombing and eventual invasion.

By the high summer of 1945, Japan's rulers wished to end the war; but its generals, together with some politicians, were still bent upon securing "honourable" terms, which included—for instance—retention of substantial parts of Japan's empire in Manchuria, Korea and China, together with Allied agreement to spare the country from occupation or war crimes indictments. "No one person in Japan had authority remotely resembling that of an American president," observes Professor Akira Namamura of Dokkyo University, a Japanese historian. "The Emperor was obliged to act in accordance with the Japanese constitution, which meant that he was obliged to heed the wishes of the army, navy and civilian politicians. He was able to take the decision to end the war only when those forces had invited him to do so." Even if this assertion was open to the widest variety of interpretations, as it remains today, it was plain that Hirohito could move towards surrender only when a consensus had evolved within Japan's leadership. This was narrowly achieved in mid-August 1945, but not a day before.

Many modern critics of the bombing of Hiroshima and Nagasaki demand, in effect, that the United States should have accepted a moral responsibility for sparing the Japanese people from the consequences of their own leaders' obduracy. No sane person would suggest that the use of the atomic bombs represented an absolute good, or was even a righteous act. But, in the course of the war, it had been necessary to do many terrible things to advance the cause of Allied victory, and to preside over enormous carnage. By August 1945, to Allied leaders the lives of their own people had come to seem very precious, those of their enemies very cheap. In those circumstances, it seems understandable that President Truman failed to halt the juggernaut which carried the atomic bombs to Tinian, and thence to Japan. Just as Hitler was the architect of Germany's devastation, the Tokyo regime bore overwhelming responsibility for what took place at Hiroshima and Nagasaki. If Japan's leaders had bowed to logic, as well as to the welfare of their own people, by quitting the war, the atomic bombs would not have been dropped.

When the nineteen-year-old Superfortress gunner Joseph Majeski saw the B-29 *Enola Gay* arrive on Tinian, specially modified to carry only tail armament and fitted with reversible-pitch propellers and other special equipment, he strolled over and asked one of its crew what they had come for. The man answered flippantly, "We're here to win the war," and of course the young airman did not believe him. A few days later, on

6 August 1945, the plane dropped "Little Boy" on Hiroshima. Its detonation generated the power of 12,500 tons of conventional explosive, created injuries of a kind never before experienced by humankind, and killed at least 70,000 people. Around the world, many people at first found the notion of what had taken place beyond the compass of their imaginations. Lt. Cmdr. Michael Blois-Brooke of the British assault ship *Sefton*, preparing to invade Malaya, said: "We heard about some wonder bomb that had been dropped on Japan and which was going to stop the war. We really took no notice, thinking that one single bomb wasn't going to alter the course of history."

Three days later "Fat Man" was dropped on Nagasaki, matching the explosive power of 22,000 tons of TNT, and killing at least 30,000 people. In the early hours of that day, the first of 1.5 million Soviet troops crossed the border into Manchuria, supported by 5,500 tanks and self-propelled guns. They swept across the region, overwhelming the hopelessly outgunned Japanese. In some places the defenders fought to the last, sustaining resistance for ten days after the war officially ended. But by 20 August the Russians had secured most of Manchuria and northern Korea. The brief campaign cost them 12,000 dead, more than the British Army lost in France in 1940, while something close to 80,000 Japanese soldiers perished.

Most of the young men bombing Japan had long since acquired a carapace of callousness about their business, matched by that which armoured their commanders. Gen. "Hap" Arnold, the USAAF's commander, wished to conclude the Superfortress offensive with a "grand finale" by a thousand fire-raising aircraft; Spaatz, now his Pacific C-in-C, preferred the idea of dropping a third atomic bomb on Tokyo. In the event, on 14 August 800 B-29s attacked the Isesaki urban area with incendiaries without losing a single plane, creating a last post-Nagasaki storm of destruction. One of the pilots, Col. Carl Storrie, said next morning of his own role: "We played alarm clock. All the rest of the aircraft carried fire bombs, but we had 4,000-pounders and went in to wake up the population of Kumugaya . . . We were at 16,000 [feet] and could feel the concussion. It was a dirty trick. We figured the Japs would think it was another atomic bomb."

Emperor Hirohito summoned a gathering of his country's military and political leaders and informed them of his determination to end the war, declared to his nation in a radio broadcast a few hours later. Not all his subjects even then accepted his conclusion. A fighter pilot, Cmdr. Haryushi Iki, said: "I never allowed myself to think about the possibility of losing the war. When the Russians invaded Manchuria, I felt terribly depressed—but even then I could not accept that we had lost." Some senior figures, including the war minister and a number of generals and admirals, committed ritual suicide, an example followed by several hundred humbler folk. "There was a clear division of opinion in the army about whether to end the war," said a General Staff intelligence officer, Maj. Shoji Takahishi. "Many of our people in China and South-East Asia favoured fighting on. Most of those in Japan accepted that we could not continue. I was sure that, once the Emperor had spoken, we must give up."

This view prevailed. At 7:00 p.m. on the evening of 14 August Washington time—already the fifteenth in Japan—Harry Truman read the announcement of Japan's unconditional surrender to a dense throng of politicians and journalists at the White House. The president then ordered the cessation of all offensive operations against the enemy. In Tokyo Bay on 1 September, Japanese and Allied representatives headed by Gen. Douglas MacArthur signed the surrender document on the deck of the battleship *Missouri*. The Second World War was officially ended.

VICTORS AND VANQUISHED

GOETHE WROTE in the early nineteenth century: "Our modern wars make many unhappy while they last and none happy when they are over." So it almost was in 1945. The war ended abruptly in Europe: sullenly or thankfully, millions of German troops surrendered, tossing away their weapons before joining vast columns of prisoners shuffling towards improvised cages, while only a small number in the east attempted to sustain resistance against the Russians. The vanquished emerged in some unlikely places and guises: a U-boat flying a white flag sailed up New Hampshire's Piscataqua River, where bewildered state police received its captain and crew. Irish prime minister Éamon de Valera, flaunting to the end his loathing of his British neighbours, paid a formal call to the German embassy in Dublin to express his condolences on the death of the Reich's head of state.

Many Germans believed themselves as much victims of Hitler as were the foreign nations he had conquered and enslaved. In Hamburg, old Mathilde Wolff-Monckeburg wrote brokenheartedly on 1 May: "We . . . mourn most deeply the fate of our poor Germany. It is as if the final bomb hit our very soul, killing the last vestige of joy and hope. Our beautiful and proud Germany has been crushed, ground into the earth and smashed into ruins, while millions sacrificed their lives and all our lovely towns and art treasures were destroyed. And all this because of one man who had a lunatic vision of being 'chosen by God.' "

Among Germans in the summer of 1945 and afterwards, self-pity was a much more prevalent sensation than contrition: one in three of their male children born between 1915 and 1924 was dead, two in five of those born between 1920 and 1925. In the vast refugee migrations that preceded and followed VE-Day, more than 14 million ethnic Germans left homes in the east, or were driven from them. At least half a million—modern estimates vary widely—perished during their subsequent odysseys; the historic problem of central Europe's German minorities was solved in the most abrupt fashion, by ethnic cleansing. Meanwhile more millions of people of a dozen nationalities, enslaved by Hitler, entered a new dark tunnel of uncertainty in displaced persons camps administered by the Allies, where some remained for years. The least fortunate were summarily consigned to Russia, their homeland, where many were categorised by the NKVD as proven or putative traitors and killed.

In Germany's cities, half the housing stock had been destroyed, including 3.8 million of 19 million apartments. Richard Johnston of the *New York Times* wrote from the ruins of Nuremberg: "Like timid ground creatures, a few Germans came up from their shelters, caves and cellars this morning to blink in strong sunlight and stare unbelieving at the awful mess that was their town . . . Nuremberg is a city of the dead." Berlin, Dresden, Hamburg were worse. The Thirty Years' War, three centuries earlier, had inflicted greater proportionate loss on Germany's population, but the physical devastation of 1945 was unparalleled in history: Europe's great cities had been spared by the First World War, and even from the rampages of Napoleon.

For two years after VE-Day, the NKVD waged a bloody counter-insurgency campaign in Poland and Ukraine to impose Stalin's will upon peoples consumed with bitterness at exchanging Nazi tyranny for that of the Soviets. Exiled Poles in the West were dismayed to be denied a place in London's victory parade, because the new British Labour government declined to upset the Russians. Gen. Władysław Anders wrote, "I felt as if I were peeping at a ballroom from behind the curtain of an entrance door through which I might not pass." Shortly before Labour took office in July, Anders encountered the U.S. ambassador and the British foreign secretary, Anthony Eden, at a banquet: "They greet me politely but without enthusiasm. Since our only crime is that we exist and thereby embarrass Allied policy, I do not consider myself obliged to hide or feel ashamed."

His bitterness was justified: he and almost 150,000 of his compatriots had fought gallantly with the Allied forces, suffering heavy casualties in Italy and northwest Europe. "We, the Poles in uniform integrated into the British armed forces, became an ugly sore on the English conscience," wrote Pilot Officer B. Lvov. In 1945 such people found themselves pariahs for the crime of rejecting a Stalinist puppet regime in their own country. The Poles ended the war as they began it, human sacrifices to the realities of power. Anders, Lvov and many of their comrades chose exile in the West rather than return home to Soviet subjection and probable execution. The Americans and British had delivered half of Europe from one totalitarian tyranny, but lacked the political will and the military means to save 90 million people of the easterly nations from falling victim to a new Soviet bondage that lasted almost half a century. The price of having joined with Stalin to destroy Hitler was high indeed.

In the victorious nations, simple people greeted the outcome of the struggle as a triumph of virtue over evil, heedless of the fashion in which liberation was blighted in many parts of the world. Painted high on the walls of several adjoining houses in the housewife Edie Rutherford's Sheffield street were the words GOD BLESS OUR LADS FOR THIS VICTORY. She and her friends spoke of Churchill: "Everyone agreed that we have been well blest in having such a leader. I felt once again great gratitude for being born British."

Millions of humble folk thought not of global issues, but of movingly personal causes for gratitude. On 7 September 1941, the nineteen-year-old gunner Bob Grafton, an east Londoner, had written to his adored girl-friend, Dot, before embarkation for the Far East: "Darling I *know* that you will wait for me. Darling do you know this. I swear that as long as we are apart I will never never touch another woman either physically or mentally. I do mean that Dot an awful lot . . . Yours Ever, with Love and Devotion so deep that the fires burn even in sleep, Bob." Before Singapore fell, Grafton escaped by junk to Sumatra, then lived wild in the jungle until he was captured by the Japanese in March 1942. Having survived a bondage which included two years on the Burma railway, in September 1945 he wrote to Dot from a homeward-bound troopship: "This I know: that it was you of the two of us who had the more difficult task. For I am a man (perhaps prematurely) and men must fight and women must weep. So my share was no exception, yours was . . . Even if we have lost four years we'll make life so that it is never regretted." Grafton's story had an unusually benign ending: he married his Dot, and they lived happily ever after.

David McCormick, a gunner, had been captured in North Africa in December 1941, and spent more than three years in Italian and German POW camps. Shortly after VE-Day his future wife met him at Salisbury station. "He was very thin, very pale and had the most enormous bump on his forehead. I wore a blue dress with white spots and bows on it, for which I had given several clothing coupons. I can't remember if we kissed. I don't think so, not until a little later on when we stopped on the back way to Ditchampton. We were both very nervous. He apologised for the bump, explaining that on his first night of freedom some Belgians had entertained a whole bunch of prisoners rather too enthusiastically, and afterwards he had met up with an anti-tank trap. He talked a great deal . . . He so desperately wanted to get four years 'in the bag' off his chest as quickly as possible."

Many others, however, returned home to discover that old ties were shattered, former passions extinct; they were obliged to content themselves with their own survival. For more millions, there was no return at all: the previous autumn Kay Kirby had become a presumed widow at twenty-one when her husband, a navigator in Bomber Command, was reported missing over Germany. In the absence of an identified corpse, she nonetheless clung to hope. "For years I expected George to turn up. I couldn't reconcile myself to the fact that he wasn't coming back . . . Before George started his tour when he came back on leave unexpectedly, he used to knock on my window with a clothes prop. After George went missing, many times I went to the door because I thought I heard him knocking at my window. Of course there was no one there."

Intellectuals reflected on the vast experience the world had undergone. Arthur Schlesinger wrote grudgingly: "It was, I suppose, a Good War. But like all wars, our war was accompanied by atrocity and sadism, by stupidities and lies, pomposity and chickenshit. War remains hell, but a few wars have been driven by decent purposes and produced beneficial results." Schlesinger's fellow historian Forrest Pogue, who had crossed northwest Europe with the U.S. Army, wrote: "The war, while giving me a chance to see more of the world and of all kinds of people, nevertheless confused me . . . I lived more thoroughly an ordinary life than ever before . . . I found how much man lives next to the animal . . . it made me tougher-minded and more tolerant and sympathetic of human frailty . . . [but also] sufficiently confused so that I have not yet been able to discover any answers."

In Asia, though handfuls of Japanese soldiers remained in hiding and even sustained guerrilla activity in the Philippines and on remote Pacific islands for months or years, MacArthur and his occupying army were received in Japan with almost slavish obeisance. Many of Hirohito's warriors who had professed themselves willing to die for their emperor admitted relief that the sacrifice was not required. Capt. Yoshiro Minamoto and thirty crewmen of a *kaiten* suicide-boat unit emerged from hiding on the island of Tokahishi, off Okinawa, on 23 August, in response to American loudspeaker appeals. "I wanted everything done properly," said Minamoto, "so I had everyone wash their fatigues and clean their weapons. I paraded the men, we bowed towards Tokyo and saluted, then I led a group with a white flag towards the American lines. They treated us very well. I felt happy to have survived."

On 15 August, all units at the island base off Japan where Toshiharu Konada commanded another suicide-boat detachment were warned to listen to the radio. Reception was so poor, however, that they could not hear Hirohito's surrender announcement and assumed that they had missed a mere patriotic harangue. Konada learned the news only after he drove to the island's mountain headquarters. His commanding officer ordered all units to remain on maximum alert. Nobody could guess what might happen next: it seemed possible the broadcast was an American trick. Stunned and bewildered, Konada chose to walk back down the mountain road to the sea, collecting his thoughts. He assumed that he and his comrades would now be told to kill themselves: if the nation had embraced defeat, no other course seemed plausible.

In the event, these young men who had volunteered to die remained in readiness to launch themselves against the Americans for a further month, while slowly accustoming themselves to the notion that they might live. Konada started classes for his men in science and English, to alleviate their boredom and teach them things useful to their future. Only at the end of November 1945 did he reach his parents' home on the mainland. His father, also a naval officer, had returned from the war convinced that his eldest son was dead: by a bureaucratic confusion, Konada had been officially listed among *kaiten* pilots lost attacking American shipping. "In those days, Japanese fathers did not show emotion," said the reprieved suicidalist. "He simply said, 'We thought we would never see you again'; but I realised that he was happy." Other such families were less fortunate: of the vast number of Japanese troops who fell into Soviet hands following the last brief campaign in Manchuria, 300,000 perished in captivity.

For months after the war ended, men continued to die through mistakes or malevolence. On 29 August, Soviet fighters shot down a USAAF B-29 dropping supplies to a POW camp in Korea, and several such fatal encounters took place in German airspace. Closure on the battlefield did nothing to alleviate starvation in many places: in the Soviet Union alone, around a million people perished between 1945 and 1947. All over the world there were accidents involving reckless abuse of vehicles or weapons, caused by young warriors casting off the shackles of discipline, killing themselves after the enemy had failed to do so.

For the most part, the conquerors and the conquered shared an overpowering relief that history's greatest bloodletting was ended. Aboard the U.S. carrier *Princeton* in the Pacific, the chief ship's clerk Cecil King exulted to have "seen it come out this way . . . just like Hollywood when the Marines come up over the horizon in the last reel." The historian of a USAAF bomb group on Saipan wrote vividly, if ungrammatically: "The ending of the war was the greatest morale factor that has befell this group since its activation." But while there were displays of rejoicing in the Allied capitals, and in the homes of families promised the return of loved ones, many people found it impossible to shake off the melancholy induced by years of suffering, fear and bereavement. After the liberation of Bucharest, Mihail Sebastian wrote: "I am ashamed to be sad. After all, this is the year that gave me back my freedom."

But what was "freedom"? A year before the Japanese surrender, the Australian minister to China warned the Advisory War Council in Canberra about widespread hostility to the restoration of white colonial rule in Asia—"It would be an error to suppose that we would be welcomed by the native populations when we return"—and he was proved right. The Malayan nationalist Mustapha Hussein said: "I cried when I heard that the Japanese had surrendered . . . simply because there were only forty-eight hours separating us from the declaration of independence for Malaya. This was indeed a tragic case of 'So near yet so far.' I regretted the matter deeply as Malaya would once again be colonised and gripped by Western Power. Even tears of blood could not rectify the situation."

Serious conflicts erupted in several countries where nationalists resisted the restoration of European hegemony, notably French Indochina and the Dutch East Indies. Lord Louis Mountbatten, the Allied supreme commander in Southeast Asia, urged returning colonial officials to concede sufficient local autonomy to avert conflict. Both the Dutch and the French declined to do this, however; instead, they plunged into long, doomed counterinsurgency campaigns. In the Banya Bini 10 internment camp on Java, the Japanese did not inform the emaciated and diseased Dutch inmates of the war's ending until 24 August. When prisoners ventured out, they found themselves threatened and sometimes fired upon by Indonesian nationalists bent upon resisting the restoration of colonial rule. Only in September did Gurkha soldiers arrive, and another two months elapsed before the Dutch were able to leave their hated place of confinement for a voyage to Holland. A thousand Japanese soldiers on Java deserted to join local communities; many of them afterwards aided nationalist guerrillas. In China, American aircraft flew Nationalist troops and some U.S. Marines into Beijing, Shanghai and Nanjing in a successful bid to forestall a communist takeover, but civil war soon engulfed the country, from which Mao Tse-tung eventually emerged victorious.

British officials returning to Burma were appalled to find destitution: public services and transport had collapsed, many people were starving and traumatised by their experiences. In Rangoon, a civil servant, T. L. Hughes, found "old friends so changed as to be unrecognisable; many were emaciated and shrunken; many were white-haired prematurely and many continued to cast an anxious eye over their shoulder on the lookout for the Japanese Gestapo." British onlookers at the Burmese capital's victory parade watched uneasily as Aung San's nationalist troops goosestepped down the central avenue in Japanese-style uniforms. It was plain to all but the most stubborn imperialists that the clock could not be set back to 1941, that the British must soon leave for good, just as they would also have to quit India. In the Philippines, too, radicalism had taken hold. A communist Huk guerrilla said of the period following the Japanese surrender: "I knew we'd have to have our peasant groups because landlords would be coming back. Life was still difficult and . . . there had been so much destruction. But I think people were hopeful. I know I was. And we little people had become stronger; we were more organised."

Each of the three principal victorious nations emerged from the Second World War confident in the belief that its own role had been decisive in procuring victory. Not for many years did a more nuanced perspective emerge, in Western societies at least. Hitler was correct in anticipating that his enemies' "unnatural coalition" must collapse and give way to mutual antagonism between the Soviet Union and the West, although this occurred too late to save the Third Reich. The Grand Alliance, the phrase with which Churchill ennobled the wartime relationship of Britain, the United States and the Soviet Union, was always a grand charade; it was a necessary fiction to pretend that the three powers fought the war as a shared enterprise directed towards common purposes.

Some modern historians have sought to argue that the entire conflict might have been avoided if in the early years of Nazism Britain and France had forged a united front with Russia against Hitler. This view seems untenable, as well as supremely cynical: how could the Western democracies have agreed on common political objectives with a Soviet regime as brutal and imperialistic as that of the Nazis? Stalin's tariff for any deal with the French and British would have been identical with that he presented in exchange for the 1939 Nazi-Soviet Pact: a free hand for his own expansionist ambitions. This was unacceptable to the Western democracies until the tumult of war enforced unforeseen obligations and realities. Powerful elements of British, French and American conservative opinion deplored communism even more than fascism, and would have resisted appeasement of Stalin with more vigour than they displayed towards appeasement of Hitler.

France, Britain and its dominions were the only major Allied nations to enter World War II as an act of principle, rather than because they sought territorial gains or were themselves attacked. Their claims upon the moral high ground were injured, however, by the fact that they declared support for embattled Poland without any intention of giving this meaningful military effect. There was little French popular appetite for a battlefield showdown with Germany in September 1939, and less in June 1940, while the British Expeditionary Force could play only a marginal role. Following France's defeat, informed British and American soldiers and politicians asserted, with truth, that many Frenchmen disliked

Churchill's nation more than Germany. Even allowing for the significant role of French troops in the final campaigns in northwest Europe, the statistical fact remains that Vichy's armies and domestic security forces made a more numerous contribution to Axis interests than those Frenchmen who later joined the Gaullists, other Resistance groups or Eisenhower's armies provided to the Allied cause.

Most French people persuaded themselves in 1940 that the Pétain regime constituted a lawful government; however uncomfortably, they indulged its rule until the eve of liberation. Once defeat in 1940 had denied the French a heroic role in the struggle against Nazism, many remained confused for the remainder of the war about the least ignoble part their nation might play. After the liberation in 1944, France indulged in an orgy of domestic recrimination, reflecting rancour about the 1940 defeat, together with a settling of national and local accounts between former collaborationists and resisters which prompted several thousand killings during *l'épuration*—the purification, as it was ironically known. Forrest Pogue wrote after a visit to Paris, "I soon found that the old bitterness against Jews and labor remained." Communist factions emerged from the war strengthened in France, as also in Italy and Greece, and for some years there were fears for the survival of democracy in all three countries. Bourgeois capitalism eventually prevailed, but political stability proved slow to achieve. To this day, France has not produced an official history of its war experience, and probably will never do so, because consensual support for any version of events would be unattainable. It is striking that the most persuasive modern studies of the French wartime era have been written by American and British authors: relatively few indigenous scholars wish to address it.

It is hard to imagine that Britain would have continued to defy Hitler after June 1940 in the absence of Winston Churchill, who constructed a brilliant and narrowly plausible narrative for the British people, first about what they might do, and later to persuade them of what they had done. The Nazi leaders, land creatures, lacked understanding of the difficulty of achieving hemispheric hegemony against a formidable sea power while themselves lacking an effective navy. Churchill owed a large debt to Hitler for a succession of unforced errors. First, by launching the Luftwaffe against the RAF's Fighter Command, Germany's leader offered Britain its only conceivable opportunity to salvage a victory from the ashes of strategic defeat in the summer of 1940. He then failed to reach agreements with Mussolini and Franco that should have enabled him to evict British forces from the Mediterranean and Middle East in 1941. After fumbling the confrontation with Britain, Hitler's invasion of Russia transformed the struggle, and ensured that Stalin's nation would bear the principal burden of combatting Nazism. Seventy-nine million Germans challenged 193 million Soviet citizens from an economic base much weaker than the Allies recognised.

Churchill displayed the highest wisdom by embracing the Soviet Union as a cobelligerent in 1941, but both he—briefly—and later Roosevelt— persistently—were foolish to suppose that a real partnership was possible. Stalin, with his usual icy clarity of vision, recognised that the common commitment of Britain, Russia and the United States to defeat Hitler did nothing to bridge the yawning divide between their other respective national objectives. He intended to sustain a tyranny which denied any vestige of freedom to his own people, and to secure territorial gains for the Soviet Union which the Western Allies would never willingly approve. Russia's vast blood sacrifice spared the lives of hundreds of thousands of British and American soldiers, but in consequence the Red Army secured physical possession of an eastern European empire. The Americans and British had no choice save to acquiesce in this, since they lacked both military means and domestic support for a new war to expel the Soviet Union from its conquests. The Russians reaped the rewards for doing most of the fighting necessary to defeat Nazism. Western material aid contributed importantly to the Soviets' 1943–45 war effort, but seems trifling alongside the destruction and slaughter they experienced.

Stalin committed many blunders in the first year after Barbarossa was launched, but thereafter learnt quickly, as Hitler did not. The Soviet Union revealed an industrial and military capability that would have enabled it to complete the destruction of Hitler's war machine even had the Western Allies never landed in Italy or France, though their interventions hastened the end. There is a powerful argument that only a warlord as bereft of scruples or compassion as Stalin, presiding over a society in which ruthlessness was even more institutionalised than in Germany, could have destroyed Nazism. Stalin proved a supremely effective tyrant, as Hitler was not. The Western Allies' manner of fighting, hampered by bourgeois sensitivity about casualties, was a chronic impediment to overcoming the Wehrmacht. In 1944, when the Italian officer Eugenio Corti first met British troops socially, he enjoyed their company, but observed in some puzzlement that "they are more like civilians than soldiers, which may account for the sluggishness of their advance." So indeed it did.

Because German and Japanese soldiers displayed high courage and tactical skill, the principal Axis powers were overrated by their enemies. From June 1940 onwards, both Berlin and Tokyo made strategy with awesome incompetence. Japan's early victories in 1941–42 reflected local

Allied weakness, not real Japanese strength; it is extraordinary that Hirohito's government entered the war without taking any convincing steps to protect its maritime lifelines from a U.S. submarine offensive. It became clear within months that Japan's gamble had failed, because its success was dependent on a German victory in Europe which was no longer attainable.

Once the British and American war efforts gained traction, the Western Allies conducted their affairs much better than the Germans and Japanese at every level save local ground combat. Whether or not the leaders of Germany and Japan were stupid men, they did many stupid things, often because their understanding of their opponents was so poor. Most of the men close to Hitler—Himmler and Göring notable among them—would have seemed to posterity ridiculous figures, save that they had licence to shed so much blood. Where Stalin's Russia was indeed a totalitarian state, a monolith, the Nazi leadership was riven by personal rivalries, its war effort weakened by competition among rival fiefdoms as well as by Hitler's insistent blunders.

The democracies mobilised the finest brains and empowered clever men to exploit their nations' scientific genius and industrial capacity. America and Britain fulfilled their strategic aims at relatively low human cost, by imaginative mobilisation of resources to generate firepower and exploit superior technologies, especially at sea and in the air. For this their governments, and above all Roosevelt and Churchill, richly earned the gratitude they received from their peoples.

Britain's defiance in 1940–41 was critical in averting Nazi triumph; but thereafter Churchill's people made only a subordinate contribution to victory. They paid a price in blood and treasure which seemed to them heavy enough, but was modest in comparison with the horrors that befell the continental nations. Even Britain's leaders were slow to realise that, while the war accelerated Britain's loss of global power, this was anyway inescapable. The British people developed a sense of grievance about their postwar privations, which included the maintenance of some food rationing until 1952. Having had an exaggerated sense of Britain's strength and wealth in 1939, its descent to diminished importance and relative impoverishment was correspondingly more painful after achieving a place among the victors of 1945.

The war became a proud national folk memory, because the British came to regard it as the last hurrah of their greatness, a historic achievement to set against many postwar failures and disappointments. Their lone stand against Nazism in 1940–41 was indeed their finest hour, for which they were empowered by Winston Churchill, the towering personality of the forces of light. Throughout the war, Britain was governed with impressive efficiency; its leaders harnessed civilian brains and scientific genius to dazzling effect, symbolised by the epic of Bletchley Park's codebreakers, the nation's greatest single achievement of the war. The Royal Navy and the RAF did many things bravely and well, though always straining to match their strengths to their commitments. The British Army's overall performance, however, seldom surpassed adequacy, and often fell short of it. As an institution, and as Alan Brooke readily acknowledged, it was deficient in competent commanders, imagination, appropriate transport and armour, and energy and professional skill, its artillery alone displaying excellence. Its shortcomings would have been even more cruelly exposed had it been obliged to bear a larger share of the burden of beating the Wehrmacht.

America's industrial might contributed more to victory than did its armies. It was apparent to German economic managers as early as December 1941 that victory was beyond Hitler's reach because of events in Russia and the accession of the United States to the Allied cause. This was long before the RAF's and USAAF's strategic air offensives attained maturity: Allied bombing of Germany hastened the end, but did not decide the outcome. Nonetheless, it is important to stress the importance of close air support, and absolute command of the skies, to the western war in 1943–45. The Western Allies created superb tactical air forces, and used them with all the skill and flair their ground operations lacked. Every man who glimpsed the armies, their convoys crowding the roads of Italy and later northwest Europe nose-to-tail without intervention from the Luftwaffe, recognised the critical contribution of air power in conferring freedom of movement, while denying it to the Wehrmacht.

The United States Navy and Marine Corps were chiefly responsible for the defeat of Japan. In pursuing that end, many battles were fought, notably in Burma and the Philippines, which were strategically redundant. But the momentum of war imposed its own imperatives, and such a judgement is much easier for historians than it was for contemporary national leaderships—as might also be said about the arguments against dropping the atomic bombs.

The United States was the only belligerent which emerged from the war without a sense of victimhood. Most of its people took pride both in their contribution to Allied victory and in their new status as the richest and most powerful nation on earth. It was characteristic of American romanticism that a war which the United States joined only because it was attacked by Japan evolved during the ensuing forty-five months into a "crusade for freedom." Thanks to Pearl Harbor, fewer of Roosevelt's people questioned the justice of their cause than in any other war their country has fought. "It was the last time most Americans thought they were innocent and good, without qualification," said Pfc. Robert Lekachman.

Americans sustained a highly effective operational relationship with the British, a notable achievement given the difficulty of sustaining alliances, together with mutual suspicions and differences of national outlook. The partnership worked best at the bottom, where British and American personnel collaborated amicably, and worsened progressively towards the summit of commands. Americans nursed a repugnance towards imperialism which intensified when some witnessed it at first hand in Egypt, India and Southeast Asia. They cherished a hubristic belief in their own virtue, and consciousness of their own dominance. In 1945, Congress's brutally abrupt closure of Lend-Lease reflected an absence of sentimentality about Churchill's nation; opinion polls showed Americans more willing to forgive Russia's Lend-Lease debt than Britain's. Relations between the two nations might have deteriorated thereafter, but for new imperatives created by the acknowledged menace of the Soviet Union. The rapidly evolving confrontation between East and West caused the United States to accept the necessity of sustaining its alliance with Britain and other European nations, somewhat to subdue its anti-imperialist scruples, and to offer the stricken Continent a portion of its vast war profits to aid economic resurrection.

Whatever Stalin's limitations as a military commander and his monstrous record as a tyrant, he presided over the creation of an extraordinary military machine, and pursued his objectives to triumphant fulfilment. In 1945, the Soviet Union seemed the only nation which had achieved its full war aims, creating a new eastern European empire to buffer its frontiers with the West, and securing important footholds on the Pacific coast. Former U.S. secretary of state Sumner Welles reported an alleged 1943 exchange between Stalin and Anthony Eden, Britain's foreign secretary. The Russian leader said: "Hitler is a genius, but doesn't know when to stop." Eden: "Does anybody know when to stop?" Stalin: "I do." Even if this conversation was apocryphal, the words reflected the reality that Stalin shrewdly judged the limits of his outrages against freedom in 1944–45, to avert an outright breach with the Western Allies, most importantly the United States. He kept just sufficient of his promises to Roosevelt and Churchill—for instance, by staying out of Greece and evacuating China—to secure his conquests in eastern Europe without precipitating a new conflict. But the Soviet Union was deluded by its military and diplomatic triumphs into a false perception of their significance. For more than forty years after 1945, it sustained an armed threat to the West at ruinous cost; the economic, social and political bankrutpcy of the system Stalin had created was eventually laid bare.

The Russians emerged from the war conscious of their new power in the world, but also embittered by the colossal destruction and loss of life they had suffered. They believed, not mistakenly, that the Western Allies had purchased cheaply their share of victory, and this perception reinforced their visceral sense of grievance towards Europe and the United States. They forgot their role as Hitler's allies between 1939 and 1941. Modern Russia maintains a stubborn, defiant denial about the Red Army's 1944–45 orgy of rape, pillage and murder: it is deemed insulting that foreigners make much of the issue, for it compromises both the nation's cherished claims to victimhood and the glory of its military triumph. In 2011, long after the Western Allies withdrew from almost all the territories they occupied in the wake of victory, Russia clings insistently to the national frontiers it claimed as war booty, embracing eastern Poland, eastern Finland and parts of East Prussia and Romania, together with Stalin's Pacific coast conquests. It seems implausible that a nation ruled by Vladimir Putin will relinquish them.

THE MILITARY COURSE of the war was more strongly influenced by mass and the comparative institutional effectiveness of rival armies than by the performance of individual commanders, important though this was; any roll call of warlords should thus include the great military managers of the United States and Britain, Marshall and Brooke, even though neither directed a campaign. Marshall showed greatness as a statesman as well as a warlord. Brooke handled Churchill superbly well, and made a notable contribution to Allied strategy between 1941 and 1943. Thereafter, however, he somewhat diminished his stature by condescension towards the Americans and stubborn enthusiasm for Mediterranean operations.

Western Allied generalship seldom displayed brilliance, though the U.S. Army produced some outstanding corps and divisional commanders. Michael Howard has written:

> There are two great difficulties with which the professional soldier, sailor or airman has to contend in equipping himself as a commander. First, his profession is almost unique in that he may have to exercise it only once in a lifetime, if indeed that often. It is as if a surgeon had to practise throughout his life on dummies for one real operation; or a barrister appeared only once or twice in court toward the end of his

career; or a professional swimmer had to spend his life practising on dry land for an Olympic championship on which the fortunes of his entire nation depended. Second, the complex problem of running an army is liable to occupy his mind and skill so completely that it is very easy to forget what it is being run *for*. The difficulties encountered in the administration, discipline, maintenance and supply of an organization the size of a fair-sized town are enough to occupy the senior officer to the exclusion of his real business: the conduct of war.

The Germans and Russians proved more successful than the Western Allies in fulfilling the requirement identified by Howard: to empower commanders who fought rather than managed. For American, British, Canadian, Polish and French troops at the sharp end, the 1944–45 northwest Europe campaign seldom seemed less than horrific. But the casualty figures, on both sides a fraction of those in the east, emphasise its relative moderation once the fighting in Normandy was over. With the exception of a few such enthusiasts as Patton, Allied commanders understood that they were mandated to win the war at the lowest possible human cost, and thus that caution was a virtue, even in victory. By pursuing such a policy, they fulfilled the will both of their societies and their citizen soldiers.

The rival claims to greatness of individual commanders are impervious to objective ranking. Circumstances decisively influenced outcomes: no general could perform better than the institutional strength or weakness of his forces allowed. Thus, it is possible that Patton—for instance—might have shown himself a great general, had he led forces with the Wehrmacht's skills or the Red Army's tolerance of casualties. As it was, especially in pursuit he displayed an inspiration and energy rare among Allied generals; but in hard fighting, his army fared no better than those of his peers. Eisenhower will never be celebrated as a strategist or tactician, but achieved greatness by his diplomatic management of the Anglo-American alliance in the field. Lucien Truscott, who finished the war commanding the U.S. Fifth Army in Italy, was arguably the ablest American officer of his rank, though much less celebrated than some of his peers. MacArthur was distinguished by the splendour of his self-image as a warlord, which it suited his nation to indulge, rather than by gifts as a battlefield commander. While he directed the 1944 phase of the New Guinea campaign with some flair, he floundered in the Philippines; superior resources, especially air support, were the deciding factors in his victories. MacArthur was a narrowly affordable luxury rather than an asset to his country's strategic purposes. The outstanding personality of the Japanese war was Nimitz, who directed the U.S. Navy's Pacific campaign with cool confidence and judgement, often displaying brilliance, especially in the exploitation of intelligence. Spruance showed himself the ablest fleet commander at sea.

On the British side Cunningham, Somerville and Max Horton were outstanding naval officers, Sir Arthur Tedder the best of the airmen. Slim, who led the Fourteenth Army in Burma, was probably the most gifted British general of the war, and certainly the most attractive command personality; his 1945 crossing of the Irrawaddy and outflanking of the Japanese at Meiktila were notable achievements. But Slim would have struggled to extract any better results from Britain's desert army in 1941–42 than did Wavell or Auchinleck, because of its collective shortcomings. Montgomery was a highly competent professional; it is unlikely that any other Allied commander could have surpassed his direction of the 1944 Normandy campaign, where attrition was inescapable, but he diminished his reputation by epic boorishness in conducting the vital relationship with the Americans. "Monty" deserves a significant part of the credit for the success of the invasion of France, but never achieved a masterstroke which would place him among history's great captains.

The Soviet Union's best generals displayed a confidence in handling large forces unmatched elsewhere on the Allied side. In the first half of the war, they suffered interference by Stalin almost as damaging to Russia's prospects of survival as was that of Hitler to Germany's cause. But from late 1942 onwards, Stalin became much more receptive to his marshals' judgements, and the Soviet war effort correspondingly more successful. Chuikov deserves full credit for the defence of Stalingrad; Zhukov, Konev, Vasilievsky and Rokossovsky were commanders of the highest gifts, though their achievements would have been impossible without their nation's tolerance of sacrifice. Soviet victories were purchased at a human cost no democracy would have accepted, and that no Western general would have been allowed to indulge. The raw aggression of Soviet commanders in 1943–45 contrasts with the caution of most American and British leaders, a reflection of their respective societies. The Red Army never showed itself superior man for man to its German opponents: until the end, the Wehrmacht inflicted disproportionate losses. Russian commanders produced their finest performances in the summer 1944 Operation Bagration, when 166 divisions attacked on a front of 620 miles. The storming of Berlin, by contrast, was conducted with a brutish clumsiness which diminished the reputation of Zhukov.

Among the Germans, von Rundstedt displayed the highest professionalism from 1939 to the end. In the desert, Rommel displayed similar gifts to those of Patton, but like the American paid insufficient attention to the critical influence of logistics. The Allies esteemed Rommel more highly than did many German officers, partly because British and American self-respect was massaged by attributing their setbacks to his supposed genius. Manstein, a superb professional, was the architect of great victories in Russia in 1941–42, and probably Germany's best general of the war, but failure at Kursk emphasised his limitations: hubristically, he accepted responsibility for launching a vast offensive which could not hope to succeed against superior Russian strength, dispositions and generalship. Kesselring's 1943–45 defence of Italy places him in the front rank of commanders. Guderian was the personification of the Wehrmacht's skill in exploiting armour. Several of Germany's generals, Model among them, merit more admiration for the manner in which they sustained defensive campaigns in the years of retreat, with inferior forces and negligible air support, than for victories in the period when the Wehrmacht was stronger than its foes. Hitler's strategic interventions prevented any German commander from claiming absolute credit for victories or accepting absolute responsibility for defeats. The institutional achievement of the German army and its staff seems greater than that of any individual general. The overriding historical reality is that they lost the war.

Yamashita, who directed the 1942 seizure of Malaya and the 1944–45 defence of the Philippines, was Japan's ablest ground-force commander. Otherwise, the energy and courage of Japanese soldiers and junior officers were more impressive than the strategic grasp of their leaders. These were hamstrung throughout by huge failures of intelligence, which transcended mere technical inadequacy and reflected a deeper cultural incapacity to consider what might be happening on the other side of the hill. The defence of successive Pacific islands reflected professional competence among some garrison commanders who lacked scope and resources to exploit any higher gifts. Afloat, though luck played an important part in the Battle of the Coral Sea and at Midway, Japan's admirals displayed astonishing timidity, and were repeatedly outguessed and outfought by their American opponents. Yamamoto merits some respect for his direction of Japan's initial 1941–42 offensives, but must bear a heavy responsibility for much that went wrong afterwards. Only his death in April 1943 spared him from presiding over the national march to oblivion he had always recognised as inevitable.

THE IMPACT of a conflict cannot be measured merely by comparing respective national tallies of human loss, but these deserve consideration, to achieve a sense of global perspective. There is no commonly agreed total of war-related deaths around the world, but a minimum figure of 60 million is accepted, and perhaps as many as 10 million more. Japan's losses were estimated at 2.69 million dead, 1.74 million of these military; two-thirds of the latter were victims of starvation or disease rather than enemy action. Germany lost 6.9 million dead, 5.3 million of these military. The Russians killed about 4.7 million German combatants, including 474,967 who died in Soviet captivity, and a substantial further number of civilians, while the Western Allies accounted for around half a million German troops and more than 200,000 civilian victims of air attack. Russia lost 27 million people, China at least 15 million. Some 5 million are reckoned to have died under Japanese occupation in Southeast Asia, including the Dutch East Indies, present-day Indonesia. Up to a million perished in the Philippines, many during the 1944–45 campaign for the islands' liberation.

Italy lost over 300,000 military dead, and around a quarter of a million civilians. More than 5 million Poles died, 110,000 in combat, most of the remainder in German concentration camps, though the Russians could also claim a substantial tally of Polish victims. France lost 567,000 people, including 267,000 civilians. Thirty thousand British troops perished in conflict with the Japanese, many of them as prisoners, out of an overall death toll of 382,700. Britain's total war loss, including civilians, was 449,000. Indian forces fighting under British command lost 87,000 dead. Total United States war losses were 418,500, slightly fewer than those of the United Kingdom, of which the U.S. Army lost 143,000 in Europe and the Mediterranean and 55,145 in the Pacific. The U.S. Navy lost a further 29,263 men in the East, the Marine Corps 19,163. It is inconsistent to account the estimated 20 million people who died of starvation and disease under Axis occupation as victims of Germany and Japan, without making the same computation on the Allied side: between 1 and 3 million Indians under British rule perished in wartime famines.

Many other nations suffered large numbers of fatalities, though all statistics should be considered suggestive rather than exact, because they remain disputed: 769,000 Romanians, many of them Jews; up to 400,000 Koreans; 97,000 Finns out of a population of less than 4 million; 415,000 Greeks from a population of 7 million; at least 1.2 million Yugoslavs from a population of 15.4 million; more than 343,000 Czechs, 277,000 of them Jews; 45,300 Canadians; 41,200 Australians; 11,900 New Zealanders from a population of 1.6 million—the highest proportionate toll of any Western ally. The most noteworthy aspect of these statistics is that the heaviest burden fell upon nations which suffered enemy occupation, or whose territories became battlefields. One in four of the world's 20 million military dead perished in German or Japanese captivity, most of them Russians or Poles.

Combatants fared better than civilians: around three-quarters of all those who perished were unarmed victims rather than active participants in the struggle. The peoples of western Europe escaped more lightly than those of eastern Europe. The best recent research suggests that 5.7 million Jews of all nationalities—out of a prewar Jewish population of 7.3 million in lands occupied by Hitler—were killed by the Nazis in their attempt to achieve a "Final Solution." Hitler's agents also murdered or allowed to die some 3 million Soviet POWs, 1.8 million non-Jewish Poles, 5 million non-Jewish Soviet citizens, 150,000 mentally handicapped people, and 10,000 homosexual men.

MOST GERMANS considered that their shattered cities, wrecked industries and millions of dead paid their dues for the crimes of Nazism. The young felt mingled bewilderment and rage that their elders whom they trusted had brought them to such a pass. "I wasn't quite sure what I ought to feel," said Helmut Lott, a teenager in 1945. "A certain world—a world I'd grown up in and believed in—was destroyed." Many Germans colluded in allowing former Nazis to meld unpunished into their postwar society. "No one believes a decent German nowadays," said the former SS officer's wife Hildegard Trutz bitterly in 1947, "but anything those dirty Jews say goes for gospel." South America became a popular destination for irreconcilables and the most heinous war criminals, some of whom were given sanctuary by the Catholic Church during their passage from Europe.

Only a tiny fraction of those guilty of war crimes were ever indicted, partly because the victors had no stomach for the scale of executions, numbering several hundred thousands, that would have been necessary had strict justice been enforced against every Axis murderer. Less than 1,000 retributive executions took place in the Western zones of occupation. Some 920 Japanese were executed, more than 300 of them by the Dutch for crimes committed in the East Indies. The Allies chose to treat Austria as a victim society rather than a partner in German war guilt, so that no serious denazification process took place there. The former Wehrmacht officer Kurt Waldheim was one of many Austrians who had been complicit in war crimes—in his case, the murder of British prisoners in the Balkans. In full knowledge of this, his countrymen eventually elected him as their chancellor.

Many German convicted mass killers served jail sentences of only a few years, or even escaped by paying a fine of fifty almost worthless Reichsmarks. The Germans and Japanese were not entirely mistaken in regarding the international war crimes trials which took place in 1945–46 as "victors' justice." Some British and Americans, and many Russians, were guilty of offences under international law, the killing of prisoners notable among them, yet very few faced even courts-martial. To have been on the winning side sufficed to secure amnesty; Allied war crimes were seldom even acknowledged. The British submarine commander "Gamp" Miers, for instance, who in 1941 distressed even some of his own crew by insisting that German soldiers struggling in the Mediterranean after the sinking of their caïques should be machine-gunned, was awarded a Victoria Cross and eventually became an admiral. American, Canadian and British troops who routinely shot snipers and Waffen SS prisoners on the battlefield, usually in supposed retaliation for similar enemy actions, went unindicted. The Nuremberg and Tokyo trials and sentences represented not injustice, but partial justice.

In both Europe and Asia from 1945 onwards, the confrontation with the Soviet Union created new strategic imperatives which were perceived to demand the enlistment of thousands of German and Japanese war criminals in U.S., British and Russian intelligence organisations and scientific research establishments. With notable cynicism, the Americans amnestied the Japanese biological warfare Unit 731's commander, Lt. Gen. Shiro Ishii, in return for his secrets. After investigation, U.S. scientists at Camp Detrick declared Ishii's data worthless. But as a result of a personal decision by the supreme commander in Japan, Gen. Douglas MacArthur, most of the 20,000 scientists and physicians engaged in Japan's wartime biological warfare programme were able to resume comfortable civilian careers, despite having been responsible for unspeakable murders in China. The only retribution for their atrocities was extracted by the Russians, who convicted twelve leading members of Unit 731 at a trial at Khabarovsk in 1949. The guilty received long terms of imprisonment; General MacArthur's headquarters in Tokyo denounced as propaganda both the trials and well-founded Soviet allegations of an American cover-up of Japan's biological warfare crimes.

Who was to blame for the catastrophe that had befallen Japan? Kisao Ebisawa, a petty officer, shrugged and said: "The brass—the people in charge." But then he added: "Really, though, one must include the whole nation, because its mood had been dragging us towards war for so long. There was a horrible inevitability about the way we just plunged deeper and deeper into the mire." After 1945 the Japanese people renounced their militarists, and indeed the soldiers who had fought in the war, with a fervour that distressed the nation's veterans, many of whom remained impenitent. Col. Hattori Takushiro, the former military secretary to Japan's war minister, wrote proudly in 1956: "The Japanese army had no peer in its terrific fighting capacity, which is a separate issue from the fact that Japan lost the war." The Japanese people embraced the postwar United States with an enthusiasm that won the hearts of most Americans who served in the occupation army. Japan's campaigns of conquest, and its treatment of its subject peoples, notably including the Chinese, became forbidden subjects of political or social exchange, and indeed of school learning. Hiroshima and Nagasaki dominated postwar Japanese perceptions; Emperor Hirohito kept his throne despite having led his country to war, which made it less plausible that his subjects should acknowledge collective guilt.

The Japanese writer Kazutoshi Hando, who survived the Tokyo firestorm, said in 2007: "In the aftermath of the war, blame was placed solely on the Japanese army and navy. This seemed just, because the civilian population had always been deceived by the armed forces about what was done. Civilian Japan felt no sense of collective guilt—and that was the way the American victors and occupiers wanted it. In the same fashion, it was the Americans who urged that no modern Japanese history should be taught in schools. The consequence is that very few people under fifty have any knowledge of Japan's invasion of China or colonisation of Manchuria." In the early twenty-first century, Hando lectured at a women's college about the Shōwa era: "I asked fifty students to list countries which have *not* fought Japan in modern times: eleven included America."

"It is important frankly to discuss what happened in the Second World War," he added, "because today relations between China and Japan are so poor. But there is a problem in starting such a discussion, because so few younger Japanese know any facts. There are many people who do not support our militant nationalists, but still find it offensive to endure endless criticism from China and Korea. They dislike those countries poking their noses into what they see as matters for the Japanese people. Most of us think that we have apologised for the war: one of our former Prime Ministers has made the most fulsome apology. I myself think that we have done enough apologising." This remains a matter of debate, and some British and American people strongly disagree with Hando. As recently as 2007, the head of the Japanese air force was obliged to resign his post after publishing a paper in which he asserted the philanthropic nature of Japan's activities in China between 1937 and 1945.

Palestine was among the lands most conspicuously influenced by the outcome of the conflict. For more than two decades of British mandatory rule, its future had been keenly debated. Capt. David Hopkinson was one among the hundreds of thousands of British soldiers who passed through the Holy Land in the course of his war service, and pondered its rightful destiny. Hopkinson had a special interest, because his wife was half Jewish. He wrote to her from Haifa in 1942, expressing a hostility to Zionism founded in his belief that "Jews are of greatest value within the countries where they have been long established. I am as impressed as everyone must be by the technical and cultural accomplishments of Jews in Palestine, but for an intensely nationalistic minority to seek to carve out for itself an independent state from territories to which others also have a claim seems to be inconsistent with the high ideas of peace and humanity in which civilized Europeans believe."

Yet in 1945, such temperate views were swamped by the ghastly revelations of the Holocaust. It is important to emphasise that, even after newsreels from liberated Belsen and Buchenwald had stunned the civilised world, the full extent of the Jewish genocide became understood only slowly, even by Western governments. But it became manifest that the Jews of Europe had fallen victim to a uniquely satanic programme of mass murder, which left many survivors homeless and dispossessed. The U.S. commissioner of immigration Earl Harrison visited the displaced persons camps of Europe and was shocked by what he found there. He reported to President Truman in August 1945: "We appear to be treating the Jews as the Nazis treated them except that we do not exterminate them." By a vast historic irony, Hitler's persecution transformed the fortunes of the Jewish people around the world. It provided an impetus to Zionism which seemed to many Westerners morally irresistible. Never again would anti-Semitism be socially acceptable in Western democratic societies; and the slaughter of Europe's Jews precipitated the 1948 creation of the state of Israel. Yet, if the Holocaust made a devastating and lasting impact upon Western culture, many other societies around the world have never identified themselves with its significance, and in some cases even deny its reality. Widespread bitterness persists that the Western powers assuaged their own guilt about the wartime fate of the Jews by making a great historic gesture in lands identified by Muslims as rightfully Arab.

There is a wider issue: some modern historians who are citizens of nations that were once European possessions regard their peoples as victims of wartime exploitation. They suggest that Britain, especially, engaged them in a struggle in which they had no stake, for a cause that was not properly theirs. Such arguments represent points of view rather than evidential conclusions, but it seems important for Westerners to recognise these sentiments, as a counterpoint to our instinctive assumption that our grandparents fought "the Good War."

Within Western culture, of course, the conflict continues to exercise an extraordinary fascination for generations unborn when it took place. The obvious explanation is that this was the greatest and most terrible event in human history. Within the vast compass of the struggle, some individuals scaled summits of courage and nobility, while others plumbed depths of evil, in a fashion that compels the awe of posterity. Among citizens of modern democracies to whom serious hardship and collective peril are unknown, the tribulations that hundreds of millions endured between 1939 and 1945 are almost beyond comprehension. Almost all those who participated, nations and individuals alike, made moral compromises. It is impossible to dignify the struggle as an unalloyed contest between good and evil, or rationally to celebrate an experience, and even an outcome, which imposed such misery upon so many. Allied victory did not bring universal peace, prosperity, justice or freedom; it brought merely a portion of those things to some fraction of those who had taken part. All that seems certain is that Allied victory saved the world from a much worse fate that would have followed the triumph of Germany and Japan. With this knowledge, seekers after virtue and truth must be content.

Acknowledgements

I feel very fortunate that the cast of colleagues and friends to whom I am indebted for assistance changes little with my successive books. At HarperCollins in London, the counsel of my editors, Arabella Pike and Robert Lacey, together with that of Andrew Miller at Knopf in New York, much enhanced the text. My agents, Michael Sissons, in London, and Peter Matson, in New York, have been steering my courses for longer than any of us care to remember. Professor Sir Michael Howard, OM, CH, MC; Don Berry; Professor N.A.M. Rodger; Richard Frank; and Dr. Williamson Murray offered immensely valuable comments on all or sections of the manuscript, and corrected some of my most egregious errors. Dr. Lyuba Vinogradova translated much Russian material, while Serena Sissons culled Italian memoirs, letters and diaries. Dr. Tami Biddle of the U.S. Army War College is wonderfully generous in passing on to me material which she gathers for her own researches. Rod Suddaby is only the foremost of the Imperial War Museum staff whose assistance contributes so much to the works of every historian of modern war, while the London Library and the National Archive provide wonderfully sympathetic settings for research. With only a brief interruption, Rachel Lawrence has been my long-suffering and peerlessly effective personal assistant for twenty-five years, an ordeal which includes collating my notes and references. My wife, Penny, is never less than a perfect partner, though I sometimes fancy that she would prefer to have lived through the Second World War than to read any more books about it written by me. To them all I offer deep gratitude, for I know that my labours would swiftly plough into sand without such sympathy, guidance and support.

Notes and References

References below to my own earlier works relate to material now lodged in the Liddell Hart Archive at King's College, London, here abbreviated as LHA. AI signifies Author Interview, meaning an eyewitness with whom I held conversations at some time over the past thirty-five years. IWM refers to manuscripts in the collections of the Imperial War Museum; BNA to the British National Archive; USNA to the United States National Archive; USMHI to the United States Military History Institute at Carlisle Barracks, Pennsylvania. References to Potsdam denote the magnificent multivolume history *Germany and the Second World War*, published by the Research Institute for Military History in Potsdam, and translated by Oxford University Press. For this work, I have consulted a manuscript narrative and some papers of Air Vice-Marshal Sir Ralph Cochrane held by his son John. I have not provided references for statements by prominent figures which have been long in the public domain.

INTRODUCTION

xviii "These are strange times": Anonymous, *A Woman in Berlin* (Virago, 2009), p. 35.

xviii "Pfc. Eric Diller's battalion": Eric Diller, *Memoirs of a Combat Infantryman* (privately published, 2002), p. 77.

xix in January 1942 Hitler: Helmuth von Moltke, ed. Beatte von Oppen, *Letters to Freya* (Collins Harvill, 1991), p. 204, 24 Jan. 1942.

CHAPTER ONE   POLAND BETRAYED

3 "Somehow, I considered": Rula Langer, *The Mermaid and the Messerschmitt* (Roy, 1942), p. 20.

3 "Like most of us": Lynn Olson and Stanley Cloud, *For Your Freedom and Ours* (Heinemann, 2003), p. 46.

3 "You aren't going to Siberia": Jan Karski, *Story of a Secret State* (Penguin, 2011), p. 5.

3 "To hear people talk": Walter Duranty, *Atlantic Monthly* (September 1939), p. 393.

4 "would quickly be turned": Galeazzo Ciano, *Diaries* (Milan, 1946), Vol. 1, 15 May 1939.

4 "If there was hardship": Norman Davies, *God's Playground* (Oxford, 1981), Vol. 2, p. 426.

4 "In view of Poland's": Edward Raczynski, *In Allied London* (Weidenfeld & Nicolson, 1962) p. 20, 30 Aug. 1939.

6 "It's a wonderful feeling": James Owen and Guy Walters, ed., *The Voices of War* (Penguin, 2004) p. 9.

6 "They were united": IWM 08/132/1 Kruczkiewitz MS, p. 163.

6 "We sang a Polish hymn": IWM 02/23/1 Ephrahim Blaichman MS.

6 "and told me he was": IWM 86/17/1 P. Fleming MS.

7 "You're alive, Witold?": Olson and Cloud, p. 52.

7 Franciszek Kornicki: IWM Kornicki MS 01/1/1.

8 "After recovering from": IWM 03/41/1 Ralph Smorczewski MS.

8 "I was awakened": Kruczkiewitz, p. 166.

9 "The stench of burning": IWM Pilot B. J. Solak MS.

9 "We saw two women": IWM 86/15/1 P. Fleming MS.

9 "Suddenly, there was the roar of an aeroplane": Wladyslaw Anders, *An Army in Exile* (Macmillan, 1949), p. 3.

10 "It was a terrible place": IWM 01/1/1 Pilot Franciszek Kornicki MS.

10 "I saw the very face": Adrian Carlton de Wiart, *Happy Odyssey* (Jonathan Cape, 1950), p. 156.

10 "news that shook": Evelyn Waugh, *Officers and Gentlemen* (Chapman & Hall, 1955), p. 5.

11 "This war has a": Moltke, p. 33.

11 "There is no excitement": William Shirer, *This Is Berlin* (Hutchinson, 1999), p. 75.

11 "None of the brave": Alexander Stahlberg, *Bounden Duty* (Brassey, 1990), p. 116.

11 "They did not feel": Stefan Zweig, *The World of Yesterday* (Pushkin Press, 2010), p. 247.

11 "I regarded England's": Louis Hagen, *Ein Volk ein Reich: Nine Lives Under the Reich* (Spellmount, 2011) pp. 32–33.

11 "have only themselves": Stuart Ball, ed., *Parliament and Politics in the Age of Churchill and Attlee: The Headlam Diaries, 1935–1951* (Cambridge, 1999), p. 167.

12 "Mother was very": Sandra Koa Wing, ed., *Our Longest Days* (Profile, 2008), p. 31.

12 "an ominous rumour": David Killingray, *Fighting for Britain* (James Currey, 2010), p. 11.

12 "The effect was": Max Hastings, *Overlord: D-Day and the Battle for Normandy*, Michael Joseph, 1984 correspondence.

12 "The mental approach": David Fraser, *Wars and Shadows* (Penguin, 2002), p. 122.

13 "It was a marvellous": Max Hastings, *Bomber Command* files, Davis to the author.

13 "How lucky you are!": Raczynski, p. 27.

13 "Are they still waiting?": Mihail Sebastian, *Journal, 1935–44* (Heinemann, 2001), p. 234.

14 "I had never experienced": IWM 02/23/1 Blaichman MS.

14 "I called out": Janusz Piekalkiewitcz, *The Cavalry of World War II* (Orbis, 1979), p. 9.

14 "The lovely Polish": Olson and Cloud, p. 52.

15 "They would hurry": Piekalkiewitcz, p. 12.

15 "I can only compare": IWM Lt. Piotr Tarczsynski MS.

16 "Boys I was at school": IWM 95/13/1 George Slazak MS.

16 "The advance of the armies": Heinz Knoke, *I Flew for the Führer* (Evans, 1979), p. 20.

17 "Run—run for your lives": IWM 78/52/1 Stefan Kurylak MS.

17 "You know the British": Olson and Cloud, p. 69.

17 "What was happening": Anders, p. 7.

18 "Fellow countrymen!": Raczynski, p. 36.

18 "It isn't right!": Adrian Ball, *The Last Days of the Old World* (Doubleday, 1963), pp. 27–28.
18 "It would seem": Janet Flanner, *New Yorker*, 10 Sept. 1939.
18 "Loathing war passionately": Leo Amery, *My Political Life* (Hutchinson, 1955), Vol. 3, p. 328.
19 "Practically everyone thinks": Simon Garfield, ed., *We Are at War* (Ebury, 2009), p. 36.
19 "And he, when the city": Davies, p. 83.
19 "The procession of wounded": Owen and Walters, p. 16.
20 "I get up at 6:30": Mungo Melvin, *Manstein*, Weidenfeld & Nicolson, 2010, p. 122.
20 "It was nice to see": ibid., p. 125.
21 "Red, glittering flames": General K. S. Rudnicki, *Last of the Old Warhorses* (Bachman & Turner, 1974), p. 49.
21 "Tomorrow morning we shall": ibid., p. 54.
21 "at variance with": ibid., p. 63.
21 "Desolate as was": IWM 91/6/1 Felicks Lachman MS.
21 "standing over the corpse": IWM 08/132/1 Adam Krusczkiewitz MS, p. 168.
22 "We are now good friends": Anders, p. 13.
22 "From this instant": IWM 99/3/1 Tadeusz Zukowski MS.
22 "You Polish, fascist lords!": Karski, p. 23.
23 "How is it possible": IWM 91/6/1 Lachman MS.
23 "Gentlemen, you have seen": John Raleigh, *Behind the Nazi Front* (Dodd Mead, 1940), p. 320.
23 "Well, your Poles": Carlton de Wiart, p. 160.
24 "encountered chaos": IWM 06/52/1 Szmulek Goldberg MS.
25 "In the household": Simon Garfield, *Private Battles* (Ebury, 2006), p. 48.
25 "Where on earth can": Raczynski, p. 34.

CHAPTER TWO NO PEACE, LITTLE WAR

28 "Seldom have I seen": Arthur Bryant, *The Turn of the Tide* (Collins, 1957), p. 71.
28 "both the French communists": IWM Kornicki MS, p. 89.
28 "The war doesn't seem": Douglas Arthur, *Desert Watch* (Blaisdon, 2000), p. 76.
29 "We went to strange beds": Norman Longmate, *The Home Front* (Chatto & Windus, 1981), p. 17.
29 "The village people objected": Koa Wing, p. 15.
29 some 18 percent: *Public Opinion 1935–1946* (Princeton University Press, 1951), p. 48.
30 Defence regulations were: E. S. Turner, *The Phoney War* (Michael Joseph, 1961), p. 53.
30 "trotted home like a gentleman": Street narrative courtesy of Miranda Corben.
30 "It certainly is breath-taking": IWM Elizabeth Belsey correspondence, 6 March 1941.
30 There was anger: Turner, p. 169.
31 "I used to wonder": Arthur Kellas, *Down to Earth* (Pentland Press, 1989), p. 11.
31 "Look at 'im, girls": Arthur, p. 28.
31 "While the [First] World War": Elliot Roosevelt, ed., *The Roosevelt Letters*, Vol. 3 (Harrap, 1952), p. 286.
32 "It would be wrong": Robert Edwards, *White Death* (Weidenfeld & Nicolson, 2007), p. 59.

32 "When one gives a gift": ibid., p. 68.
33 "Comrade Commander": ibid., p. 156.
33 "Comrades, our attack": ibid., p. 82.
34 "Our units, saturated by": Chris Bellamy, *Absolute War* (Macmillan, 2007), p. 76.
34 "The fighting was almost": Carl Mydans, *More Than Meets the Eye* (Harper, 1959), p. 119.
35 "I regard it as essential": Edwards, p. 206.
37 "The women of Finland": Harold Macmillan, Hansard 19 March 1940.
37 "In the early afternoon": Edwards, p. 232.
38 "It's particularly cold": ibid., p. 254.
38 "One thing is clear": ibid., p. 261.
38 "At least you will tell them": Mydans, p. 129.
40 "The idea was to": Francois Kersaudy, *Norway 1940* (Collins, 1990), p. 31.
40 "Everyone is getting married": Koa Wing, p. 32.
40 "We have had to suffer": ibid., p. 18.
42 "After Daladier": Julian Jackson, *The Fall of France* (Oxford, 2003), p. 127.

CHAPTER THREE   BLITZKRIEGS IN THE WEST

44 "I think of the Germans": Ruth Maier, *Ruth Maier's Diary* (Harvill Secker, 2009), p. 115.
45 "[The man] turns to me": ibid., p. 231.
45 "I am profoundly moved": Kersaudy, p. 103.
46 "You cannot conceive": Keith Jeffrey, *MI6: The History of the Secret Intelligence Service, 1909–49* (Bloomsbury, 2010), p. 374.
48 "Imagine how we felt": Robert Kershaw, *Never Surrender* (Hodder & Stoughton, 2009), p. 37.
48 "very young lads who appeared": Kersaudy, p. 169.
48 "Drunk British troops": BNA FO371/24833.
49 "The war goes on": Street diary in possession of Miranda Corben, 27 April 1940.
50 "The worst of it all": BNA W0106/1962.
50 "Those officers who had": Adrian Gilbert, *Voices of the Foreign Legion* (Skyhorse, 2010), p. 190.
51 "I am stunned": Koa Wing, p. 35.
54 "striding up and down": Jackson, p. 11.
55 "The noise of their engines": R. Balbaud, quoted in Jackson, p. 164.
55 "The gunners stopped": ibid., p. 164.
55 "A wave of terrified fugitives": ibid., p. 166.
56 "The room was barely": ibid., p. 47.
56 "sitting in tragic immobility": ibid., p. 224.
56 "with unbelieving terror": Kershaw, p. 54.
57 "We want to go home": ibid., p. 168.
57 "I saw very well": ibid., p. 169.
57 "an immediate impression": Jackson, p. 170.
57 "They told us terrible things": ibid., p. 172.
58 "Even though the reports": Irène Némirovsky, *Suite française* (Chatto & Windus, 2006), p. 3.
58 "The people are half-mad": Jackson, p. 176.
59 "They had to dress their children": Némirovsky, p. 41.
59 "After a few days' fighting": John Horsfall, *Say Not the Struggle* (Roundwood, 1977), p. 157.

59 "Armed as they were": Michael Howard, *Liberation or Catastrophe* (Hambledon, 2008), p. 9.

60 "Our soldiers just need": Horsfall, p. 54.

62 "I lost my temper": Sir Edmund Ironside, *Time Unguarded: The Ironside Diaries*, ed. Roderick MacLeod ard Denis Kelly (London, 1962), p. 321.

64 "It was evident": Horsfall, p. 57.

64 "I remember the order": Kershaw, p. 56.

64 "It was so wonderful": Owen and Walters, p. 45.

65 "When we went ashore": Peter Hart, *At the Sharp End* (Leo Cooper, 1998), p. 75.

65 "At Ramsgate we met": Horsfall, p. 151.

65 "We . . . are woken": McCormick letter in possession of Mrs. Miranda Corben.

66 "I forgot I was": Nella Last, *Nella Last's War* (Sphere, 1981), p. 62.

67 "We are really tired": Jackson, p. 178.

67 "Many of them were": Constantin Joffe, *We Were Free* (Smith & Durrell, 1943), p. 47.

68 "In these ruined villages": Alastair Horne, *To Lose a Battle* (Macmillan, 1969), p. 489.

68 "Few of my own misfortunes": Zweig, p. 149.

68 "Silently, with no lights": Némirovsky, p. 42.

68 "Their bodies had been": ibid., p. 53.

68 "We found them among": Paul Richey, *Fighter Pilot* (Cassell, 2001), pp. 69–70.

69 "A disillusioned Johnny": ibid., p. 90.

69 "All along the road": Hart, p. 47.

69 "was led astray": Jackson, p. 126.

69 "What are you waiting for": ibid., p. 144.

69 "It should really be": Barry Leach and Ian MacDonald, eds., *Command in Conflict: The Diaries and Notes of Colonel-General Franz Halder and Other Members of the German High Command* (Oxford, 1985), p. 656.

70 "I am so impatient": Roy Macnab, *For Honour Alone* (Hale, 1988), p. 59.

71 "Today among many": Jackson, p. 144.

72 The British were granted: see Max Hastings, *Finest Years* (HarperCollins, 2009), p. 45 et seq.

72 "I should . . . describe France": Jackson, p. 182.

72 "Have we suffered enough?": ibid., p. 233.

73 "For years, everything done": Némirovsky, p. 351.

74 "Stalin was in a great": Sergei Khrushchev, ed., *The Memoirs of Nikita Khrushchev* (Thomas Watson Institute, 2004), Vol. 1, p. 256.

75 To his intimates: Denis Mack Smith, *Mussolini* (Weidenfeld & Nicolson, 1981), p. 250.

75 "The C-in-C [Gen. Walter von Brauchitsch]": Halder, p. 668.

75 "The war machine rolled": Rosemary Say and Noel Holland, *Rosie's War* (Michael Mara Books, 2011), p. 86.

CHAPTER FOUR   BRITAIN ALONE

77 "I looked down on the calm": Richey, p. 155.

78 "Heard today that Hitler": Ronald Blythe, ed., *Private Words* (Viking 1991), p. 98, 19 July 1940.

80 "a regressive moral": Michael Burleigh, *Moral Combat* (HarperCollins, 2010), p. 202.

81 "All at once, crossfire": Geoffrey Wellum, *First Light* (Penguin, 2002), p. 148.
82 "Spitfire on my tail!": Stephen Bungay, *The Most Dangerous Enemy* (Aurum, 2010), p. 118.
82 "We are in the Geschwader": ibid., p. 116.
83 "It was just beer, women": ibid., p. 119.
83 "We used to booze": James Holland, *Battle Over Britain* (HarperPress, 2010), p. 548.
83 "Our hearts leapt!": Bungay, p. 179.
83 "When you seen": ibid., p. 124.
83 "There was tremendous": ibid., p. 165.
84 "People who stayed in": Robert Kershaw, p. 163.
84 "It was rather like": Beatrice Bishop Berle and Travis Beal Jacobs, *Navigating the Rapids, 1918–1971* (Harcourt Brace, 1973), p. 150.
84 "Our track across": Robert Kershaw, p. 166.
85 "I could not get": Holland, p. 383.
85 "I then said": ibid., p. 387.
85 "Oh God I do wish": IWM 97/43/1 Denis Wissler diary, 16 June 1940.
86 "The British are slowly": Holland, p. 578.
87 "I think everyone": George Barclay, *Fighter Pilot* (Kimber, 1976), p. 43.
87 "We have been up four times": ibid., p. 45.
87 "nearly jumped clean": Sandy Johnstone, *Enemy in the Sky* (Kimber, 1976), p. 118.
87 "Wherever one looks": Holland, p. 543.
88 "the pure azure-blue": ibid., p. 537.
88 "Our airmen have had": Headlam, p. 220.
89 "the troops under our command": Charles Hudson, *Journal of Major-General Charles Hudson* (Wilton 65, 1992), pp. 187–89.
90 One aristocratic housewife: Sarah Baring, *The Road to Station X* (Wilton 65), p. 20.
90 "The Sedgebury Wallop platoon": A. G. Street, *From Dusk Till Dawn* (Blandford, 1945), pp. 59–60.
91 "The bombs came down": Barbara Nixon, *Raiders Overhead* (Scolar, 1980), p. 129.
91 "I wonder what the pilots": Koa Wing, p. 60, 15 Nov. 1940.
92 "Human casualties were": Nixon, pp. 42–43.
92 "Some people . . . recall": Longmate, p. 66.
93 "I pray, Oh God!": Rev H. A. Wilson, quoted in Longmate, pp. 79–80.
93 "Neither had any idea": Nixon, p. 62.
93 "It was the old people": Owen and Walters, p. 94.
93 "as evidently her nerves": Koa Wing, p. 52.
94 "I've had really": ibid., p. 53.
94 Early in the war: James Owen, *Danger UXB* (Little Brown, 2010), passim.
94 Early one morning: ibid., pp. 115–19 and passim.
96 "The first effects": Howard Smith, *Last Train from Berlin* (London, 1942), p. 86.
98 "German command preparing": Jeffrey, p. 373.
99 It seems flippant: Ian Kershaw, *Fateful Choices* (Penguin, 2008), passim.
99 "I do not suppose": Knoke, p. 32.
99 Germany's 1940 victories: see Adam Tooze, *The Wages of Destruction* (Penguin, 2007), passim.
99 "The Prime Minister has": Johnstone, p. 161.

100 "a malevolent suspension": Evelyn Waugh, *Unconditional Surrender* (Chapman & Hall, 1961), p. 147.
100 "Sometimes I get": Koa Wing, p. 37, 4 June 1940.
101 "The British people are": Barclay, p. 73.

CHAPTER FIVE   THE MEDITERRANEAN

102 "Madam, I cannot": IWM 08/132/1 Kruczkiewitz MS, p. 150.
102 a contemptuous joke: Hagen, p. 34.
106 "We want to reach Suez": Knox MacGregor, *Mussolini Unleashed* (Cambridge, 1982), p. 153.
106 "Everyone thinks only": ibid., p. 135.
106 "We're trying to fight": Colin Smith and John Bierman, *Alamein: War Without Hate* (Penguin, 2002), p. 28.
108 "loaded with the paraphernalia": Arthur, p. 191.
108 They can't take it": Mark Johnston, *At the Front Line* (Cambridge, 1996), p. 14.
108 "All Australians now know": ibid., p. 15.
108 "One can't help": Smith and Bierman, p. 49.
108 To this end: Killingray, p. 169.
108 "It goes without saying": Sebastian, p. 320.
109 "Every day was": Arthur, p. 212.
109 "Beyond doubt Spain": Stanley Payne, *Franco and Hitler* (Yale, 2008), p. 62.
110 "it was a point of both": ibid., p. 94.
111 "We are all twenty-one": Smith and Bierman, p. 149.
112 "Here things are going": Andrea Rebora, ed., *Letters of Lt. Pietro Ostellino, N. Africa Jan. 1941 to March 1943* (Prospettiva Editrice), p. 51.
112 "Morale is very high": ibid., p. 52.
112 "The rot seemed to set in": Smith and Bierman, p. 70.
112 "We are well advanced": Ostellino, p. 73.
113 "Yesterday I received": ibid., p. 79, 3 June 1941.
113 "If anyone makes": Mack Smith, p. 357.
113 "Not having any money": C. N. Hadjipateras and M. S. Falfalios, eds., *Greece 1940–41 Eyewitnessed* (Efstathiadis, 1995), p. 35.
114 "When we've beaten": ibid., p. 33.
114 "The door of our": ibid., p. 104.
114 "Starving, soaked to the bone": ibid., p. 122.
115 "Many, many pessimists": MacGregor, p. 201.
116 "Best place we have": Tony Simpson, *Operation Mercury* (Hodder & Stoughton, 1981), p. 92.
117 "We were followed by": ibid., p. 101.
117 "It's a peculiar feeling": ibid., p. 107.
117 "the patter of feet": ibid., p. 97.
117 "They were the ones": Hadjipateras and Falfalios, p. 124.
119 "During the afternoon": Johnston, p. 29.
119 "I saw a captain": Hadjipateras and Falfalios, p. 197.
119 "George, a black night": ibid., p. 230.
119 "He began by saying": ibid., p. 255.
121 "I think . . . the masses": Koa Wing, p. 92.
122 The Vichy French authorities: for an exceptionally vivid account of Vichy's intervention in Iraq and the campaign in Syria, see Colin Smith, *England's Last*

War with France: Fighting Vichy, 1940–42 (Weidenfeld, 2009), passim, especially pp. 96–98.

123 "Churchill's policy": Warren Tute, *The Reluctant Enemies* (Collins, 1990), p. 81.

123 "My God, what is": Némirovsky, p. 347, 21 June 1941.

123 "You thought we were": Alan Moorehead, *African Trilogy* (Hamish Hamilton, 1999), p. 164.

125 "I for one have": Roald Dahl, *Going Solo* (Penguin, 1988), p. 196.

125 "So long as Britain": Sebastian, p. 358.

126 "I can only now": Ostellino, p. 140.

126 "We can *learn* from": Johnston, p. 28.

126 "In 1941 and early 1942": *Overlord* correspondence.

127 "One enemy post": Johnston, p. 43.

127 "Men of both armies": ibid., p. 44.

127 "We were sitting up": ibid., p. 46.

128 "I drew alongside": Smith and Bierman, p. 110.

129 "You are an Australian": Johnston, p. 56.

130 "The Australians regarded": John McManners, *Fusilier* (Michael Russell, 2002), p. 67.

130 "I came to realise": Arthur, p. 153.

130 "The flies plague us": Smith and Bierman, p. 32.

130 "Even the climate": Ostellino, p. 96, 5 August 1941.

131 "We . . . slowly make ourselves": Smith and Bierman, p. 134.

131 "Smooth yellow sand": Alastair Borthwick, *Battalion* (Baton Wicks, 1994), p. 39.

131 "The chief occupation": McManners, p. 46.

131 "You would think it": Ostellino, p. 54, 14 March 1941.

132 "The unreality had": Artemis Cooper, *Cairo in the War* (Hamish Hamilton, 1989), p. 80.

132 "Sweat shining, hair bleached": ibid., p. 117.

132 "Groppi's at Cairo": McManners, p. 85.

132 "not because of": Vittorio Vallicella, *Diario di Guerra da El Alamein alla tragica ritirata 1942–1943* (Edizioni Arterigere, 2009), p. 22.

132 "How many times": ibid., p. 76.

132 Italian soldiers resented: ibid., p. 59.

133 "After nearly twenty": ibid., p. 62.

133 "For those lucky enough": ibid., p. 70.

133 When Vallicella caught: ibid., p. 65.

133 about "the hell": ibid., p. 85.

133 "I had the pleasant surprise": Ostellino, p. 143, 11 Dec. 1941.

134 "We could never fire": J. Cloudsley-Thompson, unpublished MS.

135 "What a shock to find": Vallicella, p. 16.

135 Exploring the town: ibid., p. 20.

135 Some Arabs found: ibid., p. 17.

135 "Even here our allies": ibid., p. 18.

135 "We hope this nightmare": ibid., p. 19.

135 "The order came": McManners, pp. 101, 108.

CHAPTER SIX   BARBAROSSA

137 "We were all expecting": Catherine Merridale, *Ivan's War* (Faber, 2005), p. 77.

137 "Kuznetsov informed me": ibid., p. 75.

137 "Many, perhaps most": Howard, *Liberation*, p. 9.

138 "The situation is ideal": Knoke, p. 47.
138 "I accepted as natural": Henry Metelmann, *Through Hell for Hitler* (Spellmount, 1990), pp. 15, 24.
138 "Now you see how far": Potsdam, Vol. 4, p. 341.
140 "God knows, you are not": Tooze, p. 546.
140 "The war with Russia": Michael Jones, *The Retreat: Hitler's First Defeat* (John Murray, 2009), p. 23.
141 "You can tell your 'source' ": Bellamy, p. 147.
141 "The war will begin": Sebastian, p. 368.
142 "We must win": Goebbels, *Diaries*, 23 June 1941.
142 "It may so happen": Valentin Berezhkov, *Stranitsy Diplomaticheskoy Istorii* (Moscow, 1982), pp. 69, 212.
142 "We were uncritically": Martin Poppel, *Heaven & Hell* (Spellmount, 1988), p. 11.
142 "Our destination is Russia": ibid., p. 70.
143 "These days bogs": Bellamy, p. 197.
143 "As there seemed": IWM Kurylak MS.
143 "I never shot as well": Knoke, p. 45.
143 "All of a sudden": Jones, *Retreat*, p. 1.
143 "There were hundreds": ibid., p. 7.
144 "For the Motherland": Merridale, p. 69.
144 "We were following Napoleon's": Jones, *Retreat*, p. 6.
144 "The pitiful hordes": Potsdam, Vol. 9/1, p. 545.
144 "We launch wonderful attacks": ibid., p. 546.
144 "some even crawling": Jones, *Retreat*, p. 10.
145 "When the commentator": ibid., p. 55.
145 "So now Russia will get": Clare Milburn, *Mrs. Milburn's Diaries* (Harrap, 1979), p. 101.
145 "Have they entered Moscow?": Sebastian, p. 374.
145 "The war against these": Jones, *Retreat*, p. 18.
146 "I am repeatedly": ibid., p. 14.
146 "Eyes had been": Bellamy, p. 189.
148 "missed the German offensive": ibid., p. 232.
148 "They are crying": Vasily Grossman, *A Writer at War*, ed. Lyuba Vinogradova and Antony Beevor (Harvill, 2006), p. 23.
149 "We were surprised": Roderic Braithwaite, *Moscow 1941* (Profile, 2006), p. 80.
149 "What am I to say": Moskvin, quoted in *Pisma S Voiny* (Ioshkar-Ola, 1995), p. 87.
149 "some in trucks": Gabriel Temkin, *My Just War* (Presidio, 1998), p. 60.
149 "Especially those wounded": Grossman, p. 19.
152 "the Russian genius": Bellamy, p. 63.
152 "Papa, our Valik": Merridale, p. 127.
153 "The fascists drove us": *Pisma S Voiny* p. 60.
153 "It's not surprising": Merridale, p. 127.
153 "I am writing for posterity": ibid., p. 220, 25 March 1943.
153 "a courageous garrison": Bellamy, p. 187.
154 "It is increasingly clear": Halder, p. 167.
154 "I believed that Russia": Moltke, p. 151, 16 July 1941.
154 "One thing seems certain": ibid., p. 154.
154 "Everyone laughs": Grossman, p. 17.
154 "I felt an incredible": Jones, *Retreat*, p. 27.
155 "We go to look at": Grossman, p. 45.
155 "I thought I'd seen": ibid., p. 48.

155 "I have told myself": ibid., p. 96.
156 "if we do not intend": David Glanz, *Barbarossa* (Tempus, 2001), p. 82.
156 "If we don't succeed": Moltke, p. 168.
157 "It is wet and cold": Jones, *Retreat*, p. 52.
157 "From now on": ibid., p. 56.
158 "The men hauled": ibid., p. 59.
158 "Hello, Zoya!": *Pisma S Voiny*, pp. 24–25.
158 "The back wheel": Owen and Walters, p. 155.
158 "The roads have become": Jones, *Retreat*, p. 74.
159 "In essence," he said: Zhukov to Konstantin Simonov, quoted in *The Times*, 6 May 2010.
160 "The leader did not": Merridale, p. 84.
160 "Shoot me if you like": ibid., p. 85.
160 "The Führer himself": Jones, *Retreat*, p. 192
160 "Eastern campaign extended": Moltke, p. 187.

CHAPTER SEVEN   MOSCOW SAVED, LENINGRAD STARVED

162 "Soon the Germans": Konstantin Rokossovsky, *Soldatskiy Dolg* (Olun Press Moscow, 2002), p. 8.
162 "Thus we are approaching": Bellamy, p. 316, from Haupt, *Assault on Moscow*, p. 152.
163 "Relief and happiness": Jones, *Retreat*, p. 125.
163 "Out of the snowstorm": ibid., p. 141.
163 "Each time we leave": ibid., p. 193.
164 "Eighty men were brought": ibid., p. 140.
165 "methodically, precisely": Michael Jones, *The Siege of Leningrad* (John Murray, 2008), p. 74.
165 "Our soldiers are only": ibid., p. 78.
165 "You have yourself": Khrushchev, p. 256.
166 "Our guys just didn't": Jones, *Leningrad*, p. 117.
166 "It is not worth risking": ibid., p. 40.
167 "We are approaching": ibid., p. 45.
167 "grass cakes found": Lazar Brontman, *Voenny dnevnik korrespondenta "Pravdy"* [War Diary of the *Pravda* Correspondent] (Moscow, 2007), pp. 55–56, 19 Aug. 1942.
167 "I have received a letter": *Pisma S Voiny*, p. 31.
167 "All our soldiers": Jones, *Leningrad*, p. 134.
168 "Lena," he said: ibid., p. 149.
168 "It was as if that boy": ibid., p. 152.
169 In Svetlana Magaeva's: ibid..
169 "People are so weak": ibid., p. 163.
170 "I learned what war": Nikolai Nikulin, *Vospominaniya o voine* (St. Petersburg, 2009), Internet published.
170 "He fell to the ground": Jones, *Leningrad*, p. 193.
170 Lidya Okhapkina had her: ibid., p. 206.
171 "One woman, utterly": ibid., p. 215.
171 "I have often wondered": Jones, *Retreat*, p. 201.
172 "I have never heard": ibid., p. 203.
172 "When I finished": ibid.
172 "There is a serious cost": ibid., p. 235.

173   "I grabbed a saw": ibid., p. 261.
173   "He lay for a while": ibid., p. 97.
174   "As we picked our way": Jones, *Leningrad*, p. 279.
174   "The fact that we did not": Jones, *Retreat*, p. 196.
175   "The only thing holding us": ibid., p. 61.
175   "They'll kill the lot of you": Merridale, p. 99.
175   To discourage desertion: Zhadobin et al., eds., *Ogennaya Duga: Kurskaya Bitva Glazami Lubyanki* [The Salient of Fire: Kursk as Seen Through the Eyes of the Lubyanka] (Moscow, 2003), p. 25.
175   "This is no gentleman's war": Jones, *Retreat*, p. 82.
176   "They whined and grovelled": Merridale, p. 251.
176   "We have blundered": Jones, *Retreat*, p. 107.
176   "Even if we capture Moscow": ibid., p. 98.
176   "Forty per cent of our men": Mathilde Wolff-Monckeburg, *On the Other Side*, p. 57.
177   "Oh, I used to be": Grossman, p. 53.
177   "If we do win": ibid., p. 54.
178   "I never believe them Roosians": Nixon, p. 156.
178   "First, Russia is an": Wendell Willkie, *One World* (New York, 1942), p. 167.
178   "grateful recognition": *Spectator*, 19 June 1942.
178   "It hasn't half": Koa Wing, p. 122, 23 Feb. 1942.

CHAPTER EIGHT   AMERICA EMBATTLED

180   A Princeton poll: *Public Opinion*, p. 19.
180   "We over here": Roosevelt Letters, p. 286.
180   "Before the advent": Robert Sherwood, *The White House Papers of Harry L. Hopkins* (Eyre & Spottiswoode, 1948), Vol. 1, p. 132.
181   "We haven't heard": Elaine Steinbeck and Robert Wallsten, eds., *John Steinbeck: A Life in Letters* (Heinemann, 1975), p. 201.
181   "If it weren't for": ibid., p. 206.
181   "The question of whether": Berle and Jacobs, p. 314.
181   "Who among us": Donald Nelson, *Arsenal of Democracy* (Harcourt Brace, 1946), p. 85.
182   "An army post": Carson McCullers, *Reflections in a Golden Eye* (Houghton Mifflin, 1941), p. 1.
182   "slowly gathering together": Eric Sevareid, *Not So Wild a Dream* (Knopf, 1969), p. 201.
182   "The U.S. Army started": Martin Blumenson, *Parameters*, Vol. 19, No. 4, Dec. 1989.
182   "We're going to war": Carlo D'Este, *Eisenhower* (Holt, 2002), p. 264.
183   "that the United States had": *The White House Papers of Harry L. Hopkins*, Vol. 1, p. 131.
183   "I am not in a hurry": BNA PREM3/475/1.
184   "I know of no": David Kennedy, *Freedom from Fear* (Oxford, 1999), p. 232.
184   "The ability of the": Robert Dallek, *Lone Star Rising* (Oxford, 1991), p. 197.
185   "All talk centers around": IWM MP Troy Papers 95/25/1.
185   "Some of my friends": ibid., letter of 9 June 1941.
186   Historian David Kennedy: Kennedy, p. 525.
187   "afraid, unhappy and bewildered": Geoffrey Perrett, *Days of Sadness, Years of Triumph* (University of Wisconsin, 1973), p. 79.

187   "Dear Jim, When will": Roosevelt, p. 370.
188   "Fighting and death everywhere": Meirion and Susie Harries, *Soldiers of the Sun* (Heinemann, 1991), p. 222.
189   In the summer of 1939: see John Colvin, *Nomonhan* (Quartet, 1999).
190   "I understand you are": Christopher Bayly and Tim Harper, *Forgotten Armies* (Penguin, 2004), p. 71.
193   "We were flabbergasted": Alvin Kernan, *The Unknown Battle of Midway* (Yale, 2005), p. 2.
193   "the glorious news": IzumiyaTatsuro, *The Minami Organ* (Rangoon, 1967), p. 82.
193   "a country of Negroes and Jews": Mack Smith, p. 273.
194   "The attack, whatever it may": Steinbeck, p. 248, 8 Dec. 1941.
194   *Ladies' Home Journal* had published: *How America Lives* (Henry Holt, 1941).
194   "War is changing": ibid., p. 20.
195   "I knew after Pearl Harbor": Arthur Schlesinger, *A Life in the Twentieth Century* (Mariner Books, 2000), p. 287.
195   "The war was neither": John Morton Blum, *V Was for Victory* (Harcourt Brace, 1976), pp. 201, 89.
195   "We arrived in the midst": Schlesinger, pp. 287–88.
196   Geoffrey Perrett has observed: Perrett, p. 199.

CHAPTER NINE   JAPAN'S SEASON OF TRIUMPH

198   "itching to beat": John Dower, *War Without Mercy* (Pantheon, 1986), p. 242.
198   "How many really die": Emiko Ohnuki-Tierney, *Kamikaze Diaries* (University of Chicago Press, 2006), p. 62.
198   "Japan, why don't I": ibid., p. 79 et seq.
199   "Each evening we": Evelyn M. Monahan and Rosemary Neidel-Greenlee, *All This Hell* (Kentucky University Press, 2000).
199   "It was a joke": ibid., p. 8.
199   "modern Pompeiians": Bayly and Harper, p. 141.
199   There was a mutiny: ibid., p. 66.
199   "most frail, tarty": ibid., p. 111.
200   "I said to myself": Colin Smith, *Singapore Burning*, p. 123.
200   "one section of": ibid., p. 146.
201   "How is this possible?": ibid., p. 157.
201   "We now understood": Col. Masanobu Tsuji, *Japan's Greatest Victory, Britain's Worst Defeat* (Spellmount, 1997), p. 91.
201   "Brussels ball": Diana Cooper, *Trumpets from the Steep* (Hart Davis, 1960), p. 127.
204   "Every man waved": Smith, p. 220.
204   "The din was terrific": ibid., p. 238.
204   "scenes of indescribable": ibid., p. 245.
204   "A nice, good man . . . calm": ibid., p. 286.
205   "The Jitra line": Tsuji, p. 102.
206   "They took my father": Smith, p. 416.
206   "a thing which I am sure": Bayly and Harper, p. 120.
207   "The British are treating": ibid., p. 124.
207   "We have not treated": Smith, p. 426.
207   "That is the end": Bayly and Harper, p. 130.
208   "It was as if": Smith, p. 438.
208   "I don't think": ibid., p. 496.
208   "I myself only feel": ibid., p. 473.

208   "Having lost their nerve": ibid., p. 480.
209   "In civil life I am": Bayly and Harper, p. 142.
210   "Their conduct was bestial": BNA WO106/2550B.
210   "It shouldn't have happened": Smith, p. 497.
210   "Chin up, girls": ibid., p. 533.
210   "The fall of Singapore": Bayly and Harper, p. 126.
210   "had been handed over": ibid., p. 147.
210   "The area presented": Stephen Abbott, *And All My War Is Done* (Pentland, 1991), p. 31.
211   "The heavens had indeed": Bayly and Harper, p. 117.
211   "I saw them tramping": Smith, p. 550.
211   "Groups of them were": Harries and Harries, p. 264.
212   "We had cause": John Kennedy, *The Business of War* (Hutchinson, 1957), p. 198.
213   "I moved to the Nipponese": Edward Dunlop, *The Diaries of "Weary": Dunlop* (Viking, 1986), pp. 12–13.
214   In a little house: Yvonne Vaz Ezdani, ed., *Songs of the Survivors* (Noronha Goa, 2007).
214   "Out! Quick!": Daw Sein, *Les Dix milles vies d'une femme birmane* (Claude Delachet Fuillon, 1978), pp. 152–55.
215   "I'm not dead!": Edzani, p. 87.
215   "Life begins with": Bayly and Harper, p. 161.
215   "All we saw were": Julian Thompson, *Forgotten Voices of Burma* (Ebury, 2009), p. 21.
215   "among other subject": ibid., p. 164.
215   "We Europeans lived": ibid., p. 88.
216   "It is rather disheartening": KCL LHA Brooke Popham Papers File 5 7/18/2.
216   "[The Japanese] not only": John Smyth, *Before the Dawn* (Cassell, 1957) pp. 139–40.
216   "a country which had lost": Mi Mi Khaing, *A Burmese Family* (Longman, 1946), p. 130.
217   "It came to us": Tatsuro, p. 120.
217   "Has Singapore fallen?": ibid., p. 142.
217   "We didn't know what hit us": Bayly and Harper, p. 175.
217   "I sent my runner": Thompson, *Burma*, pp. 11–12.
218   "We were arrogant": ibid., p. 41.
218   "The general atmosphere": Bayly and Harper, p. 160.
218   "a Harley Street specialist": ibid., p. 163.
220   "The attitude of the army": Thompson, *Burma*, p. 34.
221   "We always felt": Bayly and Harper, p. 339.
221   "How thrilling it was": ibid., p. 173.
222   "The clearing was littered": Geoffrey Tyson, *Forgotten Frontier*, p. 79.
222   "Her voice soared clear": Ezdani, p. 80.
223   "The medical wards are": Mrs. G. Portal, quoted in Bayly and Harper, p. 189.
223   "It is the misfortune": Jawaharlal Nehru, *Selected Works of Nehru* (Orient Longman, 1980), Vol. 12, p. 269.

CHAPTER TEN   SWINGS OF FORTUNE

224   "We cannot win": James Reston, *Prelude to Victory* (Knopf, 1942), p. x.
224   "The Army . . . are aiming at": Slessor Papers File 12c.
225   "After Pearl Harbor": USMHI Forrest Pogue, *The Supreme Command* files.

225   "It will be a long, hard war": Christopher Thorne, *The Issue of War* (Oxford, 1985), p. 25.
225   "People are crazy": Blum, p. 97.
225   "The Good War myth": Schlesinger, pp. 283–84.
226   "The men have no great": Pogue, p. 335.
226   A behaviourist noted: Perrett, p. 213.
226   "Suddenly we realized": Fred Mears, *Carrier Combat* (Doubleday, 1944), p. 3.
227   "It was amazing how long": Kiernan, p. 3.
227   "Apparently it takes": Ernie Pyle, *Here Is Your War* (Pocket, 1945), p. 555.
228   "They came up the boulevards": Mydans, p. 147.
228   "I guess we are": Elizabeth Norman, *Band of Angels* (Random House, 1999), p. 66.
228   "Scores of Japs ripped": William E. Dyess, *The Dyess Story* (Putnam, 1944), p. 43.
229   "the most deplorable": John Glusman, *Conduct Under Fire* (Viking, 2007), p. 136.
229   "They were usually": Monahan and Neidel-Greenlee, p. 41.
229   The wounded often: ibid., p. 50.
229   "The argument raged": Alfred Weinstein, *Barbed Wire Surgeon* (Macmillan, 1947), p. 34.
230   "Now we knew": Donald Knox, *Death March* (Harcourt Brace, 1981), p. 121.
230   "If you fell": ibid., p. 136.
230   "just so disappointed": Glusman, p. 197.
231   "Poor Wainwright!": *The Eisenhower Diaries* (Norton, 1981), p. 54.
231   "The news commentators": Blum, p. 54.
234   "Okay, so long": Captain Walter Karig and Commander Eric Purdon, *Battle Report: Pacific War Middle Phase* (Rinehart, 1946), p. 19.
234   "It was pretty discouraging": E. T. Wooldridge, ed., *Carrier Warfare in the Pacific* (Smithsonian, 1993), p. 41.
234   "They were curious": ibid., p. 42.
234   "fires had gotten": ibid., p. 45.
237   "Many of the sailors": Kiernan, p. 13.
237   "We had a small group": Wooldridge, p. 281.
238   "I just felt at home": ibid., p. 285.
238   a sailor on the *Hornet*: ibid., p. 68.
238   "There was oil very": ibid., p. 168.
240   "There is something in": Herman Melville, *Israel Potter* (1854).
240   "After a battle is over": Walter Lord, *Incredible Victory* (New York, 1967), p. 87.
242   "The fate of the United States": John Costello, *The Pacific War* (Collins, 1981), p. 285.
243   "All of us knew": The Battle of Midway Round Table, http.//www.midway12 .org.
244   "When approximately one mile": U.S. Naval Historical Center, Esders After-Action report.
244   "I was not aware": Kiernan, p. 45.
245   "I was mad because": Wooldridge, pp. 56–57.
245   "I saw this glint": ibid., p. 58.
245   "As I looked back": Tom Cheek, *A Ring of Coral*, Battle of Midway Roundtable, http//home.comcast.net/r2russ/midway. ringcoral.htm.
246   "I was horrified": Mitsuo Fuchida and Masatake Okimuya, *Midway: The Battle That Doomed Japan* (Annapolis, 1955), p. 177.
249   "In the dirty dawn": Robert Leckie, *Helmet for My Pillow* (Ebury, 2010), p. 57.
249   "Wizard!!!": Costello, p. 177.

250 The enemy ships had: Bruce Loxton and Chris Coulthard-Clark, *The Shame of Savo* (Allen & Unwin, 1994), pp. 143–47.

251 "The navy was still": ibid., p. 265.

252 "Whether these were": Donald Miller, *D-Days in the Pacific* (Simon & Schuster, 2005), p. 68.

252 "At daybreak a couple": ibid., p. 72.

253 "Here was cacophony": Leckie, p. 78.

253 "Morale was very bad": Miller, pp. 67–68.

254 "Everything was so": James Jones, *The Thin Red Line* (Collins, 1963), p. 43.

254 "[It] was the most tremendous": Ronald Spector, *Eagle Against the Sun* (Viking, 1985), pp. 205–6.

259 "I have seen men": George Johnston, *The Toughest Fighting in the World* (Duell, Sloan & Pearce, 1943), p. 5.

259 "What a hell of a load": ibid., p. 8.

259 "This is not murder": ibid., p. 4.0

259 "I do not believe": ibid., p. 198.

260 "Confusion was the keynote": ibid., p. 45.

261 "Our troops are fighting": ibid., pp. 167–68.

261 "It was a sly and": Robert Eichelberger, *Our Jungle Road to Tokyo* (Nashville Battery Classics 1989), pp. 21–23.

CHAPTER ELEVEN   THE BRITISH AT SEA

265 "The bombers": Julian Thompson, *The War at Sea* (Sidgwick & Jackson, 1996), p. 113.

266 "I couldn't see anything": ibid., p. 149.

267 "sheer unmitigated hell": J. B. Lamb, *The Corvette Navy: True Stories from Canada's Atlantic War* (Macmillan, Toronto, 1979), p. 73.

270 "It was a continual": AI Harris 11 Oct. 1976, *Bomber Command* files.

270 An average of: Stephen Howarth and David Law, eds., *The Battle of the Atlantic, 1939–45* (Greenhill, 1994), Jurgen Rohwer, p. 411.

271 "One minute we had": ibid., p. 51.

271 "Trusting to make": Richard Woodman, *The Real Cruel Sea* (Murray, 2004), p. 166.

273 "Living and working": Howarth and Law, p. 215.

274 "race and other population": Potsdam Vol. 9/1, p. 612.

274 "There will be no": Erich Topp, quoted in Howarth and Law, p. 217.

276 "amounted almost to": Corelli Barnett, *Engage the Enemy More Closely* (Hodder & Stoughton, 1991), p. 486.

277 "This low state of efficiency": quoted in Howarth and Law, p. 199.

277 "These problems often": ibid., p. 522.

280 "While one could keep": Thompson, *War at Sea*, p. 160.

281 "I waited for the swell": Richard Woodman, *Arctic Convoys* (John Murray, 2001), p. 323.

283 "We were kept in": ibid., p. 107.

285 "The mood is bitter": ibid., p. 220.

286 "rather sad and twitchy": ibid., p. 161.

286 "The arrival in Kola": Thompson, *War at Sea*, p. 161.

287 "God knows we paid": Woodman, *Arctic*, p. 445.

289 "a fantastically wonderful": Woodman, *Malta*, p. 379.

289 "I felt indeed that": Thompson, *War at Sea*, p. 192.

289   "She presented a": ibid., p. 192.
291   "Most of us felt": ibid., p. 195.
291   "I could never have": Woodman, *Malta*, p. 403.

CHAPTER TWELVE   THE FURNACE: RUSSIA IN 1942

293   "We arrived at 8 p.m.": Brontman, p. 132.
293   "We're having a little": *Pisma S Ognennogo Rubezha 1941*, 19 May 1942.
294   "Eastern man is very": Gunther Blumentritt, quoted in *The Fatal Decisions* (Michael Joseph, 1952), pp. 37–38.
295   "One explosion next": Potsdam Vol. 6, p. 938.
295   "We wept as we retreated": Merridale, p. 133.
296   Women also policed: Brontman, p. 22, 18 June 1942.
296   "psychologically prepared for": ibid., p. 31, 4 April 1942.
298   "The night was terribly dark": Front Diary of N. F. Belov, 1941–44, in *Pisma S Ognennogo Rubezha, 1941–1945*, 23 April 1942.
298   "I have the inescapable": BNA WO208/1777.
299   In August 1942: Jeffrey, p. 376.
299   "There was, I said": Anders, p. 124.
299   "we Poles were now": ibid., p. 114.
301   "The civilians are howling": *Pisma S Ognennogo Rubezha*, pp. 271–72, 23 Oct. 1942.
301   "These fools have allowed": Grossman, p. 127.
301   "We have to learn": *Pisma S Ognennogo Rubezha*, p. 273.
302   "Results deplorable": Belov diary, 9 Sept. 1942.
302   "We ploughed over the": Potsdam, Vol. 6, p. 1097.
302   "The streets of the city": Merridale, p. 150.
303   "The officers made them": Vladimir Pershanin, *Shtrafniki, radvedchiki, pekhota* [Punishment Companies, Reconnaissance, Infantry] (Moscow, 2010), p. 177.
303   "The wounded, more than": ibid., p. 185.
303   "Approaching this place": Grossman, p. 151.
303   " 'I had been imagining' ": ibid., p. 183.
303   "I miss you very much": ibid., p. 152.
303   "There's firing and thunder": ibid., p. 170.
304   7 "cowards" and 1: Bellamy, p. 520.
305   "Courage is infectious here": Grossman, p. 174.
305   "Hello, my dear Marusya!": *Pisma S Ognennogo Rubezha*, p. 273.
306   "In connection with the": Bellamy, p. 380.
306   "During the night": Nikulin memoir.
306   "It shows in the expression": Jones, *Seige*, p. 269.
307   "This happiness": ibid., p. 276.
307   "A thought is forming": ibid., p. 279.
307   "They said that the": Merridale, p. 165.
308   "Just as I lay down": Belov diary, 8 Oct. 1942.
308   "The whole place trembled": Metelmann, p. 120.
309   "This is the most beautiful": Knoke, p. 80.
310   "Our thoughts and conversations": Poppel, p. 99.
310   "The implacable struggle": Potsdam, Vol. 11/1, p. 583.
311   "Vehicles complete with": Eugenio Corti, *Few Returned: 28 Days on the Russian Front, Winter 1942–43* (University of Missouri Press, 1997), p. 10.

311 "But how can you": ibid., p. 26.
311 "Countless instances of": ibid., pp. 30–31.
311 "the wounded were lying": ibid., p. 61.
311 "I was greeted by": ibid., p. 65.
312 "During halts on those": ibid., p. 194.
312 "We watched those aircraft": ibid., p. 76.
312 "Back in the distant *patria*": ibid., p. 78.
312 "It was extremely painful": ibid.
312 "I . . . asked myself": ibid., p. 138.
312 "in the palm of his": ibid., p. 218.
312 At the end of 1942: Mack Smith, p. 293.
313 "I'm in an exceptional": Merridale, p. 162.
313 "There's no modesty": Grossman, p. 225.
313 "The killing of thousands": Koa Wing, p. 152.
314 "The day of battle": Belov diary, 13 Feb. 1943.
314 "The man is not to my liking": Halder diaries, p. 387.
315 "Our army suddenly": G. A. Kumanyov, *Close to Stalin [Ryadom so Stalinym]* (Moscow, 1999), p. 38.

CHAPTER THIRTEEN   LIVING WITH WAR

317 "I suppose our position": Antony Hichens, *Gunboat Command* (Pen & Sword, 2007), p. 96.
318 "One of the fascinations": USMHI Pogue, *The Supreme Command* files, Morgan interview.
318 "In the early war years": Max Hastings, *Armageddon* files.
318 "Dearest Mum": Robert Kershaw, p. 203.
319 "I am absolutely fed up": Thompson, *The War at Sea*, p. 111.
319 "It must take about seven": Peter White, *With the Jocks* (Sutton, 2001), p. 37.
319 "My whole generation": Koa Wing, p. 173, 5 April 1943.
320 "After a few minutes": ibid., p. 60.
320 "I've never flirted": ibid., p. 71.
320 "After dinner I": *Pisma S Ognennogo Rubezha*, p. 210.
320 "There is nothing so": Blythe, *Private Words*, 28 July 1943.
320 "I learned to take care": AI Thompson, *Armageddon* files.
321 "We somehow hoped": AI Moody, *Armageddon* files.
321 "My comrades were mostly": Ron Davidson MS, *Armageddon* files.
321 "I accept this life": Ronald Blythe, ed., *Components of the Scene* (Penguin, 1966), p. 85.
321 "When the tents are down": USMHI Bruce Papers, Box 6.
322 "So much of this war": Harold Fennema MS, *Armageddon* files.
322 "a nightmare": Eugene Gagliardi MS, *Armageddon* files.
322 "As an urban selectee's": E.J. Kahn, *New Yorker*, 5 Dec. 1942.
322 "The personal bodily": Eugene Sledge, *With the Old Breed at Peleliu and Okinawa* (Ebury, 2010), p. 91.
322 "The damnable truth": Farley Mowat, *And No Birds Sang* (Cassell, 1980), p. 203.
323 "There was nothing subtle": Sledge, p. 72.
323 "Give a Jock a rifle": Borthwick, p. 61.
323 "Young Cutter": White, p. 155.
324 "We had learned our first": IWM 92/1/1 C. R. Eke MS, *A Game of Soldiers*.

324 "It's hard for guys my age": Mowat, p. 107.
324 "It's funny, the things": James Jones and Art Weithas, *WW II: A Chronicle of Soldiering* (Grosset & Dunlap, 1975).
325 "One learned to accept": AI Mahlo, *Armageddon* files.
325 "I was so young": AI Moser, *Armageddon* files.
325 "The man disintegrated": Roscoe Blunt, *Foot Soldier: A Combat's Infantryman's War in Europe* (Da Capo Press, 2002), p. 86.
325 "Life was so free": Norman Craig, *The Broken Plume* (IWM, 1982), p. 77.
325 "Nobody has the courage": Moltke, p. 275, 26 Jan. 1943.
325 "We weren't going to": Paul Fussell, *The Boys' Crusade* (Weidenfeld & Nicolson, 2004), p. 98.
326 "The company was": AI Gunther, *Armageddon* files.
326 "I should like": *Spectator,* 16 July 1943.
326 "The report has almost": *Spectator,* 18 Dec. 1942.
326 "If it is not accepted": David Elliott quoted in *Private Words,* p. 183, 30 April 1943.
326 "The British Army is not": Michael Foot, *Bevan* (McGibbon & Kee, 1965), p. 388.
326 "Tea from the British": Blum, p. 66.
327 "These gravely yearned-for": ibid., p. 64.
327 "a beautiful young man": AI Beavers, *Armageddon* files.
327 "I'm going home!": Schoo MS, *Armageddon* files.
327 "Any guy overseas": Blum, p. 65.
327 "I see all these thousands": Steinbeck, p. 264.
327 "I'm going to start": Blum, p. 67.
327 "They are the most": Iris Origo, *War in Val D'Orcia* (Cape, 1947), p. 58, 15 Aug. 1943.
328 "Yesterday I received": Belov diary, 31 Dec. 1942.
329 "Any personal balance": Sebastian, p. 585, 2 Dec. 1943.
329 "A pale, thin woman": *Pisma S Ognennogo Rubezha,* p. 273, 11 Sept. 1942.
329 "What is left of it?": ibid., p. 273, 1 Oct. 1942.
329 "We've got to work": ibid., 20 Oct 1942.
330 "We had no life": Braithwaite, p. 131.
330 "Farm times became": Lizzie Collingham, *The Taste of War* (Allen Lane, 2011), p. 78.
330 "People were not": Fraser, p. 183.
330 Edward McCormick: letter in possession of Mrs. Miranda Corben.
331 Gladys Skillett: *Times* obituary, 27 Feb. 2010, by Colin Smith.
332 "Now it is dawn": Miriam Mafai, *Pane Nero: Donne e vita quotidiana nella seconda Guerra mondiale* (Arnoldo Mondadori Editore, 1987), pp. 159–62.
332 "The cold and damp": ibid., p. 243.
333 "It was sad to see": Say and Holland, p. 297.
333 Stefan Kurylak: IWM Kurylak MS.
333 "We are being taken": IWM 99/9/1 Poznanski MS.
334 "The extraordinary thing": Anthony Powell, *A Writer's Notebook* (Heinemann, 2001), p. 94.
334 "Woke half drunk": Michael Davie, ed., *The Diaries of Evelyn Waugh* (Weidenfeld & Nicolson, 1976), p. 567, 1 June 1944.
334 "in comparison to": Last, p. 221, 11 Oct. 1942.
334 "Christmas is going to be": Martin Crook, ed., *Wartime Letters of a West Kent Man* (privately published, 2007).

335 "We never knew": *Spectator,* 14 Dec. 1942.

335 "His strange uniform": Blythe, *Private Words,* p. 43.

335 "Her face was wooden": Koa Wing, p. 188, 7 Sept. 1943.

336 "I had a very nice": Studs Terkel, *The Good War* (Hamish Hamilton, 1984), p. 224.

336 "I cried because": Koa Wing, p. 135, 16 June 1942.

336 "He was a soldier": Terkel, p. 118.

337 Bernice Schmidt: Janine Sinkoskey Brodine, ed., *Missing Pieces* (Hara Publishing, 2000), p. 49.

337 "What are you thinking": Koa Wing, p. 144, 9 Oct. 1942.

337 "Is it possible that": Wolff-Monckeburg, p. 35, 12 Jan. 1941.

337 "One grows ever more": ibid., p. 60, 25 June 1942.

338 "Food was our obsession": Longmate, p. 150.

338 "One morning a jar": ibid., p. 156.

338 "In this place one's mind": Tamsin Day-Lewis, ed., *Last Letters Home* (Macmillan, 1995).

339 "Imports of European delicacies": Blum, p. 98.

339 "I'm sick of the same": Collingham, p. 112.

339 In pursuit of the: ibid., p. 217.

340 "As they died the government": Theodore White and Annalee Jacoby, *Thunder Out of China* (Gollancz, 1947), pp. 166–67.

340 "were still living": Collingham, p. 116.

340 "My father had no": Mafai, p. 167.

340 "Hunger governed all": Alan Moorehead, *Eclipse* (Granta, 2000), p. 66.

341 "and had the ordinary": Norman Lewis, *Naples '44,* p. 26, 4 Oct. 1943.

341 " 'In order to win the war' ": BNA FO371 ZM257/18/22.

342 That only a relatively: an exemplary examination of these issues is found in David W. Ellwood, *Italy 1943–45* (Leicester University Press, 1985).

342 "A very different": ibid., p. 152.

343 "and is, I suspect": Koa Wing, p. 172, 25 March 1943.

343 "My initiation into": Longmate, p. 123.

343 "The airless workplace": Baring, p. 55.

345 "I suppose in everything": Koa Wing, p. 129, 15 April 1942.

345 Lazar Brontman recorded: Brontman, p. 185, 29 Aug. 1942.

345 "tears running down": Nikolai Nikutin internet MS.

345 "I went to visit": *Pisma S Ognennogo Rubezha,* 18 March 1943.

346 "The PPZh is our": Grossman, p. 120.

346 "Villages have become": Grossman, p. 119.

346 "Dear Vova!": *Pisma S Voiny,* p. 83.

346 "It sometimes seems": *Pisma S Ognennogo Rubezha,* Kalinichenko letters, 1 Dec. 1942 and 1 Feb. 1943.

348 "I push the pedals": ibid., Kalinichenko letters, 20 Feb. 1944.

348 "Maybe you should": AI Beavers, *Armageddon* files.

348 "I always believed that women": AI Harris, 14 Oct. 1976, *Bomber Command* files.

349 Air Vice-Marshal Edward: AI Addison, *Bomber Command* files.

349 "It's bloody rubbish": AI Owen, *Bomber Command* files.

349 "I was young": AI von Joest, *Armageddon* files.

349 "I am . . . almost": Koa Wing, p. 94, 17 June 1941.

349 "I did not want to": ibid., p. 104, 7 Oct. 1941.

349 "one of the happiest": ibid., p. 248, 31 Dec. 1944.

350 "Hostel life has changed": ibid., p. 257, 31 March 1945.

350 "Honey, it's pitiful": Fennema MS, *Armageddon* files.
350 "The war has shaken": *Pisma S Ognennogo Rubezha*, 1 July 1943.
350 "I would sometimes": Mafai, p. 177.

CHAPTER FOURTEEN   OUT OF AFRICA

353 "The English were kind": Dugan MS, *Overlord* files.
353 "The force of tradition": Bob Raymond, *A Yank in Bomber Command* (Moynihan, 1977), p. 101.
353 "Americans have a greater": USNA, 25 March 1942: Survey of Intelligence Materials No. 16.
353 "The Americans . . . knows us": BNA FO371/34116.
354 "The great and rich men": Keith Douglas, *Alamein to Zem Zem* (Penguin, 1967), p. 87.
354 "A whisper is": Harold Nicolson, *Diaries* (Collins, 1965), Vol. 2, 11 Feb. 1942.
354 "The conduct of our": Commons, 22 April 1942.
355 "Things here get better": Ostellino, p. 216.
355 "I assume that England": Victor Klemperer, *I Shall Bear Witness* (Weidenfeld & Nicolson, 1999), Vol. 2, p. 117.
360 "We are stuck": Vallicella, p. 39.
360 "For sixteen months": ibid., p. 46.
360 "every man for himself": ibid., p. 55.
360 "How can we keep": ibid., p. 58.
360 "We are at the end": ibid., p. 105.
360 "Before an attack": Craig, p. 75.
361 "I have seen many": Vallicella, p. 95.
361 "Officers and men": F. Formica, ed., *Account of the Battle of Deir El Murra*, Diary of Second Lieutenant Vincenzo Formica, www.fereamole.it.
362 "All our illusions": ibid., 3 Nov. 1942.
362 "As we drove, vehicles": ibid.
363 "I met Captain Bondi": ibid., 17 Nov. 1942.
363 "In the tragedy": Vallicella, p. 117.
363 "Reading this order": ibid., p. 119.
363 Panzer officer Tassilo: Hagen, pp. 176–77.
364 "In five minutes": Alfred Perrott-White, *French Legionnaire* (John Murray, 1953), p. 147.
365 "Suddenly realized": Koa Wing, p. 148.
365 "It is enormously": Moltke, p. 260.
365 "Good news came": Belov diary, 10 Nov. 1942.
365 "We hope he is right": Vallicella, p. 125.
366 "At midnight mass": ibid., p. 154.
366 "Never has a meal": ibid., p. 155.
366 "I think the Americans": Koa Wing, p. 168, 28 Feb. 1943.
368 "the pursuit of Rommel": MHI Pogue, *The Supreme Command* interview files.
368 "I think back": Formica diary, 11 Sept. 1943.

CHAPTER FIFTEEN   THE BEAR TURNS: RUSSIA IN 1943

369 "Everyone talks incessantly": Brontman, p. 62, 12 Sept. 1942.
369 "The Russians weren't very": AI Godau, *Armageddon* files.
370 "The frontal attacks": Pershanin, p. 198.

370 "Major Anoprienko": Belov diary, 13 March 1943.

370 "It was hard to": Pershanin, p. 41.

371 "For ten days": *Pisma S Voiny*, p. 199.

371 "We never heard": Guy Sajer, *The Forgotten Soldier* (Sphere, 1971), p. 171.

373 "They are so frightening": Grossman, p. 249.

373 "Not only divisions": Merridale, p. 261.

373 "I received the letter": *Pisma S Ognennogo Rubezha*, pp. 199–202.

375 "Today a Youssef": Belov diary, 13 Jan. 1943.

375 "They are greenhorns": ibid., 11 Aug. 1943.

375 "This is the first time": ibid., 2 June 1943.

375 "A German deserter": *Pisma S Ognennogo Rubezha*, 31 March 1943.

375 "a big fellow": Belov diary, 2 June 1943.

376 "How fortunate were": Merridale, p. 194.

376 "So many families": *Pisma S Voiny*, p. 194.

376 "It grew hot": Rotmistrov, quoted in Robin Cross, *Citadel* (O'Mara, 1993), p. 195.

378 "In a few hours": *Pisma S Voiny*, pp. 132–33.

378 "The 676th Rifle Regiment": *Ognennaya duga*, p. 34.

378 "Forward!": Cross, p. 214.

379 "We had been warned": ibid., p. 215.

379 "It was an awesome scene": ibid., p. 229.

380 "The Germans sent tanks": Brontman, pp. 39–40, 26 July 1942.

380 "It is a shame": Merridale, p. 183.

380 The Germans had permitted: Brontman, p. 162, 28 July 1943.

380 "It's hard now": Merridale, p. 203.

381 "We've seen no bread": Brontman, p. 153, 14 July 1943.

382 "There is no bread": *Ognennaya duga*, p. 52.

382 "Death, and only death": ibid., pp. 79–80.

383 "We passed through": *Pisma S Ognennogo Rubezha*, 9 Oct. 1943.

383 "I was shaken by": Pershanin, p. 35.

383 "[They] were a terrible": ibid., p. 27.

383 "We march in the footsteps": ibid., 1 Nov. 1943.

384 "The deputy battalion commander": Grossman, p. 247.

384 "The enemy's front": *Pisma S Ognennogo Rubezha*, 20 Sept. 1943.

385 "The weather and mud": Belov diary, 28 Nov. 1943.

385 "The soldiers with whom": *Ognennaya duga*, pp. 89–90.

385 " 'You shit!' ": Perhsanin, p. 78.

385 "This morning the combat": Cross, p. 250.

385 "Frantic men were abandoning": Sajer, p. 315.

386 "Each German soldier": Hagen, p. 181.

CHAPTER SIXTEEN   DIVIDED EMPIRES

387 "The cost in men": Nicholas Monsarrat, in his autobiographical novel *The Cruel Sea* (Cassell, 1951), pp. 151–52.

388 "My father was able": Tom Bower, *Nazi Gold* (HarperCollins, 1997), p. 13.

388 "gigantic sums" ibid., p. 58.

388 "irrelevant under Swiss law": ibid., p. 111.

389 A January 1944 opinion survey: USNA State Department Opinion Surveys, RG59, Box 11.

389 "had a very vague": Fydor Mochalasky, *Gulag Boss* (Oxford, 2010), p. 141.

389   "The Japs live like": Blum, p. 160.
390   "It was a very white": Capano MS, *Armageddon* files.
390   "The danger," they wrote: Blum, p. 92.
390   "as the Roman legions": ibid., p. 149.
391   "If we send you": AI Carullo, *Armageddon* files.
391   sergeant Henry Kissinger: AI Kissinger, *Armageddon* files.
391   "very interesting to": Hagen, p. 169.
392   "All on board felt": Commandant Bazoche Operational Report, quoted in Tute, p. 206.
394   "I must record reality": *Generazione ribelle: Diari e lettere dal 1943 al 1945 a cura di Mario Avagliano* (Einaudi Storia, 2006), p. 77.
394   "I feel that his": Anne-Marie Walters, *Moondrop to Gascony* (MPG Books, 2009), p. 233.
395   "He will not have": Peter Kemp, *The Thorns of Memory* (Sinclair-Stevenson, 1990), p. 196.
395   "As time went on": ibid., p. 200.
397   "We thought perhaps": Killingray, p. 61.
397   "When we heard about": ibid., p. 59.
398   "Sinclair . . . had the list": ibid., p. 50.
398   "*Sole, sole, sole*": ibid., p. 160.
398   "Our boss was involved": ibid., p. 54.
398   "powerful juju": ibid., p. 86.
399   A further 24: ibid., p. 122.
399   In India, segregated: ibid., p. 109.
400   "We were lucky": ibid., pp. 134–35.
400   "Poor Corporal Atang": ibid., p. 172.
400   "a white man's war": Christopher Somerville, *Our War* (Weidenfeld & Nicolson, 1998), p. 183.
401   "There's a war going": ibid., p. 29.
402   "A nasty evening": Richard Hough, *One Boy's War* (Heinemann, 1975), p. 17.
402   In August 1942: *Public Opinion*, p. 86.
402   "Our enemy was primarily": Anwar Sadat, *In Search of Identity* (Collins, 1978), p. 26.
402   "We are a group": ibid., p. 25.
403   "although his reason": Edgar Snow, *Journey to the Beginning* (Gollancz, 1959), p. 206.
403   "It [is] obvious": *Works of Nehru*, Vol. 12, p. 39, 25 Dec. 1942.
403   "We couldn't help": Smith, *Singapore Burning*, p. 57.
403   "I could see no particular": Cooper, *Trumpets*, p. 131.
403   "I have always cherished": Bayly and Harper, p. 343.
404   "Winston burbled away endlessly": Amery, p. 104.
405   Veer Damodar Savarkar: Jayakar Papers 709, 1940, National Archives of India.
405   "The present is not": *Towards Freedom: Documents on the Movement for Independence in India 1940*, Pt.1 (Oxford University Press, 1978).
405   "I am now in the army": Bayly and Harper, p. 74.
406   "Yet every nation": *Statesman*, 10 June 1940.
406   "In the summer of 1940": *Works of Nehru*, Vol. 13, p. 59, 13 Feb. 1943.
406   "there is no question": ibid., Vol. 12, p. 2.
406   "There is a large": Linlithgow, quoted in Madhusree Mukerjee, *Churchill's Secret War* (Basic, 2010), p. 63.
407   "an exhilarating departure": Bayly and Harper, p. 248.

408 "Those bloody idiots": Clive Branson, *British Soldier in India: The Letters of Clive Branson* (Communist Party London, 1944), pp. 87, 134.

408 "in the eyes of Mahatma Gandhi": Bayly and Harper, p. 303.

408 "venereal disease–ridden": ibid., p. 448.

409 "when there is tragedy": *Selected Works of Nehru*, Vol. 13, p. 19, 3 Oct. 1942.

409 "provisional Indian government": Bayly and Harper, p. 322.

409 "After being captured": Thompson, *Burma*, p. 254.

409 "I am not a doll": ibid., p. 326.

410 "I did not believe that": ibid., p. 327.

410 "We could not afford": Mukerjee, p. 282.

410 "There I saw nearly": ibid.

410 "We come home to": ibid., p. 286.

411 "A concession to one": ibid., p. 103.

411 "There is no reason": ibid., p. 117.

411 "In Sapurapota village": ibid., pp. 154, 167, 151.

412 "rickety babies": ibid., p. 287.

412 "Reports from Bengal": *Works of Nehru*, Vol. 13, p. 242.

412 "Cabinet . . . [Winston] talked": John Barnes and David Nicholson, eds., *The Empire at Bay: The Leo Amery Diaries 1929–45* (Hutchinson, 1988), p. 1026, 21 Jan. 1945.

CHAPTER SEVENTEEN   ASIAN FRONTS

414 "In her great effort": Edgar Snow, *Saturday Evening Post*, June 1936.

414 "Local people were much": Jonathan Fenby, *Generalissimo* (Free Press, 2003), p. 315.

415 The Japanese were the only: Jeffrey Lockwood, *Six-Legged Soldiers: Using Insects as Weapons of War* (Oxford, 2009), p. 108 and passim.

415 That the Japanese attempted: Daniel Barenblatt, *A Plague Upon Humanity* (Souvenir, 2004).

417 "One of them was": AI Lin Yajin, *Nemesis* files.

417 "he told me I was": AI Deng Yumin, *Nemesis* files.

418 "Terrible things were done": AI Hando, *Nemesis* files.

418 "America and Britain had been": Bayly and Harper, p. 2.

420 "in Japan the infantryman": ibid., p. 274.

420 "I am far from satisfied": Marshall Papers, Box 64/27.

420 "a gigantic system": Hugh Dalton, *Diaries*, ed. Ben Pimlott Jonathan (Cape, 1986), 4 Aug. 1944.

420 "Neither I nor my Gurkha": Thompson, *Forgotten Voices of Burma*, p. 71.

421 "I had a wounded Gurkha": ibid., p. 83.

421 "The newspapers back in India": ibid., p. 107.

423 "It was lined with amphtracs": Karl Albrecht, *Tarawa Remembered*, in *Follow Me*, November 1993, p. 28.

423 "The water never seemed": Miller, p. 105

426 Though Roosevelt and his: *Public Opinion*, p. 263.

CHAPTER EIGHTEEN   ITALY: HIGH HOPES, SOUR FRUITS

427 "How is victory possible": Evelyn Waugh, *Diaries*, p. 559.

428 "Everywhere the British": Marshall Papers, Box 64/27.

429 "A marked change": Origo, p. 55.

430 "We surrender": Carlo D'Este, *Bitter Victory* (Collins, 1988), p. 244.
430 "In my opinion": Poppel, p. 123.
430 "The Tommies obviously": ibid., p. 130.
430 "You have to hand": ibid., p. 133.
431 "in a mood of fiesta": Rick Atkinson, *Day of Battle* (Henry Holt, 2007), p. 115.
431 "A queer race": Peter Schrijvers, *The Crash of Ruin* (New York University Press, 1998), p. 120.
431 "This is *not*": Atkinson, p. 127.
431 "plodding along": David Cole, *Rough Road to Rome* (Kimber, 1983), pp. 443–44.
433 "The Italians virtually never": D'Este, *Bitter Victory*, p. 439.
433 "A ghostly old woman": Jack Belden, *Time*, 23 Aug. 1943.
434 "The end is now": Klemperer, Vol. 2, p. 303.
434 "We don't really": ibid., p. 349.
434 "With more grit": Hagen, p. 74.
435 "We hoped and hoped": Wolff-Monckeburg, p. 73.
436 "The Germans have undoubtedly": Wigram's report, a penetrating analysis of British tactical shortcomings which seems valid for the entire 1943–45 period, is printed as an appendix in Denis Forman, *To Reason Why* (André Deutsch, 1991), pp. 197–204.
437 "In the belief that": Lewis, p. 17.
437 "Shells whined swiftly": Michael Howard, *Captain Professor* (Continuum, 2004), p. 73.
437 "During the night": Peter Moore, *No Need to Worry* (Wilton 65, 2002), p. 109.
439 "Here we got our first": Hagen, p. 75.
440 "If the 'liberation' ": Origo, p. 101, 20 Oct. 1943.
440 "Italy would break": Atkinson, p. 251.
441 "The ground for fifty yards": John Guest, *Broken Images* (Hart Davis, 1949), p. 199.
441 "I hate to disillusion": Mowat, p. 137.
441 "Our boys aren't": Atkinson, p. 258.
441 "climbing a ladder": Richard Doherty, *A Noble Crusade* (Sarpedon, 1999), p. 159.
441 "I wish the people": George Biddle, *Artist at War* (Viking Press, 1944), p. 177.
442 "under a hail of fire": D. C. Bloomfield-Smith, ed., *Fourth Indian Reflections* (Larman, 1987), p. 59.
442 "The leading companies": ibid., p. 56.
442 "I feel that much": Franco Busatti, *Dal Volturno a Cassino* RSI, website.
443 "Wouldn't this be": Atkinson, pp. 288–89.
443 "I would like": ibid., p. 293.
444 "It is . . . necessary": Origo, p. 23, 1 April 1943.
444 "I won't fight on": ibid., p. 97.
444 "Half Italy is": *Generazione ribelle*, p. 25, 8 Sept. 1943.
444 "leader of a people": Eugenio Corti, *The Last Soldiers of the King* (University of Missouri Press, 2003), p. 108.
445 "We are poor wretches": *Generazione ribelle*, p. 48.
446 "All the children were": Mafai, p. 211.
446 "Whenever they take": Lewis, pp. 143–44.
447 "A woman's head appeared": Bloomfield-Smith, p. 50.
447 "Now it turns out": Mowat, p. 187.
448 "I'll be alive": Alex Bowlby, *Recollections of Rifleman Bowlby* (Leo Cooper, 1969), p. 127.
448 "Shooting in the early days": LHA Penney Papers 8/33.

448 "The peasants read these": Origo, p. 186, 21 May 1944.
448 "'Please—wouldn't the children'": ibid., p. 198.
448 "The Goums have completed": ibid., p. 236, 1 July 1944.
449 "Many had never": Milovan Djilas, *Wartime* (Secker & Warburg, 1980), p. 309.
449 "The country was very": Roderick Bailey, ed., *Forgotten Voices of the Secret War* (Ebury, 2008), p. 160.
450 Macedonia, which was: Dimitris Livanios, *The Macedonian Question* (Oxford, 2008), p. 119.
450 "The army of Mihailović": Bailey, p. 169.
451 "Sometimes [the Chetniks] would": ibid., p. 171.
451 "Unfortunately the Chetniks": ibid., p. 167.
451 "Look what you have": Djilas, p. 236.
452 "Covered with orchards": ibid., p. 139.
452 "Though quite a few": ibid., pp. 155, 160.
452 "You are fighting for": ibid., p. 170.
452 "All the villages": ibid., p. 180.
453 "It would be immoral": ibid., p. 197.
453 "They couldn't be told": ibid., p. 304.
453 "After we had been": *Diario di Guerra: Con gli Alpini in Montenegro 1941–1943* (Mursia, 2010), p. 15.
453 "We know, but there's": Djilas, p. 330.
454 "Why were doctors": ibid., p. 285
454 "He survived the war": ibid., p. 283.

CHAPTER NINETEEN   WAR IN THE SKY

455 "I saw myself as": E. P. Bone, unpublished MS, *Bomber Command* files.
455 "I experience an exhilaration": Wellum, p. 105.
455 "I would not trade": AI Dorfman, *Armageddon* files.
455 "We had all the glory": AI Wells, *Armageddon* files.
456 "I have never spoken": Day-Lewis, p. 81.
457 "Perhaps a quarter": AI Owen, *Bomber Command* files.
458 "With the start the Germans": AI Addison, *Bomber Command* files.
458 "[A] vital lesson": Alexander Seversky, *Victory Thru Air Power* (New York, 1942), p. 73.
459 In the second half: see Williamson Murray, *Luftwaffe* (Allen & Unwin, 1985), passim.
459 "We learned very early": Wooldridge, p. 196.
459 "A man approached death": Ernie Pyle, *V Was for Victory* (New York, 1945), p. 61.
459 "You were resigned": AI Bufton, *Bomber Command* files.
460 "I woke up!": *Bomber Command* correspondence.
460 "The briefings were very": AI Owen, *Bomber Command* files.
461 "In their efforts to": Hastings, *Bomber Command*, p. 104.
461 "Winston's attitude to": AI Harris, *Bomber Command* files.
462 " 'We could have kept' ": AI Brennan, *Armageddon* files.
462 "If you had losses": AI Maze, *Bomber Command* files.
462 "Good bods Pyatt, Donner": Bone MS.
462 "We learned to live": John Muirhead, *Those Who Fall* (Random House, 1986), p. 4.
463 "When I asked him": Cochrane MS, Cochrane papers.

463 "The wounds were superficial": Crafter MS, *Bomber Command* files.
463 "Thirty sorties in": Cochrane MS.
463 "I clearly remember": Raynes MS, *Bomber Command* files.
464 "You joked about": AI Owen.
464 "When a plane blew up": Harry H. Crosby, *A Wing and a Prayer* (Robson, 1993), p. 95.
465 "supported as he was": USMHI, Sir Frederick Morgan, quoted in Pogue, *The Supreme Command* files.
466 The Möhne was breached: John Sweetman, *The Dambusters Raid* (Arms & Armour, 1993), passim. This is the most authoritative account of the mission.
467 "We were told the British": Wolff-Monckeburg, p. 72.
467 Adam Tooze has made: Tooze, p. 556 and passim.
468 Adam Tooze believes: ibid., p. 603.
469 "These raids on": *Bomber Command* files.
469 "Hundreds of flak guns": Potsdam Vol. 9/1, p. 391.
470 "Our Führer ought": ibid., p. 382.
470 "often feeling that": ibid., p. 453.
470 "These elements cannot": Tooze, pp. 629–30.
471 "The white stripes moved": Potsdam, Vol. 9/1, p. 390.
472 "They were torn from": ibid., p. 75.
473 "At the front of the room": ibid., p. 427.
473 "a stupid, impudent": ibid., pp. 404–5.
473 "For two whole hours": Wolff-Monckeburg, p. 76, 24 Aug. 1943.
473 "That afternoon . . . I had": Ursula Gebel, *"November 1943 in Charlottenburg,"* quoted in Roger Moorhouse, *Berlin at War* (Bodley Head, 2010), p. 323.
474 "We stood in the fartherest": Klaus Schmidt, *Die Brandnacht* (Darmstadt, 1964), p. 91.
474 "There was a crash": ibid., p. 80.
475 "We were all petrified": ibid., p. 83.
475 "All one could see were": ibid., p. 80.
475 "What a homecoming": Metelmann, p. 180.
475 "I heard today that": Ostellino, p. 268, 9 Dec. 1942.
476 "in at the finish": unpublished MS, *Just a Gamble*, *Bomber Command* files.
476 "The planes are over": Potsdam, Vol. 9/1, p. 468.
477 "Fear and panic rule": ibid., p. 473.
477 "It is a reproach": *Spectator*, 25 Feb. 1944.
478 "It all boils down to": AI Harris, *Bomber Command* files.
478 "I have no intention": Cochrane Papers, Harris MS.

CHAPTER TWENTY   VICTIMS

480 "Eva's birthday": Klemperer, Vol. 2, p. 408.
481 "I was so far": IWM 96/55/1 ZR Pomorski.
481 "Lice bugs bugs lice": IWM Felicks Lachman MS 91/6/1.
482 "To put matters brutally": British Library India Office Records L/PJ/8/412/319. For a vivid account of the entire Polish saga, see Matthew Kelly, *Finding Poland* (Cape, 2010).
482 "I had dressed": IWM 06/52/1 Szmulek Goldberg MS.
483 "I don't believe": Guest, p. 202.
483 "The former social order": Chin Kee On, *Malaya Upside Down* (Singapore, 1946), p. 190.

483 "*Ya Njonja*": Elizabeth van Kampen memoir, Dutch East Indies website.

483 "The . . . disgusting thing": Moltke, p. 244.

484 "My dear father": IWM 95/13/1 Slazak MS.

484 "I have been to Malaya": Bayly and Harper, p. 223.

484 "Let us dance happily": ibid., p. 179.

484 "The Japanese seemed": ibid., p. 234.

485 "I've been to the American": Maier, p. 328.

485 "But we thought": AI Gabor, *Armageddon* files.

485 "In one area": Moltke, p. 175.

486 "If you shut yourself": Maier, 29 Oct. 1942.

487 In occupied western Europe: see Mark Mazower, *Hitler's Empire* (Penguin, 2008), for an exceptionally lucid exposition of many issues in this chapter.

488 "a catastrophic destruction": Tooze, p. 522.

489 "if the children aren't": Potsdam Vol. 9/1, p. 262.

489 "We are still much too": ibid., p. 267.

490 Foreign workers and slaves: Tooze, p. 537.

492 "I saw these people": Jones, *Retreat*, p. 23.

492 "must be done with": Potsdam, Vol. 9/1, pp. 349–51.

492 "If we entirely dispense": Peter Longerich, *Holocaust* (Oxford, 2010), p. 211.

493 As John Lukacs has observed: John Lukacs, *The Legacy of the Second World War* (Yale, 2010).

494 "One simply could not": Christopher Browning, *Ordinary Men* (Penguin, 1998), pp. 19–21.

495 Peter Longerich, one of the more: Longerich, p. 261 et seq.

495 "The leadership at the centre": ibid., p. 426.

496 "In autumn 1941": ibid., p. 271.

496 Hans Michaelis: Maria Sello, *Ein Familien und Zeitdokument 1933–45* (unpublished MS), Wiener Library, quoted in Roger Moorhouse, p. 178.

496 "Sadly I have to say": Potsdam, Vol. 9/1, p. 362.

497 "Voichita Aurel": Sebastian, p. 268, 28 Jan. 1940.

497 "In March 1942, Himmler": *Spectator*, 11 Dec. 1942.

498 "At least nine-tenths": Moltke, p. 285.

498 in Moscow at Easter: Brontman, p. 132.

498 "Hitler did a good job": Merridale, p. 253.

498 "an indigestible lump": Garrard, *Bones*, quoted in ibid., p. 253.

498 In 1945, when: cf. Anonymous, *A Woman in Berlin*.

498 "During the Soviet occupation": Merridale, p. 108.

499 "Two of the most": Koa Wing, p. 74, 26 March 1941.

499 Murray Mendelsohn: AI Mendelsohn, *Armageddon* files.

499 "fucking Jew": Stephen Ambrose, *Band of Brothers* (Simon & Schuster, 1992), p. 22.

499 As late as December: *Public Opinion*, p. 385.

499 "Familiar stuff": Martin Gilbert, *Auschwitz and the Allies* (Weidenfeld & Nicolson, 1981), p. 99, BNA FO 921/7.

500 "In London these": Karski, p. 393.

500 "Most of us were still": Schlesinger, p. 307.

500 "It took some time": Jeffrey, p. xiii.

501 " 'Atrocities' had come": George Orwell, *Tribune*, 31 March 1944.

501 As late as May 1945: *Public Opinion*, p. 501.

502 "After us there might": Potsdam, Vol. 9/1, p. 342.

504 On 13 July 1942: this account is taken from Browning, p. 2 and passim.

504   "In no case can I": ibid., p. 128.
505   " 'Where are my' ": ibid., p. 83.
505   "If this tragedy was": IWM 02/23/1 Frank Blaichman.
507   "Rita, you must": Moorhouse, pp. 195–96.

CHAPTER TWENTY-ONE   EUROPE BECOMES A BATTLEFIELD

508   "Hitler could think only": AI Schroder, *Armageddon* files.
509   "Everything is melting": Belov diary, 17 April 1943.
509   "the Soviet bacillus": Merridale, p. 200.
509   "They slept with Germans": Brontman, pp. 231–33, 9 Nov. 1943, and p. 262, 21 Feb. 1944.
509   "Uncle, have you": ibid., p. 271, 21 April 1944.
510   Just praise has been: see David Glanz, *Soviet Military Deception in the Second World War* (Frank Cass, 1989).
510   "The course of the war": Anders, p. 201, 16 April 1944.
511   "So back we go": Raleigh Trevelyan, *Rome '44* (Viking, 1982), p. 142.
511   "Efficiency in general": Atkinson, p. 490.
511   "This beachhead is": ibid., p. 488.
511   "I never saw so many": ibid., p. 416.
511   "The air roars": ibid., p. 386.
511   "It has become": ibid., p. 428.
512   "We could no longer see": ibid., p. 463.
512   "My heart bleeds": ibid., p. 534.
514   "evident that the project": USMHI Forrest Pogue interview, *The Supreme Command* files.
514   "Personally I couldn't": AI Harris, *Bomber Command* files.
514   "Who else is fighting": Horatius Murray, *"A Very Fine Commander,"* ed. John Donovan (Pen & Sword, 2010), p. 164.
514   "3rd Royal Tanks were virtually": Kershaw, *Overlord* correspondence.
516   "if he was hit bad": McCallum, *Overlord* correspondence.
516   "I was the first tank": Lewis, p. 117.
516   "You know, it sounds": Jon Lewis, ed., *Eyewitness D-Day* (Robinson, 1994), p. 101.
517   "No one was moving": ibid., p. 102.
517   "Eva was very excited": Klemperer, Vol. 2, p. 395.
517   "On the morning of 6 June": *Overlord* files.
518   "It turns out that": Poppel, p. 179.
518   "No landing or lodgement": von Schweppenburg, in *Spectator*, 5 June 1964.
518   "We all reckon": Poppel, p. 181.
518   "Looting by troops": F.S.V. Donnison, *Civil Affairs and Military Government: North-West Europe, 1944–46* (HMS0 1961), p. 74, report of 12 June 1944.
518   "It was an onslaught": IWM 78/35/1 Madame A. de Vigneral.
519   "The attack entailed": IWM Col. H. S. Gillies letter of June 1944.
520   "One of the scenes": Lewis, p. 173.
520   "I have often wondered": Richardson, *Overlord* correspondence.
520   "Here we encountered": Michael Reynolds, *Steel Inferno* (Spellmount, 1997), p. 75.
520   "The whole company": ibid., p. 81.
520   "We had to dig them": Lewis, p. 167.

521　"the urgent need for": USMHI First U.S. Army report of operations, 20 Oct. 1943–1 Aug. 1944.

521　"We were essentially": Kershaw, *Overlord* correspondence.

522　"A sheet of flame": J. L. Cloudsley-Thompson MS, *Overlord* files.

522　"There was, I think": Charles Farrell, *Reflections* (Pentland, 2000), p. 20.

522　"We were all rather": Cloudsley-Thompson MS.

523　"Christ!" he said: Patrick Hennessy, *Young Man in a Tank* (privately published, 1997), p. 79.

523　"There were a lot": Kerr, *Overlord* correspondence.

523　"strolling, hands in pockets": quoted in Reynolds, *Steel Inferno*, p. 36.

523　"knowing that with": Finucane, *Overlord* correspondence.

523　"The front tanks are": Ken Tout, *Tank! Forty Hours of Battle* (London, 1985), p. 39.

524　"Driver left": Andy Cropper, *Dad's War* (Anmas, 1994), p. 33.

524　"It was a hell": Lewis Keeble, *Worm's Eye View: The Recollections of Lewis Keeble*, Appendix C to Battlefield Tour: 1/4 KOYLI in the NW Europe Campaign.

524　"We discussed": Craig, p. 176.

525　"They kept saying": Pogue, p. 333, 25 Jan. 1945.

525　"The spirit of human": Craig, p. 31.

525　"On an average": Robin Hastings, *An Undergraduate's War* (Bell House, 1997), p. 104.

525　"I have drawn": Rathbone, *Overlord* correspondence.

525　"We were often": Selerie, *Overlord* correspondence.

525　"None of us were": Lapp, *Armageddon* files.

525　"I told them": Diercks, *Armageddon* files.

526　"Shit and shit": Barry Broadfoot, ed., *Six War Years* (Toronto, 1974), p. 97.

526　"War is a merry thing!": *Overlord* files.

526　"The first men to die": AI Godau, *Armageddon* files.

526　"The Russian won't": Second Army Intelligence Report, *Armageddon* files.

526　"I see worried faces": Kurt Meyer, *Grenadiers* (Fedorowiz Publishing, 1994), p. 134.

527　"From 6:30 to 8 a.m.": Zimmer, *Overlord* files.

527　"How did the poor": Poppel, p. 221.

527　"My darling Irmi": *Overlord* files.

529　"In Soviet thinking": P. H. Vigor, *Soviet Blitzkrieg Theory* (Macmillan, 1984), p. 137.

529　"This was the last": Merridale, p. 167.

529　"The enemy's use": *Armageddon* files.

531　"They all looked pitiful": Merridale, p. 242.

531　"camels on their knees": ibid., p. 259.

531　"One night you sleep": *Pisma S Voiny*, p. 188.

534　"It was incomprehensible": Reynolds, *Steel Inferno*, p. 40.

534　"There are a great many": Moltke, pp. 282–83.

534　"No one ever laughs": Wolff-Monckeburg, p. 104, 25 June 1944.

534　"For days we have": ibid., p. 107.

535　"We thought it impossible": AI Schroder, *Armageddon* files.

536　"Our nerves were shot": Cropper, p. 38.

537　"The floor of the valley": Eversley Belfield and Hubert Essame, *The Battle for Normandy* (London, 1975), p. 209.

538　"My driver was burning": Lewis, p. 271.

538 "We were shell-shocked": Michael Reynolds, *Men of Steel* (Spelmount, 1999), pp. 32–33
539 "the remainder of the war": *Spectator*, 5 June 1964.

CHAPTER TWENTY-TWO   JAPAN: DEFYING FATE

541 "Old friendships dissolve": Australian Forces Weekly Intelligence Review, No. 118 NZ External Affairs file 84/6/1, Pt.1.
541 "India is not at present": LHA Lethbridge papers, Lethbridge Report, p. 5.
542 "It is now our turn": Christopher Thorne, *Allies of a Kind*, p. 555.
542 "The physical hammering": Hart, p. 162.
543 "It was a stinking hell": ibid., p. 158.
543 "There are few things": Thompson, *Burma*, p. 219.
543 "We shot them on the tennis court": ibid., p. 215.
543 "We were attacked": ibid., p. 220.
544 "Your nerves got": ibid., p. 190.
544 "When you get to": ibid., p. 193.
544 "Come on you chaps": Hart, p. 187.
544 "Well, Sam": ibid., p. 173.
544 "Almost to a man": Raymond Cooper, *B Company* (Dobson, 1978), p. 137.
545 "In the rain, with no": ibid., p. 389.
546 "If you went out": Wooldridge, p. 132.
546 "Enemy dead were": Harry Gailey, *Bougainville, 1943–45: The Forgotten Campaign* (University of Kentucky, 1991), p. 155.
546 "Out here the war life": Fussell, p. 109.
547 "It wasn't dysentery": Gailey, p. 124.
547 "Even under the best": John Monks, *A Ribbon and a Star* (Henry Holt, 1945), p. 40.
547 "Large bogeys bearing": Wooldridge, p. 163.
548 "The carrier below": ibid., p. 177.
549 "We had hardly any": Miller, p. 147.
549 "It reminded me of": Carl Hoffman, *Saipan: The Beginning of the End* (U.S. Marine Corps, 1950), p. 223.
550 "Nowhere have I seen": *Time*, 3 July 1944.
552 "They lost all account": Norman Mailer, *The Naked and the Dead* (1948), p. 249.
554 "He was pretty shaken": Wooldridge, p. 209.

CHAPTER TWENTY-THREE   GERMANY BESIEGED

557 "You and I are both": Second Army Intelligence Report, *Armageddon* files.
557 "I have buried all": ibid.
557 "Then there'll be nothing": Wolff-Monckeburg, p. 86.
557 "I know why you want": AI Moser, *Armageddon* files.
557 "Café Kaefer": Second Army Intelligence Report, *Armageddon* files.
558 "To be nineteen": Fussell, p. 10.
558 "a walkover": Harris to Portal, 1 Nov. 1944, Cochrane Papers.
559 "Until we get Antwerp": Marshall Papers, Box 67/13, 25 Sept. 1944.
561 "This is not only true": Devers, *Military Review*, Vol. 27, No. 7, Oct. 1947, p. 6.
562 "We all thought the war": Koa Wing, p. 236, 29 Sept. 1944.
562 "This . . . is a letter": Day-Lewis, p. 19.

563 "the utter misery": John Ellis, *The Sharp End* (Pimlico, 1993), p. 30.

564 "By the winter Americans": Pogue, *The Supreme Command* files, MHI Carlisle.

564 In Montgomery's 21st: Dr. John Petty, *British Army Review* (summer, 2010), p. 89.

565 "The English, and even more": *Armageddon* files.

565 "Dear General," Eisenhower wrote: Marshall Papers, Box 67/15.

565 "What a mess": Ellis, p. 96.

567 "Words cannot describe": A. K. Altes and N.K.C.A. In't Veld, *The Forgotten Battle: Overlook and the Maas Salient, 1944–45* (Spellmount, 1995), p. 160.

567 "The war was over": Broadfoot, p. 231.

568 "I remember from": Robert Kotlowitz, *Before Their Times* (Anchor, 1998), p. 137.

568 "We strung out across": Finucane, *Overlord* correspondence.

569 "That's what I keep": ibid.

569 Alan Brooke was heard: USMHI Sir Frederick Morgan, quoted in Pogue, *Supreme Command* files.

569 "With our tent": George Neill, *Infantry Soldier: Holding the Line at the Battle of the Bulge* (University of Oklahoma Press, 2002), pp. 85, 91, 95–97.

570 "Through my vision slit": Metelmann, p. 87.

570 "your butt hurt": Schoo, *Armageddon* files.

570 "Jesus Christ!": Kotlowitz, pp. 120–21.

570 "burst into tears": AI Beavers, *Armageddon* files.

571 "If you are brave": Second Army Intelligence Report, *Armageddon* files.

571 "I wasn't scared": AI Moody, *Armageddon* files.

572 "Fear reigned": Donald Burgett, *Seven Roads to Hell: A Screaming Eagle at Bastogne* (Dell, 1999), p. 1.

572 "They looked peaceful": Lindstrom MS, *Armageddon* files.

572 "It was so foggy": Reynolds, *Men of Steel*, p. 120.

572 "Gordon got ripped": Fussell, p. 131.

573 in the small town: William Hitchcock, *Liberation: The Bitter Road to Freedom, Europe 1944–45* (Faber, 2008), pp. 87, 89.

573 "The shattered remnants": George D. Graves, *Blood and Snow: The Ardennes* [n.p.].

574 "My sergeant and I": Reynolds, *Men of Steel*, p. 113.

574 "We finished the battle": AI Schroder, *Armageddon* files.

574 "Americans are not brought up": USMHI Pogue, *The Supreme Command* files.

574 "The record of accomplishment": Blumenson, *Parameters*.

575 "I shot myself": Henry Hills narrative, p. 257, *Armageddon* files.

575 The recommendation was: Bowlby, p. 109.

576 "We left along our path": Anders, p. 251.

CHAPTER TWENTY-FOUR   THE FALL OF THE THIRD REICH

577 "Lieutenant, sir": Krisztian Ungvary, *Battle for Budapest* (Tauris, 2003), p. 20.

577 "The young soldier": ibid., p. 28.

578 "promised that Budapest": ibid., p. 41.

578 "This is the most beautiful": ibid., p. 52.

579 "would not ruin": ibid., p. 35.

579 "The Russkis": ibid., p. 111.

579 Bizarrely, a group of: ibid., p. 64.

579 "It was a girl of about": ibid., p. 141.

580 "Leaving the room": ibid., p. 142.

580 "Supply situation intolerable": ibid., p. 147.
580 "Haven't you got a mother": ibid., p. 239.
580 "In narrow Kazinczy": ibid., p. 247.
582 "Pus, blood, gangrene": ibid., p. 203.
582 "The Hitlerists continued": ibid., p. 208.
583 "They were simple": ibid., p. 293.
584 "a small, bird-like": Donald T. Peak, *Fire Mission* (Sunflower University Press, 2001), p. 148.
584 "I've had enough": Charles Felix, *Crossing the Sauer* (Burford Books, 2002), p. 153.
584 a soldier in Aaron Larkin's: MS, *Aaron's War, Armageddon* files.
584 Pfc. Harold Lindstrom: Lindstrom MS, *Armageddon* files.
584 "We were members": History Branch Office of the JAG with the U.S. Forces European Theatre, 18 July 1942–1 Nov. 1945, Vol. 1, pp. 242–49.
585 "I took aim": White, p. 102.
586 "He wore a gray wool": Fussell, p. 120.
586 "I am a deserter": AI Pflug, *Armageddon* files.
586 "The German army left": Djilas, p. 446.
587 "We are worn out": Poppel, p. 133.
588 "Rifles will be carried": Second Army Intelligence Report, *Armageddon* files.
588 he once addressed: AI Saurma, *Armageddon* files.
588 "Rations were excellent": Michael Reynolds, *Men of Steel*, p. 231.
593 "I wanted to shout": Grossman, p. 330.
595 "Estates, villages and towns": *Pisma S Ognennogo Rubezha, 1941–1945*, p. 100.
595 "At least we were young": AI Kowitz, *Armageddon* files.
595 "In these situations": AI Pflug, *Armageddon* files.
595 "The world is a very lonely": IWM 94/7/1, Mrs. S. H. Stewart MS.
596 "I don't give a fuck": Antony Beevor, *Berlin: The Downfall, 1945* (Penguin, 2002), p. 33.
596 "*Fritz, halt!*": Stanislav Gorsky, *Zapiski Navodchika SU-76* [Memoirs of an SU-76 Gunlayer] (Moscow, 2010), p. 108.
597 "We stay in all sorts": *Pisma S Ognennogo Rubezha*, p. 186.
597 "I'm sitting in my candle-lit": Fromm, *Armageddon* files.
598 "We no longer fought": Sajer, p. 382.
598 "To be an officer": Beevor, p. 164.
598 "These days I keep": Anonymous, p. 62.
598 "Hello my darling!": *Pisma S Ognennogo Rubezha*, p. 137.
598 "Silence! I've got": Beevor, p. 189.
599 "My God!": Hagen, p. 213.
599 "It's all over": Moorhouse, p. 360.
599 "Dear Fatherland, set": ibid., p. 351.
599 "as if blood": Ruth Andreas-Friedrich, *Berlin Underground, 1938–45* (Holt, 1947), p. 273.
599 "Years ago they shouted": Jacob Kronika, *Der Untergang Berlins* (Hamburg, 1946), p. 127, quoted in Moorhouse, p. 359.
600 "When we left Lieberose": Hugo Gryn with Naomi Gryn, *Chasing Shadows* (Harmondsworth, 2001), pp. 238–39.
600 "Along the whole length": Beevor, p. 219.
601 "We moved across terrain": ibid., p. 226.
601 "Why drag out": Potsdam, Vol. 9/1, p. 59.
601 "Now we're in front of": Fromm, *Armageddon* files.

602 "They all seem so miserable": Anonymous, p. 36.
602 "a mere child": Dorothea von Schwanenflugel, *Laughter Wasn't Rationed* (Alexandria, Va.), 1999, p. 342.
602 "You see very young": Anonymous, pp. 40–41.
603 "Berlin . . . presented a dreadful": Sune Persson, *Escape from the Third Reich* (London, 2010), pp. 113–14.
603 "We are vegetating": Helga Schneider, *The Bonfire of Berlin* (London, 2005), p. 55.
605 "If—instead of this": Richard Bessel, *Germany 1945* (Simon & Schuster, 2009), p. 141.
605 "No sound of man": Anonymous, p. 189.
605 "Everywhere there's filth": ibid., p. 185.
605 "The baker comes stumbling": ibid., p. 71.
605 "No one could invent": ibid., p. 230.
605 "a means of escape": ibid., p. 81.
605 "They do not speak": Bessell, p. 267.
606 "Horrifying things": Grossman, p. 327.
606 "I am a Russian": Jacob Kronika, *Der Untergang Berlins*, quoted in Moorhouse, p. 385.
608 "The pastor shot himself": quoted in Moorhouse, p. 372.
608 "They treated us with": Bailey, p. 244.
608 "Illusions about the Red Army": Djilas, p. 420.
609 "There was still too much": Fraser, p. 267.
609 "Our celebration was": Diercks MS, *Armageddon* files.
610 "instant relief": Cropper, p. 90.
610 "Within an hour the city": Detachment 14A2 BCA Regiment, *Armageddon* files.

CHAPTER TWENTY-FIVE   JAPAN PROSTRATE

612 "We shall be doing no more": Bayly and Harper, p. 431.
613 "Partisans, young men": ibid., p. 434.
613 "In all my life": U.S. Marine Corps Historical Institute, Quantico, Joseph Raspilair Papers.
614 Lt. Patrick Caruso: Patrick Caruso, *Nightmare on Iwo* (Naval Institute Press, 2001).
614 "I saw . . . destroyers get hit": Wooldridge, p. 253.
615 "I was amazed": ibid., p. 263.
616 "We took off last night": http://b-29.org/.
616 "LeMay is an operator": Steve Birdsall, *Saga of the Superfortress* (Sidgwick & Jackson, 1981), p. 143.
617 "There was surprisingly": ibid., p. 149.
617 "having visited": ibid., p. 312.
618 "To me, that means": *The Hourglass*, pp. 401–2.
619 "There have been innumerable": Rikihei Inoguchi and Tadashi Nakajima, with Roger Pineau, *The Divine Wind* (Hutchinson, 1959), p. 179.
620 "I can remember": Wooldridge, p. 110.
620 Kasuga Takeo: Kasuga Takeo, quoted in *Kamikaze Diaries*, Emiko Ohnuki-Tierney (University of Chicago Press, 2006), p. 9.
620 "Many of the new arrivals": Inoguchi and Nakajima, p. 148.
621 "a few of these pilots": ibid., p. 149.
621 "Now the wholesale": Ohnuki-Tierney, p. 88.

621 "Today the Japanese": ibid., p. 126.
621 "Mother, I am": ibid., p. 173.
621 "The other day I paid": ibid., p. 209.
623 "My comrades!": USMHI Japanese POW dox PW2050, 24 June 1945.
623 "I've got a message": Hugh Pettigrew, quoted in Thompson, *Burma*, p. 352.
623 "We thought we would": ibid., p. 356.
624 "In the forefront": Yoshida Mitsuru, *Requiem for Battleship Yamato* (Constable, 1999), p. 44.
624 "They had prepared": Laura Fermi, *Atoms in the Family* (University of Chicago Press, 1954), p. 254.
625 "I have no hope": Richard Rhodes, *Ultimate Powers* (Simon & Schuster, 1986), p. 641.
625 "Those who advocate": ibid.
626 "The sure path": Yoshijiro Umezu, *"Facing the Decisive Battle,"* *Kaikosha Kiji*, 17 May 1945.
626 "Your lectures are so": *Nemesis* files, p. 21.
627 "No one person": AI Nakamura, *Nemesis* files.
628 "We heard about": IWM RNR 95/5/1.
628 "We played alarm clock": Birdsall, p. 309.

CHAPTER TWENTY-SIX   VICTORS AND VANQUISHED

630 "We . . . mourn most deeply": Wolff-Monckeburg, p. 130.
631 "Like timid ground creatures": *New York Times*, 22 April 1945.
631 "I felt as if": Anders, p. 282.
631 "They greet me politely": ibid., p. 286.
631 "We, the Poles": IWM 90/11/1 B. Lvov.
632 "Everyone agreed": Koa Wing, p. 268 11 May 1945.
632 "Darling I *know*": Day-Lewis, p. 174.
632 David McCormick: letter in possession of Miranda Corben.
633 "For years I expected": Kevin Wilson, *Journey's End* (Weidenfeld & Nicolson, 2010), p. 392.
633 "It was, I suppose": Schlesinger, p. 353.
633 "The war, while": Forrest C. Pogue, *Pogue's War* (University of Kentucky, 2001), p. 379.
633 "I wanted everything": AI Minamoto, *Nemesis* files.
634 "In those days, Japanese": AI Konada, *Nemesis* files.
634 "seen it come out": Wooldridge, p. 286.
634 "The ending of the war": Birdsall, p. 311.
634 "I am ashamed": Sebastian, p. 628, 31 Dec. 1944.
635 "It would be an error": Christopher Thorne, *Allies of a Kind*, p. 401, 5 April 1944.
635 "I cried when I": Bayly and Harper, p. 455.
635 "old friends so changed": ibid., p. 438.
636 "I knew we'd have to": B. J. Kerkvliet, *The Huk Rebellion: A Study of Peasant Revolt in the Philippines* (Berkeley, 1977), p. 109.
637 "I soon found": Pogue, *Pogue's War*, p. 202.
638 "they are more like": Corti, *The Last Soldiers of the King*, p. 80.
641 "It was the last time": Terkel, p. 67.
641 "Hitler is a genius": Drew Pearson, *Diaries, 1939–59*, ed. Tyler Abell (New York, 1974), p. 134.
642 "There are two great": *RUSI Journal*, June 1979.

646 Germany lost: see the authoritative statistical study published in 2000 by Dr. Rudiger Overmans of the German Armed Force Military History Research Office.

647 "I wasn't quite sure": AI Lott, *Armageddon* files.

647 "No one believes": Hagen, p. 218.

648 "The brass—the people": AI Ebisawa, *Nemesis* files.

649 "The Japanese army had": article in *Bungei Shunju*, March 1956.

649 "In the aftermath": AI Hando, *Nemesis* files.

650 "Jews are of greatest": Blythe, *Private Words*, p. 33.

Bibliography

A comprehensive bibliography of the Second World War, or even of the books about it on my own shelves, is unrealistic within the compass of these pages; I have therefore listed below only titles which I have explicitly cited or quoted in my own text above. The omission of innumerable fine and great works, far from implying dismissal of their merit and importance, reflects my attempt to reprise as little as possible, especially anecdotage, from the histories and memoirs most familiar to students of the period. Titles on which I have drawn extensively for my own narrative, or which seem especially noteworthy for further reading, are shown in **bold type**. I have omitted to detail the multiple volumes of the British and American official histories, which are of course indispensable.

Abbott, Stephen. *And All My War Is Done*. Pentland, 1991.

Altes, A. K., and In't Veld, N.K.C.A. *The Forgotten Battle: Overlook and the Maas Salient, 1944–45*. Spellmount, 1995.

Ambrose, Stephen. *Band of Brothers*. Simon & Schuster, 1992.

Amery, Leo. *My Political Life*. Hutchinson, 1955. Vol. 3.

———. *The Empire at Bay: The Leo Amery Diaries, 1929–45*. Edited by John Barnes and David Nicholson. Hutchinson, 1988.

Anders, Władysław. *An Army in Exile*. Macmillan, 1949.

Andreas-Friedrich, Ruth. *Berlin Underground, 1938–45*. New York, 1947.

Anonymous. ***A Woman in Berlin***. Virago, 2009.

Arthur, Douglas. *Desert Watch*. Blaisdon, 2000.

Atkinson, Rick. ***The Day of Battle***. Henry Holt, 2007.

Avagliano Mario, ed. *Generazione ribelle: Diari e lettere dal 1943 al 1945 a cura di Mario Avagliano*. Einaudi Storia, 2006.

Bailey, Roderick, ed. *Forgotten Voices of the Secret War*. Ebury, 2008.

Ball, Adrian. *The Last Days of the Old World*. Doubleday, 1963.

Barclay, George. *Fighter Pilot*. Kimber, 1976.

Barenblatt, Daniel. *A Plague upon Humanity*. Souvenir, 2004.

Baring, Sarah. *The Road to Station X*. Wilton 65.

Barnett, Correlli. ***Engage the Enemy More Closely***. Hodder & Stoughton, 1991.

Bayly, Christopher, and Tim Harper. ***Forgotten Armies***. Penguin, 2004.

Beevor, Antony. ***Stalingrad***. Viking, 1998.

———. ***Berlin: The Downfall, 1945***. Penguin, 2002.

Belfield, Eversley, and H. Essame. *The Battle for Normandy*. London, 1975.

Bellamy, Chris. ***Absolute War***. Macmillan, 2007.

Belov, N. F. ***Front Diary of N.F. Belov, 1941–44***. Vologda, 1997.

Berezhkov, Valentin. *Stranitsy Diplomaticheskoy Istorii*. Moscow, 1982.

Berle, Beatrice Bishop, and Travis Beal Jacobs. *Navigating the Rapids, 1918–1971*. Harcourt Brace, 1973.

Bessel, Richard. *Germany 1945*. Simon & Schuster, 2009.

Biddle, George. *Artist at War*. New York, 1944.

Birdsall, Steve. *Saga of the Superfortress*. Sidgwick & Jackson, 1981.

Blair, Clay. **Hitler's U-Boat Wars**. Random House, 1996.

Bloomfield-Smith, D. C., ed. *Fourth Indian Reflections*. Larman, 1987.

Blum, John Morton. *V Was for Victory*. Harcourt Brace, 1976.

Blunt, Roscoe. *Foot Soldier: A Combat Infantryman's War in Europe*. Da Capo Press, 2002.

Blythe, Ronald, ed. *Components of the Scene*. Penguin, 1966.

———. *Private Words*. Viking, 1991.

Borthwick, Alastair. *Battalion*. Baton Wicks, 1994.

Bower, Tom. *Nazi Gold*. HarperCollins, 1997.

Bowlby, Alex. *Recollections of Rifleman Bowlby*. Leo Cooper, 1969.

Braithwaite, Roderic. *Moscow 1941*. Profile, 2006.

Branson, Clive. *British Soldier in India: The Letters of Clive Branson*. Communist Party, London, 1944.

Broadfoot, Barry, ed. *Six War Years*. Toronto, 1974.

Brontman, Lazar. *Voenny dnevnik korrespondenta "Pravdy"* [War Diary of the *Pravda* Correspondent]. Moscow, 2007.

Browning, Christopher. **Ordinary Men**. Penguin, 1998.

Bryant, Arthur. *The Turn of the Tide*. Collins, 1957.

Bungay, Stephen. *The Most Dangerous Enemy*. Aurum, 2010.

Burgett, Donald. *Seven Roads to Hell: A Screaming Eagle at Bastogne*. Dell, 1999.

Burleigh, Michael. *Moral Combat*. HarperCollins, 2010.

Busatti, Franco. *Dal Volturno a Cassino*. RSI website.

Calvocoressi, Peter, Guy Wint and John Pritchard. **Total War**. Viking, 1972.

Carlton de Wiart, Adrian. *Happy Odyssey*. Jonathan Cape, 1950.

Caruso, Patrick. *Nightmare on Iwo*. Naval Institute Press, 2001.

Cheek, Tom. *A Ring of Coral*. Battle of Midway Roundtable, http//home.comcast.net/ r2russ/midway. ringcoral.htm.

Chin Kee On. *Malaya Upside Down*. Singapore, 1946.

Ciano, Galleazo. *Diaries, 1937–43*. Edited by Redonzo de Felice. Milan, 1980.

Cole, David. *Rough Road to Rome*. Kimber, 1983.

Collingham, Lizzie. *The Taste of War*. Allen Lane, 2011.

Colvin, John. *Nomonhan*. Quartet, 1999.

Cooper, Artemis. *Cairo in the War*. Hamish Hamilton, 1989.

Cooper, Diana. *Trumpets from the Steep*. Hart Davis, 1960.

Cooper, Raymond. *B Company*. Dobson, 1978.

Corti, Eugenio. *Few Returned: 28 Days on the Russian Front, Winter 1942–43*. University of Missouri Press, 1997.

——— .*The Last Soldiers of the King*. University of Missouri Press, 2003.

Costello, John. *The Pacific War*. Collins, 1981.

Craig, Norman. *The Broken Plume*. IWM, 1982.

Cremer, Peter. *U-333*. Grafton, 1986.

Crook, Martin, ed. *Wartime Letters of a West Kent Man*. privately published, 2007.

Cropper, Andy. *Dad's War*. Anmas, 1994.

Crosby, Harry H. *A Wing and a Prayer*. Robson, 1993.

Cross, Robin. *Citadel*. O'Mara, 1993.

Dahl, Roald. *Going Solo*. Penguin, 1988.

Dallek, Robert. *Lone Star Rising*. Oxford, 1991.

Dalton, Hugh. *Diaries*. Edited by Ben Pimlott. Jonathan Cape, 1986.

Davies, Norman. *God's Playground*. Oxford, 1981. Vol. 2.

Day-Lewis, Tamsin, ed. *Last Letters Home*. Macmillan, 1995.

Dear, I.C.B., and M.R.D. Foot, eds. **The Oxford Companion to the Second World War**. Oxford, 1995.

D'Este, Carlo. **Decision in Normandy**. Collins, 1983.

———. *Bitter Victory*. Collins, 1988.

———. *Eisenhower*. Holt, 2002.

Diller, Eric. *Memoirs of a Combat Infantryman*. Privately published, 2002.

Djilas, Milovan. **Wartime**. Secker & Warburg, 1980.

Doherty, Richard. *A Noble Crusade*. Sarpedon, 1999.

Donnison, F.S.V. *Civil Affairs and Military Government: North-West Europe, 1944–46*. HMSO, 1961.

Douglas, Keith. *Alamein to Zem Zem*. Penguin, 1967.

Dower, John. *War Without Mercy*. Pantheon, 1986.

Dunlop, Edward. *The Diaries of "Weary" Dunlop*. Viking, 1986.

Dyess, William E. *The Dyess Story*. Putnam, 1944.

Echternkamp, Jorg, ed. **Germany and the Second World War**. Research Institute for Military History, Potsdam/Oxford. 9 vols, 1990–2008.

Edwards, Robert. *White Death*. Weidenfeld & Nicolson, 2007.

Eichelberger, Robert. *Our Jungle Road to Tokyo*. Nashville Battery Classics, 1989.

Eisenhower, Dwight. *The Eisenhower Diaries*. Norton, 1981.

Ellis, John. *The Sharp End*. Pimlico, 1993.

Ellwood, David W. *Italy, 1943–45*. Leicester University Press, 1985.

Farrell, Charles. *Reflections*. Pentland, 2000.

Felix, Charles. *Crossing the Sauer*. Burford Books, 2002.

Fenby, Jonathan. *Generalissimo*. Free Press, 2003.

Fermi, Laura. *Atoms in the Family*. University of Chicago Press, 1954.

Foot, Michael. *Bevan*. McGibbon & Kee, 1965.

Forman, Denis. *To Reason Why*. André Deutsch, 1991.

Formica, F., ed. *Account of the Battle of Deir El Murra*, Diary of Second Lieutenant Vincenzo Formica, www.fereamole.it.

Frank, Richard. **Downfall**. Penguin, 1999.

Fraser, David. *Wars and Shadows*. Penguin, 2002.

Fuchida, Mitsuo, and Masatake Okimuya. *Midway: The Battle That Doomed Japan*. Annapolis, 1955.

Fussell, Paul. *The Boys' Crusade*. Weidenfeld & Nicolson, 2004.

Gailey, Harry. *Bougainville, 1943–45: The Forgotten Campaign*. University of Kentucky Press, 1991.

Garfield, Simon, ed. **Private Battles**. Ebury, 2006.

———. *We Are at War*. Ebury, 2009.

Gilbert, Adrian. *Voices of the Foreign Legion*. Skyhorse, 2010.

Gilbert, Martin. *Auschwitz and the Allies*. Weidenfeld & Nicolson, 1981.

Glanz, David. *Soviet Military Deception in the Second World War*. Frank Cass, 1989.

———. *Barbarossa*. Tempus, 2001.

Glusman, John. *Conduct Under Fire*. Viking, 2007.

Gorsky, Stanislav. *Zapiski Navodchika SU-76* [Memoirs of an SU-76 Gunlayer]. Moscow, 2010.

Grossman, Vasily. *A Writer at War*. Edited by Lyuba Vinogradova and Antony Beevor. Harvill, 2006.

Gryn, Hugo, with Naomi Gryn. *Chasing Shadows*. Penguin, 2001.

Guest, John. *Broken Images*. Hart Davis, 1949.

Hadjipateras, C. N., and M. S. Falfalios, eds. *Greece 1940–41 Eyewitnessed.* Efstathiadis, 1995.

Hagen, Louis. *Ein Volk ein Reich: Nine Lives Under the Reich.* Spellmount, 2011.

Halder, Franz. ***Command in Conflict: The Diaries and Notes of Colonel-General Franz Halder and Other Members of the German High Command.*** Edited by Barry Leach and Ian MacDonald. Oxford 1985.

Harries, Meirion, and Susie Harries. *Soldiers of the Sun.* Heinemann, 1991.

Hart, Peter. *At the Sharp End.* Leo Cooper, 1998.

Hastings, Max. *Bomber Command.* Michael Joseph, 1979.

———. *Overlord: D-Day and the Battle for Normandy.* Michael Joseph, 1984.

———. *Armageddon: The Battle for Germany, 1944–45.* Macmillan, 2004.

———. *Nemesis: The Battle for Japan, 1944–45.* HarperCollins, 2007.

———. *Finest Years.* HarperCollins, 2009.

Hastings, Robin. *An Undergraduate's War.* Bell House, 1997.

Headlam, Cuthbert. *Parliament and Politics in the Age of Churchill and Attlee: The Headlam Diaries, 1935–1951.* Edited by Stuart Ball. Cambridge, 1999.

Hennessy, Patrick. *Young Man in a Tank.* Privately published, 1997.

Hichens, Antony. *Gunboat Command.* Pen & Sword, 2007.

Hitchcock, William. *Liberation: The Bitter Road to Freedom, Europe 1944–45.* Faber, 2008.

Hoffman, Carl. *Saipan: The Beginning of the End.* U.S. Marine Corps, 1950.

Holland, James. *Battle over Britain.* HarperPress, 2010.

Horne, Alastair. *To Lose a Battle.* Macmillan, 1969.

Horsfall, John. *Say Not the Struggle.* Roundwood, 1977.

Hough, Richard. *One Boy's War.* Heinemann, 1975.

Howard, Michael. *Captain Professor.* Continuum, 2004.

———. *Liberation or Catastrophe.* Hambledon, 2008.

Howarth, Stephen, and David Law, eds. ***The Battle of the Atlantic, 1939–45.*** Greenhill, 1994.

Hudson, Charles. *Journal of Major-General Charles Hudson.* Wilton 65, 1992.

Inoguchi, Rikihei, and Tadashi Nakajima, with Roger Pineau. *The Divine Wind.* Hutchinson, 1959.

Ironside, Sir Edmund. *Time Unguarded: The Ironside Diaries.* Edited by Roderick MacLeod and Denis Kelly. London, 1962.

Jackson, Julian. ***The Fall of France.*** Oxford, 2003.

Jeffrey, Keith. *MI6: The History of the Secret Intelligence Service, 1909–49.* Bloomsbury, 2010.

Joffe, Constantin. *We Were Free.* Smith & Durrell, 1943.

Johnston, George. *The Toughest Fighting in the World.* Duell, Sloan & Pearce, 1943.

Johnston, Mark. *At the Front Line.* Cambridge, 1996.

Johnstone, Sandy. *Enemy in the Sky.* Kimber, 1976.

Jones, James. *The Thin Red Line.* Collins, 1963.

———. *WW II: A Chronicle of Soldiering.* Illustrated by Art Weithas. Grossett & Dunlap, 1975.

Jones, Michael. ***The Siege of Leningrad.*** John Murray, 2008.

———. ***The Retreat: Hitler's First Defeat.*** John Murray, 2009.

Karig, Walter, and Eric Purdon. *Battle Report: Pacific War Middle Phase.* Rinehart, 1946.

Karski, Jan. *Story of a Secret State.* Penguin, 2011.

Keeble, Lewis. *Worm's Eye View: The Recollections of Lewis Keeble.* Appendix C to Battlefield Tour: 1/4 KOYLI in the NW Europe Campaign.

Kellas, Arthur. *Down to Earth.* Pentland Press, 1989.

Kelly, Matthew. *Finding Poland.* Cape, 2010.

Kemp, Peter. *The Thorns of Memory.* Sinclair-Stevenson, 1990.

Kennedy, David. *Freedom from Fear.* Oxford, 1999.

Kennedy, John. *The Business of War.* Hutchinson, 1957.

Kerkvliet, B. J. *The Huk Rebellion: A Study of Peasant Revolt in the Philippines.* Berkeley, 1977.

Kernan, Alvin. *The Unknown Battle of Midway.* Yale, 2005.

Kersaudy, François. *Norway 1940.* Collins, 1990.

Kershaw, Ian. *Fateful Choices.* Penguin, 2008.

Kershaw, Robert. *Never Surrender.* Hodder & Stoughton, 2009.

Khaing, Mi Mi. *A Burmese Family.* Longman, 1946.

Khrushchev, Nikita. *The Memoirs of Nikita Khrushchev.* Edited by Sergei Khrushchev. Thomas Watson Institute, 2004. Vol. 1.

Killingray, David. ***Fighting for Britain.*** James Currey, 2010.

Klemperer, Victor. ***I Shall Bear Witness.*** Weidenfeld & Nicolson, 1999.

Knoke, Heinz. *I Flew for the Führer.* Evans, 1979.

Knox, Donald. *Death March.* Harcourt Brace, 1981.

Koa Wing, Sandra, ed. ***Our Longest Days.*** Profile, 2008.

Kotlowitz, Robert. *Before Their Times.* Anchor, 1998.

Kronika, Jacob. *Der Untergang Berlins.* Hamburg, 1946.

Kumanyov, G. A. *Ryadom so Stalinym* [Close to Stalin]. Moscow, 1999.

Ladies' Home Journal. *How America Lives.* Henry Holt, 1941.

Lamb, J. B. *The Corvette Navy: True Stories from Canada's Atlantic War.* Macmillan Toronto, 1979.

Langer, Rula. *The Mermaid and the Messerschmitt.* Roy, 1942.

Last, Nella. ***Nella Last's War.*** Sphere, 1981.

Leckie, Robert. *Helmet for My Pillow.* Ebury, 2010.

Lewis, Jon, ed. *Eyewitness D-Day.* Robinson, 1994.

Lewis, Norman. *Naples '44.* Eland, 1983.

Livanios, Dimitris. *The Macedonian Question.* Oxford, 2008.

Lockwood, Jeffrey. *Six-Legged Soldiers: Using Insects as Weapons of War.* Oxford, 2009.

Longerich, Peter. ***Holocaust.*** Oxford, 2010.

Longmate, Norman. *The Home Front.* Chatto & Windus, 1981.

Lord, Walter. *Incredible Victory.* New York, 1967.

Loxton, Bruce, and Chris Coulthard-Clark. *The Shame of Savo.* Allen & Unwin, 1994.

Lukacs, John. *The Legacy of the Second World War.* Yale, 2010.

McCullers, Carson. *Reflections in a Golden Eye.* Houghton Mifflin, 1941.

MacGregor, Knox. ***Mussolini Unleashed, 1939–1941: Politics and Strategy in Fascist Italy's Last War.*** Cambridge University Press, 1982.

McManners, John. *Fusilier.* Michael Russell, 2002.

Macnab, Roy. *For Honour Alone.* Hale, 1988.

Mafai, Miriam. *Pane Nero: Donne e vita quotidiana nella seconda Guerra mondiale.* Arnoldo Mondadori Editore, 1987.

Maier, Ruth. *Ruth Maier's Diary.* Harvill Secker, 2009.

Mailer, Norman. *The Naked and the Dead.* New York, 1948.

Mantia, Vito. *Diario di Guerra: Con gli Alpini in Montenegro 1941–1943.* Mursia, 2010.

Mazower, Mark. ***Hitler's Empire.*** Penguin, 2008.

Mears, Fred. *Carrier Combat.* Doubleday, 1944.

Melville, Herman. *Israel Potter.* 1854.

Melvin, Mungo. *Manstein.* Weidenfeld & Nicolson, 2010.

Merridale, Catherine. ***Ivan's War.*** Faber, 2005.

Metelmann, Henry. *Through Hell for Hitler.* Spellmount, 1990.

Meyer, Kurt. *Grenadiers.* Fedorowiz Publishing, 1994.

Milburn, Clara. *Mrs. Milburn's Diaries.* Harrap, 1979.

Miller, Donald. *D-Days in the Pacific.* Simon & Schuster, 2005.

Mitsuru, Yoshida. *Requiem for Battleship Yamato.* Constable, 1999.

Mochalasky, Fydor. *Gulag Boss.* Oxford, 2010.

Moltke, Helmuth von. **Letters to Freya.** Edited by Beatte von Oppen. Collins Harvill, 1991.

Monahan, Evelyn M., and Rosemary Neidel-Greenlee. *All this Hell.* Kentucky University Press, 2000.

Monks, John. *A Ribbon and a Star.* Henry Holt, 1945.

Monsarrat Nicholas. *The Cruel Sea.* Cassell, 1951.

Moore, Peter. *No Need to Worry.* Wilton 65, 2002.

Moorehead, Alan. *African Trilogy.* Hamish Hamilton, 1999.

————. *Eclipse.* Granta, 2000.

Moorhouse, Roger. *Berlin at War.* Bodley Head, 2010.

Mowat, Farley. *And No Birds Sang.* Cassell, 1980.

Muirhead, John. *Those Who Fall.* Random House, 1986.

Mukerjee, Madhusree. *Churchill's Secret War.* Basic, 2010.

Murray, Horatius. *A Very Fine Commander.* Edited by John Donovan. Pen & Sword, 2010.

Murray, Williamson. **Luftwaffe.** Allen & Unwin, 1985.

Murray, Williamson, and Allan Millett. *A War to Be Won.* Belknap, 2000.

Mydans, Carl. *More Than Meets the Eye.* Harper, 1959.

Nehru, Jawaharlal. *Selected Works of Nehru.* Orient Longman, 1980. Vols. 12, 13.

Neill, George. *Infantry Soldier: Holding the Line at the Battle of the Bulge.* University of Oklahoma Press, 2000.

Némirovsky, Irène. *Suite française.* Chatto & Windus, 2006.

Newton, Steven H. *Kursk: The German View.* Da Capo, 2002.

Nicolson, Harold. *Diaries.* Collins, 1965. Vol. 2.

Nikulin, Nikolai. *Vospominaniya o voine.* St. Petersburg, 2009. Internet published.

Nixon, Barbara. *Raiders Overhead.* Scolar, 1980.

Norman, Elizabeth. *Band of Angels.* Random House, 1999.

Ohnuki-Tierney, Emiko. *Kamikaze Diaries.* University of Chicago Press, 2006.

Olson, Lynn, and Stanley Cloud. *For Your Freedom and Ours.* Heineman, 2003.

Origo, Iris. *War in the Val d'Orcia.* Cape, 1947.

Overy, Richard. **Why the Allies Won.** Allen Lane, 1995.

————. **Russia's War.** Allen Lane, 1997.

Owen, James. *Danger UXB.* Little, Brown, 2010.

Owen, James, and Guy Walters, eds. *The Voices of War.* Penguin, 2004.

Payne, Stanley. **Franco and Hitler.** Yale, 2008.

Peak, Donald T. *Fire Mission.* Sunflower University Press, 2001.

Pearson, Drew. *Diaries, 1939–59.* Edited by Tyler Abell. New York, 1974.

Perrett, Geoffrey. **Days of Sadness, Years of Triumph.** University of Wisconsin Press, 1973.

Perrott-White, Alfred. *French Legionnaire.* John Murray, 1953.

Pershanin, Vladimir, ed. *Shtrafniki, Radvedchiki, Pekhota* [Punishment Companies, Reconnaissance, Infantry]. Moscow, 2010.

Persson, Sune. *Escape from the Third Reich.* London, 2010.

Piekalkiewitcz, Janusz. *The Cavalry of World War II.* Orbis, 1979.

Pisma S Ognennogo Rubezha 1941–1945 [Letters from the Front, 1941–1945]. St. Petersburg, 1992.

Pisma S Viony. Ioshkar-Ola, 1995.

Pogue, Forrest. *The Supreme Command.* Office of the Chief of Military History, Washington, D.C. 1954.

———. *Pogue's War.* University of Kentucky Press, 2001.

Poppel, Martin. *Heaven and Hell.* Spellmount, 1988.

Powell, Anthony. *A Writer's Notebook.* Heinemann, 2001.

Princeton Polling. *Public Opinion, 1935–1946.* Princeton University Press, 1951.

Pyle, Ernie. *Here Is Your War.* Pocket, 1945.

———. *V Was for Victory.* New York, 1945.

Raczynski, Edward. *In Allied London.* Weidenfeld & Nicolson, 1962.

Raleigh, John. *Behind the Nazi Front.* Dodd Mead, 1940.

Raymond, Bob. *A Yank in Bomber Command.* Moynihan, 1977.

Rebora, Andrea, ed. *Letters of Lt. Pietro Ostellino: North Africa January 1941 to March 1943.* Prospettiva Editrice, 2007.

Reston, James. *Prelude to Victory.* Knopf, 1942.

Reynolds, Michael. *Steel Inferno.* Spellmount, 1997.

———. *Men of Steel.* Spellmount, 1999.

Rhodes, Richard. *Ultimate Powers.* Simon & Schuster, 1986.

Richey, Paul. *Fighter Pilot.* Cassell, 2001.

Roberts, Andrew. *Masters and Commanders.* Allen Lane, 2008.

———. *The Storm of War.* Allen Lane, 2009.

Rokossovsky, Konstantin. *Soldatskiy Dolg.* Moscow Olun Press, 2002.

Roosevelt, Franklin. *The Roosevelt Letters.* Edited by Elliot Roosevelt. Harrap, 1952. Vol. 3.

Rudnicki, General K. S. *Last of the Old Warhorses.* Bachman & Turner, 1974.

Sadat, Anwar. *In Search of Identity.* Collins, 1978.

Sajer, Guy. *The Forgotten Soldier.* Sphere, 1971.

Say, Rosemary, and Noel Holland. *Rosie's War.* Michael Mara Books, 2011.

Schlesinger, Arthur. *A Life in the Twentieth Century.* Mariner Books, 2000.

Schmidt, Klaus. *Die Brandnacht.* Reba-Verlag, 1964.

Schneider, Helga. *The Bonfire of Berlin.* William Heineman, 2005.

Schrijvers, Peter. *The Crash of Ruin.* New York University Press, 1998.

Schwanenflugel, Dorothea von. *Laughter Wasn't Rationed.* Tricor Press, 1999.

Sebastian, Mihail. *Journal, 1935–44.* Heinemann, 2001.

Sein, Daw. *Les Dix milles vies d'une femme birmane.* Claude Delachet Fuillon, 1978.

Sello, Maria. *Ein Familien und Zeitdokument 1933–45.* Unpublished manuscript, Wiener Library.

Sevareid, Eric. *Not So Wild a Dream.* Knopf, 1969.

Seversky, Alexander. *Victory Through Air Power.* Simon & Schuster, 1942.

Sherwood, Robert. *The White House Papers of Harry L. Hopkins.* Eyre & Spottiswoode, 1948. Vol. 1.

Shirer, William. *This Is Berlin.* Hutchinson, 1999.

Simpson, Tony. *Operation Mercury.* Hodder & Stoughton, 1981.

Sinkoskey Brodine, Janine, ed. *Missing Pieces.* Hara Publishing, 2000.

Sledge, Eugene. *With the Old Breed at Peleliu and Okinawa.* Ebury, 2010.

Smith, Colin. *Singapore Burning.* Penguin, 2005.

———. *England's Last War with France: Fighting Vichy, 1940–42.* Weidenfeld & Nicolson, 2009.

Smith, Colin, and John Bierman. *Alamein: War Without Hate.* Penguin, 2002.
Smith, Denis Mack. *Mussolini.* Weidenfeld & Nicolson, 1981.
Smith, Howard. *Last Train from Berlin.* London, 1942.
Smyth, John. *Before the Dawn.* Cassell, 1957.
Snow, Edgar. *Journey to the Beginning.* Gollancz, 1959.
Somerville, Christopher. *Our War.* Weidenfeld & Nicolson, 1998.
Spector, Ronald. *Eagle Against the Sun.* Viking, 1985.
Stahlberg, Alexander. *Bounden Duty.* Brassey, 1990.
John Steinbeck. *John Steinbeck: A Life in Letters.* Edited by Elaine Steinbeck and Robert Wallston. Heinemann, 1975.
Street, A. G. *From Dusk Till Dawn.* Blandford, 1945.
Sweetman, John. *The Dambusters Raid.* Arms & Armour, 1993.
Tatsuro, Izumiya. *The Minami Organ.* Rangoon, 1967.
Temkin, Gabriel. *My Just War.* Presidio, 1998.
Terkel, Studs. *The Good War.* Hamish Hamilton, 1984.
Thompson, Julian. *The War at Sea.* Sidgwick & Jackson, 1996.
———. *Forgotten Voices of Burma.* Ebury, 2009.
Thorne, Christopher. *Allies of a Kind.* Hamish Hamilton, 1978.
———. *The Issue of War.* Oxford, 1985.
Tooze, Adam. *The Wages of Destruction.* Penguin, 2007.
Tout, Ken. *Tank!: Forty Hours of Battle.* London, 1985.
Towards Freedom: Documents on the Movement for Independence in India 1940, Pt. 1. Oxford University Press, 1978.
Trevelyan, Raleigh. *Rome '44.* Viking, 1982.
Tsuji, Col. Masanobu. *Japan's Greatest Victory, Britain's Worst Defeat.* Spellmount, 1997.
Turner, E. S. *The Phoney War.* Michael Joseph, 1961.
Tute, Warren. *The Reluctant Enemies.* Collins, 1990.
Tyson, Geoffrey. *Forgotten Frontier.* Calcutta, 1945.
Umezu, Yoshijiro. "Facing the Decisive Battle," *Kaikosha Kiji,* 1945.
Ungvary, Krisztian. *Battle for Budapest.* Tauris, 2003.
Vallicella, Vittorio. *Diario di Guerra da El Alamein alla tragica ritirata 1942–1943.* Edizioni Arterigere, 2009.
Vaz Ezdani, Yvonne, ed. *Songs of the Survivors.* Goa, Noronha, 2007.
Vigor, P. H. *Soviet Blitzkrieg Theory.* Macmillan, 1984.
Walters, Anne-Marie. *Moondrop to Gascony.* MPG Books, 2009.
Waugh, Evelyn. *Officers and Gentlemen.* Chapman & Hall, 1955.
———. *Unconditional Surrender.* Chapman & Hall, 1961.
———. *Diaries.* Edited by Michael Davie. Weidenfeld & Nicolson, 1976.
Weinberg, Gerhard. *A World at Arms.* Cambridge, 1994.
Weinstein, Alfred. *Barbed Wire Surgeon.* Macmillan, 1947.
Wellum, Geoffrey. *First Light.* Penguin, 2002.
Westphal, Siegfried, ed. *The Fatal Decisions.* Michael Joseph, 1952.
White, Peter. *With the Jocks.* Sutton, 2001.
White, Theodore, and Annalee Jacoby. *Thunder Out of China.* Gollancz, 1947.
Willkie, Wendell. *One World.* Simon & Schuster, 1942.
Wilmot, Chester. *The Struggle for Europe.* Wordsworth, 1997.
Wilson, Kevin. *Journey's End.* Weidenfeld & Nicolson, 2010.
Wolff-Monckeburg, Mathilde. *On the Other Side.* Edited by Ruth Evans. Pan, 1979.
Woodman, Richard. *Malta Convoys.* John Murray, 2000.
———. *Arctic Convoys.* John Murray, 2001.

————. *The Real Cruel Sea.* John Murray, 2004.

Wooldridge, E. T., ed. *Carrier Warfare in the Pacific.* Smithsonian, 1993.

Zhadobin et al., eds. *Ogennaya Duga: Kurskaya Bitva Glazami Lubyanki* [The Salient of Fire: Kursk as Seen Through the Eyes of the Lubyanka]. Moscow, 2003.

Zweig, Stefan. *The World of Yesterday.* Pushkin Press, 2010.

Index

Note: Ranks and titles are generally the highest mentioned in the text.